MYSTERIES OF SEX

MARY P. RYAN

Mysteries of Sex

TRACING WOMEN AND MEN THROUGH

AMERICAN HISTORY

THE UNIVERSITY OF NORTH CAROLINA PRESS

CHAPEL HILL

Set in Scala type by Tseng Information Systems, Inc.

Manufactured in the United States of America

The paper in this book meets the guidelines for permanence and
durability of the Committee on Production Guidelines for Book
Longevity of the Council on Library Resources.

Library of Congress Cataloging-in-Publication Data

Ryan, Mary P.

Mysteries of sex : tracing women and men through American history /
by Mary P. Ryan.

p. cm.

Includes bibliographical references and index.

ISBN-13: 978-0-8078-3062-8 (cloth : alk. paper)

ISBN-10: 0-8078-3062-3 (cloth : alk. paper)

1. Sex role—United States—History. 2. Women—United States—
History. 3. Men—United States—History. 4. Feminism—United
States—History. 5. United States—History. 6. United States—Social
conditions. I. Title.

HQ1075.5.U6R93 2006

305.420973—dc22   2006016540

10 09 08 07 06   5 4 3 2 1

For my students and my colleagues,

with thanks for all you have taught me

CONTENTS

Introduction 1

PART I. MAKING SEX IN AMERICA: 1500–1900

Chapter 1. Where Have the Corn Mothers Gone?:
Americans Encounter the Europeans 21
*The Coordinates of Gender: Asymmetry, the Relations of the Sexes,
    and Hierarchy* 25
The Sexual Frontier 42
Warriors and Farmers on the Gender Frontier 49

Chapter 2. Who Baked That Apple Pie and When?:
How Domesticity Conquered American Culture 61
The Prehistory of Feminine Domesticity: 1620–1692 64
Between Patriarchy and Domesticity: 1750–1840 80
Homemaking in Antebellum and Victorian America 88

Chapter 3. How Did Race Get Colored?:
Gender and Sexuality in the American South 103
How Slavery Became Colored African American 105
The Gendering of Slave Society 116
Civil War and the Reconstruction of Race and Gender 124
The Sexual Politics of Jim Crow 137

PART II. DIVIDING THE PUBLIC REALM

Chapter 4. What Is the Sex of Citizenship?:
Engendering the American Political Tradition from
the Revolution to the New Deal 147
When Citizenship Was Male: 1776–1865 149
The Mother as Citizen: Segregated and Secondary 162
The Woman Citizen Goes to Washington 174
Second-Class Citizenship: Male and Female 188

PART III. WOMEN REMAKE GENDER
IN THE TWENTIETH CENTURY

Chapter 5. How Do You Get from Home to Work to Equity?:
1900–1960 201

Who Made the Woman Worker?: An Overview 203

The New Woman Goes to Work: 1890–1940 207

A Private Detour through the 1920s 214

The Next Generation Combines Work and Family: The 1940s and 1950s 227

The Mystery of the Feminine Mystique 238

Chapter 6. Where Does Sex Divide?:
Feminism, Sexuality, and the Structures of Gender since 1960 245

The Second Wave of Feminism: 1960–1970 248

Sexual Revolution and Gay Rights 265

Restructuring Gender Differences: 1980–2000 276

Chapter 7. Where in the World Is the Border between Male and Female?:
Immigration and Generation in the Twentieth Century 291

The Generations of Gender 295

New Immigrants Meet Postmodernity: 1965–2000 302

Joining Together to Remake Male, Female, and America 314

Notes 325
Bibliography 361
Acknowledgments 409
Index 411

ILLUSTRATIONS

Restroom sign, Yerba Buena Center, San Francisco 12

John L. Begay (Navajo), *Mother Earth and Father Sky* 37

Jan van der Straet, *Christopher Columbus* 45

Hearth, Williams-Hopkinson House, Philadelphia 72

The kitchen of Harriet Beecher Stowe 95

Picking Cotton on a Georgia Plantation 117

Shermantown settlement, Atlanta 133

Liberty 155

Good-by to Sumter 161

Jane Addams at the dining table of Hull House 169

Publicizing woman suffrage 180

Telephone Operators' Union Delegates at the 1917 International
Brotherhood of Electrical Workers Convention 218

Betty Friedan at home in Parkway Village, New York 240

The cover of *Notes from the Second Year* 257

Rink Foto, *At the 1978 Parade Celebration in Civic Center, San Francisco* 273

Pauli Murray, 1927 288

Pauli Murray, ca. 1977 289

E. J. Harpham, *Vision of the Virgin of Guadalupe* 292

Yolanda López, *Portrait of the Artist as the Virgin of Guadalupe* 319

MYSTERIES OF SEX

INTRODUCTION

It is the winter of 2005, a harrowing time in the history of the United States. The front pages are plastered with images of the continuing brutality and bloodshed of the war in Iraq. The catastrophic hurricanes that pounded the coastline along the Gulf of Mexico have laid waste to a region, gutted a great and beloved city, and exposed governmental inefficiency and flagrant social inequity. Even the Olympus of the American system of government, the Supreme Court, is unsettled. The appointment of two new Justices seems likely to tip the delicate balance of opinions that has held for over a decade. Those who pick up this book are apt to be attentive to patterns of sexual difference in the daily news reports. The headlines suggest that the advances of women into the public sphere heralded by the feminist movement some thirty years ago have stalled. Women hold the office of secretary of state and the governorship of beleaguered Louisiana, but they are still exceptional among political leaders. The president recommended the appointment of a woman to the Supreme Court, but her nomination was withdrawn amid conservative opposition and doubts about her qualifications. The president's second choice was a male and by no means a champion of women's rights. The ranks of soldiers in Iraq have been integrated by sex, but both the occupants of command posts and the rosters of combat fatalities remain overwhelmingly male, testimony to one of the oldest, bluntest, and deadliest examples of the sexual division of labor. Incidentally, the best-selling history books commemorate the lives of politically prominent white men.

Given the perilous condition of the nation and the world at the outset of the twenty-first century, this tabulation of sex ratios may seem a petty distraction. A look beneath the surface of the headlines, however, indicates that further attention to matters of gender is still warranted. Contemporary scholars, many of them a generation or more removed from the high tide of the feminist movement, can point to the mark of gender in each column of newsprint and every electronic image: raw wounds of masculinity and sexuality were on display at Abu Ghraib prison in Iraq; the nervous attention to the Supreme Court appointments was focused on a single issue charged with sex and gender, the right to abortion; and fundamental structures of gender, all colored by race, came to the surface with the floodwaters of New Orleans—

represented by the preponderance of single mothers, elderly women, and male prisoners among the displaced. Attention to the fault lines between male and female that reside just beneath the headlines is not a petty distraction; it should be a critical public concern.

Public discussion of questions of sex and gender is not irrelevant as the year 2005 comes to a close, but neither leaders nor journalists have found the will or a way to conduct it. Pressing gender issues seldom make the front page, and when they do it can be less than illuminating. Witness a report on page one of the *New York Times* on the future expectations of female students at Yale University. A small, selective group of elite young women were given a national platform from which to announce their intentions to interrupt careers for full-time mothering, expecting that their future husbands would assume sole financial responsibility for themselves and their children-to-be.[1] Historians, and women and men of a certain age, had heard such forecasts before; they boomed out in the 1950s and have surfaced periodically in newsmagazines and on the best-seller list ever since. The mundane reality that the wages of mothers were vital to the welfare of most American children seemed unworthy of notice. Had the powerful movements for women's rights, gender equity, and sexual freedom initiated but a few decades ago receded this far, leaving only this simplistic and sadly familiar formulation of sex difference—an upscale, updated version of man at work and mother at home? To veteran feminists, this state of affairs is more than exasperating. It poses a painful conundrum: To call attention to "women's issues" too often serves to reinscribe categorical differences between men and women, even to risk regression to the most restrictive dictates of biology—that the female role in reproduction should determine the life course of half of humankind and assign responsibility for the care of the nation's children.

For more than thirty years American scholars have worked tenaciously to foster a critical understanding of the historical differentiation of women from men. It is disappointing, to say the least, to find that all that research and writing has not dislodged the oldest categorical and social boundaries between male and female or moved women closer to the center of American history. The title of this book invites the reader to look again and yet more closely at how male and female appear in the newspapers and the history books, but from a different angle of vision. It asks readers to put aside conventional assumptions about manhood and womanhood and undertake an exploration of the "mysteries of sex." The chapters to follow do not describe two straightforward and separate tracks of men and women through past time. Rather, they are a tour of the historical record that traces the mystifying process whereby the distinction between male and female is created, adapted, and repeatedly recreated over the course of U.S. history. To illustrate, the second chapter of this book will convert the premise of that *New York Times* article about Ivy League motherhood into an interrogation of the mysterious process whereby American popular culture became so obsessed with feminine domesticity in the first place. It asks, "Who Baked That Apple Pie and When?" and prompts an investigation of family history that commences in the English colonies during the seventeenth century.

The title *Mysteries of Sex* is not intended to be titillating. Quite the contrary, it is simply the most accurate label for the subject of this book. The words "sex" and "mystery" denote the two basic premises of this search through American history. First, after prolonged thrashing through feminist theory, I have come to recognize that the term "sex" best represents the starting point of my investigation. That three-letter word is the signal for the elaborate process of differentiating women and men that will be recounted in these pages. To the extent that the terms "male" and "female" have designated different paths through human history, they have been marked off by reference (however arbitrary or mistaken) to bodies, to those zones of anatomy, desire, and reproduction commonly called sex. Sex is what distinguishes the relation between men and women from other systems of social division and inequality (like race or class) and gives it unique depth, breadth, and power. The erotic aspect of my subject, properly designated by the term "sexuality," is only one, relatively minor and subordinate element in this overarching system of social differentiation. Yet sex is not an exact, stable, predictable, easily marked, and measured compartment of humanity. American history abounds with multiple, conflicting, ever-mutating meanings attributed to sex. Just how two polarized categories of being have been derived from all the infinite variations in human populations is the overarching and forever unsolved mystery in the history of women and men. The word "mystery" evokes the enigma, contradiction, unpredictability, and treachery that surround this process.

My title also evokes some more optimistic and even playful intentions. The word "mystery" is defined in my dictionary as "anything that arouses curiosity because it is unexplained, inexplicable, or secret." To investigate the history of a cultural distinction that was left unquestioned for so long, and yet is so fundamentally entangled with the whole fabric of our past, is to undertake an intellectual project that abounds with what Virginia Woolf called the "pleasure of disillusioning."[2] For all the seriousness of this enterprise, it is also sparked with something of the fun of a detective story. Tracking down the mysteries of sex, with their mesmerizing twists and turns and stubborn continuities, can be a hypnotic exercise. In the last, most optimistic analysis, this investigation hopes to see beyond the domain of sexual danger and "gender trouble" to some more pleasing mysteries. Entangled with the relentless mystifications of male and female that will be described in this volume reside those ineluctable joys that reside in our bodies, our sexuality, and the reproduction of our species. My title connotes not just the inequities and iniquities committed in the name of gender, but also these joyful possibilities that lurk amid the mysteries of sex.

Virginia Woolf was among the first to grasp the mystery that was sex. On the eve of the Second World War she saw a historical landscape scarred with the divide between male and female: "chalk marks, within whose mystic boundaries human beings are penned in, rigidly, separately, artificially." Speaking of what she saw as the masculine imagination that patrolled the boundaries of sex, she asked ominously, "Who shall analyze the complexity of a mind that holds so deep a reservoir of time within it?"[3] Thirty years later masses of American women and many men took up Woolf's question. The mysterious powers of sex differences became the object of public attention and feverish debate in the latter half of the twentieth century. The births of the generation to be called baby boomers had been announced with the confident proclamation: "it's a boy," or "it's a girl." But over the next generation, these verities, these seemingly obvious and universal assumptions about the division of humankind, were called into question, as well they should be. Why should the course of each human life be channeled at its very outset, without hesitation or questioning, along one of two different tracks through a lifetime? Did it not restrict the freedom and individuality of each child and create a border along which conflict and inequity might grow?

Signs of doubt about the division between male and female appeared on the banner of the women's liberation movement late in the 1960s, just as the baby boomers were coming of age. Within a decade, assertions of gender equality and sexual freedom displaced the old domestic tableau—mom and dad, boy and girl—from television shows and census reports alike. Some perspicacious observers were quick to grasp the challenge to the old order of male and female. In her novel of 1977, Angela Carter put readers through a harrowing set of sex changes that left her central character, "The New Eve," in a state of profound anomie: "Masculine and feminine are correlatives which involve one another. I am sure of that—the quality and its negation are locked in necessity. But what the nature of masculine and the nature of feminine might be, whether they involve male and female . . . that I do not know. Although I have been both man and woman, still I do not know the answer to these questions. Still they bewilder me. I have not reached the end of the maze yet."[4]

The mystery of sex captured many imaginations and tapped immense creativity in the time of the New Eve. Radical challenges to the fundamental cultural divide between male and female became almost commonplace. Spearheaded by a new women's movement, the break with the orthodoxy of sex created provocative works of fiction like the novels of Carter or Gore Vidal, iconoclastic theories about "female eunuchs" and the "dialectics of sex," proposals for test-tube babies and socialized child care, and such popular icons as cross-dressing rock stars and unisex fashions. These transfigurations of male and female were not just passing fads. A quarter century later they had evolved into a whole repertoire of bending and blending male and female identities—on stage, on the streets, and potentially, in the test tubes. Who, for example, would have anticipated this television transmission at the turn of the millennium? A female reporter in a business suit interviewed a celebrant of Gay Pride Day in San Francisco. This elegantly cross-dressed member of the Sisters of Perpetual Indulgence made no pretense of masquerading as the "opposite sex": in what seems to be a local fashion, he/she sported a full beard beneath his/her immaculate eye makeup and somewhat less fastidious hairdo. Such blasé expressions of the plasticity, artificiality, and ambiguity of sex challenged the simple assumptions of the past, like "it's a boy" or "it's a girl." Granted, the streets of San Francisco were not Main Street U.S.A., where past conventions of masculinity and femininity still found many zealous adherents and concerted political support. Yet the stridency of the reaction against challenges to the traditional divide between the sexes first heard in the 1970s indicates that the meaning of male and female has not reverted to the old orthodoxy. The glossary of sex has now expanded to include such neologisms as "transgender," "gender outlaws," "virtual gender," "non-gendered sex," and "cyber sex."[5]

Even the staid custodians of the national past became caught up in a new wave of feminist consciousness in the 1970s and created, almost overnight, a whole new field of study named Women's History. In the relative quiet and privilege of feminist meetings and university classrooms, we conducted a more genteel sex change: the personages of history were transformed from generic males into women and men. I consider it my great good fortune to have joined in the exhilarating consciousness of that moment in history. In 1972, my newly minted Ph.D. in hand, I contracted to write a book entitled "A Feminist History of the United States." This project was conceived in youthful audacity heightened by the heady political possibilities of that time: it presumed to piece together a coherent history out of some frantic primary research combined with the sparse, but rapidly growing, secondary studies of women's past. The resulting book, its title chastened to simply *Womanhood in America*, appeared in 1975. My project was relatively tame, and my goal was recited in academic prose:

> The aim of this volume is to describe the making of the social and cultural category, womanhood, the artificial mold into which history has persistently shaped the female sex. This investigation is inspired by the vexing question, what is woman? and is rooted in the belief that history has invested her with a distinctive personality that greatly exaggerates and consistently distorts her simple biological characteristics. An examination of the sundry definitions of woman that have paraded through the American past will expose the destructive impositions of culture and society upon the second sex, and thus clear away the refuse of mystique that has surrounded and suppressed the human female.[6]

Those intentions were at once too grandiose and too timid. To dare to write a history of women thirty years ago seemed like a leap onto a vacant frontier; it was in fact part of a mass landing of scholars and activists that conquered academic beachheads like the history profession with relatively little effective opposition. The knowledge about the female subjects of history that began to collect haphazardly twenty-five years ago has now mounted to impressive heights. Where teachers and students of the 1970s were angered and bewildered by the neglect of female subjects in history, today's readers will encounter a mass of information about women's lives in the past that is daunting in its volume, complexity, and respectability. Simply to update my first book, undertaken as a utopian project thirty years ago, would be a conservative exercise in the twenty-first century. Moreover, this body of historical writing is no longer contained within a field called Women's History. A generation ago, men were the generic subjects of most all history books. Now they have followed women into a heightened consciousness of sex: they have been named as male and invested with the attributes of masculinity. (There is still a lot of catching up to do on the male side of American historiography, however, which accounts for some of the imbalance in the chapters that follow.[7]) A new orthodoxy now spans across the humanities and the social sciences and acknowledges the artificiality and plasticity of the divide between the sexes with the ubiquitous use of the term "gender."

The widespread acceptance of the notion of gender is the punctuation point in a major historical transition; it marks the culmination of an intellectual adventure for my generation of historians and a major revision in the meaning of male and female for my students. What we vaguely recall as the "women's movement" of the late 1960s turns out to have only dimly prefigured extraordinary changes in how women and men, mothers and fathers, and students of both genders conduct their lives. Forty years ago housewife was still the modal occupation for the female sex, the learned professions of law and medicine were virtually male preserves, and the notion of gay marriage was unimaginable. Over the last three decades the inherited meanings of male and female have become the sites of pitched political battles and unrelenting change, especially for American women, who now enroll in the paid labor force in numbers almost equal to men and have broken sundry barriers of gender, in both private and public life, from levels of extramarital sexuality to candidacy for the presidency. After living this turbulent history, all the while trying to keep abreast of the voluminous scholarship in women's and gender studies, I feel compelled to try once again to bring the accumulated scholarship into focus with the intellectual and political needs of the present.

My first reflex was to update *Womanhood in America* by incorporating this rich recent literature and rename the book "Gender in America." I ultimately rejected this strategy and therefore must confess at the outset all the things that this book is not. First of all, this is not a textbook. It does not pretend to be a comprehensive recitation of the factual history of men and women in America. I have not set out on an impossible quest to represent the history of women (and/or men) in all its variations by region, religion, age, class, race, ethnicity, and so forth. Neither is this volume a historiographical exercise: It does not present and adjudicate the debates among historians about this vast subject. These projects are difficult and essential acts of scholarship, and thankfully, other historians have done much to accomplish them.[8] I am more deeply indebted to the many colleagues who have created the fields of women's and gender history than hundreds of footnotes can ever acknowledge. This book is a conversation with their ideas and interpretations; every page is dependent upon the prodigious research of others. The wealth and sophistication of this scholarship should place it at center stage in American historiography.

While I hope my readers will taste the excitement of this recent scholarship and sense the wide sweep of women's and gender history, this book is driven by some other intellectual and political imperatives. Thirty years after the publication of *Womanhood in America*, and despite the accumulation of mountains of knowledge about its subject matter, I find the phenomenon called gender more perplexing and mysterious than ever. Hence this book is animated by my own citizen's concern and historian's fascination about the "mysteries of sex." As the reader has already detected, I am not a disinterested party to this history and would not disguise my feminist intentions or suppress my idiosyncratic personal perspective. (You will also detect that I am both angry about the crimes committed in the name of gender and optimistic that the sexes can live happily together.) For me, the political and intellectual urgency of women's history as it emerged over thirty years ago has not subsided. The discoveries and discontents that first inspired what is now a rather sedate academic field have not been put to rest. Arbitrary gender differences are still extant and still exhaust a price of injustice and personal pain (for women and men and for the significant number of people who reject both categories). This is the first reason that I have chosen to pose the chapters to follow not as a cut-and-dried report on gender in American history, but as part of a continuous engagement with the mystifications of sex differentiation, past and present. The political vigilance about matters of sex and gender initiated by feminists in the 1960s and 1970s had clearly grown lax by the close of the twentieth century and was marginalized by the national and international crises of the twenty-first, but it is needed as much or more than ever.

The battle of the sexes still goes on in popular culture and is still too often conducted in the language of fairy tales and psychobabble (for example, the assertion that "Men are from Mars, Women are from Venus"). As late as 2005 the president of Harvard University publicly espoused a naive biological explanation for the underrepresentation of women among scientists, blatantly ignorant of the research of his own faculty, not to speak of the extraordinary influx of women into fields from physics to medicine and computer science. (In each of these fields the proportion of women doctorates has increased at least fivefold over the last thirty years. Among biologists the percentage of women increased to almost 44 percent.)[9] Clearly the knowledge of sex, gender, and women's history so painstakingly produced since the 1970s still needs to be consolidated and circulated. Until we learn to walk more cautiously and wisely through the minefield of masculinity and femininity, we will find it poisoning our public, as well as private, lives. If unexamined, or taken as the obvious rather than as a mystery needing an explanation, sex becomes a public menace. Witness its apparition in the 1990s as a piteous monstrosity that began as sex play in the White House and ended as a congressional impeachment trial, or the influence of opposition to same-sex marriage on the outcome of the presidential election of 2004.

American history is stocked full of the mischief done in the name of the division between the sexes. Some of the conundrums of gender difference are small puzzles, like why do Americans color the sexes pink or blue? The little anomalies mount to bigger questions: Why did modern western politics pay so much heed to a gendered distinction between public and private? Why do so many societies invest so heavily in patrolling and prescribing lifelong heterosexual pairings? Small or colossal, the mystifications of male and female have come together for millennia to create a tedious dualism out of the wealth of human possibilities. This is one of the most excruciating enigmas of maleness and femaleness. Its painful everyday consequences assaulted Jan Morris, who, taking advantage of modern medicine, changed her sex from male to female. During the period when Morris made the transition, she found it easy to step out of her male persona and into a female one, even within the few minutes it took to move from a venue where she was known as a man to where she was taken for a woman. But to her surprise, Jan Morris found that she could not evade the differences that gender made and the demotion that came with woman's status: "No aspect of existence, no moment of the day, no contact, no arrangement, no response, which is not different for men and for women. . . . Men treated me more and more as a junior. . . . and so, addressed every day of my life as an inferior, involuntarily, month by month I accepted the condition."[10] This report does not suggest that the time has come to stop questioning the mystifying process that divides male from female. Neither can the insistent and bruising ways that men and women are divided from one another be simply assuaged by recitations of the new orthodoxy: that gender is a fiction, ever in the process of reconstruction. In the twenty-first century, even after a generation of radical challenges to gender orthodoxy, history seems to be reverting to the tired, stubborn dualism of male and female. To me, it remains imperative to confront the difference of sex squarely, in all its mystery and its potency.

This peculiar point of entry into the history of women and men accounts for the slightly unorthodox structure and chronology of this book. Each of the chapters to follow subordinates conventional notions of historical period and subject matter to what I pose as key mysteries of sex, all arranged in a rough chronology that spans the sixteenth to the twenty-first centuries. Each chapter poses a mystery with at least two dimensions, both a puzzle of gender difference and an unresolved problem in American history. Chapter 1, for example, first uses the evidence of pre-Columbian Indian tribes to interrogate the mysterious historical tenacity, some say universality, of male dominance. Then, in pursuit of the question "Where Have the Corn Mothers Gone," it puts this history of gender in play in order to help explain the outcome of the collision between Amerindian cultures and European colonizers. Six more chapters follow, culminating in an account of the gender history of the last half century when the confluence of social movements, economic transformations, and massive immigration set the stage for the most momentous mystery of sex: whether gender differences can wither away or at least be reduced in significance and disarmed of inequity and oppression.

The investigations to follow are not comprehensive historical accounts. Rather, they make strategic and selective use of the evidence available in order to solve some specific mysteries of sex. In hopes of discovering the origins of feminine domesticity, for example, chapter 2 focuses on the rich body of evidence found in the early history of Protestant New England. In pursuit of the intersection of gender and race, chapter 3 narrows in on the southern United States and the history of African Americans. (Other groups who have been categorized as races, including eastern and southern Europeans, Asians, and Latin Americans, appear in a chapter on immigration.) A chapter devoted to "How Do You Get from Home to Work to Equity" in the twentieth century is constructed around census data that separates "white" from "nonwhite." Nonetheless, this record of expanding occupational opportunities reveals that differences in age and generation may be the chief suspects in this particular mystery. The young women who laid siege to the labor force early in the last century, among them Jewish garment workers, Greenwich Village bohemians, and blues singers in Harlem, did much to solve this mystery and did so in the vivacious spirit of their fictional peer, Nancy Drew, detective.

My course through this vast historical landscape has been guided by a few simple concepts, of which I will apprise the reader as expeditiously as possible. While I have relegated questions of epistemology to the background, this historical investigation does take off from academic understandings of gender, which at the simplest level recognize that "woman" and "man" are social and cultural constructions, bearing a complex, in no way causal, relation to biological sex.[11] The distinction between sex and gender is indispensable and will be used throughout this book. The term "sex" designates a biological classification of "male" and "female," while the concept of gender refers to the social and cultural process that distinguishes "men" from "women" in any historical moment.[12] But that is not the whole of it. For almost three decades academic feminists have subjected this first premise of gender analysis to systematic, intense, and sometimes hairsplitting scrutiny. Sex is no longer seen as a physical or genital bedrock of male and female on which the gender identities of men and women are founded. Sex itself is "always already" gendered; it is a categorical supposition that is itself embedded in

INTRODUCTION

a deeply gendered human culture. Feminist philosophers vest gender not in physiological difference but in immaterial, albeit powerful, processes like language, the unconscious, and the creation of meaning through quotidian action. Those feminist theorists who regard the differentiation of men from women as a consequence of practice or performance—"the tacit collective agreement to perform, produce, and sustain discrete and polar genders" in the words of Judith Butler—are particularly useful to historians who seek to place the thought and action of women and men at the center of past events.[13]

In step with the march of feminist theory, prosaic evidence continues to pour in describing the variety and vagaries of gender, much of it voiced by marginal social groups, especially racial and sexual minorities. Patterns of manhood and womanhood are too various, too perversely contradictory, to conform to a single, universal model. Finally, often prompted by awareness of differences in erotic practices and ambiguous sexual identities, the duality of gender came under suspicion. If womanhood and manhood were so weakly anchored in either philosophy or empirical evidence, why divide humanity so bluntly into two sexes in the first place? Why not speak of one, three, none, or an infinite number of genders? In rapid succession both rubrics for dividing up the human species, gender as well as sex, seemed to topple off their ontological foundations. On the simple level of taxonomy, the move from woman to gender was complete before 1980 and operated thereafter as a powerful skepticism, progressively undermining any attribution of universal meaning to the outcome of sexual differentiation, the labels male and female, the identities of men and women.

These epistemological nuances offer essential but insufficient guidance through the long, convoluted course of women and men through history. The notion of "doing gender" enunciated by Candace West, Don Zimmerman, and Sarah Fenstermaker provides the critical step onto the stage of social history. These sociologists plot the creation of men and women as a "routine, methodical, and recurring accomplishment" done by individuals "in one sense. . . . But it is a situated doing, carried out in the virtual or real presence of others."[14] Gender is something "one *does*, and does recurrently, in interaction with others."[15] Pierre Bourdieu put it in more punishing terms when he called the practice of gender an "unremitting discipline."[16] I illustrate this principle to my students with the crudest of examples: We do gender every time we read some abstract symbols on doorways and then divide up in two different lines at the restroom. In sum, sex has been thoroughly demystified in the realm of theory, reduced to an everyday social practice.

But once the suspect ontology of sex has been acknowledged and scruti-

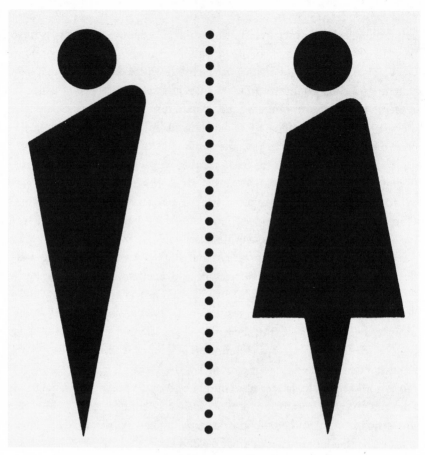

Restroom sign, Yerba Buena Center, San Francisco.

nized so exhaustively, the historian's task has hardly begun. However shaky the philosophical grounds, cultures persist in sorting out the complexity of humankind into two sexes. In defiance of both rigorous logic and the wonderful diversity of the human species, we repeatedly draw blunt lines to distinguish things male from things female. This book aggregates all sorts of these distinctions together, in their variety and perversity. In so doing, I do not intend to define what gender is, or is not, but to describe the immense amount of history that has been made in its name. This book, in other words, is not driven by a quest to know what is male or female, man or woman; it will not solve the mystery of sex. It asks instead, "What has that complicated and ever-recurring process of dividing humanity according to sex done in the world and over time?" Phrased another way, this book investigates some of those multifarious and mysterious historical deeds that produce the distinction called sex. As Howard Winant has aptly put it, gender, like race, "has a formidable inertia, a historical weight, which is crystallized in innumerable institutions, customs, and laws. It has been engraved in time and space, made into a truly 'deep structure.'"[17] Again, Pierre Bourdieu puts the mysterious and divisive power of sex most ominously: it is "exercised in very different scales, in all social spaces." It has "gone on permanently, so long as there have been men and women, and through which the masculine order has been continuously reproduced from age to age."[18]

Tracking down how sex differences operated just within the territory of the contemporary United States over the last half millennium is a preposterously tall order. After more than thirty years of trying to guide my students through the morass of trivial facts and universalistic pronouncements about men and women in history, I have found a few tools especially helpful in identifying those "deep structures" to which Winant refers. My first strategic simplification has been to sort the infinite details of everyday gender practice along three empirical coordinates—three axes along which gender operates and the sexes divide. Compiled from historical accounts and reworked according to the conceptual wisdom of social science, my operative categories of analysis are gender asymmetry, the relations of the sexes, and gender hierarchy.

The first of these, asymmetry, simply directs attention to how gender does its most familiar work, careening through society, dividing things male from things female, and creating two worlds of meaning that do not line up flush with one another. In Amerindian societies five hundred years ago, gender asymmetry was acted out by the women who planted corn while the men trapped beaver, and it is just as unmistakable along the aisles of a toy store today, where boys and girls part at the border between pink and fuchsia Barbie costumes and olive-drab plastic soldiers. My second axis of analysis focuses on the culturally sanctioned ways of relating the sexes to one another. Typified and idealized in most of American history as the nuclear family, the relations of the sexes are also easily discernible, but quite variable, from the matrifocal clans of Algonquians in the sixteenth century to the small, volatile household groupings that occupy their hunting grounds in suburban Virginia today. Tracing the third axis of gender, the hierarchical ranking of male and female, will take the reader along another meandering course, from sightings of tribal chiefs, some of them women, to a succession of forty-four male presidents of these United States. Gender hierarchy is visible on many vertical scales: it dispenses authority, honor, and material rewards in unequal portions; and up until now it has tended to cluster men at the top and women below.

While gender difference, in all three dimensions, seems remarkably stubborn over long stretches of time, the exact and specific meanings attributed to male and female are highly variable, or at least capable of running a considerable gamut, from the Indian women who first domesticated corn to the genetic engineers, more likely male, who design postmodern food products. This combination of the persistence of gender coding and the variability in actual practice presents the great conundrum of gender. It provokes an awestruck "why?" and requires that the story move beyond simple description to a world of action, of plot, of mysteries begging solution.

The description of gender is only deep background to a second objective of this book: to project the mystification and mystery of sex across time and into American history. The subjects of sex, gender, male, and female are latecomers to historical study and have seldom been subjected to the historian's battery of questions about sequence, causes, periodization, human motivation, and efficacy. Sexual differentiation is, however, clearly a historical process enacted in time and by men and women. As such, it is particularly amenable to recent social theories that employ terms like "structuration," "practice," or "habitus" to recognize human agency and acknowledge that society is ever in the making. In specific historical circumstances, men and women find ways to alter traditions, individualize institutions, and on occasion, especially when they act collectively, set social changes in motion. The anthropologist Sherry Ortner has theorized gender practice as a kind of "serious game." Like ordinary game-playing, the construction of male and female takes place in a universe of rules that clearly circumscribes and limits human freedom. But as players—active participants in the game—men and women can manipulate, stretch, and disobey the rules and occasionally exploit opportunities to change them. From the subaltern position in which women have most often played the serious game of gender, they are, as Ortner puts it, "constructed by their own culture and history and . . . in turn re-make their culture and history." Taking her cue from Marshall Sahlins's concept of historical conjuncture, Ortner also identifies a second plane of participation in the making of gender. In moments when a society and its gender culture become unstable—be it due to natural calamity, external forces, or an unprecedented convergence of events—the rules of the whole game, along with the authority that enforces the rules, can be toppled and replaced.[19]

Changes of this magnitude drive this investigation of the mysteries of sex through American history and inform the tripartite organization of this book. Coursing beneath the surface of the chapters that follow is a larger narrative of how sex has been made and unmade over the long haul of American history. The drama commences at a moment of historical conjuncture when one integral set of gender practices superseded another. This apocalyptic moment in gender history occurred when Europeans intruded into North America and introduced the changes that would unravel the intricate tribal cultures that Native Americans had finely stitched together around the roles of male warrior-hunters and female cultivator-gatherers. The wide arc of gender history that commenced from this point resulted in the construction of a modern gender regime distinctive to the United States and gives Part I its grandiose title and extended chronology, "Making Sex in America: 1500–1900." This story spans three chapters, ranges over New England and the slave South, crosses the centuries, and culminates in a particularly sharp and ideologically powerful distinction between male and female, man and woman. This way of dividing the world by sex, whose commonest emblems were "separate spheres" of feminine domesticity and male breadwinning, also made a durable mark on the American political tradition, the theme of Part II.

Consisting of only one chapter, Part II, entitled "Dividing the Public Realm," examines gender in the American political tradition between the Revolution and the New Deal and is a vital hinge of this book. First, it charts how the sharp divide between the sexes that had grown up in modern America was installed at the foundation of the American political tradition between the Revolution and the Civil War. Then it proceeds to show how the gender division between public and private life came apart at the seams of its internal contradictions. American political institutions were built along that modern divide between male and female, which turned out to be a precarious foundation. Denied entry into the formal public sphere, American women created a political domain of their own, a separate world of philanthropy and reform, which by the twentieth century had become powerful enough to undermine the sexual divide that had been the defining feature of modern American gender.

Part III extends through the whole of the twentieth century, as it describes the progressive coming apart of modern gender. By the year 2000 the border between male and female had become frayed on all sides, in the family, the workforce, the public sphere, and (with successive waves of immigrants) at the borders of the nation itself. Human agency comes to the foreground during this denouement of modern gender, acted out with special vigor by women, be they new entrants into the labor force or feminists at the barricades. The end of Part III finds the modern ways of differentiating male from female dethroned and demystified. Yet the contemporary arrangement of the sexes is still amorphous and defies any label more illuminating than the anemic term "postmodern." Just what might replace the old American way of doing gender remains a mystery, and hence a hope that in the future humanity will not be so egregiously divided by something called sex.

The historical meanings of gender are not exhausted once male and female have been named, mapped, and related to one another. As practice and as symbol, gender powerfully effects a wide set of other social, cultural, economic, and political processes—historical domains to which it would seem to have no intrinsic connection. This power of gender to influence events is repeatedly demonstrated in the pages that follow. For example, misunderstanding about the proper roles of men and women poisoned the first encounters between Europeans and American Indians and weighed heavily in the outcome; concerns specific to young single men late in the eighteenth century helped to propel a war of independence from Great Britain; relations in the bedroom and drawing room gave shape to the class differences of that historical period called "Victorian"; women's clubs drafted public policies that helped to sculpt the modern state in the Progressive Era. More generally, the distinction between male and female has served repeatedly as a way of marking the boundaries between social groups—tribes, regions, classes, races, and nations. Erotic relations (or prohibitions thereof) repeatedly serve as the symbolic and structural materials with which to erect cultural boundaries and draw tense lines between enemy and ally, belligerence and cooperation. Michel Foucault distilled this potent form of gender practice in an aphorism: "Sexuality is a major transfer point in the relations of power."[20] The most anguished social division in the history of the United States is found at the border between those groups that came to be known as races. The mystification of sex therefore will repeatedly be found haunting the history of race in America, from the origins of slavery to the constitution of citizenship. The difference of sex was complicit in all the archetypal events of American history, not just the celebrated high points like the Revolution and the Progressive Era, but also at moments of national shame such as the colonial witch hunts, the enslavement of Africans, and xenophobia against the foreign-born.

The last chapter of *Mysteries of Sex* reviews the subject of immigration from 1900 to the present. This book ends as it began, at a historical moment when different gender cultures converged on the North American continent. The most recent chapter in the global history of gender occurs at a time when the relations of men and women are being organized on an international scale and by a corporate culture that can distribute laboring families around the world and transmit cartoonlike images of male and female onto video

INTRODUCTION

screens far and wide. It is prudent to remain on the alert for new mystifications of male and female that may unfold in the twenty-first century. Yet it can also be argued that the restructuring of gender in our time has made the divide of sex less polarized and less salient than in any time in history. The volatility of the meaning of female and male over the last generation is what makes the consciousness of gender found in a book like this possible in the first place.

The repetitive pattern of gender differentiation to be described in the chapters to follow was shaped, enacted, and at times thwarted by ordinary men and women. Almost every one of the countless individuals who made American history accepted the identity of either male or female, but none of them lost their human agency in the process. The architects of gender history have many representatives in these pages. The Clan Mothers of the Seneca tribe shouted a refusal to surrender their native lands to either chiefs or Indian agents. Educated Victorian women—the spinster Catharine Beecher, the widowed Sarah Josepha Hale, the married Lydia Maria Child—devised a domestic ideology that provided them economic independence and political influence. A citizen of New York by the name of Murray Hall relished all the privileges of masculinity—exercising the vote, visiting the tavern, pursuing women—until he died of breast cancer in a woman's body. Tough-minded but care-taking leaders of the Progressive Era like Jane Addams issued some pointed reprimands to those who would dismantle the welfare state. Demands for racial justice made by Ida B. Wells in the 1890s echoed through a century of protest led by proud "colored women." Young immigrant voices—from authors like Anzia Yezierska and Abraham Cahan in the 1920s to anonymous undocumented workers and cosmopolitan novelists today—speak with many tongues and particular eloquence about the malleability, as well as the menace, of gender in America. Such polyphonic personal testimony also raises the possibility that, in time, the differences of sex might play out more sonorously, like the intrigue, excitement, and pleasure of a good mystery.

PART I

MAKING SEX IN AMERICA

1500–1900

CHAPTER I

WHERE HAVE THE
CORN MOTHERS GONE?

AMERICANS ENCOUNTER
THE EUROPEANS

In 1540 a party of Spaniards led by Hernando De Soto came upon a band of Indians in a place that is now called South Carolina. The European leader called for an audience with his local counterpart and set out "rest seats" for the headmen of the two peoples. The natives obliged, and soon a canopied boat appeared, bearing the leader of the nation of Catawba. The European explorers were startled to discover that the authoritative personage seated on that New World throne was a woman. She was designated in the colonial record as the "mistress of the town."[1] Just two years later and over three thousand miles away, emissaries of the Spanish Crown disembarked near Point Concepción in a land they would call Alta California. They were greeted and fêted by an elderly female chief of the Chumash tribe, said to command the loyalty of sixteen Indian villages. The tiny band of Iberian sailors may have been prepared for this reception for they had doubtless heard tell that the land mass to the west of North America was an island ruled by an Amazon queen named Calafia.[2] When Englishmen decamped along the Chesapeake nearly a century later, they conferred the title "queen" on the leaders of several Algonquian villages.[3]

Scraps of evidence such as these suggest that the first encounter of the peoples separated for millennia by the Atlantic Ocean was an epochal crossroads of gender. The encounter might even be imagined as a face-off between the dominant men of Europe against powerful women native to America. Scholarly prudence would dictate a retreat from such sensationalistic readings of the past, with a warning that such reports are scarce, partial, biased, and forever shrouded in mystery. Yet ethnohistorians, archaeologists, and Indian scholars have assiduously uncovered abundant evidence with which to demonstrate that the cultures native to America in the sixteenth century "did gender" in ways that would mystify European explorers. The first objective of this chapter is to describe how each axis of gender differentiation—asymmetry, the relations of the sexes, and hierarchy—was performed in myriad, unique ways across the wide landscape of North America five hundred years ago. Although not sufficient to create an exact and uniform model of primordial American gender, this fragmentary record is revealing enough to dispel the assumption that the differences between the sexes are timeless, predictable, and universal. The account of native gender practices that occupies the first half of this chapter will also serve as the background for a second investigation: how did mutual misunderstanding about the meaning of male and female affect the outcome of the confrontation between Europeans and American Indians? Not the least of these miscues concerned the distribution of power between the sexes: where Europeans saw kings and their subjects, Native Americans saw clan mothers and clan fathers. Though this chapter does not pretend to solve the quandaries of gender on the eve of European colonization, it will demonstrate that the differentiation of man from woman is a mystery of great consequence, something to wonder about and learn from as we strain to make sense of our history and our lives.

Just the first order of business is an impossibly tall one: to distill from the multiple and diverse cultures of pre-Columbian America some coherent representation of their highly complex and varied gender practices. Contrary to European imaginings of a virgin land inhabited by only a few brave young warriors and nubile Indian princesses, gender in America was a dense and wizened structure, acted out by as many as two thousand different language groups and up to eighteen million people. Together they put a human mark on virtually all the hunting and fishing grounds of North America. With roots in the hemisphere dating back twenty thousand years, *Homo sapiens* had a tumultuous if unwritten history in North America. Powerful civilizations, particularly in the Mississippi Valley and in the Southwest, had come and gone before the Europeans arrived on the scene. Tribes spread across much of the continent had been cultivating crops, especially maize, for some five thousand years.[4] Had De Soto arrived just a few centuries earlier, he might have come upon cities of up to thirty thousand residents in the lower midwest of the continent and discovered the mysteries of massive earthworks in animal shapes near the great rivers of the Mississippi Valley. Had the Spanish entourage arrived more promptly in the Southwest they might have wondered at vast systems of irrigation and high-rise dwelling units, which mounted several stories through a labyrinth of rooms.[5] But even in the year 1492, a wide

MAKING SEX IN AMERICA

range of civilizations and economies held tenacious claim to the American landscape.

Only a few blurry snapshots of this rich ethnohistory can be reproduced in this short chapter. Occasional reference will be made to the densest area of settlement, the small tribes of California, who lived in what seems like almost Edenic simplicity, camped along a web of creeks fed by the gentlest of climates and rich in easily accessible flora and fauna. There will also be occasional mention of tribes who worked out a more complex accommodation with a less generous nature. In the more hostile climates like the great midland of the north country, the Plains tribes such as the Blackfoot reshaped thousands of miles of the landscape by their expert techniques of hunting bison. Over a century after the Spanish arrival, the natives of New Mexico revolted and drove the conquistadores from their homelands, holding off full colonial domination until 1692.[6] The most intensive focus of attention in this chapter will be on tribes of the eastern part of the continent who had developed complex societies. Hundreds of years before Columbus set sail, American Indians had mastered the arts of domesticating plants and building sedentary cultures. Groups such as the Iroquois in the Northeast and another five Indian nations in the Southeast who would earn the name "Civilized Tribes" (the Creek, Cherokee, Seminole, Chickasaw, and Choctaw) boasted particularly elaborate trade networks and would develop extensive political systems—not quite states, but systems of political authority that the English translated into terms like "chiefdoms," "nations," "leagues," and "confederacies."

Before drawing a composite portrait of male and female in these multiple and intricate cultures, a fundamental question must be raised: Is gender always a salient aspect of human society, worthy of the intense scrutiny that is about to commence? When this question is posed for Native America in 1500, the answer is "yes," with only minor qualifications. It is indisputable that the humans who walked the American lands in the sixteenth century made important distinctions equivalent to the English categories, man and woman. Sex, however, may not have been the primary cultural differences among Native Americans. Age and kinship relations may have been preeminent in many native groups, just as noble and serf may have been more prominent distinctions among Europeans. It has been argued that some native groups, such as the Inuit of Alaska, saw gender as a rather fleeting distinction among humankind. For them, every living person was custodian of a soul that migrated across generations and could inhabit a male body at one time, a female's at another. This mutability of gender obviated the necessity of naming individuals according to male or female signs. Within the Algonquian languages, the dichotomy of male and female has been said to dissolve in the more powerful distinction between the animate and the inanimate. Both the weight and importance of gender difference, as well as the specific meanings attached to the male and female sides of that divide, varied markedly in 1500. Still, everywhere the distinction was recognized and acted upon. Gender dimorphism, however mysterious its ways, and whatever its rigidity or weight relative to other cultural differences, was clearly operative in pre-Columbian America. It made its power known in the discoveries of archaeologists, memories of descendants, and records of Europeans. By all these testimonies, a division between women and men was apparent in what native peoples did, where they went, and what they honored.[7]

Before proceeding to detail these gender productions, we must entertain one last preliminary question: How many genders were there, or as posed by some theorists, was there a third sex? North America was in fact quite hospitable to the species of gender versatility that went by such names as the man-woman, the manly woman, the woman warrior, and the *berdache* (a French term for cross-dressing Indians). By one estimate, Amerindian languages contain two hundred terms for alternative gender designations.[8] Especially in the Plains, the Southwest, and the Southeast, it was common to find a physiological male or female who adopted the attire, the work roles, and the ceremonial position of the opposite sex. It was most often the case that a male took on a woman's gender status, but sometimes females assumed the heroic status of "women warriors." The "manly-hearted woman" found in many Plains tribes has been described not as a deviant but as "one of several alternative roles" available to females, one that granted them such male privileges as the active role in choosing dance partners and the superior position in sexual intercourse.[9] Among the Algonquian the female who assumed a man's role acquired the chiefly status of the "sunksquaw."[10] The members of the third sex also commonly practiced what we now call homosexuality. By acknowledging a third or fourth gender, Amerindian cultures accepted and often honored those who lived in contradiction of conventional European definitions of sex difference.

Anthropologists have hypothesized that this flexibility within Native American cultures was due to the ease of lateral transfer between male and female roles, that is, their relative gender symmetry. The most fundamental characteristic of the man-woman or the woman warrior was the adoption of the work roles of the opposite sex. By this logic, a male who grew corn became a man-woman, for example, and the female who hunted was classified as a man. Because the third sex reversed rather than denied gender roles, however, this practice might have had the effect of underscoring the bipolar gender distinction to which it was a clearly marked exception.[11] Still, these variations on the theme of male and female present fascinating possibilities lurking in the mystery of sex. The Spanish translated the Indian term for the third sex in positive and pleasurable terms, simply as "*joyas*," meaning jewels.[12]

The Coordinates of Gender
Asymmetry, the Relations of the Sexes, and Hierarchy

Such jewels were set, nonetheless, in a solid and prosaic chain of gender dualism. The most fundamental divide between the sexes was written with the sweat on the brows of women and men. The fact that gender served as a rubric for dividing up the work of subsistence was so obvious that it can be described with but a few examples. Gender was ascribed to Native American infants at the very moment of birth, when a newborn male was presented with the tools of the hunt and a female child was given the implements of both gathering and planting. The Plateau tribe of the Northwest celebrated a boy's first catch of salmon and his sister's first harvest of berries. The skeletons of ancient Plainsmen were buried beside their bows, and matrons with their weaving tools. Among the Pueblo of the Southwest, males who performed cooking chores were ridiculed as women, the same epithet that was hurled at gender reversals among Huron warriors.[13] To picture the sexual division of labor in the Americas requires a depth of field that can take in the fine detail that separates the tasks of men and women and then brings them together on the same landscape of survival. In the Northwest men caught the salmon, but the women helped construct the weirs. In most horticultural tribes women may have planted, but men cleared the land and helped prepare the fields for planting. In many tribes men hunted large game, and women small.[14] Still, one slash of contrast overshadowed all these shades and mutings of the sexual division of native labor: that of man, the hunter and warrior, and woman, the gatherer and planter. The Cherokee origin myth spoke for many other cultures when it paired a first man, called Kana'ti, with a first woman named Selu. Kana'ti held the secret of providing meat from game, which he hid in a hole in the earth, and Selu produced the corn by rubbing her armpits and belly. Among their descendants men wielded the bow and women the hoe, but only together could they support the human clan. Both sexes shared a world of work; both produced subsistence goods; and no one, most certainly not women, was excused from making a hefty contribution to the material survival of the tribe.[15]

Should one want to draw an invidious distinction between male and female providers, we would have to call woman the worker and man the lord of leisure. This was in fact the recurrent complaint that European observers made about the Indian division of labor. An early English observer sighting the Amerindian farmers in the vicinity of Jamestown noted that women performed all the labor save hunting. A report similar to this English account of the mores of the Dakota might be found in almost every European American archive of Indian lore: "The men hunt a little in summer, go to war, kill an enemy, dance, lounge, sleep and smoke. The women do everything—nurse, chop wood, carry it on their back for half to a whole mile; hoe the ground for planting, plant, hoe the corn, gather wild fruit, carry the lodge, and in winter cut and carry the poles to pitch it with . . . and the men often sit and look on."[16] The familiar slander against the Indian "squaw," connoting a slavelike drudge, speaks more of the Englishman's own gender expectations than of Indian practices. The research techniques of these amateur anthropologists can also be faulted. For example, the observer cited above seems to have missed the seasonal bias of his evidence: had he visited the Dakota in winter, he might find the men on a grueling hunt and the women in relative leisure. But even these tainted observations offer important clues for solving the gender puzzles of Native America. The men of the tribe often concurred in this assessment of women's value. A Chippewa chief was quoted as saying, "women were made for labor. One of them can carry or haul as much as two men can."[17]

Regardless of invidious distinctions, be they drawn in contrast to native men or European ladies, the term "squaw" signified woman's critical contribution to the sustenance of Native America. As the cultivators and gatherers of vegetables, women provided the major sources of calories. Among Algonquians, they supplied the staple of the Indian diet, the corn that purportedly accounted for 75 percent of the tribe's nutrients.[18] Women farmers have been credited with one of the greatest inventions of human history, the domestication of plant life, which occurred in the Americas some five thousand years ago. Among the Cherokee, women added squash and beans to the local diet. Even allowing for the higher protein value of the large prey captured by hunters and fishermen, women's contribution to the native diet has been estimated as three times that of the men's. Be it Woman the Gatherer, represented by the Costanoan acorn harvester of Northern California, or Woman the Farmer, whose planting grounds nearly spanned the continent, females provided a substantial, essential, and justly recognized part of native sustenance.

Much of the meaning of gender difference was grounded in these economic imperatives, which determined not just what women and men did but where they did it. On any given day in the life of pre-Columbian Indians, women's work was likely to take them to the fields or forests, while men ventured off to the hunting or fishing grounds. The separation of male and female workers might last far longer than a day. Among the tribes who hunted large animals, like the bison, or followed the migrations of fish and game, men could be away for weeks, months, and whole seasons. Similarly, the women who cultivated corn were obliged to protect their fields from preying birds and would spend many of their summer days out in the fields in one another's company. This division of space and labor was conducive to gender solidarity and cooperation. The pleasures of the cornfield provoked the English captive Mary Jemison to extol the satisfaction, not the drudgery, of work among Indian matrons "with no master over us."[19]

All of this is to say that the differentiation of male and female divided up space as well as work. Among hunters of large game in the Great Plains, like the Hidatsa tribe, women and men seldom inhabited the same places. Tribes like the Navajo in the Southwest carried out their different tasks at different cardinal points of the compass: women's activities and women's property were consigned to the north; men orbited to the southern portion of the family compound. In tribe after tribe, the institutions of the sweathouse or the menstrual hut marked out the difference of male and female as spatial asymmetry. In the Southwest the center of the village was blocked off as a sacred space, to which men and boys gravitated for social engagement, and for sleep as well as for ceremony.[20] Among the Zuni, husbands were forbidden to even enter the storerooms of their wives.[21] The *temescal*, the Costanoan sweathouse, was, like the round house and council houses of other tribes, largely a man's space, but one where women sometimes assembled, alone or in the company of men.[22] Gender segregation extended through time as well as space. The separate identities of male and female were grounded in geography at the moment of birth, when the umbilical cord of a boy was buried outside his mother's hut and his sister's was planted near the maternal hearth. Up through the 1930s, the Seminole in Florida sent boys and girls their separate ways, off each day to toil beside fathers and mothers respectively, returning to a common hearth only at nightfall.[23] The contents of ancient gravesites scattered across North and Central America also clustered into separate gender sectors. The segregation of the sexes was never perfect, neither exact in any one culture nor characteristic of all tribes. It was sufficiently prominent, however, to imprint clear distinctions between male and female on the landscape of North America.

Was this division of space, like that of labor, just a curiosity in the museum of gender trivia? Or might it have had more consequence for those who occupied the continent before Columbus? Could gender asymmetry affect the relative physical and spiritual well-being of individuals, the quality of relations between men and women, and the equanimity of the social system? By the first standard there is abundant evidence that both the female farmer and the male hunter found abundant pride in their separate accomplishments. The material evidence speaks quietly but strongly through sacred symbols of both sexes, like the corn fetish given the girl child or flint arrows awarded to boys. Archaeologists have found poignant testimony to the value and self-esteem of women's work in the graves of the Dakota. Color-coded dots and other markings on the awls of seamstresses express the sense of accomplishment associated with each hide tanned, moccasin stitched, and tipi constructed.[24] The satisfaction of cultivating plant life so as to produce human sustenance lay heavy on the memories of Indians like Buffalo Bird Woman, an aged Dakota who recalled in 1913 how "we cared for our corn in those days, as we would care for a child; for we Indians loved our fields as mothers love their children." The California tribe's men, who well into the twentieth century were still lovingly reconstructing the council chambers and performing the dances of their forefathers, bespoke the same quiet pride of workmanship.[25]

If Native American men and women had cause to speak in a proprietary way of the tribal lands or any material goods, they would in most cases be making a gender claim. The tools and the final products of male and female labor usually remained in the hands of the sex who used and created them. The animal flesh and hides were commonly distributed by the men who hunted them, and conversely, the vegetables cultivated by women would remain in the crib or household store owned by the mother's clan.[26] Because the products wrested from nature, either by man or woman, were rarely sufficient to create a large surplus, neither gender was apt to accumulate much personal wealth. When the produce exceeded household need, both women and men bartered their wares in a relatively small trading circuit. In the less productive horticultural societies, the houses that women designed and the lands they cultivated would be abandoned for more fertile fields in a decade, if not a season. Neither men nor women could acquire sufficient material wealth to serve as durable status symbols or substantial surplus. But still, this stake in the material world brought a sense of self-worth and satisfaction, even a sense of entitlement. The sagacity of Indian chiefs in bargaining and fighting to control their hunting grounds is legendary, as was the loyalty of matrons to their lands. When, for example, Seneca matrons were confronted with the prospect that their ancestral land would be ceded to Europeans, they had no trouble grasping the vocabulary of ownership. They stepped forward and announced that "your mothers and sisters ask and beg of you not to part with any more of our lands."[27] Long before the intrusion of Europeans, the tribes of North America competed with one another to control their contiguous plots of earth and fields of game. As a consequence, women knew how to barter and men how to fight with neighboring tribes for what they claimed as the land of their mothers.

Male and female roles, no matter how clearly distinguished from one another, were not autonomous: they were integrally related to one another in a system of kinship. The preponderance of Native American tribal cultures traced descent and transferred resources through a female line. With the notable exception of some pastoral tribes in the Southwest and Great Plains, most Amerindian tribes were matrilineages. Others have been described more ambiguously, like one categorization of the Algonquian as a highly modified "patrilineage."[28] The most august and expansive Indian nations, the Iroquois and the Five Civilized Tribes of the Southeast, vested title to goods, names, households, and offices in the descendants of a common mother. Complex lines of clan and kin mapped out the primary rubric of social life in North America and formed a critical plane of gender construction. Above all, lineages sorted human beings into social relations that distributed rank and power differentially to men and women, fathers and mothers, husbands and wives, sons and daughters, brothers and sisters, aunts and uncles.

In a good number of cultures, the place of residence was also determined by maternal lines of descent. For example, all five of those sophisticated and prosperous Indian nations of the Southeast, the Chickasaw, Cherokee, Creek, Seminole, and Choctaw, as well as their northern rival in political and economic sophistication, the Iroquois, sent a newlywed groom off to live with his in-laws and labor for the bride's family. As late as the 1930s the sons who married into the farming households of the Florida Seminoles still honored the matrilineage. Seminole husbands recalled that matrilocal residency provided their gender not with a "home" but only a "dwelling place."[29] Taken together, the gender practices denoted by the kinship terms "matrilineage" and "matrilocality" created a dense nexus of sociability that clustered around the consanguineous relations of a woman, her children, brothers, and sisters.

The hub and heart of a culture converged in the mother's compound. But the extent and consequences of this gender geography did not end there. These North American societies built their distinctive civilization around women's roles and women's spaces, their cultivation of plant life, their sedentary villages and towns, the crossroads of human congress and creativity. When, as in the case of the Iroquois, the matrilineage grew prosperous, politically complex, and territorially expansive, a proud civilization formed around a matrifocal core. The Iroquois took their name from the "longhouse," a distinctive American architecture that was designed and built by women and housed the multiple families who traced their ancestry through a common mother. When the "five nations" formed themselves into a "league" at the turn of the seventeenth century, their longhouse extended metaphorically all the way from the Hudson River to Lake Ontario.[30]

To trace ancestry through females is, of course, not to create a gynocracy. Brothers and sons were members of the longhouse, and some of them were societal leaders as well. The matrilineage does, however, give a distinctive shape to the social relations of the sexes. The clan structure decreed that intergenerational ties between mothers and their descendants overshadowed the bonds between husband and wife. Among most native tribes the marital unit (around which modern kinship systems reputedly orbit) was secondary to relationships around a common mother. The matrilineage reinforced a spatial order that had already separated the Indian villages into women's fields and male hunting grounds and further displaced the married couple from the social center. Heterosexual coupling remained essential to reproductive and sexual relations, of course, but copulation did not always require co-residence and quotidian proximity. Among the Southwest tribes, for example, it was common for men and boys to use the kiva as their common sleeping quarters. To the north, the men and women of the Plateau lived completely apart for large portions of the year, as they tended their separate duties in salmon streams or forests in the exclusive company of the same sex.

The relative autonomy of men and women extended even to their sexual relations. Easy divorce, initiated by wives as well as husbands, was a common practice in Amerindian tribes. Sexual relations prior to marriage were also routine. European accounts of lascivious women (like the Jesuits' observation that Huron women took ten to fifteen lovers) can be dismissed as products of the overwrought imagination of missionaries and celibate soldiers, but it is just as unlikely that the sexual practices of Native Americans conformed to Christian standards of lifelong monogamy and extended periods of sexual abstinence. Even those tribes that were most repressive did not proscribe absolute monogamy. Among the unusually misogynist Muskogee of Georgia and Alabama, promiscuity could bring draconian consequences, including a piteous beating with switches and the severing of hair and ear, yet only for wives and their adulterous partners, not unfaithful husbands. Among the Chipewyan of the Northwest, the sacredness of conjugal relations was honored by the sport of wrestling: to the victor went his opponent's wife.[31] Even in instances where husbands dealt so harshly with their wives, women had the option of relatively simple divorce from an abusive mate. The general tolerance of adultery (at least among men), as well as premarital sex and easy divorce, loosened the conjugal bond for men and women alike. The laxness of the conjugal bond contrasted with the strength of same-sex ties in the fields and on the hunt. The sexes were intently related one to the other, but the conjugal pair was neither the solitary nor the sacrosanct social bond.

The marriage bond was thus but one link in an extended system of families and clans that constituted a society. At the point of marriage it was not the transmission of conjugal affection but a clanwide exchange of progeny and property that was critical. Or to put it more prosaically, while a young man of the hunting party and the young woman of cornfield might crave one another's intimate companionship, the concerns of their maternal kin for an exchange of labor and resources took precedence. Marriage into a matrilineal clan brought a needed hunter or fisherman and another set of arms to clear the forest into the bride's clan. An exchange of goods, more often a bride price than a dowry, sealed and balanced the bargain. Among the Choctaw the bride's family brought corn to the wedding feast, while the groom's kin brought an offering of meat. In most tribes the exchange of labor and property was arranged by kinsmen and women, chiefly mothers and maternal uncles, who were careful to guard the resources of the clan. Because marriage was also an opportunity to augment a clan's labor force, more than one wife was sometimes included in the transaction. Those hunting cultures that required intense female labor to process hides were particularly apt to practice polygamy or, as in the case of the Cherokees, wed one man to two sisters.[32]

Outside the clan and between hostile tribes, the relations of the sexes became more complicated and sometimes sinister. Neighboring tribes often greeted one another with a sexual exchange that was sometimes a general bacchanalia, but more often the barter of women's bodies. During hostile encounters, sexual tribute was sometimes taken in the form of rape. When an opponent was vanquished, the gender currency of intertribal exchanges took yet another form. Among both the Huron in the North and the Choctaw in the South, the matrons would decide the fate of those captured in warfare, anything from adoption to intermarriage to torture or genital mutilation. Most captives were absorbed into the victorious tribe by intermarriage or adoption into the matrilineage. Either way, the traffic in women and men marked the borders between clans and tribes. They were the rubric of societal separation and exchange. Within this system, the sexual relations between individual males and females mapped out critical and potentially perilous social boundaries. They required careful management. Perhaps this is why Native American tribes often restricted sexual congress at critical times. Before battle, warriors commonly observed menstrual taboos and sometimes abstained from all sexual intercourse, wary that a loss of semen might diminish martial powers. Sexual abstinence was also prescribed at the outsets of major ceremonies, hunts, and life passages.[33]

The two axes of gender differentiation examined thus far—both the relations of the sexes and gender asymmetry—indicate that Native American cultures provide a clear contrast with the conventions of the modern West. They arranged gender asymmetry so as to make woman, and not man, the preeminent farmer; they elevated the matrilineal over the conjugal relation as the pivotal social bond. In this context, the third axis of gender—hierarchy—assumes major analytic importance. In fact, case studies from Native America have supplied powerful ammunition for those who would dispute the premise of women's studies a generation ago, that male dominance was universal. Although no one has yet delivered a knockout punch against the old orthodoxy, the issue has been defused by prudent reconsiderations of the records of American aborigines. Accounts of Native American gender history do not bristle with terms like "male dominance," "the oppression of women," and "patriarchy." Quite to the contrary, they are seasoned with compromising phrases like "balanced reciprocity," "complementary but equal," and "asymmetric equality."[34]

The conclusions drawn from recent case studies are temperate in tone and open to egalitarian possibilities. Some make blunt contentions: "the genders were socially and economically equal."[35] Others are more cautious and intricate in their assessment: "By no means equal to men, whose political and religious decisions directed village life, Indian women were perhaps more powerful in their subordination than English women."[36] These more careful phrases and prudent assessments befit the seriousness of this mystery of gender: Has sex difference always been, must it ever be, a system of ranking in which men are dominant? Although the ethnographic record does not speak in modern Western measures of authority and subordination, and will remain mute if we insist on translating it directly into contemporary standards of justice and equality, it still speaks powerfully to this critical issue in the history of gender.[37] As a set of prescribed social differences, gender always has the potential to distribute human goods in unbalanced and arbitrary ways. The things of value that might fall unequally to the male or the female side of the ledger would include material resources, personal dignity, social esteem, freedom of mind and body, and societal power. The last critical value—power—is a particularly fine-textured concept. It can operate through informal influence or formal authority, and it is exercised in the creation of cultural value, in the distribution of material resources, and in making decisions that affect the whole society—a kind of power that warrants the term "political." In pre-Columbian America, gender made a difference in the distribution of all these goods.

First of all, a few ingenious archaeologists and demographers have unearthed evidence that some tribes, like the Creeks, may have dealt out basic material sustenance unequally: the sex ratios and age structure of these tribes provide material evidence of female infanticide and poorer diets among women.[38] Elsewhere, men and women seemed to share more equally in material bounty. Among the quite prosperous salmon economies of the Northwest, for example, the more fortunate women, as well as men, accumulated sufficient surplus to win the esteem of their fellows by lavish displays of generosity, the potlatches.[39] In another prosperous Indian nation, the Cherokee of the Southeast, women also had the resources to participate in the annual reconciliation ceremonies, wherein they abandoned their earthly goods to the gods of the river.[40] Arguing from social practices such as this, one anthropologist maintains that even those Native American societies that were stratified by wealth were not marked by inequities based on gender. When wealth was aggrandized by some elite families or clans, it was shared by kinsmen and kinswomen alike. In the less stratified societies so prominent in the New World, resources were either immediately consumed or, as in the case of land and tools, put under the control of those who used them to the benefit of the family, clan, and posterity. All in all, the chances of severe maldistribution of material goods were relatively slight among Native Americans.

If stocks of material goods were too small to permit extreme inequality, American native cultures were still rich in immaterial resources that could convey spiritual value in unbalanced ways. Museum-loads of objects celebrating the sexual endowments of males and females indicate that femininity, as well as masculinity, was valued. Fetish objects honored the virtues of both sexes. Among the Algonquian, for example, the red dye called *pocones* was used to mark the value and vibrancy of both male and female cultural performances: men used it as war paint, and women wore it during sexual rites.[41] The southwestern tribes looked out on the natural landscape and saw symbols of the power and majesty of male and female alike. They named natural monuments and the curvature of the earth after female anatomy, "Breast, Vagina, and Clitoris Spring."[42] The built environment of pre-Columbian America offers further clues to Native American gender culture. Most tribes built for men and for women: round houses and longhouses, sweathouses and menstrual huts. Women's withdrawal to these cloisters during menstruation was not necessarily the shameful exile of a sex deemed unclean. Some archaeologists maintain that the menstrual hut was a temple of femininity, a place that did as much honor to the female sex as the sweathouse provided for men.[43] More direct Native American testimony supports this interpretation. Among the Algonquian the huts used by menstruating women held such positive associations that the English translated their name as "gynaeceum."[44] Among the southwestern tribes, the monthly sojourn in this exclusive female space was a time of welcome leisure, which included such pampering as the delivery of prepared meals. The female reproductive cycle was honored in architecture, in quotidian practices, and of course, in legend. One Shawnee myth made a woman a superheroine who rescued a young man from a serpent's attack by a wave of her menstrual cloth. Cherokee heroines were not as potent: it took seven menstruating women to mortally wound a villain by the name of Ironclad.[45]

The tales of Indian braves that saturate popular culture testify to the heroic masculinity of native men. A contrary example is also worth mentioning. Certain Blackfoot stories feature a character who "personifies foolishness in human nature." Always a man, seldom accompanied by a woman, and named Napi, he is "impulsive, naive, lustful, scheming, . . . primordial man."[46] Chumash women in California were known to ridicule the sexual prowess of men.[47] As with all anecdotal evidence, such tales can be countered with their opposites. It was common practice for Indian warriors to shame those who were cowardly in battle with the simple epithet "woman." All told, there seems to be a certain reciprocity in the insults hurled across the divide between the sexes. The songs of Seneca girls displayed no great awe of the masculine: "you bad boys, you are all alike! Your bow is like a bent basket hoop."[48]

The rough parity of the distribution of vices and virtues to the two sexes can be tabulated in many ways, but doubtless a major reason for this relatively balanced ledger sheet is the fact that each gender had an equal chance to praise or insult the other. Positions of control over cultural production were allotted to both men and women, in roughly equal numbers. In tribe after tribe, both men and women served as the shaman and the medicine "man." In those tribes where a vivid imagination was a precious spiritual power, women and men had the gift of dreaming and reading dreams.[49] This is not to say that the goddess or the priestess reigned in solitary splendor over the Indian belief systems but rather that women shared cultural power with males. In fact, Native American cultures often honored holy couples. For example, the Blackfoot of the Plains recognized both Holy Man and Holy Woman. The Navajo of the Southwest acknowledged a host of Holy People, including Spider Woman, Earth Woman, Salt Woman, and Water Woman. The maize culture of the Americas did not forsake the goddess of the Neolithic revolution but honored Corn Mother with an annual celebration and a harvest feast. In the Southeast the female deity was a trinity: goddesses of squash, bean, and corn. And the greatest of these was the Corn Mother, celebrated with the highest ritual, the Green Corn Ceremony. On the cultural as much as the economic plane, in sum, there is enough evidence to support at least the hypothesis that parity—not hierarchy—set the initial American standard of ranking male and female.[50]

Anthropologists have come to recognize that the concepts of neither patriarchy nor matriarchy describe the gender systems of Amerindian tribes before Columbus. Some have argued that it was theoretically possible, especially in cultures with strong patterns of gender separation, for both men and women to hold to the superiority of their own sex. This hypothesis seems to fit the empirical evidence for any number of American tribes where men and women developed their own separate scales of honor and reward. Women found solidarity and esteem in the fields, men on the hunt; women drew spiritual strength from the Corn Mother, men from their war gods.[51] More recently, anthropologists have offered a variation on this separate but egalitarian hypothesis. The concept of reciprocity or complementarity offers a way of navigating across the border between the cultures of women and men without sacrificing the esteem and stature that each gender found in his or her separate roles and relations. The reciprocity between the female and male worlds operated on many levels, some of them very pragmatic. Since women had need of such things as the high protein value of men's game, their muscle power in preparing the fields, and their military skills to defend the land, an exchange was very much in women's interest. Men obliged in order to secure such essentials as women's skill in processing meats, fish, and hides and in providing a regular diet of plant food at the close of the hunting season. Obviously, reproduction, as well as production, required some communication between male and female and held the added benefit of bodily pleasures.

Reciprocity was not just self-interest; it was essential to survival in cultures that had endured for hundreds, even thousands of years, just on the margin of subsistence.[52]

This reciprocity hypothesis is not just in the minds of historical ethnologists but also appears in the legends of Native Americans themselves. The exchange between man the hunter and woman the gatherer is enacted in the mythology of California's Pomo tribe by the male founding figure, Coyote, and the female, Wood-Duck. Neither mythic character could reproduce and sustain human life until they bridged the gap between gender cultures. According to the legend, the first attempt to found the tribe was botched when the Wood-Duck sisters were contemptuous of Coyote's inept seduction. A second attempt to inaugurate Pomo civilization made the female figure of Wood-Duck the captain of the village, but only after she ceded ultimate authority to Hawk, as "we should have one head captain to govern us all."[53] Recounting the creation of the southwestern tribes also required a complex plot and a large cast of male and female characters: brothers, sisters, twins, and couples—be they animals, humans, or deities—whose cooperation was required to fructify the arid soil. These stories of gender reciprocity featured rain gods and corn mothers and recounted the origins of places like Acoma, New Mexico, the longest continuous settlement in the United States.[54]

The hundreds of cultures that claimed the continent at the time of European settlement had worked out similar gender alliances. Even a bewildered European like the Jesuit Paul Le Jeune who came upon the scene in 1632 could discern the gender reciprocity. Of the Montagnais tribe he wrote, "the women know what they are to do, and the men also; and one never meddles with the work of the other. The men make the frames of their canoes, and the women sew the bark with willow withes or similar wood. The men shape the wood of the raguettes [snowshoes], and the women do the sewing on them. Men go hunting, and kill the animals; and the women go after them, skin them, and clean the hides." Le Jeune went on to explain this everyday practice of reciprocating asymmetry not with a native myth but with a European calculation: "to live without a wife is to live without help, without home, and to be always wandering."[55]

One might argue that reciprocity trumped hierarchy in terms of politics as well as economics. In some tribes at least, chiefs shared the political stage with female leaders, and women, as well as men, raised their voices to argue about matters of war, peace, and patrimony. Among the Iroquois, where French missionaries spotted "female captainesses," anthropologists have located one of the strongest concentrations of female political power.[56] Else-

MAKING SEX IN AMERICA

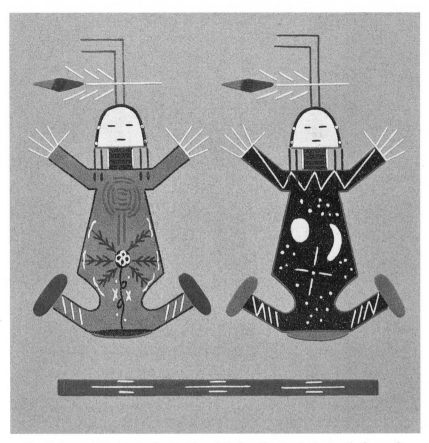

John L. Begay (Navajo), *Mother Earth and Father Sky*. Sandpainting, before 1980. (Courtesy of the National Museum of the American Indian, Smithsonian Institution [photo number 262195.00]; photo by NMAI Photo Services Staff)

where, it was not uncommon to find pairs of leaders at the helm of Native American societies. The Plateau people of the Northwest, for example, recognized male and female leadership in the personages of a salmon chief and a gathering leader, respectively.[57] The Navajo allocated decision-making power to a clan-woman and a clan-man. Their sandpaintings place the symmetrical shapes of Father Sky and Mother Earth side by side on the same plane. Similarly, the Hopi had a Clan Mother and a Clan Uncle.[58] The Blackfoot set up sodalities of every age group, each with a male and female hierarchy.[59] As late as 1830 a treaty between U.S. commissioners and the Choctaw was negotiated before a circle of seven women surrounded by sixty male councilmen.[60]

Studies of the extremely complex political order among the Iroquois tribes mark out separate political venues by sex, which gave women a jurisdiction over the village council, while men held sway over the larger tribal government. In times of crisis, these separate spheres of government operated in tandem. The Iroquois chiefs could not take to the warpath without consulting with the matrons of the tribe, who would also make decisions about the fate of any captives at the termination of battle.[61] The sexual division of labor most common in pre-Columbian North America made the segmentation of authority supremely practical: decisions about where to hunt might best be left to the hunters; the site for a garden would be a matron's choice. When the exhaustion of the soil warranted moving to fresh fields, women might make the critical decision to move the entire village. Evidence of this sort is voluminous enough to deduce that the Native American political system was a diffuse field of power in which women as well as men found stature and influence. As most of these small societies made decisions in informal local spaces, around campfires, in longhouses, round houses, and kivas, political institutions were porous structures in which both sexes and many people could participate. Practical consensus did not require specification of the gender of authority figures. In tribe after tribe, even when leadership was juridically given over to men, women were active and vocal in decision making.

But still, a shrewd gender detective will not give up the search for male supremacy too quickly. The first generation of gender anthropologists was especially astute at excavating a bedrock of male authority beneath the fine latticework of reciprocity and cooperation. In the classic formulation of Michelle Zimbalist Rosaldo and Louise Lamphere, the spatial divide between public and private was also a political ranking: it ceded formidable but informal influence to women, but the source of ultimate and overriding authority was exercised in public and by men.[62] More recently, feminist theorists have redrawn the lines of stratification between male and female in subtler ways, acknowledging that in any society power is diffuse rather than concentrated in one place, personage, or gender. Men may enjoy superiority in one sector, women in another, and absolute, totalizing domination is awarded to no one sex. Still, as Sherry Ortner and Harriet Whitehead have argued, most cultures subscribe to some overarching system of value and authority that hovers above and extends beyond the purview of separate groups or segments of society. Ortner went on to argue that this ultimate level of prestige is consistently marked off by gender. In some, and probably most, known societies, men occupy this ultimate site of political power. In other cultures males and females exercise authority jointly, relatively equally or each in their own domain. But neither ethnographers nor historians have yet discovered a society in which women monopolize political authority to the extent that men often do. In Ortner's terms, female authority is never the hegemonic form of political organization.[63]

Within this more refined, expressly political form of gender hierarchy, American corn mothers occupy an auspicious position. Their stature was not lofty enough to designate pre-Columbian America as a time and place where female authority was hegemonic. Yet at the same time, male power was never all-encompassing, and if politically hegemonic, only by a small margin. On the cross-cultural spectrum of gender hierarchy, therefore, the corn mother may have ranked among the most powerful of her sex. Based on our limited and contaminated knowledge of pre-Columbian America, we can only conclude that, compared with more modern societies, Native American gender practices leveled the gender hierarchy considerably and distributed power rather evenhandedly. If we pushed the evidence to the limit, however, it is difficult to completely erase the power differential between men and women. For example, the lack of evidence that the term "male" became the cause for ridicule among women, as the term "female" occupied in male discourse, would indicate that men had somewhat greater cultural leverage. The fact that women did not seem to conduct a trade in male sex partners is another indication that male prestige was marginally hegemonic if not absolute in Amerindian cultures. Within institutions of governing power, the scope of male authority is also clear, if relatively narrow. An occasional Indian legend, like the Pomo origin story reported above, acknowledges this complexly muted gender hierarchy: a rough balance of influence in male and female spheres combined with an ultimate and instrumental deference to men. Similarly, the Navajo charted their system of gender power as a pragmatic arrangement: the first woman and the first man argued so furiously over who was the head that the two sexes separated. They did not come together again until women agreed to abdicate the very highest, ultimately decisive levels of leadership to men.[64]

To put it in the negative, this search through pre-Columbian America has not located an ancient matriarchy. But neither has absolute male supremacy been found lurking in the forest or tipi. References in the written records to a male "chief" or a female "captainess" may not translate into positions of authority elevated one above the other. Who is to say whether the hands that planted maize or those that clasped the tomahawk had somehow grasped a rung above one another on some ladder of stratification? Amid all the lacunae, anomalies, and puzzles of gender in Native America, other representations of male and female call out a different question. Terms like "Clan Mother" and "Clan Uncle" pose this quandary: Can a culture make strong distinctions between men and women and maintain a relative balance of prestige, power, and well-being between the two? The tribute that Amerindian cultures paid to the corn mother lends some credence to that historical possibility.[65]

The idyll of the Clan Mother may not offer a simple resolution to the transhistorical quandary of sex: Is the subordination of women universal? Rather, it is the very difficulty of determining which sex was hegemonic in pre-Columbian America that is most instructive. The corn mother represents a very blunt and basic social division, between male warriors and female farmers, between cornfields and hunting grounds, between the sweathouse and the menstrual hut. Yet a steep gender hierarchy did not ensue from this asymmetry. Somehow, the men and women of Native America managed to knit their two sharply differentiated worlds together into a durable culture that had a minimum of formal political institutions and relatively faint lines of gender subordination. This unique orientation of the three axes of gender—combining strong gender asymmetry with weak relations of the sexes and relatively level stratification—makes some sense given the distinct material conditions of the American continent before 1500. This pattern developed over at least a millennium as part of a particular accommodation between man, woman, and nature. In most quarters of Native America, since the end of the first millennium, men and women had mastered the ability to support and perpetuate the species by hunting, gathering, vegetable and animal husbandry, and intertribal trade. Such survival also required a carefully worked out management of gender relations, extending even to controlling population growth through such practices as abortion and infanticide if necessary.[66]

No human culture is locked in timeless tradition, however, and American Indians were pressed to adapt to alterations in the natural environment and competition with contiguous tribes. Several historians have argued that Amerindian tribes were tilting toward male hegemony at the time of European colonization. An ethnohistorical study of one of the most sophisticated cultures native to North America, the southeastern tribes of the Muskogee (or Creek), is particularly suggestive. The Muskogee practiced intensive riverine agriculture, sustained large urban settlements, and operated complex political confederacies. They would not have sent a female to represent the matrilineage before De Soto. Neither would they have granted women much status in private life. Wives, unlike husbands, had no right of divorce and were discarded and shamed should they commit adultery. Women held no offices or positions of authority and were forbidden to enter the town plaza or rotunda, places men had claimed as public space and citadels of their authority. The men of the Muskogee tribe had stepped over into women's sphere of production and taken control of the agricultural surplus. Their control of material resources enhanced their social and political power and exaggerated the inequality between different kin groups. In this more stratified society, marriage alliances became critical to maintaining status across generations and warranted control of women's reproductive, as well as agricultural, powers.[67]

The case of the Muskogee resembles accounts of some other tribes at the time, the Huron, the northernmost Canadian tribe of Iroquois, for example, and the Algonquian in Virginia and the Choctaw farther south. In these instances an expropriation of matrilineal resources was already underway at that critical moment when intruders came from across the Atlantic to claim Indian lands. King Powhatan, the father of Pocahontas, offered the corn produced by the women of the tribe as tribute to the white man. This would suggest that Powhatan, like the Muskogee leaders to the south and Iroquois to the north, was beginning to tip the balance of reciprocity by taking control of the corn produced by the women of the clan. Perhaps these tribal leaders were acquiring an agricultural surplus that might have led to a more stratified social and gender system.[68] About the same time, the formation of intertribal confederacies also disrupted the geographical basis of women's power. The installation of a "Great Chief" among the Choctaw placed political authority at a level above the women who were formerly consulted about diplomatic and community matters.[69] Those tribes whose political alliances were beginning to spread out over vast territories, like the League of the Iroquois or the Confederacy of the Five Civilized Tribes, usually left the leading matrons behind in more parochial positions of influence. The intertribal councils that negotiated treaties and made war were located far from the home of the Clan Mothers. When some tribes distinguished between the interior and the exterior chief, they reserved the latter position, and more extensive authority in territorial terms, for men. The Indian chiefs who made a mark on written history, the likes of Powhatan, Tecumseh, and Pontiac, were not anonymous clan fathers. They were acknowledged historical actors whose power was recognized and felt by European men, as well as Indian women. In the last analysis, the detective of gender has to acknowledge the authority of numbers: those females to whom the historical record has given the title of chief, like the mistress of the Catawba town and a female leader among the Chumash mentioned in the introduction to this chapter, were relatively few.

The notoriety of male chiefs, like the suspicion that Powhatan was exploiting the matri-clan and the anomaly of Muskogee misogyny, introduces more intrigue into the mystery of Native American gender. Was the increasing concentration of power and wealth in some agricultural societies a prognosis for the future? Did it augur ill for corn mothers? If so, the arrival of the first Europeans coincided with a pivotal moment in the world history of gender. The reciprocal and relatively egalitarian relations of the sexes may have been in jeopardy. Even if these changes were prophetic, the corn mothers had left to posterity evidence of another way of doing gender, of being men and women. They point to an American past in which patriarchy was not primeval.

The Sexual Frontier

After 1492, all this was to change. Whether they set sail from Spain, France, or England, the first explorers and colonists came to America as representatives of patrilineal cultures in which patriarchy was clearly hegemonic. The Europeans did not, however, have carte blanche to impose their gender practices on what they called the New World. Colonial blueprints that called for constructing a social order around private property held in the name of male household heads could not be implemented in a single season or with the sweep and speed of manifest destiny. The sea change of gender would take hundreds of years, go through fits and starts, and meet with reversals. For at least two centuries, competing ideas about the meaning of male and female cohabitated with one another on what has been astutely characterized as a "middle ground," the time and places where neither Americans nor Europeans could dictate the future, including the reconstruction of gender.[70] It was not until well into the nineteenth century that European farmers became the absolute proprietors of the lands that Indians had held in common for millennia, most often in the name of their mothers. Even then, older matrilineal customs could still be found clinging to their ancient roots in American soil.

The transfer of land titles from matrilineages to individual husbandmen was a slow process that could only be accomplished as a part of a crisis of apocalyptic proportions that gripped North America after 1500, reduced the native population of the Americas to one-tenth its former size, and wiped fully one-half of the language groups of North America off the map.[71] In the northern province of New France, this debacle arguably took less than thirty years and was virtually completed by 1650.[72] The Spanish incursion into California did not begin in earnest until the late eighteenth century, but its demographic consequences were draconian and swift: the native population fell from three hundred thousand to thirty-two thousand by 1850. Only ten years into the Americanization of California, the decimation of the native population was complete: whole tribes had disappeared in a generation.[73] The major cause of human destruction was not military conquest under any national banner but the more sinister force of germs, bacteria, and epidemic diseases—smallpox, cholera, scarlet fever, and syphilis.[74] The relatively stable and balanced ratios of people to land that had underwritten North America's small horticultural tribes became their undoing when the Europeans invaded. Having lived for generations in the same homogeneous germ pools, Native Americans were powerless to resist the deluge of destructive microbes carried into their territory from across the Atlantic.[75]

Trailing these deadly bacteria, Europeans made their way though North America, trampling on Indian meanings of male and female as they went. Gender would be imbricated in both the short-term defeats and longer-term conquests of the European intruders. It could not be otherwise, for this historical event was an encounter between strangers in whom gender was the most obvious distinguishing characteristic. Americans met Europeans on what one historian has shrewdly called a "gender frontier," "the site of creative and destructive processes resulting from the confrontations of culturally specific manhoods and womanhoods."[76] The North American continent was crosshatched with gender frontiers as hundreds of tribes and successive waves of settlers jousted, one with the other, on a continuously shifting battleground. Every meeting brought the possibilities for exchange, mutation, or conquest of one gender culture over another. The remainder of this chapter will reduce these myriad possibilities to two dramatic performances of gender history. First, it will view the encounter between Americans and Europeans as an explicitly sexual frontier where foreign relations were conducted by way of intimate bodily connections between women and men. The second drama played out more slowly, and at a later stage in the colonizing process. At this point, the principal actors on the gender frontier were not just male and female bodies but the modal roles of colonial gender culture—Man the Warrior, Woman the Farmer, and the European Colonizer.

The first encounters of Americans and Europeans took place on a specifically sexual frontier. As the Spanish ventured north of the Rio Grande into the lands of the people they would call Pueblo, they sent back accounts of sexual exploits that read like a combination of pornography, horror story, and farce. One of the first meetings between Europe and America occurred in 1539, when a small party of Spanish missionaries and soldiers met up with the Zuni in the southwestern corner of the present-day United States. The

Zuni chieftains reportedly greeted the Spanish with a gesture of friendship: they offered their women to the strangers as a sexual welcome. The Spanish soldiers (much to the dismay of the Franciscan friars on the expedition) accepted this offering but did not reciprocate with a tribute of any sort, neither women nor portions of the turquoise and silver conspicuously displayed on their persons.[77] A misunderstanding about the appropriate sexual behavior was only one cause for this cross-cultural faux pas. Certain basic structural irregularities in gender relations were also critical to this disastrous encounter. First of all, the Spanish were handicapped by a fundamental disadvantage: they had no women to offer in exchange. Europeans in general came limping into the New World as social amputees, a tribe composed of only one gender, and even then, equipped with a very limited repertoire of masculine roles: celibate priests, stoic warriors, single-minded fortune hunters, and hell-bent adventurers. The native Californians interpreted the Spanish sex ratio as evidence that they were either grievously ill or on the warpath.[78]

The two gender cultures were off to a very bad start. In rapid succession the friars would interpret the Zuni demand for women as witchcraft and a warrant for execution. Insulted by so brutal a response to their generosity, the Zuni promptly drove the Europeans out of their territory. This incident can serve as a general advisory that the North American frontier could be a sexual minefield. The explosive first encounter stemmed in part from a simple misunderstanding of the rules that monitored sexuality in different cultures. This inevitable tension was exacerbated by the imbalanced sex ratios and by the fuse of sexual desire itself. All these combustible materials were ignited repeatedly over the next two hundred years, all across the continent, in countless encounters between the tribes of America and the nations of Europe.

The émigrés from Europe had been schooled in a sexual regime that was the antithesis of the typical native tribe. The counterreformation in the Roman Catholic Church had issued extremely repressive sexual standards to the French and Spanish clerics who ventured into the New World, where they would hold the heathen to their own exacting standards of purity. The Jesuits who set up their missions in both New Spain and New France had learned with their founder, Ignatius Loyola, to brutally suppress sexual desire. They crowned their celibacy with hair shirts and self-flagellation.[79] Not to be outdone in their repressive mission, the Franciscans appointed the California missions with whipping posts and streaked them with red paint representing the virtue of disciplining the body. To Spanish friars and French priests, the sexual behavior of the Indians, especially the women, seemed the work of the devil. Medieval theology and folklore alike had taught them that women were

MAKING SEX IN AMERICA

Jan van der Straet, *Christopher Columbus* (*"Christophorus Columbus Ligur
terroribus Oceani Superatis alterius pene Orbis regiones à se inventas Hispanis regibus
addixit"*). (Courtesy of the Print Collection, Miriam and Ira D. Wallach
Division of Art, Prints, and Photographs, New York Public Library,
Astor, Lenox, and Tilden Foundations)

intrinsically lascivious, an assessment that was not refuted by the sexual practices of the Indians. In the Jesuits' estimation, the Huron were no more than
"wild asses" for whom "to conquer one's passions is considered a great joke,
while to give free reign to the senses a lofty philosophy."[80] Plural marriage, as
practiced across much of the North American continent, was seen as licensed
adultery. The premarital sex play of native youth prompted Franciscan friars
to lock nubile women in dormitories, called *monjerios*.[81] When the Spanish
came upon the Native Americans in homosexual play, they unleashed their
own barbarity upon the "abominable and unnatural lechery." Balboa performed this scourge on the very eve of discovering the ocean he would name
the Pacific: finding some forty native men dressed as women and engag-
ing in "preposterous Venus," he commanded they "be given for a prey to his
dogges."[82]

Because these foreign relations were conducted by warriors and male chiefs, they most often put women in jeopardy. Most Amerindian tribes had a history of conflict along their borders, and some were known to rape the women of their adversaries. Routinely, however, those captured in battle, including Europeans, were adopted into the tribe as wives, husbands, or consorts of their people. Women could act as agents of hostility or reconciliation: sometimes they greeted the Europeans with offerings of food, and sex, and other times with calls for bloody sacrifice. Indian women, as well as men, resorted to sexual weapons against European intruders. A band of Virginia colonists learned as much when they bedded down with some Algonquian maidens only to awake to find their consorts had absconded with their shoes. Along the gender frontier the relations of the sexes were a risky business, and women were objects of particular suspicion and manipulation. For example, while Pueblo men offered women as tribute to the Spanish, they exiled those who conducted such sexual liaisons without tribal approval. Not all of the indigenous peoples of California stoically endured such repressive conditions. An Indian rebellion at Mission San Diego in 1775, for example, left three Spaniards dead, and the padre's face beaten to a pulp.[83]

Neither the Franciscans in the Southwest nor the Jesuits in the Northeast succeeded in reining in the appetites of the soldiers and traders they accompanied to America. By one report, their favorite recreation was to "go to the pueblos to fornicate with the Indian women." Likewise, French fur traders in the North, soldiers posted in New Orleans, even straightlaced Englishmen like John Rolfe sired a mixed-blood population all along the sexual frontier. Those who came to the Americas to trade for pelts, be they the French in the Upper Mississippi Valley or Englishmen in the Chesapeake and New England, conducted more harmonious backwoods relations with native women. With alacrity they formed partnerships with Indian women, enjoying their cooking, company, and conjugal embraces.[84]

Not all white men or Indian women acted as if the frontier were a sexual barrier between their cultures. Numerous stories of captive New England women who refused to leave an Indian mate, or of Indian women who regarded marriage *à la façon du pays* as the ideal match, or of the daughters of chiefs who refused the marital alliances proposed by their fathers testify that sexuality could become a domain of freedom, for men and for women.[85] Sometimes, it also forged a poignant bond across cultures. More touching than the myth of Pocahontas is the story of an Indian man's farewell to his captive white wife and son: "As she wanted to leave him, he would let her go, so he divided his substance equally with her, giving half ye remained to ye boy and set them both free and went with ye Woman home giving her a horse Ride."[86] As a consequence of all this mating and mingling the bloodlines could become quite complicated along the sexual frontier, as illustrated by this elite Cherokee family. A nineteenth-century chief named Chulio had taken three wives, one Cherokee, one white, and one a slave of African origin.[87]

The sexual frontier played host to a full range of erotic possibilities, all the ecstasy and perversity of intimate human contacts. But the course of sexual desire is seldom left entirely to the passions of individuals; in the age of exploration it became a matter of imperial policy and was placed under the management of monarchs. To the Spanish and their Franciscan spiritual ambassadors, the answer to the sexual excess of wanton Indian women and lusty soldiers was not to command abstinence but to encourage intermarriage. The French Crown pursued the same strategy at one point. The first vicar general of Louisiana was confident that "the blood of the Savages does no harm to the blood of the French" and promoted intermarriage with the Indians as a way of "Teaching her people to live like us." This strategy had the added advantage of producing "sons of the French king."[88] Even the English, particularly those of a more Elizabethan temperament who settled in Virginia rather than New England, contemplated interbreeding with equanimity. William Byrd put it in the strongest terms in 1728: "They had now made peace with the Indians, but there was one thing wanting to make that peace lasting. The Natives could, by no means, persuade themselves that the English were heartily their Friends, so long as they disdained to intermarry with them." The English should, in short, "have brought their Stomachs to embrace this prudent Alliance."[89]

Byrd regarded sexuality and the relations of the sexes as a strategic element of colonial relations: "the poor Indians would have had less reason to Complain that the English took away their land if they had received it by way of Portion with their Daughters."[90] American folklore put this sexual strategy more romantically, and mistakenly, in the love story of Pocahontas and the romantic hero John Smith. Pocahontas and her father, chief Powhatan, however, were probably just as calculating as Byrd. They saw material and political advantages in a marital alliance with John Rolfe, an emissary of the powerful intruders upon their lands.[91] In Georgia a native woman named Coosaponakeesa demonstrated a similar way to parlay sexual contacts into the clan's advantage and her own. The daughter of a British trader and a Creek Indian, she wed a succession of English men and thereby forged the lucrative trade alliances that elevated her to the status of "Beloved Woman" in her clan.[92] At a time when neither the Indians nor the English had established dominance along the frontier, matters of sexuality and gender could weigh heavily in the balance of power. The seventeenth century would find Pocahontas, now Mrs. John Rolfe, seated at the court of Queen Elizabeth, dressed in a fashion that fused head feathers and ruffled collars. Both the Indian princess and the English queen were privy to the sexual side of foreign relations. Each deployed her diplomatic skills and material resources adroitly at a time when the course of empire could turn in any direction. After all, the first English settlements in Virginia disappeared without a trace, and the Pueblo Indians had turned back the first Spanish incursions into the Southwest. For the time being, the European presence was just a small male encampment, a mere fragment of a distant culture. At this moment, given this sex ratio, one might even have predicted that the Europeans would be absorbed into the numerically dominant native cultures. There was certainly a precedent for such an outcome: the southern portion of the hemisphere was fast becoming a land of mestizos.

The early conflict on the gender frontier was waged on the plane of reproduction as well as sexuality. Europeans brought a lethal weapon to this battleground, the strands of disease that would decimate the native population. Venereal disease was among the most destructive European transmissions, as documented in the grisly records of the California missions. One of the most horrific ironies of the Franciscans' holy intentions was exhibited in mission dormitories. The friars locked Indian women in these cloisters, intending to protect them from both ardent young tribesmen and lecherous Spanish soldiers. Trapped in these fetid cells, they were easy prey to the deadly contagions of smallpox and measles. By 1850, women's role in perpetuating the California tribes had been eviscerated by "abduction, rape, prostitution, forced concubinage," and one more seemingly antiseptic but devastating factor.[93] The cyclone of American settlement of California that ensued after the gold rush uprooted self-sufficient Indian villages and scattered men and women along different paths. The new sexual division of labor sent Indian men to work in the gold fields, while women were dispatched as servants in Los Angeles households. The consequent imbalance of the sexes could be seen in the County of Calaveras, which was depleted not only of fish, game, and acorns but also of potential mothers: there men outnumbered women three to one. Yuba County had a genocidal sex ratio of two hundred men for every one woman. All told, these gender policies and circumstances added up to "the removal of Indian women from the reproductive cycle" and spelled the decimation of Native California.[94]

Warriors and Farmers on the Gender Frontier

As Europeans advanced ever more deeply into Indian territory, they would inflict almost lethal damage on the bonds of reciprocity between male and female that held tribal cultures together. This second front of colonization was not opened by small bands of explorers, soldiers, or traders but by planters, farmers, and merchants intent upon taking ownership of Indian lands. The confrontation would alter the roles of man and woman alike, undermining the status of both the male warrior and the woman farmer. The imperative of defending his tribe against the advancing and well-armed Europeans magnified and distorted the male's role of warrior. Initially, contact with Europeans simply multiplied the boundaries to be defended, the causes of conflict, and the sheer amount of time spent waging war. When competing European nation-states started using North America as a battleground in their imperial competition, the stakes of war and peace were raised to a point that transformed, as well as intensified, the role of Indian leader. As the French and then the British pressed deeply into Indian territory, they precipitated a more organized defense, which required a proliferation of Indian alliances both with adjoining tribes and with Europe's imperial rivals. A new kind of Indian leader emerged to act and speak for the larger, more brittle Indian confederations. Under these circumstances, the local chieftains who formerly presided alongside warrior women and corn mothers were overshadowed by the reputations of the few men who spoke for them among the Europeans.[95]

The leadership of Indian lineages had become more centralized and more masculine even in advance of the European arrival. The Iroquois formed their famed confederation just before colonization and thereby created a level of male leadership at a greater distance from the maternal longhouses. When the Virginians arrived in an Algonquian territory, they were greeted by Powhatan, who had also already won the fealty of neighboring tribes and from whom he collected tribute to expand his military operations. Intertribal rivalry had also become intense among the Iroquois and left these northeastern tribes exhausted by warfare even before they were enlisted in the hostilities between Europeans during the French and Indian War. But even in this more militarized atmosphere the job of Indian chief was more a duty than a position of power. The traditional style of Indian leadership put a premium on implementing a consensus rather than asserting authority and required more acts of conciliation and gift giving than decrees, commands, and the reaping of spoils.

In the early contact period European leaders expressed frustration with this diffused, decentralized Indian leadership. Indians, however, favored a loose set of alliances that would allow them the flexibility to obtain various European commodities, including firearms and alcohol, in exchange for their skills as hunters and warriors. This modus vivendi worked quite well early on, and particularly in relation to the French, who practiced colonization in a relatively lax and ineffectual fashion. Still, the Europeans exerted a magnetic force that would ultimately pull apart Indian communities: its effect could be seen in the clustering of deracinated warriors and refugees around military fortifications such as Detroit or in scattered, impoverished rancherías of California.[96]

As European powers and American revolutionaries contested for control of North American territory, the defense of tribal lands consumed more time, and warriors acquired more stature. The British and the French sought out authoritative native spokesmen with whom to strike an alliance and cultivated Indian leadership from among those who had traditionally presided over the tribe's foreign relations, that is, men. These clan leaders refined new male roles as diplomats, negotiators, and warlords. As they entered closer into the orbit of Europeans, chiefs became accountable for larger tribal groups and moved farther away from the Indian villages. The British and French recruited Pontiac and Tecumseh as allies in their imperial disputes and rewarded them with the coveted trophies of war, guns and alcohol. The British and Anglo-American settlers who followed the army into the Great Lakes and Midwest regions shifted the frontier balance of gender power yet further in the direction of men. They coveted more than furs to trade or recruits for an imperial battle: they came in search of farmlands. The advancing homesteaders wanted full title to Indian land and would do most anything to secure it. Meanwhile, Indian chiefs were fast losing their trust in Europeans and were amassing the arsenals with which to put up a fight for their hunting grounds and cornfields.

The fate of the Algonquian chief Pontiac illustrates the fatal mutation in Indian masculinity that accompanied these diplomatic and military operations. Pontiac rose to tribal leadership in the first instance because the British were searching for a predictable Indian ally and spokesman. At the outset, Pontiac exercised leadership in the best tradition of his tribe. When the British alliance soured, he turned back to his people, where he secured support for an Indian rebellion. Pontiac raised a force against the British in the time-honored ways: he traveled from village to village, through Illinois and Michigan, building consensus by listening, consulting, and gift giving. But soon

MAKING SEX IN AMERICA

after he had raised a force from six tribes, Pontiac began to falter as a leader of his own clan. He could be heard in 1766 to sound like an arrogant caricature of the warrior chief, presuming to act "in the name of all the Nations to the Westward whom I command."[97] When victory eluded him, Pontiac became bitter, isolated, and violent. He raged futilely against his fate, until his life ended in a grotesque parody of the warrior ideal. Given to such outbursts as ordering the drowning of a sick captive who was only ten years old, Pontiac retreated to his own tribal lands only to be stabbed in the back by a rival chief. Uprooted from the matrilineal culture, squared off against European soldiers and landgrabbers, Indian masculinity lost its former balance.

At this late date, almost two hundred years after the Algonquians first encountered Europeans and following on generations of frontier conflict, warrior culture sometimes took on a misogynist aspect. As Indian warriors became increasingly distant from the reciprocal attachments to the mothers of the clan, reports of the rape and abuse of female captives rose, and women sometimes became the scapegoats for Indian defeat. Clan strife could even turn patricidal. While presiding over the surrender of his tribe's last remaining lands, a Delaware chief named Tetapuska met his death at the hands of his own son. Incensed that the chief had deserted his mother for a younger woman, the son felled his father by tomahawk and threw him into a fire. The wrath of the Delaware was sometimes expressed in such brutal sexual gestures as the mutilation of white wombs, breasts, and penises.[98]

As the nineteenth century progressed and native cultures continued to unravel, gender relations were reconstituted in ways that jumbled up Indian traditions with European innovations. While the metamorphosis of masculinity occurred by military means in the Middle West, it transformed the role of hunter along the Great Plains. Equipped with European horses and firearms and driven by a lucrative market for hides, Indians executed their hunter role to such excess that they nearly exterminated the bison.[99] To the south the Choctaws' eagerness to trade deerskins for French arms and alcohol severely depleted the hunting grounds that fed their masculine status in the clan. Off in California, hunters driven from their creekside villages by missionaries and ranchers retaliated in bravado masculine style by becoming marauding horse thieves.[100] Such mutations of masculinity did severe damage to the former balance of male and female. When the Algonquian prophets Tenkwatawa and Tecumseh enjoined their braves to return to the ways of their ancestors, they almost reversed traditional gender asymmetry and relationships. They advised men to turn from warfare and take up the female role of farming: "you must plant corn for yourselves, for your women and for your children, and when you do it you are to help each other." When this attempt to restore the Indian lands failed, Tenkwatawa vented his disappointment with another darkly ironic twist of ancient gender culture: he attributed his failures on the warpath to being contaminated by his menstruating wife.[101]

As the sun set on this gender frontier, woman's stature and power, as well as the warrior's pride, were put in jeopardy. The expansion of European trade in the eighteenth and nineteenth centuries changed male and female, hunters and farmers alike. To man the hunter, Europeans brought the horses and guns with which to increase the bounty in meat, hides, and masculine accomplishment. The hunter's paradise was fleeting, however, as the forests and plains were depleted of game and the male's major contribution to the native diet was drastically reduced. The disruption of warfare and removal of Indians from their native lands uprooted women from their well-tended fields and eroded the foundation of the corn mother's cultural stature. At the same time Indian women found European commodities just as enticing as did their mates. They happily put down their stone-age tools and traded their corn for metal utensils—pots that eased the chores of cooking, knives that improved their butchering, needles that sped their stitches through hides and furs. The Winnebago women of Wisconsin took the advance of the French into their territory as the opportunity to develop an elaborate network for marketing maple sugar and lead.[102] In the nineteenth century Cherokees quickly learned to plant cotton and soon were bombarding traders with requests for spinning wheels, looms, and ultimately, cheap manufactured cloth. The Indian farmer was quick to adapt the agricultural methods of the European husbandman and African agriculturalists as well. Their gardens and farmsteads became a cornucopia of native and foreign foodstuffs: peas, watermelon, collards, hogs, chickens, and cows.[103]

Indians also readily bartered for those manufactured goods that would complement their rituals. Cherokee women traded corn for the manufactured cloth that could be lavishly abandoned in the reconciliation ceremony, while the Sioux wove Christian symbols like the star of Bethlehem into their native artifacts.[104] The traffic in symbols was especially heavy when corn mothers met up with Catholics. When the Spanish explorer Vizcaino encountered the Ohlone near Monterrey Bay during the expedition of 1602–3, he reported that the women "were much taken with the image of Our Lady that I showed them." In 1771 the Franciscans stationed at San Gabriel Mission near Los Angeles reported that Indians worshipped the Virgin in gendered ways: women offered her grains and seeds, and men surrendered their weapons before her image.[105] Indians embellished representations of "Our Lady of the

Conquest" with native fertility symbols such as corn plants and came to her as an intercessor when they needed rain or protection from epidemic disease. The Catholic Feast of the Virgin was timed to coincide with the harvest festivals of corn mothers. A similar syncretism evolved in New France where Indians found many resemblances between their rites and Catholic liturgy — between cannibalism and the Eucharist, for example. The Catholic "holy family" in which Mary overshadowed the distant Joseph was not unlike a matrilineage.[106] Indian women freely adapted some aspects of European gender culture and straddled the middle ground with dexterity and agility.[107]

But colonization also entailed extreme risk for women. The corn mother's most vital resource, the land she planted, was also the earthly good most coveted by the settlers who streamed ever westward during the eighteenth and nineteenth centuries. The gendered meaning of "land" was at the heart of the misunderstanding between Native Americans and Europeans. In 1620 Massasoit of the Wampanoag tribe asked of the Plymouth colonists, "What is this you call property? It cannot be the earth, for the land is our mother, nourishing all her children, beasts, birds, fish, and all men."[108] This precious trust of the matrilineage hung in the balance when warrior chieftains sat down to make treaties with Europeans. As the maternal trust was negotiated away, women often rose up to object. In 1826 a group of Cherokee matrons from Georgia circulated a petition of their own, protesting the removal of their native lands. A few years earlier, Cherokee women had called a meeting to assert, "The land was given us by the Great Spirit above as our common right, to raise our children upon and to make support for our rising generations. We, therefore, humbly petition our beloved children, the head men of warriors to hold out to the last in support of our common rights."[109]

When resistance seemed futile, women sometimes called up messianic visions to exhort their people to return to the old ways. It was an old Indian woman who fed Tecumseh's prophecies with the summons: "you are to live again as you lived before the white people came into this land." Another woman called for the return to matrifocal power among the Delaware by reviving the Big House Ceremony and enjoining her people to give up "all evil, fornication, stealing, murder and the like." By the midpoint of the nineteenth century, the depleted Native American population had been either driven off to reservations or absorbed into American culture, or was subsisting on the margins of European settlements; both women and men were uprooted from the grounds on which it was possible to enact their traditional roles. Woman the farmer, much like man the warrior, sometimes adopted new technology so obsessively that their old roles became bloated caricatures of their former selves. One Indian recalled coming home from the hunt to find wives and daughters weaving cotton in such high volume that his bounty of game seemed inconsequential by comparison. But in the last analysis neither the armed and horsebacked brave nor the industrious farmer-turned-weaver would be able to compete with the Yankee peddler and his factory-made goods.[110]

Defeated warriors and landless farmers became easy targets for those who would reform the gender culture of the "savages." During the earliest stages of contact, French missionaries took direct aim at the relations of the sexes among the Huron and Montagnais in the Great Lakes region.[111] At the outset, the Jesuits staked their chances of remodeling the relations of men and women on the reform of the marriage relationship, that is, the propagation of monogamous unions in which husbands would maintain authority. This campaign often met with resistance among women, one of whom a frustrated priest called a "little fury of hell." (The virago who thwarted baptism by trampling a vial of holy water under her feet decisively rejected the Christian invitation to heaven.)[112] But scarcely a decade after their arrival in New France, the Jesuits pronounced the native gender system basically in ruins. They displayed such trophies of conjugal reform as a wedding ceremony in which a notoriously ill tempered wife followed her mate to the altar and submitted like "a lamb" when he warned, "But thou, wilt thou continue to be proud, disobedient and ill-tempered, as in the past? Answer me; For, if thou wilt not behave better, I will not take thee for my wife. I shall easily find another."[113]

A few prelates acting as matchmakers could not overthrow the native matrilineages on their own. They required offstage assistance from the famine, epidemic, and tribal warfare that reduced the Indian population to an abject state. At this moment of cultural collapse, gender relations were particularly vital nodes from which the social fabric could come unraveled. In cultures held together by delicate relations of reciprocity between male and female sectors, a societal crisis could provoke a battle of the sexes: actions not reciprocated could provoke angry retaliation. The Huron men, for example, turned on the women as cause of their desolation in the seventeenth century. One man raged against the dying of his culture with the charge: "It is you women who are the cause of all our misfortunes." This outburst occurred at a meeting of the tribal council that had drafted a constitution disfranchising women.[114]

The battle along the gender frontier had been raging for many decades when the newly constituted government of the United States finally claimed

MAKING SEX IN AMERICA

sovereignty over Indian territory. In the nineteenth century the tribes of North America were apprised of a new national script of gender provided not by Europeans but by Anglo-Americans, including some of the founders of the republic. In 1806 Thomas Jefferson spoke before a delegation of Cherokees who were about to leave Washington after ceding their lands to the federal government. The third president of the United States did not use the occasion to speak of inalienable rights and the equality of all. Rather, he proposed a plan for invigorating Indian civilization through gender reform. He congratulated the men of the Cherokee nation for becoming farmers, for taking up the hoe and the plow to cultivate cash crops. Then he addressed the women to praise their spinning. He went on to advise Indian men and women alike that their law of inheritance should be changed from the primitive matrilineal custom to the republican ideal of private ownership, held in fee simple by the male household head. Jefferson's liberalism did not restrain him from making a policy statement about the personal relations among Indians. He urged tribesmen to withdraw their loyalties from the matri-clans: the new Indian man should esteem his nuclear family "more than he does his other relations."[115]

It was almost as if Jefferson had proposed taking a fine-pointed knife to Cherokee culture and excising the most critical gender element, the delicate lines of kinship that wedded men and women to relations with their own sex through a succession of mothers. Jefferson would suture man, woman, and child together in a nuclear family. His idealized reconstruction of gender reversed the agricultural roles of male and female, making men the farmers and putting women to the work of housewifery and the domestic production of thread and yarn. He would uproot male and female from communal land, dismantle the sexual division of labor, and disturb the solidarity of same-sex work groups. Jefferson's plan would put women to work in patrilineal and patrilocal households under the authority of their husbands.

This construction of gender relations was not just one of Jefferson's elegant architectural projects. It was a model of manhood and womanhood shared by his compatriots and enacted as national policy. A federal campaign for civilizing the Cherokee commenced in the 1790s, sending a stream of agents into Indian lands, issuing titles to property to men and the tools of spinning and sewing to women.[116] Even before 1800, Quakers were teaching Seneca matrons to spin. A commission on Indian affairs in the 1820s set up schools of gender propriety, which taught Indian girls such domestic arts as sewing and setting the table. One might find a certain resemblance to the reciprocity of native partnership in this scheme, but its context and meaning had altered fundamentally. Pairs of husbands and wives had been taken out of the matri-clan, situated in isolated, privately owned farms, and embedded in a finely graded social and political hierarchy.[117]

The course of this Jeffersonian ideal of gender relations through the British colonies, and on through Victorian America, will be traced in the next chapter. For now, its rapid and destructive path through Indian country can be encapsulated in the constitutions drafted by the Cherokee nation. Once removed from their native lands, the Cherokee set up an impressive scheme of government on an Anglo-Saxon model, which required a direct transfer of power from one gender regime to another. One of the first principles of government, which the tribe set down in writing in 1808, made children the direct heirs of their fathers and relegated their mothers to the derivative status of wives, entitled, as in the common law, to only a widow's portion of the husband's estate. The clan's matrifocal heritage was reduced to a few peripheral rights, such as protection of a woman's property should she marry a white man. Other Indian gender practices, like a woman's title to control reproduction through infanticide, were abolished in the 1820s. The constitutional order, with its exacting lines of authority, was not hospitable to the local, informal ways that women had exercised power. Collective decisions were now formalized and situated in tribal or "national" councils, presided over by men, and placed at a distance from the village meetings where the matrons once lent their voices to the politics of consensus.

When, in 1826, the General Council of the Cherokee Nation called for an election of delegates to a constitutional convention, they denied women political representation: "no person but a free male citizen who is full grown shall be entitled to vote." A year later, the constitution went on to stipulate that "no person shall be eligible to a seat on the General Council but a free Cherokee male citizen who shall have obtained the age of twenty-five years." Once the Cherokee set out to "civilize" their politics, Indian women were shunted to the sidelines of power. Not until the late date of 1964 would the Cherokee adopt woman suffrage.[118] The matrons of the Seneca tribe, perhaps the closest approximation of matriarchs ever to reign in America, took a particularly circuitous and ironic path through American political history. The year was 1848, a moment of democratic promise across the Western world and the birthday of the women's rights movement in the village of Seneca Falls, New York. For the matrons of the Seneca tribe, that date marked their official demotion in political status; their role in tribal governance was reduced to a veto over the decisions of male leaders.[119]

The piece-by-piece dismantling of one gender system and the installation of another were reenacted all along the gender frontier in the nineteenth century. By the time anthropologist Lewis Henry Morgan came upon the American Indian kinship system in the late nineteenth century, he pronounced that the former "gynocracy" of the Iroquois had been crushed, a process that Frederick Engels proclaimed a "world historic defeat of the female sex."[120] Ethnohistorians of recent times are more circumspect in their interpretations and offer a more modulated way out of this first quandary of gender in America. No social system, no matter how hierarchical, can entirely eradicate the agency of individuals and the power of subaltern groups. Although the Native American gender system was subordinated to the political regime of the United States, that more egalitarian native past was not entirely obliterated. The patriarchal gender regime to be described in the next chapter was not all-powerful. There was still room for native men and women to make a history somewhat their own—keeping old customs alive, resisting the most offensive impositions from outside, reenacting old rituals, creating syncretic blends of native and European cultural forms, and even producing microcosmic alternative worlds.

An undercurrent of alternative gender practices coursed just beneath the surface of the hegemonic culture. The most assimilated and successful members of the "civilized tribes," like Alexander McGilliway, son of a Scottish father and a Creek mother, continued to bequeath their wealth through the matrilineage, that is, to sisters, nieces, and nephews rather than wives and children.[121] The Seminole in Florida managed to resist removal from their native lands, and in their remote Florida habitat they maintained a matrilineal system into the 1930s.[122] By about that time, the population that traced its roots in America back beyond 1492 had begun to replenish itself and would eventually reach its pre-Columbian size. Liberated from the drudgery of hunting, gathering, and primitive farming, Native Americans devoted more energy to maintaining their cultural heritage and invigorated ancient arts and crafts. And not all this artistry was expended to please tourists. Among the Catawba, for example, women still etch ancient symbols into their pottery. They still keep their designs and techniques a secret of the matrilineage and take only their daughters to clandestine clay pits to collect the material for their ceramic art. The Catawba, like the Lakota, still hear their history through the dreams of a pipe mother.[123] In the villages of the Southwest, descendants of Spanish and Indians have occupied the same lands for nearly four hundred years and preserve along with their distinctive identity, which they call Hispano, such remnants of matrilineages as special protection for the property of married women. Like their Pueblo foremothers, the women of the Hispano villages proudly assume the reciprocal responsibility for plastering the earthen homes that were erected by the male work group.[124]

The Hispanos also exemplify another channel of native survival, by way of intermarriage with Europeans. While the Pueblos merged some of the matrifocal elements of their culture with the Spanish, and the Cherokees brought the English and Africans alike into their blended families, the liaisons of the Algonquians and the French of the Great Lakes made the native matrilineage the template of a Euro-American culture. These intermarriages gave birth to a subculture that vividly exemplifies how native matrilineages could become something more than the recessive strand in American ancestry. Scattered through the Midwest and southern Canada, and named after the French term for "mixed blood," the Métis are descendants of the native women who married French fur traders some two hundred years ago. The founding families of the Métis probably originated in a marital exchange along the gender frontier. The native brides of the *correur de bois* were often given in marriage by their clans in hopes of creating strategic alliances with Europeans, but these matches had much to attract the bride as well: a promise of prestige, power, geographical mobility, and access to European goods. The motivations of the French fur trader were hardy mysterious: his need for a native wife was voracious; she brought to a marriage her skills as a translator, her local contacts, her knowledge of the forest, and her ability to convert the animal carcasses he acquired into profitable furs, hides, and moccasins. Lastly, the Métis might bring to a marriage such domestic amenities as cooking, caretaking, and sexual companionship. These alliances were sometimes enduring and genuinely affectionate, at other times casually abandoned or passed on to other traders at the husband's whim. Whatever the short-term opportunism they entailed, Métis unions founded a unique and durable culture, which is traceable from the present day back to the seventeenth century, to its founding by a female ancestor.[125]

It is a culture in which Native American ways of making men and women were a powerful and visible element in a new cultural blend. The children born of these unions remained loyal to their hybrid roots: rather than marrying back into the tribe or wedding French consorts, they chose their spouses from among the mixed-blood population that settled around the trading posts of the Great Lakes region. When, by the midpoint of the nineteenth century, the homelands of the Algonquians had been turned into the private homesteads of Euro-American families, the Métis stood their ground, becoming an endogamous descent group that maintained its own ethnic boundaries and nurtured its distinctive hybrid culture. Their religion was a combina-

MAKING SEX IN AMERICA

tion of native beliefs and Catholic symbols, among which a female religious figure, a Madonna rendered in Indian beadwork, was the most revered icon. The language of the Métis was also a blend of French and Algonquian called Michif. In sum, the Métis exemplify an alternative way of crossing the gender frontier: by creating a new culture in which the balance of gender elements put the founding mothers in a hegemonic position. Here was a native matrilineage in which French men were the assimilated parties, a mixed "race" in which the dominant ancestry was a native woman, not a European man. The rugged roots of the Métis dug deep enough into American soil to survive until the late twentieth century, when the descendants of the matrilineage could claim tribal land in both Canada and the United States. Like growing numbers of U.S. citizens and members of other sovereign Indian tribes, they give living testimony to another way of doing gender.

But the case of the Métis, in its rarity and marginality, also underscores the historical landmark that was passed sometime early in the nineteenth century. As the frontier closed in on most Indian cultures, Europeans, and European men in particular, would be in the best position to dictate the terms of gender relations into the near future. This outcome was not inevitable, and its causes are neither clear nor simple, but some of the pieces of the puzzle of the gender frontier stand out. Natural history played a large part in the resiliency of Europeans: it was the fate of Native Americans to be helpless against the particular virulent germs carried into their habitat from across the Atlantic. Timing also worked against the Indians: had the encounter taken place but a few hundred years earlier, American civilizations, like the Pueblo tribes or the powerful riverine economies of the Mississippi, might have had the advantage over medieval Europeans. Once contact occurred, the position of women relative to men in both cultures became a critical factor. The power and stature of native women, while formidable, was localized around the cornfields, the longhouse, or the village council; man's sphere of warfare and diplomacy brought him into contact with European intruders, who were not incidentally members of his own sex. Power would gravitate away from the women's world to this male domain, where the vital interests of the tribe were negotiated, lost, or surrendered. Speaking of the Algonquian history, one historian has elucidated this process by staging the decisive confrontation between the Virginia Company and Chief Powhatan as a meeting and compounding of patriarchies: "On both sides, male roles intensified in ways that appear to have reinforced the patriarchal tendencies of each culture."[126]

At such a juncture the balance of the genders was lost, and much of the subsequent written history of North America would foreground men's ways of acting, seeing, and knowing. But the voices of corn mothers have not all been silenced. In fact, a renaissance of American Indian literature is now telling vibrant stories about men, women, and the survival of their people. Images of the reciprocal sovereignty of the sexes still reign in Indian memory. In Cherokee legend the world begins and ends at dawn, with the brave hunter and prolific farmer, "Kana'ti and Selu sitting together."[127]

CHAPTER 2

WHO BAKED THAT
APPLE PIE AND WHEN?

HOW DOMESTICITY CONQUERED
AMERICAN CULTURE

By the middle of the nineteenth century the icon of the clan mother had been replaced by another American idol. A family gathered around a table laden with home cooking became the ideal representation of kinship and was granted a national holiday of it own, Thanksgiving. The most widely read novelist of the nineteenth century, Harriet Beecher Stowe, celebrated Thanksgiving Day as a culinary festival featuring "pumpkin pies, cranberry pies, huckleberry pies, cherry pies, green-currant pies, peach, pear, and plum pies, custard pies, apple pies, Marlborough-pudding pies,—pies with top crusts, and pies without,—pies adorned with all sorts of fanciful flutings and architectural strips laid across and around, and otherwise varied, [which] attested the boundless fertility of the feminine mind, when once let loose to give direction."[1] A half century later, the commander of the successful campaign for woman suffrage, Carrie Chapman Catt, used a similar culinary metaphor to envision the future of her newly enfranchised sex. She anticipated that in twenty years the woman who could bake an apple pie would be as extinct as the dodo bird. Catt's prediction was at the very least premature. The domestic identity of womanhood evoked by associations with that all-American pastry would survive for some time to come. Paired with another American icon, motherhood, it also maintained a hallowed place among the platitudes of politics, foreign and domestic. "Apple pie and motherhood" have been staples of American political iconography for much of U.S. history. They even survived the onslaught of feminism in the late twentieth century when they were reincarnated as "mommy tracks," "soccer moms," and "family values." As late as the 1990s one careful study of middle-class professional women concluded that "the family, in particular, seems to have remained an island of traditional gender relations, untouched by the historical currents that lap against its edges."[2]

The title of this chapter, "Who Baked That Apple Pie and When?" poses an enigma that has long befuddled students of women's and American history. To explore this mystery is to question some basic, interdependent tenets of American culture. First of all, it will require the interrogation of the premise of Catt's mistaken prediction: Was apple pie and motherhood an apt synecdoche of the economic and social position of American women, at least up until the time she was admitted to full citizenship in the twentieth century? The answer to this preliminary question is a qualified "yes": the bulk of women's time, energy, and identity was invested in household labor of one kind or another. In the words of one recent scholar of popular culture, family attachments constituted the "primary determinant of feminine identity over the last two centuries in America."[3] Two hundred years ago, the same premise was uttered as polemic and paean; woman, it was said, was the "high priestess of the home."[4] This compact and durable cultural package contains all the elements of a distinctive gender order: the asymmetrical roles of homemaker and breadwinner, the tightly knit relations of the nuclear family, and a complicated hierarchy of the sexes that conferred moral superiority and emotional power on women but left ultimate authority to the male household head, the provider, the citizen.

Yoking womanhood to the kitchen and the nursery entailed more than just the partition of space and the allocation of gender roles. Those symbols also invested woman's place in the home with the near-sacred values of "domesticity." Dubbed a cult by historians of the antebellum period, this gender ideology not only consigned women to the job of food preparation but also enjoined her to perform that mundane task with the devotion, care, and skill that would inculcate piety, propriety, and self-discipline—all the wholesome emotional associations of the archetypal American middle-class family. Accordingly, this chapter will explore a second question: When and how did mundane household labor acquire this patina of femininity and domesticity?[5]

Third, this chapter will examine the political and cultural power that accrued to the notions of Apple Pie and Motherhood. Feminine domesticity affected more than the experience of one sex. It took meaning and acquired public value in relation to those for whom the apple pie was baked: children, husbands, and the nation. The most fulsome pronouncements of this ideology in the middle of the nineteenth century promised that women's domestic mission was to discipline husbands, socialize sons, and save the nation from the ravages of corruption and revolution. As late as the mid-twentieth century, a key rhetorical battle of the Cold War would be conducted in Moscow before a model of an American kitchen, which was, as Richard Nixon advised Nikita Khrushchev, the citadel of democracy and capitalism. Such was the political and imperial power imputed to woman, as long as she stayed beside the cradle and in the kitchen.[6]

But an icon of motherhood and apple pie, however many wreaths are laid at its feet, is still just a clay god. The national pastry was stuffed with rhetoric, not succulent fruit. In fact, the cultural utility of this icon was made to order for an imperfect and less savory world. It was held up as a warning against the social and political consequences of ill-kept homes and negligent mothers. There is, in other words, much mystification in feminine domesticity, but that is not all. The model of domestic femininity acquired its cultural power because it effectively interpreted fluid and contentious family relations. Therefore, this chapter will set apple pie and motherhood in the context of mundane parenting and housekeeping, amid the evolving social roles and shifting social spaces of real men and women. In sum, the subject of this chapter is that historical process whereby the American household was transformed into a woman-centered space and entrusted with critical emotional, psychological, and symbolic functions.

Despite the weight of tradition and nostalgia it carries, feminine domesticity was not a timeless fixture of American history. The image of mother and apple pie did not come into sharp cultural focus until the nineteenth century. To locate the origins of this gender ideology, however, it will be necessary to look back to the colonial period and follow a twisted path to the fountainheads of mainstream American culture, from the pulpits of the seventeenth century to the busy printing presses of the nineteenth. The colonial period was the critical prehistory of domesticity, the time when English settlers laid down the foundation of a family-centered culture: a political economy organized around property-owning households. The time of the American Revolution was a period of transition, when the households of the new republic came alive with possibilities of more egalitarian and reciprocal relations between men and women. Roughly between 1820 and 1850, however, the winds of family history and popular culture shifted decisively. The third section of this chapter ponders how feminine domesticity finally became installed in the kitchens of the urban middle class and the bustling marketplace of print culture. The convoluted origins of feminine domesticity are traced to specific spaces, primarily in those places where English culture first moored on the shores of North America, most especially New England. (The southern colonies will be given their due attention in chapter 3.) Although hardly ancestors to the majority of America's diverse population, New England Protestants were the primary architects of those pillars of domesticity—the cults of "home sweet home" and "true womanhood," of apple pie and motherhood.

The Prehistory of Feminine Domesticity
1620–1692

Feminine domesticity was not anticipated in the native cultures described in the previous chapter. The title of corn mother honored the progenitors of the harvest, not the purveyors of intimate services at the fireside and cradle, as conveyed by visions of apple pie and motherhood. Certainly Amerindians valued fertility as it was embodied in females, but in practice motherhood was limited primarily to childbirth and the physical care of dependent creatures, only one of the many burdens hoisted on the shoulders of woman the farmer and gatherer. Neither does it make much sense to search for the foremothers of domesticity among the advance guard of Europeans who came to North America in the sixteenth century—the explorers, conquistadores, fur traders—from Portugal, Spain, England, or France. As late as the sixteenth century, Western European writers were notably inattentive to the maternal roles. Even medical writers gave the hallowed role in procreation to men, whose more heated and active loins imprinted the characters of their progeny on the passive ovum of the female. A time when the mass of humankind lived at the margin of subsistence, vulnerable to plague, famine, and draconian infant and maternal mortality, was hardly propitious for cultivating delicate domestic sensibilities. Neither the thatch hovels of peasants nor the cavernous palaces of the nobility were breeding grounds for sentimental home associations.[7]

In the early modern era both church and state routed authority away from the domain of women and installed it along a steep hierarchy. Both in Rome and at the helm of emerging nation-states, power was channeled through male lines, among celibate priests in the first instance and from sires to sons in the second. In the fiefdom of Elizabeth I a daughter could rise to head of the dynasty, but only in the absence of a male heir; in France a lineage that did not produce male progeny forfeited the throne. Predictably, women's roles in the earliest migrations across the Atlantic were decidedly nonmaternal. Elizabeth sent the gallant Sir Francis Drake as her emissary; Isabella of Spain, the patroness of Christopher Columbus, was the consort in an opportunistic marital alliance with Ferdinand; and the Puritans named the ship that transported them to America the *Arabella*, in honor of a female patron who remained in England. The Ursuline nun Marie de L'Incarnation, the rare example of a woman venturing out into the New World on her own mission, forswore maternity: she took vows of celibacy and left her son in an orphanage.[8]

Although feminine domesticity was not visible on the horizon of sixteenth-century Europe, family relations were very much in flux. Rapid population growth combined with the enclosure of feudal lands to undermine and transform both peasant and noble households. Large estates began to splinter into small farmsteads, whose male heads took full title to the land and began producing for the local markets. Among the merchants and tradesmen of the town, the male hierarchy was modified to create what have been called "restricted" patriarchal households, which relaxed such practices as arranged marriages and conveyed the bulk of family property to the eldest son. On their family farms or in village shops, parents and children, fathers and mothers, drew closer together and often shared a material habitat that was suggestive of modern domesticity: small stone houses lit by glazed windows and warmed by central fireplaces.[9]

Under these conditions yeoman farmers, artisans, and merchants conceived new ideas about church, state, and family. The small, independent property holders of East Anglia were especially prominent among the religious sects that challenged the patrilineages of the Roman Catholic Church and the royal lines of Tudors and Stuarts. Women joined these sects more often than men; they augmented their holiness by bringing children to church, calling religious gatherings in their own homes, and even claiming to be prophets.[10] The reformed sects that set out to cleanse the Christian church of much of the pomp and luxury of the papal dynasty acquired the name "Puritan." Their ecclesiastical practices had some major gender implications. The celibate Catholic priesthood was replaced by a married ministry; marriage became a voluntary contract rather than a sacrament; worship moved from the opulence of the cathedral to the humble meetinghouse and the family hearth: "All preaching, reading catechism and other such like exercises" should take place in "private places."[11] William Gouge would invest the domestic side of worship with political consequences by proclaiming the family a "little Commonwealth" as well as a "little Church."[12] Secular writers also endorsed this reconstruction of government on a household model. The prominent political theorist of the seventeenth century Robert Filmer grounded his argument for the political legitimacy of kings on the personal authority of fathers. Puritan divines and political theorists alike had transferred male authority to a more intimate family setting.[13]

Motherhood remained in the background of these reformulations of the ideology of family and politics. Puritan practices and Filmerian pronouncements were both structured around fathers, who were admonished to over-see the household more in the manner of a governor than a loving parent. Through the seventeenth century both Reformation and Catholic catechisms vested familial authority in fathers, while the private writings of English gentry reminded wives that "you have subjected yourself to him [your husband] and made him your head."[14] English Puritans favored the kinship terminology of patriarchy, not motherhood. In their ideal family order the male household head ruled, the wife obeyed, and affectionate ties between mothers and children remained objects of some suspicion.

This family ideology proved to be a sturdy vehicle for carrying men and women into a new world. In fact, the imperative of familial social organization was not just part of the baggage of these English émigrés; it was the bark itself. Before even boarding the first ships in the ports of Bristol or London, passengers bound for New England and the Chesapeake were formed into households. The majority of the New England migrants set out as domestic units, with an unusually balanced sex ratio (for immigrants) of two women for every three men. Solitary migrants, furthermore, were not permitted to set sail until they bound themselves to established households as indentured servants. The Puritan vessels also carried unusually large numbers of married women of childbearing age. The *Mayflower*, in fact, conveyed several pregnant women, and at least one birth was celebrated on board. Title to land in the New World could only be obtained through a household connection. The passage into the English colonies during the seventeenth century operated like a kind of social sieve through which only the leaner, most domesticated, relatively young household units could pass. Husbands and wives in their peak reproductive years were particularly prevalent onboard ships headed to New England. The old, the extended relatives, the royal lines, the celibate religious, the transient, and the unattached poor were left behind.[15]

On arrival in New England these compacted families were invested with ideological authority as well as pragmatic significance. The ministers of the Massachusetts Bay Colony reminded the faithful that "the Foundation of a whole Peoples or Kingdoms REFORMATION or DEFECTION, RELIGION or REBELLION is laid in Families. Families are the Constituent Parts of Nations and Kingdoms; hence as Families are Well or Ill Disciplined, so will the whole be Well Disposed, or Ill Inclined."[16] The English colonists perceived households as political and social units bound together by exacting, and if necessary, even coercive authority. "Those who are Heads of Families" were admonished to "carry themselves very *gravely* and *soberly* in their Houses." Among the Puritans the law of obedience to the godly father and parent was evoked as the basis of all civil authority, and it was enforced scrupulously.[17] Elizabeth Perkins, appearing before the Essex County courts, would learn this painfully in 1681, when she was "severely whipped on the naked body" and made "to stand or sit in some open place in the public meetinghouse at Ipswich . . . with a paper pinned to her head on which is written in Capital letters, 'FOR REPROACHING MINISTERS, PARENTS AND RELATIONS.'"[18] Perkins's sin was grave enough to provoke a formal, legal, and punitive judgment at the level of a county court: she had claimed her minister was "more fit to be in a hogsty than in a pulpit, and that he had been a vile man in his former days." Heads of families and civil leaders were harnessed together to form one patriarchal system, whose authority was mandated by the Massachusetts Body of Liberties under the commandment to honor thy father and mother.[19]

Neither the secular leaders of Massachusetts Bay, like Governor John Winthrop, nor the spiritual fathers, like the Reverend John Cotton, hesitated to use the word "patriarch" when describing this system of government. The settlements of the New World were likened to a biblical commonwealth in which Hebrew patriarchs governed the family and the state. Women and mothers had very particular and restricted roles in this polity. Cotton reminded his parishioners that a wife should be a "meek and quiet godly spirited woman, subject and obedient to her husband and call[ing] him Lord whose daughter you are while you do well."[20] The subordination of wives in this household system was more than a simple matter of gender domination. Because the household operated as an extended system of government and was invested with major societal responsibilities, the senior women of the family shared in the administration of authority. Though subordinated to husbands, wives exacted obedience from both their children and the servants living under their roof, and they could command and punish both, be they male or female. As the mistress of the household, the wife and mother occupied a position of authority and responsibility. In the absence of her spouse, she became "the deputy husband," authorized to act in the name of the patriarch.[21]

Be it inside or outside the household unit, in relation to intimate kin or New England neighbors, adult married women operated within an intricate social hierarchy. It was customary, for example, for families to file into early New England meetinghouses according to social status. Sometimes women would take their place alongside the ascending ranks of male household heads. But should their church be divided along the nave by gender, women might proceed down the aisle separate but parallel to their kinsmen: the leaders of the women's procession would assume an auspicious position, the pews directly in front of the pulpit. This fine grain of household hier-archy was given a biblical expression in the notion of Adam's rib, deployed by a Puritan minister not as an image of dependence and subordination but as a social standing aligned "out of the side to be content with equality."[22] This was not casuistry but a reflection of the delicate registry of gender status in a family-based social order. The seventeenth-century English colonists did not conceive of social relations, either within or outside of the household, in democratic or egalitarian terms but as a scaffold of "relative duties" and "rela-tive inequality." In this system, the rank of parent, either that of male head or female mistress of the household, was invested with more power and less sentiment than prescribed by the cult of feminine domesticity, which still waited in the wings of American history.[23]

By putting such great stock in the family unit, however, the English colo-nists had built the social and political structure in which a domestic concep-tion of womanhood could eventually take up residence. The colonial house-hold was invested, first of all, with the economic imperative of making the new land productive, initially for survival and soon for profit. The English countryside had been converted from manorial estates into freehold prop-erty hardly a century earlier, when small farmers, as well as the gentry, began to claim title to the land they tilled and the homes in which their families dwelled. Only in 1670 did the common law officially abolish feudal land tenure, giving male householders the freedom to dispense with their prop-erty to subsequent generations as they saw fit. While independent landed freeholders would remain a minority in the Old World for some time, this select status was the foundation of a whole new commonwealth on the other side of the Atlantic. Despite the fiction of royal or proprietary charters to Brit-ish imperial territories, most all workable land was soon claimed by families, with rarely an acre reserved for royal titles, noble lineage, or town corpora-tions.[24]

Private, family-held property took such quick root in the New World that it strangled the utopian intent of the Pilgrim fathers. At the outset of the Puritan experiment, some of the more zealous members of Protestant re-form sects aimed to create a Christian community so perfect that all God's children shared the fruits of their toil equally and in common. But not even the devout band of Pilgrims who settled Plymouth Colony in 1620 could re-frain for very long from claiming the new land as private family property. William Bradford recalled the fatal moment as a rebellion of both genders. Men complained that they did not want to "spend their time and strength to work for other men's wives and children without any recompense."[25] Women expressed their discontent in similar terms: "men's wives . . . deemed it a kind of slavery" to be forced "to do service for other men, as dressing their meat, washing their clothes, etc. . . . neither could many husbands well brook it."[26] As Bradford told the tale, this colonial crisis was averted only when the Pilgrims were granted plots of land in the name of husbands. Then "all hands" went eagerly to work, and women in particular "now went willingly into the field, and took their little ones with them to set corn; which before would allege weakness and inability; whom to have compelled would have been thought great tyranny and oppression."[27]

Bradford's account reads like a parable of the virtues of private property and family values. Be that as it may, it also describes the economic and social structuring of the English colonies. From then until this day, the vast landscape of the North American continent has been held as private household property, channeled through the generations along narrow lines of family transmission.[28] All that remained of the utopian elements of Puritan economics was the practice of granting a generous plot from the vast landholdings of the colony to all adult heads of household who came to settle and signed a covenant of Christian community. Without hesitation and virtually without exception, the founders of the towns conveyed these plots to men, on the assumption that fathers would support their wives and children. The New England community carefully ordered and regulated the relations within and between families and across generations, relying largely on English practice and precedent, including the stipulations of the common law. First codified into a written body of legal principles by William Blackstone in the eighteenth century, the common law set down an airtight system of patriarchal descent. Property was conveyed directly by fathers to sons (patrilineal), favoring the eldest male child (primogeniture), maintaining property intact to the son's generation (entail), guaranteeing only a portion of the husband's estate to his widow (dower), and vesting control of the property a wife brought to a marriage in her husband (coverture). Coverture placed a heavy yoke on wives and mothers, who were defined by Blackstone as follows: "The very being or legal existence of the woman is suspended during the marriage or at least is . . . consolidated into that of the husband; under whose wing, protection, and *cover* she performs every thing."[29] American colonists also conformed to the common law practice of entrusting child custody to fathers rather than mothers.[30]

The few alterations that New Englanders made in the common law of inheritance worked to the benefit of sons, and younger sons in particular. Several colonies took legal steps to reduce the inheritance of the eldest from full title to his father's land to only a portion, perhaps double that of his brothers or simply an equal share. These renovations in the common law tended to equalize the familial relations among men and create what one astute synopsis of legal history has termed "abbreviated lineages," whose largesse did not extend very far "beyond the nuclear family."[31] Neither did New Englanders extend their largesse to the female members of the nuclear family. New England statutes did not mitigate the abject legal status of feme covert, expand dower rights, or increase bequests to daughters. The family law of the English colonies was less generous to women than the Spanish in the American Southwest or the Dutch in New Netherlands. The English statutes failed even to keep up with liberalization of legal practices underway at the time in Britain. The colonies of Connecticut, Massachusetts, and Pennsylvania, for example, did not create a court of equity, the English institution that afforded some women redress for legal grievances and permitted more generous marriage settlements.[32]

When it came to implementing these statutes by writing a will, the husbands and fathers of New England were even less generous to female kin than were the colonial legislatures. Probate records indicate that generous bequests of real property to younger sons were often made at the expense of women—their sisters and even their widowed mothers. Colonial courts were not scrupulously careful about monitoring property transfers among men to make sure that widows received even their one-third shares. Protective devices common in England (such as private examination of wives when family property was about to be liquidated) were rarely observed in the New World. Significantly, the wills prosecuted in the colony of Maryland, where few Puritans and greater numbers of Catholics, Quakers, and Anglicans settled, were more generous to women.[33] By shoring up the father-son connection, legal practices in most of the English colonies closed off maternal channels for transmitting family property. Women rarely came before probate courts to bequeath anything to their children. In the case of Bucks County, Pennsylvania, for example, only 12 percent of wills were drafted by women. Similarly, women became administrators of the estates of their husbands with less regularity than did their kinswomen in England.[34]

American colonists thus held landed property in a tight patriarchal grip. The property passed down by women was rarely even a small plot of land; it was more often a pittance of moveable goods, like a feather bed, crockery, or linens. This was a pale reflection of the corn mother's former glory and did not escape the notice of Indian women. Well into the nineteenth century, the Women's Council of the Cherokee resisted the imposition of En-

MAKING SEX IN AMERICA

glish common law that would deny women their ancestral claims on the land. The terms of bequests to women in America could be chilling; all too commonly, a widow would be left with no more than a minimal supply of food and firewood, or removed to a small back room in a home that had become the property of her son. It would be difficult to paint a sentimental image of maternity using evidence like this. The English colonies may have been a paradise for family property, but they were not an Eden for female heirs.[35]

Despite their limited title to property, women made vital contributions to the household economy. The mistress of the colonial household turned the role of helpmate—Adam's supportive rib—into a domain of economic value and social influence. According to William Bradford's account, the success of Plymouth Colony rested on the willingness of women to go to work for the family patrimony, even to perform the field labor to which European women were unaccustomed. In the early years of settlement, when survival required maximum effort, women's labor could not be spared. Wives and mothers were fully employed, not just in housework, but also beside their husbands in the fields, harvesting wheat and corn.[36] The bounty produced by the New England housewife was legendary: her brewed beer, her baked bread, her churned butter and rendered cheese, her homespun yarn, her handpicked herbal cures. Her larder was a cornucopia, stocked with products of her own labor or goods acquired through bartering with her neighbors. Women's trade networks created a web of local debits and credits and brought her into a busy orbit of public sociability. Mistresses of the household also appeared with some regularity at the courthouse, suing for just compensation in trade or facing accusations of fraudulent merchandising.[37]

The household mistress won her reputation as the sturdy helpmeet through the command of expansive social networks. Any surplus from the dairy, garden, or spinning wheel was likely to be the result of her supervising the work of children and servants. Thus, Martha Ballard of Maine pointed with pride to the accomplishments of her household labor force: "My girls spun 23 double skeins & wove 27¹/₂ yards last weak [sic] & did the houswork [sic] besides." Over her lifetime Ballard employed upward of thirty different young female workers in her Maine home, and at the same time she practiced the lucrative household profession of colonial women, that of midwife. Ballard converted motherhood into a career of immense social value and considerable material reward; she helped bring some eight hundred new lives into the world.[38] In all, a woman's contributions to her household and to the colonial economy, including her maternal role as the bearer and boss of household workers, was measured in very prosaic, ma-

Hearth, Williams-Hopkinson House, Philadelphia.
(Courtesy of the Library of Congress, Prints and Photographs Division,
Historic American Buildings Survey, HABS PA, 51-PHILA, 266-3)

terial terms.[39] Woman's occupation was mistress of the household, not just
wife and mother; she was more taskmaster than nurturer, the producer of
hearty brown bread rather than apple pie.

The exigencies of property and production overshadowed but did not over-
whelm the more intimate, affective, and maternal aspects of New England
womanhood. Puritan writers celebrated the helpmates of the New World and
elevated Eve a step or two on the ladder of household authority. "The Husband is to be acknowledged to hold a *Superiority* which the Wife is practically
to allow; yet in respect of all others . . . she is invested with an Authority
over them by God."[40] The climate of Massachusetts Bay tempered fatherly
authority, as depicted by the Reverend Thomas Hooker: "When a wife is
wooed and brought home and married, [the husband] gives over his right of
himselfe." A book published in 1726 conceded almost as much when its au-

thor singled out the relation of husband and wife, among "all the orders of which are unequal," as the one that was "nearest to Equality and in several respects they stand on equal ground."[41] Cotton Mather emphasized the reciprocity that inhered in the voluntary covenant of marriage, saying explicitly that "husbands owe mutual duties to their wives."[42] Sometimes, conjugality became the register for spiritual ecstasy. One of John Cotton's more memorable sermons played on the refrain, "Let him kiss me with the kisses of his mouth."[43] Though addressed to a heavenly bridegroom, such apostrophes reverberated with more earthly strains of sexual communion. What was pronounced from the pulpit was whispered in the private writings of members of the congregation who communicated tender affection and ardent desire toward their mates. Husbands and wives addressed each other as "dear partner," "yokefellowe," "best friend," and "My dear, dear, dear Friend." Governor John Winthrop recited a litany of loving salutations to his spouse: "My Love, My Joy My Faithful One," "dear heart," "my Most Sweet Heart," "My Sweet Wife."[44]

Couples like these were the progenitors of rapid population growth. On the average, the first generation of women to arrive in New England bore seven children and spent almost a quarter century caring for the young. Many gave birth early in their twenties, breast-fed each infant, and gave birth again in two to three years through the rest of their reproductive cycles, thereby exercising their maternal powers almost to the maximum. When three or four daughters replicated their mother's fecundity, the rate of population increase was exponential.[45] By the close of the seventeenth century, it was not uncommon for a New England matron to be survived by fourscore grandchildren. (The birth rate in the South, by contrast, was so weak that the first immigrants failed even to reproduce themselves. The catastrophic social implications of low fertility in the seventeenth-century South, which will be considered in the next chapter, underscore the comparative historical accomplishment of New England mothers.[46]) The long list of progeny recorded in family Bibles testified that reproduction was an awesome vocation for New England women.

Even the most somber parson described infancy as an interlude of warmth and indulgence between mothers and children. The period of nursing occupied a special place in the busy household, defining a time of tender care that defied Calvinistic doctrines of infant depravity and damnation. Until the age of six or seven (the age of reason, according to Puritan theology), children were exempted from the stern paternal authority; but then the law of the father would "break the will" of sons and daughters and set them to work as the junior helpmeets of the little commonwealth.[47] For a prolific mother, a succession of births could extend the season of infant care for decades. Though constrained within patriarchal borders, mother's realm had acquired a portentous significance and intensity in New England.[48]

The elaboration of maternity also expanded the spaces for sociability and support among women. At a time when maternal death was not an uncommon outcome of pregnancy, even in the relatively healthy conditions of New England, reproduction inspired understandable fear in mothers. To quiet those fears, women surrounded the event of birth with sisterly solace. As the fateful time approached, the midwife and a circle of women friends—four, six, even ten neighbors and kin—gathered around the expectant mother. It was a capital offense for a man to practice midwifery in New England, and even fathers were banished from the birthing room. Husbands retired a safe distance, while women friends encircled the laboring mother, whom they took under their care sometimes for as long as a month after birth.[49] Motherhood, in this physical, intimate, and affective aspect, even sparked some awe among patriarchs. Michael Wigglesworth stood watch over his wife's accouchement in such a nervous fever that he seemed to be in labor himself: "The nearnes of my bed to hers made me hear all the nois. her pangs pained my heart, broke my sleep the most off that night, I lay sighing, sweating, praying almost fainting through wearines before morning."[50]

Such were the imaginings of a patriarch of New England, who held authority, property, and power in the home, in the church, and in the town. Men like the Reverend Wigglesworth presided over a male dominion that was anchored in the household, extended hierarchically up the social order, and rendered women invisible in the domains of juridical, political, financial, and extrafamilial power. Still, he stood in awe and envy of a mother's singular power and thereby offers evidence of the intricacies of gender in Puritan New England. On one level, the asymmetry of male and female sectors of the social order was striking. Patriarchy was not just a gender system but a whole social system. The commonwealth was composed of household cells whose genetic code was stamped with the authority of the property-holding male head of household. At family worship, in the courthouse, vestry, and meetinghouse, men led and women obeyed, all in the name of the father. Yet because the basic cell structure of the New England society was composed of family units, consisting fundamentally of procreating, coproductive husbands and wives, women found their own sense of accomplishment and proximity to power in the household.

The households that New Englanders erected along the agricultural frontier, however patriarchal, were not domestic tyrannies. To the contrary, some historians have portrayed early American gender and family history in almost bucolic terms. One has written of Plymouth Colony that "this does *not* seem to have been a society characterized by a really pervasive, and operational, norm of male dominance." Another has painted everyday life of northern New England in the warmest hues, dissolving its commonplace tensions and petty quarrels in a glow of contentment that surrounded "good wives." To yet another, the head of the pious New England household exercised his authority with loving constraint, and he dispensed erotic pleasures along with the subordination of his wife.[51] New England patriarchy might seem to be doubly sugarcoated, with both a seductive religious and political doctrine of relative equality and a quotidian quotient of gratitude, courtesy, and love. The Pauline doctrine, oft repeated in New England—that there was neither male nor female, slave nor free, Greek nor Jew, for all were one in Christ Jesus— put a benevolent face on male hegemony.

The rocky shores of New England also germinated some of the most melodious expressions of conjugal love and domestic harmony. They were issued by women, as well as men, and reached sublimity in the verse of Anne Bradstreet. Bradstreet's poetry is a fulsome recital of contentment around the New England hearth. Her ode to her children—"eight birds hatched in one nest"—strikes exquisite chords of mother love.[52] The poems to her absent spouse bespeak refined pleasures of marital sexuality: "But when thou northward to me shalt return / I wish my Sun may never set, but burn / Within the Cancer of my glowing breast / The welcome house of him my dearest guest."[53] Springs of domestic affection and sexual love also fed Edward Taylor's spirituality: "O let thy lovely streams of love distill / Upon myself and spout their spirits pure / Into my viall, and my vessel fill / With liveliness."[54] Such sentiments, like Anne Bradstreet's poetic accounts of "a loving mother, and obedient wife," expressed the indubitable joys that can be found under the best domestic conditions—for mothers and fathers, for husbands and wives.[55]

But the complicated relations of the seventeenth-century household cannot be reduced to greeting-card images of contented wives, selfless mothers, and fragrant apple pies. Even the very polite verse of Anne Bradstreet tells another story as well. Her lines were also stocked with irony: "Men can do best, and women know it well / Preeminence in all and each is yours; / Yet grant some small acknowledgement of ours."[56] The flights of Bradstreet's imagination rose higher than the rank of deputy husband. In her poem to Queen Elizabeth, she clearly rankled at being barred from a larger world, "the theatre where she did act."[57] Moreover, Bradstreet espoused some political opinions of her own when she made an invidious comparison between Elizabeth and male rulers: "Since time was time, and unmanly man, / Come show me such a phoenix if you can. / Was ever people better ruled than hers?"[58] Finally, in these closing lines, Anne Bradstreet hinted of a consciousness akin to feminism as she imagined "heaven's great revolution [when] Eliza shall rule Albion once again."[59] "Now say, have women worth? or have they none? / Or had they some, but with our Queen is't gone? / Nay masculines, you have thus taxed us long, / But she, though dead will vindicate our wrong."[60]

Bradstreet's disquiet was a faint echo of the discontent that occasionally reared up in the court records of the colonies. The minority of women who were called before the magistrates for criminal offenses chafed against the patriarchal order. Most of their misdeeds were committed in the course of performing their household duties, and they expose the difficulties of producing and trading goods without access to legal rights and public authority. Wives and widows of farmers and tavernkeepers were often brought before the court for quarreling with their neighbors about the irregularities of petty transactions.[61] On a grander scale of larceny, women were more likely than men to question the whole system of religious government in New England. A study of early Salem, for example, found that more than half of those accused of heresy were women. And they often rejected the doctrines of patriarchy by questioning both husbands and parsons.[62]

The commonest offense for which women were brought to trial was sexual in nature. Charged with adultery, fornication, or infanticide, the women criminals of New England violated one of the most blatantly asymmetrical practices of the patriarchal system, the double standard of sexual morality. Because transmitting property through family lines was the lifeblood of these agricultural communities, any violation of monogamy was a grievous social threat. Accordingly, adultery and fornication were outlawed, but only when a married woman was involved, for her transgressions could lead to pregnancy and create false claims on patrilineal property. Early in the Puritan experiment, magistrates exacted the penalty for sexual crimes with an even hand, subjecting fornicating males and females alike to a whipping in the village common. But even then a pregnancy outside of wedlock exposed women more than men to prosecution; the double standard was built into the law as a hazard of maternity itself.[63]

Whether the sins of the mothers were sexual, religious, or incidental to the operation of the household economy, they provoked swift and often draconian punishment. Very early on in the history of New England, the magistrates policed the behavior of wives and mothers with special vigilance. At times, the violations of patriarchy were so extreme as to call for an epochal trial of gender, a witchcraft prosecution. Two episodes of this nature offer a particularly sobering contrast to the homily of the good wife. The first gripped the colony at the very outset of the Puritan experiment. The threat to social order in the new colony was personified by Anne Hutchinson, a fervent Puritan, a good wife, and a midwife, who gathered her neighbors to pray in her own home and raised her voice among the congregation in ways that challenged the teachings of the clergy and the magistrates. Hutchinson's crime was a classic infraction against patriarchy. Her challenge to the ministry and magistrates of the infant Massachusetts Bay Colony brought the charge, "you have stept out of your place, you have rather bine a Husband than a Wife and preacher than a Hearer and a Magistrate than a Subject."[64] Hutchinson spoke out with the most erudite and logical readings of Puritan doctrine. Called to public trial, she displayed her power of mind before the faltering patriarch John Winthrop and was banished from the colony for her efforts. Her punishment was more lenient than that of other female heretics, among whom were two Quaker women who refused to retire into decorous conformity and were summarily hanged.[65]

Allegations of witchcraft were the ultimate defensive weapon of New England patriarchs. In the late stages of her trial, it was hinted that Hutchinson was a witch, and the most incorrigible local viragos risked being charged with the capital offense of demonic possession. Mary Oliver of Salem, Massachusetts, was called six times before the magistrates. Her offenses included challenging the minister's reading of scriptures, to which she offered the belligerent retort: "I do hope to tear his flesh in pieces." For such crimes Oliver was tied to the whipping post with a split stick on her tongue and then banished from the colony.[66] Magistrates took decisive action against the first signs of female rebellion in the young colony. In the wake of Anne Hutchinson's attempted ascent to religious authority, women were told to address their religious questions only in private communications with husbands or ministers and to refrain entirely from speaking in church. Most good wives obliged. In fact, women became the most dutiful members of the church. By the close of the seventeenth century they had quietly taken up their subordinate positions in the majority of the pews in the meetinghouses of New England.[67]

Just as the second generation of New England daughters was coming of age, however, more gender troubles broke out in the heart of the colony. The site was a small farming village just inland from the shipping town of Salem. Historians have not solved the mystery of Salem Village witchcraft.

Economic crises, the devastation of frontier warfare, contagious diseases, and juridical practices have all been identified as possible causes of Salem's ignominious place in American history. But the complicity of gender in the whole turmoil is incontrovertible.[68] In New England fully 79 percent of those brought to trial for witchcraft were female, and half of the men charged with the crime were implicated by association with a woman charged with demonic possession.[69] The crimes of these women, particularly those of the first to be accused, were classic transgressions against patriarchy. Some, like Anne Hibbens, were charged with acting as if superior to their husbands or, like widow Sarah Goode, for having the temerity to marry her manservant. Others, like Bridget Bishop—who wore a red bodice—could be seen as sexually dangerous.[70] Yet others, like widow Mary Putnam, disregarded the rule of patrilineal succession in their wills.

Of all these irregular gender practices, Mary Putnam's offense was most typical of the unwomanly behavior that challenged New England patriarchy in 1692. Deft historical detective work has revealed that the women most vulnerable to charges of witchcraft were those who for one reason or another interrupted the smooth flow of property from father to sons. Their defiant assertion of a mother's claims on property provoked the full wrath of the Puritan colony.[71] But the evidence against these women is only the most obvious clue to the mystery of Salem Village witchcraft. The age and gender of their accusers are yet more intriguing. It was not thwarted patriarchs who singled out women for the charges of witchcraft but a band of young, unmarried women, ages eleven to twenty, several of whom were servants. The young women who raised the original charges resided in troubled households situated at strategic places in the community, those of minister Samuel Parris and Thomas Putnam Jr. (the sire of an extensive farming clan then engaged in a family feud with the unfortunate Mary). In terms of age and social situation, the witchcraft trials were a drama of filial and maternal relations. The accusers were Puritan daughters; those they accused were typically middle-aged married women, representatives of their mothers' generation. The "afflicted girls," as they were called, targeted women for witchcraft by acting out feelings of bodily assault: pinching, pressure, twisting, contortion, loss of breath. Their "fits" were sometimes called "the suffocation of the mother." Coming of age near the close of the seventeenth century, the afflicted girls of Salem Village directed their visceral discontent toward maternal figures, reflections perhaps of the suffocating aspects of the position of mothers and daughters in a patriarchal society.[72]

The behavior of the afflicted girls of Salem would suggest that the contradictions of gender were painfully uncomfortable for the young women of this time and place. As they waited to contract a marriage, which even in the most prosperous patriarchy would depend on the cooperation, if not control, of parents, the afflicted girls might well have become anxious. Observing the growing numbers of pariah wives and aging spinsters in the village, their anxiety might even have escalated into hysteria. By one account, the fits of demonic possession commenced after the young accusers had conducted a bit of sorcery in hopes of divining the identity of their future spouses, only to have the spectral bridegroom appear in the form of a corpse. None of the afflicted girls came from families prosperous enough to guarantee them a good match. Of the seven chief accusers, records indicate that only one would marry and live out her life in the village, two others moved away and married, and the remainder appear to have died single, one having borne a bastard child.[73] Psychic discomfort might well have arisen from such a vulnerable position in the patriarchal order, at a social place where young women nervously awaited their adult status, ideally as the mistress of a comfortable household, but with little power to determine their own fate.

Accusations of witchcraft point toward a tension lodged at the very foundation of the gender system of Puritan yeomanry. Survival within the agricultural economy required that men and women pair up to form productive households from which obedient children, compliant wives, responsible fathers, patient male heirs, and dutiful daughters would issue. The links in this chain of patriarchal succession inevitably broke on occasion: they might be fractured by niggardly or ne'er-do-well fathers, errant children, aging spinsters, black sheep, barren wives, hapless husbands, obstreperous widows, or any of the mundane calamities of family life. If compounded and concentrated in one time and place, such family crises might well produce powerful social and psychic effects. When the patriarchal order malfunctioned, the most vulnerable members—the young, single, and female—could lose their patience and, perhaps momentarily, their sanity. By some mysterious twist of social psychology, the afflicted girls of Salem turned their anxiety on the women of their mothers' or grandmothers' generation, whose lives personified the contradictions of that gender system.

To conjure their afflictions into a full-scale witchcraft trial would require the collaboration of the community and the colony, but it was initiated by a few young women and resulted in a rare public performance of colonial gender conflict. From February to May of 1692–93, the afflicted girls held forth in the meetinghouse of Salem Village and made the whole colony of Massachusetts attend to their concerns.[74] Before they were finished, their accusations implicated strangers as well as neighbors, rich men as well as poor women, and a former minister "infamous for the Barbarous usage of his two late Wifes."[75] What was it about Salem Village in the year 1692 that brought the undercurrent of gender tension so violently to the surface, and to the attention of the whole colony of Massachusetts Bay? Had the founding patriarchs and good wives inevitably fallen from grace? Or were the historical paths of women and men about to turn in an unanticipated and disquieting direction? Would the future bring European Americans closer to the standard of apple pie and motherhood?

Between Patriarchy and Domesticity
1750–1840

The trauma of Salem Village was in fact an extreme and prescient sign of a transformation that was more quietly underway throughout New England. As the third or fourth generation of native-born European Americans came of age, most agricultural towns experienced to some degree the pressure that had built up to crisis proportions in Salem Village. This conjuncture of events would activate major demographic and gender changes and speed the course of market capitalism. In the New England colonies the crisis was demographic, and the math was simple. The finite amount of farmlands within the limits of New England towns could not provide homesteads for all the sons and daughters, the products of two successive baby booms, who were coming of age late in the seventeenth century. While Salem villagers reacted to this reproductive crisis with witchcraft trials, most New Englanders adapted new ways of organizing their households and the relations of men and women.

It becomes clear in retrospect that the demographic crisis was averted because men and women, fathers and mothers, found a way to bring the population into line with local land resources. First sons, and to a lesser extent daughters, moved away from the towns of their fathers and grandfathers. Others found occupations off the homestead, in trades, commerce, or professions. The economic adjustment was facilitated by events outside the colonies. The wars that waged through European empires in the eighteenth century disrupted international commerce and created demand for American agricultural products, thereby increasing trade and infusing the local subsistence economy with cash and credit. The seaboard towns and maturing villages of the Northeast developed a more integrated and expansive trade network, a bona fide market economy that brought a modicum of growth and measure of comfort to most colonial families.[76]

MAKING SEX IN AMERICA

But this adjustment of the family economy was neither automatic, reliable, nor accomplished by all of New England's sons and daughters. The first generation of patriarchs was in quite firm control of the marriages of their progeny and regularly arranged that their sons and daughters wed in the order of their birth. Brides and grooms were older in the eighteenth century, and not every son or daughter arrived at the altar in sequence or at all. The diminishing local supply of farmland stranded a discernible class of propertyless men and their spinster sisters in the aging agrarian villages of New England. Courtships were aborted and marriages were delayed by the lack of a dowry or the absence of a deed to the family homestead. Not infrequently, failure to navigate the passage from courtship to marriage led to conception or birth outside of marriage. One parson bemoaned that "our presses are forever teeming with books and our women with bastards."[77] The statistics on premarital conception mounted steadily in the late eighteenth century, until some New England towns watched almost one-third of the local brides go to the altar pregnant. Controlling fertility was a difficult project given the levels of communication about and technology for contraception. Late in the eighteenth century only a few very modern couples began to exert control over fertility within marriage.[78]

By that date, nonetheless, the population growth and economic resources of New England had come into balance. The typical New England town settled down to the optimal size for small farming communities, between fifteen hundred and three thousand persons. The creativity and adaptability required to enact this change are best described in generational time, through a rough composite portrait of the men and women who formed families in the eighteenth century. First of all, fewer fathers could organize and underwrite new households by granting their sons a deed to family property or by purchasing new lands. Consequently, sons and daughters married less often, at later ages, and in more erratic birth order than in the past. Under these more trying circumstances, sons and daughters often acted decisively in their own interest and on their own inclinations; they married without the permission or in defiance of parents, or they became sexually intimate without benefit of wedlock. Other young men ventured out on the frontier or off to sea alone, leaving their home villages with a surplus of unmarried women. A young couple without a patrimony had to scurry to assemble resources on its own. The lucky might acquire some cheap undeveloped land far out on the frontier in New York or northern New England.

Newlyweds, united in this more independent fashion, conducted their intimate relations in novel ways. Demographers have discovered that the age at last birth began to fall in the late eighteenth and early nineteenth century, indicating that husbands and wives were taking measures to terminate the growth of their families in advance of the natural decline in fecundity. The exact mechanism of this demographic change (be it abstinence, coitus interruptus, crude modes of contraception, or abortion) is unclear, but the husbands and wives of New England were active partners in a major historical transformation. Somewhere around the year 1800, the Anglo-American communities of the Northeast passed a historic landmark, going from what demographers call a Malthusian frontier to a demographic steady state. Put in the crudest terms, regular cycles of high fertility and overpopulation, followed by famine and high mortality (the Malthusian pattern), gave way to lower fertility and a more balanced ratio between resources and reproduction. Accomplishing this demographic adjustment in English North America required considerable change in gender practices, the work of women and men together.[79]

The marriage partners of the late eighteenth century and early nineteenth century reformed the household economy with similar dexterity. Men and women entered eagerly into market agriculture. By the time of the Revolution, farms located close to seaports and market towns were exchanging as much as 40 percent of their produce for cash or credit. Farmers increasingly invested in cash crops like wheat and cultivated their lands with new intensity, at times eroding the soil but also adopting new technology, like the metal scythe, and new methods of cultivation, such as crop rotation. While woman's work was located at a greater distance from the fields, where the chief cash crop was put into production, the farmer's wife also moved with alacrity toward the marketplace. The expansion of the American dairy, poultry, and egg industry dates from this period and testifies to a flourishing woman's sector of commercial agriculture.[80]

Women's bartering in the neighborhood economy—exchanging eggs, milk, butter, garden produce, homespun yarn, even ashes and goose feathers —accelerated to meet the demand of merchants in nearby towns. Although the account books of the local tradesmen most often recorded these exchanges under the name of the male head of household, the commodities being exchanged were clearly produced by women. Furthermore, the farmer's wife often retained control of her cash earnings. Up the Hudson from New York City in the town of Nyack, wives kept a firm hand on the egg money. In the mid-Atlantic states half of all farms had a surplus available for export as of 1810, when they collectively brought fifteen million dollars into the family coffers annually. Much of this income came from women's labor. In Pennsylvania the product of women's dairies amounted to ten thousand pounds of butter, all processed in new, more efficient churns, designed by women. Some wives expanded the dairy into a thriving small business by hiring young female helpers. These commodities were taken to nearby towns or commercial centers, where other women joined the advance of the market economy. Nearly half the retailers of Philadelphia were women.[81]

Elsewhere, enterprising women took advantage of new markets and new technology by assuming the formerly male occupation of weaver. Looms began appearing not just in the households of artisan weavers but among other tradesmen, farmers, and shopkeepers; they were now operated by wives, daughters, and female servants. New England women sometimes took the initiative in home manufacturing. One Mary Tyler wrote that "having to give nine pence a yard for weaving I suggested to your father the expediency of getting a loom, and having our flax and wool wove in the house."[82] Mrs. Tyler plied her trade for a dozen years or more and recruited labor from both her children and several other young women in her employ. Eliza Wildes Bourne of Kennebunk, Maine, made a career of weaving and acquired a reputation in the local press for her ornate coverlets, valued at ten to seventeen dollars each. Homespun cloth was a major American product, and farmhouses were still stocked with looms and spinning wheels. In small towns in New York, three-quarters of all households boasted spinning wheels, and one-third had looms.[83] When industries like cloth manufacture were transferred to the small factories that dotted the rivers and streams of New England and the mid-Atlantic states, the working girls followed the path of production. Mill girls and their mothers converted female labor into family capital and cash—the makings of dowries, school expenses, or cash payment for the commodities that were bringing new comforts and small luxuries into American homes.[84]

Women were on a parallel track, and hardly a pace behind men, as the new national economy moved steadily toward market capitalism.[85] The prospects of trade and the lure of commodities loomed powerfully in the imagination of the young women who reached the threshold of adulthood late in the colonial period. Even the feverish imaginations of the afflicted girls of Salem Village fixed on visions of the wealth and fine clothes accumulating in the affluent districts of Salem Town. In the 1770s the fancy of young Sarah Welles of Connecticut also turned toward the marketplace: "Sometimes I fancy mySelf Some great Lady rideing in my Coach," and "Some times I am a poor Country farmers wife mounted on my old 'pye bawld mare' carrying fowl and eggs to market to buy my old man A holland Shirt but when I come to think in earnest about these affairs if I know my Self I shall Choose the midle way between these two 'for that which make's our lives delightfull / is A genteel Sufficiency and love.'"[86] Aware of the risks and the possibilities of the new economic order, Sarah Welles fantasized about acquiring luxuries but settled for a productive "sufficiency." Hers was not a sentimental domestic vision.

When women joined men in the marketplace after 1750, they often ventured forth with a certain swagger of equality. The late eighteenth- and early nineteenth-century period was a distinctive moment in American family history, after patriarchalism had been deposed but before the sentimental mother had been installed at the center of Victorian culture. At a time when the women of New England were actually taking action to limit their maternity, they reveled in the alternative family roles of republican wives, or daughters of liberty. Within the secular and political literature of the age of democratic revolution, enlightened husbands and fathers embraced women as friends, as rational partners in the business of life. Ben Franklin's epic autobiography had little to say about motherhood, but he acknowledged his wife Deborah as a full partner in the operation of his press and printing establishment. Deborah Franklin was not alone: the official printer for the state of South Carolina for ten critical years in the history of the young republic was a widow named Elizabeth Timothy. Mary Goddard assumed the same position in Baltimore, where she printed one of the earliest copies of the Declaration of Independence.[87]

The eighteenth century loosened ideas of patriarchy in households throughout the new nation.[88] Thomas Jefferson's letters to his daughter addressed an intellectual companion if not an equal, while the correspondence between Abigail and John Adams records the everyday courtesies of a republican marriage. The leveling of patriarchy was registered on canvases, as well as personal letters. Family portraits painted after 1760 demoted the husband from the superior elevation in the tableau and sat him down beside his wife.[89] The late eighteenth century also saw a revolution in literacy, as the native-born white women of New England achieved an ability to read and write equal to that of their brothers. Women had their own small Enlightenment in eighteenth-century America when writers like Judith Sargent Murray and Mercy Otis Warren championed women as the intellectual equals of men. In the words of one scholar, these writers depicted women "as moral and intellectual teachers capable of sharing equally with men in the pursuit of the public sphere."[90]

Motherhood and apple pie were not foremost on the mind of the busy republican wife or independent daughter. If not acquiring the education worthy

MAKING SEX IN AMERICA

of a republican, she was occupied holding up her half of the economic partnership. These busy spaces did not permit much advancement in the domestic arts. The republican diet was composed of brown bread and salted beef, and stinted on more refined pastry flour. The farmhouse was still more like a general workroom, where a huge open hearth and a few kettles were the chief culinary equipment. In the Georgian mansions growing up in places like Boston or Newport, the lady of the house was a relative stranger to the kitchen, which was commonly located out back and entrusted to servants. In sum, the innovative and dynamic little economies of the eighteenth century put relatively small stock in developing domesticity, maternity, and femininity.[91]

This fleeting image of a relatively symmetrical partnership of wife and husband was more than wishful republican rhetoric. It also took root outside the household, or at least as far as the local place of worship. After 1700, women had greater latitude to express themselves in church. A sharp tongue no longer brought suspicion of witchcraft and heresy. Rather, pious women, now the overwhelming majority of church members, were invited to lead family prayer and assume greater authority at the meetinghouse. Scarcely a generation after the Salem trials, Sarah Osbourne won respect and appreciation among Congregationalists when she convened religious meetings in her home. Women of newer sects like the Baptists and Methodists also rose to informal leadership during the upsurge of piety and expansion of church membership called the Great Awakening. Although the church fathers would not surrender their position at the top of the ecclesiastical hierarchy, they accorded women a larger place in public worship and relied on them as missionaries to their children, husbands, and neighbors.[92]

The authority of fathers was also ebbing in matters of doctrine. The Baptist sects that spread through the colonies in the years before the Revolution were founded on principles of spiritual independence. Membership in a Baptist congregation was not a legacy bequeathed by parents (who brought children forward to be christened in infancy) but rather the individual decision of an adult, often accomplished through a conversion experience that marked a break with the faith of one's father. The new converts did not practice a solitary and personal form of piety, however; on the contrary, they proclaimed their solidarity by addressing one another as "brother."[93] Growing numbers of Methodists, like Baptists, met in rapt communion outside the hierarchical spaces of the church or family—in open fields and barns and forest clearings. "Sisters" were also prominent participants in the first Baptist awakenings in the middle of the eighteenth century. They could be found exhorting others to convert and occasionally rose before the congregation to preach. Sometimes, republican mothers and their daughters even won the right to vote and participate in the formal governing of the new churches.[94]

Yet, as will be seen in a later chapter, women would not advance very far into political institutions of the new republic. Denied the vote, public office, and representation in democratic legislatures, women saw their concerns begin to slide off the agenda of public bodies. Issues once addressed by the town meeting and the established church, like the familial and sexual behavior of men and women, were of little interest to the politicians of the new nation. As a consequence, women lost public protection from domestic or sexual abuse. While men seldom faced charges of fornication and were rarely held responsible for the support of the children they fathered outside of marriage, unwed mothers were still subject to criminal prosecution, public shame, and the burden of supporting illegitimate offspring. The simultaneous increase in bastardry and infanticide did not augur well for women, mothers in particular. It was a precarious rather than a star-spangled moment for that growing class of single mothers who were regarded as a drain on community resources. Transient single mothers were warned out of town because they could not support themselves and their children. Such women accounted for the growing ranks of the "the strolling poor," brutally denied a stake in the new republic.[95]

The concentration of women, especially unwed mothers and widows, among the urban poor is chilling evidence of the gender inequality that accompanied the advances of the market economy. This omen of the sexual risks of the marketplace comes from the booming port city of Newport, Rhode Island: "Mercy Burke's child's dead. Her GMother and Mother lived together in a miserable hovel, with 4 others miserable by the lowest vices & in extreme poverty."[96] Women's entry into the brave new world of personal liberty and free trade might well have inspired anxiety, especially among those who were left unprotected by either property rights or equal access to legal redress. This unease found a variety of expressions in the late eighteenth and early nineteenth centuries. The risks of female sexuality were the theme of the first best-selling novel written and set in America, Susanna Rowson's *Charlotte Temple*. This classic seduced-and-abandoned story served as an object lesson in what might befall a young, friendless, parentless woman in Revolutionary America. Charlotte was the most pitiful of mothers. The novel's end found her penniless, unmarried, and lifeless, with a newborn daughter at her side. The hapless Charlotte, like the author herself, was of English origin, but this did not stop American readers from identifying with her

MAKING SEX IN AMERICA

plight. A gravestone in the cemetery of New York's Trinity Church that purported to mark the remains of Charlotte became a popular site for maudlin tourism.

Charlotte's predicament was more than a fanciful literary concoction. It had many analogues in the American provinces. Village gossips throughout New England and the mid-Atlantic spun more homely tales around the same plot line. Martha Ballard's diary reported on young women, daughters of stolid, churchgoing mothers, whose reckless coupling led to unwed pregnancy, poverty, and exile from the New England community. Not even the descendants of the founding Puritan families were immune to such sexual transgressions. The unwed pregnancy of Elizabeth Whitman, whose ancestors included Jonathan Edwards, was widely known. Susanna Rowson issued a fictional but well-aimed warning to young female readers who empathized with Charlotte Temple: their sexual independence came with the risks of bearing an illegitimate child. Their brothers and potential partners, meanwhile, marched on their way to wealth and independence, seemingly nonchalant about their sexual peccadilloes. Ben Franklin's autobiography, for example, was a far cry from the tale of Charlotte Temple, in style, plot, and sexual mores. Franklin jokingly confessed to many sexual "errata," while his friends seduced and abandoned with impunity on both sides of the Atlantic.[97]

The asymmetry of male and female in the age of the American Revolution inspired a story of perilous motherhood told in the American grain by Hannah Foster. Eliza Wharton, the protagonist in Foster's *The Coquette* (1797), personified the tragedy that might befall a rebellious or careless young woman in Revolutionary America. But she was a hardier heroine than Charlotte Temple. In the Franklinesque tradition she hastened to be independent: "It is *pleasure* my dear Lucy, on leaving my paternal roof. Could you have believed that the darling child of an indulgent and dearly devoted mother would feel a gleam of joy at leaving her? but it is so."[98] Eliza went on to declare her independence of the Puritan past by rejecting a minister as her suitor: "I recoil at the thought of immediately forming a connection which must confine me to the duties of domestic life and make me dependent for my happiness, perhaps too, for subsistence, upon a class of people, who will have the right to scrutinize every part of my conduct."[99] While hardly as abject and frail as Charlotte Temple (her fictional life would extend to thirty-seven years), Eliza Wharton ultimately suffered the same melodramatic fate. Seduced and abandoned, she was memorialized on the last page with the familiar epitaph: "She sustained the last painful scene, far from every friend; and exhibited an example of calm resignation."[100]

At the climactic place in the narrative where Rowson had stationed a dot-ing father at his daughter's death scene, Foster focused on another charac-ter, the mother. Eliza's fall from respectability followed from the "desperate resolution, which she formed and executed of becoming a fugitive; of desert-ing her mother's house and protection, and of wandering and dying among strangers . . . . [It] is a most distressing reflection of her friends, especially to her mother, in whose breast so many painful ideas arise, that she finds it ex-tremely difficult to compose herself to that resignation."[101] The denouement of *The Coquette* played out between bookends of maternal distress, Eliza's stricken mother on one side and the heroine's death in the throes of child-birth on the other. Foster's imagination, and that of her readers, provide clues as to the historical whereabouts of the American icon of motherhood. An avid reading audience followed Hannah Foster's characters along the risky path toward market capitalism, a world they entered without the legal protections, the property rights, or the leverage of citizenship that their brothers had won during the Revolution. Women would enter the new nation not boasting of their rights but bearing the risks of their reproductive biology.

Still, Hannah Foster, speaking through the persona of Eliza Wharton, did not greet that world with the heaving breast of the classic seduced and aban-doned maiden. Eliza left her parents' roof with a crusty Yankee indepen-dence, and even on her deathbed she heard a woman's voice raised to demand justice. Eliza's bereaved friend vowed that "my resentment at the base arts which must have been employed to complete the seduction of Eliza, I cannot suppress. I wish them to be exposed, and stamped with universal ignominy! Nor do I doubt but you will join with me in execrating the measures by which *we* have been robbed of so valuable a friend! And *society*, of so ornamental a member."[102] This last defiant message recalled the sturdy helpmates of the past and anticipated the female reformers of the future. It was an apt sym-bol of a critical moment of gender history, one pregnant with possibility and danger.

Homemaking in Antebellum and Victorian America

In the half century following the publication of *The Coquette*, women and men shaped the protean figures of the republican wives and independent daugh-ters into the icons of motherhood and apple pie. As anticipated by the last words of that novel, this major transition in gender culture was worked out in spaces of New England and the northeastern United States, and at several discursive sites—places of public worship, social reform, and print culture,

MAKING SEX IN AMERICA

as well as within the privacy of the family. All these social spaces meshed to form the springboard from which "true motherhood" would be launched into national cultural prominence.

The transition from the productive household economies of the past to the Victorian shrines of domestic femininity began in those Protestant churches where women had long been the majority of members. With each decade, women's stature in the church grew with their numbers and influence, without posing an apparent threat to either ministers or husbands. Baptist women, for example, were said to meet with men in "sweet harmony." Among Congregationalists, Presbyterians, and the upstart Methodist sects, wives led husbands, and mothers led children, into the rapid expansion of church membership. Church records indicate that beginning early in the nineteenth century children were more likely to join the faith of their mothers rather than their fathers, be it in times of revival enthusiasm or quieter Christian renewal. The cycle of evangelism called the Second Great Awakening, which commenced early in the nineteenth century, was a familial enterprise, which brought about a major cultural change: the United States of America became a nation of fervent churchgoers, with one of the highest rates of religious affiliation in the Western world.[103]

Along with the Christian gospel, the flourishing Protestant sects sent literary prescriptions for domesticity all along the frontier, into upstate New York, through the Ohio Valley, and into the South. The messages came first from ministers, but they were increasingly penned by women, packaged in magazines and funded by female missionary societies. *The Ladies' Repository* propagated the doctrines of Methodists, a sect that grew up with the new nation to become the largest American denomination by 1850. *The Ladies' Repository* pictured conversion as a family drama in which the wife and mother subtly guided husbands and children toward salvation (a telling reversal of the sex roles found in seduction literature). By the middle decades of the nineteenth century, this gentle, familial method of proselytizing had replaced the more open and democratic assemblies in which Methodist affiliation was spawned —class meetings, love feasts, camp meetings. Converts filed into formal churches, where fathers and husbands were educated in the new domestic regime of mutual respect between spouses and a gentler ministry to children. Southern Methodists, for example, gave up rowdy male entertainment —gambling, heavy drinking, and cockfighting—for a respectable and sober home life. In this chrysalis the sect grew from a band of rebellious brothers to a church of sedate families.[104]

Pious New England mothers devised novel evangelical methods for use at home and on the frontier. They founded missionary societies and female moral reform associations in which to practice and propagate their maternal influence. One of the earliest of these female moral reform societies was designed for the express purpose of cultivating motherly aptitudes. Beginning in 1815 in Maine, small groups of churchwomen formed a newfangled social institution that they called simply a "maternal association," where they regularly gathered to pray for their children and to consider how best to "raise them up in the way they should go." By the 1840s maternal associations were producing their own periodical literature. The Presbyterians hired a woman to edit their "Mothers Magazine," and the Methodists soon followed suit. Be it as bands of praying mothers or as the erudite editors of ladies' magazines, women were forging new kinds of links between the generations, traced not through the transmission of property but through immaterial influences of grace, emotional connection, and moral influence. At midcentury, the religious press was prescribing a crude psychological method of molding a child's character. One Methodist publication posed the recommended method of child-rearing as a rhetorical question: "Who can tell the power and efficiency of a mother's prayer?" The answer came close to maternal idolatry: "Her love can only be excelled by the love of God."[105] The course of grace had turned from the turbulent eruptions of revivals to the quiet but steady currents of family feeling. The model Methodist home was no longer described as a patriarchal domain; now, "rule, authority and power" had passed on to mothers. The Ladies' Repository put this theory of child-rearing and domestic influence in an appropriately feminine metaphor: the home mother was like a shrinking violet, most fragrant and captivating when she bloomed in the quiet recesses of her native woods.[106]

Not all pious mothers were so retiring. Alert to the sexual dangers that were unabated since the times of Charlotte Temple, some of them took decisive and collective action. They organized at the grass roots to change standards of sexual conduct. Chapters of Female Moral Reform Societies and Magdalene Societies grew up in some four hundred communities throughout the Northeast in the 1830s and 1840s. Working together and in cooperation with pastors and male reformers, women devised a series of methods of monitoring the sexual practices of their husbands, sons, and fellow Americans—ostracism of seducers, protests outside brothels, even campaigns to enact laws against seduction. Female Moral Reform Societies were one of the first, most aggressive, and innovative flanks of the movement to create those exacting standards of sexual self-control that have been named Victorian. Their strategies seem to have had an impact. By the 1840s, the rates of premarital conception and illegitimacy had subsided from their eighteenth-century highs. In just a generation, mothers acting collectively could at least offer a set of explicit moral guidelines to replace the legal and communal supports of the lost patriarchal authority. Ordinary women were working their way toward a new way of parenting, one that magnified the religious and social influence of motherhood. In revivals, maternal associations, and moral reform societies they strived to inoculate sons and husbands against the temptations that lurked outside their homes. The temperance movement, with its male and female contingents, also dispensed heavy doses of domestic sentimentality, especially bathetic images of the drunkard's weeping mother and frail daughter, for the same prophylactic purposes.[107]

The mothers who felt and fashioned these new maternal sentiments were still making generous economic contributions to their households.[108] The farmers' almanacs of the early nineteenth century made little of the domestic graces, and the first major manual for household management went by the title of *American Frugal Housewife*. This tidy volume was first published in 1835. Its author, Lydia Maria Child, the daughter of a New England baker and farmer, had grown up in a productive family economy. Her own marriage was not a good economic match, however, and she was called upon to help support a debt-ridden husband by her wits and her writing. No wonder, then, that she recommended frugal homemaking as the best stratagem for the young women of her time. Habits of saving, household parsimony, and ingenuity would equip America's daughters for either a lowly or a lofty rank in life, whatever might befall them in marriage.[109]

Amid recipes for brewing beer, concocting medicine, or curing beef, Child mapped the route from home to market: "Attend to all the mending in the house, once a week, if possible. Never put out sewing. If it be impossible to do it in your family, hire some one into the house, and work with them."[110] Child pointedly instructed housewives to do their own baking: "Make your own bread and cake. Some people think it just as cheap to buy of the baker and confectioner; but it is not half as cheap."[111] In these few lines Child presented women with sundry options: she could hire out—or bring in—sewing; she could bake her own bread—or purchase it in local shops. Child calculated the value of frugal housewifery as the difference between the cost of female labor and the price of a market exchange. Writing in the fourth decade of the nineteenth century, she still recalled the world of the deputy husband as she exhorted housewives to become ambidextrous contributors to the family; they could produce as well as consume, bake bread as well as occasionally make a purchase at the local dry goods store.[112]

Hardly a dozen years later, however, the frugal housewife was replaced by mother's own apple pie as the centerpiece of a booming market in domestic literature. The model of the genre was Catharine Beecher's *A Treatise on Domestic Economy*, published in 1841.[113] Beecher's ideal home was set off from public space by a filigree of gardens and picket fences. Yet this emblem of domestic sentiment disguised a thicket of connections to the marketplace. Beecher sent mothers out of the home to purchase everything from parlor furniture to kitchen utensils and, of course, treatises on domestic economy. When Beecher frowned on hiring servants or nursemaids, it was not just to save money, but also in order to stress the heightened moral power and beneficent social influence of the housewife. When performed by a loving wife and mother, mundane chores had a salutary influence on sons and husbands, reminding them to uphold the standards of comportment she represented. Seemingly forgetful of her own New England history, Beecher wrote as if the household were almost a space of idleness. Her elaborate instructions about gardening, cooking, ventilation, and family medicine gave housewives a sense of purpose at a time when productive enterprises were leaving the American woman's home: such "acquirements and information . . . may be as companions to her, whiling away the hours of solitude which would otherwise be spent in listlessness, indolence or discontent."[114] Beecher packaged the domestic labor of mothers as a vital contribution to the emotional and moral, not merely the material and economic, welfare of the American home. Women's work in the home was no less demanding and consequential, but it took a new form whose more ornamental qualities have been aptly captured in the phrase "the pastoralization of housework."[115]

Catharine Beecher made a lateral move away from the patrilineage of the Puritans and then took a giant step along the historical course toward domestic femininity. The daughter of Presbyterian minister Lyman Beecher, Catharine made a strategic detour from the New England household order only after she failed either to marry or to fully convert to the religion of her fathers. She turned away from the church toward secular pursuits, first operating a female seminary, subsequently publishing books, and ultimately sparking public controversy. Like her younger sister Harriet Beecher Stowe, with whom she coauthored an encyclopedic domestic manual called *The American Woman's Home*, Catharine Beecher forged a path to political influence. Like her sister's domestic fiction, which would become implicated in the cause of antislavery and the coming of civil war, Catharine's domestic writings had a direct and self-conscious political intent. She introduced her essay on domestic duties in 1845 with the warning that a revolution as destructive as the work of the Jacobins was imminent in America. Beecher took heed of the French in devising a remedy for the dangers she saw lurking in the aggressively democratic and fiercely partisan politics of the Jacksonian era. Citing Tocqueville, she argued that by retiring into domestic spaces, women could better mitigate the destructive passions of male citizens—their own sons and husbands. She rallied gender as a counterforce to excessive democracy: "American women! Will you save your country?"[116]

A Treatise on Domestic Economy was, therefore, far more than a manual for housewives. It was a political tract in which Beecher fine-tuned the private and feminized side of republican political theory, then updated it in response to the democratic practices of the Jacksonian period. This gender politics, which Beecher pioneered in the 1840s, was an elaboration and major reformulation of the notion of the Republican Mother. As conceived by Enlightenment thinkers like Benjamin Rush, the Republican Mother was a rather cerebral and androgynous figure, equipped with the powers of literacy and reason, which prepared her to educate her sons for citizenship. It was left to Beecher to define mother's service to the nation in a more domesticated and feminized way. Under the chapter heading "The Peculiar Responsibilities of American Women," Beecher construed the mundane domestic activities of mothering as the critical social function of training future citizens. The quotidian maintenance of a salutary home environment would, according to her theory, restrain men from riots and corruption. In sum, Beecher articulated a gender theory that not only hallowed mother and her apple pie but also appointed her the custodian of social and political order.[117]

And Beecher did not act alone. In the 1840s other authors translated Beecher's learned argument into both cookbooks and political slogans. Margaret Coxe, for example, called women "national conservatives in the largest sense," as long as they tended the home fires. The scion of another conservative New England patriarch, Theodore Sedgwick's daughter Catherine, argued that "home cultivation of the affections" was as effective a palliative to excessive democracy as was her father's conservative Federalist politics. These "natural and unchanging relations" were essential antidotes to the "morbid excitement" and "dissolute excess" of political factions. The influential minister Horace Bushnell also invested his hopes for the perpetuation of New England's founding values on the home labors of women. Before the middle of the nineteenth century, all the basic ingredients of apple pie and motherhood had been conjured up by a cohort of energetic writers, most of them women, and disseminated to a wide reading audience. By then, the adaptive strategies of grassroots associations of mothers had been collated into manuals of domesticity and a formula for political stability. The central tenets of this political and social theory were, first, the segregation and isolation of women in the home, second, the harnessing of women's domestic labor to the socialization of sons and the social control of husbands, and finally, the deployment of these conservative forces so as to modulate the excesses of democracy. This vernacular ideology (as American as you know what) was fully formed by the middle of the nineteenth century.[118]

After 1850 the new housewifery was polished into a glossy image of maternal domesticity. It traveled far out the frontier, where middle-class housewives served up such "fashionable dishes" as "waffles, cold bread, sponge cake and Washington cake," as well as a delicacy called "apple slump pies." For a sample of how this new housewifery would operate on an everyday basis, we need look no further than the letters of Harriet Beecher Stowe. Her work ledger for scarcely more than half a year had her making two sofas, a barrel chair, several bedspreads, pillowcases, and mattresses. Meanwhile, she painted rooms, refinished furniture, cajoled the landlord into installing a sink, and read the novels of Walter Scott, all the while doing the cooking and caring for a growing family. None of this secured her a pecuniary reward. This was arduous, time-consuming work, much of it highly skilled, but because it was all consumed within the home it earned no monetary reward. Perhaps that explains Stowe's incredible comment on her domestic regimen: "I am constantly pursued and haunted by the idea that I don't do anything."[119]

Mrs. Stowe and housewives like her performed work of major historical consequence. They were the architects and engineers of the political economy of domesticity. Behind the best sellers of the nineteenth century and the most profitable products of the burgeoning publishing industry—of which Stowe's domestic melodrama *Uncle Tom's Cabin* was the most popular—lurked the career strategies of determined female writers. Best-selling authors of domestic fiction like Stowe, Fanny Fern, Maria Cummins, and Susanna Warner had all embarked on their careers when their husbands or fathers failed in the role of sole provider. They had to fight for the attention of skeptical male editors and publishers, but ultimately they commanded a vast reading audience. Another needy and enterprising woman, the widowed Sarah Josepha Hale, founded *Godey's Lady's Book*, the first in a long line of highly profitable women's magazines. Once they broke into print, women writers won a popular audience, numbering hundreds of thousands of women readers, with voracious appetites for domestic literary fare. Soon the enterprising businessmen who headed publishing empires like Harper Brothers and Tichenor and Fields, or edited magazines such as the *Boston*

The kitchen of Harriet Beecher Stowe.
(Courtesy of the Harriet Beecher Stowe Center, Hartford, Connecticut)

Reporter and *The Family Ledger*, reaped the profits from a literary market in which women were both the writers and the readers, both the supply and the demand.[120]

Commodities, as well as sentiments, were distributed through the marketplace of domesticity. The country merchants of the 1830s, the managers of dry goods stores in the rising towns, and entrepreneurs like A. T. Stewart and R. H. Macy who founded department stores in the 1850s and 1860s all made their living by furnishing "the American Woman's Home." By the time Catharine Beecher and Harriet Beecher Stowe wrote the book with that title, the dwelling places of the urban middle class had taken on their classic American form—a detached, single-family residence, set in a green lawn and centered on a well-equipped kitchen. Be it a cottage or a mansion house, the floor plan of domesticity called for moving the kitchen upstairs and inside. Stowe's own kitchen was arranged as an efficient workspace and stocked with all sorts of small tools and one major piece of capital equipment, an ornate iron stove. When traced to the census of manufacturers, durable goods like this constituted a major economic sector and created jobs in machine shops and iron mills throughout the land. One economic historian has estimated that the newfangled kitchen had more machinery than the typical small factory of the time. The exterior of the home was also invested with new meaning, adornment, and care in the nineteenth century. City streets were lined with the first specialized residential buildings, often with regional charms like the row houses of Baltimore, the Garden District of New Orleans, New York's brownstones, and San Francisco's Victorians. Whole districts, the first to be set apart from spaces for mixed commercial, artisan, and residential use, were devoted to the home life of the urban middle class. Even in the rural areas, farmhouses were beginning to look more like residences than workshops. Spaces once given over to the scattered detritus of barnyards and fields now sprouted carefully tended grounds, ornamental foliage, and neatly painted frames.[121]

The women's work and market value required to maintain these domestic shrines were veiled in mists of privacy. The half-century mark had scarcely passed when hack writers could recite the mystifying new ideology of womanhood: "Her place is not on life's great battle-fields. Man belongs there. Woman must abide in the peaceful sanctuaries of home, and walk in the noiseless vales of private life. There she must dwell, beside the secret springs of public virtue. There she must smile upon the husband. There she must rear the Christian patriot and statesman, the self-denying philanthropist and the obedient citizen. There, in a word, she must form the character of the world, and determine the destiny of her race."[122] The promises of women's domestic influence became even more hyperbolic when it came to the "most important and responsible relation" ordained to women, that "which she sustains as the mother." The pious mission of the evangelical mother was repackaged as the "Empire of the Mother": "She governs the world in the capacity of mother, because in the forming period of life, the cords of love and gentleness are stronger and more prevailing than all the chains which mere force has ever forged."[123] There is a logic in all this airy geography: that the internal controls exerted through family influences on the young—attachment, guilt, and dependence on a loving parent—would somehow serve as surrogates for the old household bonds of property, inheritance, and apprenticeship. Called "gentle nurture" or "moral suasion," this new child-rearing technique was also advertised as a method of political and social control; it would moderate the passions of those young men who had been invested with awesome powers of democratic citizenship. Much of this child-rearing strategy

MAKING SEX IN AMERICA

was wishful thinking, but it did introduce an elaborate set of maternal practices, extending from using the withdrawal of love to punish disobedience to joining the Child Study Movement, which scientifically monitored every stage in the development of a son or daughter's character.[124]

The cult of motherhood has not left an obvious material imprint on American culture. Unlike the new arts of housewifery, it has not deposited domestic artifacts in antique stores or museums. Some indirect evidence about the new motherhood can be found, however, in the U.S. census, demographic records, and the statute books of the nineteenth century. The household censuses, first of all, demonstrate that a certain class of influential women had more time to devote to domestic duties. Urban, native-born, middle-class mothers very rarely worked for pay outside the home. Severed from farm and artisan production, and trained to new consumer roles, urban middle-class wives lived out the oldest cliché of family history, that modernization separated the household from the economy, and women from men. The finer details in the household census also indicate that sons and daughters remained under their mother's wings for prolonged periods.[125] Later age at marriage and low rates of employment outside the home indicate that America's daughters remained under the parental roof for especially long periods. The volatility of the male life cycle had also stabilized by the 1850s, when the census found that sons were also more likely to reside within the mother's domain until relatively late in life. These great-grandsons of New England patriarchs had been educated and supplied with the family capital, moral and educational as well as material, with which to embark on white-collar and professional jobs.[126]

The statistical record of reproduction within the urban middle class gives further credence to the evolution of domestic maternity. Total fertility rates dropped sharply over the course of the nineteenth century. One key measure of fertility, the average number of children born to married women, was cut in half, from 7 in 1800 to 3.5 in 1900. In urban middle-class districts that have been studied in detail—Utica, New York; Union Park, Chicago; the genteel neighborhoods of Philadelphia—the average completed family size of native-born families fell even earlier and at a more precipitous rate.[127] These statistics suggest that for middle-class mothers, the amount of maternal time and energy available to care for each child may have almost doubled over the century. The declining family size was like the other components of the new domestic motherhood, a purposive and arduous undertaking, with its own volatile history. In the 1830s and 1840s traditional techniques for controlling family size—abortion, coitus interruptus, condoms, and douches—

were made available through the same avenues that had circulated the other tenets of domestic femininity: the press, the post office, the marketplace. By the 1880s, this new domestic practice had created a discernible market for methods of reproduction control, from abortion, as practiced by the likes of the once fashionable Madame Restell in New York City, to fads like pessaries and devices advertised as "rubber goods for men and women." There was no silver-bullet cure for unwanted pregnancies, but determined couples could cobble together a complex of techniques that did lower their overall, long-term fertility. By lengthening the spaces between births and reducing total family size, mothers were enabled to invest more time caring for each individual child. But because it was very difficult to cut off fertility at will, and at an early age, most mothers would still have children in their homes through the bulk of their adult lives. This rudimentary "family planning" made mothering an intensive and extensive occupation.[128]

Concurrent changes in family law augment this evidence of the intensification of motherhood during the Victorian period. State by state, courts began to transfer legal responsibility for children from fathers to mothers. In the event of divorce, the father was no longer automatically awarded the custody of children, and individual judges were increasingly likely to place children under maternal care. Widowed mothers were also more often entrusted with the management of a deceased father's property. Just before the first women's rights convention convened in Seneca Falls, New York, wives won the right to control the property they brought into marriage. By 1900, most states had followed suit until married women and mothers were raised from the civil death of common law. Although often enacted in the financial interest of fathers rather than in deference to mothers, these legal reforms add further weight to the argument that the gender relations of the household had been remodeled, indeed modernized. Within two generations of the founding of the republic, the middle-class urban home had become a place were women assumed responsibility for the work of child care and were granted the legal protection necessary to execute their specialized domestic and maternal duties.[129]

By the time these new legal codes were adopted, countless anonymous American women and men had become adept at performing the new regimen of gender that historians once identified by the concept of separate spheres. Deep emotional bonds grew up around the common concerns of Victorian mothers, creating what has been called a whole "female world of love and ritual."[130] That world was set clearly apart from the masculine public sphere (the subject of a later chapter) and from sundry spaces of private male sociability such as the rowdy domains of boxing rings, fraternal lodges, and saloons.[131] While advice books urged men to adapt some of the domestic sentiments of their wives—gentler methods of fathering, for example, and prompt return to the fireside after a day's work—the masculine side of domesticity was an asymmetrical and underdeveloped sphere. The proper match to a domestic female was a "family man" known for his hard work, sobriety, and dedication to middle-class family living.[132] The man's major contribution to the household was as breadwinner, set apart from his intimate kin for most of the week with his nose to the grindstone of the job. One advice manual captured the contradictions of domesticity for the beleaguered breadwinner in this directive: "Know your business in all its details. Marry it." The major responsibility of the "family man" was to leave home in order to finance the domestic labor of mothers.[133]

Sons and husbands of the emergent middle class had taken their own path toward the modern American gender system. A survey of private diaries revealed that men and women had different reading habits. Studies of antebellum reform have found that the two sexes seldom joined the same voluntary associations. In the temperance movement, for example, women joined separate associations that were preoccupied with the welfare of their children, while male teetotalers conducted exercises in independent and self-reliant manhood.[134] At other times men sought out affection and support among their own sex. Even the male enclave of the voluntary fire department became domesticated by the middle of the nineteenth century, as the burly street fighters of antebellum fire companies settled into quiet professional quarters, where they practiced their own homemaking skills on one another. By the late nineteenth century, literally millions of men flocked to lodges, whose cozy quarters, warming firesides, and bonding rituals mimicked domesticity and expressed a certain antagonism to the opposite sex. Ritual initiation into the International Order of Redmen, for example, took new members through a cycle of birth and family formation, presided over by an old-fashioned patriarch rather than a loving mother.[135]

The relatively limited participation of men in the work and ritual of the middle-class home does not detract from the power of domesticity. In fact, it testifies to the cultural power and social utility of a new gender division of labor. The specialized domestic ministrations of mothers served to smooth the path to middle-class security amid the destabilizing conditions of market capitalism and early industrialization. Such maternal accomplishments as reduced fertility, intensive child care, cultivation of self-discipline, investment in education, and spending on domestic products and services all helped sons advance toward relatively stable and lucrative positions in the new economy—as clerks, white-collar workers, doctors, lawyers, and the more highly skilled artisans and manual laborers. When accompanied by the advantages of birth into privileged racial, ethnic, and religious groups, these techniques did in fact ease one's entry into middle-class status. By the mid-nineteenth century, white, native-born Protestants had virtually monopolized the middling ranks of the urban social structure. Motherhood was a crucible—and apple pie was a symbol—of major social, cultural, and economic consequence: it was the procreator of the American middle class, the social status still claimed by the vast majority of Americans, many of whom owned a very small piece of the economic pie.[136]

It took generations to devise the ideology of domestic femininity and then install it at the center of popular culture. The knotty roots of domesticity can be traced all the way back to the seventeenth century, and bear recapitulating. The preconditions for feminine domesticity were set down by New England colonists on the rock-solid foundation of private family property. Fenced off as separate farmsteads, presided over by patriarchs, and bequeathed to sons, the private family became a fundamental, well-fortified, and durable social institution. The mistresses of these households in the wilderness, while legally and practically subservient to men, carved out a place of economic and social usefulness for their sex. Even in the seventeenth century, the women of New England took the material and cultural products of their domestic labor out of the homestead into local meetinghouses and along neighborly trade routes.

The particular New England version of the household economy had a consequential but abbreviated life. Scarcely three generations into the family history of New England, high fertility rates set the stage for a demographic crisis. Only a minority of the prolific second and third generations could provide their progeny with a homestead in close proximity to their colonial fathers. The witchcraft hysteria in Salem Village was one extreme expression of the anxiety that devolved on the most vulnerable members of the community: young, unmarried women. Most communities, however, made an expeditious and dexterous readjustment of family practices. Husbands and wives recalibrated the balance of their productive and reproductive roles, in and outside the family. While husbands took the lead in venturing outside the farmstead into a world of commerce and mobility, revolution and republicanism, their wives advanced toward the marketplace with an increasing volume of home-produced goods in tow. Be it with egg money, frugal housekeeping, or the instruction of the young (at home or in a growing number of neighborhood schools), these republican wives and daughters subsidized the commercial farmers of the new nation.

As the nineteenth century advanced, the paths of male and female diverged more sharply, due to the ingenuity and influence of women and men alike. The powers, skills, and commitments that women had built up in the sturdy households of New England were not about to be quietly retired into social and economic insignificance. Mothers and daughters of the new republic quickly ascertained the risks, as well as the promises, of the expanding market economy. Largely without legal protection or political rights, and particularly vulnerable to unwanted pregnancy, women writers and reformers sought out new ways to protect themselves and their progeny. Mothers of the middling ranks and Protestant faith created benevolent and reform associations in which they devised ways of remodeling nearly every aspect of family life, from sexual practices to household architecture, techniques of early childhood socialization, and civics lessons for the young.

Since northern native-born women had an exceptionally high rate of literacy, almost equal to their brothers, they were ideally situated to propagate domesticity through print culture. While many middle-class women withdrew into more domestic spaces, they practiced an exacting vocation under the professional tutelage of female writers and editors. Accordingly, the domestication of women did not strand their sex in some archaic household order while men marched off to a modern, public world of politics and economics. In fact, the contents of this chapter warrant the proposition that women (in concert, of course, with their husbands, sons, ministers, and publishers) were the vanguard of one flank of modernity. They created an elaborate and innovative set of social and cultural practices, sometimes designated as a private sphere, but better termed a sphere of social reproduction.

Having secured this vantage point in Victorian culture, domestic femininity soon took on imperialistic pretensions. Middle-class reformers went studiously to work propagating domestic motherhood everywhere from Indian boarding schools, to immigrants' neighborhoods, to the far provinces of China.[137] Although (as we shall see in later chapters) domestic femininity stopped short of imperial conquest, it still maintained ideological hegemony over much of American popular culture. It became the standard against which other ways of organizing reproduction and personal life were judged. When feminine domesticity clashed with contrary gender practices, the results could be disastrous. Even in the last decade of the twentieth century, a cavalier disregard for the maternal art of baking cookies proved to be a costly political mistake for Hillary Clinton. Baking all-American apple pie could be a difficult balancing act. In the 1950s excessive, smothering maternity led to charges of "Momism," or being an overweening Jewish mother. Those mothers who erred in the other direction, by granting too much independence to children or leaving home for the labor force, risked being accused of child neglect or scolded as "black matriarchs." The white middle-class model of feminine domesticity was especially incongruent with African American experience and productive of such distorting and defaming stereotypes as the mammy, the black matriarch, or the welfare mother. These mystifying machinations of gender ideology serve as a final reminder that motherhood and apple pie, although just icons, wielded real cultural force. Among those who journeyed to America not as Pilgrims but as slaves, maternity would take on different meanings, and apple pie could have a bitter taste, as will be seen in the next chapter.

CHAPTER 3

HOW DID RACE GET COLORED?

GENDER AND SEXUALITY IN

THE AMERICAN SOUTH

Looking out to the far corners of the globe in 1758, Carl Linnaeus confidently sorted the world's population into four groups. The inhabitants of Asia, Africa, Europe, and the Americas conformed to a neat natural order, analogous to the four cardinal points of the compass, the four humors, and the four elements. Over two hundred years later, a judge presiding over a court in the state of Virginia issued another tidy pronouncement about human geography: "Almighty God created the races, white, black, yellow, malay and red, and he placed them on separate continents. . . . He did not intend the races to mix."[1] At some point between these dates, the color scheme favored by the Virginia legal code became the vernacular way of distinguishing among the peoples of the world who had come to settle on the North American continent. This separation of humankind into different lines of descent on the basis of skin color is commonly termed "race." The boundaries of race in America have long been marked off as blunt color differences, and much more. Race also designated a system of rank and power that was inscribed in law and maintained by the everyday thoughts and actions of masses of Americans. The Virginia judge quoted above, for example, insinuated these divisions into the most intimate relations: he ruled that the state could prohibit marriage between men and women whose complexions were colored differently. At the late date when the Supreme Court finally declared them unconstitutional, in 1967, laws prohibiting interracial marriage had been enacted at one time or another in forty-one states of the union.[2]

Race may appear in the spectrum of American history as a simple set of contrasting colors, yet maintaining those contrasts has required the coercive force of law and the careful surveillance of the relations of the sexes. Far murkier, more complex and varied than any simple color chart, race is also complicated by shades of gender and of sexuality. Differences in skin tone obviously play out as a spectrum of subtle gradations, especially in a nation like the United States, where the populations of the world are forever mix-ing and merging with one another. One of the first European incursions into the Americas, Coronado's expedition into the Southwest in the sixteenth cen-tury, consisted of Portuguese, Spanish, Italians, French, Germans, Africans, Mexican Indians, and slaves of various colors.[3] Those peoples called African and Indian, moreover, were composed of myriad different tribes and clans, most of whom had a long history of trading and intermarrying, as well as war-ring, with one another. As the laws against miscegenation testify, segregating the peoples of the world, by social or sexual means, has required assiduous policing. One of the most menacing mysteries of sex will be addressed in this chapter. How did sexuality and related gender practices contribute to that arduous process of constructing racial boundaries in the United States?

Race, much like gender, denotes a particular historical process—made up of countless, repeated, and variable human actions—that converts differ-ences into rigid categories, relationships, and hierarchies. The subject of this chapter is best described as the process of "racial formation" rather than an account of a specific social group or cultural identity. The historical project of coloring race in America dates back to before the time of Linnaeus, when Europeans ventured out into the world, encountering and colonizing new peoples and cultures.[4] Four hundred years later, at the time when the U.S. Supreme Court finally outlawed laws against miscegenation, the meaning of race was forming and reforming once again. For purposes of illustration, this chapter will focus on only one of many schemes for sorting out human-kind into separate races: that drawn around descendants of the African slave trade and crudely demarcated as black versus white. (Other prominent and very consequential racial formations, such as that construed around immi-grants from Asia and Latin America, will be noted in a later chapter.)

Comprehending even this single circumscribed racial formation will take this chapter through many twists and turns of history. The search for the color of race begins at a time ripe with possibilities for tribal intermingling. As described in chapter 1, the first Europeans who traveled to the Americas held open many doors to the natives of the New World, including commer-cial, sexual, and marital relations. The chapter will move quickly past these first encounters to that place, time, and institution that laid down the founda-tion of the modern racial regime: the British colonies of the American South, where Africans have mixed with Europeans since at least 1619. The legal establishment in Virginia at the close of the seventeenth century locked the descendants of Africans in bondage and coded race in the vernacular tones of black and white.

Gender played a critical role in this process of racial formation. First of all, the institutionalization and perpetuation of African American slavery was founded on a gendered pattern of inheritance: bondage was conveyed onto subsequent generations through the maternal line. Once chattel slavery was in place, it created the conditions for gender roles and relations that were distinctive to the American South, among whites as well as blacks. The contrast between the meanings of male and female in the slave quarters and in the plantation house soon became a matter of bitter contention between abolitionists and slave owners, the North and the South. The Civil War that ensued brought on further gender changes. The Emancipation Proclamation of 1863 transformed the relations between African American men and women once again, only to be buffeted by the policies of Radical Reconstruction in the late 1860s and battered by the reinstitution of conservative white domination during the 1880s. Hysteria about interracial sex and laws against miscegenation helped pave the way toward a new regime of racial subordination. At this point in time, the prohibition of sexual intimacies across racial lines became blunt and draconian. For a brief period the state of Virginia punished miscegenation with life imprisonment, and for decades allegations that African American men defied the prohibition of interracial sex excused a lynching. The vitriolic sexual rhetoric that inspired a race riot in Wilmington, North Carolina, in 1898 is a bloody marker of the racial formation that succeeded slavery and that still colors inequality in America in shades of black and white. Sex and gender did heavy and versatile labor in the complex historical process that painted this obstinate and anguished color contrast known as race.[5]

How Slavery Became Colored African American

Well before they ventured across the Atlantic, Western Europeans had made contact with peoples who lived and looked unlike themselves. Collisions of cultures were routine, be they contact between contiguous clans in Northern Europe or the advance of the Moors up from Africa onto the Iberian peninsula. And while these encounters were often belligerent, they seldom produced unassailable racial barriers between the protagonists. In fact, by taking foreign belligerents captive, Europeans and North Africans continued the genetic mixing that had long been a condition for the survival of the human species. Medieval Europeans were experienced with one form of transracial connection in particular: slave captivity. They confirmed the adage, "There is no region on earth that has not at some time harbored the institution of slavery. Probably there is no group of people whose ancestors were not at one time slaves or slaveholders."[6] When Columbus set sail in 1492, Europeans had some knowledge of the slave trade internal to Africa, as well as a long historical memory of bondage on their own continent, including the captivity of Moors, Slavs, Muslims, and fellow Christians. The characteristic that singled out certain populations for bondage was not necessarily their skin color but their vulnerability as outsiders, enemies, or strangers who could be excluded from full communion with the slave-owning society. This practice has led some theorists to describe slavery as "social death," the abrogation of claims to membership in a community or nation. At the most fundamental level, slavery operated as a denial of ties to family, clan, or lineage. As such, it was an intrinsically gendered construction, organized around one of the three major elements of this analysis of gender, the relations of the sexes.[7]

However, as seen in previous chapters, the relations of the sexes and the lines of kinship are highly plastic and flexible. While captivity broke old kin ties, it forged new ones. Those enslaved were often quickly absorbed into the clans of their captors. At the time of the European conquest, American tribes enslaved their enemies in order to build up a population that had been depleted by war and famine. This pattern of taking captives was also found on the west coast of Africa, where powerful kingdoms grew rich by capturing, trading, or accepting as tribute the human wealth of agricultural villages in the interior. In each of these cases, slavery took a form that was quite distinct from the system of forced labor that would develop in early modern America. First of all, the captives of Amerindian warriors or African kings were quickly redeemed by adoption or marriage into the enslaving culture. Some slave captives achieved a lofty status through their service as soldiers, artisans, or courtesans, and some even became slave owners themselves. As a consequence of this swift assimilation into the captors' society, African and Indian slavery was usually a temporary status. For the individual captive, it often terminated with intermarriage or adoption and rarely extended to a second generation. The children of slaves were usually born free. This form of servitude was a relatively small gradation away from common modes of labor in early modern Europe: serfdom, indenture, apprenticeship, and the impressment of seamen. It rarely lasted a lifetime, was not passed on to children, and entailed some significant social protection. As a consequence, slavery was not a particularly anomalous status at a time when "free labor" was far from universal.[8]

The incentive to enslave was all about labor, about acquiring more human energy with which to exploit the earth's bounty. Although slavery had been dying out in Europe since the eleventh century, and was deemed inhumane during the Renaissance and Enlightenment, it was given new life when the desire to exploit the resources of the New World required new sources of labor. Even then, enterprising colonizers found candidates for bondage closer at hand than in sub-Saharan Africa. The despised pagan Irish, the landless, urban poor of Europe, and the Indians of the New World provided a more immediate and cheaper source of labor than the African slave trade.

The first aborted attempt to create a slave labor force in the New World was the work of the Spanish, and the population first targeted for colonial exploitation was American. Although the Spanish had outlawed slavery in their homeland, they reintroduced a similar status for the purposes of converting Native Americans, whom they christened neophytes and subjected to forced labor as well as enrollment in the Roman Catholic Church. The Indians of the Southwest and California were put to work in Spanish mines, missions, haciendas, and pueblos. A census taken in Santa Fe, New Mexico, in 1630 already counted a population of 700 Indian slaves and mestizo servants and just 250 Spanish residents.[9] In some ways, this New World slavery resembled long-standing Indian practices. Southwestern tribes—Comanche, Navajo, and Apache—conducted regular intertribal raids, taking captives to augment their populations and sometimes selling them as laborers in Spanish households.[10] The incursion of the Spanish intensified and prolonged this traffic in Indian captives. As the native economy was undermined by colonial intrusions, Indian warriors depended increasingly on the trading of slaves for their survival. In fact, the raids would continue wreaking havoc in the Southwest until well into the nineteenth century, even after the Emancipation Proclamation.[11] Both the Spanish and Indians had multiple uses for captives. They could be traded for commodities, exchanged as part of diplomatic negotiations, or taken as wives.[12]

While the slave raids in the southwestern borderlands placed Indians in servitude to Europeans, they did not give high definition to differences of color. The closest to a racial definition of slavery among the Spanish colonizers was the term *genízaro*, an ambiguous classification that was just one of many fluid, overlapping statuses or *carta* listed in the Spanish census. *Genízaro* most often referred to an Indian who no longer lived in his or her tribal village and was often of mixed descent. Slavery retained this mark of sexual transgression in the Southwest in the eighteenth century, when an estimated 50 to 80 percent of those in forced servitude were either of illegitimate birth or children of the illegitimate.[13] Slaves were distinguished by gender attributes as well. Slave raids were often mounted from settlements of *genízaro* known for the aggressive masculinity of the bandits and warriors who resided there.[14] Those *genízaro* listed in the census of the Pueblo of Santa Fe, on the other hand, were more often women, frequently exiled from their tribes because of rape, sexual affiliations with the Spanish, or racially mixed parentage. Those slaves who owed their servitude to capture in Indian raids were also distinguished by gender: females outnumbered males among the captives two to one. Put simply, bondage among the Indians of the Southwest most often operated as traffic in women and in those of questionable birth. As a labor system, southwestern slavery was also gendered female. Women slaves garnered as much as twice the price of men in the pueblos, where they supplied domestic services in European settlements composed overwhelmingly of males.[15]

This southwestern version of slavery was relatively short-lived. The average slave woman ended her servile tenure within ten years, when she was absorbed into the mestizo population. Her status, much like that of English indentured servants, would end with marriage, and it would not extend to her children or into a second generation. As one nineteenth-century observer described it, "The system of Indian Slavery which exists in this country conduces to this state of things. The people obtain possession of their children by purchase or otherwise, whom they rear in their families as servants . . . . When they grow up to a man's or woman's estate, many of them marry with the lower class of Mexicans, and thus a new stream of dark blood is added to the current."[16] This first New World experiment with slavery was dissolved by marriage and mating and produced the mixed lineages that dominate Latin America and sections of the American Southwest today.

French attempts to enslave the native tribes of North America left a similarly slight trace in American history. A census in New Orleans in 1708 reported a population of 278, mostly French soldiers, only 28 adult French women, and 80 slaves. French colonizers did not seem to distinguish between slaves and Indian women, who were regarded as drudges assigned to menial domestic labor and maligned for their untamed sexuality: "Indian women as slaves who are always with child marrying half breeds." Native women were not much worse off than most of the French men in the region, a sorry bunch of criminals off the streets of Paris, who readily fled the thralldom of the colonial garrison to form alliances with Indians and affiliations with native consorts. The French even resorted to trafficking in women of their own nationality in order to build up the colonial population. One boatload of "*filles du roi*" was shipped to New Orleans, where the female cargo was locked up on arrival and then put on display as potential marriage partners.[17]

The French Crown was so eager to build a bastion of settlement against the English colonizers of North America that they briefly contemplated breeding subjects for Louis XIV by wedding French men to Indian women. This experiment proved to be as abortive as enslavement. The first Frenchmen to settle at the mouth of the Mississippi returned to Europe, died off, or drifted into Indian society.[18]

English colonizers were no more reluctant to enslave Indians than were the Spanish; nor were they more successful in the long term. The Massachusetts Body of Liberties permitted the enslavement of those Indians who had been captured in a just war, while Virginians conducted a trade in Indian captives during Bacon's Rebellion of 1676. Both these experiments with slavery came to naught. During the first abortive stages of European settlement, American natives were more likely to lure stray European intruders into their ranks than to permit their own capture and enslavement. By the time the English finally established viable settlements around the Chesapeake in the mid-seventeenth century, the Indian population had been marginalized and decimated by disease and warfare. Native Americans were not about to supply the labor needs of European colonists. In the crude terms of vernacular racism, slavery in America was not to be colored red.[19]

Through much of the seventeenth century, the Chesapeake colonies continued to face an acute labor shortage. The Virginia Company had ventured into the New World for the express purpose of reaping profit from the cultivation of tobacco, a highly labor-intensive process. The first scheme called for importing Englishmen who would perform the tedious work of planting, transplanting, cultivating, and harvesting the prized leaves for the international market. When few Englishmen were enticed to cross the Atlantic on the promise of shares in the company, the stockholders offered the incentive of private land grants to anyone who would immigrate. The company clearly intended to organize a labor system around household units, complete with a gender division of labor.[20] Originally, grants were issued in the name of a household head and allocated according to the number of his dependents: his wife, children, male and female servants. Recruitment did not proceed as hoped. Improvement in the English economy after 1640 drastically reduced the numbers of young men and women who were willing to migrate across the Atlantic in hopes of bettering their fortunes. Carolina Colonists courted women settlers with extravagant promises harkening back to a "Golden Age, when Men Paid a Dowry for their Wives; for if they be but Civil, and under 50 years of Age, some honest Man or other, will purchase them for their Wives."[21] Women did not rush to accept such proposals, and as late as

1704 the European population of Virginia numbered only eighty thousand, of whom only seven thousand were women.[22] The skewed sex ratio, combined with an inhospitable climate, brought about a low birth rate, high mortality, high rates of widowhood, and a plentitude of orphans, all of which contributed to what has been described as a "masculinity crisis." European settlement did not take quick domestic root around the Chesapeake. Resembling the fragile settlements in Louisiana, Florida, and the Southwest more than the fecundity of New England, the Virginia colonists were at risk of being dissolved into the native population.[23]

At this critical juncture African slavery loomed like a sinister deus ex machina to solve the problem of the colonial labor supply. Western Africa offered a singular attraction to labor-starved colonists: it already held a supply of slaves in readiness for shipping, courtesy of seafaring European merchants — Portuguese, Dutch, English and French, and a few Anglo-American colonists. One early attempt at a legal definition of slavery singled out this convenient mode of acquisition among the markers of bondage: "all servants not being christians imported into this colony *by shipping* shalbe slaves for their lives; but what shall come *by land* shall serve, if boyes or girles, untill thirty yeares of age, if men or women twelve yeares and no longer."[24] Slaves taken in Africa accompanied the first parties of Europeans to arrive in the New World. They journeyed with Columbus in 1492 and disembarked with the Virginia Company in 1619. Few of them were free agents; most bore some semblance of servitude; but neither were they utterly shackled to European owners nor defined purely by color.

Those who arrived from Africa before 1700 often disembarked in small groups, alongside European immigrants who were also held in some form of bondage, chiefly that of indenture. These first African immigrants occupied a social status that has been labeled "Creole," or the charter generation. Because they were often experienced navigators of the Atlantic world, they could translate between the cultures of Africa, Europe, and America and jockey for a position of some autonomy.[25] In Virginia, African Creoles worked alongside white indentured servants and shared some of their freedoms, notably the ability to produce their own agricultural goods, engage in petty trade, speak tribal languages, and practice their African traditions and religions, including Islam. With access to social spaces of their own, they enacted rituals like Negro Election Day or Pinkster and enjoyed Sundays of public frolic and dancing.[26] In dense settlements they developed a whole slave economy, producing and exchanging the products of gardens, hunts, and workshops. In South Carolina, where they were a majority, and in northern

MAKING SEX IN AMERICA

cities, where they constituted as much as 15 percent of the population, African Americans practiced varied occupations, acquired the skills of artisans, and served as soldiers.[27] Rural or urban, the first immigrants from Africa lived, worked, played, and loved alongside whites. Africans were clearly differentiated from European indentured servants: they arrived via the Atlantic slave trade, were unprotected by contracts, and might expect to remain in servitude for much of their lives. But their status was only a gradation away from the brutal and confining situation of indentured servants. Although African slaves learned quickly not to expect their servitude to expire within seven years, they had reason to hope they would be liberated. In the seventeenth century, manumission was a distinct possibility, legally and practically. It could be won by purchase, granted for good behavior, or obtained upon conversion to Christianity.[28]

These characteristics of African bondage in the seventeenth century were not just attributes of the Creole generation; they were also a function of gender. The early African slave trade trafficked overwhelmingly in men, and those prestigious slave occupations—soldier, artisan, Election Day king, or sacred African drummer—were all the prerogatives of males. The regularity and relative tolerance of sexual congress between Africans and whites suggest that sexual desire often overrode ethnic or "racial" differences in the formative stages of the American slave system. Sexual relations between European women and African men contributed a large part to the high rate of bastardy in the seventeenth-century Chesapeake, where as many as one-third of illegitimate children were of mixed race.[29] It was not uncommon for free white women to form liaisons and marriages with African bondmen. This masculine coloration of slavery in the seventeenth century was also consistent with the demands of the scrabbling New World economy, in particular, the need for the muscle power to cultivate the commercially profitable crops in the American South: Virginia's tobacco, South Carolina's rice and indigo, Louisiana's sugar.

In the eighteenth century the increasing world demand for these commodities coincided with the decline of emigration from Europe. Southern planters adapted by resorting to the wholesale importation of African slaves. Those coerced onto slave ships continued to be disproportionately male. Some of the slave ships arriving in Louisiana during the early eighteenth century carried three to four times as many adult males as females.[30] In the Chesapeake at the same time, male slaves outnumbered females two to one.[31] Such imbalanced sex ratios proved to be a faulty economic policy, however. Chesapeake planters failed to capitalize on a gender advantage that New Englanders had practiced so efficiently: converting relatively balanced sex ratios into rapid population growth. At the close of the seventeenth century, when New England's population had exploded into a fecund second generation, the low sex ratios among Chesapeake settlers, European and African alike, led to a stagnant population and a labor force that looked Lilliputian against the backdrop of America's vast agricultural resources.[32]

The planters' demand for labor was not the only factor at work in the Atlantic slave trade. African supply also played a powerful, and gendered, role. By the eighteenth century, African slavery was at least a thousand years old and had evolved according to intricate gender patterns. The control and distribution of slaves were centered in the urban hubs and ports of West Africa—in the great kingdoms of Mali, Zaire, and Ghana. Acquiring slaves was a military operation, the work of the male warrior class. The trade in captives was controlled by patrilineal aristocrats who dealt in precious metals and agricultural goods as well as slaves. The most prized captives were females, who brought wealth into the patrilineage in multiple ways. They served as diplomats, carriers of culture, healers, warriors, domestic servants and agricultural workers, even queens. The productive capacity of a female slave was compounded by her reproductive role and her sexuality: she bore children into the royal lineage and could serve as an additional wife for a polygamous patriarch. As the market for slaves in the New World expanded, traders also reached out to dispersed tribes, many of them matrilineal clans in which both the major agricultural workforce and the prolific source of new laborers were female. African traders calculated these gender differences into their investments; by taking women as captives they profited from both the productive and reproductive powers of female slaves. Accordingly, slave merchants preferred to retain women in Africa and send men off into the transatlantic trade.[33]

There was thus a grim reciprocity in the initial traffic of gendered labor from Africa to America. American planters demanded, and African traders supplied, a slave labor force that was disproportionately male. For a variety of reasons, however, this sex ratio became somewhat more balanced with time. As the market for slaves expanded in the eighteenth century, merchants moved ever deeper into the African hinterland and ensnared more remote agricultural tribes into the Atlantic slave trade. At this point, the sex ratio on the supply side began to shift somewhat. As they moved further and further into the agricultural hinterland, African traders encountered ethnically foreign populations and became more willing to export females as well as males. As the slave trade expanded south and east toward the Bight of Biafra, it also encountered tribes in which women performed less agricultural labor and were more expendable in local farm production. Moreover, traders found that enslaved women were easier to control under the harsh and crowded conditions of incarceration en route to the Americas. Ultimately, two of three slaves who crossed into the Americas, be they from Western or Central Africa, would be female. The increasing importation of female slaves helped ensure the reproduction of the Chesapeake slave population by the middle of the eighteenth century. The answer to the labor problems of the American colonies was a lesson in gender demography.[34]

Before the end of the seventeenth century, be it inadvertent or by calculation, Virginia planters had learned the advantages of a greater balance of the sexes among African laborers. The increasing recourse to the labor of enslaved women would have a critical effect on the subsequent history of the southern colonies. To start with, the assignment of African women to heavy field labor was one of the earliest signs of the difference between slavery and indenture and, by extension, "black" and "white." While planters were hesitant to assign menial outdoor labor to white female servants, they sent African women to work in the fields without apparent reluctance. They described African women as "hoeing machines" and as "very strong and able Wenches" who could do "as much work as any man."[35] The steady increase in slave importation into Tidewater Virginia early in the eighteenth century coincided with both the decline in white indenture and a heightened proportion of women, almost all of them of African descent, among agricultural workers. Slave masters could increasingly boast of exempting their wives and daughters from menial labor. Women's labor could be callously fungible, as when one husband regaled his wife with the Christmas gift of a slave.[36]

African American slavery worked according to a sexual division of labor that extracted the maximum productivity from both female and male labor power. When women's reproductive powers were added to their backbreaking agricultural labor, the economic value of enslaving Africans was multiplied yet again. Planters exploited the productive capacity of African slave women to the extreme, even keeping them in the fields during pregnancy. Slave owners were less apt to punish pregnancy among Africans than among white indentured servants, indicating that they regarded reproduction as an increment of rather than a subtraction from the value of female slavery. By the mid-nineteenth century, when the domestic slave market was a major business enterprise in cities like New Orleans, some planters and their wives calculated potential offspring into the relative value of purchasing male and female slaves. When a female slave was sold or bequeathed, the transfer included "her increase" or her "produce." One probate record spelled out this dehumanizing strategy for reproducing the slave labor force with bequests that included "a slave boy named Jack and a slave girle named Flora and her increase," along with "ten cows and calves and their increase." [37]

The legal foundation for such marketing in reproduction was laid down very early in American history: in 1662 Virginia adopted a statute that simultaneously legalized slavery and made it an inherited status.[38] In contrast to previous forms of slavery, and in stark contravention of Western European lineage practice, first Virginia and then Maryland declared that the status of slave would pass on through the generations from mother—not father—to child. This expedient legal practice came in response to a suit by Elizabeth Key, a mulatto slave, who sued for her freedom by claiming descent through her father, a free white man. In an instant, the pragmatic concerns of planters overruled the gender traditions of white patrilineage; Elizabeth Key's petition was summarily denied.[39] Henceforth, the official colony policy was to assign slave status according to the condition of the mother. This gender maneuver defined modern American slavery: bondage was a matrilineal kinship system. Another statute dating from 1705 created an implicit racial boundary by enslaving the children, grandchildren, and great-grandchildren of enslaved women.[40] Although the mothers with whom this slave lineage originated were of African descent, neither their "race" nor their "color" was specified. Until the very eve of emancipation, the enslavement of African Americans would be described in terms of lineage rather than pigmentation, descending in some states only as far as one slave great-grandparent. It became mathematically possible according to other state statutes for a descendant of a slave ancestor and a succession of Caucasian fathers to remain a slave even though his or her parentage was fifteen-sixteenths white.[41]

A series of changes in the relations of the sexes followed from the codification of slavery. In 1662 Virginia also began to legally patrol sexual congress between slaves and some categories of free persons. The fornication law enacted in that year exacted a double fine if the sexual partners included a "Christian" and a "negroe." Further restrictions on interracial sex were implemented in Virginia in the 1690s in order to prevent "that abominable mixture and spurious issue which hereafter may encrease in this dominion."[42] Because the "spurious issue" born of a liaison between a slave and a white woman would, by the law of matrilineage, go free, southern legislators took steps to close this loophole in the reproductive cycle of slavery. Virginia law sentenced free women of European origin who mothered mulattoes to draconian punishment: they could be enslaved for seven years, and their off-spring for thirty.[43] The Maryland statute of 1664 was more severe. It enslaved the white wives of black slaves until the husband's death. This technique for maximizing labor power exposed the planters' crude calculation of the economics of gender. Greedy for workers at the end of the seventeenth century, they were willing to sacrifice the freedom of white women, as well as their own mixed-race progeny, in order to ensure the maximum reproduction of laborers.[44]

Gender proved to be a prodigious method for recruiting, maximizing, and controlling slave labor. And it consistently operated by a double standard. Sexual relations between white men and enslaved women were not an economic risk to the planter, for they could produce offspring who inherited the status of slave from their mothers. A long lineage of southern planters fathered mixed-race children and then, by abandoning their own sons and daughters to slavery, committed an extraordinary breach of the European patriarchal tradition. Slavery suspended patrilineage, excused sexual relations between white masters and black chattel, and was bereft of chivalry toward women of humble status—English indentured servants and white mothers of mulattoes, as well as African slaves.[45] While white men violated the racial border with impunity, southern law did not protect slaves from sexual assault. Southern courts were even reluctant to enforce rape laws when the assailant was a slave and the victim a white woman of lowly social status.[46]

These extraordinary innovations in the relations of the races and the sexes were worked out in Virginia and Maryland in the late seventeenth century and were soon replicated throughout the southern colonies. They provided the framework in which the tobacco and rice economy could prosper and turned the American South into a "slave society." This social transformation was accomplished within a century of English settlement in the New World.[47] In the next century the English colonists of the South laid down the foundation for the rapid increase of the slave labor force. By 1820, the sex ratio among African Americans was balanced, and the slaves were reproducing themselves; by 1860 the enslaved population had risen to almost four million men, women, and children.[48] Although this solution to the plantation labor problem relied on the prior enslavement of African peoples, and gave a clear coloration of racial ideology to the peculiar American institution, it relied as well on stratagems of gender that stretched halfway around the world.[49]

The Gendering of Slave Society

Brought into being by the labor needs of tobacco and rice plantations during the colonial period, American slavery matured in conjunction with another momentous shift in global economics that occurred around 1800. As the tobacco fields of the Old South became depleted, the world market for cotton began to boom. The rapid expansion of textile manufacturing in Old and New England created demand for raw material that could be processed in greater volume by the cotton gin, making it profitable to open huge tracts of land in the Deep South for cotton cultivation. At the same time that slavery was gradually abolished in the urban and industrializing economy of the North, the southern demand for slave labor grew. The southern states reaffirmed their allegiance to slavery. By virtue of the South's powerful position in the federal political system and cotton's centrality to the national export economy, the United States of America was wedded to the enslavement of its people, the children of African slave mothers, regardless of who fathered them. No sooner had the foreign slave trade ended in 1808 than the domestic market in human labor began to boom, accumulating over the fifty years before the Civil War to an estimated one million transactions, most of them sending men, women, and children into the cotton fields of the Deep South.[50] The expansion of southern slavery would have a transforming effect on the relations between men and women, whatever their status or color, be they slave or free, large planters or yeoman farmers.

The growth of the Cotton Kingdom deepened the chasm between black and white. In an earlier time, planters like William Byrd could imagine intimate relations between whites, Indians, and Africans dissolving racial difference. Byrd repeated a preposterous story of how the "Blackamoor" was washed white; after three generations of incestuous breeding, the descendants of Africans became "perfectly white and very honorably descended."[51] The consequences of racial mingling could be found around the grounds of Jefferson's Monticello, where the slave quarters harbored at least five children sired by his father-in-law, one of whom, Sally Hemings, bore the founding father himself at least one enslaved child.[52] As plantation slavery grew more profitable in the Deep South, however, racial boundaries became more formidable: manumissions declined, prohibitions against interracial marriage were enforced, and the surveillance of free blacks increased. Even in places like New Orleans and Charleston, where liaisons between planters and slaves had produced casual race mixing and a large population of free blacks, color lines grew more rigid. On the plantations of the Deep South where slavery

MAKING SEX IN AMERICA

Picking Cotton on a Georgia Plantation. Ballou's Pictorial, 1858. (Courtesy of the
Library of Congress, Prints and Photographs Division, LC-USZ62-76385)

was organized on a massive industrial scale, the number of mulattoes were
few.[53] Across the South, the white mothers of black children were branded as
"unruly women," condemned for their "Lascivious & Lustfull desires."[54] The
juggernaut of modern slavery contorted the rules of gender and kinship and
built a fortress of subordination around African Americans. At the midpoint
of the nineteenth century, the census recorded that 90 percent of those of
African blood were slaves.[55] The matrilineage of slavery had converted the
vast majority of the descendants of Africans into a caste set brutally and cate-
gorically apart from other Americans.[56]

Consigned to slavery, Americans of African descent developed distinctive
insignia of gender as well as race. Despite the great variation in the conditions of bondage across the South—from the small yeoman farms of the Virginia Piedmont, to the rice plantations of the South Carolina Tidewater, to
the cotton fields of Mississippi—slaves were distinguished from free men
and women along each axis of gender differentiation: asymmetry, the relations of the sexes, and gender hierarchy. At the foundation of the slave gender
system was a distinctive sexual division of labor. Most all chattel, male and
female alike, was reduced to the status of common laborer and put to work

in remarkably similar ways. On the large plantations at least three out of four slaves, female and male, were simple field laborers, conscripted into work gangs or set to specific manual tasks in rice or cotton production. Jefferson forbid his overseers to "keep a woman out of the crop" and exempted only two female slaves (one was his father-in-law's mistress) from field labor.[57] Women performed the most onerous physical labors, including lifting heavy bales, digging steep trenches, plowing and hoeing, as well as harvesting. On large plantations with complex divisions of labor, men might be found overrepresented in some heavy jobs, such as ditchmen in rice production or "prime hands" in the cotton fields. Women were more likely to be listed as three-quarter hands or, if they were pregnant, consigned to the "trash gangs" along with children, the aged, and the infirm.[58]

Few farms or plantations developed the diversified economy that would permit a more complex sexual division of labor. The "mammy" who would become a fixture on movie sets was a rarity on the plantation.[59] Female slaves were defined by their productive capacity as field laborers. Men, in fact, may have had better chances of exemption from heavy field labor, for they were more likely to be assigned to more highly skilled jobs like that of driver, carpenter, gardener, coachman, or cooper.[60] The imperatives of cotton production overrode concern for feminine delicacy, or even the value of the planter's investment in human capital. The rates of maternal and infant mortality among slaves (twice those of free women and their progeny) suggest that planters maximized the labor of women even in the late stages of pregnancy, risking the health of mother and infant, present and future workers.[61]

The workday was especially long and hard for the majority of slaves who resided on small plantations and within yeoman farm families. One Tennessee woman recalled her servitude as "hard times. From the time [she] got up until bed-time [she] didn't have no time to eat idle bread." William Brown clocked his workday more exactly: "When I began work in the morning I could usually see a little red in the east, and I worked till ten before eating: at two I would eat again, and then work . . . until ten at night."[62] At even that late hour, a woman's work was rarely done. Women took up such domestic chores as laundry, cooking, and child care. One slave song put the gender division of labor to music: "Yo daddy ploughs ole massa's corn. Yo mammy does the cooking. She'll give dinner to her hungry chile when nobody is a lookin."[63] Larger plantations may have actually afforded slave men and women with a more relaxed and varied regimen. On the rice plantations of coastal South Carolina, for example, production was organized on a task system that permitted swift and efficient workers more time to themselves. Men and women alike used this time to work for their own benefit and that of their families. Women might stock the slave larder with products of garden plots, and men with the bounty of the hunt. In some instances, women could market their goods as peddlers, "chicken merchants," or managers of small stores, but men were more likely to claim cash wages for work outside the plantation.[64]

Though slavery bound both sexes to a life of toil, one all-important role was left exclusively to women: the physical reproduction of the labor force. Slave women practiced this gender role fervently. They had become prolific mothers by the nineteenth century, typically giving birth four to seven times. This was accomplished without much encouragement from masters.[65] With the decline of the tobacco economy in the Upper South, some planters took greater interest in the reproductive value of slave women and were brazen enough to advertise the sale of "good breeding wenches."[66] But evidence of conscious breeding is relatively rare and, at any rate, far exceeded by indications that masters were so eager to maximize agricultural production that they would put the reproductive health of women at risk.[67] Female slaves were kept in the field, subjected to the lash during pregnancy, and rarely given special incentives to marry and reproduce. As a consequence, that high rate of reproduction must be seen as testimony to slave women's own determination to bring children to life and keep them alive.[68]

Such prodigious fertility also testifies to the viability of the relations of the sexes under slavery. The gender relations of the slave quarters have been cause for much debate among historians, who have assailed the slave family as matriarchal, hailed it as patriarchal, and presented it as a model of sexual equality. Whatever the quality of gender relations, the prospects for forming strong slave families were hardly promising. The act of enslavement had broken African clan ties, and southern planters proceeded to run roughshod over the social and family bonds of their chattel. Slave marriages and the status of father were sometimes recognized by planters, but mostly in the breach. The domestic slave trade broke up hundreds of thousands of nuclear families. A study of the Appalachian South estimated that one-third of the couples who were reunited after the Civil War had been separated and sold away from one another at least once.[69] Husbands and wives found their conjugal rights violated with impunity by masters and other free men. Slave narratives and family histories are rife with reports of sexual abuse, especially from masters.

The bonds between parent and child were almost as vulnerable as those between husband and wife. In another survey of slave narratives, 82 percent of those interviewed recalled that their mothers were continuously present during their childhood, but only 42 percent had regular, but usually infrequent, contact with fathers.[70] Although the bond of mother to child was generally held intact until early adolescence, thereafter children were regularly sold away. When the slave economy shifted from the Upper South toward the Cotton Belt in the 1850s, slave families were especially vulnerable. Virginia and Maryland planters sold their surplus slaves deep into slavery, with little apparent respect for the sacred bonds of motherhood.[71] Slave sales in one Virginia county were so extensive that even the bonds between mothers and infants were in jeopardy.[72] In some cities, like New Orleans, the sex ratio was so imbalanced among African Americans that reproduction was put at risk.[73] Interviewed in the 1930s, a former slave named Caroline Hunter summed up family values under slavery with the recollection that "during slavery, it seemed lak yo' chillun b'long to ev'ybody but you."[74]

The strength of family ties, like all the gender practices of southern slavery, varied considerably according to time, place, and economic condition. The records of some large and prosperous plantations indicate that relatively stable, male-headed households were the norm. A remarkably extensive set of birth records for one plantation identified the fathers of 95 percent of the children born there. On another plantation in lowcountry South Carolina, 80 percent of births were listed with the names of both parents.[75] Other documents indicate that children were named not just for fathers but also for grandfathers, thus preserving a patrilineal family history. Historians who investigated other times and smaller farms have uncovered contrary evidence. In antebellum Loudoun County, Virginia, the majority of children lived with their mothers, and even when a father was identified, his relations to his progeny were relatively tenuous. While mothers resided with their children, fathers were likely to be entirely absent or living on a plantation located at some distance from their children.[76] For the majority of slaves who were bound to small farmers in Upcountry Carolina, as in Loudoun County, Virginia, sustaining close and regular marital ties took heroic effort. Potential mates could only be found on distant plantations, making separation from husbands and fathers routine. Narratives of former slaves commonly acknowledge this family structure by identifying absent spouses as "'broad" husbands and labeling the home the "mother's house" or "De wife house." As one husband reported, "de wife house was often eight or ten miles from de home house, and we would go there Saturday night expectin' to see de wife we had left."[77]

The fragility of slave families was largely the result of the master's labor policies. Larger planters distributed labor across a number of different satellite farms; smaller farmers could purchase only a few family members; all slave owners routinely bought and sold men, women, and children according to the fluctuations in the market and their own economic circumstances. But slave men and women were not passive pawns in the sexual division of their labor. They formed conjugal unions according to their own choices and may have found some advantages in "abroad" marriages. For both men and women, the extension of family ties across two different locations counteracted the vulnerability of depending on a single capricious master.[78] Given the likelihood that couples would be separated by sale, it might be prudent for women to rely on themselves and extended kin as much as husbands for social support. For a slave husband, visits to the plantation of his wife and children offered regular opportunities for geographical mobility. Abroad marriages, like such slave practices as a period of youthful promiscuity and serial monogamy, demonstrate the plasticity of gender relations under these most adverse circumstances. Historians have also found flexible gender practices among those African Americans who were not enslaved. A high proportion of female headed–households among free blacks suggests that women might have chosen a single status in order to protect the property rights that, according to southern family law, would be lost by marriage. As femes soles they could accumulate funds with which to purchase their children from slavery and raise them in freedom. For whatever reason, the center of family gravity shifted toward the African American mother, slave or free. This matrifocal tendency was consistent with supportive, if not legally sanctioned or protected, relations between spouses, and it may have proved a flexible adaptation to the exigencies of kinship under slavery.[79]

Extended kin ties, real or fictional, wound through the slave quarters, establishing a web of interdependence. Positions of authority within these kin networks were often determined by age as much as gender. Older slaves and longtime residents on the plantation were honored by the honorific title "aunt" and "uncle." Fictive kinship, sometimes called "swap-dog kin," extended to aunts, uncles, brothers, and sisters and designated a whole network of slaves to whom an individual owed reciprocal obligations. Unwritten rules of kinship prohibited the marriage of close relations, such as cousins, thereby broadening the network of collateral kin. The frequent use of the honorific titles "uncle" and "aunt" in slave narratives, like the salutation of "brother" and "sister," is suggestive of another distinctive gender practice among African Americans. Women and men who acquired esteem and authority were defined neither as spouses nor as parents but according to the more egalitarian lateral relations between kinsmen and women. All told, bondmen and women created a safety net out of a wide range of social relations. They could ill afford to limit their attachments to narrow heterosexual pairings. The repertoire of relationships at times resembled the practices of African clans; sometimes it was coerced by planters; and in other instances it testified to the social ingenuity of slave men and women. Whatever the medley of causes, the relations of the sexes among plantation slaves in the mid-nineteenth century took a distinctive form: men and women relaxed conjugal ties, reduced the male household authority, and gave more social prominence to mothers and female kin. One survey found that one in four titular heads of slave communities went by the name "aunt."[80]

These distinctive relations between the sexes inevitably colored the third element of gender, stratification. The relative ranking of male and female in the slave community has prompted some historians to propose that the usual gender hierarchy was inverted under slavery, that a matriarch deposed the patriarch. More recent readings of the slave records have rejected the gendered poles of patriarchy and matriarchy and have written of slavery in more egalitarian terms, speaking of the wife as "an equal partner" or marriage as "unusually egalitarian."[81] Other historians have looked unflinchingly into the inner workings of slave families and found evidence of spousal abuse and disdain for "uppity females." The master colluded in male supremacy by tolerating domestic violence in the slave quarters and by treating men and women unequally. Slave women received fewer rations, were assigned lowlier jobs, and bore the double burden of field and domestic work. In the larger order of plantation society, slave men were put in positions of authority for which women were not eligible.[82] Slave men could even rise to the status of driver and be empowered to wield force over fellow slaves. Women seldom occupied a role higher than that of the midwife, "doctoress," or the head of a small band of field hands. Similarly, community leadership fell more often to a male slave. A backwoods minister probably garnered greater prestige than a female cultural figure such as a conjurer or storyteller. The trickster tales told in the slave quarters gave the central roles to males, as did ceremonies like Pinkster, in which free blacks and slaves chose males as monarchs or governors for a day. During the slave celebrations at Congo Square in New Orleans, males drummed and chanted, while women occupied "the second line."[83]

A cautious accounting of evidence like this would conclude that the male gender was placed marginally above the female on the social hierarchy of the slave community. In the context of white domination and the diurnal violence of slavery, however, the asymmetry between the sexes was a relatively small matter. When former slaves like David Walker and Frederick Doug-

MAKING SEX IN AMERICA

lass demanded to be treated with the dignity of manhood, they were distinguishing themselves not from women but from the beasts or a piece of property. Walker recited the abolitionist call as a masculine appeal: "Are we MEN!! . . . How we could be so *submissive* to a gang of men, whom we cannot tell whether they are *as good* as ourselves or not, I never could conceive." "If ever we become men," Walker concluded, "we must exert ourselves to the full."[84] Frederick Douglass plotted his autobiography as an ascent to a standard of manhood that was sometimes generic and sometimes gendered. Shocked to see the slave treated like a species of property, he exclaimed, "Behold a man transformed into a brute!" When he emerged the victor in a savage battle with the overseer, he exalted at reclaiming "a sense of my own manhood."[85]

Douglass presented this fierce struggle with the slave master as the defense of an abused slave woman, whom he portrayed in the posture of victim, the obverse of his own heroic aggression. Women slaves were in fact more reluctant than men to engage in either fight or flight: no women, like Nat Turner, led slave rebellions, and only a small minority of runaway slaves were women. The bookend to Douglass's heroic autobiography is the slave narrative of Harriet Jacobs, who, rather than escaping with her own freedom, hid crouched in an attic for seven years, all the while watching over her children below. Jacobs told the story of slavery as a tale of maternity rather than manhood. Twice in the course of her narrative she ironically invoked the lineage of enslavement that decreed that her offspring would "follow the condition of the mother" rather than their father, a free black man. Jacobs traced the kinship of slavery not through bloodlines but through maternal relations. Observing that her mother and her mother's mistress "were both nourished at my grandmother's breast," Jacobs placed maternity at the very center of the tortured social relationships of slave households.[86]

Ties of kinship, especially to their own children, might bind slave mothers to the plantation, but they did not disempower them. Planters often complained of independent and troublesome slave women. A Mississippi slave named California was a thoroughgoing abolitionist and plague to her master, who wrote in 1847, "California especially has an idea that she is free. Goes & comes & does as she pleases, infuses a good deal of these feelings and notions in her childrens heads, has Amalgamation prints stuck up in cabin."[87] The strength of one slave mother's resistance could be heard in the recollections of her children, recorded as late as the 1930s. This female slave instructed her daughter in stalwart defiance, not docility: "I'll kill you, gal, if you don't stand up for yourself . . . . Fight, and if you can't fight, kick; If can't kick, then bite. . . . I can't tolerate you if you ain't got no back bone." Resistance to slavery was androgynous: "My mother was the smartest black woman in Eden. . . . She could do anything. . . . She made as good a field hand as she did a cook. . . . She was a demon, . . . loud and boisterous, . . . high-spirited and independent. I tell you, she was a captain." Motherhood was just as powerful a force among slaves as among the white female subjects of the previous chapter. But it was expressed not as domestic femininity but in hard physical work and the temperament of "a captain."[88]

Although some African American women may have obtained the stature of "captain" within the community of slaves, they lived in the shadow of the big house and under the power of white masters. Slaves of both sexes experienced that domination in the most immediate, quotidian, and intimate ways. Regardless of gender, slaves were in the grips of a fiercely authoritarian household system. As slave apologists would unabashedly proclaim in the 1850s, both government and families were patriarchal institutions founded on man's authority "as the head of the woman." Those subjects included wives, children, and slaves, members of what planters commonly referred to as "my family, white and black."[89] The notion that the planter class took the slave under family government was in large part hypocritical rhetoric constructed by slavery apologists in the 1850s. It was not inconsistent, however, with the organization of antebellum southern society. From the large tobacco plantations of eighteenth-century Virginia to the cotton enterprises of the Deep South just before the Civil War, even in the farm families of the Piedmont that harbored only one or two slaves, southern society was structured as a system of household authority. As one historian has put it, "Legally, slavery was a repressive extension of the household heads' established rights over other domestic dependents. The institution of slavery magnified and even transformed that authority, but it did not create the legal concept."[90]

Civil War and the Reconstruction of Race and Gender

During the 1850s, proslavery apologists and abolitionists alike cast their disagreements in terms of domestic ideology. In reaction to the abolitionist challenge, proslavery writers devised their own model for the relations of the sexes and asserted it with idolatrous rhetoric: "Her husband becomes to her a crown and a covering as soon as she sees in him the representation of God in her. . . . Her subjection to [him] takes on a religious character."[91] In defense of their peculiar institution, slave owners developed what seemed like a regressive gender ideology, a reversion to classic patriarchal beliefs. One Virginia planter proclaimed, "Like one of the patriarchs, I have my flocks

MAKING SEX IN AMERICA

and my herds, my bond-men, and bond-women." Others gave Latin names to their plantations and proudly called their distinctive political system, after the Roman model, a "Slave Republic." The classic columns and porticos that adorned the plantation houses were a facade of patriarchal pretension, behind which there stood a society built on slavery.[92] The slave owner's mansion betokened a social structure and a gender system that was very much at odds with the middle-class dwellings that symbolized gentility in the North.

In regions of the South dominated by large plantations, home and work were not set far apart from one another. The "Big House" was the center of social life, the hub of commerce, and the warehouse for the material goods that sustained the workforce and the family. It absorbed into itself much of southern society, depleting the countryside of urban institutions. Only a few regional cities, dispersed ordinaries, courthouses, and churches dotted the countryside and provided social spaces in which to develop a bourgeois counterforce to the power of the large plantation. Without extensive urban settlement or many intermediary occupations—shopkeepers, artisans, clerks, and professionals—the South was less hospitable to the development of a middle class. The gendered creations of that flourishing class in the antebellum North—the women's clubs, charities, and reform associations to be described in the next chapter—were also sparser in the South. Even yeoman farmers, whose subsistence agriculture, remote homesteads, and independent ways set them apart from large planters, maintained their political loyalties to slavery. The all-powerful plantation household was not, however, just a regression to the little commonwealth of the past. It was bloated with modern capitalist functions. The large planter, while tied to a worldwide market, operated as his own banker, financier, merchant, and manufacturer of household goods, absorbing many of those economic functions that might have expanded the middle class.[93]

Gender ideology provided one way of bridging the differences and distances between the powerful slave owners and the majority of whites who owned little property and few, if any, slaves. Powerful planters used metaphors of family authority both to justify slavery and to invite all the free, white husbands and fathers of the South to share in the planter's masculine prestige. "The peace and happiness of families," they were told, required that the husband and father be placed at the head of the household, at the helm of "a sort of domestic monarchy." Within such households of the South, women's status resembled "matrimonial slavery." By appealing to their common stakes in masculine hegemony, planter politicians obtained deference from the farmers who owned but a few slaves and the majority of men who owned none at all. In 1861, whether persuaded by this gender ideology, out of loyalty to their compatriots in the militia muster, the tavern, or the polling place, or due simply to their dependency on the slave-owning elite, men of humble status endorsed secession from the United States. Common soldiers, like this young man writing home to his parents, marched off to battle as if the Yankees were "entering your dwelling or ready to give the deadly blow to my dear wife and child."[94]

By the outbreak of the Civil War, white southern thinkers had devised a political philosophy at odds with the democratic ideals propounded in the American North and West. In the ideological place of the common man they posed a patriarch. While the women of the North were busy in their own nurseries and kitchens, southern ladies were set on pedestals and waited on by slaves. The divergence between the gender cultures of the North and the South became a powerful symbolic tributary to sectionalism and Civil War. The antislavery movement announced itself to the public by issuing a gender challenge to the southern system. Antislavery societies circulated tracts and newspapers that featured a picture of a muscular slave postured to break his chains, above the caption "Am I not a man and a brother?" William Lloyd Garrison's *The Liberator* implored readers to ransom babes about to be wrenched from their mothers' arms and sold into slavery. A black female antislavery society formed in 1832 in Salem; a white association followed in Boston in 1833. The Female Anti-slavery Society, founded in Philadelphia in 1837, boasted members from North, South, and Midwest, one-third of whom were of African descent.[95] Its motto was a slave woman's plea, "Am I not a Woman and a Sister?" The language and sentiments of domesticity suffused female abolitionism, from the public speeches of Maria W. Stewart and Angelina Grimké to the sentimental poems of Elizabeth Margaret Chandler.[96]

The most powerful antislavery polemic, *Uncle Tom's Cabin*, was a medley of images of broken families and violated womanhood. Harriet Beecher Stowe translated the antislavery message into a catalog of patriarchal brutality: the lecherous Simon Legree despoiled pure maidens; angelic girls like little Eva expired in the toxic moral climate of slave society; and the noblest embodiment of masculinity, Eva's genteel father, was impotent in the land of the patriarchs. By contrast, the happy ending of the novel was a paean to domesticity, enacted by an idealized nuclear family of former slaves who celebrated their liberation in Canada. The domestic tableau that replaced Uncle Tom's cabin was a kitchen table laid out as if it were an illustration in the domestic manual authored by Stowe or her sister Catharine Beecher. Slavery apologists retaliated ungallantly; they charged that the abolitionist woman was "made the instrument of destroying our political paradise. . . . She is to be converted into a fiend, to rejoice over the conflagration of our dwellings and murder of our people."[97]

The ideology of the Free Soil movement and the electoral strategies of the Republican Party that succeeded it set a direct collision course with the philosophy of the slave republic. The idols of the planter class were the antithesis of northern heroes, be they middle-class breadwinners or frontiersmen, laborers or farmers. The ideology of political antislavery was personified as the hegemonic masculinity of the North: "free soil, free labor, and free men." When push did come to shove with the election of Abraham Lincoln in 1860, it was largely because northern voters had been convinced that slave power intended to expand to the West, pillage the free land of yeoman democrats, send slaves northward to compete for wages with workingmen, and everywhere threaten the independence and liberty sacred to American manhood. As 1860 approached, political discourse was infested with gender images—the democrat's homestead squared off against the slave cabin, the mother's kitchen against the planter's columned porticos—and all portended more changes in the alignment of male and female, North and South, white and black.[98]

Whatever its complex causes, the Civil War would finally accomplish the abolitionism of slavery, but at a terrible cost. The war left more than 600,000 men dead, each a husband, father, and/or son. The northern victory, followed by the occupation of the South by the Union army, ordained the reconstruction of the relations of both race and gender. This irrepressible transformation was immediately apparent to Elizabeth Botume, who had gone south in order to teach the newly liberated slaves of Carolina's Sea Islands:

> Most of the field-work was done by the women and girls; their lords and masters were much interrupted in agricultural pursuits by their political and religious duties. When the days of "*conventions*" came, the men were rarely at home; but the women kept steadily at work in the fields. As we drove around, we saw them patiently "cleaning up their ground," "listing," "chopping down the old cotton stalks and hoeing them under," gathering "sedge" and "trash" from the riverside, which they carried in baskets on their heads, and spread over the land. And later, hoeing the crops and gathering them in.[99]

This one snapshot, taken from the vantage point of an abolitionist woman, prefigures both the changes and the continuity that were in store for emancipated African Americans. The meaning of gender was being rewritten in broad and basic ways, in everything from political representation (those "conventions") to such prosaic matters as gathering trash.

The transformation occurred under the spotlight of national politics and as part of a heroic effort to expand the civil rights of freedmen known to historians as Reconstruction. The most direct and dramatic achievement of the Reconstruction period was to give African American men full legal title to citizenship. With the passage of the Fourteenth and Fifteenth Amendments to the Constitution, they were entitled to exercise all the privileges and liberties of citizens, including the right to vote. For at least as long as they remained under the protection of the Union army, which would be officially withdrawn in 1877, and almost until the end of century in some southern locations, African American men practiced citizenship with authority and passion. Showing themselves to be quick studies in democracy, free men of color allied with former slaves to exert the critical force necessary to push their demands for equality onto the political agenda and into the Constitution. Scores of them rose with lightning political speed from citizens to leaders, even to the status of lieutenant governor, congressman, and senator.[100]

The immediate gender consequences of the northern victory seemed simple enough. The modern family and domestic femininity had won out over the archaic patriarchy of the slave republic. The family law of the South was brought into line with northern practices. For white planter households, that meant such things as ending the virtual immunity of southerners from prosecution for domestic abuse. Emancipation from the patriarchal slave household would also seem to welcome African American women under the mantle of Victorian purity. Liberated from the control masters had once exerted over their bodies, some freedwomen went to court to accuse former masters of rape.[101] They were no sooner emancipated from one kind of patriarchal control, however, than freedwomen became acquainted with another kind of domestic subordination. They were apprised of an obedience they owed not to the slave master but to their husbands. *The Freedman's Spelling-Book* made this new regime patently clear: "The Bi-ble con-tains ma-ny di-rec-tions to hus-bands, wives. . . . Wives, sub-mit your-selves un-to your own hus-bands."[102]

The relations of the sexes under slavery had not prepared African American women for such blatant conjugal subjugation. Some freedwomen actively rejected the biblical model of marriage. One freedwoman from Tennessee concluded that to wed was to squander her emancipation. When her

MAKING SEX IN AMERICA

betrothed announced, "I married her to wait on me," she promptly cancelled the nuptials.[103] A Georgia woman also divorced with her feet, saying, "I am my own woman and will do as I please."[104] The African American abolitionist Frances Harper observed that husbands all over the South were taking up the master's scepter of household authority. They "positively beat their wives," wrote Harper, and "their subjection has not ceased in freedom."[105] Harper went through the reconstructed South reciting the fundamentals of domestic freedom: "Part of the time I am preaching against men ill-treating their wives."[106]

Whatever the missteps along the way, former slaves quickly established and stabilized the institution of matrimony. In the process of contracting marriages according to established legal practice, former slaves became informed about the inequality and subordination of wives. Family law assured free men that they could take property in their wives, and conversely informed women that as dependents of their husbands they were required to provide sexual and personal services as recompense for material support. The U.S. Congress assured the southern states that they "may deprive women of the right to . . . contract. . . . But if you do so, or do not do so as to one race, you shall treat the other likewise. . . . If you do discriminate, it must not be on account of race, color, or former condition of slavery." One freedman affirmed the sophistical definition of "domestic freedom" as men's right "to have their own way in their families and rule their wives—that is an inestimable privilege!"[107]

Reconstruction, even at its most radical, did not directly challenge gender hierarchy. Most veterans of the antislavery movement accepted the exclusion of women from the political privileges protected by the Fifteenth Amendment. Among the abolitionists, only a few advocates of women's rights—notably Susan B. Anthony, Elizabeth Cady Stanton, and Sojourner Truth—challenged the strategy of the "Negro's hour," which would postpone enfranchising women, black and white alike, until African American men had achieved full citizenship.[108] The issue of woman suffrage was occasionally raised (during the Virginia constitutional convention, for example) but with little prospect of being enacted. Although African American women were prominent in the open-air meetings conducted at the height of emancipation euphoria, they were soon ushered into ceremonial rather than active and decisive roles in the political sphere. Men also monopolized perhaps the most powerful position in the local African American community, the pulpit. Black Baptists and Methodists claimed almost three million parishioners by the turn of the century, but they relegated women to lesser stations, like the choir or the women's committees, and denied them the right to vote on most matters of church policy and administration. Politics became racially integrated during Reconstruction, but full citizenship remained the privilege of men.[109]

Meanwhile, behind the front lines of Reconstruction politics, former slaves rewove the quotidian relations of the sexes, including their division of labor. A former South Carolina slave named Cesar expected wifely services not unlike a slave master. For the offense of "laziness & being indifferent to his comfort or welfare, and not working, washing or mending his clothes," Cesar punished his wife Laney with thirty lashes.[110] It also took some practice to solidify the family economy, as evidenced by the many husbands and wives who came before the Freedmen's Bureau complaining that their spouses had run off with a portion of the harvest.[111] Despite these initial false steps, most freedmen and women went on to establish family partnerships, and together renegotiated their roles in the agricultural economy, including their relationships with their former masters.

Agricultural records paint vivid pictures of how former slaves forced a compromise with the former slave-owning class. The conclusion of the war found the rice plantations of South Carolina deserted by the masters but occupied by bands of ex-slaves, in which women predominated. When some planters returned to take possession of their fields, they were greeted by bold moral claims to the land. One freedwoman advised her former master that the land was hers because "out o' dat black skin he got he money." The former mistress of another plantation was denied access to her homestead in the spring of 1865 by what her daughter called "a yelling mob," composed principally of women who "revolved around us, holding out their skirts and dancing—now with slow, swinging movements, now with rapid jig-motions, but always with weird chants. . . . No, no we won't let no white pusson een, . . . we'll chop um to pieces sho'."[112] On another plantation "infuriated women" reputedly sent their former master's slave driver packing, "bloodied by the assault of their hoes and clubs."[113]

If former masters had their way, freedmen and women would resume the roles assigned them under slavery, performing the same menial jobs in kitchen and fields, while residing in barracks-like quarters near the big house. Former planters quickly resumed title to their lands and recruited emancipated African Americans into gangs of field laborers with little concern for the niceties of gender difference or family relations. Postwar work gangs were composed of both sexes, irrespective of family membership, and were most often led by men. The representatives of the North condoned and

MAKING SEX IN AMERICA

even facilitated these attempts to put freedmen and women back to work in the cotton fields. The Freedmen's Bureau encouraged emancipated slaves to sign contracts with their former masters that conformed to a familiar gender protocol. They were most often signed in the hand of the male head of household but committed wives and children to labor in the fields by his side. Planters and Union officers alike were willing to disregard the most basic of family bonds: they readily apprenticed children to field work without their parents' permission. When freedwomen were unwilling to abandon their young children while they went to work in the fields, potential employers charged them with "female loaferism."[114]

Although former slaves were reluctant to accept planters' terms of employment, they were not shy of hard work. They hungered for the economic freedom to till their own land, far from the surveillance of their former masters. In the Sea Islands women went to work wherever they could make a living, in the fields, in kitchens, or in the service of the Union army. They learned the lessons of the labor market quickly and well. One woman earned enough at the cotton gin to buy twenty acres of land. Others took to wage work with alacrity: "most of the women had earned $5—the men, on an average, not so much." Lucy Gallman recalled that she "worked hard, plowed, cut wheat, split cord wood, and did other work just like a man."[115] There was no question that freedwomen would engage in productive labor, but there was considerable dispute about just when, where, and in what relationship to their former masters. The more audacious freedmen and women went to court to demand that former masters conform to their standards of economic justice. Freedwomen petitioned to rescue children from apprenticeship and to obtain such common law privileges as dower and inheritance. One Eliza Cook of North Carolina actually demanded paternal financial support for the children her master had fathered under slavery. Referring to the wife of her former master, Eliza Cook argued, "if I had my justice I had as much right here as she had."[116]

The postbellum South was besieged with conflicting economic priorities: the Freedmen's Bureau's determination to put farmers back to work, the planter's preference for work gangs, the African American husband's intention to control the labor of his wife, and the freedwoman's eagerness to labor for her own profit and the welfare of her family. A new southern labor system was reconstructed as a series of ad hoc compromises of these differing interests. The resulting gender division of labor neither reinstituted the slave's work gang nor carved out separate spheres for male and female. A few former slaves acquired farmsteads, shops, or professions of their own. Sometimes husbands and wives worked together on white-owned lands in exchange for a share of the harvest. Others pieced together their common survival through the wage labor of husbands, wives, and children. In some ways the economic circumstances of African American families resembled slavery: theirs was a sentence to heavy labor, under deplorable conditions, and for meager material reward. But the terms of employment were worked out through negotiations with begrudging former masters. In the end, former slaves succeeded, against the wishes of the planters, in escaping the old slave quarters and taking up residence in dispersed family units outside the planter's direct surveillance.

Once the Union army and the U.S. Congress ceded planters the rights to their former land, the freedmen and women of the South Carolina Low Country brokered a compromise labor policy, usually some variation on sharecropping. Household heads contracted to work on the old plantation in exchange for guaranteed access to the land and the freedom to devise their own family division of labor. The "croppers" refused to work after the harvest and rejected the most menial slave jobs, like cleaning irrigation ditches. They set their own work schedule, reserving time for themselves and their families. Although men might sign the contract, the sharecropper's wife was fully informed about family economics and agricultural practices. Husbands and wives shared the obligations of their "rent-wage." And after the harvest they sometimes went their separate ways to acquire additional income. Men often were hired off the plantations, while women stayed at home caring for children and cultivating crops for sale or home consumption. If and when wives took jobs in white households, they set limits on the terms of their employment. Rather than being at the constant beck and call of the mistress, they agreed to perform specific tasks and then returned promptly to their own families, their wages in hand.[117]

Whatever its abuses, this "work-rent system" of South Carolina's rice plantations, like the sharecropping system elsewhere, reveals how African Americans just out of slavery implemented their own notions of the roles and relations of the sexes. In the tobacco-growing areas of upcountry North Carolina, former slaves created a similarly elaborate household economy. By contracting with a landlord to produce a cash crop, tenant farmers obtained a plot of land on which they could concentrate the labor of entire families: husbands, wives, children, and aging grandparents. Their hard work may have kept them barely above subsistence, but it provided families the stability so cruelly denied them under slavery. One tenant farmer recorded the inestimable value of the reconstructed African American family in this assess-

Shermantown settlement, Atlanta. *Harper's Weekly*, 1879.

ment: "dar's dis much fer bein' free. I has got thirteen great gran'chilluns an' I knows whar dey ever'one am." [118]

African American weddings, legitimate births, and property ownership increased dramatically in the immediate aftermath of slavery. By 1915, approximately one in five African American householders were landowners. [119] Out of the battered fragments of the slave family, free men and women had created a distinctive and sturdy gender system of their own. Their families practiced a domesticity with a major difference. African American women were far more likely than white wives to labor both in the fields and outside their homes. Their rates of gainful employment were four times those of white women. African American wives in the postwar South would reenter the white woman's kitchen, but only in order to return home at the end of the day with a wage that would support their own families. African American men, for their part, claimed the right to represent their families in public, at church, and before the state. But the black public sphere was slanted toward gender balance, as can be clearly seen in the school system of the New South. At a time when college education was rare for white women (especially in the South), and generally segregated by sex, African American normal schools and colleges enrolled men and women in almost equal numbers. These places of higher learning sent out a teaching force that was predominantly female and placed women in a position of authority in black communities alongside male preachers.[120] Women also took up positions of influence and prominence in humble places. In an African American neighborhood of Atlanta called Shermantown, for example, the well around which freedwomen worked as laundresses became a central communal space.

Women slowly rose in religious stature as well. While the flourishing Baptist churches reserved the pulpit for men, they permitted women to commandeer a separate national convention that exerted real force in ecclesiastical politics. Similarly, African American women contributed to the growth of civil society among emancipated slaves. They were even known to form female militia companies. Although the African American women who marched in military formation in postwar Virginia were more ceremonial than warlike, they were an extraordinary apparition of gender symmetry. Likewise, if less spectacularly, African American fraternal orders and mutual benefit societies, usually reserved for men among whites, enrolled both sexes.[121]

These lodges, schools, and churches, as well as small businesses and a thriving press, provided the scaffolding of a growing African American middle class. The sure-footed upward mobility of some former slaves and freed blacks was exemplified by Sarah Dudley and Charles Pettey, who came to adulthood in the sunshine of emancipation and enjoyed the benefit of an education in the black seminaries of their native North Carolina. Sarah, a schoolteacher, married Pettey, a minister, and as he rose to be a bishop, she commenced writing a column for the religious journal the *Star of Zion*. Together they flourished within a black community that included lawyers, bankers, shopkeepers, minor political figures, and upstanding members of the Republican Party. The Petteys sent their sons off to fight for their country in the Spanish-American War. They shared the streets and the streetcars with whites on a daily basis. Like the sharecropper's homestead, the black middle-class household exhibited a certain egalitarianism between the sexes. Sarah and Charles Pettey were a professional team, presiding together over their congregation. On their ministerial tours through North Carolina, Sarah would often rise to speak in behalf of women's rights.[122] She was not the only feminist voice to be heard in the New South. Frances Harper, a freeborn woman of African descent, toured the South during Reconstruction, championing racial equality and women's rights on the same principle: "To prove whether I have a right to be a free woman or am rightfully the chattel of another; whether I have the right to possess all the faculties that God has given, or whether another has the right to buy and sell, exchange and barter that temple in which God enshrined my human soul."[123]

While African Americans often claimed the blessings of freedom for both sexes, men were entrusted with the representation of the family in the public arena. When African American women were insulted on the city streets, black men rose up in their defense. In one case in North Carolina, an African American man pistol-whipped the white man who insulted his sweetheart; she sued her attacker for assault, and won.[124] The editor of the local black newspaper joined in her defense: "We will remind the white editor that she is a respectable young lady, whose family is more prominent and wealthy than his. We want our ladies respected. . . . White men make us respect white ladies, and they must make white men respect ours."[125] In the act of defending "our ladies," African American men had begun to shape an identity that was at once racial and gendered. They made the protection of their womenfolk a measure of their common manhood.

Significant numbers of African American men were now educated, propertied, and entitled to vote. Enslaved only a few years before, they now claimed title to hegemonic masculinity. Those who, like the North Carolina editor, made the defense of African American women the grounds for political contestation with white men raised volatile interracial issues. After all, the recently toppled slave republic had soldered the classes together around the exclusive gender privileges of white men. They were not about to admit African Americans to the citadel of masculine privilege without a struggle.

The contest over masculine hegemony commenced at the moment of emancipation and sent a menacing undercurrent through the whole project of Reconstruction. Vanquished rebels seethed at the sight of former slaves claiming the male privileges of votes, property, and conjugal rights. A black Republican named James Rapier had put the challenge bluntly: "Nothing short of a complete acknowledgement of my manhood will satisfy me."[126] Confronted with such provocation, some white men asserted their hegemony with violence. One angry band came together in rural Tennessee, taking the Greek words for "circle" as their title. The membership of this first Ku Klux Klan represented a wide spectrum of the white male population, from planters to propertyless farmers. The targets of the Klan's menacing night rides tended to be upwardly mobile African Americans—voting Republicans, labor leaders, or men who were known to talk back to whites, break racial boundaries, and sometimes defy taboos against interracial sex. An early victim of Klan violence in central Georgia named Henry Lowther fits this profile. He was a shop owner who made a good living and who was so bold as to sue white customers who defaulted on their debts. Lowther's pretension to manly stature was not to be tolerated. A mob captured and interrogated him: "are you willing to give up your stones to save your life?" The threat was not idle; Lowther was hanged and castrated, one of the first victims of the southern lynch mob.[127]

With the end of slavery, southern whites began to patrol the sexuality of black men more diligently than in the past. Laws against "miscegenation," a term that was not coined until 1864 (and then only as part of a political parody concocted by Democratic journalists in New York City), were hastily codified across the South, as well as in some northern states.[128] Sex became linked with race in the vortex of conflict following emancipation, but it had not yet gelled into the now familiar narrative of the sexual danger black men posed to white women. While it was rumored, for example, that Henry Lowther had been the lover of a white woman, this charge was raised only in the aftermath of the lynching and was not the expressed focus of the mob's initial fury. Another case in point was that of Jourdan Ware, who was singled out for lynching because of his high profile in the political arena. Only after his death was he charged with insulting and frightening white women.[129] When the Grand Wizard of the Klan charged that "ladies were being ravished" by some escaped black prisoners, he was not invoking a strict racial code of chivalry. Not all white women, but only "ladies," were entitled to a priori protection by early chapters of the Klan.[130] Neither women nor men had yet been locked into their stereotypical roles in the deadly drama of lynching. In fact, some white women were lynched and sexually violated by avenging mobs of southern white men. In Alabama white women who sympathized with Republicans were stripped, whipped, and left to die for informing on the Klan. Others were called low-down tramps or "unruly women," time-honored epithets for those white women known to consort with blacks.[131]

For the moment, within the still unstable sexual politics of the 1860s and 1870s, white women and black men had not yet been cast in their mythic roles of pure victims and rapacious sexual predators. The occupation of the South by the Union army staved off the first barrage of racial terror and even disarmed its arsenal of sexual hysteria, temporarily. In a Tennessee case, both Confederates and Yankees floundered in their initial attempts to patrol interracial sex. When in 1864 a poor white woman accused an ex-slave of rape, it brought on not a lynch mob but a public contest between the conservative governor and the Freedmen's Bureau regarding the reliability of the white woman's charges.[132] As late as the 1880 census, the city of New Orleans re-

MAKING SEX IN AMERICA

ported over two hundred interracial marriages, twenty-nine of which united white women with black men.[133]

The Sexual Politics of Jim Crow

If the political will to construct an interracial democracy survived another generation, black institutions might have grown ever stronger, the wounds of slavery might have healed, and the regime of sex and gender that propped up that oppressive racial formation might have been discarded. Such high hopes had to be abandoned in 1877 when federal troops pulled out of the South, suspending protection of the civil rights of African Americans for eighty years and more. The way was opened for the reimposition of white supremacy in the South. In another generation, blacks would be segregated from whites, and African Americans would be stripped of their civil and political rights. The installation of the method of racial subordination known as Jim Crow was a long and exacting political process, and one in which sex and gender again played a powerful and particularly sinister role. It was not until the hard times of the 1890s that white southern politicians unsheathed the most lethal weapons of sexual hysteria. Lynchings peaked in the 1890s and by 1930 had claimed some three thousand victims, overwhelmingly black men.[134] At its height, lynching became a bloody political ritual, lit by torches and veiled by moonlight, yet publicly orchestrated and sanctioned. Ultimately, the ritual torment and murder of a black man could draw audiences of up to several thousand, men, women, and children, who sometimes arrived by train and returned home with charred body parts as souvenirs.[135] This racial terrorism went according to a sexual script. Ben Tillman, senator of South Carolina, recited it as follows: "The white women of the South are in a state of siege. . . . Some lurking demon who has watched for the opportunity seizes her; she is choked or beaten into insensibility and ravished, her body prostituted, her purity destroyed, her chastity taken from her. . . . Shall [this] be punished in the regular course of justice? So far as I am concerned he has put himself outside the pale of the law, human and divine. . . . Civilization peels off us . . . and we revert to the . . . impulses . . . to kill! kill! kill!"[136]

When Tillman delivered this diatribe in the 1920s, such racial and sexual hysteria had become formulaic. It was sexual politics with a vengeance, yet another particularly ugly way that gender was used to prop up racial inequality. Charges of interracial sex were lethal weapons in the fateful political struggles of the late nineteenth century. In pockets of the South, whites and blacks actually posed a serious threat to the conservative Democratic Party. A coalition of black and white Republicans obtained an electoral majority in Virginia in 1879, and as late as 1894 a fusion government of Republicans and Populists, black and white, came to power in North Carolina. At such moments, when the white man's republic faced a serious challenge, conservative southern politicians unleashed the hysteria about race and sex with abandon. Tillman rose to the position of senator, and the Democratic Party won its stranglehold on the southern electorate, in a fury of sexually charged political rhetoric.

Inflammatory sexual rhetoric camouflaged less prurient gender issues, matters more of masculinity than miscegenation. Not just rumors of sexual assault but the rising economic power and political status of black men were on the mind of the lynch mob. After the intervention of Radical Reconstruction put the first Ku Klux Klan in check, the advances of African American men became ever more offensive to the racial clauses of masculine hegemony. An outbreak of racial terrorism in Montgomery, Alabama, in 1887, for example, targeted an illustrious set of victims: a doctor, a lawyer, and a newspaper editor who was an upstanding member of the Baptist church and the Republican Party.[137] The vitriolic racial attack was aimed at the uplifted status of former slaves: "We deprecate any further efforts being made to introduce any such 'Educated' Romeos in our midst. . . . What State had the honor of educating this brute?"[138] A case of lynching in Memphis in 1892 targeted the proprietor of the People's Grocery Company, who was cutting into the clientele of the white competitor who would lead the mob that murdered him.[139]

The perverse logic of lynching was gendered in ways that entangled material, political, and sexual differences. Describing the 1913 lynching of the Jewish businessman Leo Frank, one historian used the concept of "reactionary populism" to capture the special utility of sexuality in this deadly politics: "Protean concerns about family and sexuality may help tame and redirect popular opposition to a dominant social order."[140] The mythology of race and rape was worked out late in the nineteenth century and served explicit political purposes.[141] In the 1880s the editor of an African American newspaper in Georgia was still rather complacent about charges of interracial rape: "The constant reports of white women in the South being raped by colored men [have] become a stale old lie. It does seem that a great many of them get off in lonesome places with colored men in a surprising degree. . . . but there seems to be a great spirit of watchfulness on the part of the white men, who somehow don't seem to trust their white sisters with the Negro."[142] This story was picked up in 1887 by another African American newspaper, the *Montgomery*

MAKING SEX IN AMERICA

Herald, whose editor, Jesse C. Duke, seemed to share this casual response to a charges about "some negro . . . outraging . . . some white women." "Why is it," he wondered in print, "that white women attract negro men now more than former days?" His answer was daring, or dangerously naive: "There is a secret to this thing, and we greatly suspect it is the growing appreciation of the white Juliet for the colored Romeo, as he becomes more and more intelligent and refined."[143]

The insouciance of these African American journalists did not pass unnoticed. Duke's editorials outraged the white leaders and journalists of Montgomery, who regarded the author as "an unmitigated fool with unparalleled effrontery."[144] The terms of the debate about race and sex were still somewhat confused and contested. Not all African Americans were on the defensive about interracial sex, which had been so often tolerated under slavery and still went on relatively undisturbed among the humbler classes of the rural South. But Reconstruction had also left white conservatives more sensitive about sexual relations across the color line. Embittered about their lost cause and emboldened by the withdrawal of northern protection for freedmen and women, white conservatives asserted hegemony with renewed fervor. A Montgomery mob extracted an apology from Duke and drove him out of town.[145] Sex, race, and politics had come together in Montgomery in 1887 but were not as yet a lethal brew. Rather than ushering in the full-fledged terror of lynching, they sparked editorial counterattacks, a meeting, and the destruction of a printing press.[146]

In Memphis a few years later, the public stakes of sexualized political combat were raised considerably, but obliquely. In 1892 vague rumors of sexual impropriety began to circulate around an African American grocer named Thomas Moss, but they only became public after his death, at the hands of a lynch mob. Once again, African American journalists rose up boldly in defense of their community. This incident inspired the brilliant journalistic and political career of Ida B. Wells, a writer for the *Memphis Free Speech*. The young journalist began her rebuttal to the lynch mob with a contemptuous dismissal of the "old thread-bare lie" that justified lynching as the protection of white women from rape.[147] Wells reported that the charge of rape was raised in only a quarter of all lynching cases, and she argued that the political and economic advancement of black men was the actual provocation for a lynching. Wells later recalled that her eyes had been opened to "what lynching really was. An excuse to get rid of Negroes who were acquiring wealth and property."[148] Wells, like Duke before her, had the political confidence to toss off a sexual challenge to white southerners. She brazenly argued that "white men lynch the offending Afro-American not because he is a despoiler of virtue, but because he succumbs to the smiles of white women."[149] And then she hurled a salacious insult at white manhood and womanhood: "If Southern white men are not careful they will over-reach themselves and a conclusion will be reached which will be very damaging to the moral reputation of their women."[150]

In response to Wells, the conservative press summoned a meeting at the Memphis Cotton Exchange. A mob formed and proceeded to the offices of the *Free Speech*, where they destroyed the offending press and warned the editor to leave town. The mob assumed that such journalistic bravado had been a man's work: "Tie the wretch who utters these calumnies to a stake and perform upon him a surgical operation with a pair of tailor's shears." Ida B. Wells left Memphis, but not before she demonstrated that the educated, middle-class black community of the reconstructed South, with its relatively balanced gender roles, was still armed with political courage, confidence, free speech, and sexual rhetoric of its own.[151]

Conservative white politicians now took the offensive in a decisive battle for racial hegemony in the South. In the closing years of the nineteenth century, the city of Wilmington, North Carolina, was the site of a deadly struggle about the relations of race and sex. The editor of the local black newspaper, Alexander Manly, issued a triple-barreled attack on the mythology of interracial rape. First, he questioned the virtue of white women who were "not any more particular in the matter of clandestine meetings with colored men than are the white men with colored women."[152] Then he put a gloss of chivalric romance on interracial unions, calling black men "sufficiently attractive for white girls of culture and refinement to fall in love with them, as is well known to all."[153] Finally, he questioned the white man's performance of his conjugal duties: "Poor white men are careless in the matter of protecting their women."[154] In the late 1890s such charges unleashed the most extreme and incendiary fuselage of sexualized racist rhetoric among whites. In response to Manly's editorial, the white press of Wilmington commenced a relentless attack on the editor. The *Wilmington Messenger* reprinted the editorial under the title "Negro Editor Slanders White Women" in every issue from late August to early November and appended accounts of "Negro Scoundrelism" such that "your daughters cannot attend church or Sunday school without having a body-guard to protect them from the lustful black brutes who roam through your county."[155] The press scoured the state for every trace of a sexual offense committed by a black man. A report that a local white Republican woman ran off with an African American man led to a lynching, and further havoc soon followed. Ultimately, an armed band demanded that Manly leave the county to avoid lynch law, and then burned his office.[156] A full-scale riot ensued and left at least ten, perhaps more than two hundred, African Americans dead.[157]

Interracial sexual relations like those publicized by Alexander Manly cannot in themselves explain the timing of the Wilmington riot or the general contagion of lynching in the 1890s. The fury of racism came home to Wilmington, a showcase of the black middle class, at a time when the mayor was a Republican and only three white Democrats served on the city council. Since 1894, the legislature of the state of North Carolina was in the control of a coalition of Republicans and Populists who owed their election to both white and African American votes.[158] The Manly incident was churned into a political advantage by conservative Democrats determined to get back into power. The alarm against sexual predators that went out in Wilmington and around the state of North Carolina was an overture to the white electorate, who would go to the polls in November. "How can any white man who remembers his mother, his sister, his wife, his daughter, vote to keep in power an administration under which such things are possible?" Democratic advocates asked. "Rise in your might white men of Brunswick. Assert your manhood. Go to the polls and help stamp out the last vestige of Republican-Populist-Negro-fusion."[159] Conservative Democrats recruited women into the partisan campaign. One Rebecca Cameron complied and cheered on her cousin, Alfred Moore Waddell, who would lead the riot: "You go forward to your bloody work, tho' it may be with the heartfelt approval of every good woman in the state."[160] Waddell put it more bluntly: "Go to the polls tomorrow, and if you find the negro out voting, tell him to leave the polls, and if he refuses, kill him."[161] The interracial Republican coalition was soundly defeated in the November election. In the aftermath of that bloody election season, only thirty of three thousand eligible black men registered to vote in the city of Wilmington.[162]

Barely four months after the 1898 election, the state legislature of North Carolina installed the mechanisms that would disfranchise black men: poll taxes, a grandfather clause, and literacy tests. White women's voices joined the chorus of racism. The scourging tongue of Rebecca Felton reached an excruciatingly high decibel before the Georgia State Agricultural Society in 1897: "If it needs lynching to protect woman's dearest possession from the ravening human beasts—then I say lynch; a thousand times a week, if necessary."[163] The myth of rape now regularly wafted through the politics of race like a seasonal hurricane. It reached its highest peak of rhetorical hysteria in the oratory of demagogues like Ben Tillman and the leaders of the second Ku Klux Klan. But the louder and the shriller the rhetoric of sexual paranoia, the fewer the lynchings, which peaked and then rapidly declined at the end of the nineteenth century. By then the mythology of interracial rape had achieved its chief political purpose; it had served as the ideological propellant for the disfranchisement and segregation of African Americans. The constrictions of Jim Crow now fell into place throughout the South. The streetcars were running with "white only" cars. Schools had been segregated, and legislatures became white bastions. The South was solidly Democratic.

Scurrilous words and images, not the actual physical acts of sex, had been decisive in stalling the quest for racial equality in the aftermath of slavery. The private and the public—the racialized body and the body politic—were yoked together to form a vice of white supremacy. The modern American racial formation had taken yet another devious turn. This time the relations of the sexes, and explicitly sexual politics, provided the essential axis of gender that propped up white supremacy. Once sexual politics had done its work, those who lived in the American South and were distant descendants of Africans were consigned to a segregated caste, now defined not by the rank of slave but by the stark contrast of signs above water fountains and restrooms across the South: "White Only," "Colored Only."

The sexual politics of segregation had an insidious effect on the relations between men and women of both races. Those Populists and Republicans who welcomed African American votes were careful to pay homage to white womanhood and impugn the virtue and racial purity of the opposition. Even someone as astute as Ida B. Wells inverted rather than uprooted the gender codes that undergirded the rape myth. Rather than simply defusing the sexualized irrationality of race politics, she raised her own slanderous counter-charge: that white women, not black men, were the seducers. The tortured logic of sexual politics could also be contorted into a challenge to white citizens, holding them to the standard of "manliness and civilization." This political script also assigned a role to educated black women who held their sisters to a high standard of sexual propriety: "it depends largely on the woman of to-day to refute such charges [of immorality and vice of blacks] by her stainless life."[164] Both black and white chapters of the Woman's Christian Temperance Union extolled the same regimen of sexual restraint, monogamy in marriage, and celibacy outside of wedlock, what Frances Willard called "the white life for two."[165] This color-coded doctrine of sexual purity provoked a confrontation between Willard and Ida B. Wells in the 1890s. To the bitter disappointment of her onetime ally, Willard could not escape the sexual mystification of the lynch mob. She repeated the slander that the black rape of white women was commonplace in the South. At the turn of the twentieth century, few could elude the sexual politics of race.

The ghosts of lynching and shadows of sex and gender would haunt American racial politics well into the twentieth century. They assumed perhaps their most bizarre form in the 1990s, when Clarence Thomas, an African American appointee to the Supreme Court, responded to charges of sexual harassment, by a woman of his own race, with an accusation of "high-tech lynching."[166] Gender was hardly the root cause of America's prolonged nightmare of racial inequality and subordination. But it did prove to be an extraordinarily flexible and durable tool for maintaining the distinctions commonly colored as race. Gender was complicit, first of all, in constructing the peculiar system of lineage that enslaved descendants of Africa and colored them black. Once slavery was firmly established, the distinctive sexual division of labor among African American bondmen and women combined with the gendered political philosophy of their masters to exacerbate the sectional antagonism that led to Civil War. Finally, sexual politics in the form of hysteria about a neologism called miscegenation helped to transform the racial formation of slavery into the white supremacy of Jim Crow.

African American women were witnesses to all these racial machinations of gender. They saw close-up how gender and sexuality were used to police the borders of racial differences, by any means necessary, including lynching. This experience equipped African American women like Ida B. Wells, Frances Harper, and Sarah Dudley Pettey to perform complex and powerful political roles. It made them stalwart pioneers in the historical process explored in Part II of this volume: the sexual differentiation of American public life.[167] Because the public realm was the central stage on which both racial and gender differences were performed and proclaimed, this next chapter is long overdue.

CHAPTER 4

WHAT IS THE SEX OF CITIZENSHIP?

ENGENDERING THE AMERICAN POLITICAL TRADITION FROM THE REVOLUTION TO THE NEW DEAL

On July 4, 1844, the female members of the Antislavery Society of Andover, Massachusetts, presented a banner to the men of the society, who raised it aloft and paraded through the streets of the town. On one side of this banner the abolitionist seamstresses had stitched the image of a male slave, along with the caption, "Am I not a Man and a Brother"; on the other side they pictured slave traders in the act of snatching a child from a mother's arms. In words, imagery, and ritual performances, the abolitionists seemed to endorse the gender dichotomy that was fast becoming the standard of the nineteenth-century middle class of the North: men marched into public space, stalwart and independent; women kept to the sidelines, draped in maternal sentiment. This distinction between male and female abolitionists was sharper in ideology than in practice. Those two sides of the banner depicted a blunt asymmetry between male and female, but the two were stitched together as one. The women and men of the abolition society shared the same civic time and place, commemorated the same national history, and in one coordinated action posed the same radical challenge to the slave society of the South. Antislavery men and women alike reached their common goal of keeping the antislavery cause "before the public eye."[1]

The gender history traversed thus far leads directly into this public and political territory. When historians scan the past, looking for events and practices that they find worthy of the label "political," they quickly encounter the gender ambiguities represented by the antislavery banner. Boundaries between the sexes weave through all of American political history, and the positions of prominence, visibility, legitimacy, and agency are most often given over to men, while women are more often consigned to passive and symbolic rather than active and leading roles. This asymmetry can be conceptualized by dividing the public realm by sex. Yet, like the members of the Andover Antislavery Society, men and women regularly and flagrantly trespassed across this border, and when they did, the historical consequences could be momentous, leading to critical turns in the course of American history, like the eventual violent end to slavery.

Complicated gender choreography like the abolitionist ceremony in Andover was performed in many places and at many times during the nineteenth and early twentieth centuries. Taken together, these political performances of gender pose the historical mystery of this chapter: what is the sex of citizenship? As Part II of this book traverses the long period between the American Revolution through the New Deal, it will provide a bewildering array of tentative and partial answers to this quandary. The citizen will assume various identities, from a sexless ideal to an exclusive male, from a maternal supplicant to a feminist insurgent. Through the whole long haul of American history, however, participation in the political process continuously fell short of the universalistic and egalitarian promises heralded by the democratic tenets of the American political tradition. The vexed relationship between sex and citizenship was rooted in the political contradiction upon which the United States was founded. The lofty principles intoned in the American creed "all men are created equal," endowed with "inalienable rights" and entitled to "self-government," illuminated a glaring contrast to actual political practices, which were rife with qualifications and exclusionary clauses, the most fundamental of which were based on sex.

From the eighteenth century into the twentieth those women who made claims on this political tradition were repeatedly rebuffed or ignored. Yet they continued to jockey for a position of civic leverage. The arena in which this gender history took place will be designated in this chapter by the term "the political public," a frame of analysis that is capacious enough to include the men and women of the Andover Antislavery Society and countless other active citizens of both sexes. The noun "public" invokes a concept in political philosophy and current debate, revolving around the work of Jürgen Habermas in particular, which invests great value in a space of unrestricted civic discussion outside of, and often critical of, the state. The ideal public is an open space in which all citizens debate and deliberate about their common welfare. The adjective "political" qualifies the noun "public" in several ways. First of all, it invests the public arena with the conflict and uncivil contestation that theorists like Habermas would expunge from the rational field of discourse designated by the term "the public sphere." Second, the term "political public" acknowledges that democratic citizenship is exercised in multiple spaces, not just a single official sphere. This chapter describes how the political public, this wider public realm, was segregated by sex through much of American history. Not even radical abolitionists could keep the male and female sides of citizenship stitched securely together. By the late nineteenth century, American women had responded to political exclusion by creating a prominent, formidable public domain of their own. In this increasingly public but woman-centered space, the mysterious political contradictions of sex became visible, a matter of public knowledge that was open to scrutiny, criticism, and change, culminating in the enfranchisement of women in 1920. At this juncture, when this political wall between men and women finally fell, gender differentiation itself faced a serious challenge, making this chapter the linchpin of this volume, the pivot between modern and postmodern ways of organizing public and private life along and across the divide of sex.[2]

When Citizenship Was Male
1776–1865

This search for the sex of citizenship commences late in the eighteenth century, when British colonists began to contemplate forming an independent nation based on republican principles of self-government.[3] In North America as in Western Europe, the rights and responsibilities of citizenship had to be wrenched from monarchical states in which kin relations were the currency of power. Although ultimate authority was most likely to be transmitted along a patriarchal line, from kings, popes, and the lords of the manor, it was not exclusively male, as the august example of Elizabeth I attests. The settlers of the New World reproduced these political hierarchies in their local charters of governance. By granting the status of freeman to adult heads of households, the British colonies denied public access to the majority of inhabitants, regardless of sex. By one estimate, more than half of all adults were household dependents—servants, slaves, or women of any age or station—and thereby barred from the colonial seat of government.[4] Although the principles of household governance denied political representation to many males on the grounds of age and condition, they ostracized women in more drastic and decisive ways. It was exceptionally rare for even a widow who headed an affluent household to darken the door of the town meeting. This patrilineal political system gave the American political tradition a powerful predisposition toward constricting the citizenship of women.

This masculine cast of early American politics became immediately apparent when the English colonists moved to form an independent government. One need read no further in the American political tradition than a few lines into the Declaration of Independence to find portentous gender references: the colonists rebelled, wrote Thomas Jefferson, in "manly firmness," while King George sanctioned savage Indian attacks on "all ages, sexes, and conditions." Like Jefferson, his ideological nemesis John Adams was a proud founding father to a republic of gender. He proclaimed a republic of all "great, manly and warlike virtues" and smiled with condescension on the call of his wife Abigail to "remember the ladies." Even the radical democrat Thomas Paine was oblivious to the political claims of women, nonchalantly equating citizenship with masculinity and branding Tories as "unmanly."[5]

In claiming the rhetorical title to manliness, American revolutionaries were not necessarily defining themselves primarily by gender or principally in opposition to women. To be manly was to advance beyond boyhood, to assume an adult, independent status among men. In America's origin story, the English patriarchy had to be overthrown if sons of liberty were to create a polity in which all men were created equal. King George, the tyrannical colonial father, and the English parliament, sometimes seen as a negligent mother, were deposed by the family metaphors so common in eighteenth-century political rhetoric. Tom Paine addressed his American reader as a "husband, father, friend or lover" and called on him to "awaken from fatal and unmanly slumbers."[6] Those who rose up in rebellion to found a polity of their own were not always gray and fatherly eminences; in 1776 George Washington and John Adams were only in their early forties, Jefferson was thirty-three, and Alexander Hamilton was a mere nineteen, and of illegitimate birth at that. While Benjamin Franklin was the elder statesman at seventy, his autobiography had installed him in American legend as an icon of strapping young manhood, breaking with his father at twelve, managing his brother's newspaper at sixteen, and finally striking out on his own at the age of seventeen. For these founding sons, entry into the public sphere was not just a matter of crossing a gender boundary but also a rite of passage into political adulthood.

Men made their way to the public sphere independent of their fathers but in the company of their brothers. These fraternal relationships thrived in "the city of brotherly love." Philadelphia was the most radically democratic bastion of the Revolutionary era and, not coincidentally, a city that was overgrown with places for male sociability. In addition to Ben Franklin's famed Junto and a bevy of voluntary men's associations, Philadelphia boasted more public houses or taverns per capita than Paris. While these spaces were virtually off-limits to respectable women, they fostered what one historian has called a "robustly popular political outlook," where gentlemen, artisans, and sailors all came together to debate public issues, plot revolution, and devise the most democratic constitution of any of the newly united states. The Yankees plotted resistance to the colonial policies in the taverns of Philadelphia, the clubs of New York, or the commons and docks of Boston; they asserted their independence from Great Britain in the name of the Sons of Liberty and won their freedom through the masculine heroics of the battlefield and the camaraderie of the militia company. The Boston rebels enacted the rites of political manhood with particular panache in 1769 when they assembled at their local Liberty Tree, downed fourteen toasts, and marched in a body to the town of Dorchester, where they raised a glass to Liberty an estimated forty-five more times before returning to Boston.[7]

Just how their wives welcomed their return has not been recorded for posterity, but we do know that women were more likely to enact their patriotism in separate spaces. They were seen only on the edges of violent protest, but they eagerly participated in the more genteel aspects of resisting British policies by boycotting English imports, appearing in the background to colonial crowds, and urging their husbands on to political defiance.[8] The matrons of Boston practiced their patriotism seated at the spinning wheel rather than by raising their glasses or shouldering a rifle. One historian has counted some forty-six of these patriotic spinning bees in New England alone. The first, dating from 1766 in Providence, reportedly brought "eighteen daughters of liberty, young ladies of good reputation" together to spin, abstain from English tea, and protest the Stamp Act. Such polite political behavior most often took place not in the tavern but in the parsonage, where rebel matrons labored to supply the goods of war and then returned home in time to do the milking. The sexual division of revolutionary labor was most dramatic on the battlefield: women made only a minor appearance in the rebel army. If not disguised as men, they trailed along behind as camp followers, laundresses, and cooks. Should a man falter in his role of citizen soldier, his shame would be marked with this customary response to gender deviance, by "being marched out of camp wearing a dress, with soldiers throwing dung at him."[9]

The War of Independence had raised the political consciousness of women as well as men. A kind of American salon took shape around the network of politicians' wives like Abigail Adams and Mercy Otis Warren, whose private correspondence offered erudite commentaries on public issues. While Abigail reminded John Adams of women's stake in the rebellion, Hannah Lee Corbin of Virginia wrote to her brother Richard Henry Lee to appeal for the political representation of tax-paying widows. In the immediate aftermath of the war, some of these educated women began to make their political opinions public. Warren, the sister of one esteemed republican politician and the wife of another, composed a history of the Revolution, introduced female characters into her political dramas, and dared to publish under her own name.[10] The 1780s and 1790s found Philadelphia's *Ladys' Magazine* championing women's rights to education, while Judith Sargent Murray addressed the reading public "On the Inequality of the Sexes." In the democratic hotbed of Philadelphia, a few stalwart females claimed the status of "freemen" and vowed to maintain their independence by remaining single.[11] As late as 1807 the single women of New Jersey were actually casting ballots. Not everyone assumed that the new republic was to be reserved for men.[12]

But as the former colonists sat down to draft a blueprint for a new government, they met as men's clubs, seemingly oblivious to women's role in the War of Independence or expectations of citizenship thereafter. The masculine predisposition of the American political tradition came back into focus once the practice of politics receded from such public space as the streets, the commons, and local assemblies and became installed instead in formal political institutions such as state legislatures and constitutional conventions. Not one state constitutional convention, not even such radical public gatherings as that of Revolutionary Pennsylvania, invited women to join in their deliberations. While some states awarded the franchise to landless whites and African American men of property, and most emancipated sons by ending primogeniture, they neither enfranchised women nor expanded women's property rights. In 1807 the state of New Jersey officially closed the loophole that had permitted a few intrepid widows to vote, seemingly without encountering any public resistance.

The federal Constitution left women even further behind on the path to full democratic citizenship. The *Federalist Papers* mentioned women once, though the authors waxed eloquent about the "band of brothers" and the "manly spirit." James Wilson of Philadelphia introduced a promising clause to the constitutional convention when he proposed that the delegates be apportioned on the basis of "the whole number of white & other free Citizens & inhabitants of every age sex & condition."[13] However, he did not intend that women (like slaves, who would be counted as three-fifths of a person for this purpose) would consent, vote, or hold official status in any electoral or governing body. Moreover, even this hint of attention to women citizens was edited out of the founding document of the United States of America. Hence, the Constitution never bothered to state officially that the franchise belonged to men, yet it used the male pronoun thirty times. When the federal government was relocated to the shores of the Potomac in 1800, the citadel of national power was erected on a landscape of male boardinghouses. Those wives of senators and congressmen who journeyed to Washington seldom stayed longer than the six-week social season. Even then, they were banished from the home of the chief architect of the United States. Jefferson's favorite White House entertainment was an intimate dinner of male politicians whom he served personally in a fashion he called "being mother." The politics of the new nation was regularly conducted in such private quarters. When political elites gathered as private cabals, in the plantation houses of Virginia or the Georgian mansions of New England merchants, for example, women were dismissed after dinner, while men retreated to the drawing rooms and the libraries to debate the issues of the day.[14]

The masculinization of early American politics was occasionally made explicit and official. The doctrine of classic republicanism held by some founding fathers offered a clear justification for the exclusion of women from the public sphere: only men were capable of exercising public virtue; the unruly passions of women made them ill equipped for rational political deportment. Jefferson was acting as a classic republican when he dismissed women who "mix promiscuously in gatherings of men" and ushered their sex behind a "domestic line."[15] The alternative ideology of the age, Lockean liberalism, was more promising for women, some of whom laid claim to the natural rights of all humankind. Mary Wollstonecraft's *Vindication of the Rights of Women* (1792) was initially well received in the United States, but in a short time these liberal voices were drowned out by the contrary doctrine of the commonsense school of moral philosophy. Coming out of Scotland, this political theory divided male from female at the portal of the public sphere and consigned the latter not just to privacy but also to the commodious social domain of feminine domesticity. One homespun political treatise assigned women a bill of rights of their own, which included such privileges as the "undoubted right to choose a husband," "to promote frugality, industry, and economy," and "to be neat and decent in her person and family."[16]

It is not that the founding fathers, sons, and brothers acted explicitly to exclude women from the public sphere; they seldom considered them eligible to apply for membership in the first place. Sometimes one hears hints of misogyny in the banishment of women from the public sphere, but more often women were rebuffed with the damning dismissal of humor. The wags of Newark, New Jersey, put it to music in 1797. A typical verse of "The Freedom of Election, A New Song" went "To Congress, lo! widows shall go, / like metamorphosed witches! / Cloath'd in the dignity of state, / and eke! in coat and breeches."[17] Cloaked in such jocular prerogatives of masculinity, one sex alone went forth into the public sphere of the new nation.

At best, women were invited to honor the public sphere by their absence and by admiring their leaders from afar. Barred from participating in elections or office holding or representative bodies, women were positioned to perform ceremonial functions in behalf of male citizens. They stood gracefully by to honor the national heroes. When Washington made his way to the seat of federal government, he was greeted along the path to the new capital by assemblages of fair ladies laden with tokens of patriotism that included garlands, wreaths, and hand-sewn banners like one presented in Trenton, New Jersey, in 1789; it read, "The Hero Who Defended the Mothers Will Protect the Daughters."[18] By virtue of being outside the circle of political protagonists, woman could represent the purest and loftiest national virtues: she impersonated the goddess of Liberty and Columbia, the icon of national unity. These symbols and a whole retinue of classic allegories sprouted up on every patriotic occasion for the century to follow—on the banners in the grand procession that celebrated the Constitution in Philadelphia in 1789, on the insignia that artisans carried in Fourth of July parades across America, and on the pediments of the public buildings that housed republican legislatures.[19]

The wives of the new nation were heralded not as citizens but as republican helpmates. The gentlemen of Philadelphia adjourned from the rowdy public sphere of the tavern to more sedate places of entertainment, where the company of "the ladies" lent order and propriety to civic life. Dolley Madison performed the same wifely service in Washington, transforming the White House into a center of genteel, decorous, mixed-gender sociability and a place where women might manipulate political relations in behalf of their husbands. The wives of presidents, senators, and congressmen conducted a very active and consequential political life, what has been called "parlor politics," just a stone's throw away from the U.S. Capitol. But women's place near the official public sphere was severely delimited and hardly autonomous. It was subordinated, as well as attached, to male roles; it operated in the private circuits of patronage and influence peddling; and it acted to conserve rather than challenge the gender status quo ante. These elite parlors were surely political places, and a domain where women wielded power, but they did not conform to the more idealized notion of the public sphere open to all. They were highly political but hardly public.[20]

When states updated their constitutions in the 1830s and 1840s, they made the rights of men and limits of women's citizenship explicit and official. All adult white men, save the criminal and the insane, were granted the

Liberty, ca. 1800–1820. (Gift of Edgar William and Bernice Chrysler Garbisch; image © Board of Trustees, National Gallery of Art, Washington, D.C.)

franchise. Women's right to such things as property, jury service, and the vote was occasionally considered in these state constitutional conventions but was never granted. The New York constitutional convention voted to confer some property rights on married women but on second thought rescinded them, and then found comic relief in debating whether to appoint a doorkeeper for the women's gallery. The idea of women voting was deemed outright ridiculous. Should women go to the ballot box, chortled the *New York Daily Tribune* in 1846, "what a time for courting, love matches, etc, an election will be."[21] Established in state jurisdictions well before the Civil War, the restriction of the franchise to one sex was affirmed in 1870 with the passage of the Fifteenth Amendment to the United States Constitution. A decade later the Supreme Court finally clarified a debate that had long befuddled politicians and legal scholars: Was citizenship equivalent to and contingent on being a voter? In *Minor v. Happersett* the Court ruled that, for women, citizenship need not confer the right to vote. This was a bitterly pyrrhic victory for women's rights and a sophistical answer to the question, "What is the sex of citizenship?" In one stroke the Court affirmed that women were citizens and then rendered them political cripples, without the means to speak for themselves or choose their representatives.

For men, meanwhile, the domain of citizenship expanded. It was practiced most exuberantly in an unanticipated addendum to constitutional politics: the party system. Winning votes had long been a masculine pastime, purchased with rum around the Virginia courthouse or exchanged for spoils and personal favors in northern towns. Factions of Jeffersonians and Federalists had by the 1820s congealed into political parties, places where men formed alliances in order to affect public opinion and the outcome of elections. Andrew Jackson's presidential campaign of 1832 brought this partisan sport to the national level. When the Whigs squared off against the party of Jackson in 1840, masses of "common men" enrolled in public political clubs. Party politics was built into the everyday life of the menfolk: it was the raison d'être of the daily press, the staple of saloon conversations, the occasion for regular meetings in city wards and rural trading posts. It was a code of tenacious loyalty handed down from father to son. Civic virtue operated at the local level as a network of familiar associations, parochial connections, and personal stakes in the outcome of elections. Periodically, partisanship propelled a phalanx of marching masculinity through the streets, chanting arcane slogans and carrying torches aloft. The campaign season culminated on election day with a public presentation of votes in a carnival spirit of routine inebriation and occasional pugnacity.

With the ascendancy of partisan electoral democracy after 1840, the most prominent public appearance of women was as an ornamental auxiliary to the mainstream parties. The Whigs welcomed women ardently to their campaign rallies. They commended the ladies for ornamenting the galleries and paraded "little girls in a Whig torchlight procession."[22] The Democrats, who were shyer of petticoat politics and firmly opposed women's rights, could still compliment the ladies in the audience: "The ladies—guardian angels that control our natures—were around us with their illuminating smiles to cheer, and their bright countenances to encourage us on to victory." Women's position among the Whigs and later the Democrats was largely a matter of ceremony, condescension, and conservatism, passively testifying to the decorum and good order of the party.[23] After 1840 roughly three-fourths of eligible voting men were exercising their franchise during presidential elections, a level of participation that would be maintained through most of the nineteenth century. With a stake in the presidency, the highest rank in the masculine political club, millions of men were connected to the pinnacle of national power. By the midpoint of the nineteenth century, politics was not just legally reserved for men; it also functioned as a crucible of masculinity. As it nurtured sociability among the members of one sex, it cultivated the political traits that would become characteristic, not just of American citizens, but of men.[24]

Although not inevitable or preordained, the masculinization of American citizenship was a predictable outgrowth of long-standing political precedents. Participation and power in colonial decision making—positions at the forefront of the church and vestry, the town meeting, the county court, and the militia company—had always been reserved for the male heads of white households. The women of the early republic were preoccupied with other matters. One woman's response to a request to sign an abolitionist petition reflected the political indifference of many others: "*didn't know* nothing about it, and didn't *care* nothing about it; it never troubled her any way; she never thought nothing about it, nor never wanted to; slavery never hurt her at all." Another declined to sign a petition (a right of citizenship long granted to her sex), saying simply, "my husband doesn't approve of it."[25]

As the women who circulated those abolitionist petitions demonstrate, however, voting, public office, and the halls of government were not the only venues of public or political significance. The political public knew no simple legalistic boundaries. From after the Revolution until well into the antebellum period, resourceful women found informal or "outdoor" methods through which to express themselves and influence public opinion. Men and women gathered in mixed-sex assemblies that posed the most controversial issues of their time—not just concerns close to home like charity, temperance, and prostitution, but also foreign affairs like the Mexican War and radical movements like antislavery and women's rights.[26]

Any illusions that the Enlightenment ideal of universal and inalienable rights applied to women had been rebutted but not entirely suppressed by the turn of the nineteenth century. The idea of sexless citizenship was reprised briefly in the 1820s by urbane coteries of "free-thinkers," many of them immigrants from England and acolytes of Tom Paine and Mary Wollstonecraft. Fanny Wright raised the most clarion call for women's equal rights and boundless freedoms, even from the institution of marriage. Her addresses before "promiscuous" audiences in New York and Philadelphia won her the title of "Red Harlot of Infidelity" and became the grist of a political backlash that swept the idea of women's rights beyond the pale of womanly purity and piety. Echoes of the Enlightenment principles of political equality were similarly heard in an out-of-the-way place two decades later, when six ordinary farm women petitioned the constitutional convention of the state of New York to award them full citizenship on the liberal grounds of "natural rights," "the defense of the individual," and "the consent of the governed." They indicted the state of New York for departing from "the true democratic principles upon which all just governments must be based by denying to the female portion of community the right of suffrage and any participation in forming the government and laws under which they live." This impeccable liberalism, untainted by sexual difference, fell on the fallow ground of antebellum politics. There is no record that the delegates to the New York state constitutional convention paid any heed to this petition for women's rights, and the petitioners were not heard from again.[27] As we shall see, the rights of women would not receive a wider hearing until they were expressed in different gender terms.

Determined women, however, found more indirect routes into the political public, especially during the antebellum period, and particularly when it came to the most divisive item on the national public agenda, the institution of slavery. Opposition to slavery was first mounted from outside the halls of the state, in sectors of civil society to which antebellum women enjoyed ready access. During the 1830s women enrolled in scores of antislavery societies in the cities of Boston, New York, and Philadelphia and small towns like Andover, Massachusetts. They founded a national political organization of their own, addressed public meetings, and provoked urban riots across the northern states. Radical abolitionism, spearheaded by the American Antislavery

DIVIDING THE PUBLIC REALM

Society and articulated through William Lloyd Garrison's newspaper *The Liberator*, was the prototype for a mixed-gender public forum: women joined men in the membership, on the podium, and among the officers of the organization. As it is well known, abolitionism was the seedbed of a women's rights movement, and not solely due to a perceived analogy between slavery and the oppression of women. The abolitionists also practiced a mode of public politics that eschewed those political institutions—elections, constitutions, parties—that had become male monopolies. Rather, the Garrisonites in particular operated on a plane of moral exhortation, in a sphere where women were often said to be the superior sex. The Grimké sisters of South Carolina, for example, found capacious public and political space in the outsider politics and moral fervor of the abolitionist movement. It welcomed them as public speakers and provided the stage for a direct challenge to the masculinization of citizenship. Before the Massachusetts legislature, armed with an abolitionist petition signed by twenty thousand women, Angelina Grimké asked, "Are we aliens because we are women . . . have women no country—no interest staked in public weal—no liabilities in common peril— no partnership in a nation's guilt and shame."[28]

The amalgam of radical antislavery and the integration of the sexes was an unstable political compound. The American Antislavery Society broke apart when one faction, including its major financial backers, the Tappan brothers, rose in opposition to the champions of women's rights such as Garrison, the Grimké sisters, and the outspoken Maria Chapman of Boston. Thereafter, opposition to slavery diverged into two channels, and the most powerful of these followed the male political course through partisan, electoral campaigns. As the antislavery cause took on the form of a political party— first the renegade Garrisonites of the Liberty Party, then the fusion with disgruntled Whigs and Democrats in the Free Soil Party, and finally, the Republicans—it shifted tactics: moral exhortation gave way to constitutional debates, legislative maneuvering, and getting out the vote. These mainstream political practices once again sidelined and subordinated women. But their voices were never entirely silenced. Two Free Soil newspapers were edited by women, Jane Grey Swisshelm of Pittsburgh and Clarina Nichols of Brattleboro, Vermont. Outspoken members of the female antislavery societies, like Sarah and Angelina Grimké, and loquacious contributors to the antislavery press, such as Elizabeth Chandler, Lydia Maria Child, and Harriet Beecher Stowe, commandeered the literary public sphere as the mouthpiece for antislavery. Women writers and editors mixed their electoral endorsements and constitutional arguments with potent domestic rhetoric, including leveling charges of "baby-stealing" and "promiscuousness" against slave owners. In the two years after its publication in 1852, *Uncle Tom's Cabin* provoked no fewer than fourteen novelistic rejoinders from proslavery writers.[29]

Americans arrived at this most cataclysmic moment in their national life through public channels that were accessible to women as well as men. However, men presided at the helm of formal government, in Washington, Richmond, and every statehouse, county court, and city hall. For all their tenacious, impassioned, and adroit politicking, women citizens remained marginalized and subordinated to the male political domain. Any ambiguities about the relation of women to the formal, practical, and most powerful government institutions had been clarified well before 1861. Women would be excluded from direct representation and active, formal citizenship, be it voting, serving on juries, holding public office, or bearing arms in the national defense. The electoral arena was gendered male in multiple ways: it had a broad and exclusive male membership; it was a bastion of male sociability; and it froze women into a feminized, second-class citizenship. The political divide between the sexes was put on full display as Yankees and Rebels marched off to war. The ladies cheered in the galleries as southern legislatures voted for secession. As men departed for the battlefield, their wives, daughters, and mothers presented regiments of both Yankees and Rebels with hand-sewn banners, a belated public and political response to the provocation issued by antislavery women in the 1830s and 1840s, but without its subversive implications for gender politics.

The Civil War would confirm and reinforce the boundaries of a male public sphere. It would deepen and rigidify this cleavage of public politics into asymmetrical and unequal male and female sectors. Fort Sumter reduced politics to perhaps the oldest and most basic masculine form, physical warfare. Locked in a fierce military conflict and armed with mutilating modern weaponry, Confederates and Yankees were allied in their fratricidal politics. The exigencies of prosecuting and financing this war also mandated the expansion and institutionalization of the federal administrative state, another political domain that was set far apart from the everyday life and concerns of women. Women labored arduously on the home front to produce, collect, and distribute some $15 million worth of supplies for the Union army, only to see the leadership of the U.S. Sanitary Commission hijacked by men.[30]

With war's end, the gender divide of American politics became even more entrenched. Confederate veterans bonded together in support of a noble lost cause, while Yankees enrolled in the Grand Army of the Republic to march off for another generation as a segregated unit of civic life. North or South,

Good-by to Sumter. Harper's Weekly, 1861.

women found their marginal political space, tending the graves of fallen heroes on a military holiday called "Decoration Day" or "Memorial Day." The militarization of the American tradition would have a long life. It endured through the life spans of Civil War veterans and was renewed for the next generation by the jingoism surrounding the Spanish-American War. The gender implications of that military adventure did not escape scrutiny from the women's quarter of the public sphere. From the Woman's Christian Temperance Union came the observation, "Many a man has not the moral courage to plead for peace, for fear he shall be accused of effeminacy or cowardice. Woman has no such fear; to be the advocate of peace is congenial to her character."[31]

The era of the Civil War and Reconstruction was in many ways the highwater mark for the masculine public sphere and the pinnacle of male political hegemony. The Fourteenth Amendment made the gender divide of the public sphere explicit for the first time: the qualifying category "male" was attached to guarantees of the right to vote and the privileges and immunities of citizens. As the Union soldiers aged and grew in public influence, they wrested from the stingy American polity over $800,000 in pension funds and widows' benefits, the major form of federal welfare before the New Deal.[32] As the restrictions on citizenship among men were progressively relinquished over the course of the nineteenth century, the male public sphere became democratized. While the Republican Party sponsored African American men for citizenship, the Democrats championed the voting rights and civil liberties of European immigrants. Eleven states in the Mid- and Far West even granted aliens the right to vote, as long as they intended to become naturalized and were male. The American political system would not necessarily fulfill these democratic promises, especially for African Americans and immigrants from Asia, but the privilege of participating in the democratic public was held up to all as a badge of manhood. Meanwhile, the increasingly vocal appeals of the women's rights movement went unheeded.

The Mother as Citizen
Segregated and Secondary

Excluded from the formal institutions of representative government, women did not abandon their civic concerns. Quite the contrary, they cultivated an autonomous female place in the larger public arena. Middle-class matrons opened up a second political front from which to voice and act upon their common concerns. As men typically congregated in a militia company or political party, women went to church or to parlor meetings to express their concerns as Christians or as mothers. In the space between home and state — civil society in theoretical terms — women, like men, articulated and solidified a gender identity. Where the tavern nurtured masculinity, the church harbored femininity. Characteristically, women's groups tended the public welfare by providing relief and education to the needy, whereas men's associations were more often dedicated to self-improvement, socializing, and making advantageous connections. White men actively discouraged women from participating in the predominant form of interest group, a mutual benefit or insurance association.[33] If there was a functional aspect to the gendered division of civil society, it drew a rough line around a sector where women's charities and church groups met the needs of others, while men pursued their mutual self-interests.

Scholars who have looked beyond Washington, election day, and the headlines have revealed that many women acted as active and effective citizens in this wider public space. From the 1790s forward, women joined enthusiastically in civil society, forming a significant fraction of those voluntary associations that were honored by Alexis de Tocqueville as the cradle of democracy in America (and recently mourned by Robert Putnam in lament for those who "bowl alone"). In 1793 African American women founded the Temple Benevolent Society of St. Thomas, two years before Isabella Graham formed what was once designated the first female benevolent association. The city of Philadelphia hosted a full agenda of female reforms, "'public meetings of women' around the most pressing political issues of the day, such as peace, capital punishment, liberty laws, prostitution, and women's rights." One historian pointedly reminds us that small but tenacious bands of women met in national women's rights conventions every year, save one, between 1848 and 1860. From public podiums of their own construction, women inserted themselves into a wide-ranging public discussion.[34]

Theirs was clearly a second-class citizenship, located in what can be called the "women's public domain" in order to distinguish it from the male-defined and -dominated public sphere. Women's public domain was not invested with the authority of either the state or the endorsement of the electorate. It did not exercise sovereignty and could only enact its will through the mediation of male representatives and rulers. It operated through "women's influence," a species of power that Virginia Woolf dismissed with the comment, "many of us would prefer to call ourselves prostitutes simply . . . rather than use it."[35] Even this segregated and second-class citizenship, moreover, was beyond the reach of many, perhaps most women, those without the economic resources, leisure time, literacy, proximity, or inclination to join an association of their peers. In point of numbers the most active and prominent women citizens were overwhelmingly white, middle-class, and Protestant.

Within this constricted domain, however, women exercised a citizenship of a second order but of major historical consequence. During and after the Civil War, women's incursions into the political public took them beyond the local arena into national associations and national consciousness, where they acquired impressive organizational acumen. As the mainstay of the United States Sanitary Commission, for example, women proved themselves capable not just of sewing blankets but also of administrating a vast supply network for the Union army. By 1890, local chapters of mothers' associations, female literary clubs, and temperance societies enrolled literally millions of women in a powerful set of interlocking associations like the General Federation of Women's Clubs, the Woman's Christian Temperance Union, and the National Congress of Mothers. Although each of these institutions commenced with a small step outside the traditional confines of womanhood, they ultimately commandeered a space that was neither domestic nor particularly homelike, but truly a public domain.[36]

The public domain that women made was drenched in the gender norms of the Victorian era. After the Civil War not even the woman suffrage movement put much stock in the Enlightenment ideals of sexless citizenship and universal rights. Women citizens increasingly pleaded their causes based on their womanly virtues and preeminently their stature as mothers. One of the largest and most enduring segments of women's public domain was the National Congress of Mothers, now the Parent-Teachers Association, which provides a good example of this respectable, womanly route to public influence. The founding meeting of the National Congress of Women in 1897 was not likely to alarm gender conservatives. Its first president, Alice Birney, vowed to remain faithful to the principle that women were "divinely appointed to be the caretaker of the child," and she called her sisters to "raise the standards of home life . . . to develop wiser, better-trained parenthood, to bring into closer relations the home and the school." The founding executive committee of the association pronounced motherhood the first duty of their sex and identified their occupations as "women of the home." The membership consisted overwhelmingly of married women who were only temporary sojourners beyond women's domestic sphere and who subordinated their public mission to their family responsibilities. The national association would never endorse woman suffrage.[37]

By the late nineteenth century, however, excursions into the public domain became easier to manage. Presiding over affluent urban homes, staffed with servants, stocked with time-saving technology, and sheltering fewer progeny, the members of the Congress of Mothers had time and energy to spare for public service. These women gathered in public and under a national spotlight to better fulfill their traditional gender roles. As one member put it, "When the birds have flown from the nest, the mother-work may still go on, reaching out to better conditions for other children."[38] From this familiar pedestal, however, the National Congress of Mothers set its sights on bigger game. The group aimed "to carry mother-love and mother-thought into all that concerns or touches childhood in home, school, church or state." At the local and the national levels, members of the Congress of Mothers sharpened their maternal skills by collectively studying child-rearing techniques in the mode of "scientific motherhood." They also extended their maternal benevolence into the community, setting up milk stations, public kindergartens, "well-baby clinics," and "better baby contests." By the 1920s, the National Congress of Mothers dared even to form coalitions with Progressive reformers on controversial public issues, before retreating into providing voluntary womanly service to the schools.[39]

As long as they stayed within a female group and conformed to an archetypal domestic role, women could create a more commodious social and political space for their sex without creating much alarm. Frances Willard, founding mother of the Woman's Christian Temperance Union, extolled women's excursions into public space in feminine terms: "Nothing is more suggestive in all the National Gatherings of the Women's Christian Temperance Union than the wide differences between these meetings and any held by men. The beauty of the decoration is especially noticeable, banners of silk, satin, and velvet, usually made by the women themselves, adorn the wall. The handsome shields of state, the great vases bearing aloft grains, fruits and flowers, the setting of a platform to present an interior as cozy and delightful as a parlor could afford are features of the pleasant scene."[40] Groups like the National Congress of Mothers and the Woman's Christian Temperance Union were the vanguard of a powerful women's domain being set up outside the home. The massive membership and nationwide jurisdiction of such groups might even suggest that women's public domain was a potential rival to the male-dominated public sphere.[41]

Still, woman's power was camouflaged in domestic and maternal rhetoric. As one historian has put it, "Virtually every female activist used motherhood rhetoric, and virtually every male politician appealed to motherhood." Moral and domestic reformers posed as "civic mothers of the race."[42] Their platforms were called "Home Protection," "Social Mothering," or a "Maternal Commonwealth." The more gritty work of urban reformers inspired rhetoric from housewifery: municipal housekeeping, social housekeeping, or (with a modern feminine accent referring to a vacuum cleaner rather than a president) "Hooverizing the world." The language of the home could also provide extended metaphors to describe the process that took women into public space on a feminine mission. Jane Addams inscribed her reform principle in a humble domestic scene: the mother who sweeps the rubbish from her private tenement kitchen into the public street cannot shield her children or neighborhood from contamination; she and her reforming helpmates had best exercise their maternal responsibility by going to city hall to demand a better public sanitation system.[43] The same message was presented graphically in a poster of the Chicago Woman's Club that drew links between every housekeeping function with a different office down at city hall. In 1898 Anna Garlin Spencer converted the domestic experience of women into a utopian and millenarian exhortation: "In so far as motherhood fitted women to give a service to the modern State which men can not altogether duplicate. . . . The earth is ready, the time is ripe, for the authoritative expression of the feminine as well as the masculine interpretation of that common social consciousness which is slowly writing justice in the State and fraternity in the social order."[44]

Contrary to Spencer's imagery, the advance of women into public life did not unfold like the natural fecundity of Mother Earth. Nor was it a simple transplantation of the avocations of middle-class mothers. Spencer also spoke the language of "the state" and "justice" and was schooled in social Darwinism, not feminine domesticity. She was well aware of ongoing mutations in women's citizenship. In the 1890s a new generation of women had risen to leadership in the women's public domain. They were rarely biological mothers at all but rather college graduates and single women who had once despaired of finding an outlet for their talents and their civic concerns. One of the leaders of that movement, the settlement house reformer Vida Scudder, described her generation of women as "ardent with hope, yet sick with half despair—bent, as no other age has ever been, on the analysis of social evil and the righting of social wrong—into this world we are born—we, the first generation of college women. In a sense, we represent a new factor in the social order . . . . we do embody a type, in some respects, hitherto unknown." A mere three years after her own graduation from Smith College, Scudder had launched a career as an academic, reformer, and public persona, roles that she pursued single-mindedly, without the distractions of either motherhood or a conventional conjugal family.[45]

In this, Vida Scudder was typical of her generation of women leaders, perhaps the most notable and politically powerful of their sex that American history has yet seen. Their collective biographies reveal that the vast majority of leading white women who would come to power in the Progressive Era remained unmarried and childless throughout their lives. Others, like Charlotte Perkins Gilman and Florence Kelley, were divorced. It proved very difficult for women to gain such public stature while maintaining a home and raising a family. The rare mothers found among the top echelon of public women, like Gilman and Kelley, gave the primary care of their offspring to others for extended portions of their working days and working lives. For one painful period in Kelley's life, when she could only secure a low-paying library job, she took up residence in a cramped single room while her children boarded in the suburban home of married friends. In this, too, the citizenship of men and women was starkly asymmetrical during the nineteenth century. Male reformers and politicians rarely found public service incompatible with marriage and fatherhood.[46]

Kelley's generation of women reformers, born before 1870, had fought their way into newly opened women's colleges and coeducational universities, only to find themselves all dressed up in their caps and gowns with nowhere to go. Addams spent eight years after her graduation from Rockford Seminary in what she called a "snare of preparation," dropping out of school, languishing on the European tour, fending off her stepmother's matchmaking. After Kelley graduated from Cornell, in whose coeducational classrooms she harbored ambitions to become a social scientist, she was denied admission to graduate school at the University of Pennsylvania because she was a woman. She found a harbor among her own sex, taking a job from the Pennsylvania Women's Club, for whom she conducted a social survey of working women. But the domain of women's philanthropy was not wide or wealthy enough to sustain her for very long. Soon Kelley's career path was stalled by what Addams had called the "family claim": however educated, talented, or ambitious, she was called to the vocation of the unmarried daughter, in Kelley's case to chaperoning her wayward brother on a tour of Europe. But once abroad, Kelley was admitted to graduate study. In Germany she married, bore children, and got back on the track to the public sphere by translating the writings of Frederick Engels. It would appear she had won a reprieve from the gender asymmetry of nineteenth-century America, both its public and private aspects. But within a few years of marriage, Kelley's husband became abusive: she fled back to the United States, a single mother, homeless and jobless. Hers was not a smooth feminine path from parlor to politics.[47]

Traversing the life course of the typical college-educated women of the 1870s and 1880s could be a risky business. Women like Kelley blazed a trail that was largely uncharted for their sex and had to improvise all along the way. Only half of all female college graduates would marry within ten years of graduation, most of these relatively late in life, and they bore few, if any, children. It was standard for the first generation of female baccalaureates to take up an occupation after graduation, most often teaching, but significant numbers ultimately found their vocations in the more prestigious fields of medicine, social science, and their own brand of politics. Perhaps the most inventive and significant stepping-stone to political efficacy was a place called the settlement house. It was at the most famous such institution, Hull House in Chicago, that Florence Kelley and her children found refuge in 1892.[48]

American social settlements were largely female institutions. In 1900, when they numbered over two hundred, a mere twenty-five were dominated by men. Hull House was home to twenty women and five men in 1896. Three-quarters of the American settlements, ultimately numbering some four hundred, were led by women.[49] The builders of the American settlements often gave a feminine and sentimental tint to their handiwork. The classic text about the settlement movement, Addams's *Twenty Years at Hull House*, first sited her reform ambitions in a childhood vow to live in a big house among all the little houses of the poor. However beguiling to Victorian sensibilities, such stories were not grounded in historical fact. The women who founded settlements broke with the domestic culture of their mothers: they not only left home and family, but they also shunned the label "philanthropist" and were less likely to be driven by expressly religious motives. Their college memoirs were written in the language of science, not religion, motherhood, or apple pie. The Hull House Women's Club adopted this public and secular language in its statement of purpose: "to discuss, investigate and act upon questions of household science, civics, and the advancement of women and the care of children."[50]

The American settlement was one preliminary answer to the dilemma of college-educated women who were barred on grounds of sex from first-class citizenship.[51] In an address Addams gave at the Rockford College junior exhibition in 1880, she came up with a novel, gender-bending metaphor for her life ambition: to become a "breadgiver," a "Saxon lady whose mission it was to give bread unto her household." For Addams, not breadwinning but breadgiving was "the only true and honorable life . . . one filled with good works and honest toil. . . . Woman's Noblest Mission."[52] Addams set out on a pioneer trail when she determined to seek a lifelong career of public service outside the private home, but she was not alone. At almost the same moment that Jane Addams and Ellen Starr moved onto Halsted Street in Chicago, Lillian Wald founded the Henry Street Settlement in New York, and graduates of the Seven Sisters schools moved into a house in New York called the College Settlement.[53] The social settlement was not some pious dream of social uplift. It was a pragmatic solution to the fundamental quandary of the more ambitious and idealistic members of the first generation of college-educated women: How were they to put their education to use and translate their civic ideals into public programs? They needed not to just get a job but to create both a new line of work and a new kind of private life. The settlement house turned out to be this ingenious invention, a woman's live-work space.[54]

Put another way, the pioneers of women's public domain lodged their vocations in a house, but it was hardly a conventional Victorian home. The social settlement had to reconstruct the relationship between everyday life,

Jane Addams at the dining table of Hull House.
(Courtesy of the Jane Addams Memorial Collection [JAMC neg. 3696],
Special Collections, University Library, University of Illinois at Chicago)

work, and gender from the floorboards up. At the most basic level, settlement workers had to arrange to pay the rent; the initial recourse was to expend the accumulated wealth of the more affluent members of the household. The household expenses on Halsted Street in Chicago were first met
by Jane Addams's legacy, which was stretched to feed some of the children in
the neighborhood. When Addams's inheritance ran out, her dear friend Mary
Rozet Smith made up the slack.[55] Smith's beneficence even extended to funding college education for Florence Kelley's children. As the residents got on
their feet, and secured paying jobs in government and the academy, they paid
their own rent and created a reliable household income pool.[56] Admittance
to Hull House was by application and peer review. Meals combined rites of
solidarity and recreation with serious business. The working day began with
a breakfast meeting at 7:30 A.M., and at dinnertime Addams presided over a

sixteen-foot-long dining table. Although that table, like all the furnishings of Hull House and other settlements, was laden with domestic artistry and affection, it also served as an executive workspace, where deliberations in the public interest were routinely conducted.[57]

The most ordinary tasks of daily life took on new meaning when they were relocated to anomalous gender spaces like the settlement house. Female friendships, those intense and affective bonds between Victorian women, grew deeper, more encompassing, and more complicated once they were no longer subordinated to the relations of marriage and biological motherhood. The leaders of the reform enterprise found personal support with intimates of their own sex with whom they shared domestic space, bank accounts, and pledges of love that could last a lifetime. For forty years, Jane Addams shared an intimate friendship with Mary Rozet Smith. Frances Kellor and Mary Dreier were companions into old age, and Vida Scudder commuted from a room at Dennison House in Boston to a fireside in Wellesley that was tended by her fellow reformer, Florence Converse. Whether or not they resided in a social settlement, the leaders of the women's public domain turned to members of their own sex for intimate companionship. The powerhouse of the Woman's Christian Temperance Union, Frances Willard, had a sequence of romantic partners that even included royalty; the Lady Somerset seems a consort whose pedigree befit the reigning monarch of American women's organizations. One survey of welfare activists identified these "Boston marriages" in 28 percent of the sample.[58]

During the early years of public womanhood, the portals of the settlement house were also open to the humble inhabitants of carefully chosen lower-class neighborhoods. Addams was said to answer the door herself and preside over her office-home with children clinging to her skirts. The internal spaces of the settlement house were communal, cross-class living rooms. In addition to welcoming immigrant mothers to the parlor, Hull House set up facilities in the basement for bathing neighborhood children and offering ritual cleansing, called *mikvahs*, for Jewish wives. Jane Addams appears in the autobiography of Hilda Satt Polacheck, a Polish American from the Nineteenth Ward, as a familiar figure in the neighborhood, standing at the threshold of Hull House, following funeral processions through the streets, and acting as the emissary between the immigrant and city hall. The neighbors brought their woes to Miss Addams's doorstep because it was said "no matter what troubles came, you could always get help at Hull-House."[59]

The settlements also provided the infrastructure that linked the voluntary activities of legions of women who remained in their private homes. The local charities that had been operating in walking distance from settlement houses now had a central office. Conversely, social scientists investigating poor neighborhoods could draw on the experience of wives and mothers who had been conducting family visits in the name of churches and charities for decades. Working-class women were also known to overcome their skepticism and made use of settlement facilities. Labor organizer Mary Kenney reluctantly took advantage of Hull House as a union hall, conceding that "we haven't a good meeting place, but we can't afford anything better." Soon, she was disarmed by Jane Addams and came to live first at Hull House, and later at Dennison House, in the company of her husband, union leader Jack Sullivan. Similarly, the members of the "Jane Club," a group of young working women, were among the longest-running tenants on Hull House property.[60]

Well before 1900 some exceptional American women had found a home away from home, a place where they could reach out beyond their kin and class, deliberate about issues of municipal, national, and international concern, practice their own kind of politics, and define and pursue their own civic goals. Surely this place was public and political, a site for the prodigious exercise of good citizenship. And it was more inclusive than the U.S. Congress. While most settlement houses were dominated by women, they seldom excluded men. Yet clearly this was a public domain designed by and for one sex. Like the male public sphere, it was built upon a separate gender history and culture. Its premier institutions, whether the National Congress of Mothers or Hull House, took their energy from women who remained dispersed in their separate homes, schools, or women's colleges and who were ostracized from ward meetings, party conventions, or public office. The political public, its culture and practice, was clearly divided by sex at the close of the nineteenth century. It remained to be seen if a public so divided could long stand.

By the dawn of the twentieth century, the forays of organized women into the public sphere were already far advanced at the local level. Nowhere were they more striking than in Chicago. Hull House was a force to be reckoned with in the Nineteenth Ward of the city, whose fifty thousand residents had emigrated from eighteen different nations and voiced a militant working-class consciousness during the massive strikes, Labor Day parades, and riots of the late 1880s. The residents of the house on Halstead Street leapt into the center of the fray. By 1890, Jane Addams had fought city hall on issues from garbage collection to civil service reform. Although she seldom won a battle, she acquired a grudging respect for the tough democracy of the immigrant neighborhoods. Hilda Satt Polacheck captured the political agility required of these municipal housekeepers in her recollection of Addams's meddling in the lucrative city patronage system and getting herself appointed the garbage inspector of the Nineteenth Ward: "I have a vision of Jane Addams, honored by the great of the world, acclaimed as the first citizen of Chicago, following a filthy garbage truck down an alley in her long skirt and immaculate white blouse."[61]

First citizen Jane Addams, and settlement workers in general, turned to other more genteel allies in the reform cause. In matters of garbage collection, for example, they would find partners not in city hall but at the Chicago Woman's Club, whose "Woman's Municipal Platform" included scientific blueprints for a citywide sanitation system.[62] Well before 1920, and without constitutional sanction, women were going regularly into the political ring to confront the denizens of the male public sphere. They countered the graft of Chicago politicians with proposals for such "virile" reforms as municipal ownership of utilities, changes in taxing policy, and management of the city debt. They also tapped into the clout of elite members of the Chicago Woman's Club such as Louise de Koven Bowen and Bertha Honoré Palmer, kin of the city's most powerful businessmen. Wherever they ventured into the gritty life of the city, women reformers drew on a pool of skilled municipal laborers among philanthropists and clubwomen. The influence of Jane Addams extended far enough by 1893 to secure the position of state inspector of factories for Florence Kelley. When Kelley assumed the job, she took a network of women with her.[63] About thirty women's organizations were at work in Illinois investigating the health conditions in the state's industries.[64] Women trained in the old charitable technique of family visiting retooled to conduct social surveys and lobby legislatures. When poor families feared the loss of income from child labor laws and restrictions on hours, Kelley sent her volunteers door-to-door explaining, cajoling, and even pledging to find well-paying adult jobs to replace the income of working children.[65]

With their networks spreading throughout the urban social structure, women's public domain looked more like a political machine than a home. And its organizational center was more like an office, indeed a whole corporate complex, than a private residence. Hull House would come to occupy four square blocks in the city of Chicago. Those offices housed social research bureaus, a major urban cartography project, and strategy sessions with political parties and government officials. Moreover, the settlement house was only one example of women's public presence on the urban landscape. The rising skyline of the Second City was also broken by a twelve-story office tower belonging to the Woman's Christian Temperance Union. The Chicago Woman's Club announced itself in civic space by setting up shop amid the architectural marvels downtown. It held its inaugural meeting in the public library and occupied office space on the seventeenth floor of a skyscraper on Wabash Avenue. Other sites of women's reform opened up a broad constituency to racial diversity. Joanna Moore's ad hoc experiment in social service opened in an African American neighborhood in Little Rock, Arkansas, several years before Hull House. Off the beaten path of reform in West Oakland, California, settlement workers and reforming matrons created what one historian has called an entire "charitable landscape." Black and white, Protestant and Catholic, women larded this working-class immigrant neighborhood with service institutions—some of them humble adaptations of existing housing stock, and others built specifically to meet the architectural needs of women's public domain.[66] Commissions to design public edifices for female clients sustained a career for the most renowned woman architect of her time, San Francisco's Julia Morgan. Morgan built no fewer than fifteen Young Women's Christian Association buildings, along with assorted women's club houses and dormitories. The women who built and presided over this reform empire had outgrown any cozy metaphorical or spatial encasement that might have served their purpose twenty years before.[67]

In fact, the paeans to motherhood, which once legitimized women's public politics, were interspersed with an alternative language and grammar of reform. The organizational abilities and leadership powers of Frances Willard and Jane Addams each inspired an occasional reversal of gender titles, winning them the status of general in a women's army of reform; Addams admitted privately that "there's power in me, and will to dominate which I must exercise."[68] Even in her college years, the head of Hull House sensed that her course to public service would take her into unknown gender territory. Young Jane Addams mused that "she wishes not to be a man, not like a man, but she claims the right to independent thought and action."[69] The mature Jane Addams was the public personification of a historic transfiguration of gender. By virtue of her leadership in a female public domain, Addams, along with legions of her sex, stood at the creative center of American politics.[70]

Building this public domain required some complex geographical maneuvers. On the one hand, women had particular political advantages at the local level, where they could weave political networks among friends, kin, and neighbors. When that locality happened to be Chicago, a hub of urban growth, capitalist enterprise, and social experiment, women's political space acquired unique energy and wide influence. On the other hand, entrenched male interests at the local level repeatedly thwarted women's civic projects. When women as wealthy and well connected as Louise Bowen went before the men's City Club, or when someone as esteemed as Jane Addams called on the mayor, they were too often treated with polite condescension and then ignored. To sidestep the bottleneck of parochial masculinity down at city hall, women began to look to more distant sites of public politics. The women of the settlements often found it more effective to work at the level of state government, and it was there that they were most successful. For example, forty-five states would enact the pet project of the women's reform constituency, the mother's pension.[71] These programs were the product of sophisticated women's organizations from the grass roots up to the state legislature. Nearly every women's organization in the United States supported the cause of mothers' pensions, a state system of direct subsidies to the needy mothers of dependent children. Everyone from the editors of the suffragist *Women's Journal* to the members of the Women's Republican Association lent their names to a project that would seem as savory as the proverbial apple pie.[72]

In fact, state mothers' pensions were more like the proverbial Trojan horse. By guaranteeing pensions to mothers, the leaders of women's public domain had succeeded in overcoming the long-standing opposition to any form of public relief on the part of partisans of laissez-faire economics. The women of Chicago had been challenging their husbands on this issue since the Great Fire of 1871. Progressive women constructed a unique welfare system at the state level that defied the sacred principles of American free enterprise. In contrast to Western Europe, where welfare legislation was sponsored by labor parties and routed through fathers, U.S. programs were usually the work of women reformers. The fine print of mothers' pensions specified that the stipends would be dispensed by the juvenile courts, state agencies that happened to be located within women's public domain. The state programs installed women on the boards of oversight for the pension programs and required that trained social workers, chiefly women, serve as the human links between the state and needy mothers. By 1911, when Illinois enacted the first state mother's pension, female civic activism had already challenged basic tenets of the American political tradition, in matters of economics as well as gender. And this was only the beginning.[73]

The Woman Citizen Goes to Washington

Early in the twentieth century women took another giant step into the political public and began to act less like mothers and more like citizens of the female sex. Well before they were awarded the franchise in 1920, women citizens had moved beyond the private realm. They climbed to the zenith of the federal system in Washington, D.C., and went quickly to work transform-ing the national way of governing. Taking the political values and methods they had devised within their own public domain, women built a place for themselves in the Progressive administrations of Theodore Roosevelt and Woodrow Wilson, and later in the New Deal. They effectively integrated pub-lic territory formerly monopolized by men. While the agenda that Progressive women brought to Washington has been called "maternalist" and remained dedicated to the welfare of families and children, it hardly operated in the ways of Victorian motherhood. Cadres of women politicians marched into Washington and catapulted ahead of many seasoned male politicians, who were more deeply mired in provincial nineteenth-century political values, especially ideological attachments to small government, states' rights, and laissez-faire economics.

In 1898 Anna Garlin Spencer prefigured this turn of gender history when she pronounced that "wherever the State touches the personal life of the in-fant, the child, the youth, or the aged, helpless, defective in mind, body or moral nature, there the State enters 'woman's peculiar sphere.'"[74] The finger-prints of women were all over the major political innovations of the early twentieth century, the expansion of the administrative state and the federal bureaucracy. The first time that the Supreme Court affirmed the constitu-tionality of federal social welfare legislation was the *Muller v. Oregon* decision of 1908, which was based on an argument formulated by Josephine Gold-mark. The court approved the Progressive agenda only if the beneficiaries were mothers or potential mothers whose health was "essential to vigorous offspring" and "an object of public interest and care in order to preserve the strength and vigor of the race."[75] Women citizens put their mark all over the social legislation of both the Progressive Era and the New Deal. The pioneer federal welfare agency, the Children's Bureau, was conceived during a break-fast meeting at Hull House and introduced in Congress three years later. Established in 1912, the bureau would process the first direct federal expen-diture for social programs as allocated by the Sheppard-Towner Act in 1925. That keystone of the American welfare state, the Social Security Act of 1935, housed a program for Aid to Dependent Children that had been drafted by veterans of Hull House, now sequestered in Washington.[76]

By the mid-1930s, public women could be justly boastful. As Democratic Party stalwart Molly Dewson put it, the passage of the Social Security Act was "the culmination of what us girls and some of you boys have been work-ing for so long, it's just dazzling."[77] That work had been underway in the na-tion's capital for more than two decades. The office of the Children's Bureau, located in the Department of Commerce and Labor, operated as a women's branch of the federal government for much of that period. At the outset, the bureau was a very small concession to women; it had a staff of only fifteen and a budget of only $25,640.[78] Still, it was a showcase of what women could do with minimal federal resources. The first director of the bureau, Julia Lathrop, would see her agency grow to a staff of over 150 employees, nine in ten of whom were women, and then pass the baton on to a second generation of female officials, first Grace Abbott and then Katharine Lenroot.[79]Lathrop's first successor represented the University of Chicago School of Social Service Administration, woman's base in the academy; the second would be called by Franklin Roosevelt to the task of drafting a children's welfare component of the Social Security Act. In the early years of its operation, the Children's Bureau would wield its state power in such a way as to be an efficient, woman-to-woman welfare delivery system: it would enlist thousands of middle-class lobbyists and family visitors in its activities and win the gratitude of countless mothers who sent a stream of thank-you notes to the Washington office. A typical missive read, "Words cannot express what I feel for you in my heart. I can only write that I thank you infinitely for your kindness towards helping me with my baby."[80] By 1929, it was estimated that half of all America's children had benefited in some way from the bureau's programs.[81]

The heyday of the Children's Bureau, and of maternal statecraft, came early in the 1920s, when the agency actually secured federal funding in the amount of $1.5 million for 1921–22 and a quarter million annually for the next five years.[82] This sum was secured through a nationwide grassroots lobbying effort that enrolled everyone from the *Ladies' Home Journal* to the Daughters of the American Revolution. One wily woman politician stooped so low as to chide recalcitrant politicians with the question, "Why does Congress wish women and children to die?" The motherly pressure group was so persistent that one exasperated legislative assistant reported, "I think every woman in the state has written to the senator." The logic was irresistible, and the appropriations bill, the Sheppard-Towner Act, passed in 1921 by a vote of 63 to 7 in the Senate and 279 to 39 in the House of Representatives. The Sheppard-Towner Act was calculated to win Uncle Sam many friends in American homes, where it relieved some parents the anguish of high infant mortality rates. In 1915 roughly 10 percent of all infants died before the age of one year.[83] The Sheppard-Towner funds financed the education of midwives and other public health initiatives that significantly reduced infant mortality among women of all classes and races. This accomplishment rested on the broad shoulders of women citizens, which now extended from the heroic Hull House generation to the growing ranks of female professionals (now formally trained in the fields of child welfare and social service) and on to masses of local volunteers. In 1927 alone, the shock troops of the women's public domain conducted more than 500,000 home visits in tenement districts and rural backwaters, where they dispensed advice and conducted medical examinations.[84] Another 1.5 million women were reached by the most popular manual on child-rearing of the time, the Children's Bureau's best seller, *Infant and Child Care*.[85]

The passage of the Sheppard-Towner Act occurred in the immediate aftermath of the ratification of the woman suffrage amendment. The suffrage victory in 1920 was in many ways not the debut of women in politics but the proof that they had already become seasoned and effective politicians. Breaking into the citadel of male citizenship had taken herculean energy and tenacity, measured in over five hundred campaigns at the state level and another nineteen before the U.S. Congress.[86] Nearly every division of women's public domain (with a few notable exceptions, like the National Congress of Mothers) endorsed the suffrage amendment to the Constitution. Washington's busy women were acutely aware that direct voting rights and office holding would simplify and expand, as well as symbolically acknowledge, their arduous public work. In the years between 1914 and 1920, woman suffrage became a mass movement, a coalition that spanned from North to South, East to West, among the wealthy and the workers, blacks, whites, and Chinese Americans, septuagenarians and college coeds. The victories of state amendments in California in 1911 and in New York in 1917 were particularly gratifying to women of intensely political temperaments like Elizabeth Cady Stanton's daughter, Harriot Stanton Blatch.[87]

The suffragist wing of the women's domain was public in a particularly precocious way, in the modern style of publicity and spectacle. When Blatch returned from London to be at her mother's bedside in 1902, she took up the mantle of suffrage and refashioned it for the twentieth century. In contrast with what she called the "the read and write fetich [*sic*]" of her elders, Blatch resorted to more contemporary and public techniques of persuasion.[88] In the 1880s, when a few brave and radical women's rights advocates took to speaking "night after night on the streets, and in the dance halls," they were excoriated as "almost a disgrace to womanhood."[89] As late as 1910, Blatch's proposal that suffragists parade down the public streets of New York struck the leadership of the National American Woman Suffrage Association as a tactic that would "set back suffrage fifty years."[90] Undeterred, Blatch established the Equality League of Self-Supporting Women, which held an open-air public meeting in Madison Square in 1907. A year later they brashly paraded all the way from 59th Street to Union Square.[91] A 1912 parade in New York City reputedly brought out twenty thousand marchers.[92] Another in Washington the next year brought out five thousand marchers and a half million onlookers. A Chicago rally was estimated to enroll thirty thousand individuals and to represent 130 different ethnic groups.[93] The eve of their victories in New York and California would find the suffragists mobilized in open-air meetings, union halls, public squares, and on street corners, even pitching their message from the running boards of automobiles. The California suffrage referendum would sail to victory in 1911 on the winds of an aggressive publicity campaign, featuring storefront offices, posters displayed in shop windows, and addresses from the roofs of automobiles.[94] Its success inspired the 1915 campaign in New York to mount its publicity not just in fashionable roadsters but atop streetcars. In one instance, advocates carried their message via an interurban trolley system all the way from Syracuse to Albany.[95]

The final lap to victory was completed at the national level but within a familiar and womanly political circuit. The National American Woman Suffrage Association (NAWSA), like the architects of the Children's Bureau, had determined that federal political structures would bend to its will more easily than the entrenched male interests at the local level. In 1914, after conducting painstaking local voting campaigns that yielded eleven state constitutional amendments and thirteen legislative victories, the national association, under the direction of the adroit politician Carrie Chapman Catt, set its sights on the United States Congress.[96] In order to usher the suffrage amendment through Congress, and on to ratification in state legislatures, the politically savvy suffragists aimed their now-renowned skills at the private persuasion of legislators. Their legislative successes led one observer to credit the suffragists for having "blazed the way for the lobbying organization in the capital."[97] The NAWSA was also capable of pragmatism, if not opportunism, for example, soft-pedaling the egalitarian rhetoric and abolitionist origins of women's rights when seeking essential southern votes. The modern-day suffragists organized into groups like the College Equal Suffrage League or Blatch's Equality League of Self-Supporting Women and went on to forge coalitions across the divides of age and class and ethnicity. They enrolled not just middle-class mothers but also a large contingent of working-class daughters. In the New York referendum of 1917, they secured sufficient support from men in working-class and immigrant neighborhoods to ensure a majority of the overall electoral vote.[98]

However modern their political tactics, the suffragists nevertheless relied on some old-fashioned rhetoric, including appeals to maternal duty. For example, American movie audiences could watch a film that portrayed woman suffrage as the road to better public health and sanitation, symbolized by a melodramatic rescue of the heroine's beloved daughter. Maternalist political values had not disappeared by 1920. Rather, they had been fired in political conflict and forged into federal policy, until they were a formidable record of effective citizenship. Only in retrospect did Lillian Wald recognize her political "awakening." She suddenly recognized that "when I was working in the interests of those babies . . . I was really in politics."[99] Within two years of taking up the direction of the Children's Bureau, Julia Lathrop, an alumna of Hull House, had consolidated her life experience into a political adage that she pronounced like a stateswomen; in her opinion the welfare of infants was simply "a profoundly important public concern," critical to "the public spirit and the democracy of a community."[100] These leading women citizens had placed the care of children in the public sphere, where it was the responsibility of both sexes.

Well into the future, however, women would bear more than their share of the political and personal responsibility for the nation's children. Harriot Stanton Blatch, among others, updated the maternalist agenda by daring to propose that the care of children should be subsidized by the state in order to free mothers from dependency on male breadwinners. Crystal Eastman, who would adopt an ideology of independent womanhood worthy of the label feminist, seconded this goal. "Every woman," said Eastman, "whether the wife of a millionaire or a day laborer, will in the world built by women, be made to feel that society honors motherhood sufficiently to raise it above sordid dependence." Fellow feminist Henrietta Rodman (whose favorite causes included the dashingly modern notion of kitchenless apartment living) concurred that motherhood "would remain largely the study and work of women."[101] Eastman and Rodman represented a younger generation of women citizens, the daughters of Progressive mothers, who would include children's interests among their myriad concerns as citizens. This new energy flowing into the suffrage movement in the 1910s was embossed on an advertisement reading, "Votes for Women. Come and hear Jane Addams speak at Carnegie Hall." The podium in this case was a motor vehicle, which also served as a platform for a dozen young, beaming, flag-waving suffragists, the daughters of us all.[102] In the flush of suffrage victory, and as women raked in such spoils as the Sheppard-Towner Act, it would appear that the

Publicizing woman suffrage. American Press Association photo. (Courtesy of the Milstein Division of United States History and Genealogy, New York Public Library, Astor, Lenox, and Tilden Foundations)

query of this chapter had been answered and could be rephrased: The citizenship of women was now recognized in the Constitution; the public realm was no longer egregiously divided by sex.

After suffrage, Progressive-minded woman wasted no time in taking their program of reform directly into the public sphere that men had made. Entry into mainstream politics would be a bracing experience for veterans of women's public domain. Their first taste of the rewards of full citizenship, the Sheppard-Towner Act, was not to be a harbinger of things to come. Several other small victories followed during the first half the 1920s, and then Progressive women lost a key battle over the passage of a constitutional amendment intended to outlaw child labor. Newly enfranchised women now faced the resistance to the Progressive social agenda head on. The American Medical Association, as well as conservative congressmen, took direct aim at the maternalists' policies, labeling them the precursors of "child control by the State . . . born out of purely socialistic brains." Others tarred the reform as the work of "the Hull House Crowd," "feminists," or "Bolsheviks." Right-wing senator James Reed opined that "it is now proposed to turn the control of the mothers of the land over to a few single ladies holding Government jobs at Washington," and for good measure, he made a sophomoric proposal to "provide for a committee of mothers to take charge of the old maids and teach them how to acquire a husband and have babies of their own."[103]

The Progressive women's agenda was buffeted by conservative political winds for the remainder of the 1920s. The administrations of Calvin Coolidge and Herbert Hoover suspended federal programs, and in the aftermath of the Russian Revolution even groups like the National Congress of Mothers were suspected of communism. The momentum of women's drive for national power subsided, and although newly enfranchised women were remarkably quick to exercise their new political privileges, they proved to be a diverse and independent electorate whose votes could not be reined into a single constituency, even around appeals to motherhood. The veterans of the women's public domain were chagrined to find that the maternalist consensus survived only a few months into the postsuffrage era. At a meeting in 1921, the National Woman's Party rejected not only Blatch's proposal for motherhood endowments but also a variety of specific legislative initiatives from voting rights for nonwhite women to birth control. The organization focused instead on a constitutional amendment that would simply outlaw all discrimination based on sex. Social welfare activists like Florence Kelley interpreted that amendment as a threat to the protective legislation for which Progressive female reformers had labored so assiduously and so long. From that moment, a rift opened down the middle of the women's movement, dividing the maternalists from the liberal feminists. It would not mend until the 1960s. In the meantime, the Democratic and Republican Parties courted the votes of women and siphoned off more recruits from women's public domain.[104]

This did not mean that politics resumed its old manly ways soon after 1920. The women who arrived at the ballot box, party headquarters, city hall, the statehouse, and the nation's capital were a different species from the "ladies" who once sat politely in the stands at party rallies and patriotic festivals. They brought considerable political experience and ideas of their own into the official public realm. In fact, seasoned participants in the women's public domain had already exercised leverage in a number of mixed-gender venues, not just around the table at settlement houses, but at party caucuses. Women had long exercised influence within third parties. When the Prohibition Party was organized in 1881, it was actually at the behest of the Woman's Christian Temperance Union, and Frances Willard would be its chief strategist. Women were a strong presence in the Socialist Party in the 1910s, and they insisted that issues like birth control, social legislation, and the cost of living be placed on the party's agenda.[105] The Populists, with fiery leaders like Mary Elizabeth Lease, also had a strong and vocal women's constituency. At the local level women had shared in the victories of several electoral coalitions. In Philadelphia in 1911, Progressive women injected "civic housekeeping" into the mayoral campaign and rode to victory. Women had won the municipal franchise in Chicago in 1914 and switched their allegiance from Republicans to Democrats when it was to their political advantage. A political sage like Ida B. Wells-Barnett was not about to let the opportunity of woman suffrage pass her by. Through her Alpha Suffrage Club she helped elect the first black alderman of the city of Chicago and would later run for office herself.[106]

The loose coalition that constituted the Progressive movement was the busiest intersection of men's politics and women's public domain, and women were so influential there that they created a kind of coeducational political party. When the Progressive movement became a formal party and put Theodore Roosevelt forward as a presidential candidate in 1912, the mark of woman was all over its platform, in its endorsements of mothers' pensions, factory safety legislation, and woman suffrage. It was Jane Addams who put the name of Roosevelt in nomination for the presidency, and she reportedly received louder applause than the former president. Addams embraced the Progressive Party as a chance to bring her long-standing concerns for "measures of industrial amelioration [and] demands for social justice . . . into the stern arena of political action." "It is inevitable," she added, that the party would "draw upon the great reservoir of [women's] moral energy so long undesired and unutilized in practical politics."[107] The Progressive Party, however, harbored a sexual division of labor all its own. While women focused on issues of child and family welfare, men favored the cause of trustbusting, and the two sexes worked together on questions like workmen's compensation. Women may not have taken control of the political public after 1920, but they did help to give it a new cast. Municipal machines and party bosses, torchlight parades and smoke-filled rooms, were fast becoming antiquated. And in their stead came some of the favorite practices of the women's public domain—commissions of experts, reform legislation, government bureaus— and a shift of attention from the local to the national political arena.[108]

Women citizens fanned out in a variety of different directions in this new

DIVIDING THE PUBLIC REALM

political system. They secured positions in the major parties, assumed the role of civic educators in the League of Women Voters, and were ceremonially appointed to public office. Most important, significant numbers of Progressive women held on another decade or more, long enough to be called back to Washington when Franklin D. Roosevelt assumed the presidency in 1933. For the first time, significant numbers of women were securely inside the executive branch of the federal government. Leading the parade of their sex into the New Deal was the first female member of the cabinet, Secretary of Labor Frances Perkins, an alumna of the settlement house and a staunch supporter of the labor movement. Under the watchful eye of Eleanor Roosevelt (herself a frequenter of social settlements in her youth and a lobbyist for maternalist causes in New York State), women were recruited for key positions in the social welfare wing of the New Deal.

When Frances Perkins was first approached about a cabinet position, she announced her determination to create a full system of welfare protection for all Americans, including old-age benefits and unemployment insurance. FDR obliged her by creating a Committee of Economic Security, which drew up the first blueprints for an American welfare state. The staffing of the committee was another case of Progressive and maternalist nepotism. Its prominent members and advisers included Elizabeth Brandeis, the daughter of Supreme Court Justice Louis Brandeis and the wife of the author of the first social insurance legislation in the state of Wisconsin. The key figure at the drafting board in Washington in 1935 was a young social welfare expert and lawyer named Barbara Nachtrieb Armstrong, who came to Washington with the clear intent of implementing a national program of social insurance. She promptly outlined a three-tiered program of benefits for the young, the aged, and the unemployed.[109]

Attempts to translate Progressive proposals into New Deal policies went most smoothly when children were the beneficiaries. This facet of public welfare was simply entrusted to the Children's Bureau, and its seasoned directors Grace Abbott and Katharine Lenroot. Because they had already devised state measures for the support of dependent children, their federal assignment was relatively easy. They drafted a policy modeled after existing mothers' pensions and designed to supplement state welfare programs. The Children's Bureau's moderate proposal called for federal stipends to be dispensed by the states, but only after case-by-case reviews to determine the eligibility and fitness of individual recipients. This was a modest proposal. Representative Ernest Lundeen of Minnesota, in league with Mary Van Kleeck of the Russell Sage Foundation, proposed more generous support for all needy and dependent children, to be financed and overseen by the federal government. Such a bold expansion of federal government overtaxed FDR's political daring. The proposal from the veterans of the Children's Bureau, by contrast, stayed within the permissible bounds of states' rights and laissez-faire economics. One of the least controversial plans in the welfare platform of 1935, the proposal was forwarded to Congress by the Roosevelt administration with little comment or revision. It remained the foundation of the federal program of Aid to Dependent Children (ADC) until even this dilute form of welfare was abolished in the 1990s.[110]

This modest but hard-fought reform was to be a last hearty hurrah for the women's public domain. First, the Roosevelt administration transferred implementation of ADC programs from the Children's Bureau to Harry Hopkins's Federal Emergency Relief Association, and then Congress passed it on to the Social Security Board. Neither agency had many women members or any experience in the public care of children. When the ADC component of the social security legislation was passed into law, its maternal origins were still apparent—both for better and for worse. The federal statute provided for direct subsidies to needy children, but unlike most state policies, it neglected to earmark any part of the funds for family caretakers. Mothers themselves were placed in the role of passive conduits of their children's welfare. Neither did the act impose any minimum standards or regulations on state use of federal funds. Nonetheless, it was assumed that women would be the essential human links between the state and the child. Mothers' unacknowledged labor alloyed with the low pay of female social workers to reduce the administrative cost of social services. The social workers also scrutinized the worthiness of mothers and provided further public savings by weeding out the "undeserving" from the welfare rolls. No state distributed these funds with largesse and permissiveness. The typical ADC subsidy was well below the sum required to support a family, and it usually came with strings attached and a prying social investigator at the door.[111]

These niggardly characteristics of the federal program of child welfare stand out in sharp relief against the other major components of the Social Security Act of 1935: old-age benefits, unemployment insurance, and the Fair Labor Standards Act. The last two programs pose an asymmetrical gender contrast with the benefits designed by and for women. Their creation was entrusted not to the Children's Bureau but to commissions in which the representatives of labor and business were the key players. While unemployment insurance began as a modest proposal like ADC, it was tended carefully by the federal bureaucrats and labor unions until it grew into a form of entitlement whose benefits were generously expanded over the years. At a time when 80 percent of all men, but only 25 percent of all women, were in the labor force, the recipients of this more generous benefit were overwhelmingly male, and they were not about to submit to interrogation by nosy social workers.[112] Male breadwinners and potential breadwinners received grants by simply registering their unemployment. Their title to unemployment benefits was so assured that it never bore the stigma of "welfare" at all.[113]

The gender asymmetry of New Deal programs was especially apparent in the Fair Labor Standards Act of 1938. By establishing federal standards for minimum wages and maximum hours, the act is still the boldest direct national intervention in the market economy. It positioned the federal government between worker and employer with the intent of guarding the former from possible exploitation by the latter. In other words, it operated in the manner of protective legislation, the kind of social reform pioneered by women citizens. Women's unions like the International Ladies' Garment Workers would be the principal backers of this legislation. Union men, on the other hand, were not as eager to place their fate in the hands of the state and thereby surrender their manly self-reliance to some federal parent figure. Preferring to fight their own battles through collective action, the major unions favored such New Deal reforms as the National Recovery Act and the Wagner Act, which guaranteed their right to strike and bargain on their own behalf. The American Federation of Labor articulated this gender ideology by rejecting protective legislation in favor of "the most essential right of free men . . . that of voluntary association for lawful purposes. . . . This priceless right and freedom to bargain collectively with employers."[114] The Fair Labor Standards Act was opposed by some male unions, and when enacted, it was stingy in its benefits, especially to women workers. It excluded those broad sectors of the labor force—domestic and agricultural work and the informal economy—where women workers were concentrated before the 1940s. And for those who were included, minimum wage rates were set at very low levels.[115]

This pattern of gender discrimination also undercut the most familiar component of the Social Security Act: old-age benefits and survival insurance. As drafted in the women's public domain, the mission of Frances Perkins and the handiwork of Barbara Armstrong, this quintessential policy of the American welfare state was originally intended to extend a blanket of well-being and dignity over the entire American population as it aged. Armstrong's initial proposal was very ambitious: it called for dispensing the reform as outright federal insurance that would provide coverage to even the lowliest ranks of the labor force, funding the program through a payroll tax, and extending benefits to the individual worker's surviving spouse. As it left the women's sector of the New Deal, this plan was calculated to achieve two goals: comprehensive coverage and a sense of entitlement, assuring all working men and women that they had earned a right to social and economic citizenship. But once it left the jurisdiction of Armstrong and Perkins, the protective blanket of social security was shredded in pieces. Their superiors in the Roosevelt administration perfunctorily removed the survivor benefits from the proposal before sending it to Congress. On arrival in the House of Representatives, and in particular at the conservative bottleneck of the House Ways and Means Committee headed by Howard W. Smith, the Social Security Bill was pruned further. The jobs of most women and blacks were cut from the program by the exclusion of agricultural and domestic workers, and benefits were set at low levels. When the old-age insurance bill was finally passed and scheduled for funding, it was weaker and less remunerative than some programs already in place at the state level. The benefits were so modest, and the beneficiaries so select, that the cost of the federal program threatened to fall far below the funds already deducted from workers' paychecks. Alarmed that their program would self-destruct, New Deal planners convened a new Social Security Advisory Council in 1937, charged with amending the original plan. The committee made the critical decision to expend the growing payroll-tax income in the form of benefits to the spouses of deceased workers.[116]

While this renovation expanded the welfare function of the federal government significantly, it also shored up conventional asymmetries in the private relations between the sexes. Rather than expanding the rolls of beneficiaries to include minorities, domestic and agricultural workers, or full-time homemakers, the amendments enacted in 1939 inflated the benefits and the familial stature of working men. The survival benefits made most women the dependents of working men, rather than social or economic citizens in their own right, even after the retirement or death of their mates. Some astute observers spied the gender bias in this policy. Mary Anderson, head of the Women's Bureau, said it this way: "On the surface it may seem that the subject of the social security program is not one that calls for consideration by sex, but that it applies alike to men and women. However, on penetrating below the phraseology of the law one soon discovers a number of factors reflecting considerable differences between men and women."[117] Some of the differences were in the fine print, and others were buried in the structures of gender. For example, the eligibility clause required an extended tenure in the labor force, a qualification that women were less likely to meet if they had devoted much of their life span to homemaking and child care. The fine print of the social security law also specified that beneficiaries could claim a subsidy only in one program—that is, either as a former worker or as a surviving spouse. Since the lifetime earnings of women were most often less than those of their husbands, it was in their economic interest to accept their spouse's stipend and surrender the benefits that might have accrued through their own labor.[118]

Women at the lowest level of the social structure, among whom African Americans were greatly overrepresented, fared especially poorly under New Deal programs. Poor women of color were expected to work, no matter how many minor children were in their care. In some southern states they were denied a mother's pension on the grounds that they were "employable." The pensions themselves were so meager that beneficiaries were often compelled to take low-paying supplementary jobs. The insufficiency of these allocations thus often functioned as a subsidy to sweated industries and stingy employers. A case culled from the welfare records of Chicago will illustrate. Mrs. Elizabeth Meyer claimed a small pension, which she supplemented by entering the paid labor force. In the words of her case worker, Meyer felt a "certain pride and exhilaration, to think that she too is a wage-earner and not so dependent as formerly." Meyer continued to work even when the state threatened to reduce her benefits in proportion to her wages and thereby wipe out the small amenities that relieved the grinding poverty of her family. But Meyer was ultimately defeated by the welfare system: she bitterly surrendered her pension rather than suffer the humiliation and surveillance that accompanied it. Most impoverished female heads of household would not be required to make Mrs. Meyer's Hobbesian choice. The system of mothers' pensions reached only a tiny portion of these needy women, be they black or white, native or foreign-born.[119]

Women were not the only group to be shortchanged in federal social programs. The segment of the population most in need of public support and social justice, poor descendants of slaves in the South, got a particularly raw deal in the welfare schemes of the 1930s. Millions were summarily excluded from federal and state programs by virtue of the exemption of their major work categories—agricultural and domestic labor. By delegating the administration of the programs to the states, including the southern jurisdictions so critical to the New Deal political coalition, federal policies sanctioned flagrant racial discrimination. African Americans, the majority of whom still resided in the South in the 1930s, were largely barred admission to the welfare state. They would not claim social citizenship until they won it through their own political actions during World War II and the civil rights movement. The state system of mothers' pensions, especially in the South, had also practiced de facto racial discrimination. The situation in Houston, Texas, was extreme but not atypical. There, in a city where more than 20 percent of the residents were black, not one of their number received a mother's pension.[120]

Second-Class Citizenship
Male and Female

The integration of women into public politics did not make citizenship blind to gender. Sex discrimination was written into public policies like the Social Security Act, routine civic practices like jury service, and legal access to property and credit. Moreover, not all women were ushered into the voting booth by the Nineteenth Amendment. The Jim Crow legislation of the southern states and increasingly restrictive voter registration laws throughout the country barred millions of American women and men from full citizenship, making them political exiles in their own land. Furthermore, the restricted citizenship of Americans of African or Asian descent was not unrelated to the difference of sex. Gender collided with race in the public sphere in myriad destructive ways: white women, from suffragists to members of the Ku Klux Klan, were guilty of racist practices, while gender ideology more generally served as a rationale for racial exclusions. The denial of full citizenship to women had long served as a convenient excuse for restricting the rights of other subaltern groups. When one delegate to the New York constitutional convention of 1846 proposed granting suffrage "without regard to color," another responded with the jocular offer of a parallel amendment that added the words "age or sex." The assembly irrupted in laughter. Whig delegate Horatio Stow was more loquacious in dismissing African American citizenship by the analogy of sex: "Wherefore the qualification of male citizenship. Why not allow it to all of both sexes, and all conditions and ages, whether alien or citizens, if it is a matter of absolute right?"[121]

Even as the privileges of women's citizenship expanded, the public realm remained compromised by the conundrums of sex. The white advocates of woman suffrage were not above playing the race card. Having failed to secure the franchise based on arguments about the inalienable rights of all humankind, some suffragists turned to arguing that women merited the vote as a privilege of gender and as the prerogative of pure, respectable mothers, who were endowed with the attributes of middle-class domestic femininity that set them clearly apart from racial and ethnic minorities. The abolitionist heritage of interracial cooperation was severely tested when the Radical Republicans abandoned women's demand for equal rights as they pressed to enfranchise freedmen. A bitter Elizabeth Cady Stanton responded by brandishing a kind of pan-racism: "American women of wealth, education, virtue and refinement, if you do not wish the lower orders of Chinese, African, German and Irish with their low ideas of womanhood, to make law for you and your daughters, awake to the dangers of your present position and demand that woman shall be represented in Government."[122] Stanton listed "Patrick, Sambo, Hans and Ung Tung" in her catalog of the males who were undeserving of citizenship, revealing that her prejudices were colored by class, ethnicity, and religion, as well as race.[123] The racial boundaries of sisterhood were transparently offensive to African American suffragists, who would be asked to turn the other cheek when they were escorted out of meetings and away from parade routes where their presence might prove a political liability.[124]

When women entered the public sphere, they were empowered to act with as much prejudice, venality, and pragmatic politicking as any citizen. As a consequence, the leaders of women's public domain have left numberless acts of racism and class prejudice in the historical record. The grand dame of the nineteenth-century women's public domain, Frances Willard of the Woman's Christian Temperance Union, bought into the perverse sexual logic of the lynch mob and was deaf to the appeals of African American members of the organization to stand up against racial terrorism. The 1920s would find women organizing their own branch of the Ku Klux Klan, even rising to leadership in an organization that was violently opposed to the racial integration of the public sphere. The architects and administrators of mothers' pensions and Aid to Dependent Children have been charged with a vulgar and vernacular sort of racism. Grace Abbott was heard to recite slurs like this: "Racial groups such as Negroes and Indians still have primitive ways of dealing with children."[125] The women who delivered welfare services to poor households could be even ruder in their bigotry. The records of Massachusetts public charities reduced their clients to such classifications as "primitive," "limited," "fairly good for a colored woman," or "a typical low-grade Italian woman."[126] Jane Addams also used the same adjective, "primitive," to describe the Italian Americans of Chicago. Maternal missionaries dispensed condescension and parochialism in the tenements. They gave instruction in subjects like the "home life of the Anglo Saxons" and tried to reform the immigrant pantry by removing garlic and spices and stocking it with American cheese (rather than mozzarella) and white bread (rather than tortillas). They have earned the label "racial essentialists" from one historian.[127]

Although Progressive women had penetrated far enough into the sphere of political power to become architects of major social programs, they had not accomplished the utopian task of erasing either the racial or class bias that still tarnished the public sphere.[128] Some women rose up from the ranks of the poor to speak up for the usually anonymous welfare beneficiaries. The fiction of the Russian immigrant Anzia Yezierska fumed with anger toward the lady do-gooders who visited the tenements of the Lower East Side of New York. She portrayed obtuse social workers trampling on the traditions of immigrant families and rending the safety net of the household economy. In a story entitled "Soap and Water," Yezierska translated the frustration of the clients of women's charity into a bitterly ironic class and gender conundrum. When the villain of this tale, by the name of "Miss Whiteside," denied a diploma to the immigrant heroine on the grounds of her unkempt appearance, Yezierska's protagonist spoke vociferously for her ethnicity, class, and gender: "I felt the suppressed wrath of all the unwashed of the earth break loose within me. . . . While they condemned me as unfit to be a teacher, because of my appearance, I was slaving to keep them clean. I was slaving in a laundry from five to eight in the morning before going to college, and from six to eleven at night, after coming from college. Eight hours of work a day, outside my studies. Where was the time and the strength for the 'little niceties of the well-groomed lady?'"[129]

While immigrants like Yezierska expressed their political protests in writing, other women, especially those who had been excluded from citizenship on the basis of race, stood up for themselves in a variety of public places. As Jim Crow closed in on African Americans, and the ghosts of Judge Lynch haunted men in particular, women sometimes took the lead in public projects. By 1900, almost every African American urban community could boast a women's group that cared for widows and orphans and operated kindergartens, libraries, clinics, and colored branches of the Young Women's Christian Association. These social service agencies resembled, and sometimes anticipated, the settlement houses of the Progressive Era, and they provided a social safety net that prefigured the modern welfare bureau. They bore names like the Atlanta Neighborhood Union. From her position of leadership in the union, Lugenia Hope, wife of the president of Morehouse College, went on to testify before the Atlanta city council, lobby the state legislature, and maintain a level of civic influence rare for her gender or her race.[130]

At a time when the political movements of black males were under strict surveillance, black women moved stealthily toward city hall, often in league with white women reformers. The story of Lula Spaulding Kelsey is a case in point. Having established herself in the black community as an undertaker, Kelsey became a civic leader among her own race and then moved on to win the cooperation of white women and the support of the mayor in her campaign to clean up urban neighborhoods.[131] Such spheres of womanly service also became avenues to national political influence for women like Nannie Burroughs, who rose to national prominence through the Baptist Woman's Convention. Burroughs organized what she called a domestic leadership program from her political headquarters in Washington, D.C. She commanded a national sisterhood armed not just with "the bible, the bath, the broom" but with social statistics, international connections, and challenges to Jim Crow. Invoking feminine domesticity was a conscious strategy for African American women leaders, what one historian has called "the politics of respectability."[132]

The trajectory of African American women into politics was more than a small step away from the household. Women of color laid claim to public authority at the greatest spectacle of nineteenth-century American culture, the World's Columbian Exposition in Chicago in 1893. It was there that Frances Harper addressed the World's Congress of Representative Women, proclaiming that "we are on the threshold of woman's era."[133] She spoke for a generation of African American women who grew up tasting the educational and material advantages of emancipation and Radical Reconstruction and was pushed into public service when black men were disfranchised. As a consequence, they often reached a level of leadership within their communities that white women scarcely imagined, or were shy of claiming.[134] Within the black community they assumed a kind of Weberian prestige: the stature to speak and act in public and before outsiders, in the name of the group as a whole. Under the banner of "Lifting as We Climb," African American women leaders assumed a position not as the second sex but as citizens for whom race and gender were integrally entwined. They were, in their own words, "race women." Mary Church Terrell, who like Ida B. Wells-Barnett, was propelled into public action in the aftermath of the lynching of Thomas Moss in Memphis, rose in small town churches and large national congresses to call on "daughters, sisters, mothers, and wives" to do more than "care for ourselves and rear our families, like all women. . . . Those of us fortunate enough to have education must share it with the less fortunate of our race. We must go into our communities and improve them; we must go out into the nation and change it. Above all, we must organize ourselves as Negro women and work together."[135] At the helm of the National Association of Colored Women (NACW), women like Terrell, Harper, and Wells-Barnett claimed a kind of sovereignty within the black community.

After launching the NACW, the first national secular association of African Americans, in 1896, Wells-Barnett and Terrell signed the call to the form the National Association for the Advancement of Colored People. The prominence of women in the earliest civil rights organizations placed them at the vanguard of an unprecedented movement in women's history. From their position of leadership they worked alongside men, and sometimes vied with them for positions of authority. In her autobiography Ida Wells-Barnett bristled with annoyance at some of the men with whom she shared the limelight, first with the ministers and editors of Memphis and ultimately with Booker T. Washington and W. E. B. Du Bois. She was not alone in her ambition and her assertiveness. One Brooklyn woman exhorted her sisters in 1922 to "Stand Up Stand up! For the Cause of Humanity, demanding our rights. The Negro man has tried for half a century with but little results." Similarly, Mary McLeod Bethune commended "the Negro woman [who] has practically carried her own man on her back, her children by the hand, while she fought off the men of other races." Women leaders did not see one another as the second sex but like the biblical figure of Sarah, able to "tower head and shoulders above the men in Israel for the magnetism of her speech, the earnestness of her appeal, the nobleness of her work."[136] Men were usually, but not always, appreciative of women's politics. John Hope, husband of the director of the Atlanta Neighborhood Union, resisted sharing leadership with women of his race. On the grounds that African Americans were "in need of men," he advised clubwomen that "the surest way for our men to become more manly is for our women to become more womanly," that is, more like Florence Nightingale than Queen Elizabeth.[137]

Elite African American women were not without prejudices of their own. Anna Jones, a clubwoman and graduate of the University of Michigan, maligned the "incompetent menials" and "lower millions" of her race. Others pointed to the "degradation and ignorance" of poor black women as "a lodestone around our necks driving us down to them." Some even proposed segregation policies of their own. The "Investigation Committee" of the Atlanta Neighborhood Union conducted a survey of "everything that seems to be a menace" in the surrounding district and proposed to clean up the neighborhood by removing unruly families and overly exuberant religious congregations. The National Colored Women's Congress went so far as to propose its own program for segregating public transportation through the creation of first- and second-class streetcars, intended to protect the middle classes, of any color from too-close contact with their social inferiors.[138] Middle-class black women also distanced themselves from women who practiced a different kind of politics, in particular, from their more brazen sisters who strutted proudly along the southern streets in flamboyant dress, waving brightly colored fans, sometimes refusing to give way to whites, even assaulting the ladies with their umbrellas. African American clubwomen targeted the haunts of such "uppity" black women—the dance halls and juke joints with their risqué sexual and music culture—for closure. The hard-won middle-class status of some African American women set them apart from the majority of former slaves and descendants of slaves, segmenting the black public sphere by class as well as gender.[139]

On occasion, women leaders in the African American public sphere allied with their peers across the color line. White and black women worked toward common goals from segregated chapters of the Young Women's Christian Association, the Woman's Christian Temperance Union, and the suffrage movement. In Atlanta they formed coalitions to better sanitary conditions and public health for all their children. Despite the insults of expedient suffragists, Ida B. Wells-Barnett still counted Susan B. Anthony as a friend and co-worker in the cause of racial and sexual equality and shared with Jane Addams a sage understanding of how politics operated in the gritty city of Chicago. Wells-Barnett saw Hull House as a model for dispensing social services in her own Chicago neighborhood.[140] Members of the Woman's Christian Temperance Union met in segregated chapters, but both promulgated sobriety and sexual purity. Just as antebellum moral reformers adopted purity as a protective strategy at the time of the market revolution, members of the Baptist Woman's Convention regarded it as a bulwark against the assaults of lynch mobs. Above all else, the African American leaders of the "woman's era" knew the value of access to the public sphere. Having seen the men of their race robbed of their votes and subject to viciously sexualized political attacks, African Americans joined the suffrage movement in larger proportions than did the white population. Once suffrage had been won, African American women registered to vote in impressive numbers and redoubled their energy to oppose the racial restrictions on the franchise in the South.

In 1921, but a few months after the ratification of the woman suffrage amendment to the U.S. Constitution, the Southeastern Federation of Colored Women's Clubs called on all women to drop the veil of feminine privacy and advance into the center of the public sphere: "We ask therefore, that white women, for the protection of their homes as well as ours indicate their sanction of the ballot for all citizens as representing government by the sober, reasoned and deliberate judgment of all the people."[141] Just a year before the Federation of Colored Women's Clubs issued this appeal, an association of white women, the Southern Branch of the Women's Council of the Methodist Episcopal Church, made public its own commitment to reforming race relations. Standing up "as women," they set about to "create a public sentiment which will uphold . . . the execution of justice."[142] They did not even flinch at the sexually charged issue of lynching, a cowardly, private form of male politics that they refused to sanction. By defying the premise of the lynch mob — that men were stalwart citizens and women their wards in need of protection — the more courageous American women, black and white, thwarted the rhetorical justification of racial terrorism and the gender assumption that lay at the foundation of the American political tradition through much of the nineteenth century. The maturation of women's public domain, combined with female suffrage, invited women of all political persuasions to come out from behind the veil of privacy, which had covered up so much gender, as well as racial, chicanery.[143]

Once the restriction of sex was removed from the citizenship, women of many social origins and political persuasions came together to take their common concerns before their representatives. Women reformers stationed in the trenches of the welfare state fought to extend benefits to nonwhites, to reduce the child mortality of African Americans, and to translate their literature into sundry foreign languages. The leaders of the Chicago Woman's Club regularly called mass "public meetings" to place their proposals before the widest possible city audience.[144] A whole cohort of union leaders was trained in the cloisters of the Bryn Mawr College labor school in the 1920s and 1930s.[145] The Women's Trade Union League, founded at Hull House and enrolling both working women and their "allies," was a diverse and democratic domain of women.

To assert that the largely white, native-born, Protestant leadership of the women's public domain was untainted by ethnic prejudices would be naive. However, to dismiss the women's public domain as just another backwater of class privilege, ethnocentrism, and racism would be to miss an extraordinary moment in the history of women and of America. The work begun in places like Hull House in the 1880s had in fact successfully challenged the lady bountiful's way of contributing to the public. Women reformers, legions strong and two generations deep, had devised political methods that made standard practices of the male public sphere, with its smoke-filled rooms, city machines, party caucuses, and the sacred cow of free enterprise, seem antiquated. The women's public domain was often the leading edge in the modernization of the American political system. Women reformers were quick to abandon the principles of political economy cherished by nineteenth-century politicians. As one veteran of the campaign for social security put it, "Laissez faire is dead! Long live social control! Social control not only to enable us to meet the rigorous demands of war, but also as a foundation for the peace and brotherhood that is to come."[146] Women also pioneered such newfangled political methods as expert testimony, organized lobbying, confrontation politics, and political spectacles.

At their best, the public-minded women who blazed this trail toward the modern state also honored social differences and democratic participation. Although the cultural democracy expounded by the best of the maternalists had its limits, it stretched the elastic divide between classes and ethnic groups about as far as their times permitted. In all these ways, the women's public domain came admirably close to fulfilling the highest standards designated in political philosophy, as extolled in the concept of the public sphere. In fact, Louise Bowen seemed to echo John Dewey and anticipate Jürgen Habermas in her assessment of the political public of Chicago:

> When a group of representative citizens come together and use their influence for the making of public opinion, it is not so difficult to swing a new project or a reform after a certain number of people have been secured as its backers. Unfortunately, one only has a limited number of interested citizens on whom to call in matters of this kind, too many people are indifferent to civic affairs, yet if every citizen could realize that the safety of his family, the honor of his wife and children, even his own happiness may be involved, we might be able to get more people who would be interested in gatherings of this kind.

Expansive political terminology—"civic," "community," "public"—abounded in the writing of women reformers like Bowen.[147] The members of the Southeastern Federation of Women's Clubs invoked the same lofty standard of publicness: "sober, reasoned, and deliberate judgment of all the people." The women reformers of the early twentieth century interposed these ideals into American politics at a time when, by Habermas's assessment, the public sphere of Western democracies had degenerated into little more than the bureaucratic infighting of interest groups.

At their best, women reformers imagined a public that was broadly democratic. Jane Addams contributed mightily, in practice as well as theory, to the project her friend and admirer John Dewey termed a movement to socialize democracy. In her lectures on *Democracy and Social Ethics*, Addams modeled a public practice that emerged from engagement with an urban, immigrant, working-class neighborhood "so heterogeneous in nationality, religion, and customs" that many middle-class reformers began to question the feasibility of self-government. But Addams pressed on, and even took lessons from saloonkeepers and corrupt city bosses: "We can only discover truth by a rational and democratic interest in life, and to give truth complete social expression is the endeavor upon which we are entering. Thus the identification with the common lot which is the essential idea of Democracy becomes the source and expression of social ethics." Less hearty democrats often become impatient with the inefficiency and contention that ensues when people are trusted to govern themselves, but Jane Addams held her course, saying "the cure for the ills of Democracy is more Democracy." Her generation of women politicians opened up an expansive space in that ever imperfect and incomplete democracy.[148]

Yet citizenship still remained sullied by sexual inequality. Women's public domain would not be easily folded into the male public sphere so as to magically smooth out the inequality of the sexes. In fact, long after the passage of the Nineteenth Amendment, and despite the impressive victories of women during the Progressive Era and the New Deal, the ideal of public democracy was fundamentally tarnished by the contradictions of gender. On every measure—of remuneration, subsidy, honor, status, and power—women's place in the public sphere was still a rung below that of men. Decades after winning the vote and working assiduously in the trenches of party politics, women still met with condescension and indifference in the public realm. Even in the year 2005 the nation's president greeted an articulate critic of his foreign policy, who had lost a son in Iraq, not by name, not with the dignity of a citizen, but as "Mom." Moreover, even today the welfare programs that were implemented during the 1930s still bear the marks of women's inequitable political origins, reducing recipients to the degraded status of "welfare *mothers*." A pragmatic amalgam of the political practices learned in the sex-segregated public realm of the nineteenth century, the resulting hybrid was not hearty enough to remove all gender inequity or social injustice from American society. Indeed, it came to appear, over time, that the unstable compound of men's and women's politics had worked a negative chemical reaction in the public sphere. Because women's public domain posed the common welfare as a problem of maternal protection, it cast a pall of feminine weakness, passivity, and suspicion on attempts to ensure social and economic welfare for all. Because women entered the official public sphere in which men had a head start of over one hundred years, they lacked the leverage to build truly comprehensive and effective welfare policies. Stranded between the male-dominated public sphere and women's public domain, the American welfare state was something of a political orphan: without parental protection it was nearly left to starve early in the twenty-first century when a campaign to privatize government functions took hold in Washington.

The utopian possibilities raised by this chapter—the hope that women's entry into the public sphere would dispel the mystifications of sex and fulfill the loftiest promises of the American political tradition—have come to a down-to-earth denouement. Democracy remains a work in progress, but as of 1930 both women and men were at least working side by side, recognized as full and equal citizens. While no longer segregated by sex, citizenship still bore the mark of gender difference. The first and guiding generation of public women never managed to completely disengage themselves from the basic gender ideology of the Victorian age into which they had been born: the belief that women, even if they entered the public sphere on their own terms, always carried with them the primary, almost exclusive, and ever sacred responsibility of caring for children and the consequent dependence on men. No matter how far Addams, Kelley, Lathrop, or even an iconoclast like Charlotte Perkins Gilman pursued the public interest, they gave hardly an inch at the gendered border of motherhood. Lathrop thought that the working mother was "the most melancholy creature in the working world."[149] While the General Federation of Women's Clubs proclaimed that "safeguarding motherhood safeguards race," its African American analogue, the National Association of Colored Women, balanced its section on "Women in Industry" with another bearing the title "Mother, Home, Child."[150] Jane Addams regarded the loosening of women's attachment to children and motherhood as a "tragedy." Conversely, it seldom occurred to these pioneers of the women's public domain that motherhood and a career of public service could be combined. Such is the historical paradox of a remarkable generation of women: at that moment when their sex had unprecedented visibility and power in the public realm, they were still defined politically as mothers rather than simply as citizens.

Some women, especially the members of a younger generation of political activists who would adopt the label "feminist," began to entertain the idea that gender difference itself needed to be examined and reconsidered. They wondered if equality could ever be achieved as long as humanity was divided into opposite sexes, be it in public or private, in the home, the workplace, or the statehouse. Their challenge will be taken up in the third, concluding part of this book. The men and women who were born into the twentieth century would confront yet more mysteries of sex. They would be pressed, in particular, to face up to some issues that their foremothers in the public domain had elided, those asymmetries and inequities that were swept under a rug called privacy, in a domain of sexual rather than civic politics. The next chapter will pursue questions of power and politics into these more private relations of men and women, bosses and workers, husbands and wives.

PART III

WOMEN REMAKE GENDER IN THE TWENTIETH CENTURY

CHAPTER 5

HOW DO YOU GET FROM HOME
TO WORK TO EQUITY?

1900–1960

The *New York Times* for February 17, 2001, printed a lengthy obituary for Rose Rosenfeld Freedman, age 107. Her death was newsworthy for several reasons, chief among them the fact that she was the last survivor of the Triangle fire of 1911. Seared in the memory of the labor movement, that fire took the lives of 146 working women who perished in a shirtwaist factory in lower Manhattan. Some of them had been locked in their hazardous workplace by the management and leapt to their deaths in flames. Ninety years later, Rose Freedman would not let the brutality of the bosses be forgotten. She testified on television, "It should never have happened. The executives with a couple of steps could have opened the door. But they thought they were better than the working people. It's not fair because material, money, is more important here than everything."[1] Rose Freedman keynotes this chapter for other, more positive, reasons as well. After surviving the Triangle fire, she enacted a more mundane history in the company of millions of American women: she found her way from home to work. In fact, she made this trip twice, once before and once after marriage. Between her two stints in the labor force—first briefly at the Triangle Shirtwaist Factory, and again beginning in 1959 as a clerk at the Manhattan Life Insurance Company—she devoted herself to raising three children. While these unexceptional facts of Rose Freedman's work history were not front-page news, they were repeated by so many American women that they caused a twofold revolution, in the economy and in family life.

In 1900 over three-quarters of all adult women were excused from "gainful employment," the Census Bureau's code for paid work outside the home. Little more than 5 percent of married women held such positions. When Rose Rosenfeld went off to a garment factory, she participated in the first stage of women's assault on the gender division of labor. Young, single women like her had been braving the world of work en masse since at least the 1890s. By 1920 it was routine for the unmarried daughters of the middle class, not just the poor, the immigrant, and the nonwhite, to enjoy a stint in the labor force. Upon marriage, however, most women of Rose Rosenfeld's generation would take up full-time domestic responsibilities. At this point, Rose Rosenfeld Freedman's life course would deviate, or at least decelerate, from that of her cohort. While she waited until widowhood to return to the labor force, the majority of her peers were back on the job by 1950, usually long before the deaths of their husbands. Within another decade Rose Freedman's cohort, joined by a younger generation of workers, would mark a second watershed in women's labor history. By 1960, the size of the female labor force had nearly doubled, now enrolling almost one in three women. The majority of women workers, fully 60 percent, were married, over 40 percent of them the mothers of school-age children, and like Rose Rosenfeld Freedman, they most often had secured white-collar rather than industrial jobs.[2]

An aggregation of anonymous actions, these statistics dryly record stories of gender change as dramatic and consequential as the Triangle fire. Just how millions of American women, without apparent coordination, direction, or cultural sanction, engineered this transformation is a mystery of major historical import. The movement of women into the workplace was the driving force behind the wholesale remodeling of gender, to be described in Part III of this book. By making their way from home to work, the women who came of age in the twentieth century effectively unraveled the seams of the modern sexual division of labor. Women like Rose Rosenfeld Freedman bridged the divide between housewife and breadwinner and thereby posed a fundamental challenge to the most basic coordinate of gender difference, the asymmetry of the sexes.

While the two terms in the title of this chapter, "home" and "work," identify the poles around which a major reorientation of gender differentiation took place, they oversimplify a complex historical process. As the previous chapters have demonstrated, American women never rested quietly in domestic space—not even during the height of the Victorian era, when they built a public domain of their own. Neither were men always the sole, self-reliant breadwinners of their families. Ironically, most working-class men did not secure that "living wage" that would support a whole family in comfort until about the same time that their wives were taking up their positions in the labor force—that is, about midway through the twentieth century. Still, the historical moment when the majority of wives and mothers secured permanent and legitimate positions in the paid labor force marks a watershed in gender history. Although jobs may not have supplanted the home in the hearts and minds of most mothers, the mass of American women were taking off to work each day, seemingly mindless of the customary gender division of labor and space. On their way out the door, they carefully tiptoed around the icon of motherhood and apple pie.

This episode of economic, as well as gender, history finds masses of ordinary women operating the levers of change. While the condition and character of the male labor force also changed significantly in the twentieth century—with the rise and decline of the unionized working class, in particular—men were more often passive and sometimes reluctant parties to this reorganization of the structures of gender and family. They held steadfastly to the title of chief breadwinner and were repeatedly summoned to the most traditional male role, that of soldier, in two world wars, in Korea, in Vietnam, in a spate of smaller conflicts, and now, for a second time, in Iraq. The concluding segment of this book places historical events like wars, depressions, and political realignments in the background to this epic drama of the twentieth century, the wholesale remaking of gender in America.

Who Made the Woman Worker?
An Overview

A social change of this magnitude warrants a high-powered scheme of causation. The first explanation to come to the minds of conventional political historians was that behemoth of twentieth-century scholarship, the Second World War. In fact, the demand for workers to produce munitions and weaponry between 1940 and 1945 brought women into the labor force in unprecedented numbers. Yet this upsurge in female employment followed increases that had been building steadily for several decades and that did not abate with the war's end, when women were summarily dismissed from jobs in the war industries. By 1952, female employment had climbed back up to the wartime high and kept climbing. Mobilization for world war was not a sufficient explanation for a pattern of female behavior that spanned a century. The mystery thickens.[3]

The next logical explanation pointed to a more general and sustained expansion in the labor force. Despite the interruption of the Great Depression, the demand for workers over the course of the century far exceeded the supply of unemployed men. Those sectors of the economy that were growing most rapidly, moreover, did not require much masculine brawn. The burgeoning service sector, especially clerical work and certain sectors of retail sales, had been marked off as a female labor market since at least the 1920s. This long-term demand for labor was clearly a necessary condition for the great gender transformation of the twentieth century. It does not explain, however, how that demand was channeled into male and female sectors, or why men and women accepted their gender assignments. We have to wonder why women acceded to employers' demands with such alacrity, without the incentive of significant wage increases. Neither will an iron law of material necessity explain the influx of women into the paid labor force, which seemed only to accelerate during the period of postwar affluence, concurrent with a rise in the real income of male household heads. The most hardnosed economists would have to resort to subtler explanations for women's labor force behavior. They would concede at least that the law of supply and demand operated through dual labor markets, separate tracks for male and female workers.[4]

To historians of women this transformation of gender roles raises another question: Why did the majority of American women throw off more than a century of conditioning and begin to act in the way of the economic man rather than the self-sacrificing mother? This historical event was propelled by more than impersonal economic and political forces. It required that millions of daughters, wives, and mothers take decisive, voluntary, and unprecedented actions. At the very least, wartime civic responsibility and labor force demands had to be transmitted into the consciousness of masses of women. Although historians cannot possibly divine the private motivations of countless, anonymous women workers, they have pored over the ideological missives and cultural signals sent their way. On close scrutiny, these popular prescriptions for the sexual division of labor appear to be mysteriously out of sync with the traffic of women in and out of the labor force. With the exception of the Second World War, when women were invited into the workplace "only for the duration," America's wives, and even mothers, went off to their jobs despite the indifference, if not the outright opposition, of American cultural commissars, high and low. The opposition was often hysterical, from indicting working wives for stealing jobs from unemployed men in the 1930s, to warnings that working mothers violated nature and undermined the free world in the 1950s. Yet the employment rate kept soaring.[5]

Gender ideology lagged behind women's actions. In the 1920s a few educated women imagined a life span that could accommodate both motherhood and labor force participation, or, in the words of journalist Dorothy Bromley, the "business of combining two careers." The theme was even picked up in ladies' magazines with articles on "The Two-Career Marriage," "The New Triangle: Wife—Husband—Work," and "Two Bites of the Cherry."[6] The prospect of combining home and work was still hemmed in by compromises, the most prominent of which was the qualification that women would spend their reproductive years at home with children. Even the modest proposal that mothers return to work when grown-up children left the parental home was not propagated very far beyond the halls of academe or the bohemian circles of Greenwich Village in the 1920s. With the devastating unemployment of the 1930s, it was quietly rescinded. Feminist pipe dreams about dual careers were largely forgotten during the revival of domesticity in the popular culture of the 1930s, 1940s, and 1950s. Presidential candidate Adlai Stevenson and college president Lynn White told women at elite colleges (Smith on the East Coast and Mills on the West) to concentrate their attention on the kitchen and the nursery, not the career ladder.[7]

And still, absent the ideological guide of feminism or the sanction of popular culture, women moved steadfastly into the labor force, and in ever greater numbers. Neither the mechanistic causal theories of the social scientists nor the linear narrative of historians can offer a simple solution to the mystery of how women got from home to work. Yet the historical change they enacted is too important to surrender either to structural determinism or an anarchy of separate and partial stories. The intent of this chapter is more modest and heuristic: to describe how ordinary women made history and remade gender according to the pace of their own life cycles. Like the biography of Rose Rosenfeld Freedman, this transformation in the everyday, elemental meaning of male and female took whole lifetimes to accomplish, lifetimes that spanned over seventy years on the average, roughly twice the typical life expectancy during the nineteenth century.

This chapter will channel the shapeless flow of millions of lives into a two-stage, two-generation story of how women got from home to work. These generations are artificial but carefully fabricated facsimiles of actual lives. They are built on statistical skeletons and then draped with the words, actions, and memories of individual women. The vanguard generation was composed of the daughters of late Victorian mothers, the junior partners of the Progressive reformers. Born around the turn of the century, they entered the labor force in their youth and had formed families of their own by 1930. The move of this birth cohort into the labor force was so massive, representing such a substantial majority of American women, that that it spanned differences of class, region, and national origin. The procession into the labor force enrolled women from the far corners of America and the world and included contingents from factory districts, farms, and suburbs. Although the Census Bureau recorded the work experience of nonwhite women separately, and found that they had advanced into the labor force in advance of and in greater proportions than the national white average, they too were a mobile labor force. African American women readily moved from agricultural work in the rural South to the service sector in northern cities. Whatever their various social backgrounds, this generation of women was on the move: immigrants crossing the Atlantic, farmers' daughters venturing into the city, African Americans escaping the Jim Crow South, bohemians fleeing the provinces, and all of them advancing stalwartly into the paid labor force.[8]

These young women entered gender history with such panache that they inscribed an all-new *esprit de femme* on American popular culture. Going by such monikers as the flapper, the new woman, or emancipated female, the new ideal of femininity was written large on the stage and the movie screen, as well as the printed page. Although this vivacious image of the modern woman faded somewhat as she aged, married, and encountered the Depression, it had a threefold historical aftereffect. First, it erased much of the sense of women's paid labor as drudgery and victimization, and thereby accustomed both employers and parents to see women's work in a positive light. Second, it afforded the youthful workers of the 1910s and 1920s the experience that would make reentry into the job market a viable option later in life, and a particularly welcome one should it be required to meet a national emergency or immediate family need. Third and finally, the women born around the turn of the century would give birth to sons and daughters who knew firsthand that women's work was not a merely domestic vocation.

The daughters who grew up roughly in the 1930s and early 1940s enacted the next stage of critical gender change. No great fanfare accompanied their march into gender history. The younger generation moved single-mindedly into the labor force but without calling much attention to their work. Eschewing any rebellious intent, these demure heroines would complete the two-stage gender transformation begun a generation earlier: they went to work before marriage, often stayed in the labor force until their children were born, and went back to work earlier than the previous generation. They seemed to be piggybacking on the rate of labor force participation achieved by their mothers. In midlife they would prove that women could combine work and family, without provoking much comment, much less great gender anxiety. Neither did they raise vocal objections to the inequalities they faced. They earned an estimated fifty-nine cents for every dollar earned by men in 1961, and they did far more than their fair share of housework.[9] They had made it from home to work, if not to equity. They solved much of the mystery of this chapter with pragmatism, determination, and fortitude, at the methodical pace of their family cycles. The year 1960 would find them along with their mothers' generation on the same eventful page of gender history, in the crowded ranks of working wives.

The New Woman Goes to Work
1890–1940

This generational story begins with a glance back to the nineteenth century, when the mothers and grandmothers of wage-earning women labored within their private households. Supporting oneself was not a likely or attractive prospect for the vast majority of women born much before 1900. Most native-born daughters still resided on farms under the employ and supervision of parents, and they would not leave home until marriage. The rare escape from the demands of the family farm was a stint as the village schoolteacher or a brief residence as a poor relation. Young urban women of the middle classes enjoyed more prolonged schooling, more varied avocations, and unchaperoned amusements, but they were tucked safely under their parental roofs at night. In a middle-class district of Chicago in the 1870s, for example, the census taker found that most young women who had left school remained unmarried, unemployed, and living with parents. So they would remain until they crossed the threshold into the homes of their grooms.[10]

While daughters of immigrants, the poor, and nonwhite often became wage laborers, they returned home at the end of a day's labor. A survey of twenty-eight cities found that only one in three wage-earning women resided outside their immediate families. Just 19 percent were boarders or lodgers. For most young women, living outside the parental home was a practical impossibility. The typical female wage fell far short of the cost of living on one's own. After long hours, pinching pennies, and doubling up on the rent, the average working girl could afford no more than a small, windowless room and a meager diet. Should she move out from under the parental roof, the working girl would not slip entirely through the cracks of familial protection. Her movements between home and work were carefully monitored by a whole army of surrogate mothers. One of the favorite projects of maternalists was the creation of homes for working girls. By 1899, there were ninety such homes in the United States. A few years later, Chicago alone boasted thirty-one women's lodging houses. Be they the creation of Progressive reformers, local charities, or African American women's clubs, these female institutions acted in *mater familias* to their residents. The Young Women's Christian Association, for example, required church attendance, excluded male callers, provided genteel parlor entertainment, and kept daughters under lock and key at night.[11]

As the nineteenth century drew to a close, young single women remained duty-bound daughters, in economic terms, just "girls." Even the imagination of independence was fettered by warnings of disastrous consequences, summed up in the title "Women Adrift." Popular literature offered up images of seduction, suicide, and that "fate worse than death" that threatened young women who embarked alone in the "frightful seething whirlpool of vice and crime" that was the city. The plot of a typical melodrama, such as "Violet the Beautiful Street Singer" (1908), revolved around a childlike heroine who was thwarted in every attempt to live on her own and ended up in the morgue. Early American movies like D. W. Griffith's *Way Down East* (1920) set the heroine, played by Lillian Gish, hurling through the frigid torrents of a frozen river fleeing the shame of bearing a child out of wedlock.[12] Only a few writers of the more highbrow sort could imagine young women taking longer, sometimes more successful, excursions outside the home. Theodore Dreiser's *Sister Carrie* (1898) was such a hardy and hardened heroine. After losing her virtue, she obtained some stature and material comfort as an actress and outlived her hapless paramour. The last chapter of Edith Wharton's *House of Mirth* (1905) found Lily Bart unemployed and expired, with an empty bottle of narcotics and a depleted checkbook at her side. Kate Chopin's Edna Pontellier took the most daring path away from home, family, even motherhood. But even the heroine of *The Awakening* (1899) enjoyed only a brief taste of sensual liberation before she joined her cohort of female characters in suicide. She disrobed and swam to her death in the Gulf of Mexico.[13]

In order to achieve independence, both daughters of privilege and working girls would have to extricate themselves from the powerful clutches of maternalism. The aspiring writer Fannie Hurst recorded a particularly tortured and prolonged struggle to separate from her Victorian mother and the provincial culture of St. Louis, Missouri. She made several attempts to leave home, each aborted by what she called a "violent maternalism": "Mama's hardy perennial cry of anguish ringing in my ears," "my baby come home to me soon."[14] By the 1920s, Hurst had found an independent and bracingly modern life for herself in New York City: she had a thriving literary career and a husband from whom she maintained a separate residence. By then, she had lots of young female company in the city. Writer Susan Glaspell had journeyed from Davenport, Iowa; journalists Neith Boyce and Louise Bryant came from Boston and from Portland, Oregon, respectively; blues singers like Ma Rainey and Bessie Smith traveled up from the South; novelists Nella Larsen and Jessie Fauset made their way to the Harlem Renaissance; painter Georgia O'Keeffe left her home in Sun Prairie, Wisconsin; and poet Edna St. Vincent Millay arrived in New York from Maine.[15] Others like Margaret Mead and Ruth Benedict flocked to urban universities like Columbia and Chicago to become pioneers of the social sciences. The growing list of women's names in the pantheon of American arts and letters heralded the avant-garde of a new womanhood. Mary Heaton Vorse recalled that an "army of women all over the country" were "out to hurt their mother [sic]" by taking off to work in the city; "More and more and more of us are coming all the time, and more of us will come until the sum of us will change the customs of the world."[16]

The statistical record indicates that women as a sex had made considerable progress toward this goal between 1900 and 1920, and that ordinary working girls, rather than modernist artists and writers, were actually in the vanguard. Two-thirds of the native-born, single women who went to work in large cities lived at home in 1900. By the 1920s, the majority of these working girls were "on their own hook."[17] The new women clearly enjoyed their growing independence. A study of working girls conducted in 1917 revealed that they preferred living alone rather than with kin by a factor of three to one. Girls' lodging houses, with all their Victorian restrictions, were not popular among such independent ingenues. The Young Women's Christian Association in Chicago had to court residents with offers of mixed-sex entertainment, the abolition of curfews, and such amenities as swimming pools. Still, women's lodging houses often stood vacant in the 1920s. A young woman alone in the city now had better options than a tawdry furnished room in a vice district or the family cloister. She and her chums might share a modern flat, like those modeled in magazines or on movie sets.[18]

If a woman worker was able to rent a comfortable room of her own, it was because she had secured a relatively well paying job. The character of the female labor force changed dramatically between 1890 and 1920 as the typical mode of employment shifted from domestic service, to factory work, to positions in the service sector. These new work destinations were likely to supply significantly better wages and be located farther away from home.[19] Manufacturing jobs relocated to relatively large and remote factories in the twentieth century, far from the farm, home production, or the neighborhood sweatshops where young women toiled alongside their kin in times past.[20] For a significant proportion of women, the journey to work led to a cosmopolitan setting that was almost the antithesis of the family hearth. That alluring site, where business, entertainment, and civic life were concentrated, was called "downtown." Young women found jobs in the central business district as sales clerks, waitresses, secretaries, stenographers, and switchboard operators. Prize jobs, like buyers in department stores, private secretaries, or supervisors at the telephone company, carried the glamorous title of businesswoman. Once the sinecure of Anglo-Saxon Protestant high school graduates, these white-collar jobs were beginning to open up to second-generation immigrants, especially Irish American ingenues, by the 1920s. Young women of diverse backgrounds made the central business district a worldly, rather than a domestic, workplace. In the process they were also rewriting the experience of class in America. They emerged from farm families and households headed by immigrant manual workers to lay claim to white-collar jobs previously held by educated, native-born men.[21]

All this is to say that women were caught up in the same forces that transformed the United States into an advanced industrial and urban economy with a booming consumer sector. Young women were not robots set abruptly down in new labor markets. Rather, they leapt exuberantly into these currents of social and economic change and contributed their own velocity to the advance of modernity. Compared with their mothers and older sisters, modern women workers were more educated, skilled, and mature and hence better prepared to maneuver through the labor force. High school enrollment among women doubled between 1900 and 1920, while college attendance rose almost to a parity with men.[22] While the immigrant generation invested in the education of sons, the second generation increasingly prepared daughters for more skilled and literate jobs. These educated entrants into the labor force were also older than the docile child laborers of the past. They were self-consciously modern women selecting new jobs, delaying marriage, and earning a modicum of social mobility.[23]

The working girl's better wages combined with a shorter workweek to expand the horizons of play as well as toil. The length of the workweek was regulated in the majority of states by 1914 and had been reduced to about fifty hours, on the average, by the 1930s. This left young working women and men ample time during which to sample the urban amusements that were beginning to line the road from work to home. Whereas a generation before, bachelors and working girls shared their precious leisure time with their elders in the supervised spaces of the parlor, church, ethnic club, or union picnic, these modern young men and women spent their free time with their peers in dance halls and social clubs. Just steps away from her desk, an office girl would find the department stores and restaurants that shared the central business district. She could window-shop in the finest stores, dine at a ladies' lunchroom, or even join in a downtown suffrage rally. After work she might tarry in the amusement district, take in the theater, or lounge in a café where wine was served. Closer to home, she might visit the neighborhood nickelodeons, of which New York City had fifty by 1900 and four hundred by the 1920s. Nickelodeons and, later, opulent movie palaces were not only affordable to working girls; they were also accessible without a family chaperone. As one daughter of immigrants put it, "The one place I was allowed to go by myself was the movies. I went to the movies for fun. My parents wouldn't let me go anywhere else, even when I was twenty-four."[24] The immigrant daughter on the Lower East Side of New York had easy access not just to movies but also to many other pleasures: within one ten-block radius she would find seventy-three soda fountains, nine dance halls, eight movie houses, two recreation centers, and one Yiddish theater.[25]

By the 1920s, American culture was electric with declarations of working girls' independence. One modern daughter went so far as to say that she and her peers craved "the freedom of being orphans for a while."[26] Among the middle-class ranks of reformers, "clubwomen" were set off from the younger generation by the label "college women," whose degrees and job titles replaced the old maternal graces. At the University of California, coeds boasted of being wine-drinking agnostics and answered the rhetorical query, "Am I the Christian gentlewoman my mother slaved to make me?" with an emphatic "No indeed."[27] The declaration of woman's independence was recited with the deepest resonance by young African American women who escaped the rural South for the social freedoms of northern cities. Ma Rainey's blues classic "No Man's Mama Now" was an anthem of liberation from the gender restrictions propounded by mothers as well as men:

I can come when I please, I can go when I please
I can flit, fly and flutter like the birds in the trees.
Because, I'm no man's mamma now. Hey, hey.
I can say what I like, I can do what I like.
I'm a girl who is on a matrimonial strike;
Which means, I'm no man's mamma now.[28]

This anthem would be anathema to the matrons of the National Association of Colored Women and the Baptist Woman's Convention, as well as many mothers of white flappers. At the movies the flapper was played by the young Joan Crawford, who in *Our Modern Maidens* bid farewell to her parents with the toast, "To myself. I have to live with me all my life."[29] By the 1920s, even the editors of ladies' magazines were sensitive to the reversal of roles in the working girl's home and advised mothers to grant their employed daughters the same respect and privileges as their sons. Mothers were now expected to act as helpmates to a generation of women who had claimed the paid labor force as a place for the young and single of their sex.[30]

The flapper, poised to take flight into a brave new world for her sex, also energized the women's public domain. By the 1910s, students at elite women's colleges were joining shirtwaist workers on the picket line. College graduates who, like Grace Abbott and Sophonisba Breckinridge, had graduate training in the social sciences took up the mantle of Jane Addams and Julia Lathrop and converted it into paying careers, in Washington and in the groves of academe. A self-conscious group of women rebels collecting in bohemian enclaves like Greenwich Village brought a sense of public mission and female solidarity to circles of aspiring writers and artists. They not only joined circles of intellectuals like the Liberal Club but also formed divisions in suffrage parades.[31]

But for all their audacity, the middle-class, college-educated rebels were latecomers to the ranks of new women. Garment factories were the first and most prominent sites of women's rebellion. A wave of strikes paralyzed the garment industry across the country, hitting Boston in the 1890s, New York and Baltimore in 1909, and Chicago in 1910. The glamorous ranks of the telephone worker became a hotbed of activism during and after the First World War, while textile factories in the South bred militant ingenues who picketed in short skirts and nylon stockings and protested from the running boards of Model T's. Clubs of working women joined the suffrage campaigns in California in 1911 and New York in 1917, winning enough votes from their fathers and brothers to secure statewide victory.[32]

The striking workers who massed on the streets of American cities before World War I staged the most dashing public display of the collective power of the burgeoning female labor force. In 1909 a charismatic Jewish immigrant named Clara Lemlich took the podium at a public meeting with all the swashbuckling swagger of a movie hero and led New York garment workers on strike. The joie de vivre of the young militants captured the attention of reporters, who greeted readers with headlines like "Girl Strikers Dance as Employers Meet." Photographs of ingenues dressed in the latest styles and carrying picket signs occupied the front pages.[33] Sarah Comstock, writing for *Collier's Magazine*, reported that the uprising of twenty thousand shirtwaist makers in 1909 was something of a "festive occasion. Lingerie waists were elaborate, puffs towered; there were picture turbans and di'mont pendants. This is a scene of gaiety and flirtation."[34] It was also a sharp contrast to earlier portrayals of the women's labor movement: "always a background of mothers wiping their eyes with their aprons vowing that they would still endure for the Great Cause."[35] While middle-class allies from the Women's Trade Union League favored the older images of hapless female workers in dire need of protection, the striking girls first took to the streets, and then to the front ranks of union men and women. Whatever their generational differences, the alliance between motherly Progressives of the Women's Trade Union League and feisty working girls of the International Ladies' Garment Workers' Union was a winning combination. A sequence of successful strikes between 1909 and the First World War swelled the ranks of organized labor with working women.[36]

In the next decade the voice of the new working woman was amplified by striking telephone workers. Irish American working girls all but monopolized the modern job of telephone operator in Boston, where they spearheaded a strike that enrolled thousands all across the continent in 1913, and again in 1917. When confronted by wages and working conditions they deemed unjust, these aggrieved working girls turned neither to Irish union fathers nor reforming mothers. In 1917 they took "matters into their own hands and fought in the street for a living wage." The telephone operators also initiated an alliance with middle-class reformers. As the story goes, some of their number happened to spy a signpost on their walk down Boylston Street, which read, "The Women's Educational and Industrial Union." The last term seemed to promise just the services they needed. With middle-class allies from that organization and the Women's Trade Union League in the back seat, the telephone workers of Boston organized in their own name, with militant Irish daughters at the wheel. Organizers like Margaret Foley, five-foot-eight with flaming red hair, agitated in behalf of women from any podium she could find—soap boxes, union halls, Jewish temples, black Baptist churches, and Catholic parishes. Foley, like Clara Lemlich, rose up without portfolio out of the ranks of working women and helped to galvanize a generation into a militant and ebullient public force. Their vivacious activism was energized by tens of thousands of brisk, self-powered journeys into the female labor force.[37]

Up to this point, this chapter seems on course toward a simple solution, even a melodramatic happy ending. The plot might go something like this: Early in the twentieth century, young women first won their independence from mothers and fathers and then found a modicum of self-reliance in the labor force. Once in the workforce they forged a collective identity and formed a formidable alliance with middle-class reformers. Finally, hoisting banners of justice and democracy, they broke down the doors of both unions and legislatures. The suffrage parade in New York in 1912 is a fitting testament to just how far they had come. Twenty thousand women marched down Fifth Avenue in divisions that were organized by occupations, from professionals to industrial workers, from doctors to domestics. The rank and file of this robust new women's movement enrolled the old and young, working class and middle class, and émigrés from rural America, the tenant farms of the South, Eastern European shtetls, and Mediterranean villages. Having crossed borders of age, class, and sex, the working girls brusquely violated the boundary between home and work, and public and private. They won the suffrage in New York State in 1917 and in the nation in 1920. With their votes in hand, they set out on an open road into the future.[38]

Having traveled so far along the path between home and work, the new woman seemed in striking distance of a gender revolution in both public and private life. As equal citizens and coworkers, the new generation of women found themselves at an extraordinary historical conjuncture: they were positioned so as make changes in both the political and economic institutions that were heretofore the monopoly of men. Optimists might even envision this generation of women taking the long-neglected concerns of their sex directly to the public sphere and the heart of capitalism, making such things as the care of children, questions of reproduction, and the demand for equal jobs and equal paychecks, public priorities.

A Private Detour through the 1920s

Such utopian imaginings began to dissipate as the new women aged and the twentieth century coursed on its tumultuous way through war and depression. After 1920 it became increasingly clear that new women would swerve from the public path opened by their mother's generation. They would take a lateral turn through gender history, distracted by such things as shopping, dating, marriage, and homemaking, the hallmarks of a new mode of privacy, better termed "personal life." One enticing route to personal satisfaction had opened early in the twentieth century, an expanding market for consumer goods. The working girl's fashionable costumes — the hats, French heels, and even furs to be found along the picket lines — may not have impeded her path to work and labor militancy, but they did train the eye and consciousness on the acquisition of consumer goods and away from the objectives of the Progressive matron: saving, sacrifice, and public service. The life course of the new womanhood was an education in consumption. Anzia Yezierska recorded it in the brash and ebullient behavior of her immigrant heroines. One character fell captive of a "sudden savage desire for clothes" and pawned her mother's feather bed for a new hat.[39] Most ominous of all, the new woman herself could become a packaged consumer item. Such was the fate of the young dancers and actresses who made careers for themselves on Broadway or in Hollywood. Although the feisty chorus girls of Broadway had gone on strike to better their wages, they could not fend off the vulgar commodification of their bodies by theatrical managers such as Florenz Ziegfeld, who arranged young women along the stage like disembodied legs and torsos on an assembly line, or director Busby Berkeley, who gilded his starlets' torsos to impersonate gold diggers in the musicals of the 1930s. The product could be painfully comic. A dance number called "The Rotisserie" lined up working girls on the Broadway stage to be cooked and consumed while a male singer named Teddy Claire sang, "We've fat chicks and tender chicks / And tough chicks and tender chicks / And chicks that are nice enough to eat / We've chicks that cost a lot / And chicks that are rather hot." The working girls were served up in the final refrain: "So try a little tender thing / How about a leg or wing / We've ev'ry kind of chick for you."[40]

The private realm offered other attractions more succulent than these. At the same time that they were turning away from their parental homes toward the marketplace, working girls also had their eyes on the intimate pleasure of male companionship. To leave home for work and for play was to move into an increasingly heterosocial culture. On the job or after work, in dance halls, at amusement parks, and at the movies, on the beaches from Coney Island to Santa Monica, women turned their attention to people of their own age and the opposite sex. On a night out in Cleveland in 1910, one sleuth estimated that up to 5,000 young women and 6,500 young men were tripping the light fantastic in one of in the city's 130 dance halls.[41] A dance hall aficionado named Belle Lindner Israels reported that getting a young swain to purchase a drink was "the acme of achievement in retailing experiences with the other sex."[42] Delicate negotiations about an escort home would soon follow. Settings like these offered women the first taste of the promiscuous sociability that had been their brothers' birthright. As Clara Lemlich explained it, "We're human, all of us girls, and we're young." Working girls found delirious relief from their labors by whirling through the dance floor in the arms of their male coworkers. College coeds rejoiced in exchanging chaperones for boyfriends or "pals."[43]

Young men and women of the working class enjoyed the promiscuous camaraderie of popular amusements long before such mixing of the sexes was made fashionable by the middle-class sophisticates of the jazz age. Models of heterosocial youth culture can be found along New York's Bowery as far back as the 1850s. But by the 1920s, the spirit of heterosocial play had secured a niche in high culture. At Greenwich Village's Liberal Club, the repartee of aspiring modernist writers was a coeducational activity. Women like Louise Bryant hightailed it from the small-town West to New York City to become a writer and hobnob with sophisticates from the Ivy League like Randolph Bourne and Eugene O'Neill. She also met up with radical women who had only recently emerged from their working-class ethnic homes, the likes of Margaret Sanger, Elizabeth Gurley Flynn, and Emma Goldman. They all stopped off for freewheeling conversation in the bohemian haunts of Greenwich Village. At the Dill Pickle Club of Chicago or obscure basement restaurants on Boston's Beacon Hill, working girls were seen in mixed company "discussing many subjects from poetry to economics." The Saturday luncheon conversations at Polly Holliday's restaurant in Greenwich Village turned the tables of heterosocial conversation. Women convened those meetings under the name of the Heterodoxy Club. They admitted men into the audience but directed the discussion to expressly feminist concerns such as birth control, companionate marriage, and woman suffrage.[44]

The Heterodoxy Club produced a written record that permits us to eavesdrop on these precocious conversations about the relations of men and women. And they offer an earful of egalitarian aspirations. Announcing themselves in 1912 as "a little band of willful women of the most unruly individuals," the members of the Heterodoxy Club began to practice "a wonderful freemasonry of women."[45] They spoke sometimes of suffrage but less often of civic or religious duties. They were most attentive to their elders in the women's movement when they proposed radical ways of reforming the private relations of men and women. Heterodoxy member Henrietta Rodman, for example, took up the cause of Charlotte Perkins Gilman and drew up plans for a kitchenless apartment building. The Greenwich Village feminists listened avidly to Margaret Sanger, who spoke not of caring for children but of the rights of women to prevent unwanted pregnancies. And they talked breathlessly of their title to pleasure rather than duty and sacrifice. Crystal Eastman issued the new woman's sexual manifesto in no uncertain terms: "Feminists are not nuns. That should be established. We want to love and be loved, and most of us want children, one or two at least. But we want our love to be joyous and free—not clouded with ignorance and fear."[46]

In their quest for intimate equality, these women organized their personal relations in strikingly various ways. Crystal Eastman chose to marry, but she

WOMEN REMAKE GENDER

lived in a separate apartment from her mate, bore two children, and then divorced. Radicals like Emma Goldman and Elizabeth Gurley Flynn lived openly outside of wedlock with a sequence of lovers. When Louise Bryant and John Reed wed, they joked of hiding the fact to avoid charges of conventionality. Grace Nail wed James Weldon Johnson and bore no children. Elsie Clews Parsons bore six without interrupting her career as an anthropologist. Sara Josephine Baker, director of the New York City Bureau of Child Hygiene, lived until her death in 1945 with two other professional women. Elizabeth Irwin ran the village's landmark, the Little Red School House, resided with a long-term female companion, and adopted two children. Clearly, the elite wing of the rising generation of women was charting a new route not just to work or to the public sphere but also through private life. Unlike the college-educated women of their mothers' generation, these modern women were not willing to trade marriage, children, and sexual pleasure for a life of single-minded public service or career success. They intended to have both work and home, on their own terms, according to a "freemasonry" of gender practices.[47]

The actions and antics of less privileged women speak with similar confidence about reshaping the relations between men and women. The daughters of immigrants who worked in the downtown offices of the New England Telephone Company, for example, left a trail of playful evidence about their relations with working boys. They were said to hang out in candlelit bohemian cafes and to entertain men in their modest apartments. They also met men on the relatively level ground of the trade union rank and file. The telephone operators formed a separate female union and elected women to positions of leadership, but they allied with the male sector of the telephone company's workforce and affiliated with the International Brotherhood of Electrical Workers (IBEW). The heterosocial space of the IBEW conventions created not just working-class solidarity but also an opportunity for young working men and women to play together. In 1917 the faces of men and women beamed out, side by side, from snapshots taken on a trip to the annual convention in Atlantic City. Another photograph captured a young couple who traveled there straddling the same motorcycle. The union's group portrait preserves whimsical testimony about how rigid gender distinctions could dissolve in the open air of a heterosocial workers' culture. A close look at a photograph dated 1917 detects a curious feature of the Sunday-best costumes of streetcar workers and telephone operators. The sexes had traded hats: the men donned plumed wide brims and velvet cloches, and the women wore jaunty fedoras and tweed fishermen's caps. The trip from home to work

Telephone Operators' Union Delegates at the 1917 International Brotherhood of Electrical Workers Convention. (Courtesy of Stephen H. Norwood)

seemed to take a detour into a symmetrical social and political life and a certain nonchalance about gender difference.[48]

From the high spirits of the electrical workers to the modern ideas of the bohemians, a generation of men and women was imagining new ways of relating to one another. This same generation reputedly fomented a sexual revolution. The massive survey of sexual behavior by Alfred Kinsey singled out the generation of women born after 1900 as the vanguard of a new sexuality. The rate of sexual intercourse outside of marriage rose dramatically for that female birth cohort and almost reached parity with men. This pathbreaking generation had also undermined the double standard. While Kinsey's sample probably overrepresented the more educated population, ordinary working men and women left their own records of sexual change. Statistics on illegitimacy began rising among the lower classes even earlier, in the 1890s. In the dance halls, saloons, and amusement parks of working-class districts, young men and women discovered new sources of sensual and erotic pleasure, and in so doing they were not thrust into the moral abyss of fallen women and lecherous men. Just to take in the music and bright lights,

WOMEN REMAKE GENDER

to touch and to dance, to exchange a kiss for the price of an admission ticket, or steal a caress in the tunnel of love could bring a sexual thrill to the working girl.[49]

The new working-girl heroines were not deterred by warnings of seduction and abandonment; they tasted erotic excitement and went back to work or school the next day. Young women charged with sexual offenses in the courts of California, for example, defended themselves frankly and shamelessly. Eighteen-year-old Margaret Emerson dressed up, ventured off to downtown Oakland with two friends, and caught the eye of several men. Emerson paired off with one of them and made a date to meet at an amusement park. The sexual dalliance that ensued preceded her marriage to this divorced man. To the south, in Los Angeles, the sexual escapades of Edna Morales did not conclude with a marriage, and as a matter of principle. Morales reported to the probation officer that "there was nothing wrong with it." She denied being coerced into premarital sex but acted, she said, out of affection for her partner. Julia Townsend, also of Los Angeles, told the probation officer that she did not believe there was any wrong in having sexual intercourse before marriage, as long as she neither took money for it nor became pregnant. Other women made a profit off such peccadilloes. In the code of behavior dubbed "treating," Chicago girls reasoned, "It won't cost us a cent if we make a killing. There's always a bunch of guys around there and it's dead easy to date up."[50]

Typically, the sensual explorations of young men and women were not so mercenary. Much reciprocal pleasure was to be found in dance halls. At the turn of the century, sexually suggestive dancing was the province of those who traveled to vice districts and frequented concert saloons or the "black and tans" and juke joints where the races could mingle. The dance steps fashioned there bore names like "Love Walk" or "Rub Me Close," featuring such pas de deux as this: "the girl with her hands around the man's neck, the man with both his arms around the girl or on her hips; their cheeks are pressed close together, their bodies touch each other."[51] Such choreography, epitomized by the infamous "Itch," "a spasmodic placing of the hands all over the body in an agony of perfect rhythm," was so infectious that it became that modern form of foreplay called the dance craze and traveled far outside the slums.[52] In the 1920s the center of sexual revolution shifted to Harlem, where authors like Zora Neale Hurston and blues singers like Ma Rainey navigated between stereotypes of African primitivism and the straitlaced standards of clubwomen to chart their own erotic subjectivity. The changes in manners and mores that signaled the "the roaring twenties" were actually a belated transmission of this new sexuality into middle-class venues — bohemia and the respectable nightclubs, mainstream amusements, the toned-down Charleston, the controlled practice of dating, and the restrained sensuality of necking and petting.[53]

Whatever the exact timing, a whole generation of women was leaving home not just to find work but to meet men and pursue desire. In the process they redefined the private as well as the public sphere. The proclamations of "feminism new style" and the conversations of the bon vivants in modernist hangouts like New York's Liberal Club were spiced with a new language of individuality. The feminist pronounced it "her twentieth century birth right to emerge from a creature of instinct into a full-fledged individual who is capable of molding her own life." The euphoric aim of modern American women, as recited by Anzia Yezierska, was "becoming a person." Her heroines vowed, "I got to work myself up for a person. I got a head. I got ideas. . . . I got to go up higher . . . by my own strength."[54]

The young men and women of the twentieth century moved together on an inward path toward the private quarters they called "personal." This social space should not be conflated with the nineteenth-century private sphere, or feminine domesticity. The private lives of young men and women were not filled up with large families and extended relatives; they did not overlap with voluntary associations and churches or extend very far into civil society. Personal life was not a feminine but a heterosexual space, invested with novel emotional and sexual expectations. While members of the Heterodoxy Club sponsored public feminist meetings, they also withdrew into a narrower "conversational community" of the like-minded and chafed at the reins of mass organizations.[55] The small circles of bohemians and writers delved into each other's innermost feelings and private relationships with such studied intensity that they charted a new social space that would be called not just personal life but "intimacy." Modernist writers and journalists like Floyd Dell and Mabel Dodge Luhan made careers out of chronicling the intimate ties and sexual jealousies that crisscrossed their coterie. Neith Boyce and Hutchins Hapgood even staged plays about their marital troubles.[56] Immigrant writers like Abraham Cahan of the *Jewish Daily Forward* wrote of "Imported Bridegrooms" and "Ghetto Weddings" and followed David Levinsky on a quest for a perfect heterosexual partnership. His social landscapes were not much broader than the immigrant settings sketched by Anzia Yezierska, which celebrated "my precious privacy" and "beautiful aloneness."[57] In *Call It Sleep* Henry Roth took excursions deep into the Oedipal and adolescent sexuality of his characters. These tales from the tenements were nonetheless a wide and populous world compared with the Long Island suburban desert on which F. Scott Fitzgerald staged the heterosexual dreaming of Jay Gatsby.[58]

Whether the work of fledgling feminists, second-generation immigrants, or modernist writers, this focus on intimacy turned the attention of the new generation away from the homosocial culture of the nineteenth century. The social networks of men, like those of women, had been constricting from at least the dawn of the new century. The high tide of the male public sphere, as measured by participation in presidential elections or fraternal orders, was the 1890s. Polling places, party caucuses, lodges, and saloons began to empty out as the new century progressed. In the 1920s young men took increasingly to dating, moviegoing, or spectator sports, and in the 1930s husbands spent more time at home listening to the radio or sitting on the front porch. Textbooks on "Marriage and the Family" alerted high school and college students to their responsibility to develop "healthy heterosexuality" and a "satisfying emotional life." Women who had devoted their lives to public service were put on the defensive, charged with being "castrated men" and obliged to assert that "a life without sexual love was not entirely without joy." Men and women alike seemed to be setting a new course, not just from home to work or private to public, but in an obliquely lateral direction, from the social to the intimate and the personal.[59]

The ideology of masculinity was adjusted to reflect the imperative of heterosexual intimacy. The old standard of manhood, which placed a premium on the virtues of the breadwinner—self-reliant, hard-working, and upright— gave way to such idols of masculine beauty as bodybuilders Bernarr MacFadden and Eugen Sandow or scantily clad heroes like Houdini and Tarzan. The new masculinity resembled the old femininity in its preoccupations with physical appearance, leisure activities, and intimate relations.[60] While the new man might exchange the ward meeting for the dance hall, he was not always comfortable in heterosexual peer culture. One dandy saw popular dancing as a game of "pursuit and capture," intended "to get a piece of tail," and complained about young women who ditched their partners "as soon as they find a man is through spending money on them." The sexual possibilities of youth culture could entail vulnerability and disappointment for both men and women.[61] Accounts of personal life, found everywhere from popular journals like *True Romance* to modernist classics like *The Sun Also Rises*, bristle with tension between the sexes. Some of their heroes abandoned the chivalry of gentlemen past with a vengeance: "She's not a woman. . . . She's lust. No brain. No heart. A stark inhuman piece of flesh with a shark's hunger inside it." Sometimes the battle of the sexes got physical, as in the case of one Fitzgerald character who confronted "that cool and impervious girl, to obtain with one magnificent effort a mastery" and then "sustained his will with violence."[62]

Real-life relationships enacted in bohemian circles of Greenwich Village or Paris were rarely conducted on level ground, and the terms of sexual experimentation were more often set by men. The well-documented relationship between Neith Boyce and Hutchins Hapgood, for example, was built on erotic asymmetry, thrown off balance by the wife's sexual reserve and the mother's inability to conduct elaborate affairs while caring for two children.[63] Obtaining what one historian has aptly called "sexual sovereignty" proved particularly difficult for women.[64] Anzia Yezierska's autobiographical fiction pictured modern heroines lapsing into a posture of sexual surrender, like one who "felt her soul swoon in ecstasy as he drew her toward him."[65] In the story "Wings," a young immigrant expressed her passion for a social and intellectual superior in a literally abased self-image: clutching his slipper, she longed to be "this leather thing only to hold his feet."[66] The discomfort of reading a scene like this is compounded by the knowledge that it was modeled on the relationship between Anzia Yezierska and the esteemed philosopher of American democracy John Dewey. Years later, Yezierska would interpret these aborted love scenes with the Dewey figure in a subtly but critically different way. In her autobiography of 1950, she wrote, "The natural delight of his touch was checked by a wild alarm that stiffened me with fear. I had the same fear of drowning in his arms that I had of drowning in the river."[67] The sexual terrain was mined with conflict and inequality between men and women, but it would not be publicly recognized—and named "sexual politics"—until the women's movement of the late 1960s.

For the time being, the road to personal life went blithely along its course away from the public sphere. The paths of intimacy and personal life led a new generation of men and women to marry and form families more frequently and earlier than their parents. Working girls retreated, at least for the moment, into the traditional sphere of their sex. The average age at marriage declined steadily between 1890 and 1950, from a peak of 22 to a nadir of 20.3 for women and three to four years older for men. The age of the bachelor and spinster was coming to an end by 1929, heralded by the popular theme song, "Wedding Bells Are Breaking Up That Old Gang of Mine."[68] Marriage spelled retirement from the labor force, by employer fiat if not the preference of the working wife. Even in advance of the Depression-era hysteria about stealing jobs from breadwinners, the majority of businesses, including the telephone company, refrained from hiring married women.

WOMEN REMAKE GENDER

In the 1930s the push homeward became brutal. One commentator put a not uncommon solution to the nation's ills this way: "Simply fire the women, who shouldn't be working anyway, and hire the men. Presto! No unemployment. No relief rolls. No depression."[69] Opinion polls during the 1930s revealed that 78 percent of Americans, male and female, opposed the employment of married women. Such assumptions about the proper gender division of labor found their way into public policy at the local and federal levels. The vast majority of school districts, as well as the federal government, prohibited the employment of wives. Although the rate of employment among married women went slowly upward in the interwar years, the typical working wife was either childless, a committed careerist, poor, or African American—that is, a woman who had seldom left the labor force after marriage in the first place. Given this rude shove away from the labor force—executed by a team of employers, husbands, Uncle Sam, and public opinion—feisty working girls went relatively quietly back home and into the time-honored roles of wives and mothers. The year 1940 found over 85 percent of America's married women outside the paid labor force.[70]

Having made what seemed to be a traditional turn in the life cycle, however, modern brides did not revert to a Victorian style of homemaking. Most now practiced some form of birth control, thereby reducing the fertility rates precipitously—within the working class and the middle class, among immigrant Catholics (who finally had been apprised of a reasonably effective rhythm method) and native-born Protestants. By 1930, the total number of children born to adult women had fallen to 2.45 from 3.56 in 1900; by 1940 it would drop to a level of only 2.10 children.[71] These prudent procreators also reaped the benefits of Progressive standards of child-rearing, which, in addition to providing advice on sanitary care and the nutritious feeding of infants, paid heed to the independent needs of mothers. The Children's Bureau's best-selling manual on infant care told mothers, "If you haven't tried putting your children to bed at six o'clock you have no idea what a relief it will be to you."[72] Academic experts upgraded motherhood from a holy Victorian mission to a job requiring efficiency and consultation with experts. Parents also delegated more of their responsibilities to professionals, from the doctors who oversaw birth and scrutinized health care to the teachers who monopolized the attention of America's children during the school day. While a generation earlier children spent an average of only 80 days a year in school, modern mothers waved good-bye to their progeny 185 days annually.[73] Although the first priority of the married woman remained the time-honored duty of bearing and raising children, that role had become streamlined to consume less time and energy. The new maternal regimen was captured by an advertisement for infant formula and bottle-feeding: "Take Baby and Run."[74]

When working women married, they also took some modern ideas and improvements to the task of housework. By 1930, two-thirds of America's homes had electricity and running water.[75] No hallowed traditions bound housewives to ancient rites like devoting all of Monday to laundry. They were delighted that washing machines could cut the time for that task in half. Feminist blueprints for kitchenless apartments or public child care did not materialize, but housewives still managed to cut their working time significantly, down to fifty-two hours a week, according to one study.[76] By 1940, modern maidens had become modern matrons. They had weathered the Depression, raised their small families, and conserved their energy and vitality. With the dramatic increase in life expectancy, the 1900 birth cohort arrived at the year 1940 with many productive years ahead of them.[77]

This pivotal generation was now about to watch their daughters and sons leave home for jobs and families of their own. Fortuitously, just as their nests were emptying, Washington issued an emergency message to women, calling them up to a domestic battle against Adolf Hitler. Uncle Sam declared that "the ultimate solution of the manpower question is women." Radio programs scripted by the federal government boomed out, "Your son—your brother—your sweetheart—the boy in the next block—they will pay with their lives for these idle machines."[78] The warmest invitations to join the labor force were sent not to mothers but to sweethearts—to the young, single, beguiling Rosie the Riveter—that is, to the daughters of now middle-aged new women. Although most advertising copy still placed mothers respectfully at home, it was older, married women who answered Uncle Sam's call to work in the greatest numbers. The majority of female employees in the war industries were middle-aged and either returning to the labor force or simply transferring from less well paying jobs. African American women rushed into the shipyards and munitions factories, welcome alternatives to domestic service. They had their own ironic perspective on wartime employment possibilities: the saying went around the Los Angeles shipyards that it took Hitler to liberate black women from white women's kitchens. Black or white, war industry workers were adamant that they wanted to remain at their lucrative workstations at war's end. And when they were summarily fired, they did not leave the labor force but moved on to other jobs. They would not go home again until it was time for retirement. These modern mothers had found their way back to work.[79]

In fact, when the temporal pattern of women's labor force participation is graphed over the life cycles of successive generations, it reveals that the last cohort of women to retire permanently from the labor force upon marriage was born before 1895. Some of these pioneer working wives had never even taken a sabbatical. They included heirs of the Progressive reformers, like Dorothy Douglas, who was mentored by Jane Addams and pursued a lifelong career as an activist and Smith College professor, undeterred by marriage, the birth of four children, and divorce. Some alumnae of the Heterodoxy Club and avant-garde couples like Georgia O'Keeffe and Alfred Stieglitz or Dorothea Lange and Paul Taylor also devised intimate partnerships that permitted both spouses to conduct illustrious careers. But ordinary working girls, especially those with a history of labor activism, were the most formidable vanguard of change. They might be represented by Bessie Abramowitz Hillman, who emigrated from Russia, helped lead the Chicago garment strike of 1910, and became a familiar figure in the Women's Trade Union League. She resigned her post in 1917, one year after her marriage to labor leader Sidney Hillman, but by 1924, three years after the birth of her second child, she was back on the job. Ruth Finkelstein was born in Russia in 1897, immigrated to Boston as a child, and became a telephone worker and member of the International Brotherhood of Electrical Workers. When she married Hyman Norwood in 1921, she was summarily fired, in keeping with company policy. But she continued her work as a labor activist and officer of the Women's Trade Union League for the next several decades. Esther Eggertsen was born in a Mormon family in Provo, Utah, and was educated at Brigham Young University. She came to the labor movement by way of Columbia Teachers' College and marriage to a working-class socialist named Oliver Peterson. She bore and raised four children without losing a step in her career of service to working women. Made visible by their public roles in union circles, these women represented the norm of their generation: over their life cycles they patched together a pragmatic strategy for combining home and work.[80]

In the coarse monetary measures of the marketplace, however, women had not yet secured equity. As of 1939, the typical woman's wage in the industrial sector was actually lower relative to men than in 1920, a mere fifty-four rather than fifty-five cents on the dollar. The measure of gender inequity would hover around sixty cents for another forty years. Steadfast labor feminists like Ruth Norwood, Bessie Hillman, Fannia Cohen, and Myra Wolfgang never made it very high in the leadership of unions, even those dominated by workers of their own sex. It would be a long time—put off, in fact, to a yet un-realized future—before women's occupation of the labor force would translate into simple parity of wages between the sexes. This continuing inequity was due in part to simple discrimination: unequal pay for the same work if performed by a woman. Some of it can be explained by the lesser work experience of married women, due especially to the interruption of child-rearing and part-time employment. The wage deficit, however, could not be attributed to the level of skills that women brought to their jobs. In fact, female educational attainment had been higher than that of men since the 1920s, when women were more likely to leave school with a high school diploma, and hence the aptitude for exacting work in the fastest growing sector of the labor force, white-collar occupations.[81]

In one of those glitches to which the free market is prone, the demand for skilled female labor did not lead employers to offer women wage increases. The major exception was during the Second World War, when women temporarily stood in for men in the war industries. This ephemeral equity required the intervention of both government and the unions. When members of the United Auto Workers saw women flocking onto their turf, threatening to drive down their wages to a female level, they saw the advantages of gender equity. Prompted by veterans in the women's labor battles of the past, industrial unions put forward demands for such modern gender reforms as equal pay for equal work and even equal pay for jobs requiring comparable skill. With war's end, however, the cause of gender equity was returned to the back burner of American politics.[82]

After the wave of Progressive legislation immediately following the passage of the suffrage amendment, both the halls of Congress and the courts of public opinion lost interest in "the Woman Question." Gender issues receded from the headlines, the congressional agenda, and the docket of laws after the mid-1920s. Although veterans of the Women's Trade Union League, the Women's Bureau, and scores of union women labored valiantly to place issues of gender equity on the public agenda, their efforts never made it into the headlines or the statute books. The women's platform of the Progressive Era faded away from public view. The first generation of women born into the twentieth century reached midlife around 1950, and continued to remodel womanhood, but they did so largely offstage in the private spaces of the marketplace and the home.[83]

WOMEN REMAKE GENDER

The Next Generation Combines Work and Family
The 1940s and 1950s

The generation of women destined to take the next critical step up the occupational ladder was born at a time of relative quiet on the gender front. As they were growing up in the 1930s, popular culture did not expend much rhetoric enforcing any particular gender role, which gave the rising generation some latitude in imagining their own futures. The front pages still had room for both career women and homemakers and were open to the tenacious reforming spirit of Eleanor Roosevelt, as well as the exploits of robust modern heroines like Amelia Earhart. The First Lady applauded the dashing young aviatrix as a champion of "the cause of women, by giving them a feeling there was nothing they could not do."[84] The *New York Times* interpreted Earhart's airborne exploits as "rebellion against a world which had been made, for women, too safe, too unexciting."[85] Born in 1897, regrettably "at a time when girls were still girls," Earhart's buoyant sprit carried the vivacious standard of modern womanhood into the 1930s. She used her celebrity status to propound such things as two-career couples, voluntary childlessness, and the wearing of pants. The children of modern mothers could not fail to get the message. One receptive twelve-year-old boy reported, "She has squarely put it up to the men that women's place is not only in the home but above the clouds."[86] There were other adventures in store for girls whose heads were in books rather than in the skies, notably the vicarious thrills of Nancy Drew mysteries that kept something of the more adventurous side of modern women alive for at least another generation.

The ladies' magazines and movie scripts of the 1930s and early 1940s delivered a more mixed, and more age-sensitive, message. Although editors admitted career women to their pages, they circumscribed their subjects' independence with reminders of the familial responsibilities of adult women. When heroines in the *Ladies' Home Journal* continued to practice their professions beyond a proper age for marriage, their ambitions became unseemly and ultimately grotesque. The transition can be measured in the rising arch of Joan Crawford's eyebrows: the peppy but feminine ingénue featured in the films of the 1920s like *Our Dancing Daughters* (1928) was transformed into a brittle, aging businesswoman by the time she appeared in *Mildred Pierce* in the 1940s. Crawford's menacing eye makeup would be her trademark for the rest of her long career. Not even the feminist director Dorothy Arzner could keep the flapper image in the air for very long. Her aviatrix heroine, played by Katharine Hepburn in the movie *Christopher Strong* (1933), flew off to her death when she discovered that she was pregnant with the child of a married man. A story in the September 1941 issue of the *Saturday Evening Post* presented a status-seeking nurse as the classic domineering female whose fate was spelled out in the title "Prescription for Murder."[87] Such draconian pronouncements were suspended when the U.S. entry into World War II increased demand for female labor on the home front. But they would emerge again with a fury in 1945, taking the ambitions of aviatrixes with them. By that time, federal regulations curtailed women's chances of getting a flying license, and ladies' magazines lowered the expectations of their readers: the story "Diapers for Flight Six" featured not an aviatrix but a stewardess, who retired at the first opportunity to start a family.[88]

Popular culture delivered an ambiguous message at best to the women growing up in the 1930s and 1940s. The yearbook prediction for Ruth Goldblum, class of 1949 at a New York City high school, captured the volatility of gender expectations: "If she doesn't succeed in becoming President of the United States she'll settle for being a housewife."[89] More systematic studies of the attitudes and behavior of this generation have indicated that young women anticipated a future in which marriage was paramount. One investigation showed that those children who experienced the greatest economic insecurity during the Depression were especially wary of deviations from the gender roles of breadwinner and housewife. The Second World War, with the showcase of the masculine warrior role and the longing to reunite families, was equally inhospitable to gender radicalism. The image of Rosie the Riveter faded into the ads for Pond's facial cream, labeled "Brides of 1942, . . . 1943 . . . 1944 . . . 1945."[90]

Although skewed toward the domestic side of female identity, the gender ideology of the 1940s did not revert to the Victorian cult of true womanhood. As the generation born to new women in the 1920s and 1930s came of age, they seldom questioned the first giant step into modern womanhood taken by their mothers; without hesitation, they would go to work before marriage. The 1930s found virtually all young single women either at school or in the labor force. The new women's progeny followed their mothers to white-collar destinations: 85 percent of New York high school students set their immediate goal after graduation as securing a secretarial job. Most of these high school graduates would get their wish. Fifty percent of second-generation Italian women in New York would hold white-collar positions, at a time when their brothers were still largely confined to blue-collar employment. By the 1940s, clerical work was the dominant job classification for white women, including the daughters of immigrants from Southern and Eastern Europe.

The positions in the white-collar world that their mother had struggled to obtain were a sinecure for daughters.[91]

Like their mothers before them, the young clerks and secretaries of the 1940s had not rejected the traditional domestic occupations of the female sex. They took it for granted that they would experience both work and maternity, but sequentially rather than simultaneously. This strategy was articulated as a commonplace entry in the high school yearbooks of the 1940s. Both Jewish and Italian girls in one New York City high school aspired to be secretaries upon graduation, but they recorded another ambition as well. Rosalie Petrullo, class of 1949, confessed "the second interest in her life / Is to become a loyal wife."[92] Her classmate Angela Carbone soared off in a more single-minded domestic direction: "A girl who's true to the sky / Therefore she wants to fly. / She's going to rocket to the moon / With a pilot very soon."[93] On leaving high school, this generation was intent on combining work and family. They would climb on their mothers' shoulders and then go one half-step further into the labor force. Having secured a niche in the white-collar sector, many of them would not retire immediately after their weddings but remain on the job until the birth of their first child.[94]

Compared with their mothers, however, the women who came of age after the Second World War were in a hurry to begin the domestic stage of their careers. They hastened both to the altar and into motherhood. The cohort of white women born between 1920 and 1929, for example, would be married by the median age of 20.8, significantly younger than their mothers.[95] They also bore slightly more children on the average, raising the total fertility rate in 1950 to 3.00, above the rates during the Depression and the war, but still shy of the 1920 figure of 3.17. Even after the boom time for babies, the 1950s, the rate would rise only to the approximate level of 1900, 3.52 to be precise. The total fertility rate of the postwar period did not indicate that American mothers were breeding with abandon. Rather, this rise in a fraction of a percentage point reflected a convergence of fertility rates across class and ethnic differences. The fecundity of both the daughters of once prolific immigrant groups and the progeny of small, middle-class families tended to bear three or four children. The prudent mothers of the 1940s and 1950s did not heed the extravagant pronatalist propaganda that urged them "to win the baby war against Hitler" or "Give us Back the Victorian Mothers of Seven to Ten Children."[96] Postwar mothers commenced their childbearing promptly and completed it with dispatch, at the tender maternal age of 30.5 on the average. All in all, this generation of women seemed to be carrying forward the modernization of womanhood at a deliberate pace and maintaining a steady equilibrium between work and homemaking. They went from middle-level, white-collar jobs to streamlined, small families, differing from their mothers primarily in the swiftness with which they advanced through the childbearing stage of their life cycle.[97]

Demographers have been quick to point out that political and economic history facilitated this accelerated timing of the twentieth-century family cycle. A confluence of events made the late 1940s and 1950s prime time for marriage and procreation. Recovery from the Depression, family reunions after the war, and conversion from wartime production to a flourishing consumer economy all came together to make it possible for more Americans to marry and start raising children. The demographic results of this convergence of family cycles and historical events goes by the name of the baby boom, a term that is justified by the raw number of births that occurred between 1946 and 1964: 76 million. But while "baby boom" may be an apt label of demographic history, it does not translate literally into women's history. Those 76 million babies were not the result of wildly inflated procreation on the part of individual women. The fact that most all the men and women of this generation married and bore children, that they started their families in synchrony (delayed by the Depression and World War II), and then had their three or four children in rapid succession concentrated the natural population growth into a relatively narrow window of chronological time. The compression of childbearing into this short postwar period acted as a multiplier effect on fertility and created a short-term population explosion. This fast-paced and efficient reproduction made perfect sense for the daughters of modern mothers, the generation that had firsthand knowledge of the strategic timing of work and family responsibilities.

Once the energy of a generation was synchronized and focused intently on raising young families, all sorts of critical changes ensued—in the marketplace, social ecology, federal policies, even foreign affairs. Demography and political economy conspired to make family formation, rather than a youthful stint in the labor force, the most celebrated moment in the life cycle of this generation of women. The effect of fertility was most obvious and immediate in the marketplace, where the wartime rationing had created pent-up demand to consume as well as reproduce. The conversion of factories to war production had denied American families the supply of durable consumer goods for which they had been building up an appetite since the 1920s. It was estimated, for example, that American consumers sacrificed 1.8 million washing machines and 2.8 million refrigerators to the production of tanks and airplanes and other military materials. Advertisements for war bonds

WOMEN REMAKE GENDER

registered these thwarted desires in images of housewives dreaming of re-deeming savings bonds for remodeled kitchens. *Business Week* assured its readers that "your future is great in a growing America." Pointing explicitly to the soaring birth rate, it said, "This means jobs, more opportunities, new business."[98] Between 1947 and 1960 consumer spending would go up a full 60 percent, and for the first time the majority of Americans would enjoy something called discretionary income, earnings that were secure and sub-stantial enough to permit them to enter sectors of the marketplace that were once reserved for the affluent.

The bulk of this surplus income was redeemed for domestic amenities. Household expenses rose at four times the rate of general consumer spend-ing, a figure of 240 percent for things like food, clothing, and items of im-mediate domestic consumption, which accounted for 30 percent of the rise in the Gross National Product. When the booming economy lagged slightly during the recession of 1958, *Life* magazine responded by placing a portrait of three dozen babies on its cover with the caption: "Kids — Built-in Recession Cure — How four million a year make millions in business."[99] The big-ticket item on the family shopping list was the house itself. The housing market had been primed for a meteoric boom during the war. Savvy entrepreneurs who held government contracts for war mobilization, like Levitt Brothers in the East and Henry Kaiser in the West, went right to work mass-manufacturing the sites of peacetime domesticity. Levittown opened on schedule in 1947 with 17,400 standardized domiciles, a production rate of thirty-five every day. Whole communities rose in the vacant spaces of the San Fernando Val-ley in Southern California, carefully planned to provide not just housing but jobs for breadwinners in nearby aircraft or automobile factories. Low-interest loans and high wages secured the deed to the American dream for blue-collar workers as well as the middle classes. The new homes rising across the coun-try were designed for domesticity: the floor plan centered on a space called a "family room."[100]

Postwar domesticity materialized not just in architecture but also as so-cial space. It was located in a habitat designed expressly for child rearing, suburban housing tracts. Between 1950 and 1970 the residential site where Americans were mostly likely to live was in one of these bedroom communi-ties outside the central cities; with 74 million residents, the suburban popu-lation surpassed that of metropolitan centers as well as rural areas.[101] Forest Park, a model suburban development in Ohio, opened with a public chris-tening presided over by the reigning "Mrs. America" and dedicated to "the wage earners and the homemakers — the families of the American Home."

The domestic meaning of this social space was also registered in such jesting monikers as "fertility valley" or "Rabbit Hutch."[102] The centrality of domesticity to the new social ecology was plotted on the streets themselves: miles upon miles of detached homes were rarely broken by public spaces and civic institutions—not a city hall, only an occasional school, not even a commercial district until strip malls and then shopping centers were belatedly established along their margins. In the late twentieth century, homemaking was the leading edge of a wholesale reshaping of space, commerce, and what came to be known as "lifestyle."[103]

The redomestication of America was underwritten by government policy. The U.S. government had already become the public purveyor of private comforts in the 1930s when the Federal Housing Authority began to guarantee low-cost mortgages and thereby equip young couples of humbler status to purchase a home of their own, to practice what has been called "consumer citizenship."[104] After World War II, the G.I. Bill extended home loans to veterans at interest rates as low as 2 percent, which propagated more homes across the vast suburban landscape. The policies of the federal housing authorities and local realtors funneled these massive subsidies to single-family dwellings rather than apartment houses and to suburbs rather than to inner cities. Major mortgage lenders like the Prudential Insurance Company followed suit. By 1948, President Harry Truman could reduce the political economy of domesticity to the slogan that "children and dogs are as necessary to the welfare of this country as is Wall Street and the railroads."[105] Soon the federal government would fortify this philosophy with programs that provided the essential infrastructure for further suburban expansion, including the Highway Act of 1956, which opened vast tracts of land to residential development.[106]

Postwar homemaking also became a matter of foreign policy. Cold War policies were couched in domestic rhetoric, from the "togetherness" of the fallout shelter to the unmanliness of communists. Even the auspicious memo in which George Kennan sketched out the Cold War policy of containment stooped to gendered language, including five uses of the term "penetration" to represent the Russian threat. The most bizarre meeting of domesticity and diplomacy took place in Moscow in 1959, when Vice President Richard Nixon debated Nikita Khrushchev before a model of an all-American kitchen. Nixon's coup de grâce: "We have many different manufacturers and many different kinds of washing machines so that the housewives have a choice . . . . Would it not be better to compete in the relative merits of washing machines than in the strength of rockets?" (Given the havoc that Cold

War foreign policy would wreak in Southeast Asia and elsewhere, one wonders whether this particular deployment of domesticity might have had some merits.) From where Nixon stood in 1959, it was already clear that the political economy of domesticity would have a major and far-flung impact.[107]

Some see the postwar domestic revival as a simple, reflexive return to the comforting stability of home after decades of depression and war, just a continuation of the ageless pursuit of the American dream. In fact, something more complicated and mysterious was at work here, including an innovative orchestration of gender difference. The recovery of America's advanced corporate economy required that both consumption and production be primed. Good economic citizens of the postwar era expended their time, energy, income, and desire in the shopping center, as well as on the job. It had been customary to track these two economic imperatives by gender: sending husbands off to earn the family wage and delegating the shopping to women. After the war and through the 1950s, both governments and advertisers operated according to these expectations, failing to take women's increasing participation in the labor force into account.

Channeling men and women into separate spheres—women dedicated to homemaking and child care, men's noses to the grindstone of breadwinning—required conscious management. First of all, the husband's fulfillment of his part of the bargain was not left to chance. By supplying veterans with college education and home loans, the G.I. Bill operated as a subsidy to male breadwinners. These government programs boosted an estimated 78 percent of the men of the postwar generation up the career ladder. Thanks to the tenacity of the labor movement, industrial workers finally secured the wages and benefits that would support their streamlined families in comfort. On the cultural front, ladies' magazines, advice books for parents, and the growing ranks of therapeutic professionals adumbrated the male domestic role. They conducted campaigns for togetherness, invited fathers to create a masculine space around the backyard barbecue, celebrated father-son athletic practice, and primed the pump of domestic consumption through a male avocation called "home improvement." The demanding jobs of middle-class professional men and long-distance commuters allowed for at least this token expression of a two-sexed domesticity.[108]

Ushering women in the direction of mothering and shopping involved other, less material incentives. Low status and low pay discouraged women workers, and the blitz of rhetoric about the joys of cooking, breast-feeding, and home care beckoned them homeward. Women were eased into their consumer roles by the pronouncements of ladies' magazines, advertisers, and television commercials, some of which were downright bullying or out-right ridiculous. Immediately after the war, books like the notorious *Modern Woman: The Lost Sex* (1947) warned those who neglected their home roles that they risked sexual frigidity and charges of treason. The ladies' magazines sometimes read like hysterical guidebooks for time travel back to the Victorian age. The titles of articles in glossy women's magazines lined up like a thoroughly domestic life course: "How to Snare a Male," "Don't Be Afraid to Marry Young," "Should I Stop Work When We Marry," "Have Babies While You're Young," "Birth: The Crowning Moment of My Life," and "I Will Have Another Baby. I Must Live that Divine Experience Again."[109] According to one statistical survey, a young mother who stayed at home with her two closely spaced children would spend one hundred hours a week at work. More intensive child care, along with higher standards of housekeeping and a substantial increase in the time spent shopping, bloated the once streamlined domestic regimen. The average housewife's workweek rose above the 1920s level, despite a massive infusion of "labor-saving devices."[110]

Much of the increase in the housewife's workload was attributable to rising standards of child care. As modeled by Doctor Benjamin Spock (after uncredited consultation with his wife), child-rearing was truly a full-time job, for which men were not invited to apply. Spock began his guide for mothers with an apology for using the male pronoun for all children, noting nonchalantly that he needed "she" for the primary caretaker. The logic of this gender grammar went as follows:

> The important thing for a mother to realize is that the younger the child the more necessary it is for him to have a steady, loving person taking care of him. In most cases the mother is the best person to give him that feeling of "belonging," safely and surely. She doesn't quit on the job, she doesn't turn against him, she isn't indifferent to him, she takes care of him always in the same familiar house. If a mother realized how vital this kind of care is to the small child it will make it easier for her to decide that the extra money she might earn or the satisfaction she might receive from an outside job is not all that important after all.[111]

Even Doctor Spock recognized that it might not be "easy" for women to give up work for exclusive child care.

Psychological studies conducted in Massachusetts and California showed how difficult it could be to toe the taut line that had been drawn between breadwinning and homemaking. To the wives surveyed, homemaking came as a welcome and fulfilling role, but with a cost they measured in such things as a loss of "achievement," "goals in life," and "personal satisfaction." The domestic lifestyle was simply not to the taste of some women: "I had kind of a drop in morale. I was ashamed that I, somehow, didn't find it altogether exciting to be tied down with [the baby], whom I had wanted, but I missed the social contacts of my job."[112] Husbands were not always understanding about women's conflicts. One particularly obtuse spouse observed, "My profession will bring in a favorable income and my work is interesting to both of us. My wife will be invaluable as an assistant in my office and has taken a keen interest in our way of earning a living."[113] Other husbands were both more understanding of their wives' grievances and envious of some aspects of the woman's role. Fathers expressed special regret when long hours of working and commuting kept them from developing close relations with their children. Moreover, the regimen of rapid reproduction could be burdensome to a lone breadwinner. One Oakland man had a nervous breakdown at the thought of a new mouth to feed. His wife reported that when he learned she was pregnant, "That was too much, you know. He couldn't face the thought of trying to raise the children—the responsibility of feeding and clothing them." The bookend to the overburdened breadwinner was the mad housewife: "They were all little at once and I about went crazy. I just couldn't cope."[114]

One close survey of upper-middle-class Boston couples indicated that women felt particularly discontent with the gender system of the 1950s. They were twice as likely as men to express unhappiness in their marriages and to consider divorce. For women, home was a workplace, with all the attendant tedium and stress; to men it was largely a place of relaxation. Likewise, men had a modicum of greater power in marriage. Despite the espoused belief in domestic democracy, most marriages gave ultimate authority, particularly in major financial decisions, to the husband. The psychological studies that eavesdropped on the young middle-class families of the 1950s exposed the fault line that lay just beneath the surface of the split-level home. It was defined by sharply dimorphic gender roles, intense and insulated relations between husbands and wives, and a hierarchy measured in men's higher status outside and inside the home. Still, as of 1960, the postwar family was given a good bill of health. The divorce rate remained low (relative to the next generation), and when asked the majority of men and women accounted themselves happy in their marriages.[115]

The causes for this relative contentment were not to be found entirely within the home. Quite the contrary, the equanimity in postwar families was due in part to women's readiness to leave home for work, to take a job that would help shoulder the responsibilities of the breadwinner. As early as the 1930s, significant numbers of married middle-class women began to reenter the labor in order to augment household income and provide such family amenities as higher education for their children. The young wives of the 1930s, 1940s, and 1950s had not rushed into retirement immediately after marriage. Some actually were stashing away their earnings in order to make down payments on their dream homes. Others were working so their husbands could stay in school to enhance their qualifications for well-paying careers. One study of Oakland, California, couples found that 30 percent of the wives were gainfully employed between marriage and the birth of their first child, and 20 percent were employed while their children were young. Most of this work carefully meshed with domestic responsibilities, was undertaken only part-time or just for a season, and redounded to the economic benefit of the family.[116]

Taken in the aggregate, these gradual adjustments in the behavior of millions of women added up to a major transformation in gender roles. By 1950, a full 52 percent of working women were married; the figure had risen to 60 percent by 1960. The overall proportion of married women in the labor force grew accordingly, from 25 percent to 32 percent in just ten years. As in the generation past, the typical working wife was approaching middle age and had completed her childbearing. Her reentry into the labor force was expedited by the dispatch with which she had borne children. Typically, the mothers of this generation bore their last child early in their thirties, and with a life expectancy of seventy-three, they could contemplate decades of economic productivity ahead. Studies that carefully tracked families over time, like that of the Institute for Human Development in Berkeley, California, found that mothers were headed back to work at the mean age of thirty-six, and the economic well-being of their families grew apace. At the close of the 1950s, one could no longer expect to find almost all adult women at home from nine to five each day. In 1960 58 percent of working women had children under eighteen, and 20 percent left children under six behind as they entered the labor force.[117]

The movement of married women and mothers into the labor force may have been hedged in by domestic priorities, but the trend was steady and decisive. In fact, if the employment rate of the generation of women born between 1926 and 1935 is graphed over time, the proportion in the paid labor force is shown to climb steadily with every age group, beginning with women in their twenties. The employment rate ascended sharply for women in their thirties. While women were interrupting their employment for mothering,

WOMEN REMAKE GENDER

it was not in sufficient numbers or for long enough intervals to reverse the overall trend: another generation of women moved decisively from home to work, taking shorter and shorter times off for motherhood.[118]

In their own good time, and on their own terms, American wives and mothers were rewriting the job description of their gender and quietly challenging the asymmetry of the sexes. The decision to reenter the paid labor force in the 1950s was not accomplished by government or the media but by women themselves. They took the initiative in reshaping the gender division of labor, usually with the acquiescence, but sometimes against the opposition, of husbands who felt a working wife reflected negatively on their manhood. Some wives tried the waters outside the home through voluntary projects or continuing education programs. Others experienced a kind of malaise that was relieved by taking a job: "As the children get older I feel I have to do something and I don't know what it is." Hardly rebelling against their home roles, the working women of the postwar era were nonetheless reaping the benefits of employment and taking something for themselves, as well as for their families, from their jobs. They claimed to "like the feeling of making my own money and doing what I want to do with it." Looking back with hindsight from the 1980s, they had a language to express their personal rewards: "It has given me self-esteem"; "I know who I am and where I am." Husbands who once were dubious about working wives also came to appreciate the extra income and the happiness of their partners. The majority of husbands queried in the Oakland longitudinal study were unequivocally supportive of their working wives. They liked the financial help, found employment "therapeutic" for their wives, and sometimes were converted to a new gender ideology. One husband put the alteration in masculinity this way in 1970: "this pride thing. I make the money and you're the mother. But I realize that women need . . . the fulfillment. It's not just women having children. It's much more than that. . . . She needs a profession."[119]

Hindsight can easily affix a feminist label to the modifications of gender underway in the families of the 1950s. At the time, however, wives and husbands made gender history in ad hoc and pragmatic ways. While hardly conspicuous revolutionaries, they were neither oblivious nor uninformed about the mysteries of sex. Even in the 1950s women's magazines registered the complaints of homebound mothers and recommended part-time jobs and volunteer work as a respite from domesticity. Social scientists also recommended some modifications in the domestic division of labor. A Ford Foundation publication entitled *Womanpower* published in 1957 explicitly advised employment for married women and mothers whenever domestic obligations permitted. In 1961 *Life* put out the alert that married women were needed in the labor force if the United States were to compete economically and militarily with Soviet Russia. A study published in 1963 as *The Employed Mother in America* amassed evidence to reassure parents that working mothers did not damage their children and in fact raised adolescent daughters who were particularly "well adjusted." Such temperate advice from the experts, the acquiescence of husbands, and the self-determined actions of American wives and mothers point to the postwar generation as accomplished "freemasons" of their own gender roles. In their matter-of-fact way, they continued the mission of modern womanhood. An informant in Oakland gave this generational accomplishment the right spin: "But everyone is too modern to go for this baloney about the wife being the housewife and that's all these days."[120]

The history of the 1950s, as documented in labor force statistics and psychological studies of marriage and the family, reads like the collective biography of a plucky generation. The working wives of postwar America carried forward the transformation of womanhood from the point where their mothers left off. Wives and mothers of moderate social standing and only high school educations made the critical break with the past by returning to work after marriage and child-rearing. A study of the working-class suburb of Southgate, California, found that female labor force participation was more than twice that of more affluent suburbs. These daughters of the working class, more than elite college graduates, pioneered dual careers for their sex. Experienced workers in their youth, often the daughters of immigrants or farmers, they entered the labor force to support themselves and families whenever time and history permitted, be that before, during, or after World War II. In the process, they were also rewriting the history of class in America, much as the designers of middle-class homes had done a century before. The typical working couples in places like Southgate united a white-collar wife with a factory worker, making it more difficult to map and measure social and economic structure. The notion of "the working-class family" took on a newly complicated meaning once wives came to the assistance of male breadwinners by taking up jobs outside the blue-collar sector.[121]

The Mystery of the Feminine Mystique

This generational history of ordinary women does not call to mind the popular icons of the 1950s like June Cleaver or Lucille Ball, and it does not conform to the critical perspective that defined the era in retrospect as the heyday of the "feminine mystique."[122] According to Betty Friedan's best seller of 1963, the women of the 1950s were under the thrall of a mystique that "says that the highest value and the only commitment for women is the fulfillment of their own femininity. It says that the greatest mistake of Western culture, through most of its history, has been the under-evaluation of this femininity. It says this femininity is so mysterious and intuitive and close to the creation and origin of life that man-made science may never be able to understand it. . . . Women tried to be like men, instead of accepting their own nature, which can find fulfillment only in sexual passivity, male domination, and nurturing maternal love."[123] Historians now conclude that Friedan's account of the gender culture of the postwar period was at best a hyperbolic and selective reading of women's magazines and popular psychology. It was also clearly race and class specific. Neither the publications nor the practices of African American women can be aligned with the feminine mystique. The ideology of psychic and sexual fulfillment was equally incongruent with the vast majority of women who had never gone to college, picked up a sex manual, or read Freud.

Still, the millions of avid readers who made Friedan's book a runaway best seller and reacted so viscerally to the critique of the "feminine mystique" cannot be ignored. The first clue to the mysterious power of *The Feminine Mystique* is in the women's history of its author. Betty Goldstein Friedan fits somewhat awkwardly into the general frame of this chapter. Born in 1921, she partook of the ambitions of new women: she went off to Smith College at the urging of her mother and was educated to both the public commitments of the political left and the personal preoccupations of the academic field of psychology. She set out to get a Ph.D. in psychology and enjoyed a stint as a New York journalist before her marriage in 1947. Although married relatively late by postwar standards, Friedan practiced the efficient fertility of the postwar period, bearing her three children in close succession. Her part-time editing job ended when a second pregnancy prompted her firing, and she moved to suburban Rockland County, New York, where she took up the joys of cooking, breast-feeding, and the Parent-Teacher Association. Family snapshots of that era show Friedan in the frazzled state of a conscientious, overworked mother. But Friedan experienced the 1950s in a unique way: as a producer as well as a consumer of the booming domestic ideology. On assignment for magazines like *McCall's* and *Redbook*, she noticed that her homebound readers responded with particular empathy to articles about runaway mothers and housewives who felt trapped. Herself a part-time working mother, Friedan sat down at her suburban kitchen table and wrote, "Gradually, with-

Betty Friedan in the kitchen of her home in Parkway Village, New York, with Daniel and Jonathan, ca. 1953. (Courtesy of the Schlesinger Library, Radcliffe Institute, Harvard University)

out seeing it clearly for quite a while, I came to realize that something is very wrong with the way American women are trying to live their lives today."[124]

Several aspects of her own situation enabled Friedan to make the critical diagnoses of postwar gender that account for the powerful cultural impact of *The Feminine Mystique*; she represented both a cohort and a class of critical import for the history of women. First, Friedan was schooled in a tradition of social criticism and protest in her youth. As a student of Dorothy Douglas's at Smith and a writer for the labor press after college, she observed the tenacious feminism of union women close up. Second, she found herself in the place and time to witness a major conjuncture in family history. She was on the cutting edge of the generation of women who returned en masse to work as their children grew up. Third and finally, Betty Friedan represented the strategic minority of wives and mothers who were college-educated and taking up positions of some influence in the popular culture industry.

Well-placed and relatively elite women like Friedan experienced the domestic interlude of the 1940s and 1950s with particular intensity. An investigation of her own college cohort, the Smith class of 1942, exposed that disquiet on the home front that Friedan would call "The Problem that Has No Name." Before the war, surveys of students at elite women's colleges like Friedan's alma mater indicated that many women of her status still intended to act the part of new women, combining careers and marriage. In 1940 63 percent of Smith faculty were women; some of them, like Dorothy Wolff Douglas, modeled a dual career for their students. For Friedan's cohort, full-time motherhood and three-child families would be seen as a deviation from earlier generations of college women, who married less frequently or later in life and bore fewer children than the average baby boom mother. Into the 1940s and through Friedan's undergraduate career, students at Seven Sisters colleges still held onto career and family goals, although surveys revealed that confidence in combining marriage and a profession had declined significantly. Friedan herself carried her high ambitions, as well as her public conscience, on through college, into the postwar era, out to the suburbs, and back into the labor force. Through it all, she retained a critical perspective that became *The Feminine Mystique* in 1963.[125]

The domestic revival did not hit the universe of the educated women with full force until the 1950s, sometime after Friedan had graduated from Smith. Fewer students owned up to strong career ambitions, and most everyone placed a profession behind the family as a life goal. This was the generation of college women who would swallow the fullest dose of prescriptions for domestic fulfillment. The *Ladies' Home Journal* began its campaign to feminize college women in earnest after the war, when the editors sent women in a homeward direction with the assurance that "certainly the happiest women have never found the secret to happiness in books or lectures. They do the right thing instinctively."[126] American colleges and universities became overwhelmingly male in the postwar years, thanks in part to the subsidies for veterans, which reserved two of every three classroom seats for men. The dropout rate was particularly high among women who left college to form asymmetrical marital pairs, where the men were older and more educated than the women. Yet the bride was often a breadwinner for the short term, earning what was called a Ph.T., for "putting husbands through."[127] Once the baby boom was in full swing, the domestic revival became a contagion that swept into the college dorms and classrooms with a fury and a fillip of psycho-logical jargon. In the 1950s it was said that college girls skipped class to at-tend wedding showers, and as many as half of all coeds ended school with a precocious Mrs. degree.[128]

The barrage of domestic messages hit some women younger than Betty Friedan with a bewildering vertigo. At the elite liberal arts college of Swarth-more, one bright coed got lost in the crossed signals between gender ide-ology and academic values. Anne Parsons filled her diary with a jumble of contradictory visions; images of electric appliances, prescriptions for pain-less childbirth, and advice about infant care competed with headlines about women working in the fields, fighting for freedom in Hungary, and going to medical school. Her head spinning, Parsons collapsed: "if somebody doesn't do something about it they are going to blow up too but it was YOU that COULD NOT COME TO TERMS WITH YOUR BASIC FEMININE INSTINCTS and want to run that electric waxer around all day and then suddenly I cracked."[129] One of Parsons's contemporaries, a member of the Smith College class of 1950, found the bombardment of the feminine mystique equally disorienting. Writ-ing under the name of Victoria Lucas, she imagined a heroine who saw her future in the shape of a fig tree, alternate branches laden with seductive fruit: husband, children, home, career, travel, fame. The choice was paralyzing; the possibility of overreaching and falling was terrifying. The novel was equal parts nightmare and comedy, a satiric and gutsy commentary on the drivel of fashion magazines, the inanity of popular psychology, and the pomposity of the narrator's suitors. At the end of this novel, the heroine had survived mad-ness and set out valiantly on a course of sexual independence. After getting fitted with a diaphragm, she congratulated herself: "I had done well by my shopping privileges, I thought. I was my own woman. The next step was to find the proper sort of man." At last, it would seem that the modern woman could find sexual sovereignty, at least in fiction.[130]

Published in January 1963, this autobiographical novel was entitled *The Bell Jar* and was the work of the poet Sylvia Plath, who died a month later by her own hand. The suicides of Sylvia Plath and Anne Parsons, both in 1963, should not be taken as homilies about the lethal toxicity of the feminine mys-tique. Most women not only survived but also thrived through the 1950s, enacting a quiet revolution in gender roles. Still, the troubled consciousness and incisive writings of women like Parsons and Plath do speak to the ex-cruciating conflicts that domestic ideology could provoke under specific cir-cumstances, in this case among college-educated women at a most sensitive time in their own life cycles. The domestic culture of postwar America posed unique difficulties for these ambitious and perspicacious graduates of elite colleges. The career prospects for their sex had fallen below the standard of their mothers' generation; the ranks of women doctors, lawyers, and elite professionals had dwindled. At the same time, the fertility rate rose to 3.5 children. For these, the "best and the brightest," leaving school could bring a precipitous loss of stature, the forfeiture of A's and accolades for secretarial jobs and diapers. For a Smith or Swarthmore graduate, the incentives to join the labor force were insulting: a college-educated woman made on the average less than a high school–educated male. For those who aimed higher and missed a step in the critical transition between home and work, the consequences could be disastrous. At the time she died, Sylvia Plath was not carefully balancing home and work in the prudent manner of her generation at large. She was furiously writing poetry and chasing after fame at the same time that she was separated from her husband and caring for two small children. Plath faced the risks of the passage from home to work alone. The acutely unhappy consciousness of women like Parsons and Plath remained shaded in privacy—a diary, a novel written under a pseudonym, a bell jar.

Most women of their generation would successfully navigate these turgid waters and live to tell quite another story. *The Feminine Mystique*, published in the year of Plath's death, rendered the domestic satire of *The Bell Jar* as a protofeminist manifesto. Graduating from Smith a decade after Friedan and just two years behind Plath was Gloria Steinem. No more sure-footed than her peers through the mysterious minefield of sex, Steinem found herself newly graduated, jobless, pregnant, and contemplating settling down to marry the unwed father. With the prospect of premature domesticity looming before her, she anticipated "going quietly crazy."[131] Gloria Steinem, however, found an abortionist in London, and she did not go crazy. She would go on to champion reproductive rights and call for a wholesale remodeling of gender called women's liberation. If college-educated women were in jeopardy during the domestic tornado of the postwar period, they also enjoyed rare opportunities. Positioned between home and work at a time of major change, and supported by working mothers on the sidelines, they became acutely conscious of the sharp edges of the gender division of labor and the blunt inequities between male and female. Some of them, like Friedan and Steinem, had the political genius to bring these issues into the public arena. Then the changes that millions of anonymous women had made over the last half century would be recognized; patterns of inequity would be discerned; and the "feminine mystique" would become not a description of how women lived, but a summons to social change. By the close of the 1950s, two generations of women, working in tandem, had gotten more than halfway there — from home to work if not to equity.

CHAPTER 6

WHERE DOES SEX DIVIDE?

FEMINISM, SEXUALITY, AND THE STRUCTURES OF GENDER SINCE 1960

In 1994 the American Psychiatric Association added a new malady to its *Diagnostic and Statistical Manual of Mental Disorders*. Code number 302.85 alerted medical practitioners to something called "gender identity disorder," defined as "a strong and persistent cross-gender identification (not merely a desire for any perceived cultural advantages of being the other sex)." Among the symptoms that might trigger such a diagnosis were the "desire to live or be treated as the other sex, or the conviction that he or she has the typical feeling and reactions of the other sex." The American Psychiatric Association delivered a mixed message to anyone who tried to locate the boundary between male and female late in the twentieth century. By employing the term "gender," the learned editors seemed to acknowledge that the difference between male and female was socially constructed and not a simple, unambiguous biological assignment of sex. They conceded as well that significant numbers of human beings did not accept the identity associated with their reproductive anatomy. Yet the psychiatric handbook also alerted mental health professionals that deviations from the biological assignment of gender were pathological and required therapeutic intervention. The professional ruling on this matter was more than an arcane semantic exercise. It prescribed correct ways of doing gender and sought to close debates about the psychological differences between men and women, the mental health of homosexuals, and the legitimacy of defying or altering the physiology of sex.[1]

The concept of "gender identity disorder" registered myriad and fundamental challenges to the conventional meanings of male and female that had been building up throughout the twentieth century and indicated that the unraveling of the modern border between the sexes had accelerated after 1960. The American Psychiatric Association was one of many cultural institutions at work redrawing the line that divided male and female. Sex was transparently mysterious on the eve of a new millennium. As one boundary of sex seemed to blur, others rose up in its place. With such "disorder" along the border between male and female in the late twentieth century, one had to ask: where, exactly, does sex divide?

In the decade of the 1990s it took some concentration to locate the lines of gender difference on college campuses, where coeds had earnestly practiced domestic femininity in the 1950s. From a distance it was hard to distinguish male from female in the parade of blue jeans and backpacks. The mark of masculinity had also faded among the faculty. The ranks of professors, once a seamless expanse of trousers and tweed jackets, were now broken by significant numbers of women, costumed in a variety of gendered or androgynous styles. Even more striking changes took place at professional schools. Women students had increased fivefold among engineers and sixfold among physicians. Over at the law school, the ranks of women had climbed tenfold until they were virtually equal to men. These apprentice lawyers had arrived at an auspicious place, the stepping-stone to positions of political leadership and financial power in America. Were we to interrogate the students of the 1990s, we would learn that men and women had very similar career aspirations: 90 percent of the women and most all of the men expected to spend their adult lives earning their own living and supporting a family. It might appear that the coeds of the class of 2000 had more in common with their male peers than with their foremothers.[2]

Before jumping to extreme conclusions, however, it would be advisable to look beyond the college campus. A glance at the front page of the morning newspaper would reveal that public affairs still looked like man's sphere. If the dateline happened to be September 7, 2000, the front page would present a portrait of gender continuity that was global in scope. That day, over one hundred heads of state had gathered at the United Nations and stopped for a group photo. Only a tiny splash of color, usually painted by the tribal garb of male chieftains from Africa or the Middle East, speckled the long lines of dark suits. On close count, only seven women (only one of whom proclaimed her gender with a bright blue suit) could be found hidden in the ranks of world leaders. A glance at the business page or a listing of the chief executive officers of the Fortune 500 would yield a similar picture. The changes so visible among the young and on college campuses had not yet percolated up to the ranks of the rich and powerful.

Gender continuity also lurked in the recesses of the private sphere. Wives and mothers still did more than their share of washing, ironing, dishes, and diapers. And in the suburbs, the signs of feminine domesticity had been inflated: Mom now conducted her parental role not in a station wagon but in an obese mode of transportation called a sport-utility vehicle. Yet the intrepid mothers of the new century also had a rate of labor force participation that was fast approaching that of fathers. If an American woman had some assistance in shouldering her double burden, it was often another woman pioneer, a cleaning lady or nanny who had journeyed into domestic service from outside the borders of the United States. A perspicacious observer who tallied up these alterations in the meaning of male and female would note that women were the major innovators. One might wonder if men, be they presidents or husbands, weren't relatively complacent bystanders, resting in their time-honored places while women created a dazzling whirlwind of change along the old gender divide. At the close of the twentieth century, great expectations glimmered amid the mysteries of sex. Was it possible that the asymmetry between male and female would diminish enough to alter the balance of power between men and women and quiet the battle of the sexes?

This chapter gathers together a panoply of changes in the meaning of male and female and arranges them into three strands of recent history. First in order of appearance (but not necessarily in analytical significance) is the dramatic emergence and powerful historical course of a second wave of feminism. Should this chapter end here, it would already have charted a major transformation in how the differences between men and women were imagined and organized. The challenges to gender conventions were only beginning, however. Almost simultaneous with the women's liberation movement, another gender debate began to rage: a contest over the meaning and practice of human sexuality, initiated by gays and lesbians. The second section of this chapter will recount how the movement for homosexual rights posed a public challenge to the normative relations of the sexes and ultimately subverted the distinction between male and female itself. These powerful social movements did not emerge from thin air; they were buoyed by transformations in the basic structuring of gender that will be described in the final section of this chapter. (An account of a fourth historical source of gender change, a powerful wave of immigration into the United States, will be reserved for another chapter.) These fundamental rearrangements of all the coordinates of gender (asymmetry, the relations of the sexes, and hierarchy) were getting underway in the 1960s and had acquired enough coherence by the year 2000 to justify a declaration of the end of the modern gender regime. Yet the course of male and female into the future remains uncharted and warrants only the tentative label, postmodern.

The Second Wave of Feminism
1960–1970

Women were the first to foment the gender disorder that would become chronic by century's end. In 1969 an advance guard of a new feminist movement took their rebellion to the steps of the Pentagon as part of a protest against the American war in Vietnam. This contingent of young women was a radical crowd. Like their male peers, they openly defied the cherished traditions of their forefathers and foremothers. While young men announced their opposition to the war by burning draft cards, the brigade of women registered their contempt for the political establishment by surrendering their voter registration cards. In callow ignorance of their feminist heritage, they actually invited aging representatives of the woman suffrage movement to preside as they gave back the right to vote. Only in hindsight would these feminist ingenues recognize the unique historical moment they occupied. They stood on the shoulders of the suffrage movement and beside their own mothers, positioned for a feminist assault on the boundary of sex.[3]

The younger generation, the leaders of what would be called "women's liberation," were largely oblivious to the tradition of women's activism that preceded them and to which they were in fact indebted. The National Woman's Party had maintained its vigil in Washington for over forty years; year after year it diligently placed the Equal Rights Amendment before Congress. Indefatigable female organizers also clung to office in the trade unions, where they tenaciously fought for gender equity and devised innovative feminist proposals for child care and comparable pay. Venerable women's organizations like the League of Women Voters, the Association of Business and Professional Women, and the American Association of University Women were fixtures on the civic landscape of most cities. Members of mainstream organizations like the Young Women's Christian Association (YWCA) and the American Friends Service Committee worked through the 1940s and 1950s for racial equality and formed alliances with African American women. The women's associations of the Friends, for example, formed an interracial "Committee of Community Leadership" that was already in place when the Supreme Court ruled against segregated schools in 1954. Within eight days this unassuming women's group had mobilized to integrate the schools of Washington, D.C. African American women maintained their stalwart position in the black public sphere, where they stood up for both their race and their sex. Pauli Murray of the National Association for the Advancement of Colored People (NAACP) made it known that her dedication to the civil rights

WOMEN REMAKE GENDER

movement was a campaign not just against racism but against what she called "Jane Crow," or the "prejudice against sex." In Montgomery, Alabama, a demure English professor named Jo Ann Gibson Robinson founded an organization called simply the Women's Political Council. The organization worked tenaciously behind the scenes to prepare another seasoned activist named Rosa Parks to challenge segregation on the city's buses.[4]

While women's social activism and gender consciousness survived through the 1950s, it seldom tampered with the conventional divide between the sexes. An ad hoc group calling itself Women Strike for Peace will illustrate. In the early 1960s an estimated fifty thousand women participated in this action protesting the arms race, nuclear testing, and its effects on the atmosphere. Women Strike for Peace played a major role in enacting a ban on nuclear testing in 1961 but did not pose their actions as a feminist offensive. To the contrary, they used feminine stereotypes to promote the cause of peace. Dressed up like model housewives, they appeared before the House Un-American Activities Committee and countered the charge of communism with a rhetorical salvo of roses, baby carriages, and mothers' milk. They acted not in the name of women's rights, much less women's liberation, but to protect their children from nuclear fallout. African American women wore similar sheep's clothing when they battled for civil rights. The civil rights organizers of Montgomery, Alabama, chose Rosa Parks to challenge the segregation of public transportation in part because of her ladylike appearance and demeanor. Through the 1950s, most women pursued their various humanitarian goals without crossing gender boundaries.[5]

This surface of gender conformity began to crack slightly early in the 1960s. The first major public breakthrough was actually a defensive maneuver on the part of the John F. Kennedy administration, the first in almost thirty years that failed to appoint a single woman to the cabinet. By way of apology to women's groups, Kennedy established the Commission on the Status of Women and staffed it with veteran reformers. Eleanor Roosevelt was the titular head of the commission; the organization's day-to-day direction was given over to Esther Peterson, who after decades of dedication to women workers was serving as director of the Women's Bureau. A staunch supporter of protective legislation, Peterson opposed the individualistic feminism of her nemesis Alice Paul, the indefatigable proponent of the Equal Rights Amendment. The civil rights movement injected some new ideas and energy into the Kennedy commission, particularly from veteran activist Pauli Murray.[6]

Although the commission's report, issued in 1963, was timid in tone and moderate in its recommendations, it did accomplish two important tasks. First, under Murray's expert legal guidance, the long-standing rift between the protectionist wing of the women's movement and the individualistic proponents of the Equal Rights Amendment was smoothed over, if not mended. Although the commission did not endorse the Equal Rights Amendment directly, it recommended a legal remedy for gender inequity that Murray had learned in the civil rights movement: appeal to the due process and equal protection clause of the Fourteenth Amendment. Second, the commission did not disband once its official bureaucratic task was completed. Rather, it continued to operate at the state level and to hold ad hoc national meetings. By the 1960s, mainstream, politically savvy women were linked to one another in a loose but extensive network, dedicated to examining the social status of their sex.[7]

That network and the protofeminist consciousness it kindled were at the ready when the issue of sexual inequality was raised before the U.S. Congress in 1964. The occasion was the debate on the Civil Rights Bill, which would create a commission on equal economic opportunity authorized to enforce prohibitions of racial discrimination. Relatively late in the congressional deliberations, the bill was amended to outlaw discrimination on the basis of sex as well. One interpretation had it that this addition was the ploy of conservative congressman Howard Smith, who calculated that the proposal to enforce sexual equality was so preposterous that it would undermine the whole bill. What actually transpired was much more complex and proactive. In fact, women from Alice Paul to Esther Peterson to Pauli Murray were very serious about adding the sex provision. And every member of the small contingent of women in Congress, led by Martha Griffiths, stood up, spoke out, and voted to uphold the principle of sexual equality. Still, the intrusion of gender issues into mainstream American politics was largely unheralded and somewhat apologetic. Esther Peterson, for example, was reluctant to enforce the sex provision, reasoning, like Radical Republicans a century before, that this was the African American's and not the woman's hour.[8]

Ordinary working women were not always so timid or as self-effacing. Within months of the bill's passage, the Equal Economic Opportunity Commission (EEOC) received more than two thousand complaints from women workers. In fact, over one-quarter of all complaints were made on the grounds of sex discrimination. Some of these complainants, like Alice Peurala, who worked at United States Steel Corporation for over twenty years, had been harboring a sense of injustice since the Second World War. When Peurala got word of the sex provision of Civil Rights Act, she thought, "here's my chance."

When the EEOC was reluctant to act on complaints like this, the former com-missioners on the status of women stepped into the breach. Meeting in Wash-ington, they determined that the EEOC was not about to enforce the sex clause of the Civil Rights Act without some concerted outside pressure. Accordingly, as the story goes, a small group of women politicians gathered in the hotel room of Betty Friedan, put pen to a paper napkin, and drafted the preamble for the National Organization for Women (NOW). They pledged "to take action needed to bring women into the mainstream of American society now with full equality of women in equal partnership with men."[9]

NOW's statement of goals, however conciliatory its tone and legalistic its reform priorities, partook of the incipient radicalism of the time. It called not for a single reform but for wholesale and wide-ranging gender equality. It dismissed the basic asymmetry between the sexes that had been the mark of modern gender with these words: "We reject the current assumption that a man must carry the sole burden of supporting himself, his wife and family . . . or that marriage, home and family are primarily woman's world and re-sponsibility—hers to dominate, his to support. We believe that a true part-nership . . . demands . . . an equitable sharing of the responsibilities of home and children and of the economic burdens of their support. . . . To these ends we will seek to open a reexamination of laws and mores governing marriage and divorce." Although the founders of NOW presented themselves as main-stream and middle class, they promptly endorsed a feminist agenda that was radical by comparison with both the women's reform groups of the past and contemporary gender culture. By 1970, NOW endorsed equal pay, the right to abortion, the public provision of day care, the rights of lesbians, and claims to justice by all races and classes of women. In a crisp professional tone, ad-dressed to middle-class Americans, the women and men of NOW had opened the first front of a new challenge to the customary ways of doing gender. They moved forward in a temperate manner, building on their professional experi-ence and distinctive political talents, to create a new feminism.[10]

The younger generation was not totally unaware of the stirrings of femi-nism among their elders. Many college students and those who were forming a radical political consciousness in the civil rights and antiwar movements had read Betty Friedan's *Feminine Mystique*, sometimes at the suggestion of their mothers. But the young Turks of the 1960s initially dismissed NOW as a bourgeois reform, a tale from the suburbs not fit for the trenches of their youthful rebellion. The search for the origins of this younger, more irrever-ent wing of the new feminism has taken historians to out-of-the-way places, deep in the American South. In 1964, not so long after Anne Parsons and

Sylvia Plath confided their despair to their diaries, another young, educated white woman tried to put her discomfort with her gender role into words. "When it came time to sit down at the typewriter," she later reported, "I was shaken with doubt. The issue was enormous. I was afraid. The reaction, I was convinced, would be one of ridicule." The tremulous author was Mary King, daughter of a Virginia minister, a graduate of Ohio Wesleyan University, a member of the Student Nonviolent Coordinating Committee (SNCC), and a veteran of the grueling and dangerous campaign to enroll African Americans in the voting registries of Mississippi. She could not bring herself to sign her name—neither could her friend and coauthor, Casey Hayden—to a list of eleven everyday inequities experienced by women in SNCC. This guarded protest was prefixed with apologies, submitted anonymously, and premised on timorous expectations: "Maybe the only thing that can come out of this paper is discussion—amidst the laughter—but still discussion. . . . And maybe sometime in the future the whole of the women in this movement will become so alert as to force the rest of the movement to stop the discrimination and start the slow process of changing values and ideas so that all of us gradually come to understand that this is no more a man's world than it is a white world."[11]

"Only," "slow," "gradual," "maybe," "some time in the future": These are not the brash words of radical agitators. King recalled, "I can never forget how lonely I felt in putting that paper out and how afraid I was of derision." The derision, and a smattering of positive responses from men and women, soon got lost in the struggle for racial equality in Mississippi. A year later, however, as white women and men were becoming marginalized within the civil rights struggle, King and Hayden took the time to translate that list of grievances into a political manifesto. Still tentative in tone and low in expectations, this document presented a cogent and radical social analysis. The authors converted those everyday inequities into evidence of a fundamental social structure, what they called the "Sex-Caste System," complete with an arbitrary division of labor, a questionable biological determinism, and a political geography that extended from personal relations to public politics. Two young civil rights workers issued an appeal in the name of women to "see basic human problems (which are now seen as private troubles) as public human problems."[12]

Mary King and Casey Hayden had translated what Friedan had called "a problem with no name" into a succinct social and political theory whose central clauses anticipated both the signature slogan of the new wave of femi-

WOMEN REMAKE GENDER

nism—"the personal is political"—and its core concept, "gender." This second memo was sent out along the circuit of the student movement, from SNCC to the Students for a Democratic Society (SDS) and the National Student Association. Printed in the SDS newsletter of December 1965, the memo provoked discussion in New Left circles across the country and led directly to the formation of a separate politically gendered space, a "women's caucus" at the national meeting of this seminal New Left group. In April of the next year, the memo was printed again in the journal *Liberation*. Soon, a summons to "women's liberation" spread beyond the New Left, took hold along the whole network of college campuses, and gave rise to small coteries called "consciousness-raising groups," which would be the seedlings of an altogether new form of gender politics.[13]

The gender consciousness that Mary King and Casey Hayden had wrenched with such effort from their struggles in the civil rights movement was not the single source of the women's liberation movement. The mass feminist movement that spread across the country in the 1970s was fed by many underground springs of discontent and by many political forces. On the other hand, in less auspicious times those memos would have been left to gather dust in the archives along with the relics of other local political groups. Conversely, in those fertile times, if not Mary King and Casey Hayden, then one of their countless, nameless peers, if not the civil rights movement, then another campus group, say, the peace movement, or perhaps even the conservative Young Americans for Freedom, might have broken the silence about gender inequity. Although hardly the single source of the second wave of feminism, this well-told story, coming out of the South in the middle of the 1960s, is a dramatic illustration of how feminism was rekindled in many places at one momentous time. It records a moment of rupture in gender history when young women braved uncharted territory and determined to take an active, collective hand in redrawing the border of sex.[14]

Like any momentous historical event, the causes of this powerful second wave of feminism can be traced back ad infinitum. Mary King's biography, for example, points back to a grandfather who insisted on a college education for his daughters and a Presbyterian father's commitment to the congregational democracy of Puritan ancestors. Selective studies reveal that most feminists of King's generation came from families who upheld a liberal-to-left social conscience and encouraged their daughters to excel in school. But at the same time, three-quarters of the new feminists grew up with conventional gender aspirations. After college they expected to marry and perhaps pursue a "fallback" career as a teacher. They rarely observed a woman in a position of professional stature and societal power who could model higher aspirations or inspire bolder dreams.[15]

The founders of women's liberation often drew inspiration from outside the American mainstream. Hayden and King found their feminist muse in the civil rights movement. Be it in northern cities or the rural South, white women activists drew inspiration from African American women who assumed a powerful status in their communities and who seemed immune to the blandishments of the feminine mystique. At ground zero in the Student Nonviolent Coordinating Committee, that inspiration was personified by the indomitable Ella Baker. When Mary King met Baker, she was executive secretary of the Southern Christian Leadership Conference (SCLC) and had over twenty years' experience in civil rights work with such groups as the YWCA, NAACP, and the Congress of Racial Equality (CORE). Miss Baker, as she was always respectfully addressed, was tactically and temperamentally more radical than the SCLC's president, Martin Luther King Jr., and it was she who championed the student radicals who sat in at the Greensboro, North Carolina, lunch counter in 1960 in direct, open defiance of Jim Crow. Ella Baker advised the young radicals to form SNCC, an independent organization outside the hierarchical structure of SCLC. This unique organization, whose membership was composed of both races and both genders, provided women like King and Hayden, as well as young African American heroines of civil rights like Diane Nash and Ruby Doris Smith Robinson, the space in which to develop into political leaders themselves.[16]

They were not alone among their gender. In the early stages of the civil rights movement, women were relatively well represented in the loose leadership structure of groups like SNCC. Such gender parity had not been seen for over a century, not since male and female, black and white, joined the ranks of another consequential reform institution, the American Antislavery Society. This political conjuncture proved to be the crucible of a new feminist consciousness. It provided women an unprecedented sense of political efficacy, followed by a bracing dose of gender subordination. That fateful memo said it graphically: "Consider why it is in SNCC that women who are competent, qualified, and experienced are automatically assigned to the 'female' kind of jobs such as typing, desk work, telephone work, field work, library work, cooking, and the assistant kind of administrative work but rarely the 'executive' kind." These contradictions were hardly unique to small coteries in the southern civil rights movement. They also arose in the community organizing projects undertaken by SDS in the North, in regional student

　　WOMEN REMAKE GENDER

rebellions like the Free Speech Movement at the University of California, Berkeley, and at encampments of Peace Corps workers around the world; that is, wherever groups of idealistic young men and men set about to right the world.[17]

In these liminal spaces, young, politically energized women became critically conscious of their gender predicament. Building their politics up from their experiences as women, the pioneers of women's liberation came to see patterns of inequality in their everyday life. King and Hayden were the first to articulate the pattern of inequity between male and female and attempt to give it a name. King recalled, "Having deeply internalized Ella Baker's lesson that the oppressed themselves must define their own freedom, I felt I could not allow the civil rights movement to overlook fundamental questions that remain unanswered by our and other movements' protest, conflicts and revolution: Who defines what it is to be a woman? Why must women form a second class? Who decides whether men or women are superior or inferior? Who determines the validity of another's existence?" Suddenly all the mysteries of sex loomed up in the consciousness of women like Mary King. Almost overnight a new movement generated a full agenda. The July 1967 issue of *New Left Notes* printed women's demands for communal child care (available for twenty-four hours a day, no less), free abortions, shared housework, and the abolition of racism and imperialism. Then, for good measure, they asserted, "We demand that our brothers recognize that they must deal with their own male chauvinism in their personal social and political relationships."[18]

The sudden proliferation of the term "chauvinism" (borrowed from left-wing politics of 1930s vintage) was one example of the centrifugal political force of women's liberation. Where there once was no name, a full vocabulary came into being: there was "male chauvinism," "sexism," "male supremacy." Quickly, even before 1970, radical women had strained for and grasped a terminology capable not just of expressing their grievances but also interrogating the very process that created woman in the first place. Hayden and King, who had pored over Simone de Beauvoir's *Second Sex* and recognized the power of her assertion that woman was made and not born, adopted the term "sex/caste" for this purpose. Others called up analogues to colonialism or internal imperialism. Shulamith Firestone called Marx and Freud to the project of women's liberation and came up with the term "dialectic of sex." It was not until 1975 that the word "gender" came into wide usage among feminists. An essay by Gayle Rubin, a young graduate student in anthropology, coined the term "Sex/Gender System" and marked out the territory that would consume feminist intellectuals for a generation. The explosion of the new language and concepts of women's liberation around the year 1970 marked a critical break with the women's politics of the past. Women's liberation burst out of the social movements of the 1960s, demanding a wholesale revolution in human thought and behavior.[19]

The embryonic feminist ideology matched societal breadth with personal depth. The slogan "the personal is political," dated 1968 and attributed to Carol Hanisch, encapsulated multiple meanings. First, it identified a set of issues that had been taboo in movements past. The contents listed on the cheap newsprint cover of the 1969 movement classic *Notes from the Second Year* bared it all: "housework," "love," and that classic, "the myth of the vaginal orgasm." The personal issues ranged through sexuality (orgasms, lesbianism, monogamy), human emotions (love, anger, and self-esteem), reproductive biology (test tube babies, obstetric practice, abortion), and everyday domestic matters (housework, child care, and the altitude of the toilet seat cover). To assert that such commonplace matters were political conveyed three principles, each of which cut incisively through American gender culture. First, it articulated the method whereby women's liberation developed a political agenda: the intensive and critical discussion of "personal" problems would reveal the predicaments that women shared and thereby identify the social problems that required a political remedy. Second, personal politics asserted that these issues, no matter how private they might seem, should be discussed and adjudicated publicly. Finally, to say that the personal is political is to contend that differences in power were lodged in the most intimate relations between men and women. This third radical postulate was given the name "sexual politics" in 1970, in a book bearing that title written by Kate Millet. This audacious signature of a new breed of feminism challenged the power of men as a gender wherever it was exerted, in the movement, at home, at work, at the statehouse.

Gathered in small groups exclusively of their own sex, women's liberationists summoned anger as a solvent for oppressive personal relations with men, abandoned the very language and pronouns and names of their early lives, and dismissed structures of authority in family, nation, and bed.[20] By 1970, tense relations between the sexes were churning beneath the surface of American politics and forming eddies of rising consciousness all across America. The rising tide of women's liberation crested first in the major universities and urban areas: fifty women's liberation groups had surfaced in New York by 1967, thirty in the San Francisco Bay area, another thirty in Chi-

The cover of *Notes from the Second Year*, 1969. (Author's copy)

cago, twenty-five in Boston. Soon, smaller cities were caught up in the second wave. Columbus, Ohio, near the campus of Ohio State University, had reaped all the fruits of consciousness-raising by 1970: rape crisis centers, abortion clinics, women's studies centers, battered women's shelters, music festivals, and auto mechanic classes for women.[21]

Mainstream feminism and women's liberation may have had different generational roots, but they germinated almost simultaneously. The first women's caucus in the New Left and the founding of NOW occurred within weeks of one another.[22] Yet, as of the early 1970s the two fronts of feminism combined enrolled only a small fraction of American women. NOW's membership was 5,800 in 1971, and women's liberation events never drew crowds of more than a few thousand people, none of whom held membership cards at all.[23] Yet the volume of their feminist voices belied their small numbers. By 1975, the majority of all Americans had heard the call of a new feminism, and almost two-thirds of them, men and women alike, endorsed the general principles on which the fledgling movement was founded.[24] The rising feminist consciousness leapt over the boundaries of race. Prominent African American women like Pauli Murray, Fannie Lou Hamer, and Shirley Chisolm were early members of NOW. A Third World Women's Alliance formed in the same year. A year later, in 1971, Mexican American women formed a caucus within the Chicano Student Movement. Meanwhile, women from forty-three tribes formed the North American Indian Women's Association.[25]

The velocity with which the feminist message spread was due in part to the brilliant theatrics of the "women's libbers." Privileged children that they were, the young radical women knew how to get adult attention. Leaders like Robin Morgan, who had acted in a television sitcom as a child, also knew something about the power of mass communication, or what was becoming known as "the media." In 1968 "women's lib" broke into prime time with an outrageous prank, a protest at the Miss America pageant in Atlantic City. This tactic was guaranteed to create photo opportunities: newspaper portraits of young women carrying giant zaftig cardboard figures, captioned "Miss America is a big Falsie," or a trash bin full of cosmetics, stiletto heels, and other items said to transform women into something they called "sex objects." Even if a brassiere was not actually burned on this occasion, such public theater made for very captivating footage on the evening news and spread the word of women's lib far and wide in record time.[26]

The radical theatricality of women's liberation went full tilt as the 1960s drew to a close. In February 1969, amid the frenzy of the cultural revolution, one New York consciousness-raising group staged a demonstration at a bridal fair. They arrived to "Confront the whore makers," carrying slogans like "always a bride never a person" and "here comes the bribe." Another group called WITCH (the acronym for "Women's International Conspiracy from Hell") recited these "unwedding" vows:

> We are gathered together here in the spirit of our passion to affirm, love and initiate our freedom from the unholy state of American patriarchal oppressors. We promise to love cherish and groove on each other and on all living things. We promise to smash the alienated family unit. We promise not to obey. We promise this through highs and bummers in recognition that riches and objects are totally available through socialism or theft. We promise these things until choice do us part. In the name of our sisters and brothers everywhere. In the name of the Revolution we pronounce ourselves free human beings.[27]

In a not-too-distant morning-after, new wave feminists would come to regret some of their more outrageous pranks, particularly those that showed insensitivity to the values of many of the women they sought to enroll in their cause. Nonetheless, these flamboyant tactics proved to be a highly effective form of cultural politics, capable of alerting masses of Americans to the discontent among their daughters. Some media-savvy women worked to publish feminism through more conventional channels. One group of Manhattan feminists took the cause to the office of John Carter, editor of the *Ladies' Home Journal*, in midtown Manhattan. They presented a set of demands that included Carter's replacement by a woman editor and reputedly denied him bathroom privileges during the negotiations. The militants left with an agreement to issue a fifteen-page supplement titled "New Feminism" to an upcoming issue. This feminist offensive was repeated in offices across town and around the nation but usually followed a more businesslike protocol. Eighty women writing for the *New York Times* presented the management with a petition in 1972, along with an exhibit of the paper's discriminatory practices in hiring, promoting, and paying women. When their complaints were ignored, they filed a class action suit on behalf of 550 employees and forced the *Times* to concede discrimination, grant compensation, and draw up a plan of affirmative action. Protests occurred simultaneously at the major news magazines, where women writers were consigned to the rank of "researcher" and denied the bylines and higher salaries of similarly qualified men. Then, in 1972 Gloria Steinem took the helm of a magazine of women's own and called it *Ms.* It would ultimately achieve a circulation of 400,000 to 500,000 and an estimated readership of 3 million. With remarkable speed, the young women, educated in the techniques of the nascent information age, were taking their expanding consciousness to a mass audience.[28]

The same fertile period spawned new feminist institutions within the senior faction of the nascent movement. The first new crop of women's organizations in fifty years, groups like NOW, the National Women's Political Caucus, and Women's Equity Action League raised the feminist membership lists to 100,000 by 1973. Combined with seasoned activists from the American Association of University Women, the League of Women Voters, and the National Federation of Business and Professional Women's Clubs, organized feminism became a formidable political constituency.[29] By 1971 women's ranks among the official delegates to the Democratic National Convention had tripled until they constituted 40 percent of those who would nominate a presidential candidate. Republican women were not far behind, constituting 30 percent of convention delegates. Women also began to break through the barriers to public office that had remained in place fifty years after suffrage. Within a decade, they occupied a third of the positions on school boards and 13 percent of state legislatures, and they had begun to take up the position of mayor in major cities. The women's caucus of the U.S. Congress linked men and women in support of the basic feminist agenda. Commissions on the Status of Women were in place in forty-nine of fifty states by 1973.[30]

Policy changes followed swiftly from this political mobilization. NOW's first project, to abolish the sex segregation of "help wanted" ads, was quickly enacted. Women won basic economic rights in rapid succession: for the first time, they could establish credit in their own names, open mortgages, and be admitted to exclusive clubs and male spaces (from the elegant Oak Room at the Plaza Hotel to the funky McSorley's pub in lower Manhattan). In 1972 the long dormant, once controversial Equal Rights Amendment passed Congress with a resounding majority. It was propelled out of committee and into legislation by support from the grass roots and direct lobbying by sundry feminist associations newly installed in Washington, D.C. The same political forces went into action against powerful lobbyists to push through Title IX of the Civil Rights Act, which outlawed sex discrimination in education, including college athletic departments. Two years later, the same pressure came very close to holding the federal government responsible for child care. A bill appropriating federal funds for this purpose, and defying sacred principles about the private sphere and the sexual division of labor, actually passed Congress in 1974, but by too small a margin to override the veto of President Richard Nixon. While the Supreme Court of the land was not amenable to such direct popular pressure, it too fell in line with the rising feminist con-

WOMEN REMAKE GENDER

sciousness, most notably by protecting women's right to abortion. The road to this decision was paved by local radical groups like the Jane Collective in Chicago, which delivered hundreds of illegal abortions annually, and grassroots activists like Patricia McGinnis in California, who arranged abortions in Mexico, lobbied the legislature in Sacramento, and formed the Society for Humane Abortion. In this atmosphere, the 1973 Supreme Court's decision in *Roe v. Wade* was both imaginable and politically tenable.[31]

The rapid takeoff of the second wave of feminism in the early 1970s was propelled by a compound of policy experience and youthful energy. Legislative success correlated directly with publicity-grabbing events staged by feminists. Still, the ranks of card-carrying women's liberationists were small. NOW remained the largest organization, enrolling 55,000 members in 1977 and 200,000 by 1982.[32] Much of the tensile strength that underlay women's political clout in the 1970s was lodged in other organized bodies. The Equal Rights Amendment was ushered through Congress, for example, after the AFL-CIO was pushed by its female membership and leadership to finally withdraw its opposition. Reforms like affirmative action and Title IX gained credibility when they were endorsed not just by NOW but by established concentrations of woman power such as the Girl Scouts, the American Association of University Women, and the United Methodist Church. Feminism welled up in these established associations at the same time that it spawned new ones. Planned Parenthood paired with the National Abortion Rights Action League; the National Association of Colored Women was joined by the National Welfare Rights Organization; and the American Association of University Women welcomed women's caucuses in nearly every profession. While unions like the American Federation of Municipal, State, and County Employees adopted a feminist agenda, the founders of the Coalition of Labor Union Women provided a feminist link between the different flanks of organized labor. This broad organizational reach, coupled with the long institutional history of many women's groups, gave a steady keel to the feminist course through the American political process. Called "new institutional feminism" by one political scientist, this species of activism could be found in such unlikely places as the U.S. Army and the Catholic Church.[33]

Call it an irresistible wave, a raging brush fire, or a grassroots movement, feminism had reached the masses by the middle of the 1970s. The breadth, diversity, and multiple facets of the new gender politics warrant speaking of feminisms in the plural. Yet the welling up of critical gender politics from so many sources at almost the same moment in time also bespeaks a remarkable historical convergence, the birth of a "feminist mass movement." Those three words denote an extremely rare phenomenon. By some calculations, a bona fide mass feminist movement had at that point arisen in only two times and places, in the United States and the Netherlands, both in the 1970s. The new gender politics met the criteria for "feminism" because it set out not just to ameliorate the condition of women but to challenge the whole process of assigning social status according to sex. One can detect such a gender ideology as early as the 1910s, but (as will be recalled from chapter 5) those early bohemian feminists were only a small fragile coterie, hardly a social "movement." To qualify as such, feminism would have to take root in multiple different locations and constituencies, which in the aggregate could effect broad social and political change. Finally, that term "mass," an elastic reference to the volume of consciousness and actions around feminist issues, was fulfilled by every measurement of public opinion in the mid-1970s. By 1975, no less than 80 percent of Americans were aware of feminism, and a slim majority actually registered support for its basic proposition of gender equality.[34]

The new wave of feminism swept through American politics and culture in less than a decade. The accomplishment was capped in 1977 with the meeting of the National Women's Conference in Houston, a kind of coming-out party for feminism as a political force to be reckoned with. The conference was instigated in the U.S. House of Representatives, where Congresswomen Bella Abzug, Patsy Mink, and Margaret Heckler secured a small appropriation to fund a kind of women's parliament. Delegates were chosen in constituent assemblies, state by state, and then gathered in Houston to endorse twenty-five planks of a "National Plan of Action" that ran the whole gamut of the women's liberation agenda: child care, welfare rights, the Equal Rights Amendment, reproductive choice, and justice and dignity for all women, including the poor, racial minorities, and lesbians. With its maturation into the mainstream of democratic politics, feminism also had to stand up to wide public scrutiny. An opposition began to form outside the Houston convention hall, which would become a well-organized right-wing challenge. For now, the opposition was a sign that feminism had come of age and had taken its place at the rough-and-tumble center of American politics.[35]

This momentous event in the history of gender—the emergence of a feminist mass movement—requires a powerful historical explanation. The historical actors encountered so far in this chapter—members of the civil rights movement, the New Left, and mainstream women's groups—however heroic, cannot carry the whole weight of a historical event of such magnitude and rarity. The velocity with which the first articulations of a feminist consciousness engulfed public opinion makes it difficult, in fact, to distinguish leaders from followers, causes from effects. Something in the general condition of American womanhood in the late 1960s and early 1970s shouted out the need for change. A quick review of the flash points of feminist consciousness suggests that many conditions for a feminist offensive were already in play by the middle of the 1960s. That peculiar dialectic of feminism that Mary King experienced in SNCC wafted through many women's places in the mid-1960s: the research staff at *Newsweek*, the seniority lists at U.S. Steel, the housewife ranks of the peace movement. In a wide range of situations, not the least of which was that mushrooming female sector of the labor force, women were experiencing the simultaneous sense of competence and constriction that formed the dialectic of feminism.

Perhaps the most strategic location of rising feminist consciousness was the American college campus. The proportion of women in U.S. colleges had gone from a low of 30 percent after World War II to over 40 percent in the 1960s; by century's end, women would occupy the majority of seats in college classrooms, most of them at coeducational institutions of higher learning. The mixing of the sexes on campus was becoming a mass experience for the first time in American history. At the same time that college women were expanding their knowledge, sharpening their skills, and getting A's, they were receiving little encouragement from an overwhelmingly male faculty. At times, professors actively discouraged their women students from pursuing professional careers. Other gender grievances were developing outside the classroom. Archaic practices like curfews imposed on women but not men generated some of the earliest battles along the boundaries of sex. They led first to the release of coeds from protective custody and then to the integration of dormitories. The late 1960s also brought changes in sexual practices. Rates of premarital sexuality began to increase along with the wide availability of reliable birth control in the form of oral contraceptives. Yet, here too, new freedom and high expectations were also accompanied by frustration and awareness of the underside of sexual freedom for women: the double standard, the objectification of the female body, the lack of reproductive rights, the high incidence of date rape. In bed, in the classroom, and in the social movement young women experienced the same dialectic: new opportunities and enhanced confidence butted up against the continuing barriers to women's freedom, equality, and pursuit of happiness.[36]

The college campus, like the civil rights movement, was only one of multiple sites where this feminist dialectic unfolded in the 1960s. All were part of a general shift in the geography of gender. Whether down South working for civil rights, away at college, or off to work, adult women were spending less time within the family and more time outside the jurisdiction of either parents or husbands. The census of 1970 recorded this lacuna in the family cycle as the growing proportion of "primary individuals": the significant portion of the population who lived alone or in households composed entirely of unrelated persons. Many of these women were widows, aging flappers continuing their independent course through history, but many others were their granddaughters, who took youthful self-reliance up a notch.[37] They had left their parental homes and remained unmarried. With more education, more sexual autonomy, and more independence from nuclear families, the children of the baby boom entered a space and time of relative gender anomaly. As they left school or home and joined the labor force, women also encountered the negative side of the gender dialectic. The late 1960s and 1970s were a low point in pay equity for women. The recent college graduate would find that, on the average, she made less than a male with just a high school diploma.

Literally millions of anonymous women experienced these structural dislocations that set the feminist dialectic in motion. The wholesale expansion of the female labor force is perhaps the most basic causal factor in the rise of feminism. It touched the majority of American women at some time, in some way. The rates of gainful employment outside the home that had been rising steadily throughout the twentieth century accelerated more rapidly in the late 1960s and 1970s, especially among educated, middle-class wives. Already in 1963, Betty Friedan had spied an advance guard of these middle-aged married women returning to school, assuming volunteer positions in their communities, and reentering the paid labor force. Offices of continuing education, established in the 1950s with the intent of utilizing female labor power to compete with Soviet Russia, quickly became hotbeds of feminism. Older married women who were making the move from home to work, no less than the young graduates, encountered the simultaneous rewards and frustrations of entering the labor force. Their earnings hovered in the range of sixty cents or less for every dollar earned by men. Should they join a union like the Amalgamated Clothing Workers, for example, they would find that over 60 percent of the workers but only 15 percent of the officials were female. The major jobs available to women were in the pink-collar ghetto, ill paid and over 95 percent female. No wonder, then, that one feminist principle quickly won widespread support: equal pay for equal work. Because the standard of fairness was violated in the personal experience of so many women, young and old, married and single, it became the staple grist for the feminist mill. Women's caucuses quickly sprouted up among clerical, professional, service, and manual workers.[38]

The dialectic of feminism operated at home as well as work during the 1960s and 1970s. At the same time that recent high school and college graduates experienced the heightened consciousness of living suspended between their parental household and their own conjugal families, their mothers were also stretched "between two worlds." Discouraged from pursuing careers of any sort in the 1950s, the educated women who returned to work in the late 1960s and 1970s were subject to discrimination in the labor force and an unfair share of work at home. Middle-aged mothers, like their youthful daughters, were primed for feminism. One returning worker said of the women's movement, "It saved my life. It explained so much of what had happened in my life. It explained my unhappiness at home when being told there was something wrong with me." Another described the synchronization of labor force reentry and feminist revival this way: it "made it easier for me to do what I am doing. It is as though I am not the only person in the world who is telling their family, 'Look now. What I have to do is important and you guys just hang tight there.'" Another wife and mother thanked the women's movement for assuring her that in going back to work she "was not fighting the tide."[39]

The late 1960s and early 1970s witnessed both a breakthrough of feminism and a breakout from families. With rates of singleness, divorce, and unwed births all on the rise, the grip of the family on a woman's life course loosened. As daughters went off to college, mothers returned to the labor force. As daughters remained single, mothers divorced. Mother and daughter could even act as mutual provocateurs, changing their lives at about the same chronological moment. This dual revolution, enacted simultaneously by two generations of ordinary women, was reflected politically in the synchronous development of women's liberation and NOW. This historical conjuncture sent a powerful wave of feminist energy crashing against the divide of sex.

Sexual Revolution and Gay Rights

The new feminism was not the only powerful force laying siege to the border of gender in the late twentieth century. Movements for sexual freedom and homosexual rights emerged at virtually the same time and delivered a second jolting blow to the modern gender system. While feminism targeted the asymmetrical roles assigned to males and females, movements of sexual liberation challenged the conventional organization of the second major axis of gender, the relations of the sexes. The coupling of individual males and females, in corporal desire, reproduction, family, and kinship, is the Gordian knot of dualistic gender systems. If the heterosexual bond should come undone, it could critically weaken the whole gender order. If male and female became independent, socially and erotically, gender asymmetry and hierarchy, as well as heterosexuality, might be undermined.

This radical potential of sexual change became apparent with the first excited eruptions of the new feminism. Anne Koedt proclaimed it in 1970 with the classic women's liberation essay, "The Myth of the Vaginal Orgasm." A potent mixture of clinical research, countercultural experimentation, and the irreverent politics of the New Left, Koedt's manifesto exploded the heterosexual assumptions that had long dominated popular psychology. The subversion began with a simple report on research published by William Masters and Virginia Johnson in 1966. By demonstrating that the most intense orgasmic pleasure centered in the clitoris, not the vagina, Masters and Johnson challenged the model of female sexuality set up by Freud. According to the Freudian script, the pleasures of clitoral stimulation were infantile and should be abandoned in favor of vaginal sensations induced by penile penetration. Coincidentally, a woman who followed the Freudian prescription would enact the entire gender system in one sexual regimen: she assumed a position in intercourse that was asymmetrical, heterosexual, and subordinate. Koedt's manifesto fomented rebellion on each of these fronts. Not only were women entitled to equal rights to sexual pleasure, they were equipped to pursue them independent of men. Heterosexual intercourse was intrinsically no more satisfying than masturbation or any of the pleasures to be shared with the opposite or the same sex. If a union of male and female was not required for sexual satisfaction, then the emotional and social necessity of heterosexuality was also placed in doubt. Soon, a chorus of women's liberationists seconded Koedt's conclusion: heterosexuality was not an imperative but an option.[40]

The swift and excited response to Koedt's essay was symptomatic of concurrent shifts in the whole culture of sexuality, spearheaded by the political mobilization among homosexuals. Late in the 1960s gay men and women in cities from New York to San Francisco began to fight back against the police harassment that they had suffered for over thirty years. This spirit of resistance had actually been building up for some time. Organizations to protect the civil rights of gays and lesbians were formed as early as the 1950s.[41] In the beginning, the gay rights movement seemed to reinforce rather than challenge conventional gender differences. Initially, advocates of gay rights, such as members of the Mattachine Society, founded in Los Angeles in the 1950s and composed primarily of men, set out to legitimize male homosexuality by disputing effeminate stereotypes and comporting themselves in a conventionally masculine manner. The first organization of homosexual women, formed a few years later in San Francisco, also professed gender conformity. Adopting the purposefully obscure sobriquet Daughters of Bilitis, this organization clothed itself in femininity. It even issued instructions to wear dresses and nylon stockings when demonstrating in behalf of job equity. When gays and lesbians came together in the same organizations, women took up their familiar gender roles, running the mimeograph machines, making the coffee, and assuming a minority of leadership positions. The early homosexual rights organizations defied the conventional relations of the sexes, but they were otherwise conservative. They conformed to the norms of masculinity and femininity and incorporated themselves into voluntary associations, chartered by the state of California.[42]

With the rise of feminism, the lesbian side of the homosexual movement entered a more militant stage. Announcing themselves as the "lavender menace," lesbians made up a prominent wing of the women's liberation movement to which they contributed the concepts of "compulsory heterosexuality" and the "woman-identified woman." Some radical gay men also construed their activism as part of a movement for gender liberation. In 1971, for example, one member of the Gay Liberation Front asserted that "the long term goal . . . is to rid society of the gender-role system which is at the root of our oppression." Another proclaimed that "gayness" was "the wedge that splits open the gender system." In this radical moment of gay liberation, some homosexual men questioned the practices of masculinity, even as they demanded their right to love members of their own sex. As one gay manifesto put it, "Gay shows the way . . . . We have already, in part at least, rejected the 'masculine' or 'feminine' roles society has designed for us." At the early meetings of the Gay Academic Union in New York City, feminism inspired heated discussions of such matters as "the problem of sexism among gay men."[43]

One gay activist described those times as the "millenarian, wildly optimistic and utopian, but inspiring early days." When the euphoria subsided in the mid-1970s, however, male homosexuals and lesbians had parted in acrimony, going off into separate, sometimes opposing, camps and momentarily losing their critical gender consciousness. While lesbians tended to adopt the androgynous gender pose of early new-wave feminists, dismissing both hyperfemininity and the masculine "butch" identity, they also trafficked in sex stereotypes. Some lesbian separatists celebrated a "woman's culture," which they saw as innately harmonious and caring, devoid of masculine traces of competition, aggression, and predatory sexuality. Meanwhile, some gay men cruised through the homosexual districts of major cities costumed as lumberjacks, sporting muscular frames and thick mustaches, and displaying cocksure masculinity. In San Francisco homosexuality went public in separate male and female divisions: lesbians threatened to bolt from the gay pride parade and complained that the gay men who dominated the Castro district were misogynists. A historian of the same-sex subcultures of Philadelphia in the 1970s and 1980s has concluded that gays and lesbians posed a radical challenge to heterosexuality but left gender conventions largely intact. Men could love men, and women could love women, but men were still men and women were still women. It would seem that the auspicious emergence of a public movement for homosexual liberation had contradictory implications for the future of gender: it challenged time-honored alignments of the relations of the sexes, but it seemed in some ways to leave gender asymmetries undisturbed, even fetishized.[44]

A brief glance back through the history of homosexuality demonstrates just how difficult it had been to get even this far toward disentangling sexuality and gender. Although evidence of homosexual behavior has been found in nearly every human culture, it seldom posed a serious challenge to reigning gender norms. It will be recalled from chapter 1 that Native American tribes often tolerated and even honored homosexual relationships, but only as long as they reinforced, rather than subverted, entrenched gender distinctions. When homosexual relations were institutionalized, as among the Zuni or the Huron, for example, one of the partners had to adopt the gender characteristics of the opposite sex. The berdache might take another man as his sexual partner, but only after he had exchanged male roles and male attire for those of a woman. These realignments of sexuality and gender resembled the practices of "passing women" often found in the ranks of patriots fighting in the Revolutionary or the Civil Wars. When nineteenth-century women impersonated men, they not only acquired female sex partners but many other benefits of the male gender role, including a family wage, a military commission, a caring wife, and the right to vote. The psychiatric files of the late nineteenth century document cases like that of Lucy Lobdel, who lived as a male, slept with a woman, and plotted his/her own course through the gender system: "I made up my mind to dress in men's attire to seek labor, of doing men's work and getting men's wages." In New York City, Murray Hall reaped a rich bounty from cross-dressing: not only a job, a wife, and sexual flings, but also access to the polling booth and the inner sanctums of Tammany Hall. Ultimately exposed as anatomically female—when Hall died of breast cancer and

Lobdel was incarcerated in a lunatic asylum—these women passed as men without openly challenging Victorian notions of gender difference.[45]

Self-identified homosexuals were more likely to reveal themselves in urban areas and modern times. In the vice districts of European cities as early as the eighteenth century, homosexuality became an overt practice in blatant defiance of the heterosexual norm. Still, these modern homosexuals honored the gender asymmetry of their times. In eighteenth-century London a homosexual was often called a "molly," taking a name from female prostitutes, with whom he shared the same brothels. Mollies organized their lives around their desire for men and clearly rejected the gender role generally prescribed by their genital anatomy. Taking names like Mary Magdelen, Garter Mary, and Princess Seraphina, addressing each other as your ladyship or madam, and assuming a passive role in the act of intercourse, mollies performed a gender reversal. To become a male homosexual was to be feminized. The molly's sex partners, often aristocrats or students who used male sex partners like prostitutes or servants, maintained a conventional masculine identity.[46]

This construction of homosexuality was still thriving during the First World War when "fairies," "queers," or "pogues" congregated in the vice districts and seaports of the eastern United States. These "effeminate" homosexuals coupled with "masculine" men, who were called "trade" and remained unscathed by charges of gender deviance. With the imposition of Prohibition, millions of Americans took to speakeasies and vice districts to obtain alcoholic beverages and, in the process, became acquainted with these illicit gender practices. In the 1930s thousands of otherwise conventional New Yorkers attended "Pansy" balls, where they watched parades of transvestites, many of whom were practicing homosexuals. Halloween pageants in cities like Philadelphia and drag shows conducted in the armed forces during the Second World War performed more of the gender charades that cloaked male homosexuality.[47]

By the 1930s, these homosexual venues also hosted same-sex love between women. Lesbians could be sighted in the libertine urban districts of the eighteenth and nineteenth centuries, where they might be called "Tommies" or "roaring girls." Near the roaring camps of the California gold rush, two picaresque female figures entered into folklore under the names Jeanne Bonnet and Blanche Buneau, leaders of a gang of thieving lesbians, said to rescue prostitutes from their pimps. But because women had so few opportunities to congregate outside the home and in the anonymity and autonomy of the city, the prospect of developing full-fledged communities of lesbians remained remote until the twentieth century. Lesbian sexual subcultures first became visible in the 1920s, and in very select places such as the privileged coterie of women gathered around Gertrude Stein in Paris, the jazz clubs and party circuits of Harlem, and bohemian haunts like the Greenwich Village Heterodoxy Club. With the increasing employment of women outside the home and more vocal public discussion of female sexual desire, the sites in which lesbian subcultures could grow proliferated. The Second World War accelerated the process, bringing women together in war industries and the Women's Army Corps.[48] After the war, cities large and small blossomed with lesbian bars, softball leagues, and social clubs.

Like gay men, lesbians defied conventional relations of the sexes but conformed to a certain gender asymmetry. The analogue to the fairy or pogue was the dyke, bull dagger, or mannish lesbian. Interviews conducted in the lesbian community of Buffalo, New York, revealed the elaborate gender theatrics involved in the bar scene. Entrants into the lesbian culture in the 1930s and 1940s were expected to identify themselves as either butch or femme, thereby colluding in a gender dimorphism not unlike a heterosexual couple. The butch dressed as a man, fought to defend her feminine date, lit her companion's cigarettes, and took the upper hand in seduction. While the butch rejected the gender assigned by her anatomy, she reenacted the conventional relations of the sexes by partnering with a femme. The masculine lover was identified as homosexual, but her feminine partner, called her "girl friend" or her "lady," was not marked as a gender deviant. The radical potential of homosexuality was contained loosely within the bounds of gender stereotypes, for the time being.[49]

Still, men went on loving men, and women loved women, even among the Victorian middle classes. Intense same-sex friendships complete with physical expressions of love were commonplace among Victorians. Not just Walt Whitman but also Ralph Waldo Emerson, Theodore Weld, Henry Ward Beecher, and Abraham Lincoln exchanged love letters and shared beds with male friends. The intimate relations of Victorian women were institutionalized at women's colleges and settlement houses late in the nineteenth century. The lifelong Boston marriages of couples like Jane Addams and Mary Smith were described in William Cullen Bryant's homage to "maiden ladies of 40 years who had slept on the same pillow and had a common purse not less sacred than the tie of matrimony."[50] Mount Holyoke president Mary Woolley and English professor Jeannette Marks pledged one another their "ardent and exclusive love," exchanged rings, and pledged to stay together for life. These couples did not require a matched pair of male and female, masculine and feminine, to enjoy intimate love. While they seemed to have accomplished "same-gender love," the sexual dimension of those relations remains unclear, and was often denied. Until female sexuality broke free of the reproductive matrix, which defined sexual relations largely as vaginal intercourse that could result in procreation, it was hard for Victorians to even imagine lesbianism.[51]

The erotic desires and embraces that passed between women were not generally identified as lesbian until quite late in the nineteenth century. Sexology, a field of study pioneered by Europeans like Richard von Krafft-Ebing, Havelock Ellis, and of course, Freud, was not popularized in the United States until the turn of the twentieth century. Ground-breaking psychologists like G. Stanley Hall charted the physical possibilities of same-sex love in medical, clinical, and often pathological terms. Within this medical paradigm, homosexuality became a perversion, defined by its negation of gender conventions. The homosexual was initially labeled an "invert" whose sex characteristics, as well as sexual behavior, were anomalous. The discrepancy was sometimes defined as an anatomical abnormality, as in the case of the hermaphrodite, or indicated by a disorder of some secondary sex characteristic, such as a woman who smoked tobacco or whistled too loudly. Erudite academic tomes cast homosexuality as a disease, a physical disorder that festered between the contrasting poles of male and female. Whether encountered as pathology in a medical textbook or scripted for performance in a gay bar, homosexuality remained constricted by the rules of gender well into the 1960s.[52]

Yet once allowed to express their sexuality openly, even in the relatively narrow spaces of urban gay networks, homosexuals began to conduct a consciousness-raising of their own. The changes within the lesbian bar culture were subtly apparent even in the 1950s. Some young women reported that they hastily, almost capriciously, chose a butch or femme persona in order to gain entry to the gay world. After trying on one role, they might adopt the other a few nights later. The same flexibility marked evolving intimate relations. The extreme role-playing of the 1930s, which ordained that a "stone butch" would assume the exclusive role of pleasuring a passive partner, proved hard to maintain as an intimate practice and soon gave way to more reciprocal sexual relations. When two lesbians formed a couple, the rigid social roles of husband and wife also proved impractical; they were simply dysfunctional when both partners were working women, each of whom had been trained to cook and clean up after herself.[53]

The expanding homosexual community of the twentieth century, especially gay bars, also had a tendency to dissolve the gender distinctions among gay men—that between the fairy and trade, for example. The end of Prohibition had altered bar culture and the social conditions of homosexuality in fundamental ways. Once the sale of alcoholic beverages became legal, state agencies vigilantly policed the taverns where homosexuals had formerly mingled with heterosexuals. Local police joined up with state liquor authorities either to demand payoffs for police protection or to mount raids on homosexual gathering places. Anyone found at a gay bar, no matter how correct his or her gender persona, was liable to be arrested, cited, fined, possibly jailed, and definitively labeled a homosexual. The carefully constructed personae of fairy and husband, femme and dyke, had no legal meaning; all were assigned a common identity as homosexuals.[54]

By the 1960s, police raids and homosexual resistance grew apace. Not coincidentally, political consciousness coalesced around bars like the famous Black Cat in San Francisco, whose habitué and camp songster Jose Sarria would run for the Board of Supervisors in 1961. The act of rebellion usually cited as the inauguration of the gay rights movement was a riot following a police raid at a bar on Christopher Street in New York's Greenwich Village. The Stonewall Inn was the haunt of male homosexuals, but the riot was hardly an effeminate act: the first stone was rumored to have been hurled by either a drag queen or a butch lesbian. Several years before, a gay gathering place called Compton's Cafeteria in San Francisco was the site of fierce resistance to police harassment. By one account, the riot began when a transvestite mounted the counterattack with a fitting gender-bending weapon, his handbag.[55]

Whoever initiated such resistance, of whatever sexual preferences or personae, the gay movement was well launched by 1971. Men and women formed scores of homosexual organizations in American cities, and rather than disguising themselves as conventional interest groups or voluntary associations, they proclaimed gay rights, gay pride, openly gay sexual expression, and a gay identity. San Francisco led the advance of gays and lesbians into the public sphere. By 1979, the city boasted some two hundred gay commercial organizations.[56] One local candidate for the Board of Supervisors, Dianne Feinstein, was courting gay voters as early as 1969. Once a guilty secret, homosexuality was an open practice, grudgingly accepted by both the American Psychiatric Association (which removed homosexuality from its lists of psychological pathologies in 1973) and general public opinion.[57]

Through much of the 1970s, gay politics operated on what has been called the ethnic identity model, with lesbians and gay men separated off into fac-

Rink Foto, *At the 1978 Parade Celebration in Civic Center, San Francisco.*
(© Rink Foto)

tions that mimicked the usual gender dimorphism. But these gender boundaries would ultimately erode. The creed of woman's culture quickly provoked heresy, as other female homosexuals asserted their tastes for less demure and feminine practices, from butch-femme role-playing to sadomasochism. Once they were well outside the closet, gay men also shed some of their gender orthodoxy and admitted drag queens to the annual gay pride parade. San Francisco's gay world became host to a more diverse cast of gender personae, not just female impersonators, but members of motorcycle clubs. Men and women began to reweave the gay and lesbian alliance around neither gender identities nor sexual practices but around the common discrimination they suffered because they violated the heterosexual imperative. Although lesbians were the least likely of any sexually active group to contract AIDS, they came to the support of the men who shared their stigma as a sexual minority. As gays and lesbians met the common political threat from conservatives and sought equivalent legal protection as parents and domestic partners, they found added reasons to form a political alliance across the divide of sex.[58]

Gay men and women built up their own institutions, became a major political constituency, and disabused the American public of any simple equivalence between sexuality and gender. By the end of the millennium, the classifications of sexual minorities had gotten far more complicated. In 1994 San Francisco's annual gay pride day, which began as a simple celebration of homosexuality, was retitled Gay, Lesbian, Bi-Sexual, and Transgender Pride Day. Those who publicly proclaimed the identity of bisexual seemed to cross the border of gender difference with uncanny ease. They spoke up in gay circles and the underground press to assert that the gender of the sex partner was not the singular and essential element of their desire. Released from the boundaries of gender, the possibilities for sexual pleasure expanded. One scholarly observer cataloged "all the many dimensions along which the genital activity of one person can be differentiated from that of another (dimensions that include preference of certain acts, certain zones or sensations, certain physical types, certain frequency, certain symbolic investments, certain relations of age, or power, a certain species, a certain number of participants etc. etc. etc. etc.)." She marveled at the "rather amazing fact" that only one of these dimensions, "the gender of the object choice, emerged from the turn of the [twentieth] century, and has remained, as *the* dimension denoted by the now ubiquitous category of 'sexual orientation.'"[59] Once the great variety of erotic possibilities had been acknowledged publicly, the correspondence between sexuality and gender was eviscerated. Eros could not be funneled into a single channel between male and female.[60]

The concept of transsexuality provoked further havoc along the gender divide. The term had been in use since the mid-twentieth century to designate individuals who exchanged a male identity for a female one, or, less frequently, vice versa. Transsexuals were not necessarily homosexual and sometimes denied any erotic reason for their compulsion to change their gender. Individuals who claimed that title at midcentury often spoke of being female minds in male bodies. The publicity surrounding the sex-change operation of Christine Jorgenson in 1952 ruffled the placid surface of postwar domesticity. Newspapers noted that "people are now wondering how uncertain and changeable a person's sex may be." The readers of *True Confessions* were said to be worrying about their own masculinity or femininity and that of their sons and daughters. Through the 1950s and 1960s the discussion of these vexing issues went on largely under the management of the medical and psychiatric professions. In the process of serving patients who were determined to change their sexual physiology, medical scientists had to devise a new language to describe the boundaries between male and female. They coined such terms as "psychological sex," "gender role and orientation," and "gender identity." Still, no one in this army of professionals (overwhelmingly male) was openly critical of the conventional ways of differentiating men from women.[61]

It would take the new feminism and movements for gay rights to convert transsexuality into a radical challenge to the polarization of male and female. When transsexuals enrolled in the gay pride processions of the 1990s, some of them paraded under the banner of a new identity entirely, a third of many genders perhaps, or at the very least a refusal to settle comfortably on one side or the other of a male/female divide.[62] In the mid-1990s the sum of all these affronts to sexual orthodoxy took the name "queer." That identity was in wide use on gay pride day in the year 2000, when an estimated one million people in San Francisco and half that number in New York City celebrated. Blazoned on the cover of the "Queer Issue" of the *Village Voice* was the portrait of an appropriately curious gender persona, neither masculine, feminine, nor androgynous, but sporting a profusion of gender fashions. The physiognomy suggested a male body; the head gear—a boyish cap—evoked the classic gay object of desire, a soldier or sailor. But the torso of the pinup was not draped with a military uniform or seaman's sweater but a low-cut lace gown. The décolletage was a hairy chest. Rendered as sexual play, and as changeable and various as a costume shop on Halloween, gender differences could be flamboyant yet frivolous. Gender polarization seemed to be relaxing its grip on sexuality.[63]

This blurring of the gender categories was not confined to homosexual cultures. It spilled over into heterosexual relations as well and appeared on prime-time television as an unlikely fashion show called *Queer Eye for the Straight Guy*. During the workday, be it at the office or on the campus, gender seemed to recede from view, muted by the unisex drab of business attire or the blue-jeans uniform of students. But at play, after dark, and in the fantasies projected for mass consumption, both males and females were invited to celebrate the new millennium as an extravagant costume drama, replete with the hourglass shapes and plunging necklines of hyperfemininity, the masculine physiques that had been pumped up to the proportions of muscle beach. Alternatively, male fashion models paraded down the runways in skirts, and women buffed up to climb mountains. The bodyworks of the twenty-first century were still asymmetrical: women were much more likely than men to invest in diets, exercise, or surgery to reconstruct themselves according to fashionable standards of their gender; but at the same time an expanding market for male cosmetics produced yet another gender neologism, the "metrosexual." Once men and women, as well as transgenders, had taken the physical construction of sex into their own hands, anatomy became not destiny but cosmetology. Which poses another mystery: When sex becomes so malleable, can gender remain asymmetrical and hierarchical? The sexual revolution of the late twentieth century had unleashed radical possibilities and would provoke an intense conservative reaction that raised a tumult in the public sphere about issues like abortion and gay marriage. But the genie had been released from the bottle, and it would prove difficult to restore the illusions of universal heterosexuality with men on top.

Restructuring Gender Differences
1980–2000

Battered by feminism and gay rights, gender conventions were clearly in disrepair by 1980 when they became the center of political controversy. Skillful maneuvering on the right blocked the ratification of the Equal Rights Amendment in 1982, and reproductive rights and sexual freedoms faced fierce opposition in the legislatures, the courts, and the media. Feminists spoke of a backlash and a postfeminist consciousness. Yet whatever way the political winds blew, and there would be a decided shift to the right, the deeply rooted changes in the meaning of male and female that surfaced in the 1960s and 1970s would not be easily reversed. The pace of gender change only picked up speed over the next two decades until it conjured up unprecedented possibilities from the unfolding mystery of sex: Could the dualism of male and female disappear? Could gender lose its sting?

A basic transformation of social and economic structure drove the course of gender changes relentlessly forward, along an uncharted but definitely postmodern course. The industrial sector continued to decline; new informational technology fundamentally altered the way Americans worked, learned, and played; medical breakthroughs revolutionized reproduction; and the global economy lurched forward across troubled national borders. There was no way of restoring the antiquated barricade that once divided America into homemakers and breadwinners; it had been crumbling for almost a century and was registered in the decadal census as a sequence of watersheds. The trends in labor force participation were most dramatic. In 1980 — for the first time ever recorded — the majority of all adult women were in the formal labor force. By 1985, the majority of American wives were on the job. In the following decade this standard would apply to mothers of school-age children. The rate of employment among mothers of children under six more than doubled between 1970 and 1992. And before the twentieth century closed, the majority of mothers were back on the job within a year of giving birth. Women of all ranks and races were vacating the last major bastion of a separate sphere: a mother's station at the side of her infant child. Two-thirds of the college-educated mothers of infants were in the labor force in the 1990s, in the same decade that the suspension of Aid to Families with Dependent Children made it imperative that poor mothers leave the newly born to take a job. With such high rates of female employment, men lost the role of sole breadwinner by default. By 1996, nearly half of families with children had two workers, and women constituted over 46 percent of the labor force.[64]

For the vast majority of women who were or aspired to be mothers, a job outside the home required significant trade-offs, most notably a careful planning and curtailment of fertility. Up until the last half of the twentieth century, a woman's employment history was set by the family clock: wives and mothers went back to work when the children entered school. By the year 2000, the order of decision making was reversed. Working women put off childbearing until later in their twenties, even their thirties, timing their first births according to economic necessity or career prospects, and then rushing back to the job before a newborn reached his or her first birthday. As a consequence, America's working women reined in their reproductive capacity until the total fertility rate fell to 2.1, barely high enough to replace the population.[65] This tight scheduling soon became a mundane exigency of family life. The economic pressures induced by the inflation of the 1970s and recession in the 1980s converted the two-worker household into a routine and a necessity. One woman who would have preferred to be a full-time housewife put it bluntly: "I started to work because I had to . . . the bills started piling up. So, I had to do something."[66] During periodic recessions, in the 1980s and again in the 1990s, families clung desperately to middle-class status. They calculated the gender division of labor in simple terms: "I mean, yeah, I've got a husband, but I'm not working for my health. We need the money, and every dollar I make helps."[67]

The long arm of the job began to encroach upon the portion of the female life cycle that was once consumed with domesticity. In 1959 approximately two out of three women over the age of eighteen were married and living with their husbands; in 1980 a minority of 43 percent could be found in this once quintessential social setting of adult womanhood. The median age at marriage rose to twenty-seven for men and twenty-five for women. For a sizable and ever-growing number of women, marriage was not the necessary social context for motherhood. The rate of unwed births rose dramatically: from 10 percent in 1970 to 32.2 percent of all live births in 1995. The divorce rate accelerated apace: it took off in the 1970s, and for the remainder of the century 50 percent of all marriages were terminated. The census for the year 2000 reported the statistical obituary of the classic middle-class family: less than one in four American households harbored two parents and their children. The nostalgic family norm of stay-at-home wife, male breadwinner, and their two children accounted for only one in ten families. At any given moment in the new millennium, the majority of adults would be living outside of blessed wedlock: single, divorced, widowed, or homosexual partners.[68]

The relations of the sexes appeared to be something of a shambles by the late 1970s. During the Jimmy Carter administration, the White House had to cancel a conference on the "family" because the organizers could not agree on a definition of that protean institution. Family pluralism had devolved into a giddy anarchy, as pictured in an ethnographic study conducted in the heartland of the new economy, Silicon Valley, California. It would require a rococo kinship chart to describe the family that gathered for the 1986 wedding of Pamela and Albert Gama. The bride and groom (given fictional names) had "cohabited intermittently since 1975 and [had] been legally married since 1980, [and] were about to celebrate their reborn marriage with a Christian wedding ceremony." Moreover, "Serving as the official wedding photographer was Pam's ex-husband, Don Franklin, who was accompanied by Shirley Moskowitz, his live-in lover and would-be third wife. All of the wedding attendants were step kin and step-in-laws to the groom. . . . More than half of the pews were filled with members of four generations from the 'confusing tangle' of former, step-, dual, and in-law relatives of Pamela and Al's divorce-extended family."[69] Family portraits like this led social scientists to fumble for new terms for that time-honored institution. Some called it the "recombinant family," the "accordion matrifocal family," the "blended family," or just a "site of disorder, a contested domain."[70] Whatever its name, the volatility in the relations of the sexes destabilized a second fundamental structural linchpin of gender systems past.[71]

It is not that women and men had rejected marriage and the family. Fully 90 percent of all Americans would ultimately wed, and most women would bear children. The increase in life expectancy meant that these marriages endured, on the average, longer than ever. In some ways the commitment to family had actually grown stronger and more pervasive. Highly educated women, who once forfeited children for careers of private accomplishment or public service, now chose to become mothers, despite the double burden it entailed. Gay men and lesbians also claimed and exercised the right to form families and raise children. (In the twenty-first century they could even secure a marriage license in some states.) At any one moment, furthermore, over 70 percent of school-age children still lived with both their parents. The nuclear family had hardly disappeared; it had simply come to occupy a relatively smaller space and time in the long, busy, and varied lives of postmoderns. Marriage, in the words of one sociologist, had become "de-institutionalized," a voluntary choice not a social or cultural necessity.[72]

Most women, like most men, wanted a balanced life, both a secure family and a satisfying job. These were reasonable desires, and not necessarily contradictory. Bridging the distance between home and work, however, had become a complicated task and too often a double burden for women. Sometimes it entailed excruciating conflict, like that experienced by this single mother: "on the way home from the office, I would panic whenever the train made an unscheduled stop between stations. That meant I would have even less time with my daughter." Or witness this mother who was threatened with firing if she left work to attend a school ceremony honoring her daughter: "I didn't want to lose the job. But I cried through the rest of the afternoon because I was missing it." Scenes like this were repeated thousands of times every working day, on the way home, outside the school door, whenever the call came in to pick up a sick child. At issue here was not a divide between a job and a child, but how all this necessary labor, the joys and the burdens of both, were organized and distributed between the sexes and across society.[73]

In other words, recent changes in both the roles and the relations of men and women raised fundamental questions of equity. With one axis of the gender system quite thoroughly remodeled, and the other in considerable disrepair, the third—the age-old hierarchy of men over women—no longer appeared invincible. Until late in the 1970s, however, scaling the gender hierarchy still seemed a Sisyphean task. Women had been flocking into the labor force for decades, but they were still making fifty-nine cents for every dollar men earned, and they still constituted 99 percent of the secretaries and 2 percent of all construction workers.[74] This gender barricade finally began to crack in the 1980s. The number of female engineers rose sixfold in that decade; the proportion of female managers climbed from 4 percent to 33 percent in the 1990s; among veterinarians the ratio of women to men went from one in twenty to seven in ten. The composition of the labor force was being shaken up at every level of the economy. In the insurance industry, for example, 5,500 men were dismissed and 8,900 women were hired in a single two-year period.[75] The cumulative effects of this diminution in the sex segregation of the labor market were soon registered on the wage scale. By 1987, full-time working women were earning seventy cents for every dollar men took home: the figure rose to seventy-two cents in 1990 and stood as high as seventy-five cents by the end of the century. While substantial inequity remained, women had clearly mounted an ascent of the wage hierarchy. Their overall earnings, adjusted for inflation, had gone up 17 percent, almost twice the rate for men. Young women graduating from college, where they slightly outnumbered men, faced especially bright prospects. They began their careers without family encumbrances and at wage rates equal to men. At this pace of change, it was not entirely utopian to expect that the last vestige of the patriarchy might wither away.[76]

Expectations of such a coup d'état were forecast in the television scripts of the late twentieth century. The 1970s brought the first models of female independence and upward mobility to the small screen: the spunky journalist of the *Mary Tyler Moore Show* was followed into prime time in the 1980s by the gun-toting police officers Cagney and Lacey and the sundry women doctors who took up their stations in hospital dramas. At the same time that some men made room for female partners in law firms and newsrooms, others became objects of ridicule, like the comic working-class antihero Archie Bunker or the parade of amiable, low-key characters such as Jerry Seinfeld, who shuffled through a world of single friends, including a politely contemptuous female peer. Only a half century after *Father Knows Best*, the males had toppled from the television hierarchy, leaving a far more complicated representation of gender, as well as class.[77]

The political picture also displayed a perceptible leveling of gender equality. Between the 1970s and the 1990s the number of female municipal officers rose by 269 percent, elected mayors rose from 1 percent to 17 percent, the female ranks of state legislators quadrupled until women filled 20 percent of the seats. As of 1960, women had virtually disappeared from high-profile positions in Washington; by the end of the century, they were a sizable minority presence in Congress and the cabinet and on the Supreme Court. Although the highest elective offices remained a male monopoly, women were becoming viable candidates for even the presidency. The proportion of Americans who considered women qualified to become president rose from 41 percent in 1974 to 67 percent in 1996.[78] If still grossly underrepresented at the higher echelons of political power, women were fully enfranchised and active participants in the political process. Still trailing men in voter participation as late as 1960, they had become the majority of voters by 1980. (Fifty-eight percent of eligible women and 56 percent of men recorded a vote for president in that year.) Women also exercised those votes in an independent fashion. A gap of about ten percentage points between the votes of males and females emerged in 1980 and endured through the 2000 presidential election. In politics as in economics, the second sex was at the forefront of a swift and continuous sea change.[79]

Each of the three dimensions of the modern constellation of gender had been seriously eroded by the year 2000. First, the gender division of space and labor had lost the high definition of the past: the old pairings of breadwinner and homemaker applied to only a small minority of men and women and for only a small slice of the life cycle. Second, the relations of the sexes had become so distended that the marital dyad had lost much of its centrality in the social web of intimacy, parenting, mutuality, and personal interdependence. Third and finally, the women of the late twentieth century had made a major assault up the steep cliffs of gender hierarchy, although substantial measures of gender inequality remained.

At the beginning of the twenty-first century, the boundaries between the sexes, be they measured on a vertical or horizontal axis—as asymmetry or as hierarchy—had weakened and become more difficult to discern and describe. No longer a single, deep canyon, the dividing line between male and female has stretched across a whole landscape of meandering hills and gullies. The simple, blunt divisions that had mapped the relations of male and female during the modern era, themselves always a gross simplification of reality, were fast becoming illegible. Accordingly, any profile of postmodern womanhood is distorted and incomplete until it is set in a larger context.

First of all, the recent history of women must be set alongside the history of men. Second, it must be seen against the backdrop of race and class.

American men were hardly insulated from the whole cycle of changes recounted in this chapter. They had been at the helm of the social movements that cradled women's liberation and had placed their own personal issues on the public agenda. In fact, the sons of the baby boom were destined to undergo a very personal political trial during the 1960s and 1970s, the Vietnam War. The resistance to the war in Vietnam on the part of hundreds of thousands of young men had a gender dialectic all its own. While sometimes expressed with a masculine swagger of street protest, opposition to the war violated a male gender rule as old and hallowed as motherhood and apple pie—the ethic of the stoic warrior-patriot. Men of every political stripe—soldiers, draft resisters, veterans against the war, contrite policymakers, deposed presidents—found masculinity confused, if not threatened, by the divisive war and defeated peace. The literary legacy of Vietnam was bleaker than earlier war stories, say, by Ernest Hemingway for World War I, or Norman Mailer for World War II. Memoirs like Ron Kovic's *Born on the Fourth of July* presented the ethic of the warrior-patriot as a cruel hoax to which he sacrificed his young body and his naive patriotism. Films like *The Deer Hunter* and *Full Metal Jacket* featured male characters who were casualties rather than heroes, broken in spirit as well as body. To this day, veterans of that war make up a disproportionately large segment of America's homeless and mentally ill. Others returned more conventional heroes, but still haunted by the ghosts of war. Twenty years of silence, a Medal of Honor, and a Bronze Star could not shield former U.S. senator Robert Kerrey from ultimately confronting the trial and the travesty of masculinity that was the Vietnam War. He would ultimately be held to public account as the commanding officer in a military exercise that had slaughtered women and children. Beginning in 1992, every presidential candidate had to account for his whereabouts during the Vietnam War.[80]

Although masculinity was severely tested in the late 1960s and early 1970s, men seldom became critics of gender conventions. While women sought parity in military obligations and opportunities, men rarely complained that an all-male draft was sex discrimination. The men's organizations that emerged sporadically in the late twentieth century were either feminist auxiliaries or male defense groups. Perhaps 100,000 men participated in what was called the mytho-poetic men's movement, whose purpose was more therapeutic than political. This men's movement, like two other significant mobilizations on the male side of the gender system—the conservative Christian group called the Promise Keepers and the African American Million Man March—disbanded very quickly, regrettably without ever systematically challenging the gender divide from a male perspective.[81] An army of self-conscious agents of change comparable to feminists has not assembled on the male side of the border between the sexes. To the contrary, the gender-bending images of masculinity characteristic of the counterculture—the longhaired, beaded youth who made love and not war—soon competed with hypermasculinized heroes modeled by a movie character called Rambo, who marauded through the jungles of Vietnam like a vengeful Tarzan. An unabated flood of male action movies followed and is still pouring out of Hollywood, prompting one feminist critic to lament the "remasculinization of America."[82]

Off the silver screen, most American men have been valiant but something less than heroic on the home front. The average husband's contribution to housework and parenting has begun to increase significantly. Some were as gallant as the African American husband who acknowledged, "I figure it's my job, too."[83] But wives were seldom compensated fully for their second shift in the labor force. They were left to shoulder more than their share of housework, delegate chores to children, reduce their standards, or purchase relief through commercial vendors. Meanwhile, literally millions of men were actually withdrawing from the whole process of social reproduction. With the marriage rate precipitously down, the divorce rate up, and single mothers abounding, men overall were assuming less responsibility for the next generation, and some left the care of their own biological children entirely to mothers. Out of wedlock births rose from 11 percent in 1970 to 30 percent in 1992, when only 27 percent of unwed pregnancies led to marriage. This withdrawal from paternity left one in four children in what is called a female-headed household; moreover, it is estimated that nearly half of all children will spend some portion of their youth living apart from their fathers.[84]

The resistance to change on the male side of the gender divide is manifested in many mundane but curiously unacknowledged ways. Amid the fanfare over women becoming doctors and police officers, men are not rushing proudly into the ranks of nurses and secretaries; they have not adopted suitdresses to match women's pantsuits. Yet while most men may have been rather passive bystanders to the gender revolution, they share in both its causes and consequences. At the most basic level, women's position squarely within the labor force, where many occupy well-paying professional, managerial, and industrial posts, has created unaccustomed competition for men.

That rivalry has become fierce in the elite ranks of doctors and lawyers and at the admissions offices of Ivy League universities, where successful women applicants went from virtually zero to almost half. The consequences for men of equal opportunity for women could be very personal. In as many as one in four households, the wife now commanded a higher income than her mate. Thirty-five percent of young female college graduates have married men of lower educational standing. The increasing competition between the sexes hit different segments of the population in very different ways. Among managers and professionals, men still out-earned women by a comfortable margin; among manufacturing workers, by contrast, women's wages were on a par with men's. The intricate interweaving of male and female in the postmodern labor force can no longer be ironed out into a simple scheme of male dominance. Almost every American man—in some capacity, at some time—is subordinate to a woman: his boss, his senator, his better-paid wife, a president-to-be.[85]

The precipitous decline in the industrial sector of the economy has eliminated hundreds of thousands of well-paying union jobs and left countless men in an unaccustomed and uncomfortable position. At the same time that women's income was increasing 17 percent, the real wages of men actually declined by three percentage points. By one estimate, 48 percent of the reduction in this wage ratio was due to a decline in male earnings.[86] In some working-class neighborhoods, the consequent blight on male breadwinning became epidemic: "My brother's been out of a job for a long time; now my brother-in-law just got laid off. It seems like every time I turn around, somebody's losing his job. I've been lucky so far, but it makes you wonder how long it'll last."[87] Men of little education, and those equipped with only manual skills and experience, occupied a very precarious position along the ladder of gender hierarchy. Their sector of the labor force, once the mainstay of a family wage, was rapidly shrinking. The postindustrial economy put African American men at especially acute risk. Black workers never fully recovered from the loss of industrial jobs after the war industries closed in 1945. They and their sons often remained trapped in rust belt cities with their empty factories and faced rising rates of unemployment, double that for whites. In some cities half of all young black males were without jobs. While a remarkable proportion of poor African Americans kept their households intact against these odds, the toll on their families and communities was very costly. In the 1980s inner-city black neighborhoods were hit by record unemployment, dwindling social services, and fierce drug traffic. Under the direst of circumstances, families divided into two devastated gender fragments: imprisoned men and impoverished single mothers.[88]

It was clear at century's end that shifts in the sexual division of labor were altering the structures of both class and race. As long as it could be assumed that the majority of wives and mothers were not wage-earners, it was possible to define the class position and material condition of any given household: it could be transcribed from the occupation and income of the male breadwinner without too much misrepresentation. The influx of women of all ages, marital statuses, and occupational standing into the labor force made such a calculation difficult and distorting. How would one categorize the household of a blue-collar husband and a pink-collar wife, a not uncommon social unit? The consequences of women's integration into the labor force were far-reaching. First of all, it produced a new social hierarchy: a pyramid of status and income among women. A century ago, when almost all white mothers, Victorian ladies as well as poor immigrants, stayed at home caring for their children, they shared a position within the structure of gender, if hardly the same class privileges. Once women took up positions in the paid labor force, the female gender became divisible by class, along a scale that ran from the chief executive officer to the maid. The earnings of women began to become polarized as educated women entered elite professions and the unskilled were locked into low-paid service jobs. As some women got richer, others became relatively poorer. Racial differences further complicated the inequality between women. A century ago, African American mothers were far more likely than white women to enter the labor force. That ratio began to turn around in the 1960s, when the labor force participation rate of African American women declined, not because they chose to stay at home, but because they could not find jobs.

The trend toward increasing inequality between women shows no sign of abating, and for many it is more than an abstract statistic. It often means that women are directly subordinated one beneath the other, in the office and in the home, as the secretary and her boss or as the nanny and the "working mother."[89] In fact, the inequality between women could make the difference between affluence and impoverishment in America. When mothers of young children entered the labor force, they required household assistance and child care, a demand that was usually supplied by a cheap pool of female labor. For well-paid women workers the low cost of child care buoyed up an affluent lifestyle. But among low-wage workers, child care absorbed a substantial chunk of their meager income. For these less fortunate working mothers (many of whom were recent immigrants who will be described in the next chapter), the cost of child care reduced their families close to the poverty level, however hard they worked.[90]

The increasing inequality between women is but one way gender has contributed to the emergence of what has been called a "new class society." Since the 1970s, during the same time that women have been taking up long-term positions in the labor force, the gulf between the rich and poor has been growing wider, by a measure of 20 to 30 percent.[91] Such gender factors as marital status, the extent of women's employment, and the relative earnings of men and women played a significant role in determining just where a household would fall along this increasingly steep scale of inequality. Among the wealthy, it was possible to live luxuriously on a single male income, to afford a non-working wife, or to permit a professional woman to interrupt her career for childbirth and parenting. In the year 2000 households earning more than $100,000 were the most likely to have stay-at-home wives and mothers. The majority of working mothers, 52 percent, contributed their earnings to comfortable, middle- or upper-middle-class households (with an income between $50,000 and $100,000).[92] In other words, two incomes were the signature of the postmodern middle class. Gender was just as critical to the achievement of this middling status as it had been in the past, but now mothers went to work so that they might purchase, rather than bake, an apple pie. Meanwhile, the surest sentence to the bottom of the American class structure was to be born into a female-headed household. The median income of a female-headed household was approximately one-third that earned by a married couple with two workers. Factoring race into the scale of household income further exacerbates what has been called the postmodern "configuration of inequality." In 1995 over 50 percent of all black children and almost 30 percent of nonwhite Hispanics were living in female-headed households, and the vast majority of them were sentenced to poverty.[93]

These vagaries of gender contribute to the new class society in multiple ways. First, gender still operates as simple inequity between men and women. On the average, white men still occupy the pinnacle of the social structure. Among the four hundred wealthiest Americans, there are only sixty-nine women, only six of whom made their fortunes without the help of a male partner. Although gender asymmetry and inequality have become less dramatic lower down the social ladder, 80 percent of all women still make less than the *average* male wage. Second, the complexity of the new gender/class system is compounded by the precarious status of many men, particularly members of the old industrial working class and racial minorities. Finally, because male and female workers marry, divorce, and procreate with one another, gender contributes mightily to the social economic status of children and families. The offspring born to a power couple face very different prospects than the children of a single mother. Husbands, sons, and daughters benefit from the earnings of highly educated women, while nearly one in four of the families in poverty have two low-wage workers.[94]

Given these complications of American social structure, gender hierarchy can no longer be measured by the simple yardsticks used in the past. In its conventional meaning as a division between men and women, gender inequality has declined significantly; however, measured along a scale of differences among women it has increased. Meanwhile, family instability has placed low-income women workers and their children in the greatest jeopardy. In sum, continuing gender asymmetry has combined with unstable relations between the sexes to widen the gulf between affluent and poor households. The mysteries of sex continue and compound one another. Just as in the past gender shaped such major historical processes as the cultural production of domesticity and the institutionalization of slavery, it is altering American social structure and race relations in the twenty-first century.

At the turn of the millennium, the divide between male and female is less blunt than in the past, but it is as consequential as ever. Gender retains its postmodern plasticity, still subject to feminist scrutiny, challenged by sexual pluralism, and weakened by the increasingly symmetrical relations of the sexes. The border between the sexes may be more open than ever before, raising the possibility that men and women can relate to one another in ways that would be more equitable and pleasurable for all. Yet the headlines are also haunted by contrary prospects. The contemporary mystifications of sex were projected onto the front pages in shocking and grotesque imagery in 2004, when women soldiers, from a general to a private, appeared among those implicated in the brutal torture of male prisoners in Iraq. Although the secretary of state was a woman of African American descent, the war machinery was still primarily in male hands. Given such complications of gender in the present, and the resilience of male dominance in the past, it is prudent to assume that the divide between the sexes is in the process of reconstruction rather than disintegration.

Whatever the future of gender, wherever the border of male and female is to be drawn in the twenty-first century, it cannot be contained within the political borders of the United States of America. The increasing volume of

Pauli Murray, at the time of her graduation from Richmond Hill High School, New York, 1927. (Courtesy of the Schlesinger Library, Radcliffe Institute, Harvard University)

Pauli Murray, ca. 1977. (Courtesy of the Schlesinger Library,
Radcliffe Institute, Harvard University)

immigration and the integration of the world economy raise yet more quandaries and possibilities about where sex divides and warrant one brief parting chapter.

This current chapter cannot conclude, however, without a tribute to those who enacted gender changes in the late twentieth century: feminists, gay men and lesbians, hardworking women and men. No one testifies more poignantly to this heroism and the hope it inspires than Pauli Murray. Born in 1910, the great-granddaughter of a slave and her master's son, Murray led her life within the racial category that she preferred to call Negro and the gender classification of female. She battled tenaciously against the injustices attendant to both social conditions. At different times in her life of seventy-five years, Pauli Murray was denied admission to the University of North Carolina because of her race and to Harvard Law School because of her sex. At Howard University Law School, she confronted an African American institution that practiced what she called the "prejudice of sex." Pauli Murray overcame each of these setbacks, received her college education and her law degree, and devoted a lifetime to improving the opportunities for those who would follow her. She has been applauded for "nearly single-handedly" ensuring that sex discrimination would be included in the Civil Rights Act of 1964. Murray took up this political challenge in the 1920s, ahead of her time, but at the end of her life she would share in the rewards of a century of hard-won social change and fulfill her own private dream. At over seventy years of age, Pauli Murray became the first African American woman to be ordained an Episcopal priest. She celebrated her first Eucharist in the church where her great-grandmother had occupied the slave balcony. The elation of this moment and her words on this occasion crystallize the legacy of positive gender changes left to us by the women of the twentieth century, the promises in our keeping: "All the strands of my life had come together. Descendant of a slave and of slave owner, I had already been called poet, lawyer, teacher, and friend. Now I was empowered to minister the sacrament of One in whom there is no north or south, no black or white, no male or female—only the spirit of love and reconciliation drawing us all toward the goal of human wholeness."[95]

CHAPTER 7

WHERE IN THE WORLD IS THE BORDER BETWEEN MALE AND FEMALE?

IMMIGRATION AND GENERATION IN THE TWENTIETH CENTURY

On Sunday afternoons a group of Aztec dancers regularly perform in the Plaza of Los Angeles, a modest open space set beside a freeway and not far from the skyscrapers of downtown and the brashly postmodern Disney Concert Hall. The brawny dancers and drummers are led by a graceful, middle-aged woman who wears a garment crafted in bright yellow leather and embossed on the back with the image of the Virgin of Guadalupe. The first apparition of the Virgin took place outside Tenochtitlan (now Mexico City) in 1531. As legend has it, the Madonna appeared not far from the shrine of a native goddess and offered succor to a humble Indian devastated by the European invasion. Over the years, the Virgin of Guadalupe, called Tonantzin by the Aztecs, took on a Mexican identity; her skin tones deepened, her veil brightened, corn and other native plants clustered around her.[1] The Virgin has reigned over Los Angeles since the plaza was laid out in 1781 by émigrés from Mexico, most of them Indians or Mestizos. More recent immigrants from Latin America still worship her at the Catholic Church founded there in the 1820s.

The Virgin of Guadalupe has been carried north from Mexico by streams of migrants, and she still presides in the center of the nation's second-largest city. Men wear T-shirts printed with her name; old women light candles before her likeness; teenagers spray-paint her image on low-riding automobiles. This female allegory, approaching five hundred years of age, rubs shoulders with Hollywood starlets and is at home in the glittering capital of American popular culture. In her long history and contemporary vitality, the Virgin of Guadalupe evokes mysteries of gender that still hover over American culture. For one thing, this durable female icon reprises the mystery of the corn mother, who, reincarnated as the Catholic virgin, did not exit the stage of history upon the arrival of colonists from Europe. That this ancient

E. J. Harpham, *Vision of the Virgin of Guadalupe*, Our Lady Queen of Angels
Church, Los Angeles. (Courtesy of E. J. Harpham; photo by the author)

maternal spirit survives in the city of Los Angeles, whose economy is dedicated to refashioning gender imagery according to the latest hedonistic standards, raises another quandary: Given the heterogeneity of contemporary
standards of femininity or masculinity, can gender still be described in the
simple binary terms of male and female? Finally, the Virgin of Guadalupe
poses a fundamental question about the geography of gender. Because this
representation of womanhood crossed into the United States along with the
largest and most diverse wave of immigration in the history of the nation,
one has to ask: Where in the world can we locate some foundational border
between the sexes?

At the close of the twentieth century, the putative objects of this investigation—women, men, and America—were suspended in time and in space,
caught up in a global whirlwind of migration. Before returning to the postmodern shrine of the Virgin of Guadalupe, this chapter will retrace some of
the multiple, twisted paths of immigration into the United States, encountering yet more various and changing gender distinctions. This tour of the
world is necessitated by the global restructuring of economy and society that

WOMEN REMAKE GENDER

sped up late in the twentieth century when capital broke free of national borders. Giant corporations and upstart entrepreneurs located their production in cheap labor markets outside their native lands; financial institutions spread their tentacles around the globe and concentrated their offices in a few international cities; hard-pressed governments offered tax incentives to foreign investors; and countries joined together to create mega-economies like the North American Free Trade Agreement and the European Union. This worldwide reorganization of the economy reshuffled the human population, male and female alike. In 1965, the same year that the first free-trade zones opened along the Mexican border, the United States revised its immigration policy. The federal statute admitted permanent residents from abroad regardless of their national origins, as long as they met at least one of three criteria: a close family connection to a legal resident, the status of political refugee, or the possession of skills deemed necessary but scarce within the United States. Under this rubric, the volume of documented immigration rose explosively. More than 3 million arrived in the 1960s; the number rose to 4.5 million in the 1970s; and more than 7 million joined the flow of immigrants in the 1980s. By the mid-1990s the official tally of legal immigrants had risen to 1 million a year. Meanwhile, the waves of undocumented arrivals were estimated at 300,000 annually.[2]

Social scientists have acknowledged the worldwide integration of the economy and high volume of immigration by proposing a new geographical terminology. The adjectives "global" or "transnational" are affixed to everything from financial power to ethnic identity and political allegiance. Historians are quick to point out that the massive movement of peoples around the globe is hardly unique to the late twentieth century. The written history of this nation commenced after a major migration across the Atlantic, with cataclysmic consequences for the native-born population. The most tortuous chapters of our history were also inaugurated with a brutal transport of people, the forced migration of slaves out of Africa. The flow of largely unrestricted immigration before 1920 brought upward of 40 million new citizens into the United States, mostly from Europe.[3] Finally, migrants from Asia set down roots in the United States well before the Civil War. They were greeted with hostility and the Chinese Exclusion Act of 1882, the first federal restriction on immigration and the source of another distinctive coloration to race in America. Whatever the technical term—international, global, or transnational—this persistent worldwide flow of population made the process of doing gender even more complicated and contested.

This final chapter focuses on two successive stages of immigration into the United States, one coming out of Eastern and Southern Europe at the turn of the nineteenth century and a second from Asia and Latin America more recently. The chapter begins with a general description of the multiple, unfamiliar, and competing patterns of gender differentiation that immigrants brought into their adopted country. It goes on to consider the ways in which the process of immigration disrupted the meaning and altered the practice of gender within the United States. Those who leapt across the continents experienced a kind of gender shock, a collision between different meanings of male and female that necessitated rapid adaptation. Immigration infused American gender culture with bracing doses of individual transformation as well as social diversity. Despite the great variety of immigrant origins, certain patterns of gender change were repeated all along the transnational circuit of peoples. Pausing at such dissimilar historical sites as the Jewish shtetls of the nineteenth century and the Laotian villages of the twentieth, this chapter describes recurrent challenges to gender orthodoxy. For example, the economic hardships of immigration repeatedly disrupted both the sexual division of labor and the patterns of family authority. The adaptations and transformations required of immigrants were paced according to the family cycle, and they unleashed other common gender consequences, including conflicts between parents and children about the norms of manhood and womanhood.

While the process of immigration almost always destabilizes the meanings of male and female, the specific outcome of gender shock varies over time. Therefore, the chapter concludes by focusing on one historical period, from 1965 until the year 2000. The most recent wave of immigration collided with postmodernism and magnified the force of gender change. Men and women from all around the world were now adapting to postmodern conditions in familiar ways, most notably by sending wives and mothers into the paid labor force. Whether they came from Latin America or Asia, women devised new strategies to support themselves and provide for their families. In this recent period, the relations between husbands and wives, not just parents and children, became especially vulnerable to the transformative effects of immigration. The immigrants who arrived in the United States after 1965 compounded the mystery of sex and multiplied the possibilities of further change. They prompt the query: Do the many peoples that are coming together in the United States in the twenty-first century bring with them the leaven of alternative gender imagery and practices that might dissolve the obstinate and monotonous dichotomy between male and female?

The Generations of Gender

The process of immigrating to America is often dramatized as a conflict with the patriarchs of the Old World. This story has been told many times in ethnic literature by American daughters, whose protagonists might face a Jewish father who piously studies the Talmud while she slaves in the garment factory, or a Chinese parent who arranges a marriage against the heroine's romantic inclinations. Anzia Yezierska used both tropes in the classic immigration tale *Bread Givers*, published in 1925. By forcing his daughters to support his studies with their sweatshop labor and then marrying them off to the highest bidder, Yezierska's Reb Smolinsky won the compliment of being "more tyrannical than the Tsar."[4] Maxine Hong Kingston retold this tale as a memoir of growing up in California in the 1950s, haunted by such archaic visions of Chinese gender as bound feet, female infanticide, and marital slavery.[5] A half century later, young female refugees from the mountains of Laos were still complaining to ethnographers about gender oppression, which took such forms as polygamy and the male domination of public life. Sons also wrestled with parental authority: one dutiful American son conformed to his mother's plea that he date only Chinese women until he experienced a familiar immigrant epiphany: a "kind of revelation. I thought, 'I can't marry a person just to please someone else.'"[6]

Historians have assembled evidence to support such narratives of ancestral patriarchy. The most conservative practitioners of Judaism questioned whether women had souls and, according to I. J. Singer, were known to flog a young father for siring a female child.[7] It was her beloved mother who sent Rosa Cavalleri from Italy to her husband in America with the remonstrance: "You must go. However bad that man is, he is your husband, he has the right to command you."[8] The immigration file of Lee Puey You, dated 1955, recalled a perilous process of immigration decades earlier when she was sold to a Hong Kong merchant and forced into concubinage, slavish domestic service, and involuntary marriage.[9] Such contracts with transnational merchants in female sexuality had stocked San Francisco's Chinatown with brothels in the 1850s. The horrors visited on women whose American journey began in the killing fields of Cambodia, or as victims of rape in the refugee camps of Thailand or Bosnia, lend substance to the dramatization of immigration as an escape from patriarchy. Some of these examples of gender hierarchy were grounded in social structure. Many of the men and women caught up in the second, as well as the first, wave of immigration embarked from economies that were built on patrilineal property and patri-local residence. Whether they came from Sicily or Guangdong Province in China, peasant households were often reluctant to squander their resources on daughters.

Yet this patriarchal narrative is too brittle to serve as the springboard from which to launch a full tide of immigration. In each of these societies, changes in gender roles and relations were underway well in advance of departure for America. Immigration did not become a routine economic strategy until the old household order was no longer viable, be it from famine, popula-tion growth, political instability, or local innovations. Those who made their way to the United States were already adept at refashioning the meaning of male and female. Back in Italy, daughters of domineering Italian fathers could find work outside the bounds of patriarchal surveillance in local gar-ment and textile factories. The Jewish families of Eastern Europe, wracked by pogroms and state repression, had already left their villages for the cities where daughters and sons flourished in the ambience of modernity. Two of the seven founders of the modern and secular socialist organization the Jew-ish Socialist Labor Bund were women.[10] China sent republican ideas about gender across the Pacific with political figures like Sieh King who rose before a San Francisco audience in 1902 to proclaim, "Men and Women are equal and should enjoy the privileges of equals."[11] Certainly those who emigrated from Southeast Asia in the 1970s had a potent foretaste of the American gen-der system, which populated their homeland with a half million soldiers and the most advanced weaponry. Bona fide revolutionaries who had toppled a dictator could be found among the Korean immigrants of the 1980s.[12] Immi-gration was born of change, not tradition: it sent an especially venturesome population of women and men to the United States and opened the way for a new world order of male and female.

Deployed in a flexible way, gender could serve as a highly effective im-migration strategy. Families often organized immigration as a geographical extension of the sexual division of labor. In some instances, notably among the Irish and Jews, emergencies like famine or ethnic persecution necessi-tated that whole families, both genders, depart the Old World. Relatively even sex ratios within migrating groups generally guaranteed permanent settle-ment and a firm implantation of immigrant culture in America. Neither Irish nor Jewish immigrants returned to the old sod in great numbers. But in most cases the complementary roles of male and female were not trans-ported to the United States intact. Before 1914, when immigration met the labor needs of American industrialization, the sex ratio was out of balance.

WOMEN REMAKE GENDER

Seventy-five percent of non-Irish immigrants were male, and approximately one-third of them would return to their country of origin.[13] Among some groups, notably the Chinese, the sex ratio was even more askew. In 1900 men outnumbered women twenty to one among Chinese Americans; only after the Second World War would the sex ratio become reasonably balanced.[14] With the two sexes separated and scattered across the globe, it was imperative that immigrants find new ways of doing gender.

Italian immigrants arriving in the United States between 1815 and 1914 managed an efficient, if taxing, transnational division of labor. At least 60 percent of those arriving in the United States were male, half of whom would ultimately return to Italy. The women who stayed behind were called white widows, and they adapted to male absence by assuming Herculean labor in support of their children. They recalled working like slaves, serving virtually as beasts of burden in order to supply the household necessities in the absence of husbands and fathers. Meanwhile, across the Atlantic, men settled into makeshift boardinghouses, fended for themselves as housekeepers, made do with a diet of "rice, pasta, bread and vegetables," and abstained from the meat that was a badge of masculinity for all-American working men. Mutual sacrifice and flexibility on the part of both male and female often paid off with a "family reunion in Sicily," and perhaps the purchase of a bit of land and a more comfortable home. For these Italian families, the journey to America was just a way station, a temporary expedient, in the process of reorganizing the Italian household economy.[15]

The United States, the fabled Gold Mountain, served a similar function for many Chinese households. While the dramatically skewed sex ratio among Chinese Americans was dictated by exclusionary policies (that left very few loopholes for female migration in particular), family practices back in China were also a critical contributing factor. Such customs as polygamy among elites and the vesting of land in the eldest son left many Chinese men with little hope of finding a wife and founding a household. Immigration dispersed these unmarriageable males or impecunious husbands to the United States.[16] Over time, many of these American sojourners acquired the means to visit their homeland, arrange a marriage, and father children back in China. Husbands returned to the United States, and their "split households" endured indefinitely, maintained by the wives who remained in China, raising subsistence crops and livestock and serving as "acting heads of household" or "*gam saan poh*."[17] Otherwise known as the spouses of Gold Mountain men, these wives and mothers practiced gender in an elastic fashion, stretched all the way across the Pacific. This dexterous sexual division of labor was also manifest in other extraordinary gender practices back in China, among them religious cults that celebrated spinsterhood among silk workers.[18]

The first wave of immigration resounded with gender change on both sides of the transnational divide. While migration shored up families at the place of origin, it also left sufficient numbers of immigrants within the United States to provide the makings of new ethnic and gender identities. The fact that ethnic differences did not melt rapidly away on arrival in the United States is testament to the resiliency of immigrant gender practices. The maintenance of ethnic identity required that immigrant men and women intermarry, procreate, and collaborate. The close economic cooperation of the sexes was essential in American cities at the turn of the twentieth century when few jobs, be they for males or females, could support an entire family. The typical unskilled job available to adult males seldom paid a living wage and was repeatedly interrupted by seasons of unemployment. Census surveys from 1875 through the 1910s demonstrated that families seldom got by on a father's income alone. Every ounce of labor power was put to use. Children, regardless of sex or nationality, went off to work at an early age. Even protective Italian fathers sent their teenage daughters into the labor force. In immigrant neighborhoods fourteen- and fifteen-year-olds were found at work, not at school, while their younger siblings did piecework in the tenements. Even six-year-olds could sew tags on garments or stitch ribbons into corsets.[19]

By contrast, the employment of mothers outside the home did not prove to be an effective allocation of family labor before the 1930s. The energies of adult women were better allocated to frugal housework, bearing and raising child laborers, and performing such lucrative domestic tasks as taking in boarders or washing. Among Asian Americans, wives and mothers put in long hours in the family business, the laundries and restaurants of San Francisco's Chinatown or the Japanese farms in the Central Valley of California.[20] The assiduous pooling of family income remained critical to immigrant survival in postmodern cities. A Vietnamese father of eight children practiced this gender strategy with aplomb. He took on two or three janitorial jobs, while his wife was employed in an electronics factory, the grandfather worked as a grocery vendor, and teenage children held part-time jobs. Cobbled together, this income became the nest egg with which the Nguyen family opened a restaurant and sent a son to medical school. A sociologist has given this persistently gendered immigrant strategy an appropriate American name: "patch-working." Women were as likely as men to stitch the pieces

WOMEN REMAKE GENDER

of the family economy together. In Vietnam, in fact, family members commonly gave one-third of their earnings to mothers.[21]

Such a deployment of family resources was more ingenious and flexible than a simple reproduction of ethnic mores, be they European or Asian, patriarchal, matrifocal, or egalitarian. Piecing together a common survival from the independent efforts and separate paychecks of husbands, wives, and children required a measure of individual sacrifice, voluntary contribution, mutual loyalty, and conscious choice. Oral historians have collected gripping stories of conflicts over young women's contributions to the household's income. One Italian girl recalled the consequences of reserving one penny of her wages for herself: her father beat her with a towel and threatened, "Girl I'll break you if you don't change." The wisdom of such harsh exercise of patriarchal power was called into question when the daughter responded, "And I said in my heart, my father, we shall see."[22] A Jewish garment worker named Sophie Abrams who raided the family treasury by steaming open her pay envelope was overcome with fear and ethical ambivalence: "Boy, was I scared. But, it worked. I lived in fear my mother would catch me, that she would find out I was cheating. I didn't think I was cheating. I was just taking some of what was mine."[23]

Some family recollections suggest a more effective method of ensuring that daughters contributed their wages to the household pool. Another Italian daughter recounted that "my father was a stonemason. You know how it is. He didn't have steady work and my mother used to talk all the time about how poor we were. So I had my mind on work all the time. I was thinking about how I could . . . bring my money home to my mother."[24] In this case, family loyalty short-circuited patriarchal power and was relayed directly from daughter to mother. Anzia Yezierska pictured the Jewish families of the Lower East Side operating on similar principles, out of mother love rather than patriarchal authority. Her heroine Sara Smolinsky explained her precocious wage-earning this way: "I was about ten years old then. But from always it was heavy on my heart the worries for the house as if I was mother."[25] Her filial piety was echoed in the report of Oi Kwan "Annie" Lai, who left Hong Kong in the 1980s: "I gave all my salary to my parents because our family was very poor. . . . My mom didn't have the $8 a month it cost to go to school."[26]

These recollections warrant some revisions in the usual account of family economics. The division of labor in immigrant families did not conform to the model of Old World patriarchy, the middle-class American breadwinner, or the working-class family wage. These immigrant families might better be described as matrifocal home economies. When the reproduction of the immigrant line depended not just on the male wage but on the pooling of resources within the domestic unit, then the moral force that held the family together, so often that of the mother, became the critical economic factor. Motherhood may have been the most powerful adhesive that bonded the various elements of the household economy—the facets of sex, age, and generation—into a functioning whole. This alternative reading also finds support in the literature of American immigration: not just in the icon of the Jewish mother, as lauded by the founding generation of writers—including Elizabeth Stern, Rose Schneiderman, Anzia Yezierska, Abraham Cahan, Herbert Gold, and Henry Roth—but in the world of the Italian don as well. Mario Puzo's first novel, *The Fortunate Pilgrim*, was a paean not to the godfather but to the heroic mother figure whom he lauded as "ready to murder anyone who stood in the way of so much as a crust of bread from themselves or their children, the implacable enemies of death."[27]

The authority of the immigrant mother was not just a figment of the literary imagination. It also abided in the institutions and practices of ethnic communities and was fervently celebrated by Roman Catholic immigrants. The Virgin of Guadalupe was only one example of the veneration of the Madonna figure, worshiped at Italian festivals from East Harlem to Monterey, California. Rosa Cavalleri turned to the Madonna as her first intercessor whenever she was in need, be it in Tuscany or Chicago: "The Madonna is the mother of us poor women. She helps us all the time. In the old time there were more miracles than now, but I see lots of miracles—in Chicago too. The Madonna and the Saints, they all the time make miracles—in Chicago too."[28] Statues of the Madonna were treasured objects in Italian parishes, and they were carried through the streets in annual neighborhood celebrations such as the feast of Our Lady of Mount Carmel in New York in July, the blessing of the fishing fleet in Monterey Bay in September, and the Feast of the Immaculate Conception in Whittier, California's Vietnamese community.[29] The second wave of immigration carried the Madonna figure to other locations—that Vietnamese church in Whittier, California, the Church of Mary, Queen of Vietnam in New Orleans, and Mission Católica, Nuestra Señora de Las Americas in the suburbs of Atlanta, Georgia. Not coincidentally, the pluralistic aspect of American nationalism is also draped in maternal symbolism. The ample, rounded form of the Statue of Liberty, "Our Lady of the Harbor," promises world-weary immigrants a warm and motherly refuge in her voluptuous skirt.[30]

The Madonna figure reigned most powerfully during the period of peak immigration from Europe, which happened to coincide with the heyday of Progressive maternalism. Like women's public domain, the immigrant manifestation of the symbolic power of motherhood had its generational and historical limits. Ultimately, mothers were succeeded by their sons and daughters, the second immigrant generation. At certain moments in history, moreover, the second generation enacted a rebellion against the first and effected another transformation in gender. The 1910s and 1920s, as described in chapter 5 of this volume, was such a time. The daughters of immigrants enrolled enthusiastically in the ranks of the new women who exchanged the maternal standards of womanhood for models of independence and modernity. Recall Anzia Yezierska's revolt against the Russian Jewish patriarch and her insistence that she would make herself "a person, an American." Yezierska's peer Sarah Reznikoff was incensed by the dismissal of female education in her Jewish family and vowed "not to listen to Mother or Grandmother and learn as much as I could."[31]

These rebellious daughters could be found among Asian immigrants as well. Yezierska's declaration of independence seemed to echo in the memoirs of Jade Snow Wong. Writing as a *Fifth Chinese Daughter*, Wong declared her independence from her immigrant father with an impassioned oration: "I can't help being born a girl. Perhaps, even being a girl, I don't want to marry, just to raise sons! I am a person, besides being a female! Don't the Chinese admit that women also have feelings and minds?"[32] A generation later, Maxine Hong Kingston recited a very similar speech to her mother: "Not everybody thinks I'm nothing. I am not going to be a slave or a wife."[33] At some point in their personal stories, each of these articulate immigrant daughters would make peace with parents, both mothers and fathers, and season their youthful independence with respect for their origins and ancestors. But in their youth they all joined in a chorus that swelled American gender culture with possibilities of liberation from the rusty shackles of modern gender.

The second generation, Jewish, Italian, Chinese, and Japanese alike, bristled at the yoke of the family economy. The breach was monitored in Jewish literature by the figure of the "ghetto girl," berated for spending her wages on gaudy finery and fashion: "listen to the voice of one of you—don't endeavor to mimic the pampered pet of material fortune. . . . For the price of one silken rag, your mother, your toiling father and your little sisters and brothers can have better, purer food, warmer and better garments, comfortable rooms in a better neighborhood and a dozen other things that they haven't now, and suffer because of the lack of it."[34] An Italian daughter succumbed to similar temptations: "I'll never forget the time I got my first pay . . . . I went downtown, first, and I spent a lot, more than half my money . . . . I just went hog wild."[35] The daughters of Japanese immigrants provoked a familiar parental disapproval. The Japanese American press reproved the young generation as "short-skirted baby dolls with their artificial rosebud lips and their languishing, mascara'ed eyes."[36] Whereas the immigrant mother was the personification of familial survival and ethnic solidarity, her daughter stood indicted for unraveling both with her rebellious, selfish, American ways. Each generation of immigrant women kindled change in the meaning of gender in America. The restriction of immigration enacted in 1924 slowed this brushfire but did not extinguish it in the long term.

New Immigrants Meet Postmodernity
1965–2000

When the Immigration Act of 1965 reopened the United States to a new flood of immigrants, the challenge to gender orthodoxy was raised anew. A young woman named Shui Mak Ka recently reenacted the drama of filial rebellion at a banquet table in New York's Chinatown, which was teeming anew with immigrants. It was customary to have men and boys eat first at Chinese ceremonial dinners, leaving smaller, less appealing portions to women. Shui Mak Ka, soon to be a labor activist, defied this family custom by threatening a hunger strike: "It's unfair for girls to get inferior food. We should have the same food as everyone else, or we won't eat." Her father's angry response to this outburst at the dinner table eventually subsided, and the tradition was abandoned. A voice from San Francisco's Chinatown similarly chimed in, in a baritone key. Frank Chin's novel *Donald Duk* reimagined Chinese American history as the restoration of patrilineage between a teenage son and his father, the master chef of the New Year's banquet. But even here the daughters' voice could not be suppressed. Chin also gave a memorable background role to Donald's feisty sisters, fourteen-year-old twins, who interrupted their brother to condemn "old-fashioned, insensitive, machismo, chauvinist pigs." Donald's father had to intervene: "Hold it, girls, let him talk."[37] The leavening of second-wave feminism, which gave rise to chapters of the women's liberation movement among Asian Americans, compounded the volatility of gender among recent immigrants.

Through the 1980s the most voluminous waves of immigration flowed from the east and the south, making Los Angeles International Airport and the U.S.-Mexican border the Ellis Islands of the late twentieth century. European sources of immigration sped up with the fall of the Soviet Union in 1989. For the first time in history, America's borders were permeable from every side and could be accessed from every direction. The Asian sources of the new immigration seemed to be closing the circle of world history begun more than ten thousand years ago when the first human inhabitants of the present-day United States arrived from across the Pacific. Africa began to send a small stream of voluntary immigrants across the Atlantic, some of whom, like the Islamic Mourides of Senegal, displayed an enterprising and merchandising acumen that resembled the first British colonists more than their African slave predecessors. The human race that originated in Africa was reassembling in the United States at the end of the second millennium.[38]

Whatever their country of origin, the newest immigrants were a very diverse lot. They included not just the tired, poor, and homeless but also highly trained professionals. Immigration into the United States was part of a worldwide exchange of peoples, crossing in many directions and—thanks to the ease of transportation and communication—maintaining strong connections with the cultures left behind. In 1990, 30 million residents of the United States claimed Hispanic origins, over 60 percent of them from Mexico and most of the remainder from Central America and the Caribbean. Many moved regularly back and forth across the nation's southern border.[39] The links of the family economy also wrapped around the world. A recent feature article in the *New York Times*, for example, described how Chinese American mothers who worked in the city's sweatshops sent their children back to China to obtain affordable child care within their extended families.[40] In Los Angeles a sociologist encountered domestic workers who left their children back in the Philippines while they pursued better-paying jobs in the United States.[41] In the late twentieth century, international migration seemed to implicate everyone. It enrolled male and female in almost equal numbers.[42] Men dominated the worldwide flow of migration by a small margin, but slightly more than 50 percent of the immigrants into the United States were, for the first time, women. In New York City in the 1990s, there were only ninety-two men for every one hundred women in the immigrant population.[43]

The immigrants who arrived in America in the late twentieth century often discovered that their predecessors had remodeled the gender systems of the old world. Third-generation Chinese Americans, for example, had vaulted from peasant patriarchy to the vanguard of postmodern womanhood. By 1970, the granddaughters of Chinese immigrants had reached levels of education and rates of employment about equal to the national average.[44] In San Francisco 51 percent of the women of Chinese descent were in the labor force in 1970, a rate 10 percent higher than the mean.[45] Already in the second generation, Japanese American women and men conformed to American middle-class marriage patterns and raised a yet more independent generation. Their children stepped decisively beyond their parental cultures: nearly half of them married outside their ethnic group.[46]

Some of the immigrants who arrived after 1965, especially those admitted under the category of skilled workers, were already full-fledged postmodernists. With the fall of Soviet Communism in 1989, Russians and Eastern Europeans added a very contemporary element to the medley of gender changes. They were a world apart from their countrymen and women who had disembarked on Ellis Island a century before. In the Russia of the late twentieth century, 75 percent of all adult women were paid workers, often highly educated and highly skilled.[47] Women constituted 85 percent of all medical personnel, for example, including 50 percent of physicians and executives in medical institutions.[48] In fact, Russian women might well look to the American gender system for a reduction in their workload. They were refuges from a draconian double day that sentenced them to virtually all the household work, along with their jobs outside the home.[49] Immigrants from South India in the 1990s were also up-to-date in their gender practices. Sixty percent of the men and 55 percent of the women held graduate degrees.[50] The Philippine case illustrates the convolutions of gender migration in this century. Three generations past, men led the migration from the Philippines to the United States, only to find their chances of marrying and reproducing cut short by the scarcity of women among them, the restriction of further immigration, and imposition of antimiscegenation statutes. Thousands of them were left to age and die as bachelors in an inhospitable land. When immigration from the Philippines resumed in 1965, women were in the majority and brought with them a thoroughly updated gender culture. Drawing on a long tradition of bilateral kinship, relatively egalitarian property rights, and economic opportunities, Filipino American women posted among the highest rates of education and professional stature among U.S. women. They also led the advance of women into the labor force: with 55 percent of them on the job outside the home, they overtook native-born white women.[51]

The Korean immigrants who migrated about the same time as the Filipinos brought cultural baggage of another sort. In one regard, these migrants had much in common with their host culture. Slightly more than half of them (as opposed to 20 percent of those who stayed at home in Korea) were Christians. Most came as middle-class, Protestant families seeking economic gain. While women were the majority of Korean immigrants, they were rarely independent: if not wives of immigrant men, they were brides of U.S. soldiers

WOMEN REMAKE GENDER

or children adopted into American families. Korean immigrants took exception to postmodern gender roles. In their nation of origin, men and women occupied very separate spheres: men regarded domestic tasks with distaste, while married women were reluctant to take jobs outside the home.[52] Whatever the gender norms Korean immigrants carried to America, they would soon be tested by postmodern exigencies. When their husbands found limited employment opportunities, Korean wives quickly entered the labor force or pitched in running the family businesses.[53]

Many recent immigrants fled their homelands with greater urgency than the enterprising Korean merchants or the ambitious women of the Philippines. Few had the resources of the young Indian couples taking up high-tech jobs in the computer industry, while hundreds of thousands were admitted to the United States as penniless political refugees. The nearly one million immigrants exiled from Southeast Asia after the U.S. defeat in the Vietnam War experienced the most extreme gender shock. The widest gulf between national cultures was straddled by the mountain tribesmen of Laos, the Hmong. In the 1950s the Hmong lived three thousand feet above sea level, subsisted on slash-and-burn agriculture, and resided in extended households, some of which were formed by the age-old customs of wife kidnapping and polygamy.[54] The women did much of the hard agricultural labor, while men cleared the land and defended the clan. Then, in the 1960s, after selling their warrior skills to the French during the colonial wars in Indochina, the Hmong tribesmen became the mercenary army of the Central Intelligence Agency. When the U.S. Army withdrew from Southeast Asia in defeat, the Hmong had little choice but to emigrate with them. Resettled in places like California, Hmong women and men were forced to make remarkable changes in rapid order. The Xiong family, for example, found the housing laws of Goleta, California, inhospitable to their conjoined extended families, which totaled twenty-seven residents, and scraped together the money to purchase larger and cheaper accommodations in the Central Valley. Middle-aged peasant women accustomed to driving water buffalo through rice fields had to learn to navigate freeways to take their children to school. (One cheerfully reported that she failed her driver's test the first time, perhaps because she was given the Spanish version.) Some men could not adapt at all and succumbed to a mysterious illness that took their lives as they slept. For the Hmong men and women alike, gender change was imperative and immediate. One woman put it simply: "Here in America, both the husband and wife must work simultaneously to earn enough money to live on."[55]

The resourcefulness of refugees and the particular adaptability of women immigrants were also displayed by émigrés from Vietnam. The Vietnamese gender heritage blended the patriarchal ideology of ancient Confucian texts with local folk traditions that were less rigidly hierarchical.[56] Confucius reminded women of the four virtues of their sex—"to be a good housewife, to have a beautiful appearance, to speak well and softly, and to be of good character"—and the threefold obediences owed to father, husband, and then sons. But folk tradition permitted Vietnamese daughters to inherit property and elevated wives to the role of "Chief of the Interior."[57] More to the point, Vietnamese gender practices had been constantly modified and updated by centuries of anticolonialist struggles—against the Chinese, the French, and the United States. The men who migrated to the United States from Vietnam in the 1970s had long ago given up their traditional roles to take on military duties as soldiers in the South Vietnamese army, or as allies and employees of the U.S. military. While the men practiced this militarized masculinity, women assumed expanded roles in the family economy. As the war dragged on, and husbands and fathers were off on the battlefields for prolonged periods, women became the economic support of their families. They sharpened their linguistic tools and took up government jobs (under the Vietnamese, French, or Americans), ran the family businesses, operated much of the commercial sector, and took advantage of the opportunities to trade with American servicemen. Once evacuated into the United States, Vietnamese women would be prepared to assume modern and postmodern gender roles. Among early migrants from Vietnam (those most likely to have close ties with the Americans), women had a higher rate of employment in sales and clerical work than did men—only 7 percent called themselves housewives—and they had obtained an educational level almost equal to their mates.[58]

In the last decade of the twentieth century, the path of immigration had come full circle; it had extended through Asia and Latin America and returned to the European sites of the previous wave. Immigrants from all around the globe were strategically stationed and well prepared to take part in gender changes underway within the United States. With alacrity immigrant women became up-to-date with the postmodern fashion of womanhood; promptly on arrival, wives and mothers (not just teenage daughters as in the early wave of immigration) marched into the labor force. With the notable exception of Russian and Jamaican women, who had already maximized their work potential, the pace of labor force participation quickened on entry into the United States. Among Russian Jewish immigrants, 61 percent of women, as opposed to just under 68 percent of men, entered the U.S. labor force, the highest proportion of any ethnic group.[59] The majority of émigrés from Jamaica were women who headed to the United States on their own in pursuit of specific employment opportunities in fields like nursing.[60] Cuban refugees also adopted the postmodern sexual division of labor. On arrival in the United States, the rate of female employment among one group of émigrés rose to 68 percent, in contrast to 48 percent in Cuba.[61] Among Mexican women, 69 percent of undocumented women immigrants and 44 percent of the documented came with the intention of working. Forty to 60 percent of the wives joined the labor force, even though two-thirds of their countrymen said, "women's place is in the home."[62] In New York 40 percent of Korean wives and 50 percent of husbands worked sixty hours a week or more, mostly in their family businesses.[63] In the Vietnamese community the ratio of employment between men and women kept declining until the differential was as low as 21 percent by 1980.[64]

Immigrant wives and mothers were rushing to work with the same determination as the native-born. A study of Portuguese and Colombian workers in the textile industry of New England chronicled the remodeling of the immigrant family economy. Restrictions on child labor and home work, along with compulsory education, prohibited sons and daughters from supplementing the small income of working-class fathers; it was left to wives to provide this critical second income in the 1990s.[65] Like young immigrants from Southern and Eastern Europe before them, Asian and Hispanic women often took the first giant step from home to work by entering the needle trades. The garment shops were humming again after 1965, often in the same dilapidated buildings in lower Manhattan where Jewish working girls had once served their apprenticeships. In Chinatown six of ten families contained a garment worker, usually a woman and often a wife and mother. These were not the working girls of old. Their employers, union representatives, and co-workers called them "aunts and grannies"; to their families they were the margin of survival.[66]

Whether immigrant women joined the labor force as independent migrants, as the wives of poor men, or as eager professionals, work outside the home became an essential part of their identity. Cuban wives, for whom employment initially marked a humiliating descent from the middle class to manual labor, took satisfaction in their jobs outside the home: "I love to work. Working makes me feel independent and in control of my life."[67] "I work to help my family," another continued. "But besides that, I couldn't stand the loneliness if I stayed home."[68] Jamaican healthcare workers found both self-esteem and social worth on the lowliest rungs of the occupational ladder: "I like to help people. People don't realize how hard it is to work in the home and deal with sick people. Have to please them, make them comfortable, keep them happy. I like to work and I love my job. I love housework, yes, but I love nursing better. I may not be an R.N., but I help people."[69] Another Jamaican woman found her work compensated by a new sense of autonomy. "We were brought up to think we have to depend on a man, do this for a man, listen to your man," said this New York secretary, "but here you can be on your own, more independent."[70] Recalling the pleasure of cultivating corn and potatoes in the Azores, a Portuguese immigrant quickly adjusted to her American workplace. "I have always liked working," she said.[71] Now she cherished the factory job that supplied her with the financial wherewithal to "set up a new life."[72]

Like the generations before them, the new immigrants adjusted the sexual division of labor to the economic conditions of their adopted land. However, the immigrants of the late twentieth century exercised their gender dexterity in distinctively postmodern ways and with different consequences. For example, reports of generational conflict are rarer and less intense in the writings and oral histories of recent immigrants. The later-day second generation has not mounted a concerted rebellion against their elders. Typically, daughters trouble their parents with the usual adolescent annoyances — their tastes in music, styles of dress and undress, and procrastination on their homework. The fact that the younger or second-generation immigrants are to be found at school or college rather than in the labor force probably accounts for the relative quiet on the generation front. In the postmodern global economy, wives have replaced children as the principal supplementary workers, and as a consequence the pressures attendant to immigration now bear down on the relations between husbands and wives, rather than parents and children.

Wives and mothers met the challenge of immigration with resilience and resourcefulness. In fact, their willingness to assume responsibility for the material welfare of themselves and their families often initiated immigration in the first place. After 1930 women made up a slight majority of immigrants into the United States. Some of them, like Kyung Park, set out for the United States as an act of independence: "I came to the U.S. in 1990 without my husband. He stayed in Korea. At the time we were having big problems." She would send his divorce papers back to Korea. Lucrecia Tamayo told a similar postmodern immigration story: "I got married in Mexico, but the person I married was treating me bad, so I moved here 15 years ago in 1982. I came by myself . . . [through the mountains], with a coyote. Oh, it was scary!"[73] Almost all the new women immigrants — divorced, married, or single, émigrés from the more traditional or most postmodern gender cultures — braved the

WOMEN REMAKE GENDER

labor force soon upon arrival in the United States. One Vietnamese daughter reported this extraordinary but not atypical work history of her mother: "Since we moved to the United States in 1979, my mother has worked in an assembly line, at a factory, operated a mom-and-pop Oriental food market, transported garment pieces between the factories and seamstresses who sewed from their homes, served Chinese fast food at the mall, and become a beautician, an occupation she still maintains. In Vietnam she worked as a waitress at a restaurant and as a maid in a hotel."[74] However overworked and underpaid, wives seldom complained about a conflict between the family and the workplace. The two were indivisible parts of everyday life among new immigrants to the United States. Long hours of wage labor fulfilled family obligations and were the mother's milk of immigrant family economics.

Grateful children are good informants about the internal dynamics of these households. The son of a New York Chinatown garment worker spoke for many children when he expressed his appreciation for his hard-working mother. Blending his American savvy and his Asian heritage, he commended her as a "superwoman" and the embodiment of a Chinese proverb about the "greatness of cows": "they eat grasses but produce milk."[75] The latest, voluminous wave of immigration has extended the matrifocal household economy far beyond the family residence. In order to provide for their children, the new immigrant mothers ventured across national boundaries, sometimes leaving their families behind. Motherhood stretched and strained from the United States to places like the village of Miraflores in the Dominican Republic, where nearly two-thirds of all families had members in Boston, Massachusetts. For some immigrants from Miraflores, motherhood was compressed painfully into an annual Christmas visit.[76] Filipinas extended the bonds of motherhood all the way across the Pacific. Domestic workers who resided in Southern California typically sent over 50 percent of their earnings to families back in the Philippines.[77] One Filipina described the emotional pains of this transnational mothering as "that guilty feeling. You know you're supposed to be there, beside them."[78] Another wrestled with her maternal conscience: "It's worth it you know, because I can give [them] whatever [they] like. Not really everything, because I'm not there, but I can send them to good schools, I can buy them what they like. . . . I miss their growing up. But what can I do? I sacrifice."[79]

While mothers took up the responsibility of earning income away from home, with all the anguish it might entail, fathers and husbands had their own difficulties adjusting to the changing gender order. One Colombian man who worked in a New England textile town reported commonplace injuries to immigrant masculinity: "In our country the wife is not accustomed to working because it's a dishonor."[80] A compatriot added, "It is a right of feeling oneself to be a man, a male. Well, he thinks himself more powerful, right?"[81] Vietnamese men who migrated to Philadelphia in the 1970s often saw their stature plummet from high military positions to unemployment. Some of them complained bitterly about the damage to their masculinity: "In Vietnam the man of the house is king. Below him the children, then the pets of the home, and then the women. Here the woman is the king and the man holds a position below the pets."[82] The initial years of resettlement also entailed downward mobility for Korean men. In both immigrant communities this crisis of masculinity correlated with high rates of domestic violence.[83] Immigrant families often broke apart under this pressure. One Hmong wife told this story: "We needed two incomes and I went to work. I know my husband did not like it, but it could not be helped. . . . I could work easier than he could and I began to do well and I supported the family. I became the breadwinner. He had bad feelings about this. . . . Eventually, we were divorced."[84]

For immigrants, like the native-born, postmodernity brought opportunities, as well as risks, for women, for men, and for the relations of the sexes. The gender flexibility required by immigration often had a modestly egalitarian effect. Prosperous Indian husbands of working women were reluctant to take equal responsibility for housework and child care, but at times they picked up some of the chores that would have fallen to servants back in India: "My wife started working also and I cannot expect the same kind of service [as] from the non-working wife. If she is cooking, I wash the dishes or cut the vegetables or some other kind of help. I kind of share the responsibility."[85] That small gesture of reciprocity was about all to be expected from husbands in middle-class, two-income households. More radical alterations in the sexual division of labor were required of men who arrived in the United States without financial resources or marketable skills. Some working wives were the beneficiaries of the husbandly care extended by this Cambodian refugee: "My husband says to the kids, 'Your Mommy is so tired. Let her sleep a little while. Can you come with me, please?' He's so busy with the kids. He helps me a lot when he's home. When he's home, I just sit down."[86] A minority of Dominican wives surrendered their earnings to husbands, and some couples formed egalitarian consumer partnerships: "On Saturdays we would do the shopping together. If there was anything extra we had to buy, we would decide we'll save this much and put this much aside so we can buy that new chair in a few months."[87] Some impoverished men in New York's Chinatown accommodated their working wives in more arduous ways.

They worked nights in restaurants, sometimes doing dishes till midnight, and supervised children when their wives went off to the sweatshop. Other husbands acceded only begrudgingly to a wife's working outside the home. Immigrant men and women were often caught in the sharpest dislocation in the postmodern economy, the shift from an industrial to a service economy. The men who were expelled from the former seldom sought employment in the garment industry or in the personal service sector where women took up their low-paying jobs. A few unemployed immigrant men did venture into the garment shops of Chinatown, but they assumed the few better-paying jobs to be found there.[88] While immigrant men expressed remorse for their loss of patriarchal authority, both sexes suffered the burden of supporting a family during hard times in a strange land.

It would be impossible to predict how the relations of the sexes would stand up to the massive reshuffling of the world's population. Moreover, the future of gender in America would unfold under the uncertain conditions of a new millennium, in a nation whose economy and politics were in flux, if not crisis. A look at the most advanced sector of the new economy, the capital of the electronics and computer industry in Santa Clara County, California, offers a prescient glimpse at how gender, class, and ethnicity operated at the vortex of economic change. Not surprisingly, the upper ranks of the computer industry in the Silicon Valley were dominated by white, native-born men. In 1990 men constituted over 73 percent of the managers, 80 percent of professional employees, and 77 percent of the technicians. At the pinnacle of the electronics industry, however, at Hewlett-Packard, the company where the computer revolution began a half century ago, there briefly stood a symbol of gender revolution and immigrant origins, a chief executive officer named Carly Fiorina (a medieval history major, by the way).[89] After a brief tenure, however, she was deposed and replaced by another of the native-born white males who predominated at the helm of the most dynamic economic sector. During the boom years of the 1990s, a buffed-up masculinity reigned over Silicon Valley, personified by the engineers and designers who had an insatiable appetite for work. At Apple Computer, with its whiz-kid leaders Steve Jobs and Steve Wozniak, it was said that "the cult of the macho workaholic is alive and well." Although Apple had family-friendly policies and day care centers, there were still few women in the top management.[90]

Recent immigrants were not excluded from the higher economic echelons of Silicon Valley. Natives of China, Hong Kong, and India were among the leading entrepreneurs in the electronics industry. They, too, were overwhelmingly male, however, and were said to be so hard-working that their wives referred to themselves as "computer widows," consigned to suburban homes while their husbands roamed the stratosphere of the global economy.[91] Most recent immigrants and racial minorities, however, fared poorly in the silicon economy: they were 12 percent of managers, 16 percent of professionals, and 18 percent of technicians.[92] Immigrant women were crowded together at the bottom of the income scale. In the few remaining manufacturing jobs in Silicon Valley, women constituted 50 to 75 percent of the operatives, at least three-quarters of whom had been born abroad.[93] According to one study, 80 percent of these low-paid women workers were the highest earners in their households and the major source of family income.[94] Making a living in high-tech California threw the poor and the foreign-born back on such old-fashioned economic strategies as home production and child labor. This report was dated June 1999: "Tong, a Vietnamese immigrant, leans over the family dining table to inspect his work as his ten-year-old son, Nam, piles a handful of transistors by his side. . . . Down the back hallway, Tong's daughters—three of them teenagers—can be heard, chatting and moving about the family bedroom. They are working on boards, too."[95]

Gender could act like salt in the wounds of immigration and economic restructuring. The managers of electronic assembly plants attempted to buy off the women operatives with compliments and flirtation. They reasoned that "the gals . . . even though they do unfeminine work, they really are still feminine." The women worked for other stakes: to support their families and maintain a fragile gender balance in beleaguered immigrant households. One woman even conveyed part of her pay to her son, that he might pass it on to her spouse without damaging the pride of the breadwinner. Others excused domestic violence: "He doesn't want to hurt me, but he is so hurt inside because he feels he has failed as a man."[96] At the bottom of the social structure, at a time of increasing economic inequality in America, male and female shared the same hardships and gender pain.

Despite all the variations, twists, turns, and reversals of postmodernity, immigrant women and racial minorities clustered toward the bottom rungs of the social structure. Concentrated at the lowest ranks were immigrants from south of the Rio Grande, designated in the census as ethnically Hispanic. Tides of emigrants from Mexico plunged into the postmodern stream of gender change: wives and mothers enrolled in the labor force in proportions comparable to the national average, but they usually found work in America grueling and ill paid. In the San Francisco Bay area women workers pieced together less than a living wage cleaning private homes that were strewn along a vast sprawl of freeway. Working mothers returned from these household labors only to take up another, unpaid, domestic job in their own homes. Still, immigrant women often counted their blessings to social investigators: "Here, with one week's pay we can buy shoes for all three children, clothes, pants, or whatever we need, and being there [in Mexico], no, we can't. . . . and we have always the refrigerator full of milk. Also, the milk over there is not as good as it is here. If you are going to take your children from a place where they are better off to take them elsewhere, where they will suffer more, where they will have few opportunities to study for a career, it's difficult, it's very difficult."[97] Like most of the women interviewed in a community called Oakview, this Mexican immigrant mother was more determined than her husband to stay in the United States.[98]

Men who emigrated from Mexico found fewer opportunities for steady work in the service-oriented economy and often longed to return to Mexico and to what they recalled as its masculine privileges. The postmodern global economy treated Hispanic men especially unkindly. One Southern California employer calculated gender into his personnel practices as follows: "Mexican women, especially the foreign-born, will do anything for their families. They work hard and they don't ask for much, they don't give you any hassles. So men could do the same job but are more ambitious and what we have is handiwork; that's women's work."[99] One Oakview man became despondent in describing his family life: "Well, each person orders oneself here, something like that. . . . Back there, no. It was still whatever I said that was. I decided matters."[100] This imperiled male hegemony took its toll in a rising tide of divorces and female-headed households.

Masculinity may have remained a hegemonic ideology in large parts of America, but it often poisoned the relations of the sexes in both the barrio and the silicon suburbs. While manhood still conveyed power and pride to the executives at the top, it brought a sense of defeat to men who emigrated from Mexico to find only menial, irregular employment and fewer job opportunities than many of the women who followed the same immigrant path. The meaning of male and female was volatile and somewhat blurry, but the power of gender had not subsided. It might seem that the power of sex to create meaning and organize society had only grown more mysterious, sophisticated, and wily. Gender not only divided men from women but also created bewildering layers of inequity that extended from the female-headed households of the poor, to the two-income families of the middle class, to the trophy wives of the rich. The Latinas who journeyed each working day from their barrio homes to the kitchens of affluent employers, like the day laborers who cleared the debris from suburban lawns, viewed this gender/class system at painfully close quarters.[101]

The strains of male and female stretched from the poor districts of the United States to all around the globe in the late twentieth century. The work history of Bo Yee, born in Guangdong Province, China, illustrates this small world of postmodern gender. She traveled from the People's Republic of China to Hong Kong and then to California, but she never escaped the snares of the sweatshop. The 1980s found her in Oakland, working for a pittance, seven days of week, locked in a windowless "sealed cage," forbidden to go to the bathroom or talk loudly.[102] These working conditions resembled the sweatshops of the Lower East Side a century ago, the maquiladores set up on the Mexican border in the 1960s, and the free-enterprise zones proliferating through South Asia today.[103] In Malaysia, Mexico, the Philippines, and Sri Lanka, 80 percent of the workers in these transnational factories are young women.[104] The outsourcing of American jobs was a postmodern twist on the familiar quest for cheap female labor: it led to places like Bangladesh, where young women earned as little as twenty cents an hour sewing clothes for Wal-Mart.[105] Compilations of statistics by the United Nations documented a worldwide contagion of the maladies of postmodern gender: sweated labor, divorce, desertion, unwed motherhood, inadequate child care, female-headed households, and the woman's double day plagued the first world and the third, north and south, east and west.[106]

Joining Together to Remake Male, Female, and America

The global reorganization of gender raises one last urgent question: Where in the world is there a space of citizenship, a public place where women and men can act together for their common good? The immigrants who disembarked in the United States a century ago invigorated the nation's politics. While many sons and daughters of the Eastern European shtetls reveled in socialism, anarchism, and communism, others swelled the ranks of the labor and the suffrage movements. Mary Antin, who arrived in 1894, embraced the mainstream American political tradition. She spoke for "the creature with the untidy beard [who] carries in his bosom his citizenship papers" and "the rag picker's daughters [who] are hastening over the ocean to teach your children in the public school." Antin recalled the zenith of her own "civic pride and personal contentment" as "the bright September morning when [she] entered the public school."[107] By the close of the twentieth century, the daughters and granddaughters of European immigrants had taken up posts in the U.S. Congress. For example, the California congressional delegation for the 108th Congress was led by Senators Dianne Feinstein and Barbara Boxer, and the minority leader of the House of Representatives was Nancy Pelosi of San Francisco. At the same time, new immigrants from south of the Rio Grande rushed to send women into positions of political authority. The 47th District of California first sent Loretta Sanchez, a daughter of Mexican immigrants, to the U.S. Congress in 1996. The nearby 39th District sent her sister, Linda T. Sánchez, to the House of Representatives six years later.

The second wave of immigration hit the shores of the United States at an auspicious time, at the height of the civil rights and feminist movements. In the showcase of the electronic age, Silicon Valley, California, women had actually laid claim to the local public sphere. They took over the mayor's office, the majority of seats on the county Board of Supervisors, and the city council of San Jose and proceeded to put their imprint on public policy. Calling their city the feminist capital of America, the woman-dominated city government enacted the first comparable pay statute for the public sector. The feminist politicians were pushed toward this feminist policy by striking workers and assisted in this accomplishment by an energetic service sector union, the American Federation of State, County, and Municipal Employees. The Labor Council of San Mateo County was also headed by a woman. In this most futuristic outpost of America, it seemed as if the busy managers of the private sector had conceded the public sphere to women.[108]

Feminism energized politics in the late twentieth century from the local to the international level. Having leapt over national boundaries since the days of Mary Wollstonecraft, women's rights were first institutionalized internationally with the 1946 Commission on the Status of Women and then grounded in international law with the Universal Declaration of Human Rights in 1948. Fueled by the second wave of feminism, which still waxes strong in many portions of the world, the United Nations sponsored three international forums on women's issues, culminating with a congregation of some 50,000 women and 250 nongovernmental organizations in Beijing in 1995.[109]

Gender politics garnered strength all along the route of postmodern migration. In the Indian American community of Pittsburgh, women initiated a campaign to create a multimillion-dollar temple, and they held at least half the positions on its board of directors.[110] Women also played leading roles in articulating a political identity for Indian Americans by creating an Indian Nationality Room at the University of Pittsburgh.[111] Some South Asian daughters practiced a brazenly feminist politics by founding an organization called Sahki to combat domestic violence within the immigrant community. They earned the rancor of their fathers and, along with a contingent of lesbians, were denied the right to march in the forty-seventh annual Indian Independence Day celebration in New York City.[112] Immigrant women and their daughters were also becoming more prominent in the unions. In New York's Chinatown during the 1980s, women initiated a demand for day care centers and then a successful garment strike.[113] When in 1986 the United States granted amnesty to resident undocumented workers, thousands of women came forward to claim citizenship.

Those women and men who migrated into the United States from Mexico acted out a transnational politics of gender in particularly vibrant and dynamic ways. Under the banner of the Virgin of Guadalupe, they carried their own heritage of gender difference and their own sense of the common good with them across the border. Early in the nineteenth century, when Alta California was Mexican territory, women were constrained by both Spanish codes of honor and gender roles of domestic servitude, but they also enjoyed stronger property rights than Anglo-American women, retained their dowries and their names after marriage, and enjoyed equal interest with their husbands in community property.[114] A century later, though still very much a minority among Mexican migrants, women flocked into the workforce in fields and canneries, and they played significant roles in the labor movement. Relatively well represented on some slates of union officers, they put matters of child care on the agenda of the West Coast labor movement.[115]

The prominent role of Chicanas in the labor struggles of the 1930s expanded in the 1960s, when Dolores Huerta shared the leadership of the United Farm Workers union with César Chávez. Huerta, a mother of nine, a single parent, and former teacher, became the super-mom of what has been termed the "political familialism" of Mexican Americans.[116] Huerta encapsulated this political strategy in a simple vignette: "When I had my younger children and I was still negotiating, I would take nursing breaks . . . everybody would have to wait while the baby ate. Then I would go back to the table and started negotiating again. . . . I think it made employers more sensitive to the fact that women were talking about benefits and the terms of a contract, we're talking about families and we're talking about children."[117] In the 1970s the daughters of Mexican immigrants would be organizing feminist caucuses in the Chicano Student Movement, while cannery workers were making demands for equal pay and equal work. In 1976, when women workers of Santa Clara County, California, won a contract that overthrew discriminatory job

WOMEN REMAKE GENDER

classifications, one of the beneficiaries reported that "ever since women have been able to do 'men's jobs' we have it easier."[118] The wage increase that came with the opening of heavy industrial jobs to her sex bought this woman a divorce. She credited her political activism with helping her win "freedom from a bad marriage."[119]

When these benefits disappeared along with the canneries in the next decade, the Latinas moved out of the fields and factories and into the cities and the expanding service sector of the economy. In the 1990s women became a sizable presence in the previously male ranks of janitors. Employed by large agencies that had contracted to perform these services throughout the country, immigrant women and men cleaned the office towers, sports stadiums, airports, and public buildings of global cities. Latinos quickly converted these postmodern places of employment into a place of labor activism. In Los Angeles in 1988 the Service Employees International Union began mobilizing men and women in a campaign called Justice for Janitors. Latinas filed onto picket lines and into leadership positions and helped to secure union representation for a vast and growing segment of the labor force. The collaboration of women and men during the Los Angeles janitors' strike demonstrated that gender could be a political resource rather than a liability.[120]

The women and men who came up from Mexico to help write the most recent chapter of U.S. gender history are closing the cycle that began to unfold five hundred years ago. The blood of the conquistadores had long ago merged with the Indian majority and created a population that is now the largest single ethnic minority in the United States and the majority in some of the nation's major cities. Latinos and Latinas represent both the poorest social strata and a vibrant cultural presence. They carry onto city streets, plazas, and political stages the promise of a more inclusive politics that is symbolized by the protean image of the Virgin of Guadalupe. Transported to the United States by Mexican immigrants, the Virgin has become a summons to political activism, as well as piety. In 1934 in the city of Los Angeles, forty thousand Angelenos defied both the Mexican consulate and the Anglo mayor by parading behind a statue of the Virgin, on her feast day, December 8.[121] Young and old, men and women, took the Virgin as the insignia of their ethnic identity. During an outbreak of xenophobia in the 1990s, the Virgin's image was emblazoned on the walls of the barrio, effaced by vandals, and painted again.[122]

Feminists also commandeered the symbol of the Mexican American Madonna. In the 1970s Chicana artists interpreted the Virgin of Guadalupe not as their intercessor before male power but as a model of independent womanhood. Ester Hernández posed the Virgin defending the "*derechos de los Xicanos,*" and Yolanda López painted a "portrait of the artist as the Virgin of Guadalupe." In the first the Virgin had donned a martial arts costume and in the second a pair of running shoes. In both images the Virgin's veil waved as a banner of liberation for her sex. By the 1990s, the mantle of the Virgin of Guadalupe was capacious enough to shelter even sexual revolutionaries. A small northern California press issued a volume of Latina lesbian literature under a blasphemous cover image: the Virgin of Guadalupe was tattooed on the back of a female nude. This chameleon-like gender symbolism evoked all the multiplicity and possibility of postmodern gender.[123]

Through symbols like this, the men and women who came across the border from Mexico in the late twentieth century spoke eloquently of the maelstrom of migration and the malleability of gender. With each new movement of peoples across the porous borders of North America, women and men made themselves anew and then knit themselves together again into families, communities, and trade unions. Behind the banner of the Virgin of Guadalupe, immigrants from Mexico have moved beyond some of the dualism that has so long divided male from female, home from work, family from community, and public from private. The writer Richard Rodriguez retrieved this message from his childhood worship before the Virgin: the Mexican American church bridged the intimacy of his family and the remote public territory of the Anglo world. The Virgin, the special counsel of his mother, also spoke to him personally. She was "someone like us. And she appeared, I could see from her picture, as a young Indian maiden—dark just like me."[124] Juana Gutierrez, who served her neighborhood and fought city hall in an association named simply "The Mothers of East Los Angeles," framed her political philosophy this way: "The mother is the soul of the family; but the child is the heartbeat. We must fight to keep the heart of our community beating. Not just for our children, but for everyone's children."[125]

Maternal allegories, like the Virgin of Guadalupe, have the rhetorical power to bring public and private, family and society, male and female together under a mantle of mutual care. But they also have their political liabilities. Consider the less savory aspects of the apple pie described in chapter 2 and recall how the maternalism of the Progressive Era also camouflaged class inequities and institutionalized a dependent, childlike status for women in need. Madonna symbolism, with its foundation in family and kinship, can also set narrow ethnic boundaries on the common good and inhibit the political interchange and coalition-building necessary in a diverse, democratic society. Fortunately, the heterogeneous immigrant population of global cities like Los Angeles also shows some signs of a more pluralistic and expansive

Yolanda López, *Portrait of the Artist as the Virgin of Guadalupe.*
(Courtesy of Yolanda M. López)

political activism. Los Angeles garment workers have formed ad hoc groups like the Thai and Latino Workers Organizing Committee of the Retailers Accountability Campaign. The Korean Immigrant Workers Advocates was founded in 1992, when Korean waitresses joined with Latino kitchen staff to resist the oppressive working conditions in the restaurants of Korea Town.[126] This coalition organized laborers in low-paying sectors of janitorial, construction, and garment work regardless of ethnicity and gender.[127] Meanwhile, to the north in Oakland, Asian Immigrant Women Advocates united different generations and classes in support of American workers of both Asian and Latin American ancestry.[128] By joining together regardless of national origin and embracing both genders, these grassroots organizations are outgrowing the metaphor of maternalism.

Postmodern feminists also have reason to distrust Madonna complexes. At a time when women still bear more than their share of the cost of parenting, and as long as the public sector is stingy in its benefits for mothers and children, equating the public good with maternity has dubious financial implications. It is reassuring, therefore, to see that the Mexican American Madonna has been rewritten by the young and the second generation, even tattooed on the backs of lesbians. Like the kaleidoscopic images of the Virgin of Guadalupe, Mexican American writing varies by generation as well as class. The stories told by immigrant daughters late in the twentieth century quaked with the excitement of gender change. The voice of the second-generation Chicana became an anthem of independence in 1984 when Sandra Cisneros's *The House on Mango Street* won a wide following among young women readers. The author herself was an immigrant's daughter, highly educated, a teacher of Latino high school students in Chicago, and a stylish and urbane poet. She presented her poetry and fiction not as autobiography but as "a collective story peopled with several lives from my past and present, placed in one fictional time and neighborhood."[129]

Cisneros populated the place called Mango Street with a large cast of Spanish-speaking characters—from Mexico, Central America, Puerto Rico, and Chicago, Illinois. Almost all her characters, girls and women, boys and men, lived just outside the American dream. There was Sally, to whom she wrote the apostrophe: "Do you wish your feet would one day keep walking and take you far away from Mango Street, far away and maybe your feet would stop in front of a house, a nice one with flowers and big windows and steps for you to climb up two by two upstairs to where a room is waiting for you?" Or Minerva, who "has two kids and a husband who left. Her mother raised her kids alone and it looks like her daughters will go that way too." And then there was Elenita, who resorted to voodoo, tarot cards, and magic potions, as well as prayers to the Virgin, all in hopes of divining some hope in her future. The Mango Street of Cisneros's imagination, however, was not a woman's sphere. The street was full of sympathetic male characters. There was the single father who went off to work before dawn, "papa who wakes up tired in the dark," and the young immigrant who died anonymously in the North. His transnational family "never saw the kitchenettes. They never knew about the two-room flats and sleeping rooms he rented, the weekly money orders sent home, the currency exchange."[130]

One central figure escorted the reader along Mango Street: Esperanza, whose name in English "means hope. In Spanish it's too many letters." When readers asked Cisneros if Esperanza speaks for the author she responded, "Yes. And no. And then again, perhaps maybe." And finally: "you the reader, are Esperanza." Esperanza's parting words are these: "One day I will pack my bags of books and paper. One day I will say good bye to Mango. I am too strong for her to keep me here forever." And when friends and neighbors ask, "Why did she march so far away? They will not know I have gone away to come back. For the ones I left behind. For the ones who cannot [get] out."[131] Such a posture is one resourceful way to face the unfolding mysteries of sex: alert with hope, loyal to memory, and acutely attentive to the great variety of men and women to be found along the streets we share. Esperanza remembers the long history of inequity and injustice that adheres so stubbornly to the most polarized and dualistic distinction within human populations. But Esperanza also imagines another future. If women and men can edge closer toward equality, our differences might become matters of reciprocal understanding, mutual pleasure, and a few invigorating arguments.

Cisneros was not alone among the daughters and sons of immigrants who have been reimagining the divide between men and women in America. In a nation of immigrants, these challenges to the tired old ways of doing gender have been repeated many times. The short stories of M. Evelina Galang pictured young South Asian women bounding across borders in a relay of personae: an exotic dancer and a corporate grind, an unwed, pregnant filmmaker and a studious applicant to Johns Hopkins University, chaste obedient daughters and lusty, love-struck adolescents. Galang's new immigrant heroines chafed against both ethnic and gender identity as they proclaimed a "wild American self, a woman who speaks with a nasal twang, drinks beer with brats and rice, and dances when no one's looking." Perhaps the most powerful solvent of gender orthodoxy is the sense of humor demonstrated by a small but ebullient third wave of feminism. In one postmodern parable written by Gish Jen, a Chinese-born mother gave voice to the everyday trials of gender as experienced by her daughter, an ambitious professional, anxious parent, and wife to a hapless mate—of Irish parentage: "These days my beautiful daughter is so tired she can just sit there in a chair and fall asleep. John lost his job again, already, but still they rather hire a baby-sitter than ask me to help, even they can't afford it." The grandmother retreats from this hothouse of gender gone awry and takes up residence with her daughter's mother-in-law: "Now I am become honorary Irish myself, according to Bess. Me! Who's Irish? I say, and she laugh."[132]

A whimsical query like "Who's Irish?" raises a playful mystery of sex and a critical open question. At a time when China, Ireland, the United States of America, and the wide world are all bound up together on the same fragile globe, it would be wasteful to confine the energy and talent of another generation within arbitrary boundaries of ethnicity, nationality, or sex. The last tumultuous half century opened many fissures in the gender divide and has shown that men and women can be extremely flexible and inventive in converting the restrictions of the past into resources for positive change. Unraveling the mystery of sex is a fitting exercise of mind and imagination in these times. It teaches us to see differences as interdependency.

Only a present-minded Pollyanna, however, would expect the youthful defiance of a few postmodern immigrant writers to finally topple the hierarchy of gender. This moment in American history, when the public domain is in considerable disarray, when military masculinity is again hegemonic, and when popular culture is still stocked with both momism and misogyny, does not seem to be propitious for feminist revolution. The public discussion necessary to realign male and female in more equitable ways is hardly audible in the twenty-first century. But history has not stopped, and the present is always alive with possibilities of change. The ardor of movements for women's rights and sexual freedom has not totally subsided. Feminist institutions, some of them international in scale, remain in place to advocate gender justice and defend the rights of sexual minorities. And multitudes of women and men are bridging the gender divide every day, in the workforce, in the home, and in the public sphere. Perhaps the most auspicious aspect of this present unsettled moment in the history of gender in America is the opening of the public sphere to significant numbers of women and to the issues that their particular history has prepared them to articulate.

At the beginning of the twenty-first century, as enacted with special vigor by the new immigrants, gender often serves not as a straitjacket but as a set of resources that can be adapted in flexible ways in behalf of families, communities, and the public good. By adopting new work roles, women, and some men, cushioned the shock of transplanting their families to the United States. Leaders of unions, and men and women of the rank and file, championed the needs of working parents and children. Postmodern mothers are of necessity attentive to the public interest on two fronts, both on the job and in the home. When a second generation of immigrants, feminists, and sex radicals assail the tyranny of sex difference, the possibilities of gender change redouble yet again. Much of the dualism of sex dissolves in this effervescent multiplicity of postmodern America. The immigrant neighborhoods of East Los Angeles or Queens, New York, suburbs, and cities across the United States are exploding with differences that cannot be reduced to black or white, us or them, or to that persistent and mystifying simplification: male versus female. For all these reasons, sex is not a mandate but a mystery. By vigilantly resisting the impulse to divide humans according to this single aspect of our complex humanity, we might learn to abide peaceably together in the whole thicket of differences that crisscrosses this earth.

This attempt to trace women and men through American history began at another time of ambiguity, possibility, and change: the moment when the clan mothers met the conquistadores. Like most all of us, the descendants of clan mothers traveled through streams of history that were marked off as separate channels labeled male and female but also came together in eddies of change. In the 1970s, after 150 years of exile, Choctaw women returned to a position once occupied by the corn mothers, a place on the tribal council.[133] While half the Pueblo tribes of New Mexico still barred women from participation in tribal politics, others elevated women to leadership positions, from which they acted on what one of their number called "the true teachings of our people [that] the mother is the most important, the most sacred thing there is. . . . All I was doing was just bringing it back [full] circle."[134] Today, young Indian women can be found in all the ordinary places where American history is being made—for example, at the powwows that will gather across America this summer. In a parking lot outside a casino, you might hear the music of an all-girl band of Navajo drummers: they have reclaimed the right to play an instrument said to have been brought to the tribe by "Thunderbird Lady." You can listen to Karen Ann Coffey, the newly crowned Princess of the Comanche tribe, describe her plans for the future. After traveling the country learning the problems of Indians, she hopes to become a lawyer, the better to serve her people: "Being a lawyer is kind of out of the rank of being a princess but still it is very helpful. . . . You talk in public, meet Indian people

. . . you get to hear about different tribes and their problems. Now with water rights, tribal sovereignty, and our religious freedom. They take it away from us. And I'm not gonna allow that to happen for my children."[135]

The descendants of the clan mothers also raise a powerful, distinctively postmodern voice in contemporary fiction and poetry. When N. Scott Momaday inaugurated a renaissance of Indian literature in the 1960s, he invoked a tradition in which "The earth is our mother. The sky is our father"[136]; by the close of the century, a host of Indian authors, speaking in a multiplicity of tribal tongues, testified to the mutability of gender. The novels of Louise Erdrich drew on history and myth to create characters who could glide between the poles of male and female. Her imaginary landscape was peopled not just by Indians but by German, French, and Polish Americans, and especially Métis, the mixed ancestry that accounts for well over half of those who are now registered as members of Indian tribes.[137] The central character of her 2001 novel *The Last Report on the Miracles at Little No Horse* was born Miss Agnes De Witt but lived most of her life as Father Damien, pastor of an Ojibwe congregation. Erdrich's heroine changed her gender with the ease of a "manly-hearted woman" of yore: "She decided to miss Agnes as she would a beloved sister, to make of Father Damien her creation. He would be loving, protective, remote, and immensely disciplined. He would be Agnes's twin, her masterwork, her brother."[138] In *Four Souls* (2004) Erdrich cast a man as the cross-dresser. Nanapush dared to appear before the tribal council in a sacred garment fashioned by his wife and publicly proclaimed, "I am not afraid, as others may be, that my manhood will be compromised by such a little thing as wearing a skirt. My manhood is made of stiffer stuff. No, I was not concerned for that. Rather, I worry that I, like so many other men who boast of their superiority and revel in their brute strength, cleverness, or power, was unworthy to wear the dress of a woman."[139]

Erdrich's fiction is emblematic of a time when "all things familiar dissolve into strangeness," even the dichotomy between things male and female.[140] Sex has not disappeared, but seen in its "strangeness" it can become less rigid, less oppositional, and less restricting. Diffused in an array of cultural differences, individual eccentricities, and varieties of love and pleasure, sex becomes an enticing mystery.

NOTES

Introduction

1. Louise Story, "Many Women at Elite Colleges Set Career Path to Motherhood," *New York Times*, September 20, 2005, A1.

2. Quoted in Bourdieu, *Masculine Domination*, 109.

3. Woolf, *Three Guineas*, 105.

4. Carter, *Passion of New Eve*, 149–50.

5. Vidal, *Myra Breckinridge*; Greer, *Female Eunuch*; Firestone, *Dialectic of Sex*; O'Farrell and Vallone, *Virtual Gender*.

6. Ryan, *Womanhood in America*, 1st ed., 3.

7. Ditz, "New Men's History and the Peculiar Absence of Gendered Power."

8. DuBois and Dumenil, *Through Women's Eyes*; Hewitt, *Companion to American Women's History*; Cott, *No Small Courage*; Woloch, *Women and the American Experience*.

9. W. Michael Cox and Richard Alm, "Scientists Are Made, Not Born," *New York Times*, February 28, 2005, A25.

10. Morris, *Conundrum*, 148–49.

11. Gayle Rubin, "Traffic in Women."

12. Zillah Eisenstein, *Sexual Decoys*.

13. Butler, *Gender Trouble*, 178; see also Butler, *Bodies That Matter*; Laqueur, *Making Sex*.

14. West and Zimmerman, "Doing Gender," 4.

15. Ibid., 16.

16. Bourdieu, *Masculine Domination*, 27.

17. Winant in Collins, Maldonado, Takagi, Thorne, Weber, and Winant, "Symposium on West and Fenstermaker's 'Doing Difference,'" 74.

18. Bourdieu, *Masculine Domination*, 106, 82.

19. Ortner, *Making Gender*, 18; Joan Scott, "Gender"; Joyce, *Social in Question*.

20. Foucault, *History of Sexuality*, 1:103.

Chapter 1

1. Merrell, *Indians' New World*, 8.

2. Bouvier, *Women and the Conquest of California*, 7–10, 24.

3. W. Stitt Robinson, "Conflicting Views on Landholding," 90, 92.

4. McNickle, *Native American Tribalism*; Salisbury, "Indians' Old World"; Thornton, "Demography of Colonialism."

5. Upton, *Architecture in the United States*, 187–91.

6. Gutiérrez, *When Jesus Came, the Corn Mothers Went Away*, 130–40.

7. Guemple, "Gender in Inuit Society"; Kehoe, "Blackfoot Persons," 120.

8. Bouvier, *Women and the Conquest of California*, 41.

9. Medicine, "'Warrior Women,'" 271.

10. Roscoe, *Changing Ones*, 97.

11. Whitehead, "Bow and the Burden Strap."

12. Bouvier, *Women and the Conquest of California*, 41; see also Roscoe, *Changing Ones*.

13. Albers and Medicine, *Hidden Half*; Gutiérrez, *When Jesus Came, the Corn Mothers Went Away*; Ackerman, "Complementary But Equal"; Lamphere, *To Run After Them*; Scadron, *On Their Own*.

14. Laura Klein, "Mother as Clanswoman."

15. Theda Perdue, *Cherokee Women*.

16. Spector, "What This Awl Means," 392.

17. Van Kirk, *"Many Tender Ties,"* 18; Kupperman, *Indians and English*, 149–53.

18. Kathleen Brown, "Anglo-Algonquian Gender Frontier," 29.

19. Jensen, *With These Hands*, 22.

20. Gutiérrez, *When Jesus Came, the Corn Mothers Went Away*, 21–23.

21. Sarah Nelson, "Widowhood and Autonomy in the Native American Southwest," 32.

22. Albers and Medicine, *Hidden Half*, chap. 4; Lamphere, *To Run After Them*, 9.

23. Spoehr, *Florida Seminole Camp*, 123–45.

24. Spector, "What This Awl Means," 392–95.

25. Jensen, *With These Hands*, 22 (quotation); Heizer and Elsasser, *Natural World of the California Indians*.

26. Klein and Ackerman, *Women and Power in Native North America*; Albers and Medicine, *Hidden Half*.

27. Demos, "Tried and the True," 40; Jensen, "Native American Women and Agriculture."

28. Richard White, *Middle Ground*, 17.

29. Spoehr, *Kinship System of the Seminole*, 102–3.

30. Richter, *Ordeal of the Longhouse*, 12.

31. Sharp, "Asymmetric Equals," 46–47; Merritt, *At the Crossroads*, 140–43.

32. Pesantubbee, *Choctaw Women in a Chaotic World*, 102.

33. Karen Anderson, *Chain Her by One Foot*; Gutiérrez, *When Jesus Came, the Corn Mothers Went Away*, 176–240; Hurtado, *Intimate Frontiers*, chap. 1; Pesantubbee, *Choctaw Women in a Chaotic World*, 45–46.

34. Klein and Ackerman, *Women and Power in Native North America*, 14, 46–100.

35. Ackerman, "Complementary But Equal," 78.

36. Brown, "Anglo-Algonquian Gender Frontier," 31.

37. Albers and Medicine, *Hidden Half*, chap. 4; Lamphere, *To Run After Them*, 9.

38. Sattler, "Women's Status among the Muskogee and Cherokee"; Claassen and Joyce, *Women in Prehistory*.

39. Klein, "Mother as Clanswoman."

40. Mary Young, "Women, Civilization, and the Indian Question."

41. Brown, "Anglo-Algonquian Gender Frontier," 30.

42. Gutiérrez, *When Jesus Came, the Corn Mothers Went Away*, 17.

43. Galloway, "Where Have All the Menstrual Huts Gone?"; Pesantubbee, *Choctaw Women in a Chaotic World*, 120–21.

44. Brown, "Anglo-Algonquian Gender Frontier," 31.

45. Theda Perdue, *Cherokee Women*, 4, 30.

46. Kehoe, "Blackfoot Persons," 121.

47. Hurtado, *Intimate Frontiers*, 4.

48. Jensen, *With These Hands*, 22.

49. Anderson, *Chain Her by One Foot*, 178–85; Klein, "Mother as Clanswoman."

50. Kehoe, "Blackfoot Persons," 116–20; Mary Shepardson, "The Gender Status of Navajo Women," in *Women and Power in Native North America*, ed. Klein and Ackerman, 170–73; Pesantubbee, *Choctaw Women in a Chaotic World*, 117–28.

51. Rogers, "Female Forms of Power and the Myth of Male Dominance."

52. Ackerman, "Complementary But Equal."

53. Victoria Patterson, "Evolving Gender Roles in Pomo Society," 130–32.

54. Gutiérrez, *When Jesus Came, the Corn Mothers Went Away*, xxix, 3–36.

55. Devens, *Countering Colonization*, 10.

56. Green, "Gender and the Longhouse."

57. Ackerman, "Complementary But Equal."

58. Schlegel, "Hopi Family Structure and the Experience of Widowhood."

59. Kehoe, "Blackfoot Persons," 119–24.

60. Pesantubbee, *Choctaw Women in a Chaotic World*, 1.

61. Judith Brown, "Economic Organization and the Position of Women among the Iroquois"; Bilharz, "First among Equals?" 104–5.

62. Rosaldo, Zimbalist, and Lamphere, *Women, Culture, and Society*.

63. Ortner and Whitehead, *Sexual Meanings*; Ortner, "Gender Hegemonies."

64. Petersen, "Women Dreaming."

65. Leacock, *Myths of Male Dominance*; Sanday, *Female Power and Male Dominance*; Sacks, *Sisters and Wives*; Collier, *Marriage and Inequality in Classless Societies*.

66. Hurtado, *Indian Survival on the California Frontier*, 187–88.

67. Sattler, "Women's Status among the Muskogee and Cherokee," 214–29.

68. Anderson, *Chain Her by One Foot*, 217–20; Brown, "Anglo-Algonquian Gender Frontier," 31.

69. Pesantubbee, *Choctaw Women in a Chaotic World*, 138–39.

70. White, *Middle Ground*.

71. McNickle, *Native American Tribalism*, 4–5.

72. Anderson, *Chain Her by One Foot*.

73. Hurtado, *Indian Survival on the California Frontier*.

74. Robert Jackson, *Indian Population Decline*.

75. Stannard, *Death in America*.

76. Brown, "Anglo-Algonquian Gender Frontier," 27.

77. Gutiérrez, *When Jesus Came, the Corn Mothers Went Away*, 39–40.

78. Bouvier, *Women and the Conquest of California*, 18–32.

79. Anderson, *Chain Her by One Foot*, 16–19.

80. Ibid., 22.

81. Hurtado, *Intimate Frontiers*, 1–21; Bouvier, *Women and the Conquest of California*, 43–44.

82. Goldberg, "Sodomy in the New World," 14; Bouvier, *Women and the Conquest of California*, 42–43.

83. Brown, "Anglo-Algonquian Gender Frontier"; Hurtado, *Intimate Frontiers*, 14.

84. Gutiérrez, *When Jesus Came, the Corn Mothers Went Away*, 51; Van Kirk, *"Many Tender Ties"*; Godbeer, "Eroticizing the Middle Ground"; Spear, "'They Need Wives.'"

85. White, *Middle Ground*, 60–75.

86. Ibid., 262.

87. McLoughlin, *Cherokee Renascence in the New Republic*, 152–54.

88. Jerah Johnson, "Colonial New Orleans," 23, 31, 35.

89. Byrd, *William Byrd's Histories of the Dividing Line Betwixt Virginia and North Carolina*, 3; Kathleen Brown, *Good Wives, Nasty Wenches, and Anxious Patriarchs*; Theda Perdue, *"Mixed Blood" Indians*, 73–78.

90. Byrd, *William Byrd's Histories of the Dividing Line Betwixt Virginia and North Carolina*, 4.

91. Richter, *Facing East from Indian Country*, 70–78.

92. Barker, "Princesses, Wives, and Wenches."

93. Hurtado, *Indian Survival on the California Frontier*, 212.

94. Ibid.; Jackson, *Indian Population Decline*, 132; Hurtado, *Intimate Frontiers*.

95. White, *Middle Ground*, chaps. 6–7.

96. Richter, "War and Culture."

97. Ibid.

98. Ibid.; Merritt, *At the Crossroads*, 178–80.

99. Andrew Isenberg, *Destruction of the Bison*.

100. Hurtado, *Indian Survival on the California Frontier*, 45–46, 345.

101. White, *Middle Ground*, 515.

102. Murphy, "Autonomy and the Economic Roles of Indian Women of the Fox-Wisconsin Riverway Region."

103. Perdue, *Cherokee Women*; Devens, *Countering Colonization*; McLoughlin, *Cherokee Renascence in the New Republic*, chap. 16.

104. Hill, *Weaving New Worlds*; Albers, "Sioux Women in Transition."

105. Bouvier, *Women and the Conquest of California*, 25, 48, 49.

106. Nancy Shoemaker, "Kateri Tekakwitha's Torturous Path to Sainthood," 51.

107. Taylor, "Virgin of Guadalupe in New Spain."

108. Linklater, *Measuring America*, 44.

109. Jensen, *With These Hands*; Eldridge, *Women and Freedom in Early America*, 17; McLoughlin, *Cherokee Renascence in the New Republic*, chap. 16.

110. White, *Middle Ground*, 503; McLoughlin, *Cherokee Renascence in the New Republic*, 63.

111. Anderson, *Chain Her by One Foot*; Devens, *Countering Colonization*, 7.

112. Anderson, *Chain Her by One Foot*, 94.

113. Ibid., 1.

114. Devens, *Countering Colonization*, 7.

115. McLoughlin, *Cherokee Renascence in the New Republic*, 106. See also Onuf, *Jefferson's Empire*.

116. Perdue, *Cherokee Women*, 110–34.

117. Jensen, *With These Hands*; McLoughlin, *Cherokee Renascence in the New Republic*; Dowd, "North American Indian Slaveholding and the Colonization of Gender"; Perdue, *Cherokee Women*; Nancy Shoemaker, *Negotiators of Change*.

118. McLoughlin, *Cherokee Renascence in the New Republic*, 398.

119. Wellman, *Road to Seneca Falls*, 185–86.

120. Lerner, *Creation of Patriarchy*, 21.

121. Dowd, "North American Indian Slaveholding and the Colonization of Gender."

122. Spoehr, *Florida Seminole Camp*; Spoehr, *Kinship System of the Seminole*.

123. Merrell, *Indians' New World*; St. Pierre and Long Soldier, *Walking in the Sacred Manner*.

124. Deutsch, *No Separate Refuge*; Jensen and Miller, *New Mexico Women*.

125. Petersen, "Women Dreaming"; Jennifer Brown, *Strangers in Blood*; Van Kirk, *"Many Tender Ties"*; White, *Middle Ground*; Murphy, *Gathering of Rivers*; Widder, *Battle for the Soul*.

126. Brown, "Anglo-Algonquian Gender Frontier," 41.

127. Ortiz, "Chocheno and Rumsen Narratives"; Perdue, *Cherokee Women*, 15.

Chapter 2

1. Stowe, *Oldtown Folks*, 340.

2. Dinnerstein, *Women between Two Worlds*, 182.

3. McHugh, *American Domesticity*, 6.

4. Plante, *Women at Home in Victorian America*, 35.

5. Welter, "Cult of True Womanhood"; Boydston, *Home and Work*; Diana Wall, *Archaeology of Gender*.

6. May, *Homeward Bound*, 16–20.

7. Ariès, *Centuries of Childhood*; Ryan, *Womanhood in America*; Ryan, *Cradle of the Middle Class*.

8. Pavla Miller, *Transformations of Patriarchy in the West*; Natalie Zemon Davis,

Women on the Margins, 63–139; Crowley, "Women, Religion, and Freedom in New France."

9. Miller, *Transformations of Patriarchy in the* West; Stone, *Family, Sex, and Marriage in England*; Fletcher, *Gender, Sex, and Subordination in England*; Robert Shoemaker, *Gender in English Society*.

10. Wiesner, *Women and Gender in Early Modern Europe*, 186–95; Davis, *Women on the Margins*; McKeon, "Historicizing Patriarchy."

11. Porterfield, *Female Piety in Puritan New England*, 24; Demos, *Little Commonwealth*; Axtell, *School upon a Hill*, 19 (quotation).

12. Porterfield, *Female Piety in Puritan New England*, 24.

13. Mary Beth Norton, *Founding Mothers and Fathers*.

14. Fletcher, *Gender, Sex, and Subordination in England*, 173; Miller, *Transformations of Patriarchy in the West*.

15. Horn, *Adapting to a New World*.

16. Gildrie, *Profane, the Civil, and the Godly*, 85.

17. Ibid.

18. Ibid., 41.

19. Ibid., 89, chap. 2; Helena Wall, *Fierce Communion*.

20. Porterfield, *Female Piety in Puritan New England*, 38.

21. Ulrich, *Good Wives*, chap. 2.

22. Ryan, *Womanhood in America*, 3d ed., 20.

23. Ibid., 35–37.

24. Salmon, *Women and the Law of Property in Early America*; Dayton, *Women before the Bar*; Shammas, Salmon, and Dahlin, *Inheritance in America*.

25. Demos, *Little Commonwealth*, 61.

26. Ibid.

27. Norton, *Founding Mothers and Fathers*, 7; Ryan, *Womanhood in America*, 3d ed., 23; Bradford, *Of Plymouth Plantation*, 120.

28. T. P. Schwartz, "Durkheim's Prediction about the Shift from Family to Organizational Inheritance."

29. Dayton, *Women before the Bar*, 19–20.

30. Shammas, "Anglo-American Household Government in Comparative Perspective"; Dayton, *Women before the Bar*, 19.

31. Shammas, Salmon, and Dahlin, *Inheritance in America*, 21.

32. Salmon, *Women and the Law of Property in Early America*, chap. 1; Shammas, Salmon, and Dahlin, *Inheritance in America*, 3–22.

33. Meyers, *Common Whores, Vertuous Women, and Loveing Wives*, chap. 5.

34. Shammas, Salmon, and Dahlin, *Inheritance in America*, 43, 119; Salmon, *Women and the Law of Property in Early America*, chap. 7; Ulrich, *Good Wives*.

35. Shammas, "Anglo-American Household Government in Comparative Perspective"; Dunaway, "Rethinking Cherokee Acculturation"; McLoughlin, *Cherokee Rena-*

scence in the New Republic, 330–31; Theda Perdue, *Cherokee Women*, 145; Ulrich, *Good Wives*.

36. Ulrich, *Good Wives*, 37–38, chap. 1.

37. Ibid.; Ryan, *Womanhood in America*.

38. Ulrich, *Midwife's Tale*, 39, 80, 82.

39. Ibid., 33.

40. Edmund Morgan, *Puritan Family*, 45.

41. Ulrich, *Good Wives*, 107, chap. 6; Norton, *Founding Mothers and Fathers*; Ryan, *Womanhood in America*, 3d ed., 36.

42. Ryan, *Womanhood in America*, 3d ed., 37.

43. The "Song of Solomon," cited in Porterfield, *Female Piety in Puritan New England*, 38; see also p. 74.

44. Godbeer, "Love Raptures"; Lisa Wilson, "Marriage 'Well-Ordered,'" 79, 80.

45. Main, *Peoples of a Spacious Land*; Virginia Anderson, *New England's Generation*; Berkin, *First Generations*.

46. Carr and Walsh, "Planter's Wife"; Menard, "Immigrants and Their Increase."

47. Demos, *Little Commonwealth*, 135.

48. Ryan, *Womanhood in America*, 3d ed., 48–51; Mason, *From Father's Property to Children's Rights*.

49. Leavitt, *Brought to Bed*.

50. Lisa Wilson, *Ye Heart of a Man*, 84–85.

51. Demos, *Little Commonwealth*, 95; Ulrich, *Good Wives*; Godbeer, "Love Raptures."

52. Bradstreet, *Writings of Mrs. Anne Bradstreet*, 275.

53. Gilbert and Gubar, *Norton Anthology of Literature by Women*, 89.

54. Godbeer, "Love Raptures," 60.

55. Bradstreet, *Writings of Mrs. Anne Bradstreet*, 248.

56. Gilbert and Gubar, *Norton Anthology of Literature by Women*, 84.

57. Ibid., 85.

58. Ibid., 87.

59. Ibid.

60. Ibid.

61. Ulrich, "'Friendly Neighbor'"; Dayton, *Women before the Bar*, chap. 2.

62. Gildrie, *Salem, Massachusetts*, 78–80.

63. Dayton, *Women before the Bar*, chap. 3; Ryan, *Womanhood in America*, 3d ed., 43.

64. Koehler, *Search for Power*, 222.

65. Gildrie, *Salem, Massachusetts*, 81–83.

66. Ibid., 82.

67. Ulrich, *Good Wives*, 215–16.

68. Oldridge, *Witchcraft Reader*; Boyer and Nissenbaum, *Salem Possessed*; Mary Beth Norton, *In the Devil's Snare*; Carlson, *Fever in Salem*.

69. Karlsen, *Devil in the Shape of a Woman*, 48–49.

70. Ryan, *Womanhood in America*, 3d ed., 63.

71. Karlsen, *Devil in the Shape of a Woman*; Norton, *In the Devil's Snare*; Ryan, *Womanhood in America*, 3d ed., 62–66.

72. David Hall, *Witch-Hunting in Seventeenth-Century New England*, 284; Ryan, *Womanhood in America*, 3d ed., 62–66.

73. Norton, *In the Devil's Snare*, 309–11.

74. Ibid., 3.

75. Ibid., 247.

76. See Ryan, *Womanhood in America*, 3d ed., chap. 2; Sellers, *Market Revolution*; Vickers, *Farmers and Fishermen*.

77. Cowing, "Sex and Preaching in the Great Awakening," 624.

78. Ibid.

79. Berry, "From Malthusian Frontier to Demographic Steady State."

80. Lemon, *Best Poor Man's Country*.

81. Nordstrom, *Frontier Elements in a Hudson River Village*, 51; Ryan, *Womanhood in America*, 3d ed., 73–85.

82. Ulrich, *Good Wives*, 32.

83. Ibid.; Wermuth, "New York Farmers and the Market Revolution"; Ulrich, "Wheels, Looms, and the Gender Division of Labor in Eighteenth-Century New England"; Jensen, *Loosening the Bonds*.

84. Dublin, *Transforming Women's Work*.

85. Banson, "Women and the Family Economy in the Early Republic"; Boydston, "Woman Who Wasn't There."

86. Dayton, *Women before the Bar*, 64.

87. Kerber, *Women of the Republic*, chap. 9; Martha King, "'What Providence Has Brought Them to Be'"; Christopher Young, "Mary K. Goddard."

88. Wulf, *Not All Wives*.

89. Lovell, "Reading Eighteenth-Century American Family Portraits."

90. Lewis, *Pursuit of Happiness*, 147; Kritzer, "Playing with Republican Motherhood."

91. Bushman, *Refinement of America*; Plante, *American Kitchen*.

92. Juster, *Disorderly Women*, 68.

93. Schneider, *Way of the Cross Leads Home*, chap. 9.

94. Juster, *Disorderly Women*.

95. Dayton, *Women before the Bar*; Farber, *Guardians of Virtue*; Ryan, *Womanhood in America*, 3d ed., 82–83, 97–98; Douglas Jones, "Strolling Poor."

96. Farber, *Guardians of Virtue*, 144–45.

97. Ulrich, *Midwife's Tale*, 240–42; Hannah Foster, *The Coquette*; Smith-Rosenberg, "Domesticating 'Virtue.'"

98. Foster, *The Coquette*, 5.

99. Ibid., 29.

100. Ibid., 169.

101. Ibid., 162.

102. Ibid., 163–64; Smith-Rosenberg, "Domesticating 'Virtue.'"

103. Schneider, *Way of the Cross Leads Home*, 154; Ryan, *Cradle of the Middle Class*.

104. Schneider, *Way of the Cross Leads Home*.

105. Quoted in ibid., 177.

106. Ibid., 159; Ryan, *Cradle of the Middle Class*, chaps. 3–4.

107. Ryan, *Cradle of the Middle Class*, 125–27, 155–58; Smith-Rosenberg, "Beauty and the Beast and the Militant Woman."

108. Dublin, *Transforming Women's Work*; Karen Hansen, *Very Social Time*; Boydston, *Home and Work*.

109. Child, *American Frugal Housewife*.

110. Ibid., 9.

111. Ibid.

112. McHugh, *American Domesticity*; Child, *American Frugal Housewife*, 66–69; Ryan, *Empire of the Mother*.

113. Beecher, *Treatise on Domestic Economy*.

114. Ryan, *Empire of the Mother*, 36.

115. Boydston, *Home and Work*, chap. 7.

116. Beecher, *Treatise on Domestic Economy*; McHugh, *American Domesticity*; Ryan, *Empire of the Mother*, 40.

117. Beecher, *Treatise on Domestic Economy*; McHugh, *American Domesticity*; Ryan, *Empire of the Mother*, 39–43.

118. Beecher, *Treatise on Domestic Economy*; McHugh, *American Domesticity*; Ryan, *Empire of the Mother*, 40; Ulrich, *Age of Homespun*, 14–17; Cott, *Bonds of Womanhood*.

119. Kelly, "'Well Bred Country People,'" 461–62; Boydston, *Home and Work*, 159–62; Kerber, "Separate Spheres, Female Worlds, Woman's Place."

120. Richard Brown, *Knowledge Is Power*; Baym, *Woman's Fiction*; Kelley, *Private Woman, Public Stage*.

121. Matthews, *"Just a Housewife"*; Lopata, *Occupation: Housewife*; Cowan, *More Work for Mother*; Plante, *Women at Home in Victorian America*; McHugh, *American Domesticity*; Wall, *Archaeology of Gender*; Spencer-Wood, "Feminist Historical Archaeology."

122. Plante, *Women at Home in Victorian America*, 39.

123. Ibid., 70.

124. Ibid., chap. 3; Ryan, *Empire of the Mother*, chap. 2.

125. Sennett, *Families against the City*; Blumin, *Emergence of the Middle Class*; Katz, *People of Hamilton, Canada West*.

126. Ryan, *Cradle of the Middle Class*, chap. 4.

127. Brodie, *Contraception and Abortion in Nineteenth-Century America*, 2.

128. Ibid., 2.

129. Grossberg, *Governing the Hearth*; Hartog, *Man and Wife in America*.

130. Ryan, *Womanhood in America*; Smith-Rosenberg, "Female World of Love and Ritual"; Hansen, *Very Social Time*, 56.

131. Rotundo, *American Manhood*, 51; Blumin, *Emergence of the Middle Class*; Yacovone, "Surpassing the Love of Women"; Herman, "Other Daniel Boone"; Ruppel, "Gender Training."

132. Johansen, *Family Men*.

133. Hilkey, *Character Is Capital*, 146.

134. Brown, *Knowledge Is Power*, chap. 7; Dorsey, *Reforming Men and Women*, chap. 3.

135. Blumin, *Emergence of the Middle Class*; Carnes and Griffen, *Meanings for Manhood*; Greenberg, *Cause for Alarm*; Carnes, *Secret Ritual and Manhood in Victorian America*; Dumenil, *Freemasonry and American Culture*.

136. Ryan, *Cradle of the Middle Class*; Blumin, *Emergence of the Middle Class*; Mahoney, *Provincial Lives*; Kelly, "'Well Bred Country People.'"

137. Sanchez, "'Go After the Women'"; Orsi, *Madonna of 115th Street*; Carol Chin, "Beneficent Imperialists"; Jane Hunter, *Gospel of Gentility*.

Chapter 3

1. Pascoe, "Miscegenation Law, Court Cases, and Ideologies of 'Race,'" 480.

2. Ibid., 467, 486 n. 15; Wacquant, "For an Analytic of Racial Domination."

3. Brooks, *Captives and Cousins*, 46–47.

4. Wacquant, "For an Analytic of Racial Domination," 223.

5. Omi and Winant, *Racial Formation in the United States*; Williamson, *New People*; Winant, *World Is a Ghetto*; Wacquant, "For an Analytic of Racial Domination"; Sollors, *Interracialism*, 24; Wallenstein, *Tell the Court I Love My Wife*; Cecelski and Tyson, *Democracy Betrayed*.

6. Orlando Patterson, *Slavery and Social Death*, vii.

7. Blackburn, "Old World Background to European Colonial Slavery"; Patterson, *Slavery and Social Death*.

8. Robertson, "Africa into the Americas?"; Jalloh and Maizlish, *African Diaspora*; Bay, "Servitude and Worldly Success in the Palace of Dahomey"; Broadhead, "Slave Wives, Free Sisters."

9. Gutiérrez, *When Jesus Came, the Corn Mothers Went Away*, 104.

10. Ibid., 158.

11. Brooks, *Captives and Cousins*, 180–93, 241–50.

12. Barr, "From Captives to Slaves."

13. Gutiérrez, *When Jesus Came, the Corn Mothers Went Away*, 199–201.

14. Brooks, *Captives and Cousins*, 132.

15. Gutiérrez, *When Jesus Came, the Corn Mothers Went Away*, 149–56, 180–90; Brooks, *Captives and Cousins*, 132–33.

16. Brooks, *Captives and Cousins*, 298.

17. Spear, "'They Need Wives,'" 49; Spear, "Colonial Intimacies."

18. Gwendolyn Hall, *Africans in Colonial Louisiana*; Spears, "'They Need Wives,'" 42. See also Berlin, *Many Thousands Gone*, 79–80.

19. Edmund Morgan, *American Slavery, American Freedom*, chaps. 15–16; Melish, *Disowning Slavery*.

20. Wood, *Origins of American Slavery*, 68–69; Kathleen Brown, *Good Wives, Nasty Wenches, and Anxious Patriarchs*, 83–88.

21. Jennifer Morgan, *Laboring Women*, 75.

22. Carr and Walsh, "Planter's Wife," 543.

23. Brown, *Good Wives, Nasty Wenches, and Anxious Patriarchs*, chap. 5; Morgan, *American Slavery, American Freedom*, 405, chaps. 16–17. See also Menard, "Immigrants and Their Increase"; and Carr and Walsh, "Planter's Wife."

24. Higginbotham and Kopytoff, "Racial Purity and Interracial Sex in the Law of Colonial and Antebellum Virginia," 89 (emphasis mine).

25. Berlin, *Many Thousands Gone*, chaps. 1–3.

26. Ibid., 191–92.

27. Ibid., 143, 178–79, chaps. 6–7.

28. Ibid.; Williamson, *New People*, 21; Research Department of the Association for the Study of Negro Life and History, "Free Negro Owners of Slaves in the United States in 1830," 41–42; Wood, *Origins of American Slavery*; Johnson and Roark, *Black Masters*.

29. Brown, *Good Wives, Nasty Wenches, and Anxious Patriarchs*, 198–99.

30. Berlin, *Many Thousands Gone*, 83.

31. Ibid., 111; Gomez, *Exchanging Our Country Marks*, 35–36; Eltis, *Rise of African Slavery in the Americas*. See the *William and Mary Quarterly*, 3d ser., 58 (January 2001), for the most recent estimates of the volume of the slave trade.

32. Hall, *Africans in Colonial Louisiana*; Carr and Walsh, "Planter's Wife"; Deborah White, *Ar'n't I a Woman?* 64–65.

33. Coquery-Vidrovitch, *African Women*; Meillassoux, *Maidens, Meal, and Money*; Bay, "Servitude and Worldly Success in the Palace of Dahomey"; Broadhead, "Slave Wives, Free Sisters"; Eltis, *Rise of African Slavery in the Americas*, chap. 4; Nwokeji, "African Conceptions of Gender and the Slave Traffic"; Lovejoy, "Impact of the Atlantic Slave Trade on Africa."

34. Jaffe, *History of Africa*; Lovejoy and Richardson, "Competing Markets for Male and Female Slaves"; Eltis, *Rise of African Slavery in the Americas*; Amadiume, *Reinventing Africa*; Meillassoux, *Maidens, Meal, and Money*; Bay, "Servitude and Worldly Success in the Palace of Dahomey"; Broadhead, "Slave Wives, Free Sisters"; Nwokeji, "African Conceptions of Gender and the Slave Traffic."

35. Morgan, *Laboring Women*, 146, 161, chap. 5.

36. Walter Johnson, *Soul by Soul*, 200.

37. Edmund Morgan, *American Slavery, American Freedom*; Wood, *Origins of American Slavery*; Brown, *Good Wives, Nasty Wenches, and Anxious Patriarchs*; Jennifer Morgan, *Laboring Women*, 91.

38. Brown, *Good Wives, Nasty Wenches, and Anxious Patriarchs*, chap. 4; Higginbotham and Kopytoff, "Racial Purity and Interracial Sex in the Law of Colonial and Antebellum Virginia," 85–86.

39. Brown, *Good Wives, Nasty Wenches, and Anxious Patriarchs*, 132; Morgan, *American Slavery, American Freedom*, 334.

40. Brown, *Good Wives, Nasty Wenches, and Anxious Patriarchs*, 215–16.

41. Wood, *Origins of American Slavery*; Morgan, *American Slavery, American Freedom*; Brown, *Good Wives, Nasty Wenches, and Anxious Patriarchs*; Higginbotham and Kopytoff, "Racial Purity and Interracial Sex in the Law of Colonial and Antebellum Virginia"; Wallenstein, *Tell the Court I Love My Wife*; Johnson, *Soul by Soul*, 53.

42. Williamson, *New People*, 8; Bardaglio, "'Shamefull Matches,'" 115.

43. Bardaglio, "'Shamefull Matches,'" 114; Brown, *Good Wives, Nasty Wenches, and Anxious Patriarchs*, 197, 205.

44. Brown, *Good Wives, Nasty Wenches, and Anxious Patriarchs*, 123; Morgan, *American Slavery, American Freedom*; Bardaglio, *Reconstructing the Household*, 48–73; Wallenstein, *Tell the Court I Love My Wife*, 53.

45. Sommerville, "Rape Myth in the Old South Reconsidered"; Bardaglio, "'Shamefull Matches'"; Hodes, *White Women, Black Men*.

46. Sommerville, *Rape and Race*, chap. 4.

47. Philip Morgan, "British Encounters with Africans and African-Americans," 199; Berlin, *Many Thousands Gone*.

48. Farley, *Growth of the Black Population*, 30. See also Johnson, *Soul by Soul*.

49. Farley, *Growth of the Black Population*; Eltis, *Rise of African Slavery in the Americas*.

50. Johnson, *Soul by Soul*, 5.

51. Brown, *Good Wives, Nasty Wenches, and Anxious Patriarchs*, 333.

52. Lewis and Onuf, *Sally Hemings and Thomas Jefferson*.

53. Hall, *Africans in Colonial Louisiana*, esp. chap. 8.

54. Bynum, *Unruly Women*; Williamson, *New People*, 10.

55. White, *Ar'n't I a Woman?* 69.

56. Dominguez, *White by Definition*; Williamson, *New People*.

57. Shammas, "Black Women's Work and the Evolution of Plantation Society in Virginia," 15.

58. Hudson, *To Have and to Hold*, 188 n. 9, chap. 3; Jacqueline Jones, *Labor of Love, Labor of Sorrow*, 15; Stevenson, *Life in Black and White*, 186–93; White, *Ar'n't I a Woman?* 94, 100; Joyner, *Down by the Riverside*; Shammas, "Black Women's Work and the Evolution of Plantation Society in Virginia."

59. White, *Ar'n't I a Woman?* 46–61.

60. Dunaway, *African-American Family in Slavery and Freedom*, 163; Joyner, *Down by the Riverside*, chap. 2.

61. Dunaway, *African-American Family in Slavery and Freedom*, 141; Steckel,

"Women, Work, and Health under Plantation Slavery in the United States"; White, *Ar'n't I a Woman?* 68–71, 113.

62. Dunaway, *African-American Family in Slavery and Freedom*, 278.

63. Ibid., 177.

64. Ibid., 153–60; Schwalm, *Hard Fight for We*, 62–63; Hudson, *To Have and to Hold*; Stevenson, *Life in Black and White*, chap. 7; Sheridan, "Domestic Economy," 63.

65. Dunaway, *African-American Family in Slavery and Freedom*, 129–30; Jennings, "'Us Colored Women Had to Go Through Plenty'"; Stevenson, *Life in Black and White*.

66. Stevenson, *Life in Black and White*, 245.

67. Jennings, "'Us Colored Women Had to Go Through Plenty,'" 49–51, 54–58; White, *Ar'n't I a Woman?* 177–78 n. 22; Dunaway, *African-American Family in Slavery and Freedom*, 128–29; Stevenson, *Life in Black and White*, 245.

68. White, *Ar'n't I a Woman?* 99–102; Jennings, "'Us Colored Women Had to Go Through Plenty.'" On child mortality see Stevenson, *Life in Black and White*, 248–49.

69. Johnson, *Soul by Soul*, 19; Dunaway, *African-American Family in Slavery and Freedom*, 56.

70. Stevenson, *Life in Black and White*, 398 n. 44; Perdue, Barden, and Phillips, *Weevils in the Wheat*.

71. White, *Ar'n't I a Woman?* 95–99; Stevenson, *Life in Black and White*, 224.

72. Stevenson, *Life in Black and White*, 256–57.

73. Gould, "'House That Never Was a Home,'" 92.

74. Perdue, Barden, and Phillips, *Weevils in the Wheat*, 150; see also Jennings, "'Us Colored Women Had to Go Through Plenty'"; and Gould, "'House That Never Was a Home.'"

75. Schwalm, *Hard Fight for We*, 51.

76. Stevenson, *Life in Black and White*, 211–12.

77. Dunaway, *African-American Family in Slavery and Freedom*, 64, 76. On slave families and abroad marriages see Herbert Gutman, *Black Family in Slavery and Freedom*, 145–55; Schwalm, *Hard Fight for We*, 50–69; Stevenson, *Life in Black and White*, chaps. 7–8; and Wilma King, "Suffer with Them Till Death," 148. On the "structured absence" of men from slave families, see Dunaway, *African-American Family in Slavery and Freedom*, 62–67.

78. See Stevenson, *Life in Black and White*, 256–57.

79. Lebsock, *Free Women of Petersburg*; Lebsock, "Free Black Women and the Question of Matriarchy." On women's (forced) autonomy during the Civil War due to the impressment of males, see Schwalm, *Hard Fight for We*, chap. 3; and Stevenson, *Life in Black and White*, chaps. 7–8.

80. Gutman, *Black Family in Slavery and Freedom*, 87–93, chap. 5; Stevenson, *Life in Black and White*, 324–26, chap. 8; see also White, *Ar'n't I a Woman?* 65–66.

81. White, *Ar'n't I a Woman?* 158; Farnham, "Sapphire? The Issue of Dominance in the Slave Family"; Hine, *Black Women in American History*; Frazier, *Free Negro Family*;

Gutman, *Black Family in Slavery and Freedom*; Lebsock, *Free Women of Petersburg*; Lebsock, "Free Black Women and the Question of Matriarchy."

82. Jones, *Labor of Love, Labor of Sorrow*, chap. 1; White, *Ar'n't I a Woman?* chap. 2, and 151–53; Dunaway, *African-American Family in Slavery and Freedom*, 163–76.

83. Shane White, "'It Was a Proud Day'"; Levine, *Black Culture and Black Consciousness*, chap. 2, esp. 121–33; Jones, *Labor of Love, Labor of Sorrow*; Dunaway, *African-American Family in Slavery and Freedom*, 163–76.

84. Walker, *David Walker's Appeal*, 16, 62.

85. Douglass, *Narrative of the Life of Frederick Douglass*, 62, 68.

86. Jacobs, *Incidents in the Life of a Slave Girl*, 486, 447, 449.

87. Camp, *Closer to Freedom*, 97–98.

88. Lerner, *Black Women in White America*, 34–35.

89. Fox-Genovese, *Within the Plantation Household*, 100, 101.

90. McCurry, *Masters of Small Worlds*, 217; Edwards, "Law, Domestic Violence, and the Limits of Patriarchal Authority in the Antebellum South," 68.

91. McCurry, *Masters of Small Worlds*, 217.

92. Brown, *Good Wives, Nasty Wenches, and Anxious Patriarchs*, 265, and chap. 8; McCurry, "Two Faces of Republicanism"; Michael Johnson, "Planters and Patriarchy."

93. Fox-Genovese, *Within the Plantation Household*; McCurry, *Masters of Small Worlds*; McCurry, "Two Faces of Republicanism"; Johnson, "Planters and Patriarchy."

94. McCurry, *Masters of Small Worlds*, 88; McCurry, "Two Faces of Republicanism"; Johnson, "Planters and Patriarchy"; McCurry, "Citizens, Soldiers' Wives, and 'Hiley Hope Up' Slaves," 97–98.

95. Yee, *Black Women Abolitionists*, 87, 90; Dorsey, *Reforming Men and Women*, 166–67.

96. Ryan, "American Society and the Cult of Domesticity"; Yellin, *Women and Sisters*, chap. 6; Tompkins, "Sentimental Power"; Elizabeth Young, "Wound of One's Own."

97. Yellin, *Women and Sisters*, 3.

98. Eric Foner, *Free Soil, Free Labor, Free Men*.

99. Elsa Barkley Brown, "To Catch the Vision of Freedom," 130–31.

100. Eric Foner, *Reconstruction*; Dailey, *Before Jim Crow*; Thomas Holt, "Marking Race."

101. Basch, *In the Eyes of the Law*; Stanley, *From Bondage to Contract*; Edwards, *Gendered Strife and Confusion*.

102. Stanley, *From Bondage to Contract*, 48.

103. Ibid., 49.

104. Ibid., 54.

105. Ibid., 47.

106. Ibid., 53; Schwalm, *Hard Fight for We*; Edwards, *Gendered Strife and Confusion*; Fahs, "Gendering of Reconstruction."

107. Stanley, *From Bondage to Contract*, 58, 49.

108. DuBois, *Feminism and Suffrage*.

109. Ryan, *Women in Public*; Brown, "Negotiating and Transforming the Public Sphere"; DuBois, *Feminism and Suffrage*; Dailey, *Before Jim Crow*.

110. Schwalm, *Hard Fight for We*, 262; Higginbotham, *Righteous Discontent*, 6.

111. Stanley, *From Bondage to Contract*; Zipf, "Reconstructing 'Free Woman'"; Schwalm, *Hard Fight for We*; Litwack, *Been in the Storm So Long*.

112. Schwalm, *Hard Fight for We*, 129, 160.

113. Ibid., 192–93.

114. Ibid., 205.

115. Weiner, *Mistresses and Slaves*, 194, 204, 203–33.

116. Zipf, "Reconstructing 'Free Woman,'" 16.

117. Schwalm, *Hard Fight for We*, 226–31.

118. Sharon Holt, *Making Freedom Pay*, 132.

119. Schweninger, *Black Property Owners in the South*.

120. Gilmore, *Gender and Jim Crow*, 36–40.

121. Ibid.; Higginbotham, *Righteous Discontent*; Brown, "Womanist Consciousness."

122. Gilmore, *Gender and Jim Crow*, 10–12, 16–17.

123. Stanley, *From Bondage to Contract*, 30.

124. Gilmore, *Gender and Jim Crow*, 74–75.

125. Ibid., 75.

126. Hodes, *White Women, Black Men*, 166.

127. Ibid., 151–59; Waldrep, *Many Faces of Judge Lynch*, 74.

128. Bardaglio, "'Shamefull Matches,'" 124–25; Bardaglio, *Reconstructing the Household*, chap. 6.

129. Hodes, *White Women, Black Men*, 153–55.

130. Ibid., 161. For other, similar cases in various states, see also ibid., 161–65.

131. Ibid.; Bynum, *Unruly Women*.

132. Edwards, "Disappearance of Susan Daniel and Henderson Cooper."

133. Sollors, *Interracialism*; Wallenstein, *Tell the Court I Love My Wife*; Edwards, "Disappearance of Susan Daniel and Henderson Cooper"; Blassingame, *Black New Orleans*, 206–7.

134. Bederman, *Manliness and Civilization*, 47. See also Wells-Barnett, *Crusade for Justice*, xi–xii.

135. On such a case in Atlanta, see Hodes, *White Women, Black Men*, 207.

136. Wiegman, "Anatomy of Lynching," 460.

137. Hodes, *White Women, Black Men*, 188–90.

138. Ibid., 188.

139. Bederman, *Manliness and Civilization*, 53–54; Wells-Barnett, *Crusade for Justice*; Gilmore, *Gender and Jim Crow*; Cash, *Mind of the South*.

140. MacLean, "Leo Frank Case Reconsidered," 921.

141. Cash, *Mind of the South*.

142. Hodes, *White Women, Black Men*, 187.

143. Ibid., 188.

144. Ibid.

145. Ibid., 189.

146. Gilmore, *Gender and Jim Crow*.

147. Wells-Barnett, *Crusade for Justice*, 65.

148. Ibid., 64.

149. Hodes, *White Women, Black Men*, 191.

150. Wells-Barnett, *Crusade for Justice*, 66.

151. Bederman, *Manliness and Civilization*, 53–57; Wells-Barnett, *Crusade for Justice*, 56, chap. 8. See also Hodes, *White Women, Black Men*, 191.

152. Yarborough, "Violence, Manhood, and Black Heroism," 228.

153. Prather, "We Have Taken a City," 23; Yarborough, "Violence, Manhood, and Black Heroism," 228.

154. Gilmore, *Gender and Jim Crow*, 106.

155. See Gilmore, *Gender and Jim Crow*, 269 n. 70; Prather, "We Have Taken a City," 23; and Kirshenbaum, "Vampire that Hovers over North Carolina," 13.

156. Hodes, *White Women, Black Men*, 196.

157. Kirshenbaum, "Vampire that Hovers over North Carolina," 6; Gilmore, *Gender and Jim Crow*, chap. 4; Cecelski and Tyson, *Democracy Betrayed*.

158. Gilmore, *Gender and Jim Crow*, 78.

159. Kirshenbaum, "Vampire that Hovers over North Carolina," 12, 13.

160. Ibid., 21.

161. Gilmore, "Murder, Memory, and the Flight of the Incubus," 84.

162. Gilmore, *Gender and Jim Crow*, 124.

163. Whites, "Love, Hate, Rape, Lynching," 149. See also Yarborough, "Violence, Manhood, and Black Heroism," 228.

164. Wells, *Memphis Diary of Ida B. Wells*, 188.

165. Whites, "Love, Hate, Rape, Lynching," 159.

166. Morrison, *Race-ing Justice, En-Gendering Power*; Bederman, *Manliness and Civilization*.

167. Jacquelyn Hall, *Revolt against Chivalry*.

Chapter 4

1. Jeffrey, "Permeable Boundaries," 86.

2. Habermas, *Structural Transformation of the Public Sphere*; Calhoun, *Habermas and the Public Sphere*; Ryan, *Civic Wars*, introduction; Light and Smith, *Philosophy and Geography II*; Weintraub and Kumar, *Public and Private in Thought and Practice*.

3. Levy and Applewhite, "Women, Radicalization, and the Fall of the French Monarchy"; Landes, *Women and the Public Sphere in the Age of the French Revolution*; Good-

man, *Republic of Letters*; Habermas, *Structural Transformation of the Public Sphere*, 5–19; Calhoun, *Habermas and the Public Sphere*; Arendt, *Human Condition*; Kerber, *Women of the Republic*.

4. Shammas, "Anglo-American Household Government in Comparative Perspective," 123.

5. Adams, "Thoughts on Government," 669; Abigail Adams to John Adams, March 31, 1776, in Butterfield, *Adams Family Correspondence*, 369–70; Rogers Smith, *Civic Ideals*, 76.

6. Cited in Kerber, "'I Have Don . . . Much to Carrey on the Warr,'" 232; see also Fliegelman, *Prodigals and Pilgrims*; and Burrows and Wallace, "American Revolution."

7. Thompson, *Rum Punch and Revolution*, 127; Ulrich, "'Daughters of Liberty,'" 226.

8. Ulrich, "'Daughters of Liberty'"; Andrew Young, "Women of Boston"; Kerber, "'I Have Don . . . Much to Carrey on the Warr.'"

9. Ulrich, "'Daughters of Liberty,'" 215; Kerber, "'History Can Do It No Justice,'" 32.

10. Young, "Women of Boston," 212.

11. Wulf, *Not All Wives*, 191.

12. Lewis, "Revolution for Whom?" 88; Young, "Women of Boston," 212, 217; Kerber, "'I Have Don . . . Much to Carrey on the Warr,'" 236–38.

13. Lewis, "Revolution for Whom?" 88, 90.

14. Allgor, *Parlor Politics*, 24; Kross, "Mansions, Men, Women, and the Creation of Multiple Publics in Eighteenth-Century British North America"; Smith, *Civic Ideals*, 110–13.

15. Allgor, *Parlor Politics*, 21–22.

16. Bloch, *Gender and Morality in Anglo-American Culture*, 136–53; Zagarri, "Rights of Man and Woman in Post-Revolutionary America," 220–21.

17. Zagarri, "Rights of Man and Woman in Post-Revolutionary America," 220.

18. Kerber, *Women of the Republic*, 108–9.

19. Ryan, *Women in Public*.

20. Thompson, *Rum Punch and Revolution*, 150–51, 170; Allgor, *Parlor Politics*, chap. 2.

21. Ginzberg, *Untidy Origins*, 8.

22. Thompson, *Rum Punch and Revolution*, 150–51, 170.

23. Varon, *We Mean to Be Counted*, 77, 96; Pierson, "'Guard the Foundation Well.'"

24. Paula Baker, "Domestication of Politics," 627; Joanne Freeman, *Affairs of Honor*, 259–60; James Young, *Washington Community*; Altschuler and Blumin, *Rude Republic*; Jean Baker, *Affairs of Party*; Ryan, *Women in Public*; McGerr, *Decline of Popular Politics*; Paula Baker, *Moral Frameworks of Public Life*; Ryan, *Civic Wars*.

25. Zaeske, *Signatures of Citizenship*, 107, 109.

26. Greenberg, *Manifest Manhood and the Antebellum American Empire*.

27. Ginzberg, "'Hearts of Your Readers Will Shudder,'" 195; Cogan and Ginzberg,

"1846 Petition for Woman's Suffrage, New York State Constitutional Convention," 439.

28. Dorsey, *Reforming Men and Women*, chap. 4; Nancy Isenberg, *Sex and Citizenship in Antebellum America*, 59–64; Yellin, *Women and Sisters*; Wellman, *Road to Seneca Falls*; Zaeske, *Signatures of Citizenship*, 120–21.

29. Pierson, "Gender and Party Ideologies," 58; Varon, *We Mean to Be Counted*, 107–14.

30. Attie, *Patriotic Toil*, 3; Whites, *Civil War as a Crisis in Gender*, chaps. 6–7.

31. Hoganson, *Fighting for American Manhood*, 178, and chap. 5.

32. Skocpol, *Protecting Soldiers and Mothers*; Gaines Foster, *Ghosts of the Confederacy*; Clinton, *Other Civil War*; Whites, *Civil War as a Crisis in Gender*.

33. Melder, *Beginnings of Sisterhood*; Ginzberg, *Women and the Work of Benevolence*; Ryan, *Cradle of the Middle Class*; Kaufman, *For the Common Good?*

34. Putnam, *Bowling Alone*; Isenberg, *Sex and Citizenship in Antebellum America*, 20–21, 69; Dorsey, *Reforming Men and Women*, 12.

35. Woolf, *Three Guineas*, 15.

36. Bordin, *Woman and Temperance*; Blair, *Clubwoman as Feminist*; O'Neill, *Feminism in America*; Baker, "Domestication of Politics"; Anne Scott, *Natural Allies*; Giesberg, *Civil War Sisterhood*.

37. Ladd-Taylor, *Mother-Work*, 45, 47.

38. Ibid., 40, 45, 46, chap. 2.

39. Ibid., 45, 52, chaps. 1–2.

40. Evans, *Born for Liberty*, 128–29.

41. Ryan, *Womanhood in America*.

42. Ladd-Taylor, *Mother-Work*, 43, 60.

43. Addams, "Women's Conscience and Social Amelioration," 253. See also Allen Davis, *American Heroine*, 187.

44. Anthony and Harper, *History of Woman Suffrage*, 4:309; Mary Beth Norton, *Major Problems in American Women's History*, 256–57.

45. McManus, "'From Deep Wells of Religious Faith,'" 106–7.

46. Sklar, *Florence Kelley and the Nation's Work*; O'Neill, *Everyone Was Brave*; McManus, "'From Deep Wells of Religious Faith.'"

47. Addams, *Twenty Years at Hull-House*, chap. 13; Sklar, *Florence Kelley and the Nation's Work*, 195, chaps. 3–5.

48. Solomon, *In the Company of Educated Women*; Sklar, *Florence Kelley and the Nation's Work*, 171–72.

49. Allen Davis, *Spearheads for Reform*, 21.

50. Bowen, *Growing Up with a City*, xvii.

51. Addams, *Twenty Years at Hull-House*, chap. 6; Scudder, *Relation of College Women to Social Need*. See McManus, "'From Deep Wells of Religious Faith,'" 104–8.

52. Davis, *American Heroine*, 20.

53. Davis, *Spearheads for Reform*.

54. Davis, *American Heroine*; Elshtain, *Jane Addams Reader*, 8–9.

55. Elshtain, *Jane Addams Reader*, xxvi.

56. Matthews, *"Just a Housewife,"* 149.

57. Kerber, Cott, Gross, Hunt, Smith-Rosenberg, and Stansell, "Beyond Roles, Beyond Spheres"; Polacheck, *I Came a Stranger*; Sklar, *Florence Kelley and the Nation's Work*.

58. Gordon, "Black and White Visions of Welfare," 574; Cook, "Female Support Networks and Political Activism."

59. Polacheck, *I Came a Stranger*, 70, chap. 11; see also Shannon Jackson, *Lines of Activity*.

60. Sklar, *Florence Kelley and the Nation's Work*, 197; McManus, "'From Deep Wells of Religious Faith.'"

61. Sklar, *Florence Kelley and the Nation's Work*, 172; Polacheck, *I Came a Stranger*, 71.

62. Sklar, *Florence Kelley and the Nation's Work*, 207.

63. Ibid., 235–36.

64. Ibid., 211, chap. 9; Norton, *Major Problems in American Women's History*, 274.

65. Sklar, *Florence Kelley and the Nation's Work*, chap. 9, 237–40, chap. 10; Flanagan, *Seeing with Their Hearts*.

66. Polacheck, *I Came a Stranger*, 70; Marta Gutman, "On the Ground in Oakland," chap. 3; Higginbotham, *Righteous Discontent*; Scott, *Natural Allies*; Boris, "Power of Motherhood," 224–25; Bohlmann, "'Our "House Beautiful."'"

67. Wadsworth, *Julia Morgan*, 122–23; Shannon Jackson, *Lines of Activity*.

68. Muncy, *Creating a Female Dominion in American Reform*, 3.

69. Elshtain, *Jane Addams Reader*, 8.

70. Davis, *American Heroine*, 184–97.

71. Ladd-Taylor, "Mothers and the Making of the Sheppard-Towner Act," 330; Ladd-Taylor, *Mother-Work*, chap. 5.

72. Gordon, *Pitied But Not Entitled*, 98, 212–13; Skocpol, *Protecting Soldiers and Mothers*.

73. Ladd-Taylor, *Mother-Work*, chap. 5; Michel, *Children's Interests/Mothers' Rights*.

74. Norton, *Major Problems in American Women's History*, 257.

75. Ladd-Taylor, *Mother-Work*, 123.

76. Mettler, *Dividing Citizens*, chap. 5; Norton, *Major Problems in American Women's History*, 257.

77. Ware, *Partner and I*, 233.

78. Ladd-Taylor, *Mother-Work*, 77.

79. Muncy, *Creating a Female Dominion in American Reform*, 51.

80. Ladd-Taylor, *Mother-Work*, 85.

81. Ladd-Taylor, "Mothers and the Making of the Sheppard-Towner Act," 336; Ladd-Taylor, *Mother-Work*; Muncy, *Creating a Female Dominion in American Reform*.

82. Ladd-Taylor, *Mother-Work*, 175.

83. Ibid., 18–19.

84. Muncy, *Creating a Female Dominion in American Reform*, 2.

85. Ladd-Taylor, *Mother-Work*, 18–19, 84, 170–75.

86. Jean Baker, "Introduction," 5.

87. DuBois, *Harriot Stanton Blatch and the Winning of Woman Suffrage*; Gullett, *Becoming Citizens*; Jean Baker, *Votes for Women*.

88. Marilley, *Woman Suffrage and the Origins of Liberal Feminism*, 190.

89. Finnegan, *Selling Suffrage*, 52.

90. Ibid.; DuBois, *Harriot Stanton Blatch and the Winning of Woman Suffrage*, 111–12. See also Finnegan, *Selling Suffrage*, 186 n. 26.

91. DuBois, *Harriot Stanton Blatch and the Winning of Woman Suffrage*, 102–3.

92. Glenn, *Female Spectacle*, 147.

93. Flanagan, *Seeing with Their Hearts*, 127.

94. Gullett, *Becoming Citizens*, 184–87; Finnegan, *Selling Suffrage*, 54–55.

95. Glenn, *Female Spectacle*, 129, 132; Deutsch, *Women and the City*; Flanagan, *Seeing with Their Hearts*, 127–34; DuBois, *Woman Suffrage and Women's Rights*, 197.

96. Marilley, *Woman Suffrage and the Origins of Liberal Feminism*, 226.

97. Ibid., 216.

98. Gullett, *Becoming Citizens*; DuBois, *Harriot Stanton Blatch and the Winning of Woman Suffrage*; Finnegan, *Selling Suffrage*.

99. Ladd-Taylor, *Mother-Work*, 80.

100. Ibid., 74.

101. Ibid., 81, 115, 118, 145; DuBois, *Harriot Stanton Blatch and the Winning of Woman Suffrage*, 216–19.

102. DuBois, *Harriot Stanton Blatch and the Winning of Woman Suffrage*; Marilley, *Woman Suffrage and the Origins of Liberal Feminism*; Finnegan, *Selling Suffrage*, 73.

103. Ladd-Taylor, *Mother-Work*, 172–77; Harvey, *Votes without Leverage*.

104. DuBois, *Harriot Stanton Blatch and the Winning of Woman Suffrage*, 221; Norton and Alexander, *Major Problems in American Women's History*, 326–27, 333–48; Cott, "Feminist Politics in the 1920s." See also Cott, *Grounding of Modern Feminism*, chap. 2.

105. Rebecca Edwards, *Angels in the Machinery*, 41–42; Buhle, *Women and American Socialism*.

106. Gustafson, Miller, and Perry, *We Have Come to Stay*, 15, 33, 55–63; Bowen, *Growing Up with a City*, chap. 8.

107. Davis, *American Heroine*, 186; Davis, *Spearheads for Reform*.

108. Gustafson, Miller, and Perry, *We Have Come to Stay*; Muncy, "Trustbusting and White Manhood in America."

109. Ware, *Beyond Suffrage*; Ladd-Taylor, *Mother-Work*; Mettler, *Dividing Citizens*, chap. 3.

110. Mettler, *Dividing Citizens*, chap. 4, 133–35.

111. Ladd-Taylor, *Mother-Work*, 199–200.

112. Barbara Nelson, "Origins of the Two-Channel Welfare State," 132.

113. Ibid., 123–51. See also Sapiro, "Gender Basis of American Social Policy."

114. Mettler, *Dividing Citizens*, 191.

115. Ibid., 176, 191; Mink, "Lady and the Tramp."

116. Kessler-Harris, *In Pursuit of Equity*, chap. 3.

117. Mettler, *Dividing Citizens*, 81.

118. Ibid. See also Gordon, *Women, the State, and Welfare*; Sapiro, "Gender Basis of American Social Policy"; Mink, "Lady and the Tramp"; and Nelson, "Origins of the Two-Channel Welfare State."

119. Ladd-Taylor, *Mother-Work*, 151–55; Mettler, *Dividing Citizens*.

120. Ladd-Taylor, *Mother-Work*, 149; Mettler, *Dividing Citizens*; Gordon, *Women, the State, and Welfare*; Gordon, *Pitied But Not Entitled*.

121. Ginzberg, *Untidy Origins*, 151.

122. DuBois, *Feminism and Suffrage*, 178.

123. Eric Foner, *Short History of Reconstruction*, 193.

124. Giddings, *When and Where I Enter*.

125. Muncy, *Creating a Female Dominion in American Reform*, 117.

126. Gordon, *Heroes of Their Own Lives*, 14–15.

127. Mink, "Lady and the Tramp," 106.

128. Gordon, *Heroes of Their Own Lives*; Mink, *Wages of Motherhood*.

129. Yezierska, *Hungry Hearts*, 105.

130. Gilmore, *Gender and Jim Crow*; Elsa Barkley Brown, "Negotiating and Transforming the Public Sphere"; Brown, "Womanist Consciousness"; Deborah White, *Too Heavy a Load*, 66–67.

131. Gilmore, *Gender and Jim Crow*, 165–69.

132. Higginbotham, *Righteous Discontent*, chaps. 6–7; Boris, "Power of Motherhood," 227; Anne Scott, "Most Invisible of All"; Lake, "Politics of Respectability."

133. Carby, *Reconstructing Womanhood*, 262.

134. Ibid., 1; White, *Too Heavy a Load*.

135. White, *Too Heavy a Load*, 21–22.

136. Ibid., 60–61, 73.

137. Ibid., 56–58, 60; Giddings, *When and Where I Enter*.

138. Gilmore, *Gender and Jim Crow*, 26–27; White, *Too Heavy a Load*, 71–72; Hunter, *To 'Joy My Freedom*, 136–40.

139. Gilmore, *Gender and Jim Crow*, 102–3; Hunter, *To 'Joy My Freedom*.

140. Wells-Barnett, *Crusade for Justice*, 274–76, chaps. 31, 40.

141. Norton and Alexander, *Major Problems in American Women's History*, 325.

142. Ibid., 323; Jacquelyn Hall, *Revolt against Chivalry*.

143. MacLean, *Behind the Mask of Chivalry*.

144. Polacheck, *I Came a Stranger*; Wells-Barnett, *Crusade for Justice*; McManus, "'From Deep Wells of Religious Faith.'"

145. Bauman, *Women of Summer*.

146. Muncy, *Creating a Female Dominion in American Reform*, 95.

147. Bowen, *Growing Up with a City*, 23–24.

148. Addams, *Democracy and Social Ethics*, 11–12, 225; Ross, "Gendered Social Knowledge."

149. Michel, "The Limits of Maternalism," 292.

150. Ibid., 297; Boris, "Power of Motherhood," 218.

Chapter 5

1. "Rose Freedman, Last Survivor of Triangle Fire, Dies at 107," *New York Times*, February 17, 2001, B8.

2. Goldin, *Understanding the Gender Gap*, 10, 17; Opdycke, *Routledge Historical Atlas of Women in America*, 132; Woloch, *Women and the American Experience*, 608; Matthaei, *Economic History of Women in America*, 120–21; Baxandall and Gordon, *America's Working Women*, 405; Taeuber, *Statistical Handbook on Women in America*, 72.

3. Goldin, *Understanding the Gender Gap*; Chafe, *American Woman*; Kessler-Harris, *Out to Work*; Milkman, *Gender at Work*.

4. Goldin, *Understanding the Gender Gap*; Milkman, *Gender at Work*; Oppenheimer, *Female Labor Force in the United States*; Wandersee, *Women's Work and Family Values*.

5. Honey, *Creating Rosie the Riveter*; Oppenheimer, *Female Labor Force in the United States*; Chafe, *American Woman*.

6. Antler, "Feminism as Life Process"; Rosenberg, *Beyond Separate Spheres*; Elizabeth Adams, *Women Professional Workers*, 31–32.

7. Oppenheimer, *Female Labor Force in the United States*; Komarovsky, *Women in the Modern World*; Chafe, *American Woman*; Solomon, *In the Company of Educated Women*, 192.

8. See Elder, *Children of the Great Depression*; Baird, *Family Life Course and the Economic Status of Birth Cohorts*.

9. Goldin, *Understanding the Gender Gap*, 62.

10. Sennett, *Families against the City*, 206–7.

11. Meyerowitz, *Women Adrift*, 35; Kessler-Harris, *Out to Work*; Pascoe, *Relations of Rescue*; Knupfer, "'If You Can't Push, Pull, If You Can't Pull, Please Get Out of the Way.'"

12. Meyerowitz, *Women Adrift*; Enstad, *Ladies of Labor, Girls of Adventure*; Ryan, "Projection of a New Womanhood."

13. Dreiser, *Sister Carrie*; Wharton, *House of Mirth*; Chopin, *The Awakening*.

14. Hurst, *Anatomy of Me*, 76, 143, 213.

15. Stansell, *American Moderns*, 19.

16. Ibid., 29; Hurst, *Anatomy of Me*; Cheryl Wall, *Women of the Harlem Renaissance*.

17. Goldin, *Understanding the Gender Gap*, 93, 186; Kessler-Harris, *Out to Work*, 125.

18. Yezierska, *Bread Givers*; Meyerowitz, *Women Adrift*; Ryan, "Projection of a New Womanhood."

19. Amott and Matthaei, *Race, Gender, and Work*, 322.

20. Brissenden, *Earnings of Factory Workers*, 10.

21. Benson, *Counter Cultures*; Deutsch, *Women and the City*; Ryan, *Womanhood in America*, 3d ed., 223–31.

22. Solomon, *In the Company of Educated Women*, 62–64; Norwood, *Labor's Flaming Youth*.

23. Miriam Cohen, *Workshop to Office*; Fass, *Damned and the Beautiful*; Goldin, *Understanding the Gender Gap*, 106; Sassler, "Women's Marital Timing at the Turn of the Century."

24. Enstad, *Ladies of Labor, Girls of Adventure*, 178; Ewen, "City Lights."

25. Sarah Eisenstein, *Give Us Bread But Give Us Roses*; Enstad, *Ladies of Labor, Girls of Adventure*; Sewell, "Gendering the Spaces of Modernity"; Deutsch, *Women and the City*.

26. Enstad, *Ladies of Labor, Girls of Adventure*, 73.

27. Cott, *Grounding of Modern Feminism*, 36.

28. Carby, "'It Jus Be's Dat Way Sometime,'" 246.

29. Ibid.; Ryan, "Projection of a New Womanhood"; Ryan, *Womanhood in America*, 3d ed., 228–29; Deutsch, *Women and the City*.

30. Ryan, *Womanhood in America*, 3d ed., 229; Norton and Alexander, *Major Problems in American Women's History*, 288–91; Ewen, "City Lights," 56; Smith, *Family Connections*; Eisenstein, *Give Us Bread But Give Us Roses*.

31. Stansell, *American Moderns*.

32. Benson, *Counter Cultures*; Deutsch, *Women and the City*; Jacquelyn Hall, "Disorderly Women"; DuBois, "Working Women, Class Relations, and Suffrage Militance"; Stansell, *American Moderns*; Wertheimer, *We Were There*, part 5; Argersinger, *Making the Amalgamated*.

33. Enstad, *Ladies of Labor, Girls of Adventure*, 96.

34. Ibid., 84.

35. Ibid.

36. Ibid.; Deutsch, *Women and the City*; Kessler-Harris, *Out to Work*, chap. 8.

37. Deutsch, *Women and the City*; Norwood, *Labor's Flaming Youth*, chap. 4.

38. Glenn, *Female Spectacle*, 147; Finnegan, *Selling Suffrage*.

39. Yezierska, *Hungry Hearts*, 16.

40. Glenn, *Female Spectacle*, 194.

41. McBee, *Dance Hall Days*, 60.

42. Ibid., 75.

43. Enstad, *Ladies of Labor, Girls of Adventure*, 146; Mary Beth Norton, *Major Problems in American Women's History*, 324; McBee, *Dance Hall Days*, 75; Odem, *Delinquent Daughters*.

44. Deutsch, *Women and the City*, 98; Stansell, *City of Women*; Judith Schwartz, *Radical Feminists of Heterodoxy*.

45. Schwartz, *Radical Feminists of Heterodoxy*, 1; Schwartz, Peiss, and Simmons, "'We Were a Little Band of Willful Women,'" 118.

46. Schwartz, *Radical Feminists of Heterodoxy*; Cott, *Grounding of Modern Feminism*, chap. 1; Cook, *Crystal Eastman on Women and Revolution*, 47.

47. Schwartz, *Radical Feminists of Heterodoxy*; Stansell, *American Moderns*.

48. Norwood, *Labor's Flaming Youth*, photos following p. 170.

49. Peiss, *Cheap Amusements*; Paul Robinson, *Modernization of Sex*; Ryan, *Womanhood in America*, 3d ed., 231–38; Crane, *Maggie, A Girl of the Streets*.

50. Meyerowitz, *Women Adrift*, 103; Odem, *Delinquent Daughters*, 48–55; Ullman, *Sex Seen*; Peiss, *Cheap Amusements*, 108–14.

51. Peiss, *Cheap Amusements*, 102.

52. Hunter, *To 'Joy My Freedom*, 177.

53. Mumford, *Interzones*; Hunter, *To 'Joy My Freedom*, 176, chap. 8; Erenberg, *Steppin' Out*; Batker, "'Love Me Like I Like to Be'"; Powers, "Women and Public Drinking"; Peiss, *Cheap Amusements*, chap. 4.

54. Stansell, *American Moderns*, 89–90; Norton and Alexander, *Major Problems in American Women's History*, 326; Yezierska, *Hungry Hearts*, 40.

55. Stansell, *American Moderns*, 88–90.

56. Ibid., 303–4.

57. Cahan, *Rise of David Levinsky*; Yezierska, *Bread Givers*, 241.

58. Roth, *Call It Sleep*; Fitzgerald, *Great Gatsby*.

59. Ryan, *Womanhood in America*, 3d ed., 238–44; Marsh, "Suburban Men and Masculine Domesticity"; Laipson, "'Kiss without Shame, for She Desires It'"; Jessica Weiss, "'Drop-In Catering Job'"; LaRossa, *Modernization of Fatherhood*.

60. Kasson, *Houdini, Tarzan, and the Perfect Man*.

61. McBee, *Dance Hall Days*, 157.

62. Kevin White, *First Sexual Revolution*, 44, 50; Pendergast, "'Horatio Alger Doesn't Work Here Anymore.'"

63. Stansell, *American Moderns*, 261–62.

64. Haag, "In Search of 'the Real Thing'"; McBee, *Dance Hall Days*, chap. 5.

65. Yezierska, *Hungry Hearts*, 22.

66. Ibid., 23. See also Yezierska, *Salome of the Tenements*.

67. Yezierska, *Red Ribbon on a White Horse*, 113.

68. McBee, *Dance Hall Days*, 179.

69. Kessler-Harris, *Out to Work*, 256.

70. Chadwick and Heaton, *Statistical Handbook on the American Family*, 44; Opdycke, *Routledge Historical Atlas of Women in America*, 104; Ryan, *Womanhood in America*, 3d ed., 249–51; Wandersee, *Women's Work and Family Values*, chaps. 2–4; Chafe, *American Woman*, 56–57; Scharf, *To Work and to Wed*, 48; Ware, *Beyond Suf-*

frage, 129–30; Oppenheimer, *Female Labor Force in the United States*, 42–49; Komarovsky, *Unemployed Man and His Family*, 49; McBee, *Dance Hall Days*, 179; Chudacoff, *Age of the Bachelor*.

71. Woloch, *Women and the American Experience*, 606; Kurian, *Datapedia of the United States*, 39.

72. Ryan, *Womanhood in America*, 3d ed., 247.

73. Snyder, *Digest of Education Statistics*, 50.

74. Ryan, *Womanhood in America*, 3d ed., 244–47; Wright, *Moralism and the Model Home*, part 3; Vanek, "Time Spent in House Work"; Uhlenberg, "Cohort Variations in Family Life Cycle Experiences of U.S. Females"; Litoff, *American Midwives*; Wertz and Wertz, *Lying-In*; Watson, *Psychological Care of Infant and Child*; Lindquist, *Family in the Present Social Order*; Nancy Weiss, "Mother, the Invention of Necessity"; Daniel Smith, "Number and Quality of Children"; Snyder, *Digest of Education Statistics*, 50.

75. Opdycke, *Routledge Historical Atlas of Women in America*, 92; Matthaei, *Economic History of Women in America*, 38.

76. Berch, *Endless Day*, 98.

77. Vanek, "Time Spent in House Work."

78. Straub, "Women in the Civilian Labor Force," 206, 215.

79. Honey, *Creating Rosie the Riveter*, 125; Ryan, *Womanhood in America*, 3d ed., 255–56; Straub, "Women in the Civilian Labor Force"; Karen Anderson, *Wartime Women*, 59; Gluck, *Rosie the Riveter Revisited*, 23.

80. Argersinger, *Making the Amalgamated*; Cobble, *Other Women's Movement*, 26–28; Norwood, "Reclaiming Working-Class Activism"; Kessler-Harris, *Out to Work*; Goldin, *Understanding the Gender Gap*; Lynn Weiner, *From Working Girl to Working Mother*.

81. Goldin, *Understanding the Gender Gap*, 106–7.

82. Ibid., 60–61; Cobble, "Recapturing Working-Class Feminism"; Milkman, *Gender at Work*, 74–77.

83. Ethel Klein, *Gender Politics*; Cobble, *Other Women's Movement*.

84. Ware, *Still Missing*, 24.

85. Ibid., 29.

86. Ibid., 130.

87. Honey, *Creating Rosie the Riveter*, 71.

88. Ware, *Still Missing*; Honey, *Creating Rosie the Riveter*, 97, chap. 2; Ryan, *Womanhood in America*, chap. 6.

89. Cohen, *Workshop to Office*, 188.

90. Elder, *Children of the Great Depression*; Jessica Weiss, *To Have and to Hold*; May, *Homeward Bound*; Cohen, *Workshop to Office*, 187–88; Ryan, *Womanhood in America*, 3d ed., 257.

91. Cohen, *Workshop to Office*, 161–77.

92. Ibid., 180–86.

93. Ibid., 170–82 (quotation on p. 180).

94. Ibid., 187; Van Horn, *Women, Work, and Fertility*; Goldin, *Understanding the Gender Gap*; Weiss, *To Have and to Hold*.

95. Taeuber, *Statistical Handbook on Women in America*, 258; Weiss, *To Have and to Hold*, 4.

96. Ryan, *Womanhood in America*, 3d ed., 259, 261.

97. Ibid., 267–78, Easterlin, *Birth and Fortune*.

98. Landon Jones, *Great Expectations*, 41.

99. Oppenheimer, *Female Labor Force in the United States*; Chafe, *American Woman*; Ryan, *Womanhood in America*, 3d ed., 269; Jones, *Great Expectations*, 41; Wright, *Building the Dream*, 246.

100. Kenneth Jackson, *Crabgrass Frontier*, 234–38; Hise, *Magnetic Los Angeles*; Wright, *Building the Dream*; Ryan, *Womanhood in America*, 3d ed., 268–69; Lizabeth Cohen, "From Town Center to Shopping Center."

101. Opdycke, *Routledge Historical Atlas of Women in America*, 104.

102. Zane Miller, *Suburb*, 48.

103. Jackson, *Crabgrass Frontier*, 235; Miller, *Suburb*.

104. Lizabeth Cohen, *Making a New Deal*; Lizabeth Cohen, *Consumer's Republic*; Jackson, *Crabgrass Frontier*.

105. Wright, *Building the Dream*, 246.

106. Jackson, *Crabgrass Frontier*, 238; Wright, *Building the Dream*; Hanchett, "Financing Suburbia," 312.

107. May, *Homeward Bound*, 16–18; Zarlenga, "Civilian Threat"; Costigliola, "Nuclear Family."

108. Weiss, "Drop-In Catering Job"; Pendergast, "'Horatio Alger Doesn't Work Here Anymore.'"

109. Lundberg and Farnham, *Modern Woman*; Friedan, *Feminine Mystique*, 38.

110. Ryan, *Womanhood in America*, 3d ed., 259–67, 271–74; Friedan, *Feminine Mystique*, 20, 38, chap. 2; Komarovsky, *Women in the Modern World*, 7–8, 108–9; Vanek, "Time Spent in Housework"; Friedan, *It Changed My Life*; Mokyr, "Why 'More Work for Mother?'"

111. Spock, *Baby and Child Care*, 563.

112. Weiss, *To Have and to Hold*, 38.

113. May, *Homeward Bound*, 54–55.

114. Weiss, *To Have and to Hold*, 35–38; Dinnerstein, *Women between Two Worlds*, chap. 4; May, *Homeward Bound*.

115. May, *Homeward Bound*, 83–89.

116. Wandersee, *Women's Work and Family Values*; Weiss, *To Have and to Hold*.

117. Taeuber, *Statistical Handbook on Women in America*, 110; Berch, *Endless Day*, 9.

118. Goldin, *Understanding the Gender Gap*; Oppenheimer, *Female Labor Force in the United States*; Ryan, *Womanhood in America*; Chafe, *American Woman*.

119. Goldin, *Understanding the Gender Gap*; Weiss, *To Have and to Hold*, 60, 71–73, 78; Dinnerstein, *Women between Two Worlds*, 170–75.

120. Meyerowitz, "Beyond the Feminine Mystique"; Weiss, *To Have and to Hold*, 34; Dinnerstein, *Women between Two Worlds*.

121. Nicolaides, *My Blue Heaven*, 199–200.

122. Meyerowitz, *Not June Cleaver*, 1–18; Meyerowitz, "Beyond the Feminine Mystique"; Goldin, *Understanding the Gender Gap*, 68.

123. Friedan, *Feminine Mystique*, 37.

124. Ibid.; Friedan, *It Changed My Life*, 13; Friedan, *Life So Far*; Horowitz, *Betty Friedan and the Making of the Feminine Mystique*.

125. Solomon, *In the Company of Educated Women*, 200–201.

126. May, *Homeward Bound*, 140.

127. Friedan, *Feminine Mystique*, 12.

128. Solomon, *In the Company of Educated Women*, chap. 12.

129. Breines, *Young, White, and Miserable*, 183.

130. Plath, *Bell Jar*, 251.

131. Marcia Cohen, *Sisterhood*, 106.

Chapter 6

1. Scholinkski, *Last Time I Wore a Dress*, 205–6; Meyerowitz, *How Sex Changed*.

2. Jonathan D. Glater, "Women Are Close to Being Majority of Law Students," *New York Times*, March 26, 2001, A1, A16; Costello, Miles, and Stone, *American Woman*; Granrose and Kaplan, *Work-Family Role Choices for Women in Their 20s and 30s*.

3. Rosen, *World Split Open*; Flora Davis, *Moving the Mountain*; Echols, *Daring to Be Bad*, 12; Mary King, *Freedom Song*, 78; Evans, *Personal Politics*, 122.

4. Rupp and Taylor, *Survival in the Doldrums*; Lynn, "Gender and Post–World War II Progressive Politics"; Ware, "Dialogue: Pauli Murray's Notable Connections"; Jo Ann Robinson, *Montgomery Bus Boycott and the Women Who Started It*; Cobble, "Recapturing Working-Class Feminism."

5. Swerdlow, *Women Strike for Peace*.

6. Cobble, *Dishing It Out*; Deslippe, *Rights Not Roses*; Harrison, *On Account of Sex*, chaps. 7–8.

7. Harrison, *On Account of Sex*.

8. Ibid.; Deslippe, *Rights Not Roses*.

9. MacLean, "Hidden History of Affirmative Action"; O'Farrell and Kornbluh, *Rocking the Boat*, chap. 12; Friedan, *It Changed My Life*, 91–92, 119.

10. Rosen, *World Split Open*, 78–84; Ryan, *Womanhood in America*, 3d ed., 309–10.

11. King, *Freedom Song*, 443; Evans, *Personal Politics*, 234.

12. King, *Freedom Song*, 450, 571–74; Olson, *Freedom's Daughters*.

13. Evans, *Personal Politics*, 98–101; Jo Freeman, *Politics of Women's Liberation*; Echols, *Daring to Be Bad*, 23–50; Rosen, *World Split Open*, 120–22; Evans, *Tidal Wave*.

14. Klatch, *Generation Divided*, chap. 6.

15. Ibid., 151–61; Evans, *Personal Politics*; Dinnerstein, *Women between Two Worlds*; Olson, *Freedom's Daughters*.

16. King, *Freedom Song*, 74, 42–46; Evans, *Personal Politics*, 33–36, 52–53; Mueller, "Ella Baker and the Origins of Participatory Democracy"; Fleming, *Soon We Will Not Cry*; Olson, *Freedom's Daughters*.

17. Evans, *Personal Politics*, 234; Rothschild, "White Women Volunteers in the Freedom Summers."

18. King, *Freedom Song*, 471; Robin Morgan, *Sisterhood Is Powerful*; Evans, *Personal Politics*, 240–41.

19. Firestone, *Dialectic of Sex*; Gayle Rubin, "Traffic in Women."

20. Rosen, *World Split Open*, 196.

21. Ibid., 129–33; Davis, *Moving the Mountain*, chap. 4; Whittier, *Feminist Generations*, chap. 1.

22. Freeman, *Politics of Women's Liberation*, 86; Carden, *New Feminist Movement*.

23. Carden, *New Feminist Movement*, 59–67, 105.

24. Ryan, *Womanhood in America*, 3d ed., 317.

25. Olson, *Freedom's Daughters*; Hartmann, *From Margin to Mainstream*, 17, 69–70; Benita Roth, *Separate Roads to Feminism*.

26. Rosen, *World Split Open*, 159–60.

27. Robin Morgan, *Going Too Far*, 80–81.

28. MacLean, "Hidden History of Affirmative Action," 52–53; Rosen, *World Split Open*, 208–17, 300–301.

29. Carden, *New Feminist Movement*, 140–47.

30. Hartmann, *From Margin to Mainstream*; Ries and Stone, *American Woman*, 408–18; Farrell, *Yours in Sisterhood*, 1.

31. Hartmann, *From Margin to Mainstream*; Solinger, "Pregnancy and Power before *Roe v. Wade*"; Reagan, *When Abortion Was a Crime*.

32. Hartmann, *From Margin to Mainstream*, 138.

33. Katzenstein, "Feminism within American Institutions"; Hartmann, *From Margin to Mainstream*, 138; MacLean, "Hidden History of Affirmative Action."

34. Chafetz and Dworkin, *Women's Movements in World and Historical Perspective*; Buechler, *Women's Movements in the United States*.

35. Hartmann, *From Margin to Mainstream*; Ethel Klein, *Gender Politics*.

36. Fass, *Outside In*, 157; Dinnerstein, *Women between Two Worlds*, 63; Solomon, *In the Company of Educated Women*.

37. See Ryan, *Womanhood in America*, 3d ed., 329.

38. MacLean, "Hidden History of Affirmative Action"; Deslippe, *Rights Not Roses*; Goldin, *Understanding the Gender Gap*; Costello, Miles, and Stone, *American Woman*.

39. Dinnerstein, *Women between Two Worlds*, 87–88, 102.

40. Gerhard, "Revisiting the 'Myth of the Vaginal Orgasm'"; Allyn, *Make Love, Not War*.

41. D'Emilio, *Sexual Politics, Sexual Communities*; Stryker and Van Buskirk, *Gay by the Bay*; Armstong, *Forging Gay Identities*, chap. 2.

42. D'Emilio, *Sexual Politics, Sexual Communities*; Stein, *City of Sisterly and Brotherly Loves*; Armstrong, *Forging Gay Identities*.

43. D'Emilio, *Sexual Politics, Sexual Communities*; Segal, *Slow Motion*, 146–48; D'Emilio, *Universities and the Gay Experience*, 9–20.

44. Segal, *Slow Motion*, 146–48; Stein, *City of Sisterly and Brotherly Loves*; Poirier, *Last Call at Maud's*; Armstrong, *Forging Gay Identities*.

45. Duggan, "Trials of Alice Mitchell"; Katz, *Gay American History*, 214–25, 232–38; Herdt, *Third Sex, Third Gender*; San Francisco Lesbian and Gay History Project, "She Even Chewed Tobacco."

46. Duggan, "Trials of Alice Mitchell"; Trumbach, "Birth of the Queen."

47. Chauncey, "Christian Brotherhood or Sexual Perversion?"; Chauncey, *Gay New York*; Berube, *Coming Out under Fire*; D'Emilio, *Sexual Politics, Sexual Communities*.

48. Berube, *Coming Out under Fire*.

49. Kennedy and Davis, *Boots of Leather, Slippers of Gold*; Boyd, *Wide-Open Town*.

50. Faderman, *Odd Girls and Twilight Lovers*, 1.

51. Faderman, *Surpassing the Love of Men*, 228–30. See also Smith-Rosenberg, "Female World of Love and Ritual"; and Faderman, *Scotch Verdict*. For a discussion of the reproductive matrix, see D'Emilio and Freedman, *Intimate Matters*.

52. Bert Hansen, "American Physicians' 'Discovery' of Homosexuals"; Katz, *Invention of Heterosexuality*.

53. Kennedy and Davis, *Boots of Leather, Slippers of Gold*; Dell Martin and Phyllis Lyon interviewed in Poirier, *Last Call at Maud's*.

54. Boyd, *Wide-Open Town*; Chauncey, *Gay New York*, chap. 12.

55. Chauncey, *Gay New York*; Stryker and Van Buskirk, *Gay by the Bay*; Armstrong, *Forging Gay Identities*, 62.

56. Armstrong, *Forging Gay Identities*, 121.

57. Armstrong, *Forging Gay Identities*; Seidman, *Difference Troubles*, 120–30.

58. Escoffier, *American Homo*.

59. Sedgwick, *Epistemology of the Closet*, 8.

60. Faderman, *Odd Girls and Twilight Lovers*, 1; National Museum and Archive of Lesbian and Gay History, *Gay Almanac*; Sedgwick, *Epistemology of the Closet*.

61. Meyerowitz, *How Sex Changed*, 91, 99, chap. 3.

62. Ibid., 91.

63. "Queer Issue," *The Village Voice*, June 27, 2000.

64. Costello, Miles, and Stone, *American Woman*, 5, 264; Casterline, Lee, and Foote, *Fertility in the United States*, 202–4; Bergmann, *Economic Emergence of Women*; Goldin, *Understanding the Gender Gap*; McCall, *Complex Inequality*, 170–71; May, *Homeward Bound*; Opdycke, *Routledge Historical Atlas of Women in America*; Hacker,

Mismatch; Stacey, *In the Name of the Family*, chap. 1; Ries and Stone, *American Woman*, 244–66; Hertz and Marshall, *Working Families*, chap. 1.

65. Casterline, Lee, and Foote, *Fertility in the United States*, 52; Stacey, *In the Name of the Family*, 29–31.

66. Lillian Rubin, *Families on the Faultline*, 81.

67. Ibid., 83; Dinnerstein, *Women between Two Worlds*.

68. Kimmel, *Gendered Society*, chap. 6; Stacey, *In the Name of the Family*, chap. 2; Casterline, Lee, and Foote, *Fertility in the United States*; Ries and Stone, *American Woman*, 244–63; "Poll Reveals More Acceptance of a Changing American Family," *New York Times*, November 26, 1999, A41; Cherlin, "De-institutionalization of American Marriage."

69. Stacey, *Brave New Families*, 64–67, 78–82.

70. Ibid., chap. 1.

71. Ibid., 64.

72. Cherlin, "De-institutionalization of American Marriage."

73. Jennifer Johnson, *Getting by on the Minimum*, 124; Ehrensaft, "Kindercult," 306; Thorne, "Pick-Up Time at Oakdale Elementary School"; Rubin, *Families on the Faultline*.

74. Costello, Miles, and Stone, *American Woman*.

75. Hacker, *Mismatch*, 2–3, 168, chap. 11; Baran and Teegarden, "Women's Labor in the Office of the Future."

76. Goldin, *Understanding the Gender Gap*, 75; Spain and Bianchi, *Balancing Act*.

77. Ella Taylor, *Prime Time Families*.

78. Bennett and Bennett, "Changing Views about Gender Equality in Politics."

79. Costello, Miles, and Stone, *American Woman*; Manza and Brooks, "Gender Gap in U.S. Presidential Elections."

80. Kovic, *Born of the Fourth of July*; Kerry, *Call to Service*; Vistica, "What Happened in Thanh Phong"; Stone, *Born on the Fourth of July*; Cimino, *Deer Hunter*; Kubrick, *Full Metal Jacket*. See also Susan Jeffords, *Remasculinization of America*.

81. Kimmel, *Manhood in America*; Schwalbe, *Unlocking the Iron Cage*.

82. Braudy, *From Chivalry to Terrorism*, 519–41.

83. Rubin, *Families on the Faultline*, 92.

84. Costello, Miles, and Stone, *American Woman*; Hochschild, *Second Shift*; Mokyr, "Why 'More Work for Mother?'"; Hacker, *Mismatch*, chaps. 3–4.

85. Hacker, *Mismatch*, chaps. 5, 11.

86. Bernhardt, Morris, and Handcock, "Women's Gains or Men's Losses?"; Hacker, *Mismatch*.

87. Rubin, *Families on the Faultline*, 105.

88. Ibid.; "Black Women Graduates Outpace Male Counterparts," *New York Times*, October 31, 1994, A12; Costello, Miles, and Stone, *American Woman*; Sugrue, *Origins of the Urban Crisis*; William Julius Wilson, *When Work Disappears*.

89. Bernhardt, Morris, and Handcock, "Women's Gains or Men's Losses?"; Mc-

Call, *Complex Inequality*; Pleck, "Mother's Wages"; Goldin, *Understanding the Gender Gap*.

90. McCall, *Complex Inequality*; Benería and Stimpson, *Women, Households, and the Economy*, parts 2–3.

91. Perrucci and Wysong, *New Class Society*, 13.

92. Hacker, *Mismatch*, 181.

93. Costello, Miles, and Stone, *American Woman*, 223; Perrucci and Wysong, *New Class Society*, 13; Bernhardt, Morris, and Handcock, "Women's Gains or Men's Losses?"; Hacker, *Mismatch*, 181, chap. 11; Rubin, *Families on the Faultline*, 28–35; Ries and Stone, *American Woman*, 390.

94. Costello, Miles, and Stone, *American Woman*; Bernhardt, Morris, and Handcock, "Women's Gains or Men's Losses?"; McCall, *Complex Inequality*, chap. 2; Perrucci and Wysong, *New Class Society*.

95. Murray, *Song in a Weary Throat*, 435; Eleanor Norton, "Introduction," xi; Ware, "Dialogue: Pauli Murray's Notable Connections."

Chapter 7

1. This predecessor to the Virgin of Guadalupe was also known as Teteoinnan, and Toci or Tozi. William Taylor, "Virgin of Guadalupe in New Spain."

2. Rumbaut, "Origins and Destinies," 591.

3. Mazumdar, "What Happened to the Women?" 59.

4. Yezierska, *Bread Givers*, 25, 65.

5. Kingston, *Woman Warrior*.

6. Kibria, *Becoming Asian American*, 172.

7. Weinberg, *World of Our Mothers*, 15, 33.

8. Ets, *Rosa*, 160.

9. Yung, "'Bowlful of Tears,'" 131–34.

10. Weinberg, *World of Our Mothers*, 54–55.

11. Yung, *Unbound Feet*, 52–53; Yung, "'Bowlful of Tears.'"

12. Min and Song, "Demographic Characteristics and Trends of Post-1965 Korean Immigrant Women and Men," 49.

13. Mazumdar, "What Happened to the Women?" 61; Gabaccia, "When the Migrants Are Men."

14. Mazumdar, "What Happened to the Women?" 60.

15. Gabaccia, "When the Migrants Are Men," 190, 192, 196–99.

16. Mazumdar, "What Happened to the Women?"

17. Yung, *Unbound Voices*, 107–12.

18. Ibid.

19. Ryan, *Womanhood in America*, 3d ed., 167–82; Judith Smith, *Family Connections*, chap. 2.

20. Yung, *Unbound Feet*; Matsumoto, *Farming the Home Place*; Louie, *Sweatshop Warriors*, 52.

21. Portes and Rumbaut, *Legacies*, 71; Kibria, *Family Tightrope*, chap. 4.

22. Smith, *Family Connections*, 60–61.

23. Ewen, *Immigrant Women in the Land of Dollars*, 198.

24. Ryan, *Womanhood in America*, 3d ed., 176.

25. Yezierska, *Bread Givers*, 1.

26. Louie, *Sweatshop Warriors*, 52.

27. Orleck, *Common Sense and a Little Fire*; Puzo, *Fortunate Pilgrim*, 286.

28. Ets, *Rosa*, 242–43.

29. See Portes and Rumbaut, *Legacies*, plate 6, pp. 112–13.

30. Ibid.; Orsi, *Madonna of 115th Street*; McKibben, "'Of All the Gifts You Gave Me the Most Important One Is That I Belong.'"

31. Weinberg, *World of Our Mothers*, 48.

32. Wong, *Fifth Chinese Daughter*, 109–10.

33. Kingston, *Woman Warrior*, 201.

34. Prell, *Fighting to Become Americans*, 38–39.

35. Gabaccia, "When the Migrants Are Men," 202.

36. Matsumoto, "Japanese American Girls' Clubs in Los Angeles during the 1920s and 1930s," 174.

37. Bao, *Holding Up More Than Half the Sky*, 188; Frank Chin, *Donald Duk*, 148.

38. Simon and Brettell, *International Migration*.

39. U.S. Bureau of the Census, *We, the American—: Hispanics*.

40. "Squeezed by Debt and Time, Mothers Ship Babies to China," *New York Times*, September 14, 1999, A1.

41. Parreñas, "Migrant Filipina Domestic Workers and the International Division of Reproductive Labor," 572.

42. Gabaccia, *Immigration and American Diversity*, 241; Tung, "Caring across Borders," 308.

43. Nancy Foner, "Benefits and Burdens," 2; Hondagneu-Sotelo, *Doméstica*.

44. "Selected Statistics on the Status of Asian American Women," 136.

45. Ibid., 135.

46. Hollinger, "Amalgamation and Hypodescent," 1385; Yanagisako, *Transforming the Past*; Matsumoto, "Japanese American Women during World War II"; Lamphere, Zavella, and Gonzales, *Sunbelt Working Mothers*; Matsumoto, *Farming the Home Place*; "Selected Statistics on the Status of Asian American Women"; Yung, *Unbound Feet*.

47. Simon, Shelley, and Schneiderman, "Social and Economic Adjustment of Soviet Jewish Women in the United States," 78.

48. Ibid., 79.

49. Ibid., 77–78.

50. Rayaprol, *Negotiating Identities*, 26.

51. "Selected Statistics on the Status of Asian American Women," 136, 138, 135.

52. Min and Song, "Demographic Characteristics and Trends of Post-1965 Korean Immigrant Women and Men," 53–60; Chang and Moon, "Work Status, Conju-

gal Power Relations, and Marital Satisfaction among Korean Immigrant Married Women," 75.

53. Kim and Hurh, "Burden of Double Roles"; Song and Moon, *Korean American Women.*

54. Chan, *Hmong Means Free,* esp. chaps. 1–2, 9.

55. Ibid., 74–75, 116, 126, 85; Parreñas, "Asian Immigrant Women and Global Restructuring"; Chan, "Scarred, yet Undefeated."

56. Kibria, *Becoming Asian American,* 45, 48.

57. Ibid.

58. Ibid., 67–68, 56–60; Kibria, *Family Tightrope;* Haines, "Vietnamese Refugee Women in the U.S. Labor Force," 65, 67.

59. Simon, Shelley, and Schneiderman, "Social and Economic Adjustment of Soviet Jewish Women in the United States," 86.

60. Foner, "Sex Roles and Sensibilities," 138–40.

61. Prieto, "Cuban Women and Work in the United States," 102–3.

62. Simon and DeLey, "Undocumented Mexican Women," 128.

63. Kim and Kim, "Family and Work Roles of Korean Immigrant Wives and Related Experiences," 108; Min, "Burden of Labor in Korean American Wives," 94.

64. Haines, "Vietnamese Refugee Women in the U.S. Labor Force," 70.

65. Lamphere, "Working Mothers and Family Strategies."

66. Simon and Brettell, *International Migration;* Hondagneu-Sotelo, *Gendered Transitions;* Rayaprol, *Negotiating Identities;* Bao, *Holding Up More Than Half the Sky,* 68, 97, 129, 161.

67. Prieto, "Cuban Women and Work in the United States," 108.

68. Ibid.

69. Foner, "Sex Roles and Sensibilities," 145.

70. Ibid., 143–44.

71. Lamphere, "Working Mothers and Family Strategies," 274.

72. Ibid.

73. Louie, *Sweatshop Warriors,* 138, 78.

74. Vô, "Managing Survival," 237.

75. Bao, *Holding Up More Than Half the Sky,* 78.

76. Levitt, *Transnational Villagers,* 2.

77. Tung, "Caring across Borders," 301, 307.

78. Ibid., 307.

79. Ibid., 306.

80. Lamphere, "Working Mothers and Family Strategies," 273.

81. Ibid., 271.

82. Kibria, *Family Tightrope,* 108.

83. Ibid., 10, 61, 123–24, chap. 5; Song and Moon, "The Domestic Violence against Women in Korean Immigrant Families"; Hondagneu-Sotelo, *Gendered Transitions;* Bao, *Holding Up More Than Half the Sky,* 8.

84. Chan, "Scarred, yet Undefeated," 265.

85. Rayaprol, *Negotiating Identities*, 113.

86. Chan, "Scarred, yet Undefeated," 265.

87. Levitt, *Transnational Villagers*, 102.

88. Bao, *Holding Up More Than Half the Sky*, 97, 116–18.

89. Matthews, *Silicon Valley, Women, and the California Dream*, 222.

90. Ibid., 210.

91. Ong, *Flexible Citizenship*, 110–36.

92. Hossfeld, "'Their Logic against Them,'" 155.

93. Ibid.

94. Ibid., 163.

95. Matthews, *Silicon Valley, Women, and the California Dream*, 245.

96. Hossfeld, "'Their Logic against Them,'" 160, 164, 165.

97. Hondagneu-Sotelo, *Gendered Transitions*, 100.

98. Ibid., 98–104; Simon and Brettell, *International Migration*.

99. Poster, "Dangerous Places and Nimble Fingers"; Croucher, *Globalization and Belonging*, 169.

100. Hondagneu-Sotelo, *Gendered Transitions*, 119.

101. Hondagneu-Sotelo, *Doméstica*, 17.

102. Louie, *Sweatshop Warriors*, 48–51.

103. Ibid., 66–71.

104. Croucher, *Globalization and Belonging*, chap. 6.

105. Naples, "Changing the Terms," 11.

106. Ibid.; Louie, *Sweatshop Warriors*, 48–51; United Nations, *World's Women 1995*; Matthews, *Silicon Valley, Women, and the California Dream*, 142, 145; Ehrenreich and Hochschild, *Global Woman*.

107. Antin, *Promised Land*, 156, 168.

108. Matthews, *Silicon Valley, Women, and the California Dream*, 183; Stacey, *Brave New Families*, 25.

109. Desai, "Transnational Solidarity," 28; "Chinese Jostle Thousands of Women at Forum," *New York Times*, September 7, 1995, A11.

110. Rayaprol, *Negotiating Identities*, 41, 93–94.

111. Ibid., 140.

112. Dasgupta, *Patchwork Shawl*, 166.

113. Bao, "Politicizing Motherhood."

114. Ruiz, *From Out of the Shadows*, 5.

115. Ibid., 101; Ruiz, *Cannery Women, Cannery Lives*; Zinn, "Political Familialism"; Zinn, "Family, Feminism, and Race in America"; del Castillo, *La Familia*.

116. Zinn, "Political Familialism."

117. Ruiz, *From Out of the Shadows*, 134.

118. Zavella, *Women's Work and Chicano Families*, 64–66, 106.

119. Ibid., 147.

120. Cranford, "Gender and Citizenship in the Restructuring of Janitorial Work in Los Angeles," 32, 42; Zinn, "Family, Feminism, and Race in America"; Ruiz, *From Out of the Shadows*, 134–35; Lamphere, Zavella, and Gonzales, *Sunbelt Working Mothers*; Louie, *Sweatshop Warriors*, 210.

121. Sanchez, *Becoming Mexican American*, 167–68.

122. William Taylor, "Virgin of Guadalupe in New Spain"; Jeanette Rodriguez, *Our Lady of Guadalupe*; Poole, *Our Lady of Guadalupe*; Sanchez, *Becoming Mexican American*.

123. Farris, *Women Artists of Color*; Trujillo, *Chicana Lesbians*.

124. Richard Rodriguez, *Hunger of Memory*, 85.

125. Ruiz, *Las Obreras*, 29.

126. Louie, *Sweatshop Warriors*, 149–50, 209–11.

127. Ibid., 209–11.

128. Ibid., 204–6.

129. Cisneros, *House on Mango Street*, xi–xx.

130. Ibid., 103, 105, 76–79, 68–69, 82.

131. Ibid., 11, xix, xx, 134.

132. Galang, *Her Wild American Self*, 184; Jen, *Who's Irish?*, 15, 16.

133. Valaskakis, "Chippewa and the Other."

134. Prindeville and Gomez, "American Indian Women Leaders," 25–26.

135. Buff, *Immigration and the Political Economy of Home*, 170, 136–37.

136. Momaday, *Man Made of Words*, 33.

137. Connie Jacobs, *Novels of Louise Erdrich*, 7.

138. Erdrich, *Last Report on the Miracles at Little No Horse*, 77.

139. Erdrich, *Four Souls*, 155.

140. Ibid., 210.

BIBLIOGRAPHY

Ackerman, Lillian. "Complementary But Equal: Gender Status in the Plateau." In
  Women and Power in Native North America, edited by Laura F. Klein and
  Lillian A. Ackerman, 75–100. Norman: University of Oklahoma Press, 1995.

Adams, Elizabeth Kemper. *Women Professional Workers: A Study Made for the
  Women's Educational and Industrial Union*. New York: Macmillan, 1921.

Adams, John. "Thoughts on Government." In *The Founders' Constitution*, edited by
  Philip B. Kurland and Ralph Lerner, 669. Chicago: University of Chicago Press,
  1987.

Addams, Jane. *Democracy and Social Ethics*. Edited by Anne Firor Scott. Cambridge,
  Mass.: Belknap Press of Harvard University Press, 1964.

———. *Twenty Years at Hull-House*. Foreword by Henry Steele Commager. New
  York: New American Library, 1961.

———. "Women's Conscience and Social Amelioration." In *The Jane Addams
  Reader*, edited by Jean Bethke Elshtain, 252–63. New York: Basic Books, 2002.

Albers, Patricia. "Sioux Women in Transition: A Study of Their Changing Status in
  a Domestic and Capitalist Sector of Production." In *The Hidden Half: Studies of
  Plains Indian Women*, edited by Patricia Albers and Beatrice Medicine, 175–234.
  Washington, D.C.: University Press of America, 1983.

Albers, Patricia, and Beatrice Medicine, eds. *The Hidden Half: Studies of Plains
  Indian Women*. Washington, D.C.: University Press of America, 1983.

Allgor, Catherine. *Parlor Politics: In Which the Ladies of Washington Help Build a City
  and a Government*. Charlottesville: University Press of Virginia, 2000.

Allyn, David. *Make Love, Not War: The Sexual Revolution, an Unfettered History*.
  Boston: Little, Brown, 2000.

Altschuler, Glenn C., and Stuart M. Blumin. *Rude Republic: Americans and Their
  Politics in the Nineteenth Century*. Princeton, N.J.: Princeton University Press,
  2000.

Amadiume, Ifi. *Re-inventing Africa: Matriarchy, Religion, and Culture*. New York: Zed
  Books, 1997.

Amott, Teresa, and Julie Matthaei. *Race, Gender, and Work: A Multi-Cultural
  Economic History of Women in the United States*. Boston: South End Press, 1996.

Andersen, Kristi. *After Suffrage: Women in Partisan and Electoral Politics before the
  New Deal*. Chicago: University of Chicago Press, 1996.

Anderson, Karen. *Chain Her by One Foot: The Subjugation of Native Women in
  Seventeenth-Century New France*. New York: Routledge, 1991.

Anderson, Karen L. *Wartime Women: Sex Roles, Family Relations, and the Status of Women during World War II.* Westport, Conn.: Greenwood Press, 1981.

Anderson, Virginia D. *New England's Generation: The Great Migration and the Formation of Society and Culture in the Seventeenth Century.* New York: Cambridge University Press, 1991.

Anthony, Susan B., and Ida Husted Harper, eds. *The History of Woman Suffrage.* Vol. 4. Indianapolis, Ind.: Hollenbeck Press, 1902.

Antin, Mary. *The Promised Land.* Boston: Houghton, Mifflin, 1912.

Antler, Joyce. "Feminism as Life Process: The Life and Career of Lucy Sprague Mitchell." *Feminist Studies* 7 (Spring 1981): 134–57.

Applewhite, Harriet B., and Darline G. Levy, eds. *Women and Politics in the Age of the Democratic Revolution.* Ann Arbor: University of Michigan Press, 1990.

Arendt, Hannah. *The Human Condition.* Chicago: University of Chicago Press, 1998.

Argersinger, JoAnn E. *Making the Amalgamated: Gender, Ethnicity, and Class in the Baltimore Clothing Industry, 1899–1939.* Baltimore, Md.: Johns Hopkins University Press, 1999.

Ariès, Philippe. *Centuries of Childhood: A Social History of Family Life.* Translated by Robert Baldick. New York: Knopf, 1962.

Armstrong, Elizabeth A. *Forging Gay Identities: Organizing Sexuality in San Francisco, 1950–1994.* Chicago: University of Chicago Press, 2003.

Attie, Jean. *Patriotic Toil: Northern Women and the American Civil War.* Ithaca, N.Y.: Cornell University Press, 1998.

Axtell, James. *The School upon a Hill: Education and Society in Colonial New England.* New Haven, Conn.: Yale University Press, 1974.

Baird, Allen Jan. *Family Life Course and the Economic Status of Birth Cohorts: The United States and Western Europe, 1950–1976.* New York: Garland, 1989.

Baker, Jean H. *Affairs of Party: The Political Culture of Northern Democrats in the Mid-Nineteenth Century.* New York: Fordham University Press, 1998.

———. "Introduction." In *Votes for Women: The Struggle for Suffrage Revisited*, edited by Jean H. Baker, 3–20. New York: Oxford University Press, 2002.

———, ed. *Votes for Women: The Struggle for Suffrage Revisited.* New York: Oxford University Press, 2002.

Baker, Paula C. "The Domestication of Politics: Women and American Political Society, 1780–1920." *American Historical Review* 89 (June 1984): 620–47.

———. *The Moral Frameworks of Public Life: Gender, Politics, and the State in Rural New York, 1870–1930.* New York: Oxford University Press, 1991.

Banson, Susan. "Women and the Family Economy in the Early Republic: The Case of Elizabeth Meredith." *Journal of the Early Republic* 16 (Spring 1996): 47–72.

Bao, Xiaolan. *Holding Up More Than Half the Sky: Chinese Women Garment Workers in New York City, 1948–92.* Urbana: University of Illinois Press, 2001.

————. "Politicizing Motherhood: Chinese Garment Workers' Campaign for Daycare Centers in New York City, 1977–1982." In *Asian/Pacific Islander American Women: A Historical Anthology*, edited by Shirley Hune and Gail M. Nomura, 286–300. New York: New York University Press, 2003.

Baran, Barbara, and Suzanne Teegarden. "Women's Labor in the Office of the Future: A Case Study of the Insurance Company." In *Women, Households, and the Economy*, edited by Lourdes Benería and Catharine R. Stimpson, 201–24. New Brunswick, N.J.: Rutgers University Press, 1987.

Bardaglio, Peter W. *Reconstructing the Household: Families, Sex, and the Law in the Nineteenth-Century South*. Chapel Hill: University of North Carolina Press, 1995.

————. "'Shamefull Matches': The Regulation of Interracial Sex and Marriage in the South before 1900." In *Sex, Love, Race: Crossing the Boundaries in North American History*, edited by Martha Hodes, 112–38. New York: New York University Press, 1999.

Barker, Eirlys M. "Princesses, Wives, and Wenches: White Perceptions of Southeastern Indian Women to 1770." In *Women and Freedom in Early America*, edited by Larry D. Eldridge, 44–61. New York: New York University Press, 1997.

Barr, Juliana. "From Captives to Slaves: Commodifying Indian Women in the Borderlands." *Journal of American History* 92 (June 2005): 19–46.

Basch, Norma. *In the Eyes of the Law: Women, Marriage, and Property in Nineteenth-Century New York*. Ithaca, N.Y.: Cornell University Press, 1982.

Batker, Carol. "'Love Me Like I Like to Be': The Sexual Politics of Hurston's *Their Eyes Were Watching God*, the Classic Blues, and the Black Women's Club Movement." *African American Review* 32 (Summer 1998): 199–214.

Bauman, Suzanne. *The Women of Summer: The Bryn Mawr Summer School for Women Workers, 1921–1938*. New York: Filmakers Library, 1985.

Baxandall, Rosalyn, and Linda Gordon, eds., with Susan Reverby. *America's Working Women: A Documentary History, 1600 to the Present*. New York: Norton, 1995.

Bay, Edna G. "Servitude and Worldly Success in the Palace of Dahomey." In *Women and Slavery in Africa*, edited by Claire C. Robertson and Martin A. Klein, 340–67. Madison: University of Wisconsin Press, 1983.

Baym, Nina. *Woman's Fiction: A Guide to Novels by and about Women in America, 1820–1870*. Ithaca, N.Y.: Cornell University Press, 1978.

Bederman, Gail. *Manliness and Civilization: A Cultural History of Gender and Race in the United States, 1880–1917*. Chicago: University of Chicago Press, 1995.

Beecher, Catharine. *A Treatise on Domestic Economy, for the Use of Young Ladies at Home, and at School*. Boston: Marsh, Capen, Lyon, and Webb, 1841.

————. *A Treatise on Domestic Economy*. Introduction by Kathryn Kish Sklar. New York: Schocken Books, 1977.

Benería, Lourdes, and Catharine R. Stimpson, eds. *Women, Households, and the Economy*. New Brunswick, N.J.: Rutgers University Press, 1987.

Bennett, Linda L. M., and Stephen E. Bennett. "Changing Views about Gender

Equality in Politics: Gradual Change and Lingering Doubts." In *Women in Politics: Outsiders or Insiders? A Collection of Readings*, edited by Lois Duke Whitaker, 46–56. Upper Saddle River, N.J.: Prentice Hall, 1999.

Benson, Susan Porter. *Counter Cultures: Saleswomen, Managers, and Customers in American Department Stores, 1880–1940*. Urbana: University of Illinois Press, 1986.

Bercaw, Nancy, ed. *Gender and the Southern Body Politic*. Jackson: University Press of Mississippi, 2000.

Berch, Bettina. *The Endless Day: The Political Economy of Women and Work*. New York: Harcourt Brace Jovanovich, 1982.

Bercovitch, Sacvan, and Myra Jehlen, eds. *Ideology and Classic American Literature*. New York: Cambridge University Press, 1986.

Bergmann, Barbara R. *The Economic Emergence of Women*. New York: Basic Books, 1986.

Berkin, Carol. *First Generations: Women in Colonial America*. New York: Hill and Wang, 1996.

Berlin, Ira. *Many Thousands Gone: The First Two Centuries of Slavery in North America*. Cambridge, Mass.: Belknap Press of Harvard University Press, 1998.

Bernhardt, Annette, Martina Morris, and Mark S. Handcock. "Women's Gains or Men's Losses? A Closer Look at the Shrinking Gender Gap in Earnings." *American Journal of Sociology* 101 (September 1995): 302–28.

Berry, Brian J. L. "From Malthusian Frontier to Demographic Steady State: The Concordian Birth Rate, 1635–1993." *Population and Development Review* 22 (June 1996): 207–29.

Berube, Allan. *Coming Out under Fire: The History of Gay Men and Women in World War Two*. New York: Free Press, 1990.

Bilharz, Joy. "First among Equals? The Changing Status of Seneca Women." In *Women and Power in Native North America*, edited by Laura F. Klein and Lillian A. Ackerman, 101–12. Norman: University of Oklahoma Press, 1995.

Blackburn, Robin. "The Old World Background to European Colonial Slavery." *William and Mary Quarterly* 54 (January 1997): 65–102.

Blair, Karen J. *The Clubwoman as Feminist: True Womanhood Redefined, 1868–1914*. New York: Holmes and Meier, 1980.

Blassingame, John W. *Black New Orleans, 1860–1880*. Chicago: University of Chicago Press, 1973.

Bloch, Ruth. *Gender and Morality in Anglo-American Culture, 1650–1800*. Berkeley: University of California Press, 2003.

Blumin, Stuart M. *The Emergence of the Middle Class: Social Experience in the American City, 1760–1900*. New York: Cambridge University Press, 1989.

Bohlmann, Rachel E. "'Our "House Beautiful"': The Woman's Temple and the WCTU Effort to Establish Place and Identity in Downtown Chicago, 1887–1898." *Journal of Women's History* 11 (Summer 1999): 110–34.

Bordin, Ruth. *Woman and Temperance: The Quest for Power and Liberty, 1873–1900.*
Philadelphia: Temple University Press, 1981.

Boris, Eileen. "The Power of Motherhood: Black and White Activist Women
Redefine the 'Political.'" In *Mothers of a New World: Maternalist Politics and the
Origins of Welfare States,* edited by Seth Koven and Sonya Michel, 213–45. New
York: Routledge, 1993.

Bourdieu, Pierre. *Masculine Domination.* Translated by Richard Nice. Stanford,
Calif.: Stanford University Press, 2001.

Bouvier, Virginia M. *Women and the Conquest of California, 1542–1840: Codes of
Silence.* Tucson: University of Arizona Press, 2001.

Bowen, Louise de Koven. *Growing Up with a City.* Introduction by Maureen A.
Flanagan. Urbana and Chicago: University of Illinois Press, 2002.

Boyd, Nan Alamilla. *Wide-Open Town: A History of Queer San Francisco to 1965.*
Berkeley: University of California Press, 2003.

Boydston, Jeanne. *Home and Work: Housework, Wages, and the Ideology of Labor in
the Early Republic.* New York: Oxford University Press, 1990.

———. "The Woman Who Wasn't There: Women's Market Labor and the
Transition to Capitalism in the United States." *Journal of the Early Republic* 16
(Summer 1996): 183–207.

Boyer, Paul, and Stephen Nissenbaum, eds. *Salem Possessed.* New York: MJF Books,
1997.

Bradford, William. *Of Plymouth Plantation, 1620–1647.* Notes and introduction by
Samuel Eliot Morison. New York: Knopf, 2001.

Bradstreet, Anne. *The Writings of Mrs. Anne Bradstreet.* Introduction by Charles
Eliot Norton. New York: Duodecimos, 1897.

Braudy, Leo. *From Chivalry to Terrorism: War and the Changing Nature of
Masculinity.* New York: Knopf, 2003.

Breines, Wini. *Young, White, and Miserable: Growing Up Female in the Fifties.* Boston:
Beacon Press, 1992.

Brissenden, Paul. *Earnings of Factory Workers, 1899–1927: An Analysis of Pay-Roll
Statistics.* Washington, D.C.: Government Printing Office, 1929.

Broadhead, Susan Herlin. "Slave Wives, Free Sisters: Bakongo Women and Slavery,
c. 1700–1850." In *Women and Slavery in Africa,* edited by Claire C. Robertson
and Martin A. Klein, 160–81. Madison: University of Wisconsin Press, 1983.

Brodie, Janet Farrell. *Contraception and Abortion in Nineteenth-Century America.*
Ithaca, N.Y.: Cornell University Press, 1994.

Brooks, James. *Captives and Cousins: Slavery, Kinship, and Community in the
Southwest Borderlands.* Chapel Hill: University of North Carolina Press, 2002.

Brown, Elsa Barkley. "Negotiating and Transforming the Public Sphere: African
American Political Life in the Transition from Slavery to Freedom." *Public
Culture* 7 (Fall 1994): 107–47.

———. "To Catch the Vision of Freedom: Reconstructing Southern Black Women's Political History, 1865–1880." In *Unequal Sisters: A Multicultural Reader in U.S. Women's History*, edited by Ellen Carol DuBois and Vicki L. Ruiz, 124–46. 3d ed. New York: Routledge, 2000.

———. "Womanist Consciousness: Maggie Lena Walker and the Independent Order of Saint Luke." *Signs* 14 (Spring 1989): 610–33.

Brown, Jennifer S. H. *Strangers in Blood: Fur Trade Company Families in Indian Country.* Vancouver: University of British Columbia Press, 1980.

Brown, Judith K. "Economic Organization and the Position of Women among the Iroquois." *Ethnohistory* 17 (1970): 151–67.

Brown, Kathleen. "The Anglo-Algonquian Gender Frontier." In *Negotiators of Change: Historical Perspectives on Native American Women*, edited by Nancy Shoemaker, 26–48. New York: Routledge, 1995.

———. *Good Wives, Nasty Wenches, and Anxious Patriarchs: Gender, Race, and Power in Colonial Virginia.* Chapel Hill: University of North Carolina Press, 1996.

Brown, Richard. *Knowledge Is Power: The Diffusion of Information in Early America, 1700–1865.* New York: Oxford University Press, 1989.

Buechler, Steven M. *Women's Movements in the United States: Woman Suffrage, Equal Rights, and Beyond.* New Brunswick, N.J.: Rutgers University Press, 1990.

Buff, Rachel. *Immigration and the Political Economy of Home: West Indian Brooklyn and American Indian Minneapolis, 1945–1992.* Berkeley and Los Angeles: University of California Press, 2001.

Buhle, Mari Jo. *Women and American Socialism, 1870–1920.* Urbana: University of Illinois Press, 1981.

Burrows, Edwin G., and Michael Wallace. "The American Revolution: The Ideology and Psychology of National Liberation." *Perspectives in American History* 6 (1972): 167–306.

Bushman, Richard L. *The Refinement of America: Persons, Houses, Cities.* New York: Knopf, 1992.

Butler, Judith. *Bodies That Matter: On the Discursive Limits of "Sex."* New York: Routledge, 1993.

———. *Gender Trouble: Feminism and the Subversion of Identity.* New York: Routledge, 1999.

———. *Undoing Gender.* New York: Routledge, 2004.

Butterfield, L. H., ed. *Adams Family Correspondence.* Cambridge, Mass.: Belknap Press of Harvard University Press, 1963.

Bynum, Victoria E. *Unruly Women: The Politics of Social and Sexual Control in the Old South.* Chapel Hill: University of North Carolina Press, 1992.

Byrd, William. *William Byrd's Histories of the Dividing Line Betwixt Virginia and North Carolina.* New York: Dover, 1987.

Cahan, Abraham. *The Rise of David Levinsky, A Novel.* New York: Harper, 1917.

Calhoun, Craig, ed. *Habermas and the Public Sphere*. Cambridge, Mass.: MIT Press, 1992.

Camp, Stephanie M. H. *Closer to Freedom: Enslaved Women and Everyday Resistance in the Plantation South*. Chapel Hill: University of North Carolina Press, 2004.

Carby, Hazel. "'It Jus Be's Dat Way Sometime': The Sexual Politics of Women's Blues." In *Unequal Sisters: A Multicultural Reader in U.S. Women's History*, edited by Ellen Carol DuBois and Vicki L. Ruiz, 238–49. New York: Routledge, 1990.

———. "'On the Threshold of Woman's Era': Lynching, Empire, and Sexuality in Black Feminist Theory." *Critical Inquiry* 12 (Autumn 1985): 262–77.

———. *Reconstructing Womanhood: The Emergence of the Afro-American Woman Novelist*. New York: Oxford University Press, 1987.

Carden, Maren Lockwood. *The New Feminist Movement*. New York: Russell Sage, 1974.

Carlson, Laurie Winn. *A Fever in Salem: A New Interpretation of the New England Witch Trials*. Chicago: I. R. Dee, 1999.

Carnes, Mark C. *Secret Ritual and Manhood in Victorian America*. New Haven, Conn.: Yale University Press, 1989.

Carnes, Mark C., and Clyde Griffen, eds. *Meanings for Manhood: Constructions of Masculinity in Victorian America*. Chicago: University of Chicago Press, 1990.

Carr, Lois Green, and Lorena S. Walsh. "The Planter's Wife: The Experience of White Women in Seventeenth-Century Maryland." *William and Mary Quarterly* 34 (October 1977): 542–71.

Carter, Angela. *The Passion of New Eve*. New York: Harcourt Brace Jovanovich, 1977.

Cash, W. J. *The Mind of the South*. New York: Knopf, 1941.

Casterline, John B., Ronald D. Lee, and Karen A. Foote, eds. *Fertility in the United States: New Patterns, New Theories*. New York: Population Council, 1996.

Cecelski, David S., and Timothy B. Tyson, eds. *Democracy Betrayed: The Wilmington Race Riot of 1898 and Its Legacy*. Chapel Hill: University of North Carolina Press, 1998.

Chadwick, Bruce, and Tim B. Heaton, eds. *Statistical Handbook on the American Family*. 2d ed. Phoenix, Ariz.: Oryx Press, 1999.

Chafe, William H. *The American Woman: Her Changing Social, Economic, and Political Roles, 1920–1970*. New York: Oxford University Press, 1972.

Chafetz, Janet Saltzman, and Anthony Gary Dworkin. *Women's Movements in World and Historical Perspective*. Totowa, N.J.: Rowman and Allanheld, 1986.

Chan, Sucheng. "Scarred, yet Undefeated: Hmong and Cambodian Women and Girls in the United States." In *Asian/Pacific Islander American Women: A Historical Anthology*, edited by Shirley Hune and Gail M. Nomura, 253–67. New York: New York University Press, 2003.

———, ed. *Hmong Means Free: Life in Laos and America*. Philadelphia: Temple University Press, 1994.

Chang, Hye Kyung, and Ailee Moon. "Work Status, Conjugal Power Relations, and

Marital Satisfaction among Korean Immigrant Married Women." In *Korean American Women: From Tradition to Modern Feminism*, edited by Young I. Song and Ailee Moon, 75–87. Westport, Conn.: Praeger, 1998.

Chauncey, George, Jr. "Christian Brotherhood or Sexual Perversion? Homosexual Identities and the Construction of Sexual Boundaries in the World War I Era." In *Hidden from History: Reclaiming the Gay and Lesbian Past*, edited by Martin Duberman, Martha Vicinus, and George Chauncey Jr., 294–317. New York: New American Library, 1989.

———. *Gay New York: Gender, Urban Culture, and the Makings of the Gay Male World, 1890–1940*. New York: Basic Books, 1994.

Cherlin, Andrew J. "The De-institutionalization of American Marriage." *Journal of Marriage and the Family* 66 (November 2003): 848–61.

Child, Lydia Maria. *The American Frugal Housewife*. Mineola, N.Y.: Dover, 1999.

Chin, Carol C. "Beneficent Imperialists: American Women Missionaries in China at the Turn of the Twentieth Century." *Diplomatic History* 27, no. 3 (2003): 327–52.

Chin, Frank. *Donald Duk*. San Francisco: Coffee House Press, 1991.

Chopin, Kate. *The Awakening*. New York: H. S. Stone and Company, 1899.

Chudacoff, Howard. *The Age of the Bachelor: Creating an American Subculture*. Princeton, N.J.: Princeton University Press, 1999.

Cimino, Michael. *The Deer Hunter*. Universal Pictures and EMI Films, 1985.

Cisneros, Sandra. *The House on Mango Street*. New York: Knopf, 1994.

Claassen, Cheryl, and Rosemary A. Joyce, eds. *Women in Prehistory: North America and Mesoamerica*. Philadelphia: University of Pennsylvania Press, 1997.

Clinton, Catherine. *The Other Civil War: American Women in the Nineteenth Century*. New York: Hill and Wang, 1999.

Cobble, Dorothy Sue. *Dishing It Out: Waitresses and Their Unions in the Twentieth Century*. Urbana: University of Illinois Press, 1991.

———. *The Other Women's Movement: Workplace Justice and Social Rights in Modern America*. Princeton, N.J.: Princeton University Press, 2004.

———. "Recapturing Working-Class Feminism: Union Women in the Postwar Era." In *Not June Cleaver: Women and Gender in Postwar America, 1945–1960*, edited by Joanne Meyerowitz, 57–83. Philadelphia: Temple University Press, 1994.

Cogan, Jacob Katz, and Lori D. Ginzberg. "1846 Petition for Woman's Suffrage, New York State Constitutional Convention." *Signs* 22 (Winter 1997): 427–39.

Cohen, Lizabeth. *A Consumer's Republic: The Politics of Mass Consumption in Postwar America*. New York: Knopf, 2003.

———. "From Town Center to Shopping Center: The Reconfiguration of Community Marketplaces in Postwar America." *American Historical Review* 101 (October 1996): 1050–81.

———. *Making a New Deal: Industrial Workers in Chicago, 1919–1939*. New York: Cambridge University Press, 1990.

Cohen, Marcia. *The Sisterhood: The True Story of the Women Who Changed the World.* New York: Simon and Schuster, 1988.

Cohen, Miriam. *Workshop to Office: Two Generations of Italian-American Women in New York City, 1900–1950.* Ithaca, N.Y.: Cornell University Press, 1993.

Collier, Jane Fishburne. *Marriage and Inequality in Classless Societies.* Stanford, Calif.: Stanford University Press, 1988.

Collins, Patricia Hill, Lionel A. Maldonado, Dana Y. Takagi, Barrie Thorne, Lynn Weber, and Howard Winant. "Symposium on West and Fenstermaker's 'Doing Difference.'" In *Doing Gender, Doing Difference: Inequality, Power, and Institutional Change,* edited by Sarah Fenstermaker and Candace West, 81–94. New York: Routledge, 2002.

Cook, Blanche Wiesen. "Female Support Networks and Political Activism: Lillian Wald, Crystal Eastman, Emma Goldman." In *A Heritage of Her Own,* edited by Nancy F. Cott and Elizabeth Pleck, 412–44. New York: Simon and Schuster, 1979.

———, ed. *Crystal Eastman on Women and Revolution.* New York: Oxford University Press, 1978.

Coquery-Vidrovitch, Catherine. *African Women: A Modern History.* Translated by Beth Gillian Raps. Boulder, Colo.: Westview Press, 1997.

Costello, Cynthia B., Shari Miles, and Anne J. Stone, eds. *The American Woman, 1999–2000: A Century of Change—What's Next?* New York: Norton, 1998.

Costigliola, Frank. "The Nuclear Family: Tropes of Gender and Pathology in the Western Alliance." *Diplomatic History* 21 (Spring 1997): 163–83.

Cott, Nancy F. *The Bonds of Womanhood: "Woman's Sphere" in New England, 1780–1835.* New Haven, Conn.: Yale University Press, 1977.

———. "Feminist Politics in the 1920s: The National Woman's Party." *Journal of American History* 71 (June 1984): 43–68.

———. *The Grounding of Modern Feminism.* New Haven, Conn.: Yale University Press, 1987.

———, ed. *No Small Courage: A History of Women in the United States.* New York: Oxford University Press, 2000.

Cott, Nancy F., and Elizabeth Pleck, eds. *A Heritage of Her Own.* New York: Simon and Schuster, 1979.

Cowan, Ruth Schwartz. *More Work for Mother: The Ironies of Household Technology from the Open Hearth to the Microwave.* New York: Basic Books, 1983.

Cowing, Cedric B. "Sex and Preaching in the Great Awakening." *American Quarterly* 20 (Autumn 1968): 624–44.

Crane, Stephen. *Maggie, A Girl of the Streets, and Other Tales of New York.* New York: Penguin, 2000.

Cranford, Cynthia. "Gender and Citizenship in the Restructuring of Janitorial Work in Los Angeles." In *Immigrant Women,* edited by Rita James Simon, 21–47. New Brunswick, N.J.: Transaction, 2001.

Crawford, Vicki L., Jacqueline Anne Rouse, and Barbara Woods, eds. *Women in the Civil Rights Movement: Trailblazers and Torchbearers, 1941–1965*. New York: Carlson, 1990.

Croucher, Sheila L. *Globalization and Belonging: The Politics of Identity in a Changing World*. Lanham, Md.: Rowman and Littlefield, 2004.

Crowley, Terrence A. "Women, Religion, and Freedom in New France." In *Women and Freedom in Early America*, edited by Larry D. Eldridge, 109–26. New York: New York University Press, 1997.

Dailey, Jane Elizabeth. *Before Jim Crow: The Politics of Race in Postemancipation Virginia*. Chapel Hill: University of North Carolina Press, 2000.

Dasgupta, Shamita Das, ed. *A Patchwork Shawl: Chronicles of South Asian Women in America*. New Brunswick, N.J.: Rutgers University Press, 1998.

Davis, Allen Freeman. *American Heroine: The Life and Legend of Jane Addams*. New York: Oxford University Press, 1975.

———. *Spearheads for Reform: The Social Settlements and the Progressive Movement, 1890–1914*. New Brunswick, N.J.: Rutgers University Press, 1984.

Davis, Flora. *Moving the Mountain: The Women's Movement in America since 1960*. New York: Simon and Schuster, 1991.

Davis, Natalie Zemon. *Women on the Margins: Three Seventeenth-Century Lives*. Cambridge, Mass.: Harvard University Press, 1995.

Dayton, Cornelia Hughes. *Women before the Bar: Gender, Law, and Society in Connecticut, 1639–1789*. Chapel Hill: University of North Carolina Press, 1995.

De Cunzo, Lu Ann, and Bernard L. Herman, eds. *Historical Archaeology and the Study of American Culture*. Knoxville: University of Tennessee Press for the Winterthur Museum, 1996.

del Castillo, Richard Griswold. *La Familia: Chicano Families in the Urban Southwest, 1848 to the Present*. Notre Dame, Ind.: University of Notre Dame Press, 1984.

D'Emilio, John. *Sexual Politics, Sexual Communities: The Making of a Homosexual Minority in the United States, 1940–1970*. Chicago: University of Chicago Press, 1983.

———. *The Universities and the Gay Experience: Proceedings of the Conference Sponsored by the Women and Men of the Gay Academic Union*. New York: Gay Academic Union, Inc., 1974.

D'Emilio, John, and Estelle B. Freedman. *Intimate Matters: A History of Sexuality in America*. New York: Harper and Row, 1988.

Demos, John. *A Little Commonwealth: Family Life in Plymouth Colony*. New York: Oxford University Press, 1970.

———. "The Tried and the True: Native American Women Confronting Colonization." In *No Small Courage: A History of Women in the United States*, edited by Nancy Cott, 3–50. New York: Oxford University Press, 2000.

Desai, Manisha. "Transnational Solidarity: Women's Agency, Structural Adjustment, and Globalization." In *Women's Activism and Globalization: Linking*

Local Struggles and Transnational Politics, edited by Nancy A. Naples and Manisha Desai, 15–33. New York: Routledge, 2002.

Deslippe, Dennis A. *Rights, Not Roses: Unions and the Rise of Working-Class Feminism, 1945–1980.* Urbana: University of Illinois Press, 2000.

Deutrich, Mabel E., and Virginia C. Purdy, eds. *Clio Was a Woman: Studies in the History of American Women.* Washington, D.C.: Howard University Press, 1980.

Deutsch, Sarah. *No Separate Refuge: Culture, Class, and Gender on an Anglo-Hispanic Frontier, 1880–1940.* New York: Oxford University Press, 1987.

———. *Women and the City: Gender, Space, and Power in Boston, 1870–1940.* New York: Oxford University Press, 2000.

Devens, Carol. *Countering Colonization: Native American Women and Great Lakes Missions, 1630–1900.* Berkeley: University of California Press, 1992.

Dinnerstein, Myrna. *Women between Two Worlds: Midlife Reflections on Work and Family.* Philadelphia: Temple University Press, 1992.

Ditz, Toby L. "The New Men's History and the Peculiar Absence of Gendered Power: Some Remedies from Early American Gender History." *Gender and History* 16 (April 2004): 1–35.

Dominguez, Virginia R. *White by Definition: Social Classification in Creole Louisiana.* New Brunswick, N.J.: Rutgers University Press, 1986.

Dorsey, Bruce. *Reforming Men and Women: Gender in the Antebellum City.* Ithaca, N.Y.: Cornell University Press, 2002.

Douglass, Frederick. *Narrative of the Life of Frederick Douglass, Written by Himself.* Edited and with an introduction by Deborah E. McDowell, notes by John Charles. New York: Oxford University Press, 1999.

Dowd, Gregory Evans. "North American Indian Slaveholding and the Colonization of Gender: The Southeast before Removal." *Critical Matrix* 3 (Fall 1987): 152–53.

Dreiser, Theodore. *Sister Carrie.* New York: Doubleday, 1900.

Duberman, Martin, Martha Vicinus, and George Chauncey Jr., eds. *Hidden from History: Reclaiming the Gay and Lesbian Past.* New York: New American Library, 1989.

Dublin, Thomas. *Transforming Women's Work: New England Lives in the Industrial Revolution.* Ithaca, N.Y.: Cornell University Press, 1994.

DuBois, Ellen Carol. *Feminism and Suffrage: The Emergence of an Independent Women's Movement in America, 1848–1869.* Ithaca, N.Y.: Cornell University Press, 1978.

———. *Harriot Stanton Blatch and the Winning of Woman Suffrage.* New Haven, Conn.: Yale University Press, 1997.

———. *Woman Suffrage and Women's Rights.* New York: New York University Press, 1998.

———. "Working Women, Class Relations, and Suffrage Militance: Harriot Stanton Blatch and the New York Woman Suffrage Movement, 1894–1909." *Journal of American History* 74 (June 1987): 34–58.

DuBois, Ellen, and Lynn Dumenil. *Through Women's Eyes: An American History with Documents*. Boston: Bedford/St. Martin's, 2005.

DuBois, Ellen Carol, and Vicki L. Ruiz, eds. *Unequal Sisters: A Multicultural Reader in U.S. Women's History*. 3d ed. New York: Routledge, 2000.

Duggan, Lisa. "The Trials of Alice Mitchell: Sensationalism, Sexology, and the Lesbian Subject in Turn-of-the-Century America." *Signs* 18 (Summer 1993): 791–815.

Dumenil, Lynn. *Freemasonry and American Culture, 1880–1930*. Princeton, N.J.: Princeton University Press, 1984.

Dunaway, Wilma. *The African-American Family in Slavery and Freedom*. New York: Cambridge University Press, 2003.

———. "Rethinking Cherokee Acculturation: Agrarian Capitalism and Women's Resistance to the Cult of Domesticity, 1800–1838." *American Indian Culture and Research Journal* 21 (Winter 1997): 155–82.

Easterlin, Richard A. *Birth and Fortune: The Impact of Numbers on Personal Welfare*. New York: Basic Books, 1980.

Echols, Alice. *Daring to Be Bad: Radical Feminism in America, 1967–1975*. Minneapolis: University of Minnesota Press, 1989.

Edwards, Laura F. "The Disappearance of Susan Daniel and Henderson Cooper: Gender and Narratives of Political Conflict in the Reconstruction-Era U.S. South." In *Sex, Love, Race: Crossing Boundaries in North American History*, edited by Martha Hodes, 294–312. New York: New York University Press, 1999.

———. *Gendered Strife and Confusion: The Political Culture of Reconstruction*. Urbana: University of Illinois Press, 1997.

———. "Law, Domestic Violence, and the Limits of Patriarchal Authority in the Antebellum South." In *Gender and the Southern Body Politic*, edited by Nancy Bercaw, 63–86. Jackson: University Press of Mississippi, 2000.

Edwards, Rebecca. *Angels in the Machinery: Gender in American Party Politics from the Civil War to the Progressive Era*. New York: Oxford University Press, 1997.

Ehrenreich, Barbara, and Arlie Russell Hochschild, eds. *Global Woman: Nannies, Maids, and Sex Workers in the New Economy*. New York: Owl Books, 2002.

Ehrensaft, Diane. "The Kindercult: The New Child Born to Conflict between Work and Family." In *Working Families: The Transformation of the American Home*, edited by Rosanna Hertz and Nancy L. Marshall, 304–22. Berkeley: University of California Press, 2001.

Eisenstein, Sarah. *Give Us Bread But Give Us Roses: Working Women's Consciousness in the United States, 1890 to the First World War*. Boston: Routledge and Kegan Paul, 1983.

Eisenstein, Zillah. *Sexual Decoys*. London: Zed Books, forthcoming.

Elder, Glen H., Jr. *Children of the Great Depression: Social Change in Life Experience*. Chicago: University of Chicago Press, 1974.

Eldridge, Larry D., ed. *Women and Freedom in Early America*. New York: New York University Press, 1997.

Elshtain, Jean Bethke, ed. *The Jane Addams Reader*. New York: Basic Books, 2002.

Eltis, David. *The Rise of African Slavery in the Americas*. New York: Cambridge University Press, 2000.

Enstad, Nan. *Ladies of Labor, Girls of Adventure: Working Women, Popular Culture, and Labor Politics at the Turn of the Twentieth Century*. New York: Columbia University Press, 1999.

Erdrich, Louise. *Four Souls*. New York: Harper Collins, 2004.

————. *The Last Report on the Miracles at Little No Horse*. New York: Harper Collins, 2001.

Erenberg, Lewis A. *Steppin' Out: New York Nightlife and the Transformation of American Culture, 1890–1930*. Westport, Conn.: Greenwood Press, 1981.

Escoffier, Jeffrey. *American Homo: Community and Perversity*. Berkeley: University of California Press, 1998.

Estrada, William David. "Sacred and Contested Space: The Los Angeles Plaza." Ph.D. diss., University of California, Los Angeles, 2003.

Ets, Marie Hall. *Rosa: The Life of an Italian Immigrant*. Minneapolis: University of Minnesota Press, 1970.

Evans, Sara. *Born for Liberty: A History of Women in America*. New York: Free Press, 1989.

————. *Personal Politics: The Roots of Women's Liberation in the Civil Rights Movement and the New Left*. New York: Knopf, 1979.

————. *Tidal Wave: How Women Changed America at Century's End*. New York: Free Press, 2003.

Ewen, Elizabeth. "City Lights: Immigrant Women and the Rise of the Movies." *Signs* 5, Suppl. (Spring 1980): 45–65.

————. *Immigrant Women in the Land of Dollars: Life and Culture on the Lower East Side, 1890–1925*. New York: Monthly Review Press, 1985.

Faderman, Lillian. *Odd Girls and Twilight Lovers: A History of Lesbian Life in Twentieth-Century America*. New York: Columbia University Press, 1991.

————. *Scotch Verdict: Miss Pirie and Miss Woods v. Dame Cumming Gordon*. New York: Morrow, 1983.

————. *Surpassing the Love of Men: Romantic Friendship and Love between Women from the Renaissance to the Present*. New York: Morrow, 1981.

Fahs, Alice. "The Gendering of Reconstruction: Contests over the Private and Public in North Carolina." *Reviews in American History* 27 (March 1999): 73–78.

Farber, Bernard. *Guardians of Virtue: Salem Families in 1800*. New York: Basic Books, 1972.

Farley, Reynolds. *Growth of the Black Population: A Study of Demographic Trends*. Chicago: Markham, 1970.

Farnham, Christie. "Sapphire? The Issue of Dominance in the Slave Family, 1830–

1865." In *"To Toil the Live-Long Day": America's Women at Work, 1780–1980*, edited by Carol Groneman and Mary Beth Norton, 63–83. Ithaca, N.Y.: Cornell University Press, 1987.

Farrell, Amy Erdman. *Yours in Sisterhood: Ms. Magazine and the Promise of Popular Feminism.* Chapel Hill: University of North Carolina Press, 1998.

Farris, Phoebe, ed. *Women Artists of Color: A Bio-Critical Sourcebook to 20th Century Artists in the Americas.* Westport, Conn.: Greenwood Press, 1999.

Fass, Paula S. *The Damned and the Beautiful: American Youth in the 1920s.* New York: Oxford University Press, 1977.

———. *Outside In: Minorities and the Transformation of American Education.* New York: Oxford University Press, 1989.

Fenstermaker, Sarah, and Candace West, eds. *Doing Gender, Doing Difference: Inequality, Power, and Institutional Change.* New York: Routledge, 2002.

Finnegan, Margaret Mary. *Selling Suffrage: Consumer Culture and Votes for Women.* New York: Columbia University Press, 1999.

Firestone, Shulamith. *Dialectic of Sex: The Case for Feminist Revolution.* New York: Bantam, 1970.

Fischer, Kirsten. *Suspect Relations: Sex, Race, and Resistance in Colonial North Carolina.* Ithaca, N.Y.: Cornell University Press, 2002.

Fitzgerald, F. Scott. *The Great Gatsby.* New York: Scribner's Sons, 1925.

Flanagan, Maureen. *Seeing with Their Hearts: Chicago Women and the Vision of the Good City, 1871–1933.* Princeton, N.J.: Princeton University Press, 2002.

Fleming, Cynthia Griggs. *Soon We Will Not Cry: The Liberation of Ruby Doris Smith Robinson.* Lanham, Md.: Rowman and Littlefield, 1998.

Fletcher, Anthony. *Gender, Sex, and Subordination in England, 1500–1800.* New Haven, Conn.: Yale University Press, 1995.

Fliegelman, Jay. *Prodigals and Pilgrims: The American Revolution against Patriarchal Authority, 1750–1800.* Cambridge, Eng.: Cambridge University Press, 1982.

Foner, Eric. *Free Soil, Free Labor, Free Men: The Ideology of the Republican Party before the Civil War.* New York: Oxford University Press, 1970.

———. *Reconstruction: America's Unfinished Revolution, 1863–1877.* New York: Harper and Row, 1988.

———. *A Short History of Reconstruction, 1863–1877.* New York: Harper and Row, 1990.

Foner, Nancy. "Benefits and Burdens: Immigrant Women and Work in New York City." In *Immigrant Women*, edited by Rita James Simon, 1–20. New Brunswick, N.J.: Transaction, 2001.

———. "Sex Roles and Sensibilities: Jamaican Women in New York and London." In *International Migration: The Female Experience*, edited by Rita James Simon and Caroline B. Brettell, 133–51. Totowa, N.J.: Rowman and Allanheld, 1986.

Foster, Gaines M. *Ghosts of the Confederacy: Defeat, the Lost Cause, and the Emergence of the New South, 1865 to 1913.* New York: Oxford University Press, 1987.

BIBLIOGRAPHY

Foster, Hannah Webster. *The Coquette*. New York: Oxford University Press, 1986.

Foucault, Michel. *History of Sexuality*. Vol. 1: *An Introduction*. New York: Pantheon, 1980.

Fout, John C., and Maura Shaw Tantillo, eds. *American Sexual Politics: Sex, Gender, and Race since the Civil War*. Chicago: University of Chicago Press, 1993.

Fox-Genovese, Elizabeth. *Within the Plantation Household: Black and White Women of the Old South*. Chapel Hill: University of North Carolina Press, 1988.

Frazier, Edward Franklin. *The Free Negro Family*. New York: Arno Press, 1968.

Freeman, Jo. *The Politics of Women's Liberation*. New York: David McKay Company, 1975.

Freeman, Joanne. *Affairs of Honor: National Politics in the New Republic*. New Haven, Conn.: Yale University Press, 2001.

Friedan, Betty. *The Feminine Mystique*. New York: Dell Publishing, 1976.

————. *It Changed My Life: Writings on the Women's Movement*. New York: Random House, 1976.

————. *Life So Far*. New York: Simon and Schuster, 2000.

Friedman, Jean, and William Shade, eds. *Our American Sisters: Women in American Life and Thought*. Boston: Allyn and Bacon, 1976.

Gabaccia, Donna R. *Immigration and American Diversity: A Social and Cultural History*. Malden, Mass.: Blackwell, 2002.

————. "When the Migrants Are Men: Italy's Women and Transnationalism as a Way of Life." In *Women, Gender, and Labour Migration: Historical and Global Perspectives*, edited by Pamela Sharpe, 190–208. London and New York: Routledge, 2001.

Galang, M. Evelina. *Her Wild American Self: Short Stories*. Minneapolis, Minn.: Coffee House Press, 1996.

Galloway, Patricia. "Where Have All the Menstrual Huts Gone? The Invisibility of Menstrual Seclusion in the Late Prehistoric Southeast." In *Women in Prehistory: North America and Mesoamerica*, edited by Cheryl Claassen and Rosemary A. Joyce, 47–62. Philadelphia: University of Pennsylvania Press, 1997.

Gaspar, David Barry, and Darlene Clark Hine, eds. *More Than Chattel: Black Women and Slavery in the Americas*. Bloomington: Indiana University Press, 1996.

Gates, Henry Louis, ed. *The Classic Slave Narratives*. New York: Penguin Putnam, 2002.

Gerhard, Jane. "Revisiting the 'Myth of the Vaginal Orgasm': The Female Orgasm in American Sexual Thought and Second Wave Feminism." *Feminist Studies* 26 (Summer 2000): 449–77.

Gero, Joan M., and Margaret W. Conkey, eds. *Engendering Archaeology: Women and Prehistory*. Cambridge, Mass.: Blackwell, 1991.

Giddings, Paula. *When and Where I Enter: The Impact of Black Women on Race and Sex in America*. New York: W. Morrow, 1984.

Giesberg, Judith Allen. *Civil War Sisterhood: The U.S. Sanitary Commission and Women's Politics in Transition.* Boston: Northeastern University Press, 2000.

Gilbert, Sandra M., and Susan Gubar, eds. *The Norton Anthology of Literature by Women: The Traditions in English.* 2d ed. New York: W. W. Norton, 1996.

Gildrie, Richard P. *The Profane, the Civil, and the Godly: The Reformation of Manners in Orthodox New England, 1679–1749.* University Park: Pennsylvania State University Press, 1994.

———. *Salem, Massachusetts, 1626–1683: A Covenant Community.* Charlottesville: University Press of Virginia, 1975.

Gilmore, Glenda Elizabeth. *Gender and Jim Crow: Women and the Politics of White Supremacy in North Carolina, 1896–1920.* Chapel Hill: University of North Carolina Press, 1996.

———. "Murder, Memory, and the Flight of the Incubus." In *Democracy Betrayed: The Wilmington Race Riot of 1898 and Its Legacy,* edited by David S. Cecelski and Timothy B. Tyson, 73–93. Chapel Hill: University of North Carolina Press, 1998.

Ginzberg, Lori D. "'The Hearts of Your Readers Will Shudder': Fanny Wright, Infidelity, and American Free Thought." *American Quarterly* 46 (June 1994): 195–226.

———. *Untidy Origins: A Story of Woman's Rights in Antebellum New York.* Chapel Hill: University of North Carolina Press, 2005.

———. *Women and the Work of Benevolence: Morality, Politics, and Class in the Nineteenth-Century United States.* New Haven, Conn.: Yale University Press, 1990.

Glenn, Susan A. *Female Spectacle: The Theatrical Roots of Modern Feminism.* Cambridge, Mass.: Harvard University Press, 2000.

Gluck, Sherna Berger. *Rosie the Riveter Revisited: Women, the War, and Social Change.* Boston: Twayne, 1987.

Godbeer, Richard. "Eroticizing the Middle Ground: Anglo-Indian Sexual Relations along the Eighteenth-Century Frontier." In *Sex, Love, Race: Crossing Boundaries in North American History,* edited by Martha Hodes, 91–111. New York: New York University Press, 1999.

———. "Love Raptures." In *A Shared Experience: Men, Women, and the History of Gender,* edited by Laura McCall and Donald Yacovone, 51–77. New York: New York University Press, 1998.

Goldberg, Jonathan. "Sodomy in the New World: Anthropologies Old and New." In *Fear of a Queer Planet: Queer Politics and Social Theory,* edited by Michael Warner, 3–18. Minneapolis: University of Minnesota Press, 1993.

Goldin, Claudia. *Understanding the Gender Gap: An Economic History of American Women.* New York: Oxford University Press, 1990.

Gomez, Michael Angelo. *Exchanging Our Country Marks: The Transformation of African Identities in the Colonial and Antebellum South.* Chapel Hill: University of North Carolina Press, 1998.

Goodman, Dena. *The Republic of Letters: A Cultural History of the French Enlightenment*. Ithaca, N.Y.: Cornell University Press, 1994.

Gordon, Linda. "Black and White Visions of Welfare: Women's Welfare Activism, 1890–1945." *Journal of American History* 78 (September 1991): 559–90.

———. *Heroes of Their Own Lives: The Politics and History of Family Violence: Boston, 1880–1960*. New York: Viking, 1988.

———. *Pitied But Not Entitled: Single Mothers and the History of Welfare, 1890–1935*. Cambridge, Mass.: Harvard University Press, 1995.

———, ed. *Women, the State, and Welfare*. Madison: University of Wisconsin Press, 1990.

Gould, Virginia Meacham. "'The House That Never Was a Home': Slave Family and Household Organization in New Orleans, 1820–1850." *Slavery and Abolition* 18 (August 1997): 90–103.

Granrose, Cherlyn Skromme, and Eileen E. Kaplan. *Work-Family Role Choices for Women in Their 20s and 30s: From College Plans to Life Experiences*. Westport, Conn.: Praeger, 1996.

Green, Gretchen. "Gender and the Longhouse: Iroquois Women in a Changing Culture." In *Women and Freedom in Early America*, edited by Larry D. Eldridge, 7–25. New York: New York University Press, 1997.

Greenberg, Amy S. *Cause for Alarm: The Volunteer Fire Department in the Nineteenth-Century City*. Princeton, N.J.: Princeton University Press, 1998.

———. *Manifest Manhood and the Antebellum American Empire*. New York: Cambridge University Press, 2005.

Greene, Jack P., and J. R. Pole, eds. *Colonial British America: Essays in the New History of the Early Modern Era*. Baltimore, Md.: Johns Hopkins University Press, 1984.

Greer, Germaine. *The Female Eunuch*. New York: McGraw-Hill, 1971.

Grossberg, Michael. *Governing the Hearth: Law and the Family in Nineteenth-Century America*. Chapel Hill: University of North Carolina Press, 1985.

Guemple, Lee. "Gender in Inuit Society." In *Women and Power in Native North America*, edited by Laura F. Klein and Lillian A. Ackerman, 17–27. Norman: University of Oklahoma Press, 1995.

Gullett, Gayle. *Becoming Citizens: The Emergence and Development of the California Women's Movement, 1880–1911*. Urbana and Chicago: University of Illinois Press, 2000.

Gustafson, Melanie, Kristie Miller, and Elisabeth I. Perry, eds. *We Have Come to Stay: American Women and Political Parties, 1880–1960*. Albuquerque: University of New Mexico Press, 1999.

Gutiérrez, Ramón. *When Jesus Came, the Corn Mothers Went Away: Marriage, Sexuality, and Power in New Mexico, 1500–1846*. Stanford, Calif.: Stanford University Press, 1991.

Gutman, Herbert George. *The Black Family in Slavery and Freedom, 1750–1925.* New York: Pantheon Books, 1976.

Gutman, Marta Ruth. "On the Ground in Oakland: Women and Institution Building in an Industrial City." Ph.D. diss., University of California, Berkeley, 2000.

Haag, Pamela S. "In Search of 'the Real Thing': Ideologies of Love, Modern Romance, and Women's Sexual Subjectivity in the United States, 1920–1940." In *American Sexual Politics: Sex, Gender, and Race since the Civil War*, edited by John C. Fout and Maura Shaw Tantillo, 161–92. Chicago: University of Chicago Press, 1993.

Habermas, Jürgen. *The Structural Transformation of the Public Sphere: An Inquiry into a Category of Bourgeois Society.* Translated by Thomas Burger. Cambridge, Mass.: MIT Press, 1989.

Hacker, Andrew. *Mismatch: The Growing Gulf between Women and Men.* New York: Scribner, 2003.

Haines, David W. "Vietnamese Refugee Women in the U.S. Labor Force: Continuity or Change?" In *International Migration: The Female Experience*, edited by Rita James Simon and Caroline B. Brettell, 62–75. Totowa, N.J.: Rowman and Allanheld, 1986.

Hall, David D., ed. *Witch-Hunting in Seventeenth-Century New England: A Documentary History, 1638–1693.* 2d ed. Boston: Northeastern University Press, 1999.

Hall, Gwendolyn Midlo. *Africans in Colonial Louisiana: The Development of Afro-Creole Culture in the Eighteenth Century.* Baton Rouge: Louisiana State University Press, 1992.

Hall, Jacquelyn Dowd. "Disorderly Women: Gender and Labor Militancy in the Appalachian South." *Journal of American History* 73 (September 1986): 354–82.

———. *Revolt against Chivalry: Jessie Daniel Ames and the Women's Campaign against Lynching.* Rev. ed. New York: Columbia University Press, 1993.

Hanchett, Thomas. "Financing Suburbia: Prudential Insurance and the Post–World War II Transformation of the American City." *Journal of Urban History* 26 (March 2000): 312–29.

Hansen, Bert. "American Physicians' 'Discovery' of Homosexuals, 1880–1900: A New Diagnosis in a Changing Society." In *Framing Disease: Studies in Cultural History*, edited by Charles E. Rosenberg and Janet L. Golden, 104–33. New Brunswick, N.J.: Rutgers University Press, 1996.

Hansen, Karen V. *A Very Social Time: Crafting Community in Antebellum New England.* Berkeley: University of California Press, 1994.

Harrison, Cynthia. *On Account of Sex: The Politics of Women's Issues, 1945–1968.* Berkeley: University of California Press, 1988.

Hartmann, Susan. *From Margin to Mainstream: American Women and Politics since 1960.* New York: Knopf, 1989.

Hartog, Hendrik. *Man and Wife in America: A History*. Cambridge, Mass.: Harvard University Press, 2000.

Harvey, Anna L. *Votes without Leverage: Women in American Electoral Politics, 1920–1970*. New York: Cambridge University Press, 1998.

Heizer, Robert F., and Albert B. Elsasser. *The Natural World of the California Indians*. Berkeley: University of California Press, 1980.

Herdt, Gilbert, ed. *Third Sex, Third Gender: Beyond Sexual Dimorphism in Culture and History*. New York: Zone Books, 1994.

Herman, Daniel J. "The Other Daniel Boone: The Nascence of a Middle-Class Hunter Hero, 1784–1860." *Journal of the Early Republic* 18 (Fall 1998): 428–57.

Hertz, Rosanna, and Nancy L. Marshall, eds. *Working Families: The Transformation of the American Home*. Berkeley: University of California Press, 2001.

Hewitt, Nancy, ed. *A Companion to American Women's History*. Malden, Mass.: Blackwell, 2002.

Higginbotham, A. Leon, Jr., and Barbara K. Kopytoff. "Racial Purity and Interracial Sex in the Law of Colonial and Antebellum Virginia." In *Interracialism: Black and White Intermarriage in American History, Literature, and Law*, edited by Werner Sollors, 81–139. New York: Oxford University Press, 2000.

Higginbotham, Evelyn Brooks. *Righteous Discontent: The Women's Movement in the Black Baptist Church, 1880–1920*. Cambridge, Mass.: Harvard University Press, 1993.

Hilkey, Judy. *Character Is Capital: Success Manuals and Manhood in Gilded Age America*. Chapel Hill: University of North Carolina Press, 1997.

Hill, Sarah H. *Weaving New Worlds: Southeastern Cherokee Women and Their Basketry*. Chapel Hill: University of North Carolina Press, 1997.

Hine, Darlene Clark, ed. *Black Women in American History: From Colonial Times through the Nineteenth Century*. Brooklyn, N.Y.: Carlson, 1990.

Hirsch, Arnold R., and Joseph Logsdon, eds. *Creole New Orleans: Race and Americanization*. Baton Rouge: Louisiana State University Press, 1992.

Hise, Greg. *Magnetic Los Angeles: Planning the Twentieth-Century Metropolis*. Baltimore, Md.: Johns Hopkins University Press, 1997.

Hochschild, Arlie, with Anne Machung. *The Second Shift*. New York: Viking, 1989.

Hodes, Martha Elizabeth. *White Women, Black Men: Illicit Sex in the Nineteenth-Century South*. New Haven, Conn.: Yale University Press, 1997.

———, ed. *Sex, Love, Race: Crossing Boundaries in North American History*. New York: New York University Press, 1999.

Hoffman, Ronald, and Peter J. Albert, eds. *Women in the Age of the American Revolution*. Charlottesville: University Press of Virginia for the United States Capitol Historical Society, 1989.

Hoganson, Kristin L. *Fighting for American Manhood: How Gender Politics Provoked the Spanish-American and Philippine-American Wars*. New Haven, Conn.: Yale University Press, 1998.

Hollinger, David A. "Amalgamation and Hypodescent: The Question of Ethnoracial Mixture in the History of the United States." *American Historical Review* 108 (December 2003): 1363–90.

Holt, Sharon Ann. *Making Freedom Pay: North Carolina Freedpeople Working for Themselves, 1865–1900.* Athens: University of Georgia Press, 2000.

Holt, Thomas C. "Marking Race: Race-Making and the Writing of History." *American Historical Review* 100 (February 1995): 1–20.

Hondagneu-Sotelo, Pierrette. *Doméstica: Immigrant Workers Cleaning and Caring in the Shadows of Affluence.* Berkeley: University of California Press, 2001.

———. *Gendered Transitions: Mexican Experiences of Immigration.* Berkeley: University of California Press, 1994.

Honey, Maureen. *Creating Rosie the Riveter: Class, Gender, and Propaganda during World War II.* Amherst: University of Massachusetts Press, 1984.

Horn, James P. *Adapting to a New World: English Society in the Seventeenth-Century Chesapeake.* Chapel Hill: University of North Carolina Press, 1994.

Horowitz, Daniel. *Betty Friedan and the Making of the Feminine Mystique.* Amherst: University of Massachusetts Press, 1998.

Hossfeld, Karen. "'Their Logic against Them': Contradictions in Sex, Race, and Class in Silicon Valley." In *Women Workers and Global Restructuring*, edited by Karen Ward, 149–78. Ithaca, N.Y.: ILR Press, 1990.

Hudson, Larry E., Jr. *To Have and to Hold: Slave Work and Family Life in Antebellum South Carolina.* Athens: University of Georgia Press, 1997.

Hune, Shirley, and Gail M. Nomura, eds. *Asian/Pacific Islander American Women: A Historical Anthology.* New York: New York University Press, 2003.

Hunter, Jane. *The Gospel of Gentility: American Women Missionaries in Turn-of-the-Century China.* New Haven, Conn.: Yale University Press, 1984.

Hunter, Tera W. *To 'Joy My Freedom: Southern Black Women's Lives and Labors after the Civil War.* Cambridge, Mass.: Harvard University Press, 1997.

Hurst, Fannie. *Anatomy of Me.* New York: Arno Press, 1980.

Hurtado, Albert L. *Indian Survival on the California Frontier.* New Haven, Conn.: Yale University Press, 1988.

———. *Intimate Frontiers: Sex, Gender, and Culture in Old California.* Albuquerque: University of New Mexico Press, 1999.

Isenberg, Andrew. *The Destruction of the Bison: An Environmental History, 1750–1920.* Cambridge, U.K.: Cambridge University Press, 2000.

Isenberg, Nancy. *Sex and Citizenship in Antebellum America.* Chapel Hill: University of North Carolina Press, 1998.

Jackson, Kenneth. *Crabgrass Frontier: The Suburbanization of the United States.* New York: Oxford University Press, 1985.

Jackson, Robert H. *Indian Population Decline: The Mission of Northwestern New Spain, 1687–1840.* Albuquerque: University of New Mexico Press, 1994.

Jackson, Shannon. *Lines of Activity: Performance, Historiography, Hull-House Domesticity.* Ann Arbor: University of Michigan Press, 2000.

Jacobs, Connie A. *The Novels of Louise Erdrich: Stories of Her People.* New York: Peter Lang, 2001.

Jacobs, Harriet. *Incidents in the Life of a Slave Girl, Written by Herself.* In *The Classic Slave Narratives,* edited by Henry Louis Gates, 437–668. New York: Penguin Putnam, 2002.

Jaffe, Hosea. *A History of Africa.* Totowa, N.J.: Biblio Distribution Center, 1985.

Jalloh, Alusine, and Stephen E. Maizlish, eds. *The African Diaspora.* College Station: Texas A&M University Press, 1996.

Jeffords, Susan. *The Remasculinization of America: Gender and the Vietnam War.* Bloomington: Indiana University Press, 1989.

Jeffrey, Julie Roy. "Permeable Boundaries: Abolitionist Women and Separate Spheres." *Journal of the Early Republic* 21 (Spring 2001): 79–93.

Jen, Gish. *Who's Irish?* New York: Vintage Books, 2000.

Jennings, Thelma. "'Us Colored Women Had to Go Through Plenty': Sexual Exploitation of African-American Slave Women." *Journal of Women's History* 1 (Winter 1990): 45–74.

Jensen, Joan M. *Loosening the Bonds: Mid-Atlantic Farm Women, 1750–1850.* New Haven, Conn.: Yale University Press, 1986.

———. "Native American Women and Agriculture: A Seneca Case Study." *Sex Roles* 3 (1977): 423–41.

———. *With These Hands: Women Working on the Land.* Old Westbury, N.Y.: Feminist Press, 1981.

Jensen, Joan, and Darlis Miller, eds. *New Mexico Women: Intercultural Perspectives.* Albuquerque: University of New Mexico Press, 1986.

Johansen, Shawn. *Family Men: Middle-Class Fatherhood in Early Industrializing America.* New York: Routledge, 2001.

Johnson, Jennifer. *Getting by on the Minimum: The Lives of Working-Class Women.* New York: Routledge, 2002.

Johnson, Jerah. "Colonial New Orleans: A Fragment of the Eighteenth-Century French Ethos." In *Creole New Orleans: Race and Americanization,* edited by Arnold R. Hirsch and Joseph Logsdon, 12–57. Baton Rouge: Louisiana State University Press, 1992.

Johnson, Michael P. "Planters and Patriarchy: Charleston, 1800–1860." *Journal of Southern History* 46 (February 1980): 45–72.

Johnson, Michael P., and James L. Roark. *Black Masters: A Free Family of Color in the Old South.* New York: Norton, 1984.

Johnson, Walter. *Soul by Soul: Life inside the Antebellum Slave Market.* Cambridge, Mass.: Harvard University Press, 1999.

Jones, Douglas Lamar. "The Strolling Poor: Transiency in Eighteenth-Century Massachusetts." *Journal of Social History* 8 (Spring 1975): 28–54.

Jones, Jacqueline. *Labor of Love, Labor of Sorrow: Black Women, Work, and the Family from Slavery to the Present*. New York: Basic Books, 1985.

Jones, Landon Y. *Great Expectations: America and the Baby Boom Generation*. New York: Coward, McCann, and Geoghegan, 1980.

Joyce, Patrick, ed. *The Social in Question: New Bearings in History and the Social Sciences*. New York: Routledge, 2002.

Joyner, Charles W. *Down by the Riverside: A South Carolina Slave Community*. Urbana: University of Illinois Press, 1984.

Juster, Susan. *Disorderly Women: Sexual Politics and Evangelicalism in Revolutionary New England*. Ithaca, N.Y.: Cornell University Press, 1994.

Kamensky, Jane. *Governing the Tongue: The Politics of Speech in Early New England*. New York: Oxford University Press, 1997.

Karlsen, Carol F. *The Devil in the Shape of a Woman: Witchcraft in Colonial New England*. New York: Norton, 1987.

Kasson, John. *Houdini, Tarzan, and the Perfect Man: The White Male Body and the Challenge of Modernity in America*. New York: Hill and Wang, 2001.

Katz, Jonathan. *Gay American History: Lesbians and Gay Men in the U.S.A., A Documentary*. New York: Avon Books, 1978.

———. *The Invention of Heterosexuality*. New York: Dutton, 1995.

Katz, Michael B. *The People of Hamilton, Canada West: Family and Class in a Mid-Nineteenth-Century City*. Cambridge, Mass.: Harvard University Press, 1975.

Katzenstein, Mary. "Feminism within American Institutions: Unobtrusive Mobilization in the 1980s." *Signs* 16 (Autumn 1990): 27–55.

Kaufman, Jason. *For the Common Good? American Civic Life and the Golden Age of Fraternity*. New York: Oxford University Press, 2002.

Kehoe, Alice B. "Blackfoot Persons." In *Women and Power in Native North America*, edited by Laura F. Klein and Lillian A. Ackerman, 113–25. Norman: University of Oklahoma Press, 1995.

Kelley, Mary. *Private Woman, Public Stage: Literary Domesticity in Nineteenth-Century America*. New York: Oxford University Press, 1984.

Kelly, Catherine E. "'Well Bred Country People': Sociability, Social Networks, and the Creation of a Provincial Middle Class, 1820–1860." *Journal of the Early Republic* 19 (Autumn 1999): 451–79.

Kennedy, Elizabeth Lapovsky, and Madeline D. Davis. *Boots of Leather, Slippers of Gold: The History of a Lesbian Community*. New York: Routledge, 1993.

Kerber, Linda K. "'History Can Do It No Justice': Women and the Reinterpretation of the American Revolution." In *Women in the Age of the American Revolution*, edited by Ronald Hoffman and Peter J. Albert, 3–42. Charlottesville: University Press of Virginia for the United States Capitol Historical Society, 1989.

———. "'I Have Don . . . Much to Carrey on the Warr': Women and the Shaping of Republican Ideology after the American Revolution." In *Women and Politics in*

the Age of the Democratic Revolution, edited by Harriet B. Applewhite and
Darline G. Levy, 227–57. Ann Arbor: University of Michigan Press, 1990.

———. "Separate Spheres, Female Worlds, Woman's Place: The Rhetoric of
Women's History." *Journal of American History* 75 (June 1988): 9–39.

———. *Women of the Republic: Intellect and Ideology in Revolutionary America.*
Chapel Hill: University of North Carolina Press, 1980.

Kerber, Linda K., Nancy F. Cott, Robert Gross, Lynn Hunt, Carroll Smith-
Rosenberg, and Christine M. Stansell. "Beyond Roles, Beyond Spheres:
Thinking about Gender in the Early Republic." *William and Mary Quarterly* 46
(July 1989): 565–85.

Kerry, John. *A Call to Service.* New York: Viking, 2003.

Kessler-Harris, Alice. *In Pursuit of Equity: Women, Men, and the Quest for Economic
Citizenship in Twentieth-Century America.* New York: Oxford University Press,
2001.

———. *Out to Work: A History of Wage-Earning Women in the United States.* New
York: Oxford University Press, 1987.

Kibria, Nazli. *Becoming Asian American: Second-Generation Chinese and Korean
American Identities.* Baltimore, Md.: Johns Hopkins University Press, 2002.

———. *Family Tightrope: The Changing Lives of Vietnamese Americans.* Princeton,
N.J.: Princeton University Press, 1993.

Kim, Kwang Chung, and Won Moo Hurh. "The Burden of Double Roles: Korean
Wives in the U.S.A." *Ethnic and Racial Studies* 11 (April 1988): 151–67.

Kim, Kwang Chung, and Shin Kim. "Family and Work Roles of Korean Immigrant
Wives and Related Experiences." In *Korean American Women: From Tradition to
Modern Feminism*, edited by Young I. Song and Ailee Moon, 103–12. Westport,
Conn.: Praeger, 1998.

Kimmel, Michael S. *The Gendered Society.* New York: Oxford University Press,
2000.

———. *Manhood in America: A Cultural History.* New York: Free Press, 1996.

King, Martha J. "'What Providence Has Brought Them to Be': Widows, Work, and
the Print Culture of Colonial Charleston." In *Women and Freedom in Early
America*, edited by Larry D. Eldridge, 147–66. New York: New York University
Press, 1997.

King, Mary. *Freedom Song: A Personal Story of the 1960's Civil Rights Movement.* New
York: William and Morrow, 1987.

King, Wilma. "Suffer with Them Till Death: Slave Women and Their Children in
Nineteenth-Century America." In *More Than Chattel: Black Women and Slavery
in the Americas*, edited by David Barry Gaspar and Darlene Clark Hine, 147–68.
Bloomington: Indiana University Press, 1996.

Kingston, Maxine Hong. *The Woman Warrior: Memoirs of a Girlhood among Ghosts.*
New York: Vintage International, 1989.

Kirshenbaum, Andrea Meryl. "The Vampire that Hovers over North Carolina: Gender, White Supremacy, and the Wilmington Race Riot of 1898." *Southern Cultures* 4 (Fall 1998): 6–30.

Klatch, Rebecca. *A Generation Divided: The New Left, the New Right, and the 1960s.* Berkeley: University of California Press, 1999.

Klein, Ethel. *Gender Politics: From Consciousness to Mass Politics.* Cambridge, Mass.: Harvard University Press, 1984.

Klein, Laura F. "Mother as Clanswoman: Rank and Gender in Tlingit Society." In *Women and Power in Native North America,* edited by Laura F. Klein and Lillian A. Ackerman, 28–45. Norman: University of Oklahoma Press, 1995.

Klein, Laura F., and Lillian A. Ackerman, eds. *Women and Power in Native North America.* Norman: University of Oklahoma Press, 1995.

Knupfer, Anne Meis. "'If You Can't Push, Pull, If You Can't Pull, Please Get Out of the Way': The Phyllis Wheatley Club and Home in Chicago, 1896 to 1920." *Journal of Negro History* 82 (Spring 1997): 221–31.

Koehler, Lyle. *A Search for Power: The "Weaker Sex" in Seventeenth-Century New England.* Urbana: University of Illinois Press, 1980.

Komarovsky, Mirra. *The Unemployed Man and His Family.* New York: Dryden Press, 1940.

———. *Women in the Modern World: Their Education and Their Dilemmas.* Boston: Little, Brown, 1953.

Koven, Seth, and Sonya Michel, eds. *Mothers of a New World: Maternalist Politics and the Origins of Welfare States.* New York: Routledge, 1993.

Kovic, Ron. *Born on the Fourth of July.* New York: McGraw-Hill, 1976.

Kritzer, Amelia Howe. "Playing with Republican Motherhood: Self-Representation in Plays by Susanna Haswell Rowson and Judith Sargent Murray." *Early American Literature* 31 (Spring 1996): 150–66.

Kross, Jessica. "Mansions, Men, Women, and the Creation of Multiple Publics in Eighteenth-Century British North America." *Journal of Social History* 33 (Winter 1999): 385–408.

Kubrick, Stanley. *Full Metal Jacket.* Warner Brothers, 1987.

Kupperman, Karen Ordahl. *Indians and English: Facing Off in Early America.* Ithaca, N.Y.: Cornell University Press, 2000.

Kurian, George T. *Datapedia of the United States, 1790–2000: America Year by Year.* Lanham, Md.: Bernan Press, 2001.

Kurland, Philip B., and Ralph Lerner, eds. *The Founders' Constitution.* Chicago: University of Chicago Press, 1987.

Ladd-Taylor, Molly. "Mothers and the Making of the Sheppard-Towner Act." In *Mothers of a New World: Maternalist Politics and the Origins of Welfare States,* edited by Seth Koven and Sonya Michel, 321–42. New York: Routledge, 1993.

———. *Mother-Work: Women, Child Welfare, and the State, 1890–1930.* Urbana: University of Illinois Press, 1994.

Laipson, Peter. "'Kiss without Shame, for She Desires It': Sexual Foreplay in American Marital Advice Literature, 1900–1925." *Journal of Social History* 29 (Spring 1996): 507–25.

Lake, Marilyn. "The Politics of Respectability: Identifying the Masculinist Context." *Historical Studies* 22 (April 1986): 116–31.

Lamphere, Louise. *To Run After Them: Cultural and Social Bases of Cooperation in a Navajo Community.* Tucson: University of Arizona Press, 1977.

———. "Working Mothers and Family Strategies: Portuguese and Colombian Women in a New England Community." In *International Migration: The Female Experience,* edited by Rita James Simon and Caroline B. Brettell, 266–83. Totowa, N.J.: Rowman and Allanheld, 1986.

Lamphere, Louise, Patricia Zavella, and Felipe Gonzales. *Sunbelt Working Mothers: Reconciling Family and Factory.* Ithaca, N.Y.: Cornell University Press, 1993.

Land, Aubrey C., Lois Green Carr, and Edward C. Papenfuse, eds. *Law, Society, and Politics in Early Maryland: Proceedings of the First Conference on Maryland History, June 14–15, 1974.* Baltimore, Md.: Johns Hopkins University Press, 1977.

Landes, Joan. *Women and the Public Sphere in the Age of the French Revolution.* Ithaca, N.Y.: Cornell University Press, 1988.

Laqueur, Thomas. *Making Sex: Body and Gender from the Greeks to Freud.* Cambridge, Mass.: Harvard University Press, 1990.

LaRossa, Ralph. *The Modernization of Fatherhood: A Social and Political History.* Chicago: University of Chicago Press, 1997.

Leacock, Eleanor. *Myths of Male Dominance: Collected Articles on Women, Class, and Inequality.* New York: Monthly Review Press, 1981.

Leavitt, Judith Walzer. *Brought to Bed: Childbearing in America, 1750 to 1950.* New York: Oxford University Press, 1986.

Lebsock, Suzanne. "Free Black Women and the Question of Matriarchy: Petersburg, Virginia, 1784–1820." *Feminist Studies* 8 (Summer 1982): 270–92.

———. *The Free Women of Petersburg: Status and Culture in a Southern Town, 1784–1860.* New York: Norton, 1984.

Lemon, James T. *The Best Poor Man's Country: Early Southeastern Pennsylvania.* Baltimore, Md.: Johns Hopkins University Press, 2002.

Lerner, Gerda. *Black Women in White America: A Documentary History.* New York: Pantheon Books, 1972.

———. *The Creation of Patriarchy.* New York: Oxford University Press, 1986.

Levine, Lawrence W. *Black Culture and Black Consciousness: Afro-American Folk Thought from Slavery to Freedom.* New York: Oxford University Press, 1977.

Levitt, Peggy. *The Transnational Villagers.* Berkeley: University of California Press, 2001.

Levy, Darline G., and Harriet B. Applewhite. "Women, Radicalization, and the Fall of the French Monarchy." In *Women and Politics in the Age of the Democratic*

Revolution, edited by Harriet B. Applewhite and Darline G. Levy, 81–107. Ann Arbor: University of Michigan Press, 1990.

Lewis, Jan E. *The Pursuit of Happiness: Family and Values in Jefferson's Virginia.* New York: Cambridge University Press, 1983.

———. "A Revolution for Whom? Women in the Era of the American Revolution." In *A Companion to American Women's History*, edited by Nancy Hewitt, 83–99. Malden, Mass.: Blackwell, 2002.

Lewis, Jan Ellen, and Peter S. Onuf, eds. *Sally Hemings and Thomas Jefferson: History, Memory, and Civic Culture.* Charlottesville: University Press of Virginia, 1999.

Light, Andrew, and Jonathan M. Smith, eds. *Philosophy and Geography II: The Production of Public Space.* Lanham, Md.: Rowman and Littlefield, 1998.

Lindquist, Ruth. *The Family in the Present Social Order: A Study of Needs of American Families.* Chapel Hill: University of North Carolina Press, 1931.

Linklater, Andro. *Measuring America: How the United States Was Shaped by the Greatest Land Sale in History.* New York: Walker and Company, 2002.

Litoff, Judy Barrett. *American Midwives, 1860 to the Present.* Westport, Conn.: Greenwood Press, 1978.

Litwack, Leon F. *Been in the Storm So Long: The Aftermath of Slavery.* New York: Knopf, 1979.

Lopata, Helena Znaniecka. *Occupation: Housewife.* New York: Oxford University Press, 1971.

Louie, Miriam Ching Yoon. *Sweatshop Warriors: Immigrant Women Workers Take on the Global Factory.* Cambridge, Mass.: South End Press, 2001.

Lovejoy, Paul E. "The Impact of the Atlantic Slave Trade on Africa: A Review of the Literature." *Journal of African History* 30 (1989): 365–94.

———. "The Volume of the Atlantic Slave Trade: A Synthesis." *Journal of African History* 22 (1982): 473–501.

Lovejoy, Paul E., and David Richardson. "Competing Markets for Male and Female Slaves: Prices in the Interior of West Africa, 1780–1850." *International Journal of African Historical Studies* 28 (1995): 261–93.

Lovell, Margaretta M. "Reading Eighteenth-Century American Family Portraits: Social Images and Self-Images." *Winterthur Portfolio* 22 (Winter 1987): 243–64.

Lundberg, Ferdinand, and Marynia F. Farnham. *Modern Woman: The Lost Sex.* New York: Harper and Brothers, 1947.

Lynn, Susan. "Gender and Post–World War II Progressive Politics: A Bridge to the Social Activism of the 1960s U.S.A." *Gender and History* 4 (Summer 1992): 215–39.

MacLean, Nancy. *Behind the Mask of Chivalry: The Making of the Second Ku Klux Klan.* New York: Oxford University Press, 1994.

———. "The Hidden History of Affirmative Action: Working Women's Struggles in the 1970s and the Gender of Class." *Feminist Studies* 25 (Spring 1999): 42–78.

————. "The Leo Frank Case Reconsidered: Gender and Sexual Politics in the Making of Reactionary Populism." *Journal of American History* 78 (December 1991): 917–48.

Mahoney, Timothy R. *Provincial Lives: Middle-Class Experience in the Antebellum Middle West.* New York: Cambridge University Press, 1999.

Main, Gloria L. *Peoples of a Spacious Land: Families and Cultures in Colonial New England.* Cambridge, Mass.: Harvard University Press, 2004.

Mancall, Peter, and James Merrell, eds. *American Encounters: Native and Newcomers from European Contact to Indian Removal, 1500–1850.* New York: Routledge, 2000.

Manza, Jeff, and Clem Brooks. "The Gender Gap in U.S. Presidential Elections: When? Why? Implications?" *American Journal of Sociology* 103 (March 1998): 1235–66.

Marilley, Suzanne M. *Woman Suffrage and the Origins of Liberal Feminism in the United States, 1820–1920.* Cambridge, Mass.: Harvard University Press, 1996.

Marsh, Margaret. "Suburban Men and Masculine Domesticity, 1870–1915." In *Meanings for Manhood: Constructions of Masculinity in Victorian America,* edited by Mark C. Carnes and Clyde Griffen. Chicago: University of Chicago Press, 1990.

Mason, Mary Ann. *From Father's Property to Children's Rights: The History of Child Custody in the United States.* New York: Columbia University Press, 1994.

Matsumoto, Valerie J. *Farming the Home Place: A Japanese American Community in California, 1919–1982.* Ithaca, N.Y.: Cornell University Press, 1993.

————. "Japanese American Girls' Clubs in Los Angeles during the 1920s and 1930s." In *Asian/Pacific Islander Women: A Historical Anthology,* edited by Shirley Hune and Gail M. Nomura, 172–87. New York: New York University Press, 2003.

————. "Japanese American Women during World War II." In *Unequal Sisters: A Multicultural Reader in U.S. Women's History,* edited by Ellen Carol DuBois and Vicki L. Ruiz, 436–49. 2d ed. New York: Routledge, 1994.

Matthaei, Julie. *An Economic History of Women in America: Women's Work, the Sexual Division of Labor, and the Development of Capitalism.* New York: Schocken Books, 1982.

Matthews, Glenna. *"Just a Housewife": The Rise and Fall of Domesticity in America.* New York: Oxford University Press, 1987.

————. *Silicon Valley, Women, and the California Dream: Gender, Class, and Opportunity in the Twentieth Century.* Stanford, Calif.: Stanford University Press, 2003.

May, Elaine Tyler. *Homeward Bound: American Families in the Cold War Era.* New York: Basic Books, 1988.

Mazumdar, Sucheta. "What Happened to the Women? Chinese and Indian Male Migration to the United States in Global Perspective." In *Asian/Pacific Islander*

American Women: A Historical Anthology, edited by Shirley Hune and Gail M. Nomura, 58–74. New York: New York University Press, 2003.

McBee, Randy D. *Dance Hall Days: Intimacy and Leisure among Working-Class Immigrants in the United States.* New York: New York University Press, 2000.

McCall, Laura, and Donald Yacovone, eds. *A Shared Experience: Men, Women, and the History of Gender.* New York: New York University Press, 1998.

McCall, Leslie. *Complex Inequality: Gender, Class, and Race in the New Economy.* New York: Routledge, 2001.

McCurry, Stephanie. "Citizens, Soldiers' Wives, and 'Hiley Hope Up' Slaves: The Problem of Political Obligation in the Civil War South." In *Gender and the Southern Body Politic,* edited by Nancy Bercaw, 95–129. Jackson: University Press of Mississippi, 2000.

———. *Masters of Small Worlds: Yeoman Households, Gender Relations, and the Political Culture of the Antebellum South Carolina Low Country.* New York: Oxford University Press, 1995.

———. "The Two Faces of Republicanism: Gender and Proslavery Politics in Antebellum South Carolina." *Journal of American History* 78 (March 1992): 1245–64.

McGerr, Michael E. *The Decline of Popular Politics: The American North, 1865–1928.* New York: Oxford University Press, 1986.

McHugh, Kathleen Anne. *American Domesticity: From How-To Manual to Hollywood Melodrama.* New York: Oxford University Press, 1999.

McKeon, Michael. "Historicizing Patriarchy: The Emergence of Gender Difference in England, 1660–1760." *Eighteenth-Century Studies* 28 (Spring 1995): 295–322.

McKibben, Carol Lynn. "'Of All the Gifts You Gave Me the Most Important One Is That I Belong': The Sicilians: Chain Migration, Gender, and the Construction of Identity in Monterey, California, 1920–1999." Ph.D. diss., University of California, Berkeley, 1999.

McLoughlin, William. *Cherokee Renascence in the New Republic.* Princeton, N.J.: Princeton University Press, 1986.

McManus, Margaret M. "'From Deep Wells of Religious Faith': An Interpretation of Vida Scudder's Activism, 1887–1912." Ph.D. diss., Graduate Theological Union, 1999.

McNickle, D'Arcy. *Native American Tribalism: Indian Survivals and Renewals.* New York: Oxford University Press, 1973.

Medicine, Beatrice. "'Warrior Women': Sex Role Alternatives for Plains Indian Women." In *The Hidden Half: Studies of Plains Indian Women,* edited by Patricia Albers and Beatrice Medicine, 267–80. Washington, D.C.: University Press of America, 1983.

Meillassoux, Claude. *Maidens, Meal, and Money: Capitalism and the Domestic Community.* Cambridge, U.K.: Cambridge University Press, 1981.

Melder, Keith. *Beginnings of Sisterhood: The American Woman's Rights Movement, 1800–1850.* New York: Schocken Books, 1977.

Melish, Joanne Pope. *Disowning Slavery: Gradual Emancipation and "Race" in New England, 1780–1860.* Ithaca, N.Y.: Cornell University Press, 1998.

Menard, Russell R. "Immigrants and Their Increase: The Process of Population Growth in Early Colonial Maryland." In *Law, Society, and Politics in Early Maryland: Proceedings of the First Conference on Maryland History, June 14–15, 1974,* edited by Aubrey C. Land, Lois Green Carr, and Edward C. Papenfuse, 88–110. Baltimore, Md.: Johns Hopkins University Press, 1977.

Merrell, James Hart. *The Indians' New World: Catawbas and Their Neighbors from European Contact through the Era of Removal.* Chapel Hill: University of North Carolina Press, 1989.

Merritt, Jane T. *At the Crossroads: Indians and Empires on a Mid-Atlantic Frontier, 1700–1763.* Chapel Hill: University of North Carolina Press, 2003.

Mettler, Suzanne. *Dividing Citizens: Gender and Federalism in New Deal Public Policy.* Ithaca, N.Y.: Cornell University Press, 1998.

Meyerowitz, Joanne. "Beyond the Feminine Mystique: A Reassessment of Postwar Mass Culture, 1946–1958." *Journal of American History* 79 (March 1993): 1455–82.

———. *How Sex Changed: A History of Transsexuality in the United States.* Cambridge, Mass.: Harvard University Press, 2002.

———. *Women Adrift: Independent Wage Earners in Chicago, 1880–1930.* Chicago: University of Chicago Press, 1988.

———, ed. *Not June Cleaver: Women and Gender in Postwar America, 1945–1960.* Philadelphia: Temple University Press, 1994.

Meyers, Debra. *Common Whores, Vertuous Women, and Loveing Wives: Free Will Christian Women in Colonial Maryland.* Bloomington: Indiana University Press, 2003.

Michel, Sonya. *Children's Interests/Mothers' Rights: The Shaping of America's Child Care Policy.* New Haven, Conn.: Yale University Press, 1999.

———. "The Limits of Maternalism: Policies toward American Wage-Earning Mothers during the Progressive Era." In *Mothers of a New World: Maternalist Politics and the Origins of Welfare States,* edited by Seth Koven and Sonya Michel, 277–320. New York: Routledge, 1993.

Milkman, Ruth. *Gender at Work: The Dynamics of Job Segregation by Sex during World War II.* Urbana: University of Illinois Press, 1987.

Miller, Pavla. *Transformations of Patriarchy in the West: 1500–1900.* Bloomington: Indiana University Press, 1998.

Miller, Zane. *Suburb: Neighborhood and Community in Forest Park, Ohio, 1935–1976.* Knoxville: University of Tennessee Press, 1981.

Min, Pyong Gap. "The Burden of Labor on Korean American Wives in and outside the Family." In *Korean American Women: From Tradition to Modern Feminism,* edited by Young I. Song and Ailee Moon, 89–101. Westport, Conn.: Praeger, 1998.

Min, Pyong Gap, and Young I. Song. "Demographic Characteristics and Trends of Post-1965 Korean Immigrant Women and Men." In *Korean American Women: From Tradition to Modern Feminism*, edited by Young I. Song and Ailee Moon, 45–63. Westport, Conn.: Praeger, 1998.

Mink, Gwendolyn. "The Lady and the Tramp: Gender, Race, and the Origins of the American Welfare State." In *Women, the State, and Welfare*, edited by Linda Gordon, 92–122. Madison: University of Wisconsin Press, 1990.

———. *The Wages of Motherhood: Inequality in the Welfare State, 1917–1942*. Ithaca, N.Y.: Cornell University Press, 1995.

Mokyr, Joel. "Why 'More Work for Mother'? Knowledge and Household Behavior, 1870–1945." *Journal of Economic History* 60 (March 2000): 1–41.

Momaday, N. Scott. *The Man Made of Words: Essays, Stories, Passages*. New York: St. Martin's, 1997.

Morgan, Edmund S. *American Slavery, American Freedom: The Ordeal of Colonial Virginia*. New York: Norton, 1975.

———. *The Puritan Family: Religion and Domestic Relations in Seventeenth-Century New England*. New York: Harper and Row, 1966.

Morgan, Jennifer L. *Laboring Women: Reproduction and Gender in New World Slavery*. Philadelphia: University of Pennsylvania Press, 2004.

Morgan, Philip D. "British Encounters with Africans and African-Americans, circa 1600–1780." In *Strangers within the Realm: Cultural Margins of the First British Empire*, edited by Bernard Bailyn and Philip D. Morgan, 157–219. Chapel Hill: University of North Carolina Press, 1991.

Morgan, Robin. *Going Too Far: The Personal Chronicle of a Feminist*. New York: Vintage, 1977.

———, comp. *Sisterhood Is Powerful: An Anthology of Writings from the Women's Liberation Movement*. New York: Random House, 1970.

Morris, Jan. *Conundrum*. New York: Harcourt Brace Jovanovich, 1974.

Morrison, Toni, ed. *Race-ing Justice, En-Gendering Power: Essays on Anita Hill, Clarence Thomas, and the Construction of Social Reality*. New York: Pantheon Books, 1992.

Mueller, Carol. "Ella Baker and the Origins of Participatory Democracy." In *Women in the Civil Rights Movement: Trailblazers and Torchbearers, 1941–1965*, edited by Vicki L. Crawford, Jacqueline Anne Rouse, and Barbara Woods, 51–70. New York: Carlson, 1990.

Mumford, Kevin. *Interzones: Black/White Sex Districts in Chicago and New York in the Early Twentieth Century*. New York: Columbia University Press, 1997.

Muncy, Robyn. *Creating a Female Dominion in American Reform, 1890–1935*. New York: Oxford University Press, 1991.

———. "Trustbusting and White Manhood in America: 1898–1914." *American Studies* 38 (Fall 1997): 21–42.

Murphy, Lucy Eldersveld. "Autonomy and the Economic Roles of Indian Women of the Fox-Wisconsin Riverway Region, 1763–1832." In *Negotiators of Change: Historical Perspectives on Native American Women*, edited by Nancy Shoemaker, 72–89. New York: Routledge, 1995.

———. *A Gathering of Rivers: Indians, Métis, and Mining in the Western Great Lakes, 1737–1832*. Lincoln: University of Nebraska Press, 2000.

Murray, Pauli. *Song in a Weary Throat*. New York: Harper and Row, 1987.

Naples, Nancy A. "Changing the Terms: Community Activism, Globalization, and the Dilemmas of Transnational Feminist Praxis." In *Women's Activism and Globalization: Linking Local Struggles and Transnational Politics*, edited by Nancy A. Naples and Manisha Desai, 3–14. New York: Routledge, 2002.

Naples, Nancy A., and Manisha Desai, eds. *Women's Activism and Globalization: Linking Local Struggles and Transnational Politics*. New York: Routledge, 2002.

National Museum and Archive of Lesbian and Gay History. *The Gay Almanac*. New York: Berkley Books, 1996.

Nelson, Barbara J. "The Origins of the Two-Channel Welfare State: Workmen's Compensation and Mother's Aid." In *Women, the State, and Welfare*, edited by Linda Gordon, 123–51. Madison: University of Wisconsin Press, 1990.

Nelson, Sarah M. "Widowhood and Autonomy in the Native American Southwest." In *On Their Own: Widows and Widowhood in the American Southwest, 1848–1939*, edited by Arlene Scadron, 22–41. Urbana: University of Illinois Press, 1988.

Nicolaides, Becky M. *My Blue Heaven: Life and Politics in the Working-Class Suburbs of Los Angeles, 1920–1965*. Chicago: University of Chicago Pres, 2002.

Nordstrom, Carl. *Frontier Elements in a Hudson River Village*. Port Washington, N.Y.: Kennikat Press, 1973.

Norton, Eleanor Holmes. "Introduction." In *Song in a Weary Throat*, by Pauli Murray. New York: Harper and Row, 1987.

Norton, Mary Beth. *Founding Mothers and Fathers: Gendered Power and the Forming of American Society*. New York: Random House, 1996.

———. *In the Devil's Snare: The Salem Witchcraft Crisis of 1692*. New York: Knopf, 2002.

———, ed. *Major Problems in American Women's History: Documents and Essays*. Lexington, Mass.: D. C. Heath, 1989.

Norton, Mary Beth, and Ruth M. Alexander, eds. *Major Problems in American Women's History*. Lexington, Mass.: D. C. Heath, 1996.

Norwood, Stephen H. *Labor's Flaming Youth: Telephone Operators and Worker Militancy, 1878–1923*. Urbana: University of Illinois Press, 1990.

———. "Reclaiming Working-Class Activism: The Boston Women's Trade Union League, 1930–1950." *Labor's Heritage* 10 (Summer 1998): 20–35.

Nwokeji, G. Ugo. "African Conceptions of Gender and the Slave Traffic." *William and Mary Quarterly* 58 (January 2001): 47–68.

Odem, Mary. *Delinquent Daughters: Protecting and Policing Adolescent Female Sexuality in the United States, 1885–1920*. Chapel Hill: University of North Carolina Press, 1995.

O'Farrell, Brigid, and Joyce Kornbluh, eds. *Rocking the Boat: Union Women's Voices, 1915–1945*. New Brunswick, N.J.: Rutgers University Press, 1996.

O'Farrell, Mary Ann, and Lynne Vallone, eds. *Virtual Gender: Fantasies of Subjectivity and Embodiment*. Ann Arbor: University of Michigan Press, 1999.

Oldridge, Darren, ed. *The Witchcraft Reader*. London: Routledge, 2002.

Olson, Lynne. *Freedom's Daughters: The Unsung Heroines of the Civil Rights Movement from 1830 to 1970*. New York: Scribner, 2001.

Omi, Michael, and Howard Winant. *Racial Formation in the United States: From the 1960s to the 1980s*. New York: Routledge and Kegan Paul, 1986.

O'Neill, William L. *Everyone Was Brave: A History of Feminism in America*. New York: Quadrangle, 1971.

———. *Feminism in America: A History*. New Brunswick, N.J.: Transaction, 1989.

Ong, Aihwa. *Flexible Citizenship: The Cultural Logics of Transnationality*. Durham, N.C.: Duke University Press, 1999.

Onuf, Peter. *Jefferson's Empire: The Language of American Nationhood*. Charlottesville: University Press of Virginia, 2000.

Opdycke, Sandra, ed. *The Routledge Historical Atlas of Women in America*. New York: Routledge, 2000.

Oppenheimer, Valerie Kincade. *The Female Labor Force in the United States: Demographic and Economic Factors in Governing Its Growth and Changing Composition*. Berkeley: University of California Press, 1970.

Orleck, Annelise. *Common Sense and a Little Fire: Women and Working-Class Politics in the United States, 1900–1965*. Chapel Hill: University of North Carolina Press, 1995.

Orsi, Robert A. *The Madonna of 115th Street: Faith and Community in Italian Harlem, 1880–1950*. New Haven, Conn.: Yale University Press, 1985.

Ortiz, Beverley. "Chocheno and Rumsen Narratives." In *The Ohlone Past and Present: Native Americans of the San Francisco Bay Region*, compiled and edited by Lowell John Bean, 99–163. San Francisco: Ballena Press, 1994.

Ortner, Sherry B. "Gender Hegemonies." In *Making Gender: The Politics and Erotics of Culture*. Boston: Beacon Press, 1996.

———. *Making Gender: The Politics and Erotics of Culture*. Boston: Beacon Press, 1996.

Ortner, Sherry B., and Harriet Whitehead, eds. *Sexual Meanings: The Cultural Construction of Gender and Sexuality*. New York: Cambridge University Press, 1981.

Parreñas, Rhacel Salazar. "Asian Immigrant Women and Global Restructuring,

1970s–1990s." In *Asian/Pacific Islander American Women: A Historical Anthology*, edited by Shirley Hune and Gail M. Nomura, 271–85. New York: New York University Press, 2003.

———. "Migrant Filipina Domestic Workers and the International Division of Reproductive Labor." *Gender and Society* 14 (2000): 560–81.

Pascoe, Peggy. "Miscegenation Law, Court Cases, and Ideologies of 'Race' in Twentieth-Century America." In *Sex, Love, Race: Crossing Boundaries in North American History*, edited by Martha Hodes, 464–90. New York: New York University Press, 1999.

———. *Relations of Rescue: The Search for Female Moral Authority in the American West, 1874–1939*. New York: Oxford University Press, 1990.

Pateman, Carol. *The Sexual Contract*. Stanford, Calif.: Stanford University Press, 1988.

Patterson, Orlando. *Slavery and Social Death: A Comparative Study*. Cambridge, Mass.: Harvard University Press, 1982.

Patterson, Victoria D. "Evolving Gender Roles in Pomo Society." In *Women and Power in Native North America*, edited by Laura F. Klein and Lillian A. Ackerman, 126–45. Norman: University of Oklahoma Press, 1995.

Peiss, Kathy. *Cheap Amusements: Working Women and Leisure in Turn-of-the-Century New York*. Philadelphia: Temple University Press, 1986.

Peiss, Kathy, and Christina Simmons, eds., with Robert A. Padgug. *Passion and Power: Sexuality in History*. Philadelphia: Temple University Press, 1989.

Pendergast, Tom. "'Horatio Alger Doesn't Work Here Anymore': Masculinity and American Magazines, 1919–1940." *American Studies* 38 (Spring 1997): 55–80.

Perdue, Charles L., Jr., Thomas E. Barden, and Robert K. Phillips, eds. *Weevils in the Wheat: Interviews with Virginia Ex-Slaves*. Bloomington: Indiana University Press, 1980.

Perdue, Theda. *Cherokee Women: Gender and Culture Change, 1700–1835*. Lincoln: University of Nebraska Press, 1998.

———. *"Mixed Blood" Indians: Racial Construction in the Early South*. Athens: University of Georgia Press, 2003.

Perrucci, Robert, and Earl Wysong. *The New Class Society*. Lanham, Md.: Rowman and Littlefield, 1999.

Pesantubbee, Michelene E. *Choctaw Women in a Chaotic World: The Clash of Cultures in the Colonial Southeast*. Albuquerque: University of New Mexico Press, 2005.

Petersen, Jacqueline. "Women Dreaming: The Religiopsychology of White Indian Marriage and the Rise of Métis Culture." In *Western Women, Their Land, Their Lives*, edited by Lillian Chisel, Vicki L. Ruiz, and Janice Monk, 49–80. Albuquerque: University of New Mexico Press, 1988.

Pierson, Michael D. "Gender and Party Ideologies: The Constitutional Thought of Women and Men in American Antislavery Politics." *Slavery and Abolition* 19 (December 1998): 46–67.

————. "'Guard the Foundation Well': Antebellum New York Democrats and the Defense of Patriarchy." *Gender and History* 7 (April 1995): 25–40.

Pitkin, Hanna Fenichel. *Fortune Is a Woman: Gender and Politics in the Thought of Niccolò Machiavelli.* Berkeley: University of California Press, 1984.

Plante, Ellen M. *The American Kitchen, 1700 to the Present: From Hearth to Highrise.* New York: Facts on File, 1995.

————. *Women at Home in Victorian America: A Social History.* New York: Facts on File, 1997.

Plath, Sylvia. *The Bell Jar.* New York: Harper and Row, 1971.

Pleck, Elizabeth A. "A Mother's Wages: Income Earning among Married Italian and Black Women, 1896–1911." In *The American Family in Social-Historical Perspective,* edited by Michael Gordon, 490–510. 2d ed. New York: St. Martin's Press, 1978.

Poirier, Paris. *Last Call at Maud's.* The Maud's Project, 1993. Videorecording.

Polacheck, Hilda Satt. *I Came a Stranger: The Story of a Hull-House Girl.* Edited by Dena J. Polacheck Epstein, with an introduction by Lynn Y. Weiner. Urbana: University of Illinois Press, 1989.

Poole, Jean Bruce, and Tevvy Ball. *El Pueblo: The Historic Heart of Los Angeles.* Los Angeles: Getty Conservation Institute and the J. Paul Getty Museum, 2002.

Poole, Stafford. *Our Lady of Guadalupe: The Origins and Sources of a Mexican National Symbol, 1531–1797.* Tucson: University of Arizona Press, 1995.

Porterfield, Amanda. *Female Piety in Puritan New England: The Emergence of Religious Humanism.* New York: Oxford University Press, 1992.

Portes, Alejandro, and Rubén G. Rumbaut. *Legacies: The Story of the Immigrant Second Generation.* Berkeley: University of California Press, 2001.

Poster, Winifred. "Dangerous Places and Nimble Fingers: Discourses of Gender Discrimination and Rights in Global Corporations." *International Journal of Politics, Culture and Society* 15, no. 1 (2002): 77–105.

Powers, Madelon. "Women and Public Drinking, 1890–1920." *History Today* 45 (February 1995): 46–53.

Prather, H. Leon, Sr. "We Have Taken a City: A Centennial Essay." In *Democracy Betrayed: The Wilmington Race Riot of 1898 and Its Legacy,* edited by David S. Cecelski and Timothy B. Tyson, 15–41. Chapel Hill: University of North Carolina Press, 1998.

Prell, Riv-Ellen. *Fighting to Become Americans: Jews, Gender, and the Anxiety of Assimilation.* Boston: Beacon Press, 1999.

Prieto, Yolanda. "Cuban Women and Work in the United States: A New Jersey Case Study." In *International Migration: The Female Experience,* edited by Rita James Simon and Caroline B. Brettell, 95–112. Totowa, N.J.: Rowman and Allanheld, 1986.

Prindeville, Diane-Michele, and Teresa Braley Gomez. "American Women Leaders,

Public Policy, and the Importance of Gender and Ethnic Identity." *Women and Politics* 20 (Summer 1999): 19–31.

Putnam, Robert D. *Bowling Alone: The Collapse and Revival of American Community.* New York: Simon and Schuster, 2000.

Puzo, Mario. *The Fortunate Pilgrim.* New York: Atheneum, 1965.

Rayaprol, Aparna. *Negotiating Identities: Women in the Indian Diaspora.* New York: Oxford University Press, 1997.

Reagan, Leslie. *When Abortion Was a Crime: Women, Medicine, and Law in the United States, 1867–1973.* Berkeley: University of California Press, 1997.

Reiter, Rayna R., ed. *Toward an Anthropology of Women.* New York: Monthly Review Press, 1975.

Research Department of the Association for the Study of Negro Life and History. "Free Negro Owners of Slaves in the United States in 1830." *Journal of Negro History* 9 (January 1924): 41–85.

Richter, Daniel K. *Facing East from Indian Country: A Native History of Early America.* Cambridge, Mass.: Harvard University Press, 2001.

———. *The Ordeal of the Longhouse: The Peoples of the Iroquois League in the Era of European Colonization.* Chapel Hill: University of North Carolina Press, 1992.

———. "War and Culture: The Iroquois Experience." In *American Encounters: Native and Newcomers from European Contact to Indian Removal, 1500–1850,* edited by Peter Mancall and James Merrell, 283–310. New York: Routledge, 2000.

Ries, Paula, and Anne J. Stone. *The American Woman, 1992–93 Status Report.* New York: Norton, 1992.

Robertson, Claire. "Africa into the Americas? Slavery and Women, the Family, and the Gender Division of Labor." In *More Than Chattel: Black Women and Slavery in the Americas,* edited by David Barry Gaspar and Darlene Clark Hine, 3–40. Bloomington: Indiana University Press, 1996.

Robertson, Claire C., and Martin A. Klein, eds. *Women and Slavery in Africa.* Madison: University of Wisconsin Press, 1983.

Robinson, Jo Ann Gibson. *The Montgomery Bus Boycott and the Women Who Started It: The Memoir of Jo Ann Gibson Robinson.* Edited by David Garrow. Knoxville: University of Tennessee Press, 1987.

Robinson, Paul. *The Modernization of Sex: Havelock Ellis, Alfred Kinsey, William Masters, and Virginia Johnson.* New York: Harper and Row, 1976.

Robinson, W. Stitt. "Conflicting Views on Landholding: Lord Baltimore and the Experiences of Colonial Maryland with Native Americans." *Maryland Historical Magazine* 83 (Summer 1988): 85–97.

Robinson, W. W. *Los Angeles from the Days of the Pueblo: A Brief History and Guide to the Plaza Area.* Revised and with an introduction by Doyce B. Nunis Jr. North Hollywood: California Historical Society/Chronicle Books, 1981.

Rodriguez, Jeanette. *Our Lady of Guadalupe: Faith and Empowerment among Mexican-American Women.* Austin: University of Texas Press, 1994.

Rodriguez, Richard. *Hunger of Memory.* New York: Bantam, 1983.

Rogers, Susan C. "Female Forms of Power and the Myth of Male Dominance: A Model of Female/Male Interaction in Peasant Society." *American Ethnologist* 2, no. 4 (1975): 727–56.

Rosaldo, Michelle Zimbalist, and Louise Lamphere, eds. *Women, Culture, and Society.* Stanford, Calif.: Stanford University Press, 1974.

Roscoe, Will. *Changing Ones: Third and Fourth Genders in Native North America.* New York: St. Martin's Press, 1998.

Rosen, Ruth. *The World Split Open: How the Modern Women's Movement Changed America.* New York: Viking, 2000.

Rosenberg, Charles E., and Janet L. Golden, eds. *Framing Disease: Studies in Cultural History.* New Brunswick, N.J.: Rutgers University Press, 1996.

Rosenberg, Rosalind. *Beyond Separate Spheres: Intellectual Roots of Modern Feminism.* New Haven, Conn.: Yale University Press, 1982.

Ross, Dorothy. "Gendered Social Knowledge: Domestic Discourse, Jane Addams, and the Possibilities of Social Science." In *Gender and American Social Science: The Formative Years,* edited by Helene Silverberg, 235–64. Princeton, N.J.: Princeton University Press, 1998.

Roth, Benita. *Separate Roads to Feminism: Black, Chicana, and White Feminist Movements in America's Second Wave.* New York: Cambridge University Press, 2004.

Roth, Henry. *Call It Sleep: A Novel.* 1934; Patterson, N.J.: Pageant Books, 1960.

Rothschild, Mary Aickin. "White Women Volunteers in the Freedom Summers: Their Life and Work in a Movement for Social Change." *Feminist Studies* 5 (Fall 1979): 466–95.

Rotundo, E. Anthony. *American Manhood: Transformations in Masculinity from the Revolution to the Modern Era.* New York: Basic Books, 1993.

Rowson, Susanna. *Charlotte Temple: A Tale of Truth.* Edited by Clara M. Kirk and Rudolf Kirk. New Haven, Conn.: College and University Press, 1964.

Rubin, Gayle. "The Traffic in Women: Notes on the Public Economy of Sex." In *Toward an Anthropology of Women,* edited by Rayna R. Reiter, 157–210. New York: Monthly Review Press, 1975.

Rubin, Lillian. *Families on the Faultline: America's Working Class Speaks about the Family, the Economy, Race, and Ethnicity.* New York: Harper Collins, 1994.

Ruiz, Vicki L. *Cannery Women, Cannery Lives: Mexican Women, Unionization, and the California Food Processing Industry, 1930–1950.* Albuquerque: University of New Mexico Press, 1987.

———. *From Out of the Shadows: Mexican Women in Twentieth-Century America.* New York: Oxford University Press, 1998.

———, ed. *Las Obreras: Chicana Politics of Work and Family.* Los Angeles:

University of California, Los Angeles, Chicano Studies Research Publications, 2000.

Rumbaut, Ruben G. "Origins and Destinies: Immigration to the United States since World War II." *Sociological Forum* 9 (December 1994): 583–621.

Rupp, Leila J., and Verta Taylor. *Survival in the Doldrums: The American Women's Rights Movement, 1945 to the 1960s*. New York: Oxford University Press, 1987.

Ruppel, Tim. "Gender Training: Male Ambitions, Domestic Duties, and Failure in the Magazine Fiction of T. S. Arthur." *Prospects* 24 (1999): 311–37.

Ryan, Mary P. "American Society and the Cult of Domesticity, 1830–1860." Ph.D. diss., University of California, Santa Barbara, 1971.

———. *Civic Wars: Democracy and Public Life in the American City during the Nineteenth Century*. Berkeley: University of California Press, 1997.

———. *Cradle of the Middle Class: The Family in Oneida County, New York, 1790–1865*. New York: Cambridge University Press, 1981.

———. *The Empire of the Mother: American Writing about Domesticity, 1830 to 1860*. New York: Institute for Research in History and the Haworth Press, 1982.

———. "The Projection of a New Womanhood: The Movie Moderns of the 1920s." In *Our American Sisters: Women in American Life and Thought*, edited by Jean Friedman and William Shade, 366–85. Boston: Allyn and Bacon, 1976.

———. *Womanhood in America: From Colonial Times to the Present*. 1st ed. New York: New Viewpoints, 1975.

———. *Womanhood in America: From Colonial Times to the Present*. 3d ed. New York: Franklin Watts, 1983.

———. *Women in Public: Between Banners and Ballots, 1825–1880*. Baltimore, Md.: Johns Hopkins University Press, 1990.

Sacks, Karen. *Sisters and Wives: The Past and Future of Sexual Equality*. Urbana: University of Illinois Press, 1982.

Salisbury, Neal. "The Indians' Old World: Native Americans and the Coming of Europeans." *William and Mary Quarterly* 53 (July 1996): 435–58.

Salmon, Marylynn. *Women and the Law of Property in Early America*. Chapel Hill: University of North Carolina Press, 1986.

Sanchez, George J. *Becoming Mexican American: Ethnicity, Culture, and Identity in Chicano Los Angeles, 1900–1945*. New York: Oxford University Press, 1993.

———. "'Go After the Women': Americanization and the Mexican Immigrant Woman, 1915–1929." In *Unequal Sisters: A Multicultural Reader in U.S. Women's History*, edited by Ellen Carol DuBois and Vicki L. Ruiz, 250–63. New York: Routledge Press, 1990.

Sanday, Peggy. *Female Power and Male Dominance: On the Origins of Sexual Inequality*. New York: Cambridge University Press, 1981.

San Francisco Lesbian and Gay History Project. "She Even Chewed Tobacco: A Pictorial Narrative of Passing Women in America." In *Hidden from History: Reclaiming the Gay and Lesbian Past*, edited by Martin Duberman, Martha

Vicinus, and George Chauncey Jr., 183–94. New York: New American Library, 1989.

Sapiro, Virginia. "The Gender Basis of American Social Policy." In *Women, the State, and Welfare,* edited by Linda Gordon, 36–54. Madison: University of Wisconsin Press, 1990.

Sassler, Sharon L. "Women's Marital Timing at the Turn of the Century: Generational and Ethnic Differences." *Sociological Quarterly* 38 (Fall 1997): 567–86.

Sattler, Richard A. "Women's Status among the Muskogee and Cherokee." In *Women and Power in Native North America,* edited by Laura F. Klein and Lillian A. Ackerman, 214–49. Norman: University of Oklahoma Press, 1995.

Scadron, Arlene, ed. *On Their Own: Widows and Widowhood in the American Southwest, 1848–1939.* Urbana: University of Illinois Press, 1988.

Scarry, Elaine, ed. *Literature and the Body: Essays on Populations and Persons.* Baltimore, Md.: Johns Hopkins University Press, 1988.

Scharf, Lois. *To Work and to Wed: Female Employment, Feminism, and the Great Depression.* Westport, Conn.: Greenwood Press, 1980.

Schlegel, Alice. "Hopi Family Structure and the Experience of Widowhood." In *On Their Own: Widows and Widowhood in the American Southwest, 1848–1939,* edited by Arlene Scadron, 42–64. Urbana: University of Illinois Press, 1988.

Schneider, A. Gregory. *The Way of the Cross Leads Home: The Domestication of American Methodism.* Bloomington: Indiana University Press, 1993.

Scholinkski, Daphne, with Jane Meredith Adams. *The Last Time I Wore a Dress.* New York: Riverhead Books, 1997.

Schwalbe, Michael. *Unlocking the Iron Cage: The Men's Movement, Gender Politics, and American Culture.* New York: Oxford University Press, 1996.

Schwalm, Leslie A. *A Hard Fight for We: Women's Transition from Slavery to Freedom in South Carolina.* Urbana: University of Illinois Press, 1997.

Schwartz, Judith. *Radical Feminists of Heterodoxy: Greenwich Village, 1912–1940.* Norwich, Vt.: New Victoria Publishers, 1986.

Schwartz, Judith, Kathy Peiss, and Christina Simmons. "'We Were a Little Band of Willful Women': The Heterodoxy Club of Greenwich Village." In *Passion and Power: Sexuality in History,* edited by Kathy Peiss and Christina Simmons with Robert A. Padgug, 118–37. Philadelphia: Temple University Press, 1989.

Schwartz, T. P. "Durkheim's Prediction about the Shift from Family to Organizational Inheritance: Evidence from the Wills of Providence, 1775–1985." *Sociological Quarterly* 36 (1996): 503–19.

Schweninger, Loren. *Black Property Owners in the South, 1790–1915.* Urbana: University of Illinois Press, 1990.

Scott, Anne Firor. "Most Invisible of All: Black Women's Voluntary Associations." *Journal of Southern History* 56 (February 1990): 3–22.

————. *Natural Allies: Women's Associations in American History*. Urbana: University of Illinois Press, 1991.

Scott, Joan Wallach. "Gender: A Useful Category of Historical Analysis." *American Historical Review* 91 (December 1986): 1053–75.

Scudder, Vida. *The Relation of College Women to Social Need*. Publication of the Association of Collegiate Alumnae, Series II, no. 30. N.p., 1891.

Sedgwick, Eve Kosofsky. *Epistemology of the Closet*. Berkeley: University of California Press, 1990.

Segal, Lynne. *Slow Motion: Changing Masculinities, Changing Men*. New Brunswick, N.J.: Rutgers University Press, 1990.

Seidman, Steven. *Difference Troubles: Queering Social Theory and Sexual Politics*. New York: Cambridge University Press, 1997.

"Selected Statistics on the Status of Asian American Women." *Amerasia* 4 (1977): 133–40.

Sellers, Charles Grier. *The Market Revolution: Jacksonian America, 1815–1846*. New York: Oxford University Press, 1991.

Sennett, Richard. *Families against the City: Middle-Class Homes of Industrial Chicago, 1872–1890*. Cambridge, Mass.: Harvard University Press, 1970.

Sewell, Jessica Ellen. "Gendering the Spaces of Modernity: Women and Public Space in San Francisco, 1890–1915." Ph.D. diss., University of California, Berkeley, 2000.

Shammas, Carole. "Anglo-American Household Government in Comparative Perspective." *William and Mary Quarterly* 52 (January 1995): 104–44.

————. "Black Women's Work and the Evolution of Plantation Society in Virginia." *Labor History* 26 (Winter 1985): 5–28.

Shammas, Carole, Marylynn Salmon, and Michel Dahlin, eds. *Inheritance in America: From Colonial Times to the Present*. New Brunswick, N.J.: Rutgers University Press, 1987.

Sharp, Henry. "Asymmetric Equals: Women and Men among the Chipewyan." In *Women and Power in Native North America*, edited by Laura F. Klein and Lillian A. Ackerman, 46–74. Norman: University of Oklahoma Press, 1995.

Sharpe, Pamela, ed. *Women, Gender, and Labour Migration: Historical and Global Perspectives*. London and New York: Routledge, 2001.

Sheridan, Richard B. "The Domestic Economy." In *Colonial British America: Essays in the New History of the Early Modern Era*, edited by Jack P. Greene and J. R. Pole, 43–87. Baltimore, Md.: Johns Hopkins University Press, 1984.

Shoemaker, Nancy. "Kateri Tekakwitha's Torturous Path to Sainthood." In *Negotiators of Change: Historical Perspectives on Native American Women*, edited by Nancy Shoemaker, 49–71. New York: Routledge, 1995.

————, ed. *Negotiators of Change: Historical Perspectives on Native American Women*. New York: Routledge, 1995.

Shoemaker, Robert. *Gender in English Society, 1650–1850*. New York: Longman, 1998.

Silverberg, Helene. *Gender and American Social Science: The Formative Years.* Princeton, N.J.: Princeton University Press, 1998.

Simon, Rita James, and Margo Corona DeLey. "Undocumented Mexican Women: Their Work and Personal Experiences." In *International Migration: The Female Experience*, edited by Rita James Simon and Caroline B. Brettell, 113–32. Totowa, N.J.: Rowman and Allanheld, 1986.

Simon, Rita James, Louise Shelley, and Paul Schneiderman. "The Social and Economic Adjustment of Soviet Jewish Women in the United States." In *International Migration: The Female Experience*, edited by Rita James Simon and Caroline B. Brettell, 76–94. Totowa, N.J.: Rowman and Allanheld, 1986.

Simon, Rita James, ed. *Immigrant Women*. New Brunswick, N.J.: Transaction, 2001.

Simon, Rita James, and Caroline B. Brettell, eds. *International Migration: The Female Experience*. Totowa, N.J.: Rowman and Allanheld, 1986.

Sklar, Kathryn Kish. *Florence Kelley and the Nation's Work: The Rise of Women's Political Culture, 1830–1900*. New Haven, Conn.: Yale University Press, 1995.

Skocpol, Theda. *Protecting Soldiers and Mothers: The Political Origins of Social Policy in the United States*. Cambridge, Mass.: Belknap Press of Harvard University Press, 1992.

Smith, Daniel Scott. "The Number and Quality of Children: Education and Marital Fertility in Early Twentieth-Century Iowa." *Journal of Social History* 30 (Winter 1996): 367–93.

Smith, Judith E. *Family Connections: A History of Italian and Jewish Immigrant Lives in Providence, Rhode Island, 1900–1940*. Albany: State University of New York Press, 1985.

Smith, Rogers M. *Civic Ideals: Conflicting Visions of Citizenship in U.S. History*. New Haven, Conn.: Yale University Press, 1997.

Smith-Rosenberg, Carroll. "Beauty and the Beast and the Militant Woman: A Case Study in Sex Roles and Social Stress in Jacksonian America." *American Quarterly* 23 (October 1971): 562–84.

———. *Disorderly Conduct: Visions of Gender in Victorian America*. New York: Knopf, 1985.

———. "Domesticating 'Virtue': Coquettes and Revolutionaries in Young America." In *Literature and the Body: Essays on Populations and Persons*, edited by Elaine Scarry, 160–84. Baltimore, Md.: Johns Hopkins University Press, 1988.

———. "The Female World of Love and Ritual: Relations between Women in Nineteenth-Century America." *Signs* 1 (1976): 1–29.

Snyder, Thomas D. *Digest of Education Statistics, 1996*. Washington, D.C.: U.S. Department of Education, Office of Educational Research and Improvement, National Center for Educational Statistics, 1996.

Solinger, Rickie. "Pregnancy and Power before *Roe v. Wade*, 1950–1970." In

Abortion Wars: A Half Century of Struggle, 1950–2000, edited by Rickie Solinger. Berkeley: University of California Press, 1998.

———, ed. *Abortion Wars: A Half Century of Struggle, 1950–2000*. Berkeley: University of California Press, 1998.

Sollors, Werner, ed. *Interracialism: Black and White Intermarriage in American History, Literature, and Law*. New York: Oxford University Press, 2000.

Solomon, Barbara M. *In the Company of Educated Women: A History of Women and Higher Education in America*. New Haven, Conn.: Yale University Press, 1985.

Sommerville, Diane Miller. *Rape and Race in the Nineteenth-Century South*. Chapel Hill: University of North Carolina Press, 2004.

———. "The Rape Myth in the Old South Reconsidered." *Journal of Southern History* 61 (August 1995): 481–518.

Song, Young I., and Ailee Moon. "The Domestic Violence against Women in Korean Immigrant Families: Cultural, Psychological, and Socioeconomic Perspectives." In *Asian/Pacific Islander American Women: A Historical Anthology*, edited by Shirley Hune and Gail M. Nomura, 161–73. New York: New York University Press, 2003.

———, eds. *Korean American Women: From Tradition to Modern Feminism*. Westport, Conn.: Praeger, 1998.

Spain, Daphne, and Suzanne Bianchi. *Balancing Act: Motherhood, Marriage, and Employment among American Women*. New York: Russell Sage Foundation, 1996.

Spear, Jennifer M. "Colonial Intimacies: Legislating Sex in French Louisiana." *William and Mary Quarterly* 55 (January 2003): 75–98.

———. "'They Need Wives': Metissage and the Regulation of Sexuality in French Louisiana, 1699–1730." In *Sex, Love, Race: Crossing Boundaries in North American History*, edited by Martha Hodes, 35–59. New York: New York University Press, 1999.

Spector, Janet. "What This Awl Means: Toward a Feminist Archaeology." In *Engendering Archaeology: Women and Prehistory*, edited by Joan M. Gero and Margaret W. Conkey, 388–407. Cambridge, Mass.: Blackwell, 1991.

Spencer-Wood, Suzanne M. "Feminist Historical Archaeology and the Transformation of American Culture by Domestic Reform Movements, 1840–1925." In *Historical Archaeology and the Study of American Culture*, edited by Lu Ann De Cunzo and Bernard L. Herman, 397–446. Knoxville: University of Tennessee Press for the Winterthur Museum, 1996.

Spewack, Bella. *Streets: A Memoir of the Lower East Side*. New York: Feminist Press, 1995.

Spock, Benjamin. *Baby and Child Care*. New York: Pocket Books, 1970.

Spoehr, Alexander. *The Florida Seminole Camp*. Chicago: Field Museum of Natural History, 1944.

———. *Kinship System of the Seminole*. Chicago: Field Museum of Natural History, 1942.

Stacey, Judith. *Brave New Families: Stories of Domestic Upheaval in Late-Twentieth-Century America*. Berkeley: University of California Press, 1990.

———. *In the Name of the Family: Rethinking Family Values in the Postmodern Age*. Boston: Beacon Press, 1996.

Stanley, Amy Dru. *From Bondage to Contract: Wage Labor, Marriage, and the Market in the Age of Slave Emancipation*. New York: Cambridge University Press, 1998.

Stannard, David, ed. *Death in America*. Philadelphia: University of Pennsylvania Press, 1974.

Stansell, Christine. *American Moderns: Bohemian New York and the Creation of a New Century*. New York: Henry Holt, 2000.

———. *City of Women: Sex and Class in New York, 1789–1860*. New York: Knopf, 1986.

Steckel, Richard. "Women, Work, and Health under Plantation Slavery in the United States." In *More Than Chattel: Black Women and Slavery in the Americas*, edited by David Barry Gaspar and Darlene Clark Hine, 43–60. Bloomington: Indiana University Press, 1996.

Stein, Marc. *City of Sisterly and Brotherly Loves: Lesbian and Gay Philadelphia, 1945–1972*. Chicago: University of Chicago Press, 2000.

Stevenson, Brenda E. *Life in Black and White: Family and Community in the Slave South*. New York: Oxford University Press, 1996.

Stone, Lawrence. *The Family, Sex, and Marriage in England, 1500–1800*. New York: Harper and Row, 1979.

Stone, Oliver. *Born on the Fourth of July*. Universal Pictures, 1989.

Stowe, Harriet Beecher. *Oldtown Folks*. Boston: Fields, Osgood, and Company, 1869.

St. Pierre, Mark, and Tilda Long Soldier. *Walking in the Sacred Manner: Healers, Dreamers, and Pipe-Carriers—Medicine Women of the Plains Indians*. New York: Simon and Schuster, 1995.

Straub, Eleanor F. "Women in the Civilian Labor Force." In *Clio Was a Woman: Studies in the History of American Women*, edited by Mabel E. Deutrich and Virginia C. Purdy, 206–26. Washington, D.C.: Howard University Press, 1980.

Stryker, Susan, and Jim Van Buskirk. *Gay by the Bay: A History of Queer Culture in the San Francisco Bay Area*. San Francisco: Chronicle Books, 1996.

Sugrue, Thomas. *The Origins of the Urban Crisis: Race and Inequality in Postwar Detroit*. Princeton, N.J.: Princeton University Press, 1996.

Swerdlow, Amy. *Women Strike for Peace: Traditional Motherhood and Radical Politics in the 1960s*. Chicago: University of Chicago Press, 1993.

Taeuber, Cynthia, ed. *Statistical Handbook on Women in America*. Phoenix, Ariz.: Oryx Press, 1991.

Taylor, Ella. *Prime Time Families: Television Culture in Postwar America*. Berkeley: University of California Press, 1989.

Taylor, William B. "The Virgin of Guadalupe in New Spain: An Inquiry into the

Social History of Marian Devotion." *American Ethnologist* 14 (February 1987): 9–33.

Thompson, Peter. *Rum Punch and Revolution: Taverngoing and Public Life in Eighteenth-Century Philadelphia*. Philadelphia: University of Pennsylvania Press, 1999.

Thorne, Barrie. "Pick-Up Time at Oakdale Elementary School: Work and Family from the Vantage Point of Children." In *Working Families: The Transformation of the American Home*, edited by Rosanna Hertz and Nancy L. Marshall, 354–76. Berkeley: University of California Press, 2001.

Thornton, Russell. "The Demography of Colonialism and 'Old' and 'New' Native Americans." In *Studying Native America, Problems and Prospects*, edited by Russell Thornton, 17–40. Madison: University of Wisconsin Press, 1998.

Tompkins, Jane. "Sentimental Power: Uncle Tom's Cabin and the Politics of Literary History." In *Ideology and Classic American Literature*, edited by Sacvan Bercovitch and Myra Jehlen, 267–92. New York: Cambridge University Press, 1986.

Trujillo, Carla. *Chicana Lesbians: The Girls Our Mothers Warned Us About*. Berkeley, Calif.: Third Woman Press, 1991.

Trumbach, Randolph. "The Birth of the Queen: Sodomy and the Emergence of Gender Equality in Modern Culture, 1660–1750." In *Hidden from History: Reclaiming the Gay and Lesbian Past*, edited by Martin Duberman, Martha Vicinus, and George Chauncey Jr., 129–40. New York: New American Library, 1989.

Tung, Charlene. "Caring across Borders: Motherhood, Marriage, and Filipina Domestic Workers in California." In *Asian/Pacific Islander American Women: A Historical Anthology*, edited by Shirley Hune and Gail M. Nomura, 301–18. New York: New York University Press, 2003.

Uhlenberg, Peter. "Cohort Variations in Family Life Cycle Experiences of U.S. Females." *Journal of Marriage and the Family* 36 (May 1974): 284–92.

Ullman, Sharon. *Sex Seen: The Emergence of Modern Sexuality in America*. Berkeley: University of California Press, 1997.

Ulrich, Laurel Thatcher. *The Age of Homespun: Objects and Stories in the Creation of an American Myth*. New York: Knopf, 2001.

———. "'Daughters of Liberty': Religious Women in Revolutionary New England." In *Women in the Age of the American Revolution*, edited by Ronald Hoffman and Peter J. Albert, 211–43. Charlottesville: University Press of Virginia for the United States Capitol Historical Society, 1989.

———. "'A Friendly Neighbor': Social Dimensions of Daily Work in Northern New England." *Feminist Studies* 6 (Summer 1990): 392–405.

———. *Good Wives: Image and Reality in the Lives of Women in Northern New England, 1650–1750*. New York: Random House, 1982.

———. *A Midwife's Tale: The Life of Martha Ballard, Based on Her Diary, 1785–1812.* New York: Vintage Books, 1991.

———. "Wheels, Looms, and the Gender Division of Labor in Eighteenth-Century New England." *William and Mary Quarterly* 55 (January 1998): 3–38.

United Nations. *The World's Women, 1995: Trends and Statistics.* New York: United Nations, 1995.

U.S. Bureau of the Census. *We, the American—: Hispanics.* Washington, D.C.: U.S. Department of Commerce, Economics, and Statistics Administration, 1993.

Upton, Dell. *Architecture in the United States.* New York: Oxford University Press, 1998.

Valaskakis, Gail Guthrie. "The Chippewa and the Other: Living the Heritage of Lac Du Flambeau." *Cultural Studies* 2 (1988): 267–93.

Vanek, Joann. "Time Spent in House Work." *Scientific American* 231 (November 1974): 116–20.

Van Horn, Susan Householder. *Women, Work, and Fertility, 1900–1986.* New York: New York University Press, 1987.

Van Kirk, Sylvia. *"Many Tender Ties": Women in Fur-Trade Society, 1670–1870.* Winnipeg: Watson and Dwyer, 1980.

Varon, Elizabeth R. *We Mean to Be Counted: White Women and Politics in Antebellum Virginia.* Chapel Hill: University of North Carolina Press, 1998.

Vickers, Daniel. *Farmers and Fishermen: Two Centuries of Work in Essex County, Massachusetts, 1630–1850.* Chapel Hill: University of North Carolina Press, 1994.

Vidal, Gore. *Myra Breckinridge.* Boston: Little, Brown, 1968.

Vistica, Gregory L. "What Happened in Thanh Phong." *New York Times Magazine.* April 29, 2001, 50–57, 66–68, 133.

Vô, Linda Trinh. "Managing Survival: Economic Realities for Vietnamese American Women." In *Asian/Pacific Islander American Women: A Historical Anthology,* edited by Shirley Hune and Gail M. Nomura, 237–52. New York: New York University Press, 2003.

Wacquant, Loïc J. D. "For an Analytic of Racial Domination." *Political Power and Social Theory* 11 (1997): 221–34.

Wadsworth, Ginger. *Julia Morgan, Architect of Dreams.* Minneapolis, Minn.: Lerner Publications, 1990.

Waldrep, Christopher. *The Many Faces of Judge Lynch: Extralegal Violence and Punishment in America.* New York: Palgrave Macmillan, 2002.

Walker, David. *David Walker's Appeal in Four Articles; Together with a Preamble, to the Coloured Citizens of the World.* Introduction by Sean Wilentz. Rev. ed. New York: Hill and Wang, 1995.

Wall, Cheryl A. *Women of the Harlem Renaissance.* Bloomington: Indiana University Press, 1995.

Wall, Diana diZerega. *The Archaeology of Gender: Separating the Spheres in Urban America.* New York: Plenum Press, 1994.

Wall, Helena M. *Fierce Communion: Family and Community in Early America*.
Cambridge, Mass.: Harvard University Press, 1990.

Wallenstein, Peter. *Tell the Court I Love My Wife: Race, Marriage, and Law—An American History*. New York: Palgrave, 2002.

Wandersee, Winifred. *Women's Work and Family Values, 1920–1940*. Cambridge, Mass.: Harvard University Press, 1981.

Ward, Karen. *Women Workers and Global Restructuring*. Ithaca, N.Y.: ILR Press, 1990.

Ware, Susan. *Beyond Suffrage: Women in the New Deal*. Cambridge, Mass.: Harvard University Press, 1981.

———. "Dialogue: Pauli Murray's Notable Connections." *Journal of Women's History* 14 (Summer 2002): 54–57.

———. *Partner and I: Molly Dewson, Feminism, and New Deal Politics*. New Haven, Conn.: Yale University Press, 1987.

———. *Still Missing: Amelia Earhart and the Search for Modern Feminism*. New York: Norton, 1993.

Watson, John B. *Psychological Care of Infant and Child*. New York: Norton, 1928.

Weinberg, Sydney Stahl. *The World of Our Mothers: The Lives of Jewish Immigrant Women*. Chapel Hill: University of North Carolina Press, 1988.

Weiner, Lynn Y. *From Working Girl to Working Mother: The Female Labor Force in the United States, 1820–1980*. Chapel Hill: University of North Carolina Press, 1985.

Weiner, Marli Frances. *Mistresses and Slaves: Plantation Women in South Carolina, 1830–80*. Urbana: University of Illinois Press, 1997.

Weintraub, Jeffrey, and Krishan Kumar, eds. *Public and Private in Thought and Practice: Perspectives on a Grand Dichotomy*. Chicago: University of Chicago Press, 1997.

Weiss, Jessica. "'A Drop-In Catering Job': Middle-Class Women and Fatherhood, 1950–1980." *Journal of Family History* 24 (Fall 1999): 374–90.

———. *To Have and to Hold: Marriage, the Baby Boom, and Social Change*. Chicago: University of Chicago Press, 2000.

Weiss, Nancy Pottishman. "Mother, the Invention of Necessity: Dr. Benjamin Spock's *Baby and Child Care*." *American Quarterly* 29 (Winter 1977): 519–46.

Wellman, Judith. *The Road to Seneca Falls: Elizabeth Cady Stanton and the First Woman's Rights Convention*. Urbana: University of Illinois Press, 2004.

Wells-Barnett, Ida B. *Crusade for Justice: The Autobiography of Ida B. Wells*. Edited and with an introduction by Alfreda M. Duster. Chicago: University of Chicago Press, 1991.

———. *The Memphis Diary of Ida B. Wells*. Edited by Miriam DeCosta-Willis. Boston: Beacon Press, 1995.

Welter, Barbara. "The Cult of True Womanhood." *American Quarterly* 18 (Summer 1966): 151–74.

Wermuth, Thomas S. "New York Farmers and the Market Revolution: Economic

Behavior in the Mid-Hudson Valley, 1780–1830." *Journal of Social History* 32 (Fall 1998): 179–96.

Wertheimer, Barbara. *We Were There: The Story of Working Women in America*. New York: Pantheon, 1977.

Wertz, Richard W., and Dorothy C. Wertz. *Lying-In: A History of Childbirth in America*. New York: Free Press, 1977.

West, Candace, and Don H. Zimmerman. "Doing Gender." In *Doing Gender, Doing Difference: Inequality, Power, and Institutional Change*, edited by Sarah Fenstermaker and Candace West, 3–23. New York: Routledge, 2002.

Wharton, Edith. *House of Mirth*. New York: Scribner's Sons, 1933.

Whitaker, Lois Duke, ed. *Women in Politics: Outsiders or Insiders? A Collection of Readings*. Upper Saddle River, N.J.: Prentice Hall, 1999.

White, Deborah G. *Ar'n't I a Woman? Female Slaves in the Plantation South*. New York: Norton, 1985.

———. *Too Heavy a Load: Black Women in Defense of Themselves, 1894–1994*. New York: Norton, 1999.

White, Kevin. *The First Sexual Revolution: The Emergence of Male Heterosexuality in Modern America*. New York: New York University Press, 1993.

White, Richard. *The Middle Ground: Indians, Empires, and Republics in the Great Lakes Region, 1650–1815*. New York: Cambridge University Press, 1991.

White, Shane. "'It Was a Proud Day': African Americans, Festivals, and Parades in the North, 1741–1834." *Journal of American History* 81 (June 1994): 13–50.

Whitehead, Harriet. "The Bow and the Burden Strap: A New Look at Institutionalized Homosexuality in Native North America." In *Sexual Meanings: The Cultural Construction of Gender and Sexuality*, edited by Sherry B. Ortner and Harriet Whitehead, 80–115. New York: Cambridge University Press, 1981.

Whites, LeeAnn. *The Civil War as a Crisis in Gender: Augusta, Georgia, 1860–90*. Athens: University of Georgia Press, 1995.

———. "Love, Hate, Rape, Lynching: Rebecca Latimer Felton and the Gender Politics of Racial Violence." In *Democracy Betrayed: The Wilmington Race Riot of 1898 and Its Legacy*, edited by David S. Cecelski and Timothy B. Tyson, 143–62. Chapel Hill: University of North Carolina Press, 1998.

Whittier, Nancy. *Feminist Generations: The Persistence of the Radical Women's Movement*. Philadelphia: Temple University Press, 1995.

Widder, Keith R. *Battle for the Soul: Métis Children Encounter Evangelical Protestants at Mackinaw Mission, 1823–1837*. East Lansing: Michigan State University Press, 1999.

Wiegman, Robyn. "The Anatomy of Lynching." *Journal of the History of Sexuality* 3 (January 1993): 445–67.

Wiesner, Merry E. *Women and Gender in Early Modern Europe*. New York: Cambridge University Press, 1993.

Williamson, Joel. *New People: Miscegenation and Mulattoes in the United States*. New York: Free Press, 1980.

Wilson, Lisa. "A Marriage 'Well-Ordered': Love, Power, and Partnership in Colonial New England." In *A Shared Experience: Men, Women, and the History of Gender*, edited by Laura McCall and Donald Yacovone, 78–97. New York: New York University Press, 1998.

———. *Ye Heart of a Man: The Domestic Life of Men in Colonial New England*. New Haven, Conn.: Yale University Press, 1999.

Wilson, William Julius. *When Work Disappears: The World of the New Urban Poor*. New York: Knopf, 1996.

Winant, Howard. *The World Is a Ghetto: Race and Democracy since World War II*. New York: Basic Books, 2001.

Woloch, Nancy. *Women and the American Experience*. 3d ed. Boston: McGraw-Hill Higher Education, 2000.

Wong, Jade Snow. *Fifth Chinese Daughter*. New York: Harper and Row, 1950.

Wood, Betty. *The Origins of American Slavery: Freedom and Bondage in the English Colonies*. New York: Hill and Wang, 1997.

Woolf, Virginia. *Three Guineas*. San Diego, Calif.: Harcourt Brace Jovanovich, 1938.

Wright, Gwendolyn. *Building the Dream: A Social History of Housing in America*. New York: Pantheon, 1981.

———. *Moralism and the Model Home: Domestic Architecture and Cultural Conflict in Chicago, 1873–1913*. Chicago: University of Chicago Press, 1980.

Wulf, Karin. *Not All Wives: Women of Colonial Philadelphia*. Ithaca, N.Y.: Cornell University Press, 2000.

Yacovone, Donald. "Surpassing the Love of Women." In *A Shared Experience: Men, Women, and the History of Gender*, edited by Laura McCall and Donald Yacovone, 195–221. New York: New York University Press, 1998.

Yanagisako, Sylvia. *Transforming the Past: Tradition and Kinship among Japanese Americans*. Stanford, Calif.: Stanford University Press, 1985.

Yarborough, Richard. "Violence, Manhood, and Black Heroism: The Wilmington Riot in Two Turn-of-the-Century African American Novels." In *Democracy Betrayed: The Wilmington Race Riot of 1898 and Its Legacy*, edited by David S. Cecelski and Timothy B. Tyson, 225–51. Chapel Hill: University of North Carolina Press, 1998.

Yee, Shirley J. *Black Women Abolitionists: A Study in Activism, 1828–1860*. Knoxville: University of Tennessee Press, 1992.

Yellin, Jean Fagan. *Women and Sisters: The Antislavery Feminists in American Culture*. New Haven, Conn.: Yale University Press, 1989.

Yezierska, Anzia. *Bread Givers: A Novel: A Struggle between a Father of the Old World and a Daughter of the New*. Introduction by Alice Kessler-Harris. New York: Persea Books, 1975.

———. *Hungry Hearts.* New York: Penguin, 1997.

———. *Red Ribbon on a White Horse.* New York: Persea Books, 1987.

———. *Salome of the Tenements.* Urbana and Chicago: University of Illinois Press, 1995.

Young, Andrew. "The Women of Boston: 'Persons of Consequence' in the Making of the American Revolution, 1765–76." In *Women and Politics in the Age of the Democratic Revolution,* edited by Harriet B. Applewhite and Darline G. Levy, 181–226. Ann Arbor: University of Michigan Press, 1990.

Young, Christopher. "Mary K. Goddard: A Classical Republican in a Revolutionary Age." *Maryland Magazine of History* 96 (January 2001): 4–27.

Young, Elizabeth. "A Wound of One's Own: Louisa May Alcott's Civil War Fiction." *American Quarterly* 48 (September 1996): 439–74.

Young, James Sterling. *The Washington Community, 1800–1828.* New York: Harcourt, Brace and World, 1966.

Young, Mary E. "Women, Civilization, and the Indian Question." In *Clio Was a Woman: Studies in the History of American Women,* edited by Mabel E. Deutrich and Virginia C. Purdy, 98–110. Washington, D.C.: Howard University Press, 1980.

Yung, Judy. "'A Bowlful of Tears': Lee Puey You's Immigration Experience at Angel Island." In *Asian/Pacific Islander Women: A Historical Anthology,* edited by Shirley Hune and Gail M. Nomura, 123–37. New York: New York University Press, 2003.

———. *Unbound Feet: A Social History of Chinese Women in San Francisco.* Berkeley: University of California Press, 1993.

———. *Unbound Voices: A Documentary History of Chinese Women in San Francisco.* Berkeley: University of California Press, 1999.

Zaeske, Susan. *Signatures of Citizenship: Petitioning, Antislavery, and Women's Political Identity.* Chapel Hill: University of North Carolina Press, 2003.

Zagarri, Rosemarie. "The Rights of Man and Woman in Post-Revolutionary America." *William and Mary Quarterly* 55 (April 1998): 203–30.

Zarlenga, Kristina. "Civilian Threat: The Suburban Citadel and Atomic Age American Women." *Signs* 24 (Summer 1999): 925–58.

Zavella, Patricia. *Women's Work and Chicano Families: Cannery Workers of the Santa Clara Valley.* Ithaca, N.Y.: Cornell University Press, 1987.

Zinn, Maxime Baca. "Family, Feminism, and Race in America." *Gender and Society* 4 (March 1990): 68–82.

———. "Political Familialism: Toward Sex Role Equality in Chicano Families." *Aztlán* 8 (1995): 13–26.

Zipf, Karin L. "Reconstructing 'Free Woman': African-American Women, Apprenticeship, and Custody Rights during Reconstruction." *Journal of Women's History* 12 (Spring 2000): 8–31.

ACKNOWLEDGMENTS

Every sentence of this book is a debt to other historians. With each paragraph come my thanks and my apologies for any misunderstandings and misuses I have made of the research and writing of my colleagues. My debt to those with whom I have worked side by side for some thirty years in the field of women's and gender history is yet deeper. This book was conceived in the classrooms of the University of California, Berkeley, where I co-taught first with the anthropologist Aihwa Ong and then with European historians Thomas Laqueur and Carla Hesse. They made me see the history of women in the United States with new clarity as well as complexity. The American Studies reading group at Berkeley gave me the courage to move forward on what seemed like a foolhardy project; Paul Groth, Richard Hutson, Larry Levine, Margaretta Lovell, Kathy Moran, Louise Mozingo, Carolyn Porter, Chris Rosen, and Dell Upton offered critical interdisciplinary perspectives and sharp readings of several chapters. My graduate students at Berkeley offered research assistance as well as inspiration all along the way; most recently I have especially to thank Amanda Littauer and Karen McNeill.

The History Department of Johns Hopkins provided the bracingly supportive environment in which the book was completed. "The Seminar" invigorated its author on successive Mondays for the last three years, while teaching along side Toby Ditz, Tobie Meyer-Fong, and Judy Walkowitz broadened and enriched my understanding of gender history. Without the research assistance from Zhao Ma, computer help from Clayton Haywood, and the historical and practical wisdom of Katherine Hijar, the manuscript would never have made it to press.

The early draft of the manuscript benefited immensely from tolerant and toughly sympathetic readings by Kathleen Brown, Nancy Cott, Linda Gordon, Linda Kerber, and Jan Lewis. Jane Dailey, James Brooks, and David Henkin offered invaluable readings of individual chapters. The anonymous readers for the University of North Carolina Press, two of whom turned out to be Nancy Hewitt and Stephanie McCurry, offered strategic editorial advice, as well as their expertise. At UNC Press, Kate Torrey pushed me, again and again, to get it better, and she was always right. These scholars kept me from sundry mistakes and misconceptions: I only wish I could correct them all and respond more adeptly to their criticism.

I have my colleagues and coworkers to thank for the excitement that still surrounds the field of women's history. Closer to home, my daughter Anne Busacca-Ryan and the trail of wonderful young friends who seem always to follow her are to be credited with infusing my sense of the present and future of gender with such hopefulness. I have Robert Roper to thank for the pleasures that begin and end each of our writing days. The book is dedicated to my students and colleagues too numerous to name. But I remember you vividly: the alert faces in the front of the lecture hall, tough questions from the back rows, brilliant exegesis in seminars, incisive commentaries at scholarly conferences, the intense satisfaction of working together (especially on the journal *Feminist Studies*), and the raucous celebrations that followed our successful struggles to put women, sex, and gender on the curriculum—from the State University of New York, Binghamton, to the University of California at Santa Barbara, Irvine, and Berkeley. It has been a pleasure and a privilege. I cannot thank you enough.

INDEX

Abbott, Grace, 176, 183, 189, 212

Abolitionists: and meanings of male and female, 105; proslavery writers' reaction to, 124; and woman suffrage, 129, 178; and gender dichotomy, 147–48, 149; women circulating petitions for, 157–58; and radical abolitionism, 158–59. *See also* Antislavery movement

Abortion rights, 1, 82, 97, 98, 251, 255, 261, 276

Abrams, Sophie, 299

Abzug, Bella, 262

Adams, Abigail, 84, 150, 151

Adams, John, 84, 150, 151

Addams, Jane: and welfare state, 17; and motherhood, 165, 197; preparation of, 167; reform ambitions of, 168; and Hull House, 169–74; relationship with Smith, 170, 270; and democracy, 171, 195–96; and woman suffrage, 179; and Progressive Party, 182; on immigrants, 189; and Wells-Barnett, 193; and Douglas, 225

Africa: internal slave trade of, 104, 106, 110, 112–13, 115; late twentieth century immigrants from, 303

African American men: and white women, 111, 114–15, 117, 136, 137; slave men, 111–12, 114–15, 117, 118–19; citizenship for, 128, 129–30, 162, 188, 189; religious authority of, 129–30, 134; and hegemonic masculinity, 135–36, 138; and Million Man March, 283; unemployment rate of, 284, 287

African Americans: subordination of, 117; and men's religious authority, 129–30; post–Civil War employment of, 131–33; and public sphere, 133–34, 135, 162, 192–93; and middle class, 134, 140, 141, 193;

press of, 138–39; disenfranchisement of, 141–42; rights of, 162; and New Deal programs, 186, 187–88; restricted citizenship for, 188; and voting rights, 252; and unemployment in black inner-city neighborhoods, 284–85. *See also* Slaves and slavery

African American women: and feminine domesticity, 102, 191; and domestic subjugation, 128–29; as women workers, 131, 133, 202, 205–6, 211, 223, 224, 285; and civil society, 134, 163; and feminism, 134, 258; and regimen of sexual restraint, 142; and New Deal programs, 187; and woman suffrage, 189, 193; and political public, 190–94, 248; and civil rights, 192, 248–49; prejudices of, 192–93; alliances with white women, 193, 248; and relations between the sexes, 219–20; and feminine mystique, 239; as inspiration for white women activists, 254; unemployment of, 285; and female-headed households, 286. *See also* Slave women

Age relations: and Amerindians, 23; and kinship ties among slaves, 121; and immigrants, 295–302, 308, 320

AIDS, 274

Aid to Dependent Children, 175, 184, 189

Aid to Families with Dependent Children, 277

Algonquian people, 13, 21, 24, 26, 29, 33–34, 41, 46, 51, 58–59

Alpha Suffrage Club, 182

Amalgamated Clothing Workers, 264

American Antislavery Society, 158–59, 254

American Association of University Women, 248, 260, 261

American Federation of Labor, 185, 261

American Federation of Municipal, State, and County Employees, 261, 315
American Friends Service Committee, 248
American Medical Association, 180–81
American Psychiatric Association, 245–46, 272
American Revolution, 16, 63, 87, 151–52
Amerindian societies: and female chiefs, 13, 21; and gender asymmetry, 13, 28, 32, 40, 51–52; and gender practice, 15, 16, 22–25; political systems of, 23, 36–41, 56, 59, 323; and alternative gender designations, 24, 45, 57; and homosexuality, 24, 45, 268; and sexual division of labor, 25–27, 28, 30, 38, 48, 55; and gender segregation, 27–28, 30, 35; and gender hierarchy, 28, 29, 32–41, 57, 59; and relations of the sexes, 28, 30–32, 34–36, 40, 51–52, 55–56; wealth accumulation in, 28–29, 33, 57; and gender reciprocity, 35–36, 38, 39, 41, 49, 54, 60; population of, 42–43, 54, 57, 107, 109; and women as agents of hostility or reconciliation, 46; alliances of, 49, 50; and leadership, 49–50; and gendered meaning of land, 53; motherhood practices of, 64; resistance to English common law, 70–71; enslavement of enemies, 106; as source of slave labor, 107–9
Amerindian women: and gender hierarchy, 39; and European encounter with Native Americans, 44–45, 46, 47, 48, 52–53, 54, 55–56, 58–59; as *genízaro*, 108. *See also* Corn mothers; Female farmers
Anderson, Mary, 186
Andover Antislavery Society, 147–48
Anthony, Susan B., 129, 193
Antin, Mary, 314
Antislavery movement, 126–27, 147, 158–60. *See also* Abolitionists
Apache tribe, 107
Apple pie: and feminine domesticity, 61, 62, 93, 101–2; as icon, 88, 92, 93, 100, 102, 203, 318

Armstrong, Barbara Nachtrieb, 183, 185–86
Arzner, Dorothy, 227
Asian Americans: and racial formation, 104; rights of, 162; restricted citizenship of, 188, 189; immigrants of pre–Civil War period, 293; as women workers, 294, 298, 307; immigrants of late twentieth century, 294, 303; sex ratio balance of, 297–98; and family relations, 299, 301, 309
Asian Immigrant Women Advocates, 320
Association of Business and Professional Women, 248
Atlanta Neighborhood Union, 190, 192
Atlantic slave trade, 111–13, 116
Aviation, 227–28

Baby boom, 230, 241
Baker, Ella, 254, 255
Baker, Sara Josephine, 217
Ballard, Martha, 71, 87
Baptists, 85, 89, 129–30, 134
Baptist Woman's Convention, 191, 193, 211
Beauvoir, Simone de, 255
Beecher, Catharine, 17, 92–93, 95, 126
Beecher, Henry Ward, 270
Beecher, Lyman, 92
Benedict, Ruth, 209
Berdache, 24, 268
Bethune, Mary McLeod, 192
Birney, Alice, 164
Birth control, 223, 263
Bisexual identity, 274
Bishop, Bridget, 78
Blackfoot tribe, 23, 34, 35, 37
Blackstone, William, 69
Blatch, Harriot Stanton, 177–78, 179, 181
Bonnet, Jeanne, 269
Botume, Elizabeth, 127
Bourdieu, Pierre, 11, 13
Bourne, Eliza Wildes, 83
Bourne, Randolph, 216
Bowen, Louise de Koven, 172, 173–74, 195
Boxer, Barbara, 315

Boyce, Neith, 208, 220, 222
Bradford, William, 68–69, 71
Bradstreet, Anne, 75–76
Brandeis, Elizabeth, 183
Brandeis, Louis, 183
Breckinridge, Sophonisba, 212
Bromley, Dorothy, 204
Brown, William, 118
Bryant, Louise, 208, 216, 217
Bryant, William Cullen, 270
Buneau, Blanche, 269
Burroughs, Nannie, 191
Bushnell, Horace, 93
Butler, Judith, 11
Byrd, William, 47, 116

Cahan, Abraham, 17, 220, 300
California: Amerindians of, 21, 23, 26, 28;
    and European encounter with Native
    Americans, 42–43, 46, 48, 50, 51; Amer-
    indians as slave labor in, 107; and woman
    suffrage, 177, 178; housing in, 231
Cambodian immigrants, 310
Cameron, Rebecca, 141
Carter, Angela, 4–5
Carter, Jimmy, 278
Carter, John, 259
Catawba nation, 21, 57
Catt, Carrie Chapman, 61, 62, 178
Cavalleri, Rosa, 295, 300
Census records, 97, 205–6, 264, 298
Chandler, Elizabeth Margaret, 126, 159
Chapman, Maria, 159
Chávez, César, 316
Cherokee tribe, 23, 25–26, 29, 33–34, 52–53,
    55–56, 58, 60, 70–71
Chicago Woman's Club, 165, 172–74, 194
Chicano Student Movement, 258, 316
Chickasaw tribe, 23, 29
Child, Lydia Maria, 17, 91, 159
Child care: and feminist union members,
    248; and National Organization for
    Women, 251; and women's liberation
    movement, 255, 256, 262; bill on, 260;

and inequality between women, 285–86;
    and immigrants, 303, 310, 314, 316
Child custody, 69, 98
Child-rearing. See Parenting
Children: and female wages, 2; Puritan at-
    titudes toward, 73–74; and Methodist
    ministry, 89; of slaves, status of, 106,
    108, 114–15, 116, 123; and bonds with par-
    ents during slavery, 119–20, 123–24; and
    post–Civil War labor arrangements, 131;
    and child labor, 172, 180, 298, 299, 307,
    312; social welfare programs for, 175–76,
    183–84; African American social services
    for, 190; women's responsibility for, 197;
    women workers interrupting work for,
    205, 206, 229, 234–35, 236, 237; and
    relations of the sexes, 217; streamlined
    care of, 223–24; and women's social activ-
    ism, 249; and family pluralism, 279;
    and female-headed households, 286; and
    immigration, 294, 298, 299, 304, 309,
    310, 313. See also Illegitimate children
Children's Bureau, 175–76, 177, 178, 179,
    183–84, 223
Child Study Movement, 97
Chin, Frank, 302
China, 101, 296
Chinese Americans, 297–98, 301, 302, 303,
    307, 309, 310–11, 314
Chinese Exclusion Act of 1882, 293, 298
Chipewyan tribe, 31
Chippewa tribe, 26
Chisolm, Shirley, 258
Choctaw tribe, 23, 29, 31–32, 37, 41, 51, 323
Chopin, Kate, 208
Chumash tribe, 21, 34
Cisneros, Sandra, 320–21
Citizenship: constitution of, 16; and Amer-
    indian societies, 56; and gender hier-
    archy, 62; and feminine domesticity, 93,
    94, 96–97, 101; for African American
    men, 128, 129–30, 162, 188, 189; gender
    identity of, 148, 149, 150, 152, 188; and
    patrilineal political system, 149; equated

with masculinity, 149, 150, 152, 157, 159, 162; and state constitutions, 154–55; relationship to suffrage, 156; and mark of gender difference, 197; and immigration, 314, 316. *See also* Women's citizenship

Civil rights: and Jim Crow, 137, 141, 254; and African American's social citizenship, 188; and African American women, 192, 248–49; and women's liberation movement, 252, 253, 254, 262; and immigration, 315

Civil Rights Act, 250–51, 260, 261, 290

Civil society, 134, 158, 162–64, 165, 166, 168, 176

Civil War, 105, 126, 127, 128–29, 160, 268. *See also* North; South

Claire, Teddy, 215

Clan Mothers, 17, 40, 41, 61, 323–24

Clan structure, 29–30

Clinton, Hillary, 101

Coalition of Labor Union Women, 261

Coffey, Karen Ann, 323–24

Cohen, Fannia, 225

Cold War, 62–63, 232–33

College Equal Suffrage League, 178

College Settlement, 168

Colonial period: witch hunts of, 16, 77–80, 100; and gender frontier, 43; as prehistory of feminine domesticity, 63, 64–80; and common law, 69–71; women's social networks in, 71–72, 74; birth rate in, 73; conjugal bond in, 73, 75; illegitimate children in, 81; and racial formation in South, 104; labor shortages of, 109–10; and formation of independent government, 149–50. *See also* European encounter with Native Americans; New England Protestants

Columbus, Christopher, 64, 106, 110

Comanche tribe, 107

Commissions on the Status of Women, 249–50, 251, 260, 315

Committee of Economic Security, 183

Common law, 69–71

Communism, 181

Computer industry, 311–12

Comstock, Sarah, 212

Confederacy of the Five Civilized Tribes, 41

Confrontation politics, 195

Congregationalists, 85, 89

Congress of Racial Equality (CORE), 254

Conjugal bond: in Amerindian societies, 30–31, 32; in colonial society, 73, 75; and slave families, 119, 121, 122; and freedwomen, 128–29. *See also* Marriage

Consciousness-raising groups, 253, 258–59

Consumer goods, 214–15, 230–31, 233–34

Converse, Florence, 170

Cook, Eliza, 131

Coolidge, Calvin, 181

Corbin, Hannah Lee, 151

Corn mothers: and gender parity, 35, 39, 40, 42, 60; and European encounter with Native Americans, 49, 52; and land, 53, 70; feminine domesticity contrasted with, 64; and Virgin of Guadalupe, 291

Corporate culture, 16–17

Costanoan tribe, 26, 27

Cotton, John, 67, 73

Coxe, Margaret, 93

Crawford, Joan, 211, 227

Credit, 188, 260

Creek tribe, 23, 29, 33

Cuban immigrants, 307

Cummins, Maria, 94

Dakota tribe, 26, 28

Dance halls, 211, 219–20

Dating, 220, 263

Daughters of Bilitis, 267

Daughters of liberty, 84–88, 101, 151

Daughters of the American Revolution, 176

Declaration of Independence, 150

Delaware tribe, 51, 53

Dell, Floyd, 220

Democracy, 93, 94, 171, 195–96, 253

Democratic National Convention, 260

Democratic Party, 138, 141–42, 157, 159, 162, 175, 181–82, 260

Demography, 80–82, 97, 100, 230

De Soto, Hernando, 21, 22, 40

Dewey, John, 195, 222

Dialectic of sex, 255

Divorce: in Amerindian societies, 30–31, 40; and freedwomen, 129; rate of, 235, 265, 278, 283; and gender equality, 251; and immigration, 310, 313, 314, 317

Domesticity: post–World War II, 231–33, 242–43; masculine, 233, 235. *See also* Feminine domesticity

Domestic service, 209, 224, 247, 285, 303, 309, 312–13

Domestic/sexual abuse, 86, 122, 128, 129, 310, 312, 316

Domestic slave market, 113–14, 116, 119

Douglas, Dorothy, 225, 240, 241

Douglass, Frederick, 122–23

Drake, Francis, 64

Dreier, Mary, 170

Dreiser, Theodore, 208

Du Bois, W. E. B., 192

Duke, Jesse C., 139

Dutch colonies, 70

Earhart, Amelia, 227

Eastern European immigrants, 294, 296, 304, 307, 314

Eastman, Crystal, 179, 216–17

Edwards, Jonathan, 87

Eggertsen, Esther, 225

Elizabeth I (queen of England), 64, 75–76, 149

Ellis, Havelock, 271

Emancipation Proclamation, 105, 107

Emerson, Margaret, 219

Emerson, Ralph Waldo, 270

Engels, Frederick, 57, 167

English colonies, 69–71, 109–10, 149–50

Enlightenment, 158, 164

Equal Economic Opportunity Commission (EEOC), 250–51

Equality League of Self-Supporting Women, 177–78

Equal Rights Amendment, 248, 249, 250, 260, 261, 262, 276

Erdich, Louise, 324

Ethnic groups, 229, 295, 298, 300–301, 317–18, 320–22, 324. *See also* Immigrants and immigration; Racial minorities

European encounter with Native Americans: and gender history, 9–10, 15; and gender roles, 16; and gender practice, 21–22; and gender hierarchy, 22, 41, 42; and relations of the sexes, 22, 44, 46, 51, 54, 59; and Amerindian sexual division of labor, 26; and gender frontier, 42–48, 59; and epidemic diseases, 43, 48, 54, 59, 109; and sexuality, 43–48, 104; and intermarriage, 46–47, 58, 104; and Amerindian leadership, 49–50; and syncretism of religious symbols, 52–53; and racial formation, 104

Europeans: landless urban poor as labor source, 107; as immigrants, 293–94, 296, 300–302, 304, 307, 314, 315

European Union, 293

Fair Labor Standards Act, 184, 185

Family relations: and feminine domesticity, 3, 63, 68; and relations of the sexes, 61; and feminine identity, 62; in early modern era, 65; and political issues, 65–67, 68; and position of women in Puritan households, 67–68, 72; and New Englanders' alterations to common law, 69–70; and icons of motherhood, 89; and slavery, 119–22; and freedmen and women, 129, 130, 131, 132; and women workers, 203, 206, 225, 227–38, 241; and homemaker/breadwinner roles, 235, 237; and married women workers, 237; women's independence from, 264, 265; and family pluralism, 278–79; and family instability, 287; and immigration, 294, 298–99, 301, 309. *See also* Kinship relations

Fatherhood, 65–66, 69, 85, 98, 119–22, 283. *See also* Motherhood

Fauset, Jessie, 290

Federal Emergency Relief Association, 184

Federal Housing Authority, 232

Federation of Colored Women's Clubs, 194

Feinstein, Dianne, 272, 315

Felton, Rebecca, 141

Female Anti-slavery Society, 126

Female farmers, 26, 32, 40, 43, 49, 51–54, 64

Female-headed households, 121, 149, 283, 285, 286, 287, 313, 314

Female Moral Reform Societies, 90–91, 101

Female wages: and welfare of children, 2; and cost of living, 207; and independence, 209–10; and leisure, 210–11; and strikes, 212, 213; gender inequity in, 225–26, 243, 248, 264, 280, 286; as discouragement for women workers, 233; and equal pay, 251, 264; and feminism, 259; increases in, 284; and immigrants, 312–13

Female warriors, in Amerindian societies, 24–25, 49

Feminine domesticity: and family relations, 3, 63, 68; and popular culture, 3, 100, 101, 205; and Protestant New England, 10, 63–64, 89; as separate sphere, 15; and motherhood, 61, 62, 93, 96, 100, 124; values of, 62; and household labor of women, 62, 63, 91–92, 94; and middle class, 62, 63, 94, 95, 97, 100, 101, 102; cultural power of, 62–63, 99–100, 102; and Cold War, 62–63, 232–33; and print culture, 63, 89, 90, 92–95, 96; religious influence on, 89–90; imperialistic pretensions of, 101–2; and African American women, 102, 191; and antislavery movement, 126; and Civil War, 128; and commonsense school of moral philosophy, 153; and woman suffrage, 188; revival of, 205; post–World War II, 231–33, 242–43; and women's education, 246; and women's social activism, 249

Femininity: conventions of, 5; as social construction, 10; and Amerindian societies, 33, 34; and family attachments, 62; and women workers, 206; and feminine mys

tique, 238–44, 254; and lesbians, 267; heterogeneous standards of, 292

Feminists and feminism: and women's advances, 1; and sex difference, 2, 3; and gender analysis, 8, 10–11, 197–98, 287, 290; and Amerindian societies, 38; and feminine domesticity, 61; and Bradstreet, 76; and African American women, 134, 258; and rift with maternalists, 181; and women workers, 205; and maternalism, 207; and Heterodoxy Club, 216; and modernism, 220; and housework, 224; and trade unions, 225–26, 240; second wave of, 247, 248–65, 302, 315; and protectionists and individualists, 249, 250; and protofeminist consciousness, 250; youthful, 251–52; background of new, 253–54; ideology of, 256; as mass movement, 261–63; and transsexuality, 275; backlash against, 276; and lack of male counterparts, 283; and immigration, 315; and Virgin of Guadalupe, 317–18; third wave of, 321. See also Women's liberation movement

Fenstermaker, Sarah, 11

Fern, Fanny, 94

Fertility rates, 223, 229–30, 243, 277

Fifteenth Amendment, 128, 129, 156

Filmer, Robert, 65

Fiorina, Carly, 311

Firestone, Shulamith, 255

Fitzgerald, F. Scott, 221, 222

Five Civilized Tribes, 23, 29, 41

Flappers, 206, 211–12, 227, 264

Flynn, Elizabeth Gurley, 216, 217

Foley, Margaret, 213

Ford Foundation, 237–38

Foster, Hannah, 87–88

Foucault, Michel, 16

Fourteenth Amendment, 128, 161, 250

Franciscans, 44, 45, 46, 47, 48, 52

Frank, Leo, 138

Franklin, Benjamin, 84, 87, 150

Franklin, Deborah, 84

Free blacks, 116, 121, 122

Freedman, Rose Rosenfeld, 201, 202, 205
Freedmen and women, 128–32
Freedmen's Bureau, 130, 131, 136
Free Soil movement, 127
Free Soil Party, 159
Free Speech Movement, 255
French and Indian War, 49
French colonies, 108–9
Freud, Sigmund, 239, 255, 266, 271
Friedan, Betty Goldstein, 239–43, 251, 252, 264

Galang, M. Evelina, 321
Gallman, Lucy, 131
Garment factories, 212–13, 225
Garrison, William Lloyd, 126, 159
Gay Academic Union, 267
Gay Liberation Front, 267
Gay men: and practice of human sexuality, 247; rights of, 265–76; gender distinctions among, 269, 271–72; and formation of families, 279; and gender changes, 290. *See also* Lesbians
Gender: use of term, 6, 253, 255; acceptance of notion of, 6–7; as social construction, 9, 10; duality of, 9, 11; sex distinguished from, 10–11, 245; as performative, 11, 245; historical weight of, 13; and postmodernism, 16, 247, 277, 281, 287, 290, 294; changes in, 105, 128–29, 276–87, 290, 294, 296, 298, 305, 322–23; and passing women, 268–69; lack of correspondence with sexuality, 274
Gender asymmetry: and sex difference, 13; and Amerindian societies, 13, 28, 32, 40, 51–52; and European encounter with Native Americans, 22; and homemaker/breadwinner roles, 62, 99, 202, 228, 233, 235, 237, 251; in Puritan households, 74; and sexual morality, 76; during American Revolutionary era, 87; and masculine side of domesticity, 99; of slavery, 117, 122–23; and antislavery movement, 147; and public sphere, 147–48, 160–63, 165, 166–67, 171, 246; in

New Deal programs, 184–87; and privacy, 198; and women workers, 202; and women's education, 241; and changes in balance of power, 247, 281, 286; and National Organization for Women, 251; and feminism, 265; and homosexuality, 266, 268, 269, 270
Gender continuity, 246–47
Gender dimorphism, 24, 270, 274
Gender equality, 251, 255, 262, 281, 321
Gender geography, 30, 263–64, 292
Gender hierarchy: and European encounter with Native Americans, 22, 41, 42; and Amerindian societies, 28, 29, 32–41, 57, 59; and political issues, 33, 84, 281; complex nature of, 62, 287; and religion, 64, 66, 77, 85–86, 129–30, 134; in early modern era, 64–65; and Puritans, 65–68, 72–76, 79; and slavery, 117, 122–23; of planters, 125–26; and Reconstruction, 129–30; fundamental rearrangements of, 247; and gay rights, 266; and female wages, 280, 286; and immigration, 295–96, 322; and computer industry, 311–12
Gender history, 7, 14–15, 33
Gender identities: blending of, 5, 275, 276; and sex as gendered, 10–11; acceptance of, 17; and immigration, 17, 298, 321; and Amerindian societies, 27; of citizenship, 148, 149, 150, 152, 188; and social reform, 173; social construction of, 245; challenges to, 245–46; and gay identity, 272, 274; and transsexuality, 275; and popular culture, 276, 282, 283
Gender identity disorder, 245–46
Gender outlaws, 5
Gender practice: as discipline, 11–12; and rules of the game, 14; and Amerindian societies, 15, 16, 22–25; and power relations, 16; and European encounter with Native Americans, 21–22; and racial boundaries, 104; and slavery, 121; and relations of the sexes, 217; effect of immigration on, 294, 298. *See also* Gender

asymmetry; Gender hierarchy; Relations of the sexes

Gender reciprocity: and Amerindian societies, 35–36, 38, 39, 41, 49, 54, 60; and marriage, 73

Gender segregation: and Amerindian societies, 27–28, 30, 35; of political public, 149; in labor market, 280

Gender shock, 294

General Federation of Women's clubs, 163, 197

Genízaro, 107–8

George III (king of England), 150

G.I. Bill, 232, 233

Gilliway, Alexander, 57

Gilman, Charlotte Perkins, 166, 197, 216

Girl Scouts, 261

Gish, Lillian, 208

Glaspell, Susan, 208

Global restructuring of economy, 290, 292–93, 314

Goddard, Mary, 84

Gold, Herbert, 300

Goldblum, Ruth, 228

Goldman, Emma, 216, 217

Goldmark, Josephine, 175

Gold Mountain, 297–98

Goode, Sarah, 78

Gouge, William, 65

Graham, Isabella, 163

Grand Army of the Republic, 160

Great Awakening, 85

Great Depression, 203, 204, 205, 222, 223, 228

Great Fire of 1871, 174

Griffith, D. W., 208

Griffiths, Martha, 250

Grimké, Angelina, 126, 159

Grimké, Sarah, 159

Gross National Product, 231

Gutierrez, Juana, 318

Habermas, Jürgen, 148, 195

Hale, Sarah Josepha, 17, 94

Hall, G. Stanley, 271

Hall, Murray, 17, 268–69

Hamer, Fannie Lou, 258

Hamilton, Alexander, 150

Hanisch, Carol, 256

Hapgood, Hutchins, 220, 222

Harper, Frances, 129, 134, 143, 191–92

Hayden, Casey, 252–53, 254, 255

Heckler, Margaret, 262

Hemings, Sally, 116

Hemingway, Ernest, 282

Henry Street Settlement, 168

Hepburn, Katharine, 227–28

Hermaphrodites, 271

Hernández, Ester, 317–18

Heterodoxy Club, 216, 220, 225, 270

Heterosexuality, 9, 266, 267, 268, 274, 276

Heterosocial culture, 215–21

Hibbens, Anne, 78

Hidatsa tribe, 27

Highway Act of 1956, 232

Hillman, Bessie Abramowitz, 225

Hillman, Sidney, 225

Hispanics: and female-headed households, 286; as immigrants, 303, 307. *See also* Mexican Americans

Hitler, Adolf, 224, 229

Hmong immigrants, 305, 310

Homemaker/breadwinner roles: and separate spheres, 15, 233, 277; and gender asymmetry, 62, 99, 202, 228, 233, 235, 237, 251; and masculinity, 221; and women workers, 222, 241; costs of, 234–35, 237; breaking down of, 277, 278, 281, 284

Homosexuality: and Amerindian societies, 24, 45, 268; and mental health, 245; and gay rights, 247, 265–76; and gender asymmetry, 266, 268, 269, 270; history of, 268–72; and gender distinctions, 269–71, 272; and homosexual partners, 278. *See also* Gay men; Lesbians

Homosocial culture, 221

Hooker, Thomas, 72

Hoover, Herbert, 181

Hope, John, 192

Hope, Lugenia, 190

Hopi tribe, 37

Hopkins, Harry, 184

Household labor of women: and feminine domesticity, 62, 63, 91–92, 94; proportion of, 62, 283, 314; and trade, 71, 76, 82–84, 91, 92, 100–101; in colonies, 71–72; post–World War II increase in, 234; women's discontent with, 235, 265; and gender continuity, 246–47; and immigration, 298, 304

Households: restricted patriarchal, 65; connection necessary for land, 66; position of women in Puritan, 67–68, 72; female-headed, 121, 149, 283, 285, 286, 287, 313, 314; authority over, in South, 124; status of freeman to adult heads of, 149; two-worker, 278, 286, 287, 305, 307, 308, 310, 313

Housework, 206, 224, 234, 255, 256, 283, 310. See also Household labor of women

Huerta, Dolores, 316

Hull House, 167–71, 172, 175, 193, 194

Hunter, Caroline, 120

Huron tribe, 25, 30, 31–32, 41, 45, 54, 268

Hurst, Fannie, 208

Hurston, Zora Neale, 219

Hutchinson, Anne, 77

Illegitimate children: in colonial period, 81; and criminal prosecution of mothers, 86; and risks of sexual independence, 87, 101; and forced servitude of Amerindians, 107, 108; and white women's relationships with African bondmen, 111, 117; rise of, in 1890s, 218; rise of, in twentieth century, 265, 278, 283; and immigration, 314

Immigrants and immigration: and sex difference, 16; and gender identities, 17, 298, 321; and feminine domesticity, 101; and racial formation, 104; and voting rights, 162; and settlement houses, 170, 171, 173; and woman suffrage, 178; and condescending social reform, 189–90;

and women's education, 210, 301, 303, 306; and birth control, 223; and fertility groups, 229; and gender changes, 290, 294, 296, 298, 305, 322–23; and religion, 291–92, 298, 300, 316, 317–18; and U.S. immigration policy, 293; and sexual division of labor, 294, 296, 297–300, 307, 308, 310; and patriarchy, 295–96, 299, 301, 303, 306, 311; and generations of gender, 295–302, 308, 320; and sex ratio balance, 296–97, 303, 304; and post-modernity, 302–14; diversity of, 303; and two-worker households, 305, 307, 308; and trade unions, 314, 316–17, 318, 320, 323

Immigrant women workers: unmarried daughters as, 202; and white-collar jobs, 210, 228–29, 238; and leisure, 211; and heterosocial culture, 217; and domestic service, 247; and child care costs, 286; and postmodern conditions, 294; and working mothers, 298, 303, 307, 309, 313; and patch-working, 298–99; educational level of, 304; adaptability of, 305–6; and working identity, 307–8; independence of, 308–9; and relation of the sexes, 310–11; and female wages, 312–13; and trade unions, 316–17

Immigration Act of 1965, 302

Imperialism, 101–2, 255

Indenture, 106, 108, 110, 111, 113, 115

Indian Americans, 305, 310, 311, 315

Industrialization, 99, 116

Infanticide, 40, 86

Infant mortality, 118, 176

Inheritance laws, 69–71, 76, 78, 114

Institute for Human Development, 236

International Brotherhood of Electrical Workers (IBEW), 217, 225

International Ladies' Garment Workers' Union, 185, 213

International Order of Redmen, 99

Intimacy, 220, 221–22

Inuit tribe, 23–24

Iraq war, 1

Irish Americans, 107, 210, 296

Iroquois, 23, 29, 30, 36, 37–38, 41, 49, 57

Irwin, Elizabeth, 217

Isabella I (queen of Spain), 64

Israels, Belle Lindner, 215

Italian immigrants, 189, 228, 229, 296, 297, 298, 299, 301–2

Jackson, Andrew, 156

Jacobs, Harriet, 123

Jamaican immigrants, 306–8

Jane Club, 171

Jane Collective, 261

Japanese immigrants, 301, 302, 304

Jefferson, Thomas, 55, 56, 84, 116, 118, 150, 153

Jemison, Mary, 27

Jen, Gish, 322

Jesuits, 44, 45, 46, 54

Jewish Socialist Labor Bund, 296

Jews, 10, 102, 229, 294, 295, 296, 299, 300, 301, 306

Jim Crow system, 137, 141, 142, 188, 191, 206, 254

Jobs, Steve, 311

Johnson, James Weldon, 217

Johnson, Virginia, 266

Jones, Anna, 192

Jorgenson, Christine, 275

Ka, Shui Mak, 302

Kaiser, Henry, 231

Kelley, Florence, 166, 167, 169, 172, 181, 197

Kellor, Frances, 170

Kelsey, Lula Spaulding, 191

Kennan, George, 232

Kennedy, John F., 249

Kenney, Mary, 171

Kerrey, Robert, 282

Key, Elizabeth, 114

Khrushchev, Nikita, 63, 232

King, Martin Luther, Jr., 254

King, Mary, 252–53, 254, 255, 263

King, Sieh, 296

Kingston, Maxine Hong, 295, 301

Kinsey, Alfred, 218

Kinship relations: and Amerindian societies, 23; and maternal lines of descent, 29–30, 55; and Thanksgiving Day, 61; and patriarchy, 66–67; flexibility of, 106; and slavery, 114, 121–22; and monarchical states, 149. See also Family relations

Koedt, Anne, 266

Korean immigrants, 296, 304–5, 307

Korean Immigrant Workers Advocates, 318

Kovic, Ron, 282

Krafft-Ebing, Richard von, 271

Ku Klux Klan, 135, 136, 138, 142, 188, 189

Labor force: and incentive to enslave, 106–9; recruitment from Europe, 109; shortages of, in colonial period, 109–10; and masculine nature of seventeenth slavery, 111; and African Americans in post–Civil War period, 131–33; changes in, 202–3, 277–78, 280, 284; factors affecting, 203–4; and two-worker households, 278, 286, 287, 305, 307, 308, 310, 313; and global restructuring of economy, 293. See also Men workers; Women in labor force; Women workers

Labor movement. See Trade unions

Ladies' Home Journal, 176, 227, 241, 259

Ladies' Repository, The, 89, 90

Laissez-faire economics, 174, 175, 184, 195

Lakota tribe, 57

Lamphere, Louise, 83

Land: Amerindian ownership of, 29; gendered meaning of, 53; household connection necessary for, 66; as private family property, 68–71, 100; patriarchal inheritance of, 69–71, 76, 78; and demographic crisis in New England, 80–81

Lange, Dorothea, 225

Laotian immigrants, 294, 295, 305

Larsen, Nella, 209

Lathrop, Julia, 176, 179, 197

Latin American immigrants, 104, 294, 303

League of Women Voters, 183, 248, 260

Lease, Mary Elizabeth, 182

Lee, Richard Henry, 151

Leisure, 210–11, 215–20

Le Jeune, Paul, 36

Lemlich, Clara, 212, 213, 215

Lenroot, Katharine, 176, 183

Lesbians: and practice of human sexuality, 247; rights of, 251, 262, 266, 274; and femininity, 267; in urban areas, 269–70; in Victorian period, 270–71; and rigid social roles, 271; and formation of families, 279; and gender changes, 290; and immigrants, 316; and Virgin of Guadalupe, 318, 320. *See also* Gay men

Levinsky, David, 220

Liberal Club, 212, 216, 220

Liberalism, 153, 158

Liberty Party, 159

Life expectancy, increase in, 224, 279

Life magazine, 231, 238

Lincoln, Abraham, 127, 270

Linnaeus, Carl, 103, 104

Literacy, 84, 101

Literacy tests, 141

Lobdel, Lucy, 268–69

Locke, John, 153

López, Yolanda, 318

Lowther, Henry, 135–36

Lucas, Victoria, 242

Luhan, Mabel Dodge, 220

Lundeen, Ernest, 183–84

Lynching, 105, 136, 137, 138, 139–43, 189, 191, 194

Madison, Dolley, 154

Madonna figures, 300–301, 318, 320

Mailer, Norman, 282

Male breadwinning. *See* Homemaker/ breadwinner roles

Male chauvinism, 255

Male dominance, 9–10

Male supremacy, 255

Male wages, 202, 284, 298

Male warriors, in Amerindian societies, 15, 43, 49, 50–51, 53–54

Mammy stereotype, 102, 118

Manly, Alexander, 140–41

Man-woman, in Amerindian societies, 24–25, 324

Market capitalism, 80, 83–84, 88, 99–100, 101, 125, 230, 290, 292–93

Marks, Jeannette, 270

Marriage: same-sex, 7, 8, 276; in Amerindian societies, 30–31, 45, 54; and Europeans' intermarriage with Native Americans, 46–47, 58, 104; and Puritans, 65; and women's legal rights, 70; and gender reciprocity, 73; arrangement of, 81; age of women at, 97, 222, 229, 278; interracial, 103, 104, 116, 137; and redemption of captive into enslaving culture, 106; enslavement of Amerindians ending with, 108; slave, 119, 120–21; abroad, 120, 121; and freedwomen, 128–29; "Boston marriages," 170, 270; women workers' delay of, 210, 227; importance of, in 1950s, 228; and gender equality, 251; and family pluralism, 278–79; declining rate in 1990s, 283; and immigrants, 304, 317. *See also* Conjugal bond

Married women workers: and working mothers, 197, 204, 236, 238, 239–40, 277, 285–86, 287; and return to domestic responsibilities, 202, 222, 225, 236–37; lack of, in work force, 223; and World War II employment opportunities, 224; lesser work experience of, 226; in post–World War II period, 235–38, 241–42; numbers of, in 1960s and 1970s, 264; numbers of, in 1980s, 277

Marx, Karl, 255

Maryland, 70, 115, 120

Masculine domesticity, 99, 233, 235

Masculinity: conventions of, 5, 282–83; as social construction, 10; and Amerindian societies, 33, 34, 50–52; and domesticity, 99, 233, 235; and political philosophy of North, 127; and African American men, 135–36, 138; citizenship equated with, 149, 150, 152, 157, 159, 162; and bodybuilding, 221; and heterosexual intimacy, 221; and gay men, 267, 268; and Vietnam War protests, 282; heterogeneous standards of, 292; and immigration, 310, 313; and computer industry, 311; military, 322

Massachusetts Bay Colony, 66, 67–68, 72

Massachusetts Body of Liberties, 67, 109

Masters, William, 266

Mather, Cotton, 73

Matrilineal structures: of Amerindian societies, 29–30, 42–43, 51, 53, 54, 55–59; of slavery, 114, 115, 117, 119, 121, 122, 123, 143; of immigrant families, 299–300, 309

Mattachine Society, 266–67

Mayflower, 66

McGinnis, Patricia, 261

Mead, Margaret, 209

Media: and women's liberation movement, 258, 259–60; and sexual freedoms, 276

Men: as subject of history, 6; and settlement houses, 171; and woman suffrage, 178; federal benefits for, 185, 186; and women workers, 203; and intimacy, 221–22; and Vietnam war protests, 248, 282; and gender changes, 282, 283–84, 290; and housework contributions, 283, 310. *See also* African American men

Men's movement, 282

Men workers: in urban areas, 210; and heterosocial culture, 215–17; and private realm, 220; and immigration, 298–99, 303, 306, 307, 309–10, 313–14, 317

Methodists, 85, 89, 90, 129–30, 194, 261

Métis, 58–59, 324

Mexican Americans: and feminism, 258; as immigrants, 312–14, 316–18. *See also* Hispanics

Meyer, Elizabeth, 187

Middle class: and feminine domesticity, 62, 63, 94, 95, 97, 100, 101, 102; and women's legal rights, 98; and masculine domesticity, 99; lack of development in South, 125; planters compared to,

125; and African Americans, 134, 140, 141, 193; gender dichotomy of, 147; and women in civil society, 163, 166, 176; and woman suffrage, 178, 188; and women workers, 201–2, 207, 211, 212, 236; and trade unions, 213; and leisure, 216; and birth control, 223; and fertility rates, 229; and women's discontent with household labor, 235; and National Organization for Women, 251; and homosexuality, 270; and two-worker households, 278, 286, 310, 313; and immigrants, 304

Midwife profession, 71, 74, 122, 176

Millay, Edna St. Vincent, 209

Millet, Kate, 256

Million Man March, 283

Mink, Patsy, 262

Minor v. Happersett (1874), 156

Miscegenation, 103, 104, 105, 136, 143, 304

Misogyny, 31, 42, 51, 153, 268, 322

Mixed-blood population, 46–47, 58–59, 107–8

Modernity, and women workers, 210, 220, 221

Momaday, N. Scott, 324

Montagnais tribe, 36, 54

Moore, Joanna, 173

Moral superiority: and gender hierarchy, 62; and sexual morality, 76; and impact of female moral societies, 90–91; and feminine domesticity, 92; and Progressive Party, 182

Morgan, Julia, 173

Morgan, Lewis Henry, 57

Morgan, Robin, 258

Morris, Jan, 9

Mortgages, 232, 260

Moss, Thomas, 139, 191

Motherhood: and working mothers, 2, 197, 204, 236, 238, 239–40, 277, 285–86, 287, 298, 303, 307, 309, 313; and feminine domesticity, 61, 62, 93, 96, 100, 124; in Amerindian societies, 64; and Puritan practices, 65–66, 73–74; icons of, 88–89, 91–92, 93, 102, 165, 203; and maternal associations, 90, 91; social and religious influence of, 91; and declining family size, 97–98; and changes in family law, 98; and slavery, 119–20, 121, 122, 123–24; and antislavery movement, 147; and civil society, 162, 163–65; and National Congress of Mothers, 163, 164–65; rhetoric of, 165–66, 173, 175, 179; and mothers' pensions, 174, 182, 183, 187, 188, 189; and federal social welfare, 175; and maternal statecraft, 176–77, 180–81, 196–97, 207, 301, 318; and professional advice for mothers, 223; streamlining of, 223–24; post–World War II promotion of, 233; and single mothers, 283; and immigrants, 300–301, 302, 309, 318. *See also* Fatherhood

Ms., 259

Muller v. Oregon (1908), 175

Murray, Judith Sargent, 84, 152

Murray, Pauli, 248–49, 250, 258, 290

Muskogee tribe, 31, 40–41, 42

Nail, Grace, 217

Nash, Diane, 254

National Abortion Rights Action League, 261

National American Woman Suffrage Association, 177, 178

National Association for the Advancement of Colored People (NAACP), 192, 248–49, 254

National Association of Colored Women, 192, 197, 211, 261

National Colored Women's Congress, 192–93

National Congress of Mothers, 163, 164–65, 171, 177, 181

National Federation of Business and Professional Women's Clubs, 260

National Organization for Women (NOW), 251, 258, 260, 261, 265

National Welfare Rights Organization, 261

National Woman's Party, 181, 248

National Women's Political Caucus, 260

Native Americans. *See* Amerindian societies; European encounter with Native Americans

Navajo people, 27, 35, 37, 39, 107

Negro Election Day, 110, 111

Netherlands, 262

New Deal, 175, 183, 184–87

New England Protestants: and feminine domesticity, 10, 63–64, 89; and family ideology of households, 66–68; and private property, 68–71, 100; and alterations to common law, 69–70; and household labor of women, 71–73, 100; and population growth, 73, 112; patriarchal authority in, 74–75, 76, 77; and women's criminal offenses, 76–77; and demography, 80–82, 100; and icons of motherhood, 88–89

New Jersey, 152

New Left, 253, 258, 262, 266

New Mexico, 23

New woman, 206, 214, 215, 239, 241

New York, 156, 158, 177, 178

Nichols, Clarina, 159

Nineteenth Amendment, 188, 196

Nixon, Richard, 63, 232, 233, 260

North: and meanings of male and female slaves, 105; African Creoles in, 110–11; gradual abolition of slavery in, 116; planters' patriarchal society compared to, 125; gender hierarchy in, 126; and miscegenation laws, 136

North Africans, 105

North American Free Trade Agreement, 293

North American Indian Women's Association, 258

North Carolina, 132, 135, 138, 141

Norwood, Hyman, 225

Norwood, Ruth Finkelstein, 225

Notes from the Second Year, 256

O'Keeffe, Georgia, 209, 225

Oliver, Mary, 77

O'Neill, Eugene, 216

Ortner, Sherry, 14, 38, 39
Osbourne, Sarah, 85

Paine, Thomas, 150, 158
Palmer, Bertha Honoré, 172
Parenting: and feminine domesticity, 63,
    96–97, 101, 102; and Puritan households,
    68; and religious press, 90; and religious
    and social influence of motherhood, 91;
    and parent/child bonds during slavery,
    119–20; and National Congress of Moth-
    ers, 164; and Progressive Era, 223; and
    residential site, 231; and rising standards
    of child care, 234; men's contributions to,
    283; and immigration hardships, 294. *See
    also* Fatherhood; Motherhood
Parent-Teachers Association, 164
Park, Kyung, 308
Parks, Rosa, 249
Parris, Samuel, 78
Parsons, Anne, 242, 243, 251
Parsons, Elsie Clews, 217
Patriarchy: and colonial witch hunts, 16,
    77–80, 100; and restricted patriarchal
    households, 65; kinship terminology
    of, 66–67; and patriarchal descent in
    common law, 69–71; as social system,
    74, 124; leveling of, 84; and patrilineal
    slave trade in Africa, 112; and slavery as
    suspension of patrilineal descent, 115;
    and slave families, 119, 120, 122; and
    planters' patriarchal beliefs, 124–25,
    128; and antislavery movement, 126–
    27; and monarchical states, 149, 150; and
    women's liberation movement, 259; and
    immigration, 295–96, 299, 301, 303,
    306, 311
Paul, Alice, 249, 250
Peace, women as advocates of, 161, 163, 263
Peace Corps, 255
Pelosi, Nancy, 315
Perkins, Elizabeth, 67
Perkins, Frances, 183, 185, 186
"Personal is political," 253, 256
Peterson, Esther, 249, 250

Peterson, Oliver, 225
Pettey, Charles, 134
Pettey, Sarah Dudley, 134
Peurala, Alice, 250–51
Philippines, 303, 304, 309
Pink-collar ghetto, 264, 285
Plains tribes, 23, 24, 25, 27, 29, 51
Planters: and meanings of male and female,
    105; productive capacity of slave women
    exploited by, 113, 119; and matrilineal
    descent of slaves, 114, 115; and sexual
    relations with slaves, 116, 119, 131; labor
    policies' effect on slave families, 120–
    21; unequal treatment of slave men and
    women, 122; slave women as trouble-
    some to, 123–24; slaves under family
    government of, 124; patriarchal beliefs of,
    124–25, 128; gender hierarchy of, 125–26;
    and post–Civil War labor arrangements,
    130–32
Plateau people, 25, 30, 37
Plath, Sylvia, 242, 243, 252
Plymouth Colony, 71, 75
Pocahontas, 46, 47, 48
Polacheck, Hilda Satt, 170, 171–72
Political issues: and women's history, 7, 8;
    and separate spheres, 15; and gender hier-
    archy, 33, 84, 281; and immigration, 37,
    314–15, 320; and feminine domesticity,
    62–63; and family relations, 65–67, 68;
    of new republic period, 86, 152; and
    motherhood, 92–94; and planters' mas-
    culine prestige, 125–26; and Civil War,
    126; and sexual hysteria of lynching era,
    137–43; and public realm, 147–48; and
    women's liberation movement, 253, 255–
    56, 259–60, 262; and homosexuality,
    266; and gay rights, 272, 274
Political parties, 156–57, 159, 196
Political public: as wider public realm, 148–
    49, 157–58, 162–63; segregation by sex,
    149; of women in revolutionary era, 151–
    52; and antislavery movement, 158–60;
    and women's gender identity, 162; and
    national associations, 163–65, 174; and

rhetoric of motherhood, 165–66; and settlement houses, 167–74; division by sex, 171; and federal government programs, 174–77, 178, 182, 183; and woman suffrage, 177–81; and influence in third parties, 181–82; women's new roles in, 182–83; and African American women, 190–94, 248; and social reform, 194–96; and Steinem, 243; and rhetoric of feminine stereotypes, 249

Pomo tribe, 36, 39

Pontiac (chief), 41, 50–51

Popular culture: and feminine domesticity, 3, 100, 101, 205; and battle of the sexes, 8; and women workers, 206, 208, 211–12, 227–28, 241; and gender roles, 227–28, 233–34, 241, 242; and gender identities, 276, 282, 283; and gender hierarchy, 280; and Virgin of Guadalupe, 291; and misogyny, 322

Population growth: in colonial period, 73. *See also* Fertility rates

Populists, 138, 141, 142, 182

Portuguese immigrants, 308

Post–World War II domesticity, 231–33, 242–43

Poverty: and strolling poor, 86; women's groups concern with, 162; and settlement houses, 170, 171; and mothers' pensions, 174, 182, 183, 187, 188, 189; and African American women leaders, 192–93; and women workers, 201–2, 223; and women's liberation movement, 262; and working mothers, 277; and child care costs, 286; and two-worker households, 287; and immigration, 313–14

Power relations: and gender practice, 16; and gender hierarchy, 33, 38, 56, 59; and race, 103; and women's influence, 163; and gender asymmetry, 247; and relations of the sexes, 256; and women's liberation movement, 256

Powhatan (chief), 41–42, 47, 49, 59

Premarital conception, 81, 86–87, 90–91, 101

Presbyterians, 89, 90

Print culture, 63, 88–89, 90, 91–95, 96

Progressive Era: and women's clubs, 16; women leaders of, 17, 166–67, 175, 182, 190; and National Congress of Mothers, 165; and women's influence in federal government, 174–76; maternalism of, 176–77, 180–81, 196–97, 207, 301, 318; priorities of, 214; and parenting, 223; and Woman Question, 226

Progressive Party, 182

Prohibition, 269, 272

Prohibition Party, 181–82

Promise Keepers, 283

Property rights, 69, 70, 71, 98, 152, 156, 316

Proslavery apologists, 124, 127, 160

Public sphere: and women's advances, 1, 15, 16, 322; and women in public office, 7, 260, 281, 315; and American political tradition, 15; and African Americans, 133–34, 135, 162, 192–93; and African American women, 143; and gender asymmetry, 147–48, 160–63, 165, 166–67, 171, 246; and men's fraternal relationships, 150–51, 162; women's exclusion from, 153–54, 160, 161–62; and women's ceremonial function, 154; and Children's Bureau, 179; sexual inequality of, 196–97; and gay rights movement, 272. *See also* Political public

Pueblo people, 25, 43, 46, 57–58, 59, 323

Puritans, 64–71, 72, 73–74, 77–79, 92, 253

Putnam, Mary, 78

Putnam, Robert, 163

Putnam, Thomas, Jr., 78

Puzo, Mario, 300

Quakers, 55

Race and racism: and structures of gender, 1; and history of African Americans, 10, 16; and racial justice, 17; concepts of, 103; and shades of skin tone, 103–4; and violence, 135, 136; of women leaders, 189–90; and women's liberation move-

ment, 255; and feminism, 258; and sexual
division of labor, 285; and female-headed
households, 286
Racial boundaries, 103–5, 114–16, 135, 139,
143, 188–89
Racial discrimination, 187–88, 250
Racial equality, 248, 252
Racial formation, 104, 105, 142
Racial minorities, 11, 188–89, 262, 287. *See
also specific minorities*
Racial subordination, 137
Radical Republicans, 189
Rainey, Ma, 209, 211, 219
Rapier, James, 135
Reconstruction, 105, 128, 129–30, 135–36,
138, 139, 161–62
Reed, James, 181
Reed, John, 217
Relations of the sexes: and sex difference, 3,
13; and European encounter with Native
Americans, 22, 44, 46, 51, 54, 59; and
Amerindian societies, 28, 30–32, 34–36,
40, 51–52, 55–56; and family relations,
61; and American Revolution, 63; and
New England Protestants, 75–76, 79–80;
and women's legal rights, 98; and race,
103, 104, 114–15; and Emancipation Proclamation, 105; and slavery, 106, 117, 119,
121–22; and codification of slavery, 114;
and former slaves, 130; and sexual politics of segregation, 142–43; and private
realm, 198, 216–17, 218, 220–22, 253,
256; and homemaker/breadwinner roles,
235; and homosexual rights movement,
247, 265–76; and sex discrimination,
252; and women's liberation movement,
256; and family pluralism, 278, 279–80,
281; and competition, 283–84; symmetry
in, 287; and immigration, 296, 310, 313
Religion: and European encounter with Native Americans, 52–53; and civilizing of
Amerindians, 55; and gender hierarchy,
64, 66, 77, 85–86, 129–30, 134; and
feminine domesticity, 89–90; and civil
society, 162, 168; and political public,

191, 193; and working girls' indepen-
dence, 211; and immigration, 291–92,
298, 300, 316, 317–18. *See also* New
England Protestants; Roman Catholic
Church
Religious authority, 77, 85–86, 88–89,
129–30, 134
Religious press, 90
Reproduction control, 81, 82, 98
Reproductive rights, 243, 256, 262, 263,
276
Republicanism, 153
Republican Party, 127, 134, 138, 141–42, 159,
162, 181–82, 260
Republican wives, 84–88, 93, 101, 154
Reznikoff, Sarah, 301
Right: and challenge to feminism, 262; and
Equal Rights Amendment, 276
Robinson, Jo Ann Gibson, 249
Robinson, Ruby Doris Smith, 254
Rodman, Henrietta, 179, 216
Rodriguez, Richard, 318
Roe v. Wade (1973), 261
Rolfe, John, 46, 47, 48
Roman Catholic Church, 44, 52–53, 59, 64,
66, 107, 261, 291, 300
Roosevelt, Eleanor, 183, 227, 249
Roosevelt, Franklin D., 176, 183, 184, 185,
186
Roosevelt, Theodore, 175, 182
Rosaldo, Michelle Zimbalist, 38
Roth, Henry, 220–21, 300
Rowson, Susanna, 86–87, 88
Rubin, Gayle, 255–56
Rush, Benjamin, 93
Russell Sage Foundation, 183
Russian Revolution, 181

Sahlins, Marshall, 14
Salem witchcraft trials, 77–80, 100
Same-sex marriage, 7, 8, 276
Sánchez, Linda T., 315
Sanchez, Loretta, 315
Sanger, Margaret, 216
Sarria, Jose, 272

Schneiderman, Rose, 300
Scott, Walter, 94
Scudder, Vida, 166, 170
Second Great Awakening, 89
Sedgwick, Catherine, 93
Sedgwick, Theodore, 93
Segregation: by sex, 27–28, 30, 35, 149, 280; by race, 142, 143, 248
Seminole tribe, 23, 27, 29, 57
Seneca tribe, 29, 34, 55, 56
Separate spheres, 15, 98–99, 151, 202–3, 233, 277, 305
Service Employees International Union, 317
Service sector, 203–4, 206, 209–10, 285, 311, 313, 317
Settlement houses, 166, 167–74, 270
Sex changes, and sex difference, 4–5, 9
Sex difference: historical differentiation of, 2–3, 8, 11, 12–13, 14, 15–16; mysterious powers of, 4, 9; and women's liberation movement, 4–5; and gender axes, 13; and gender history, 22; and Amerindian societies, 24, 32; and racial restrictions on citizenship, 188; and homosexual rights movement, 247; and women's social activism, 249. *See also* Gender asymmetry; Gender hierarchy; Relations of the sexes
Sex discrimination, 250, 252–53, 259, 260, 265, 290
Sexism, 255
Sexology, 271
Sexual division of labor: and warfare, 1; and Amerindian societies, 25–27, 28, 30, 38, 48, 55; and feminine domesticity, 99–100; and slavery, 113, 117–19, 118, 122, 127–28; and freedmen and women, 130–32; in revolutionary period, 151; and Progressive Party, 182; and women workers, 202, 204, 285; and dual labor markets, 204; in post–World War II period, 237; and gender inequity, 243–44; and sex discrimination, 252; and child care, 260; and two-worker households, 278; and race and class structures, 285;

and immigration, 294, 296, 297–300, 307, 308, 310
Sexual equality, 250
Sexual frigidity, 234
Sexuality: and sex difference, 3; and power relations, 16; and Amerindian societies, 30–31, 32, 44–45; and European encounter with Native Americans, 43–48, 104; and women's criminal offenses, 76; risks of female, 86–88, 90; and standards of sexual conduct, 90–91, 101; and interracial sex, 105, 114–15, 136, 137–41; of Amerindian women slaves, 108; of white women and African American men, 111, 114–15, 117, 136, 137; and codification of slavery, 114; and relations of the sexes, 218–22; and feminine domesticity, 234; altering physiology of, 245; contest over practice of, 247; and women's liberation movement, 256; premarital, 263; and gay rights, 265–76; lack of correspondence with gender, 274; and immigration, 295. *See also* Heterosexuality; Homosexuality; Transsexuality
Sexual minorities, 11, 274, 322
Sexual orientation, 274. *See also* Heterosexuality; Homosexuality
Sexual politics, 222, 256
Sexual tribute, 31
Shawnee tribe, 34
Sheppard-Towner Act (1925), 175, 176, 177, 179, 180
Singer, I. J., 295
Sioux tribe, 52
Slave men, 111–12, 114–15, 117, 118–19
Slave rebellions, 123
Slaves and slavery: origins of, 16, 105–10; and bondage conveyed through maternal line, 105; as labor source, 106–7, 110; racial definition of, 107, 113; legal definitions of, 110; characteristics of, 110–12; indentured servants compared to, 111, 113; sex ratio of, 111–13, 115; and matrilineal descent of, 114, 115, 117, 119, 121, 123, 143; and interracial sex restrictions, 114–15;

population of, 115; and forced migration, 293. *See also* Planters; Slave men; Slave women

Slave trade: internal African, 104, 106, 110, 112–13, 115; Atlantic, 111–13, 116; and domestic slave market, 113–14, 116, 119

Slave women: Amerindian, 108; and internal African slave trade, 112; and Atlantic slave trade, 112–13; and sexual division of labor, 113, 117–19, 118, 122, 127–28; reproductive capacity of, 113, 118, 119; workday of, 118–19; and motherhood, 119–20, 121, 122, 123–24; and gender hierarchy, 122; reluctance of, to fight or flight, 123; resistance of, 123–24

Smith, Bessie, 209

Smith, Howard, 250

Smith, Howard W., 186

Smith, John, 47

Smith, Mary Rozet, 169, 170, 270

Social class: and settlement houses, 170; and class prejudice of women leaders, 189–90, 192–93; and women workers, 210, 285; and fertility rate, 229; and inequality between women, 285–86; and new class society, 286–87; and immigrants, 303, 305, 312. *See also* Middle class; Poverty; Working class

Socialist Party, 182

Social networks: of colonial women, 71–72, 74; of slavery, 121–22

Social reform: and icons of motherhood, 88–89, 165; and maternal associations, 90, 196; and settlement houses, 167–74; and African Americans, 173; and mothers' pensions, 174, 182, 183, 187, 188, 189; and state welfare system, 174, 183; and federal welfare system, 175, 183–88, 196–97; and trade unions, 194, 213; and political public, 194–96

Social Security Act (1935), 175, 176, 184, 185–87, 188

Social Security Advisory Council, 186

Social Security Board, 184

Social spaces, and feminine domesticity, 63, 94

Society for Humane Abortion, 261

Sons of Liberty, 151

South: birth rate in colonial period, 73; and feminine domesticity, 89; racial formation in colonial period, 104; and meanings of male and female slaves, 105; conditions for gender roles in, 105; labor needs of, 111, 115, 116; and increase in slave labor force, 115; and system of household authority, 124; plantations dominant in, 125; gender hierarchy in, 125–26; Union army's occupation of, 127–28, 131, 136, 137; post–Civil War economic priorities of, 131–32; and miscegenation laws, 136; battle for racial hegemony in, 140–41; and mothers' pensions, 188

South Carolina, 110–11, 118–19, 120, 132

Southeast Asia, 296, 305

Southeastern Federation of Colored Women's Clubs, 193

Southeast tribes, 23, 24, 29, 35

Southern Christian Leadership Conference (SCLC), 254

Southern European immigrants, 294, 307

South Indian immigrants, 304

Southwest tribes, 22–24, 27, 29, 34, 36, 57, 107, 108

Soviet Union, 238, 264, 302, 304

Spaniards, and European encounter with Native Americans, 21, 22, 23, 25

Spanish-American War, 161

Spanish colonies, 70, 107

Spatial asymmetry, 27–28, 30

Spencer, Anna Garlin, 165–66, 175

Spock, Benjamin, 234

Stanton, Elizabeth Cady, 129, 177, 189

Starr, Ellen, 168

Stein, Gertrude, 270

Steinem, Gloria, 243, 259

Stern, Elizabeth, 300

Stevenson, Adlai, 205

Stewart, Maria W., 126

Stieglitz, Alfred, 225

Stonewall riot, 272

Stow, Horatio, 188

Stowe, Harriet Beecher, 61, 92, 94, 95–96, 126–27, 159, 160

Strikes, 212–13, 225

Student Nonviolent Coordinating Committee (SNCC), 252, 253, 254, 263

Students for a Democratic Society (SDS), 253, 254

Sullivan, Jack, 171

Swisshelm, Jane Grey, 159

Tamayo, Lucrecia, 308

Tappan brothers, 159

Taylor, Edward, 75

Taylor, Paul, 225

Tecumseh (chief), 41, 50, 51, 53

Telephone workers, 212, 213, 217, 225

Temperance movement, 91, 99. *See also* Woman's Christian Temperance Union

Temple Benevolent Society of St. Thomas, 163

Tenkwatawa (Algonquian prophet), 51–52

Terrell, Mary Church, 191–92

Textile factories, 116, 212

Thai and Latino Workers Organizing Committee, 320

Third World Women's Alliance, 258

Thomas, Clarence, 143

Tillman, Ben, 137, 138, 142

Timothy, Elizabeth, 84

Tocqueville, Alexis de, 93, 163

Townsend, Julia, 219

Trade: and Amerindian societies, 23, 29, 40; and European encounter with Native Americans, 51, 52, 104; and household labor of women, 71, 76, 82–84, 91, 92, 100–101; and growth of market capitalism, 80; and feminine domesticity, 95–96; and slave women, 119. *See also* Slave trade

Traders, 46, 58

Trade unions: and social reform, 194, 213; and Triangle fire of 1911, 201; rise of, 203; and strikes, 212–13, 225; and heterosocial culture, 217–18; and wages and benefits, 233; and feminism of union women, 240, 261; and female organizers' leadership, 248; and declining union jobs, 284; and immigrants, 314, 316–17, 318, 320, 323

Transgender, 5, 274

Transsexuality, 275

Transvestites, 269, 272

Triangle Shirtwaist Factory fire of 1911, 201

True womanhood, 164, 228

Truman, Harry, 232

Truth, Sojourner, 129

Turner, Nat, 123

Tyler, Mary, 83

Union army, 127–28, 131, 136, 137, 163

Unions. *See* Trade unions

Union veterans, 161–62

United Auto Workers, 226

United Farm Workers, 316

United Nations, 315

U.S. Army, 261, 305

U.S. Congress, 178, 184, 260, 281, 315

U.S. Constitution, 152–53, 154, 177. *See also specific amendments*

U.S. government: and Indian territory, 54–55; impact of Civil War on, 160; women's Progressive Era influence on, 174–76; and federal welfare, 183–86; and women in labor force, 224; and low-cost mortgages, 232; women's presence in, 281; and immigration policy, 293, 302

U.S. Sanitary Commission, 160, 163

U.S. Supreme Court: and women's advances, 1; and interracial marriage, 103, 104; and Thomas, 143; definition of citizenship, 156; and federal social welfare legislation, 175; and school segregation, 248; and feminism, 260–61; and women's presence, 281

Universal Declaration of Human Rights, 315

Universal rights, 158, 164

Urban areas: residential architecture of, 96; and feminine domesticity, 97, 100; and women's legal rights, 98; of South, 125; and women workers, 207, 208–11; and women's liberation movement, 256, 258; and police harassment of homosexuals, 266, 272; overt homosexuality in, 269–70, 271; and African American unemployment, 284–85

Van Kleeck, Mary, 183–84
Venereal disease, 43, 48
Victorian period, 16, 17, 164, 170, 197, 202, 228, 234, 270–71
Vidal, Gore, 5
Vietnamese immigrants, 298–99, 306, 307, 309, 310
Vietnam War, 248, 282, 305
Violence: and race, 135, 136; and lynching, 137–41
Virginia, 103–5, 109–11, 113, 114–15, 120
Virginia Company, 59, 109, 110
Virgin of Guadalupe, 291–92, 300, 316, 317–18, 320
Vorse, Mary Heaton, 209

Waddell, Alfred Moore, 141
Wagner Act, 184
Wald, Lillian, 168, 179
Walker, David, 122–23
Wampanoag tribe, 53
Ware, Jourdan, 136
Warfare, as male realm, 1, 160–61, 203, 228
Warner, Susanna, 94
War of Independence, 151–52
Warren, Mercy Otis, 84, 151, 152
Washington, Booker T., 192
Washington, George, 150, 154
Wealth: in Amerindian societies, 28–29, 33, 57; and inequality between women, 286
Weber, Max, 191
Weld, Theodore, 270
Welfare: and mothers, 102, 196; state system

of, 174, 183; and federal system of, 175, 183–88, 196–97; rights, 262
Welles, Sarah, 83–84
Wells-Barnett, Ida B., 17, 139–40, 142–43, 182, 191–92, 193
West, Candace, 11
West, political philosophy of, 126, 127
Wharton, Edith: *House of Mirth*, 208
Whigs, 156, 157, 159
White, Lynn, 205
White-collar jobs, and women workers, 210, 226, 228–29, 230, 238, 264, 284, 285
White domination, 105, 122–23
Whitehead, Harriet, 38
White supremacy, 137, 142, 143
Whitman, Elizabeth, 87
Whitman, Walt, 270
Widows, 69–71, 86, 98, 149, 151, 190, 202, 264
Wigglesworth, Michael, 74
Willard, Frances, 142–43, 165, 170, 173, 182, 189
Wills, 70, 78. *See also* Inheritance laws
Wilmington, N.C., riot in, 140–41
Wilson, James, 152
Wilson, Woodrow, 175
Winant, Howard, 13
Winnebago tribe, 52
Winthrop, John, 67, 73, 77
WITCH (Women's International Conspiracy from Hell), 259
Witch hunts, 16, 77–80, 100
Wolfgang, Myra, 225
Wollstonecraft, Mary, 153, 158, 315
Womanpower, 237–38
Woman's Christian Temperance Union, 142, 161, 163, 165, 170, 172–73, 182, 189, 193
Woman suffrage: and abolitionists, 129, 178; achievement of, 149, 177–80, 226; lack of consideration for, 153–54, 156; and liberalism, 158, 164; and women distinguished from racial minorities, 188–89; and African American women, 189, 193; and women workers, 212, 214;

and second wave of feminism, 248; and
immigrants, 314

Women in labor force: and feminine domesticity, 102; and Fair Labor Standards Act,
185; and unemployment insurance, 185;
and Social Security Act, 186; and causation schemes, 203–6; opposition to, 204,
223, 225, 227; and census records, 205–
6, 207; in post–World War II period, 233,
235–36; in early twenty-first century, 247;
and feminism, 263, 264; in late twentieth century, 277; as competition for men,
283–84; and sexual division of labor, 285;
inequality between, 285–86, 287; and
outsourcing of American jobs, 314. *See
also* Slave women; Women workers

Women's Army Corps, 270

Women's Bureau, 186, 226, 249

Women's citizenship: and patrilineal political
system, 149; in republican era, 150–
54; state constitutions' limits on, 154,
156; and woman suffrage, 156, 177; and
marginalization of women, 160, 163, 188;
and civil society, 162–64, 165, 166; and
women's education, 166, 168; and gender asymmetry, 166–67; and settlement
houses, 171; and federal government,
174–75; and children's interests, 179; and
sex discrimination, 188–89

Women's Council of the Methodist Episcopal
Church, 194

Women's criminal offenses, 76–77

Women's education: women's rights to,
152; and women's citizenship, 166, 168;
and women reformers, 167; and urban
women of middle classes, 207; and immigrants, 210, 301, 303, 306; and gender
practice, 217; and female wages, 226;
and feminine mystique, 240–43; and
feminine domesticity, 246; commitment
to, 253; sex discrimination in, 260; and
coeducation, 263

Women's Educational and Industrial Union,
213

Women's Equity Action League, 260

Women's history: as field of study, 5–6, 7;
and political issues, 7, 8

Women's Journal, 174

Women's legal rights: and property rights,
69, 70, 71, 98, 152, 156, 316; and common law, 69–70, 74, 76; and changes
in family law, 98; and miscegenation
laws, 114–15; and freedwomen, 129, 131;
and state constitutions, 156; and sex
discrimination, 188

Women's liberation movement: and sex difference, 4–5; effects of, 7, 247; and sexual
politics, 222; and Steinem, 243; and tradition of women's activism, 248, 256; and
consciousness-raising groups, 253; and
gender inequality, 255; and child care,
255, 256, 262; growth of, 256, 258; and
media, 258, 259–60; theatrics of, 258–59,
261; and lesbians, 267; and immigrants,
302. *See also* Feminists and feminism

Women's Political Council, 249

Women's Republican Association, 174

Women's rights: convention at Seneca Fall,
New York, 98; and African American
women, 134–35; and women's education,
152; and liberalism, 153, 158; and Enlightenment principles, 158; and abolitionism,
159, 178; vocal appeals of, 162, 163

Women's Trade Union League, 194, 213, 225,
226

Women Strike for Peace, 249

Women workers: and careers, 2, 166, 167,
197, 217, 227, 241, 242, 243, 277; and
combining work and family, 2, 225, 227–
38; African American, 131, 133, 202,
205–6, 211, 223, 224, 285; statistics on,
201–2, 205; and separate spheres, 202–
3; and World War II, 203, 204, 224; and
family relations, 203, 206, 225, 227–38,
241; compromises of, 205, 279; in nineteenth century, 207–8; independence of,
208–9, 211, 213; and trade unions, 212–
13, 225–26; and private realm, 214–16,

220–22; and interwar years, 223; and sex
  discrimination, 250; and feminism, 264;
  and delay of childbearing, 277; and gen-
  der changes, 290. *See also* Female wages;
  Immigrant women workers; Married
  women workers
Wong, Jade Snow, 301
Woolf, Virginia, 3, 4, 163
Woolley, Mary, 270
Working class: and settlement houses, 171;
  and woman suffrage, 178; and trade
  unions, 203; and leisure, 215–16
Working-class men, 202, 238, 284, 285, 298
Working-class women, 223, 238
Working girls, 207, 211
World's Columbian Exposition (1893), 191
World's Congress of Representative Women,
  191

World War I, 269, 282
World War II, 203, 204, 224, 226, 228, 269,
  270, 282, 297
Wozniak, Steve, 311
Wright, Fanny, 158

Yee, Bo, 314
Yezierska, Anzia, 17, 190, 214–15, 220, 222,
  295, 299, 300, 301
You, Lee Puey, 295
Young Americans for Freedom, 253
Young Women's Christian Association, 173,
  190, 193, 207–8, 209, 248, 254

Zimmerman, Don, 11
Zuni tribe, 27, 43–44, 268